PROCONSUL IN POLITICS

MILNER

Proconsul in Politics

a study of Lord Milner
in Opposition and in Power

by

A. M. GOLLIN

With an Introductory Section,
1854 - 1905

THE MACMILLAN COMPANY
NEW YORK
1964

Library of Congress Number 64—13121

Printed in Great Britain by The Garden City Press Limited,
Letchworth, Hertfordshire.

Contents

(v)

213571

Illustrations

Acknowledgment and Author's Preface

I have to acknowledge the gracious permission of Her Majesty the Queen to publish a document from the Royal Archives, reproduced in the text. In this connection I must also express my thanks to the Librarian at Windsor Castle, Mr. Robert Mackworth-Young, for his courtesies.

Access was granted for me to the Milner Papers in the Library of New College Oxford during two separate periods of study. I wish to express my thanks to Mr. David Ogg and Mr. H. E. Bell, successively Librarians of the College, who arranged for me to examine Milner material. Mr. Bell in particular during the second period of study made the most pleasant arrangements on my behalf. I have also to thank Mr. R. L. Rickard of the New College Library for his help and advice.

I owe a very great debt to Lord Beaverbrook who generously supplied me with material from the Lloyd George Papers, and from other sources that he owns. He also helped the work in a private correspondence, and in conversation.

Sir Evelyn Wrench, Lord Milner's biographer, did a great deal to help, with the charm and courtesy that is typical of him.

Mr. Julian Amery very kindly allowed me to study his father's collection of papers, and I must express my appreciation of his generosity.

Mr. Dermot Morrah generously gave access to the Round Table archives and to the papers of Lionel Curtis; The Hon. Mrs. Celia Dawson allowed me to see material from the collection of her husband, Geoffrey Dawson; Sir Geoffrey Harmsworth supplied letters from the Northcliffe collection.

As an American engaged in the study of recent British political history I wish to record my thanks to the following for their help either in supplying information; or in giving me permission to exploit papers in which they possess the copyright; or in helping me to obtain access to unpublished material: the late Viscountess Milner; the late Lord Elibank; the late Sir Maurice Bonham Carter; Lady Violet Bonham Carter; Mr. John Strachey; Lord Altrincham; Lord Lansdowne; Lord David Cecil; Mr. A. J. P. Taylor; Colonel Maxwell; the Late Lord Winterton; Mr. Stanley Morison; the late Lord Hankey.

I have also to thank the officials of the British Museum, the British Museum Newspaper Library at Colindale, the Librarian of *The Times* Newspaper Library, and the Librarian of the *Daily Express* Newspaper Library.

The use I made of all this material is clearly indicated in the footnote references in the text. My object, with the footnotes, has been to demonstrate exactly how my sources were exploited.

I must also express my sincere thanks to the John Simon Guggenheim Memorial Foundation and to the American Council of Learned Societies for the financial assistance that enabled me to prepare this study.

Finally, I wish to acknowledge my debt to my friend Mr. Maurice H. Smith, of H.M. Customs and Excise, who kindly read the book in typescript; Mr. D. Dutton typed the manuscript with great skill; Mr. Dennis J. Nisbet was kind enough to prepare the Index.

* * * * *

This book is not a biography of Lord Milner. Rather, as the subtitle suggests, it is a study of Lord Milner in action in the political life of his time. In order to carry out my purpose, it has been necessary to analyse the political characters of Lord Milner's friends and opponents, and to describe with some care the political conditions in which he acted. To neglect these aspects would be to sacrifice genuine understanding of the subject, for no valid reason. By design, therefore, Lord Milner does not appear on every page of this book, though he is never forgotten.

When I began this study a friend who may be described as a distinguished member of the Liberal Party asked me why I wanted to become concerned with "that vile brute", while another acquaintance of great charm told me that I should discover what a great and good man Lord Milner was. It seemed clear that the subject was not devoid of controversy. My purpose has been to shed further light upon the matter, and not to add to the heat that still surrounds the name of Lord Milner, in so far as such a course is possible.

A. M. GOLLIN

Bibliographical Note

This book is based upon several collections of papers; upon a study of the contemporary Press; and upon other published works in the field. The most helpful books, in this latter category, are indicated in the footnote references to the text. The following collections of papers, in private possession, were studied: L. S. Amery's Papers; Lionel Curtis's Papers; the Round Table Archives; St. Loe Strachey's Papers; Geoffrey Dawson's Papers; Lord Northcliffe's Papers; material in the collection of Lord Lansdowne; Lord Astor's Papers; J. L. Garvin's Papers; material in the Lloyd George collection; material in Lord Elibank's Papers. In public archives resort was had to: the Balfour Papers and the Campbell-Bannerman Papers in the British Museum; H. H. Asquith's Papers in the Bodleian Library at Oxford; and Lord Milner's Papers in the Library at New College, Oxford.

PART I
INTRODUCTORY
1854-1905

I. A Curious Man

I

AN air of mystery hovers over the figure of Lord Milner.
With the passage of time and the advance of historical
scholarship we are coming to understand his contemporaries of the early years of the present century. Asquith
and Balfour, Lloyd George and Birkenhead, Churchill and
Chamberlain, Campbell-Bannerman and Bonar Law, Curzon
and Carson—the list "is as sonorous as Homer's catalogue
of the ships". They are beginning to take their places in the
classic array of British statesmen. Almost alone in this
company of governors of men, Alfred Milner remains a
figure of extreme controversy.

This quality of mystery that clings to Lord Milner's
political personality is not a result of ignorance. Men have
never been able to agree about him. In the course of his
lifetime he won to his side ardent friends at the same time
that he created for himself bitter and violent enemies. Lord
Milner attracted controversy and aroused passion.

When he retired as High Commissioner for South Africa

in 1905 the *Daily News* of 2nd March declared: "Lord Milner's retirement was inevitable . . . He stands for everything this country abhors . . . It is a happy omen that that sinister rule is over . . . South Africa has proved the grave of his, as of so many other reputations . . ."

In the first of its Editorial Notes *The Outlook* of 4th March remarked that "Lord Milner's resignation has taken effect . . . posterity will have it to say of him . . . that 'England had been a long time in labour, but had brought forth a man'. In intellectual strength and moral force he has no equal among the politicians of his generation. These qualities have saved the Empire in South Africa. They may yet play as large a part in saving the cause of Empire at home".

There could be no middle ground where Lord Milner was concerned. In the opinion of some of his countrymen his ideas, his statesmanship and his policies seemed harsh, brutal and un-English; for others, these same designs had the simplicity and straightforwardness of genius.

His contemporaries, however, were all partisans. Lord Milner, by reason of his pedigree and experience, was a curious and complicated man; no easy platitudes can be applied to him.

II

Even the circumstances of his birth became a matter for criticism and contention. Alfred Milner was born in Germany in 1854. For this reason he was subjected to the attacks of Liberals, Radicals, Conservatives and Irish Nationalist politicians whenever they had cause to disagree with him. Throughout his career as a public man Milner was vulnerable to the charge that he was a German foreigner, different from his fellow politicians and for that reason unworthy of public trust.[1]

[1] British Radicals do not like to believe that their party could ever attack a man because of his origins. In this connection see, for example, R. B. McCallum, *Public Opinion and The Last Peace* (London, 1944), p. 100—"Lord Milner had been much more German in his education . . . but as an eminent Conservative statesman

4

Milner's grandfather, James Richardson Milner, an English businessman from Manchester, settled in Germany in 1805. There he married Sophia von Rappard, the daughter of a German official. Charles Milner, their eldest son, married an English widow named Mary Ready, a woman nearly twenty years his senior in age. Alfred Milner was the only child of their union.

Mary Ready Milner, a sturdy product of the English middle class, came from a family of soldiers and administrators. In 1852 her first husband, St. George Cromie, was killed in Ireland; in order to educate her two sons on a limited income the frugal widow travelled to Bonn in 1853. She engaged Charles Milner, then a young medical student, as their tutor. Within a very short time the couple were married at the British Consulate in Cologne.

In the spring of 1860 Dr. Milner brought his small family to London where he began to practise medicine. The venture was not a success from the financial point of view. The Milners were poor when they arrived and during the six years of their stay in London one financial crisis regularly followed another. In 1866, in consequence of his failure as a doctor, Charles Milner accepted an academic post at Tübingen University and the family, in the autumn of that year, returned with him to Germany.

---

he was immune from the persecution which bore upon Haldane". While this statement is correct in an immediate sense we have to notice that Milner was not immune from persecution on the score of his German connections, as this history will show. Even the Christian names of his father aroused controversy, as a few random examples suggest. Milner liked to refer to his father as Charles Milner. In the *New Age* for 20th June 1901, however, we find the following reference to an article in the Leipzig *Neuste Nachtrichten* for 11th June 1901 ". . . the writer even calls Milner's father 'Charles'; though he should be aware that the correct Christian name . . . is 'Karl'. The logic of facts compels us to insist that our good German friends shall accept Milner as a fellow citizen". In the *Daily Chronicle* for 24th December 1915 Milner's father is referred to as "Karl". In the *Star* for 4th January 1916 he is called "Carl". These periodicals were all on the Radical side. R. C. K. Ensor, a radical journalist in his youth, in his standard work *England 1870–1914* (Oxford, 1949), p. 217 (n.) (1) refers to the father as "Karl Milner". It is perhaps fair to point out in this connection that Milner suffered less than Haldane from "persecution" of this kind for the simple reason that his friends stood by him more staunchly than did those of the Liberal statesman.

Then, as now, academic salaries for the lower ranks were inadequate. Dr. Milner's meagre income had to be supplemented by his taking into his home, as boarders, British students who wished to learn German in an Anglo-German family.

Despite the fact that she no longer lived in England, Mary Milner was determined that her boy should be brought up as an Englishman. A crisis came in 1869. She had been ill for some time when it was at last realised that her disease was mortal. In these painful circumstances she acted with the resolution typical of her class. Her brother, Colonel Charles Ready, was summoned to Tübingen where it was arranged that Alfred should be put in his charge after she died, and that he should not remain with his father in Germany. Within ten days of her death in August 1869, Dr. Milner, Colonel Ready and Alfred were in London in order to arrange the circumstances of the boy's new life.

Mary Milner's sons by her first husband had already established themselves in the world, one in India and the other in China. These half-brothers played little or no part in Alfred Milner's life. John Cromie, the older of the two brothers, died soon after his mother while Charles lived out his days at the other end of the earth.

It was decided that Alfred should live with his mother's cousin, John Malcolm, a widower. Although Malcolm and his daughter Marianne welcomed Milner into their home, this period of the young man's life was miserable and unhappy. The catalogue of his youthful hardships was not yet complete. His mother's death was a bereavement he felt very keenly; it has been called the "greatest tragedy of his life". London itself was a vast and unpleasant change from the country atmosphere which had become familiar to him in Germany. On his visits to Tübingen during these years the boy found Dr. Milner rendered sleepless by indifferent health and distracted by monetary worries. In 1872 when John Malcolm died it was discovered that his finances were in complete disorder. He had been given the charge of a small sum Alfred inherited from his mother but the boy's money disappeared with the rest in the general confusion of his affairs. After Malcolm's death, the cousins Alfred and Marianne shared an establishment for more than a decade until Marianne's drunken habits drove the young man to withdraw from her society into bachelor quarters of his own.

Meanwhile, however, in that one sphere where Alfred's native ability could make itself felt great strides were being taken. At King's College School in London he impressed his masters with his truly extraordinary powers. Although one of his contemporaries, who later became Speaker of the House of Commons (Lord Ullswater), regarded Milner as a "grave, serious and thoughtful boy", his teachers rightly looked upon him as one of their most brilliant pupils. In 1872 in his final year at the school he won a whole battery of prizes, medals and academic awards.

Despite the fact that Milner had no family connections with any university he was advised to try for the Balliol Scholarship, then looked upon as the finest open scholarship offered at the University of Oxford. From Tübingen Dr. Milner urged the safer if more pedestrian idea of the Indian Civil Service but Alfred's imagination had been fired by the thought of Oxford and all that it implied in the eighth decade of the nineteenth century.

The summer of 1872 was given over to strenuous preparation. Every hope for the future depended upon the result of this one examination. The boy's meagre reserves of money were raided in order to pay for the coaching of an expert, and in November the trial began.

If it is too much to say that Alfred Milner went up to his Balliol scholarship examination unfellowed, friendless and alone, it is not far off the mark. He seems to have been accompanied by one friend, Philip Gell, a colleague from King's College. The results were announced in the Hall. As each successful candidate was called, his school friends cheered and applauded. When the name of Alfred Milner

7

was read out as the winner of the first scholarship there
was an awful silence until Gell astonished the company of
Wykehamists, Etonians, and the like with his solitary shouts
of joy. It was a noble and romantic achievement. The
triumph seemed to wipe out the dreary experiences of
adolescence.

III

In Milner's day Balliol enjoyed a pre-eminent place
among the Oxford colleges. This was the result, in good
part, of the efforts and influence of Dr. Benjamin Jowett,
the celebrated Master of Balliol. His Senior Common
Room boasted an assemblage of personalities that glittered.
In addition to the Master himself, "the greatest of them all",
it included Thomas Hill Green, Lewis Nettleship, Baron de
Paravicini, and others of that lofty quality. In time each of
these men was impressed by the charm of Milner's personality while they observed with satisfaction his development
as a scholar of the very highest order. The tale of Oxford
scholarships and prizes which fell to Milner's assaults
became a legend in his own lifetime. Once, when he failed
to win a coveted scholarship by an unhappy mischance,
Jowett himself remarked that he need not worry because
there could be no doubt that he had a splendid career
before him. The "scholarship-hunter", as he once referred
to himself, came by degrees to the realisation that his future
course was more or less assured.

The high opinions of his tutors were echoed by those of
his fellow undergraduates. It became the boast of Balliol
men to declare that Alfred Milner was "made of no common clay". In the wider society of the university as in
Balliol itself Milner demonstrated, in addition to his
intellectual pre-eminence, an extraordinary capacity for
making friends. In many cases, the friendships he began at
Oxford lasted throughout his life. In 1875 he served as
Treasurer of the Union and in 1876 he gained the distinction of being elected unanimously as President of that

society. Three years later, in 1879, Milner brought his university career to its culmination when he was elected to an open Fellowship at New College.

IV

We must now pause in order to notice, if we desire to understand Lord Milner, that his marvellous achievements at Oxford were not won without the payment of a heavy price.

His efforts to establish his superiority over his colleagues drew tremendously upon his reserves of vitality and nervous energy. The iron control which was required, if the unknown young aspirant were to succeed at Oxford, at once affected his health and his attitude to life in general.

Tenseness is the key to much of his life in these years. One example of the mood occurred when he sat for the "Ireland" Scholarship. The incident, though well known, has sometimes been misunderstood. Milner explained his failure to win the prize in a letter to his cousin, Marianne Malcolm:[1]

> . . . The first three days I got on well . . . But by this time I had got all the work that was in me out of myself. The next day I felt my head muddled and the morning of the fifth day I had got all the work that was in me out of myself. I was excited and forgetful . . . I got up, tore up my papers and hoped to hear no more about the "Ireland" . . . That night . . . Jowett sent for me and struck me all of a heap by telling me that I had been a long way ahead . . . and if I could have shown up some papers, *any* papers that last day, the thing would have been mine . . .

For Milner, each scholarship examination was a crucial test. His limited stock of nervous energy was consumed in the preparations for the test, in the writing of it, and in the anxiety that accompanied each of these ordeals. That he succeeded brilliantly in almost every case could never alleviate the tension and consequent exhaustion of a man who depended upon his own exertions in order to gain the high place among his fellows that he coveted.

[1] See Cecil Headlam ed., *The Milner Papers* (London, 1931), vol. I, p. 11, hereafter cited as Headlam.

We must realise in this connection that Milner himself and his Balliol contemporaries recognised this aspect of his position. When he first came up to Oxford he explained to Jowett that he would be obliged to supplement his income by taking pupils in the vacations. The Master agreed to this course and arranged for him to tutor W. H. Grenfell, later Lord Desborough. By this means, Milner expanded the circle of his aristocratic connections. At the same time it was obvious to his contemporaries by this and other details of daily life that Milner was burdened in his career by the lack of that kind of family support which eased the way for so many of them. He was almost, but not quite, one of them. St. John Brodrick, later the Earl of Midleton, a Balliol friend, had no doubt that Milner was "handicapped by straitened means", and when Jowett expressed a different view Brodrick was convinced that the Master "wise as he was . . . knew little of the world".[1]

Brodrick recognised something else that those close to Milner were able to perceive. He saw that his health "was never very robust". This condition of delicate health also impressed itself upon W. T. Stead of the *Pall Mall Gazette* who came to know Milner well when he joined the staff of the paper shortly after he came down from Oxford. Stead observed that Milner was liable to feel the strain of his work and that he was easily exhausted. Writing in 1899 of their earlier association, Stead said of Milner: "In those days he was a weaker man physically than he is today. He suffered much from indigestion, had to be careful about his food, and if he ever had a long morning's work he wilted considerably under the strain. . . His physical energy was deficient. He often suffered from sleeplessness, and he needed to take care of himself".[2]

By that time Milner knew that he could provide for

---

[1] The Earl of Midleton, *Records & Reactions* (London, 1939), p. 31.

[2] W. T. Stead, "Sir Alfred Milner" in *Review of Reviews*, vol. XX, July 1899, pp. 19–22. See also in this connection John Buchan, *Memory Hold The Door* (London, 1945), p. 101, who writes of Milner that "Early in life he became aware that he had a limited stock of vitality, bodily and mental".

himself in life. He saw that people like John Morley and Stead of the *Pall Mall Gazette* were anxious to associate him with their newspaper; and there was always the security provided by his New College Fellowship. Nevertheless, the tenseness we have already noticed was still there. It was in this period that he decided to live apart from his cousin, Marianne Malcolm. When he explained the decision to her, he recognised the importance of their relationship; but he had to leave her—not because he was angered by her drinking habits—but because, as he made it clear, he had to have the absolute disposal of his own time ". . . if I am not to steer straight into failure . . ."[1] This is not the reason that would be advanced by a young man content with himself and convinced of his power to master events as they arose. It is the argument of a man who is still impressed with the fact that he has to struggle mightily, however capable he may be, to get whatever he wants from the world.

This aura of uneasiness also impressed itself on L. S. Amery who knew Milner many years later. Toward the end of his life Amery put his collection of private papers in order; when he came to the Milner file, in July 1951, he wrote a short note with the object of summing up his old political chief, and he saw to it that this docket was preserved together with the letters he had received from Milner. No one admired Lord Milner more than Leo Amery did, and we must look upon his note as the comment of an intimate friend and disciple. Nevertheless, he fixed on Milner's earliest experiences in order to explain his personality and he wrote that:[2]

Milner had the nature of an aristocrat but the feeling that he had to make his beginning here with no social connections and with the suggestion that he was not quite English contributed to his extreme restraint about himself and to what was almost agoraphobia.

[1] The letter to Marianne is printed in J. E. Wrench, *Alfred Lord Milner* (London, 1958), pp. 57–9, hereafter cited as Wrench, *Milner*.
[2] Amery Papers, Note dated 6th July 1951 in L. S. Amery's handwriting.

V

In addition to absorbing the course of preparation Oxford provided for the cadets of the ruling class, Milner fell under the influence of two remarkable contemporaries. These young men, Arnold Toynbee and George Parkin, determined in their different spheres much of Milner's outlook after he came down from Oxford.

Arnold Toynbee was the son of a famous surgeon of the day. Early in life he hoped to become an army officer but a delicate constitution forced him to abandon the idea. Instead, he came up to Oxford in order to study law; he found, however, that economics and economic history were more compelling subjects for a man with his interests. Although he began his Oxford career at Pembroke College, he transferred after a time to the more congenial atmosphere of Balliol where he was well liked by Jowett and others. Eventually, he was appointed as a lecturer and tutor in the College. His devotion to the study of economic history was part of an enthusiastic concern for and a selfless interest in the working-classes of his time, especially those in the East End of London. As a result of his inspiring example, his friends at Oxford took an active part in his social work on behalf of the poor. It is fair to say that he coloured the outlook of a generation of University men who became concerned with social questions at this time.

Alfred Milner was one of this number. No one ever charmed him to the extent that Arnold Toynbee did. Few human beings were more reticent about their personal feelings that Milner but in a brief *Memoir* of Toynbee he took pains to admit that "No man has ever had for me the same fascination . . ." while in an article he wrote on Toynbee for the *Dictionary of National Biography* he emphasised that the chief source of Toynbee's influence lay in his charm.[1]

---

[1] Alfred Milner, *Arnold Toynbee* (London, 1895), p. 20, and the article on Toynbee in the *D.N.B.*

For Milner, this personal attraction led to an interest in Toynbee's political philosophy. By the 1870s Toynbee and a good number of others were no longer able to maintain that confident faith in the political and economic organisation of society which had been, until then, a principal feature of English life in the middle of the nineteenth century. For those who thought as Toynbee did, the old conviction that the *laissez faire* system was at once miraculous and providential could no longer be accepted without question. It was at last recognised that the Liberal methods of the early nineteenth century were not universally applicable to every possible national contingency and condition.

If free competition and the pursuit of economic self-interest were no longer valid and socially acceptable ideals, Toynbee helped to provide Milner with others; ". . . it was a distinguishing mark of those who came under Toynbee's influence", Milner wrote, "that they were deeply impressed with their individual duty as citizens, and filled with an enthusiasm for social equality, which led them to aim at bridging the gulf between the educated and the wage-earning class. . ."[1]

We have now to notice exactly what it was that Alfred Milner came to believe in as a result of the influence exerted upon him by Toynbee. The sense of duty that Toynbee inspired led Milner into the East End of London to work with other young men of his class in the University Settlements of those days. It prompted him to undertake the study of Marx and Lassalle at a time when they were scarcely known in this country, and it left him with a permanent interest in socialism and social reform. It did not turn him into a socialist.

Milner was never attracted by those collectivist theories which came to dominate Continental socialism; nor did he approve of all the policies and objects which were eventually fastened upon by the British Labour Party and which led,

[1] Milner, *Arnold Toynbee*, p. 27.

13

in the fullness of time, to the establishment of the welfare state. In describing Toynbee's ideas, Milner took care to express his own suspicion of ". . . the paternal government of an omnipotent all-absorbing state . . ." He was afraid that such a State would, in the exercise of its unlimited powers, destroy the sturdy independence of the individual citizen. He wrote, with approval, of Toynbee's opinion that "nothing that tended to discourage self-reliance or to weaken character could possibly lead even to material well-being".[1]

At the same time, however, Milner recognised the failure of nineteenth-century England to establish that good, harmonious social order which was the object of any rational society. He was particularly attracted by Toynbee's emphasis upon the need for social reorganisation. The Industrial Revolution had shattered the old social system; corporate effort was required to create a new one; "the pursuit of economic self-interest would never evolve order out of the existing chaos".[2]

In other words, the object of Milner's "socialism" was to avoid at the same time the waste and inefficiency that seemed to him typical of his country in the nineteenth century, and also those extremes of collectivist theory which would invest government with too much power and influence over the lives of men.

He was distressed by the haphazard squandering of the nation's most precious resources; in particular, he regretted the effects of the Industrial Revolution upon the mass of ordinary Englishmen who had been crowded off the land and into the slums where they lost their physical strength, their moral values and even the material standards of an earlier generation. Milner was already an Imperialist who feared that these denizens of the nineteenth-century towns would be unable to perform their duty to the nation and the Empire because of their physical debility and the decay

[1] *Ibid.*, p. 55.
[2] *Ibid.*, p. 53.

of that moral fibre which had carried the English people so far in the past. He therefore came to advocate state and municipal intervention of the kind that was called "Gas and Water Socialism". The object was to preserve health, strength and intelligence in order to avoid national degeneration.

This does not mean, of course, that Milner's appreciation of socialism was limited to these aspects of the idea. In a series of lectures delivered in 1882 at Toynbee Hall, the famous social settlement named after his friend, Milner explained other phases of the subject to his audience. In a moving passage he said that the ultimate success of socialism depended upon the gradual growth of "individual unselfishness, of a higher sense of the value and the beauty of common work and common enjoyment and of nobler aims than of individual money getting . . . a self-development that will lead men to seek that kind of wealth in obtaining which they are despoiling no one, which will be to the advantage and not to the detriment of others. . ."

He took care to emphasise, however, that in our imperfect condition such ideals had not yet proven themselves attractive to a predominant number of men, and until they did society could not dispense with "the present harsh and mean stimulants to personal exertion". Socialism, he maintained, was a noble ideal which could not yet be realised.[1]

We have to observe in this connection that in spite of the genuine attraction of the socialist principle for him, Milner never tried to work together with the leaders of either the advanced Radical or Labour Parties though, as we shall see, the idea did occur to him. He prided himself, above all things, on the realism of his outlook; and nothing in his experience ever suggested to him that his fellow men

[1] Milner's lectures were posthumously published in six articles in the *National Review*, January–June, 1931; Leo Maxse, editor of the *National Review*, was the brother of Lord Milner's widow.

were ready to abandon these base, carnal and unscrupulous appetites which prevented them from becoming worthy of the promised land.

VI

In the same way that Toynbee turned Milner's thoughts in the direction of social reform, George Parkin quickened in him those Imperial feelings which became the great passion of his public life.

Parkin was a Canadian schoolmaster who came up to Oxford in 1873. He was an Imperial patriot but in England at that time there was not much enthusiasm for the Empire. This lack of interest was a result of the fact that Britain still enjoyed an easy dominion over the markets of the entire world; as yet, no country had offered any real challenge to her commercial or political supremacy. In such a condition of affairs Imperial matters were of little consequence to many Englishmen because it seemed to be clear that Britain had no need of an Empire in order to prosper.

In a speech at the Oxford Union, however, Parkin attracted attention by urging, in terms that were novel to his audience, the cause of a united Empire and "such . . . Imperial Federation as will secure the representation of the more important Colonies in the Imperial Councils". Parkin's ideas were explained in those energetic transatlantic tones which can sometimes charm an English audience. At the end of the debate Milner came up to him in order to express interest in his "new and curious" ideas and to arrange for further discussions of this exciting subject of Empire Federation.[1]

This was the beginning of Parkin's fantastic influence on the development of the Imperial idea in England. For, from the 1870s onward Englishmen did become aware of the serious competition of foreign rivals in every sphere of international activity. As the old complacency of the mid-

[1] For the incident see Wrench, *Milner*, p. 44.

Victorian era disappeared Imperial sentiments became increasingly popular. More and more people in the United Kingdom began to consider closer relations with the Colonies as one method to maintain and bolster up the position Britain had enjoyed for so many years as the paramount power in the world. In 1884 an Imperial Federation League was formed to promote this idea of Empire integration; Parkin accepted a position as a travelling speaker for the League and became, in Lord Rosebery's phrase, "the bagman of Empire". Such was the effect of Parkin's personality that Winston Churchill and Leo Amery, who listened to his lectures as Harrow schoolboys in 1889, could recall his exact words and phrases more than half a century later. In his *Autobiography* Amery recalled the incident and explained that: "No history of the growth of the Imperial idea in the last century would be complete that failed to do justice to the influence of George Parkin upon his generation".[1]

Parkin, with roots in New Brunswick and bred in the proud tradition of those United Empire Loyalists who had done so much to mould the history of Canada, was an Empire patriot in the very widest sense. He was less concerned with the maintenance of the old position of the United Kingdom than he was with his dreams for a mighty and powerful Greater Britain. In the introduction to his book, *Imperial Federation*, he explained the nature and essence of his Imperial aspirations: ". . . United with all others of their own race and language, British people might have been able, in self-sufficing strength, to withdraw almost a hundred years earlier than could otherwise be possible from the entanglements of European politics, and to be free to devote all their energies to the maintenance of peace,

---

[1] L. S. Amery, *My Political Life* (London, 1953), vol. I, p. 37. Historians will do well to reflect upon the fact that Parkin's name does not even appear in the index to the 3rd volume of the *Cambridge History of the British Empire*, published in 1959. This volume, entitled "The Empire-Commonwealth 1870–1919", deals with the growth of the Imperial idea in these years. It is, of course, a massive, brilliant and standard source for its subject.

and the development of industry, commerce, and civilisation".[1]

As this passage suggests, Parkin, like so many nationalists and Imperialists of the late nineteenth century, believed in the idea of race. He was convinced that the united British Empire of his dreams, bound into a single formidable unit by means of some kind of Federal system of government, was a possibility of world politics because "A special capacity for political organisation may, without race vanity, be fairly claimed for Anglo-Saxon people".[2]

These were the ideas and this the message which Parkin brought with him from Canada to Oxford and pressed upon Milner and his other English friends. His opinions and aspirations turned out to be immensely attractive to the general company of young Imperialists at the University; in Milner's case they were decisive in determining the direction and bias of his life. Just as we must reckon with Arnold Toynbee as one who roused in Milner an interest in social reform, so must we look upon George Parkin as the first of those to stimulate Milner's interest in the Empire and in that race patriotism which became the great cause of his life.

VII

The young man who came down from Oxford in 1879 in order to read for the Bar was looked upon as the pride of his university. The old background of poverty and insecurity seemed far behind him; instead, men saw a dignified, polished and handsome youth who was bound to succeed in London in the same way that he had triumphed at Oxford.

In addition to preparing for the Bar, Milner added to his

[1] George R. Parkin, *Imperial Federation* (London, 1892), p. 6. It is not without significance that Lord Beaverbrook, like Parkin an Empire patriot from New Brunswick, picked on exactly these themes when he tried to sum up Milner. See Lord Beaverbrook, *Men and Power* (London, 1956), p. xxi, where he writes of Milner that "... the unity of the Empire, political and economic, was his goal. That Britain was no part of Europe was his conviction".

[2] George R. Parkin, *Imperial Federation*, p. 1.

income by dabbling in political journalism. As early as 1880, however, in less than a year, he realised that neither journalism nor the legal profession were particularly attractive to him. In October 1880 he wrote to his friend E. T. Cook, later Sir Edward Cook, in order to tell him of the dreary condition of life in London:[1]

> You at Oxford can have little idea of a busy life in London. . . I find I am doing hard dull work all day with a view to a highly prob-lematical supply of bread and cheese in the future, and then in the evening I read—the papers! A man's mind, like his body, does not thrive on even the most liberal allowance of bran, so after a while there ensues a condition of mental feebleness hardly describable.

It is thus clear that the acquisitive life of the many could hold no attraction for the man who had been trained at Balliol under Jowett, and exposed to Toynbee's moral fervour.

Since these professions failed to satisfy, Milner was plagued by the question of his future. Like so many young men he mused on his fate and wondered about his choice of a career. After contemplation, he decided to devote his life to politics, and public service. In consequence, he gave up his legal work and joined the *Pall Mall Gazette* as a regular member of its staff. At the same time he made it clear to W. T. Stead, the assistant editor, that "I don't want to give myself up to journalism, but it would be helpful to me to give some time to it and I would rather do it regularly than spasmodically".[2]

The political opportunity Milner sought came in 1885. After lengthy preparations and careful calculation an invita-tion was secured for him to stand for Parliament as the Liberal candidate for the Harrow division of Middlesex.

No incident in Lord Milner's long career has been more misunderstood than his electoral campaign of 1885. It was an episode of vital importance in his life but because he himself tried in later years to dismiss it as a momentary

---

[1] The letter is printed in J. Saxon Mills, *Sir Edward Cook* (London, 1921), p. 42.
[2] See J. W. Robertson Scott, *Life and Death of a Newspaper* (London, 1952), p. 207.

aberration of no significance, its real meaning has not been
appreciated.

We are usually told that Milner was interested in obtaining a seat in Parliament in the very brief period 1884–5.
This was not the case; he was in a position to contest a
constituency for at least four years, and during that time
he was prepared to accept considerable sums of money
from a friendly patron in order to pursue his parliamentary
ambitions.

In February 1882 he wrote to Jowett at Balliol in order
to explain that he had given up all thought of devoting his
life to the legal profession. He emphasised that he was not
"dazzled" by the prospect of a great political career; as a
poor man he realised that he could not, in the ordinary
course, hope to become a Member of Parliament. However,
he could aspire to "many useful careers outside Parliament".[1]

Despite this letter to Jowett, Milner was not content to
begin his new course as a non-Parliamentary politician.
At this turning point in his life he entertained a valid hope
that he could overcome his lack of money and embark
upon the traditional road to political power in England,
the road that begins with a place in the House of Commons.
On the very day that he wrote to Jowett, Philip Gell, his
old friend, also sent a letter to the Master; he revealed that
Milner already possessed the funds that would enable him
to stand for Parliament. Writing in the excited tones of one
who reveals a vital secret, Gell told the Master the latest
news of Milner:[2]

. . . What he craves and what alone will hold him are strong human
interests. . . As secretary to a Royal Commission, or to a leading politician, or to some political association, he would render most loyal
and helpful service. . .

There is a secret also which I feel I should tell you . . . A friend has
guaranteed his expenses if he will stand for Parliament at the next election, and has already lodged £1,000 for this purpose and no other . . .

[1] Milner's letter, dated 2nd February 1882, is published in Geoffrey Faber,
Jowett (London, 1957), pp. 362–3.
[2] *Ibid.*, pp. 364–5.

We have to notice that when Milner abandoned the Bar at the end of 1881 in order to devote his life to politics, he knew that he had the funds that would enable him to fight for a seat in the Commons. Within two months of his decision, his friends could reveal the fact that his electoral expenses were already guaranteed.

It was only natural for Milner to point out to his friends that he was not intoxicated or "dazzled" by his new course. Jowett and his other teachers might question, with reason, this radical decision to throw over the profession they had trained him for. Their fears would be mollified, however, if he stressed the sober aspects of his plan, if he emphasised that he was looking for a private secretaryship or a post with a political association, and that he was not giving up all merely to chase parliamentary day dreams.

In this way Milner made it clear that he proposed to seek a new life in politics by more than one method; on the one hand, he was looking for the sort of position a young man of his high ability could reasonably hope to secure, and on the other he could still pursue his plan to try for the great prize, a seat in Parliament.

The next step was taken with scrupulous care. In March 1884 he was invited to become the Liberal candidate for the Borough of Cheltenham. After consultation with his political friends, Milner declined the offer because Cheltenham was regarded as a very doubtful opportunity for a Liberal candidate; he also refused the Liberal nomination for Oxford in this period. In 1885, however, a General Election took place and Milner agreed to stand for Harrow, in the Liberal interest. Harrow was hardly a safe seat but the opportunity had to be grasped.

Milner fought his campaign hard. All his other work was abandoned. Between June and November he made more than ninety public speeches. His Oxford friends came in cohorts to support his effort. H. H. Asquith, Alfred Lyttelton, G. W. E. Russell and others trooped out to Harrow to speak on his behalf. Despite their exertions and his own industry, Milner was unsuccessful at the poll; and in the opinion of contemporaries he was "beaten, and beaten badly".

The effect of this experience was profound. Often enough in English politics the young candidate who loses an election maintains his interest in party politics and tries a second time when another opportunity offers. This was not the case with Alfred Milner. He never contested an election again. "I am afraid I should never make a good party man", he liked to say in later years, "but I hope to make a fairly decent Englishman".

From this time Milner looked to non-elected posts to furnish him with the public and political work he still desired. Later on in life he was always ready to express his disgust and loathing for party politics and the English political system as a whole.

After 1885, Alfred Milner sought political power elsewhere than at elections.

VIII

Milner's enthusiasm for his campaign was so strong that he gave up almost every other duty in order to pursue the electors in complete freedom. Since February 1884 he had been employed as a private secretary by George Joachim Goschen, later Viscount Goschen, a leading politician of the day, but this work was suspended for the sake of the contest in the Harrow division. Although he was still a member of the Liberal Party, Goschen was already regarded at this time as one of those discontented Whigs who were no longer in touch with the mainstream of Liberal policy. After his rebuff at Harrow, the connection with Goschen was re-established and became Milner's chief occupation.

The two men became fast friends. One unkind critic said of their association that "Goschen would be remembered because Milner had been his secretary". Nevertheless, it was this friendship which decided the direction of Milner's career and put him on the certain path to high administrative influence and power.

Although there could be no suggestion of failure up to this point in Milner's life there was, equally, no sign of genuine success despite the clear evidence of outstanding ability. He had been elected a Fellow of New College, but he refused a tutorship, which meant that he did not propose to devote himself to teaching; he had begun work as a lawyer, but he chose to leave the Bar; he had been welcomed into the profession of Journalism by men of the calibre of John Morley and Stead, but he made it clear to them that newspapers would never occupy the whole of his time; he had tried his hand at a Parliamentary election, but the voters preferred the other candidate.

Now, with Goschen, he was on a more certain course in an occupation that was congenial to his talents. From this moment we can observe the steady and regular advance of his fortunes.

In 1886 the English political scene was convulsed by Gladstone's decision to grant Home Rule to Ireland. Goschen joined the minority faction of Liberals who abandoned the party in order to defy their old leader. He subscribed most of the funds for the creation of a Liberal Unionist Committee. His secretary was put in charge of the London office of this group; there, Milner's experience as a journalist was especially valuable in the efforts to win Liberal and other public opinion for the Unionist cause. In this post Milner demonstrated for the first time those outstanding administrative powers which were to carry him so far in the public service.

A General Election brought Lord Salisbury to power in the summer of the year. The even course of his Ministry was at once disturbed by the activities of Lord Randolph Churchill, his Chancellor of the Exchequer, who sought to defy his colleagues in order to assert his own authority in national affairs. Lord Randolph's challenge became Goschen's opportunity; when Salisbury asked him to become Chancellor in Churchill's place, he accepted. As Chancellor of the Exchequer Goschen selected Milner as his Official Private Secretary.

These Olympian struggles carried Milner in their train to the very centre of the Government machine. At a step he was removed, within a space of months, from the dreary hustings at Harrow to one of the most important offices of state in Whitehall. The lesson inherent in these developments was one that Alfred Milner never forgot.

IX

Goschen's warm opinion of his young assistant was now enhanced by Milner's ready display of another facet of his mental powers, an easy but exact mastery of finance. As a matter of course their relationship was watched very closely; Milner soon established a reputation, among those who counted in such high matters, for outstanding ability and extraordinary capacity. In 1888, as a result of these opinions, he was invited to become private secretary to the Viceroy of India. After reflection, the dazzling prize was refused, gracefully, because Milner decided that he was better equipped to serve at the Treasury than in India.

By the end of the following year, however, the time had come to take the next forward step. Although he was distressed to part with him, Goschen recommended Milner for the post of Director-General of Accounts in Egypt. The duties of the new position were soon mastered; the change from an office in Whitehall to an outpost of Empire presented Milner with no problems. In less than a year he was advanced in rank to the very responsible post of Under-Secretary for Finance. Milner's three years in Egypt were turned into yet another series of personal triumphs and achievements.

All was not work, however, in this Egyptian adventure. We must now mark an incident which played some part, however indefinable, in Milner's personal life and also in his political career. Among the many visitors who travelled to Egypt while he was there was Margot Tennant, a vivacious young lady who was able to charm a veritable host of men belonging to the English ruling class. On the occasion of her Egyptian tour, Milner was added to the impressively long list of her admirers. It was a radical blow to the plan of his life. Years before, in 1881, he had decided that because of his poverty he would have to remain celibate in order to devote all his energies and resources to his public career. Resolve melted in Margot's company and Milner fell in love. Margot Tennant was also moved by the association but in the end she refused to marry him, though their friendship continued. About a year later she wrote to tell him that she was engaged to marry H. H. Asquith. There is no need for us to seek to penetrate the secret recesses of Milner's mind in order to realise that this development affected, to a greater or lesser degree, his relationship with Asquith. For many years they remained warm friends. Later on, as we shall see in this history, they became mortal political enemies, and when Asquith was dragged down from the Premiership in 1916 no one was more elated by the crash than Milner. This does not imply that Milner's grave political differences with Asquith in later years were in any way the result of this curiously private episode. It is only fair, however, to record the incident in a study of Lord Milner's political career. Toward the end of his life Asquith took pains to declare publicly that he and Milner maintained to the end of the latter's life "perfectly friendly relations". This statement contains only an aspect of the truth; far more accurate is the conclusion of an acute political observer who summed up the relationship by referring to Milner as Asquith's "lifelong, devoted enemy".[1]

---

[1] Asquith's statement is to be found in The Earl of Oxford and Asquith, *Memories and Reflections* (London, 1928), vol. I, p. 178. The second quotation comes from an article by Roger Fulford in the *Manchester Guardian*, 28th August 1958.

X

Early in 1892 the Chancellor brought his young friend home when he appointed him Chairman of the Board of Inland Revenue at Somerset House. This position, one of the most responsible in the Permanent Civil Service of the country, established Milner on an eminence in the official world of Westminster and Whitehall. He at once proceeded to create a reputation for himself in wider spheres.

It had long been his purpose to write a book about Egypt; despite the press of his new duties he managed to write *England in Egypt* before the year was out. The book was received as a classic presentation and justification of the English case in Egypt; more than a dozen editions were printed. Something of the excitement caused by Milner's volume was captured by a young officer who wrote a classic book of his own a few years later; in his marvellous account of *The River War* Winston Churchill wrote of the effect of *England in Egypt* upon an Imperial people: ". . . the book was more than a book. The words rang like a trumpet-call which rallies the soldiers after the parapets are stormed, and summons them to complete the victory".

Milner served for five years at Somerset House. As Chairman of the Board of Inland Revenue he worked, as a matter of course, in close contact with several Chancellors of the Exchequer. His most notable accomplishment in this period was the work he performed for Sir William Harcourt; Milner was the chief authority in the preparation of Harcourt's famous "Death Duty Budget" of 1894, a milestone in the history of British taxation. His high services were not unappreciated by authority. In 1894 he received the award of the C.B., and in the following year he became Sir Alfred Milner, K.C.B.

Sir Alfred was now recognised as an official of the very first rank; he had been closely and successfully associated with statesmen of every political complexion; he had served with Goschen at the Treasury, with Cromer in

Egypt, with Sir Michael Hicks-Beach and Harcourt at the
Board of Inland Revenue. Each of these official chiefs
competed with the others in their tributes to him as a servant
of the State. He enjoyed the confidence of every political
party—Liberals, Conservatives, and Liberal Unionists.

It was to this official paragon that Joseph Chamberlain,
the Colonial Secretary, turned when affairs in South
Africa were boiling up to a crisis in 1897. The Unionist
Administration had lost confidence in their chief officer at
the Cape, Lord Rosmead, because of what they looked
upon as his weakness and vacillation. In casting about for
a man to take his place at what was clearly recognised as a
point of danger, their attention was directed to Milner by
several important advisers of government.

The appointment was not easily made. Sir Michael
Hicks-Beach, the Chancellor, was anxious to retain so
capable a subordinate at Somerset House. "Black Michael"
was not the man to allow anyone, even Chamberlain, to
tamper with his staff. It remained for Milner to decide the
matter by a demonstration of that iron will he could show to
even the highest authorities. On 3rd February he wrote to
Chamberlain in no uncertain terms:[1]

3 . 2 . 97   Somerset House

Confidential

Dear Mr. Chamberlain,

Sir Michael Hicks-Beach spoke to me today with reference to my
going to South Africa and seemed much annoyed . . .

I have a great wish to go . . . it was not my intention to stay inde-
finitely or indeed very much longer, at the Inland Revenue in any case
. . . I always hoped that it might lead to some appointment such as
Egypt or the present one. . . It was my fixed intention, if it did not
lead to anything better . . . to retire. . . That intention will only be
strengthened if I find, that my work at Somerset House . . . is a hind-
rance to me in the desire to devote the best years of my life to the
Imperial interests of my country. . .

Without being a rich man, I am pecuniarily quite independent, and
though I should not dream of resigning in a huff or a hurry, I should

---

[1] This letter and the one following are reproduced from previously unpublished
copies in the Amery papers.

feel that there was not much more time to be lost in freeing myself from a position in which the harder I worked the more I was removing myself from the only kind of career for which I care.

Yours very truly,
A. Milner.

In the face of such resolution even a Chancellor had to give way. Sir Michael delayed for a time, but then wrote to Chamberlain in order to acquiesce in the appointment. His letter, dated 12th February 1897, revealed his high opinion of Milner:

. . . Milner is unquestionably one of the ablest men who ever was Chairman of the Inland Revenue. I know now, what I always suspected, that Harcourt could never have framed the Finance Act without him. . . But now, even if he did not go to South Africa, he has been made restless by the offer of a career which in itself he would prefer— and of course he *will* go there. . .

More than anything else in life, Alfred Milner yearned to serve the State and the Empire. He was now to be given an opportunity to gratify his desires on a field that would, in the opinion of contemporaries, decide the Imperial future.

II. Milner in South Africa

Object of the chapter – Significance of the South African situation – Background of the struggle between Britain and the Transvaal – The Uitlanders and the Jameson Raid – Milner's invitation to the Colonial Office – Powers of the High Commissioner – Political significance of the farewell dinner of March 1897 – The "cross-bench mind" –Milner's conclusions after a year at Capetown – Significance of the Graaf-Reinet speech – The Colonial Office applies a brake – Milner's reaction – His dislike of public opinion – Effect of the "Helot" Dispatch upon political parties in England – How the coming of war changed Milner's public status – Milner is dragged into the whirlpool of party politics – A picture of Milner at the end of the war – South African reconstruction – The Milner Kindergarten –Balfour's high opinion of Milner – Milner's reason for refusing to become Secretary of State – Viceroy of India – A man with a problem – Lord Lothian's opinion.

I

MERCIFULLY, the rights and wrongs of the Transvaal War form no part of the present study. We have, however, to notice in brief outline the part Milner was called upon to play as the principal British officer in South Africa during the great crisis of 1897–1905. By this means, we will be able to observe the development of his political personality, the way in which he was measured by the rulers of the State in London, and the public reputation he acquired as a result of his services at the frontier of Empire. These matters form the indispensable background to the course he pursued after 1905, which is the subject of this volume.

29

When the Secretary of State first invited Milner to come to the Colonial Office on 18th January in order to explain his proposition, both men realised that Chamberlain was offering his visitor the chance to attain greatness.

The South African situation was the most vital of their time. Later, Chamberlain described it in the following dramatic terms: "What is now at stake is the position of Great Britain and with it the estimate formed of our power and influence in our Colonies and throughout the world . . ."[1] This aspect of the matter was crystal clear to both men on that January day.

The relations between Great Britain and the South African Republic (the Transvaal) had been strained for decades past. The essence of their difference was a question of power. Both sides were struggling for the mastery of a vast area, the South African sub-continent.

For a long time the aspirations of the Boers seemed ridiculous, in the face of British Imperial power. In the 1880s, however, gold was discovered in the Transvaal. The discovery had a revolutionary effect upon the South African situation.[2]

When the richness of the Transvaal mines was proven, the Afrikaner nationalists among the Boers felt that they were at last in a position to achieve their dream of a United States of South Africa, independent of the British Empire. The immense wealth of the goldfields was the key to their plan; with it, they hoped to attract the other South African States into an Afrikaner Union, which they would dominate. The British feared, with reason, that their Colonies would be lured into the Transvaal sphere. So far as the Colonial Office experts could see, after the discovery of gold the time factor in South Africa upon which they had always relied was no longer working in Britain's favour.

For British Imperialists the pretensions of the Transvaal

---

[1] Quoted in J. S. Marais, *The Fall of Kruger's Republic* (Oxford, 1961), p. 318, a recent and powerful study of the subject. See also J. L. Garvin, *Life of Joseph Chamberlain* (London, 1934), vol. III, p. 459.

[2] See Marais, *op. cit.*, pp. 327 ff.

constituted a crisis of Empire that extended far beyond South Africa. In their eyes the difficulty with the Boers was a test, and on its outcome depended the fate and future course of Greater Britain. If they failed in this case, the Imperial movement would be discredited, not only in South Africa and in the Dominions, but also at home.

At the time of Milner's visit to the Colonial Office, the British had recently suffered a major defeat in this South African contest when the Jameson Raid, a misguided attempt to overthrow the Transvaal government, ended in complete and absolute failure. It has been well described as the one "spasm of madness which ruined the British case for a time".

In London, Joseph Chamberlain was determined to retrieve the British position. It soon became apparent, however, that his chief agent in South Africa, Lord Rosmead, was not the man to carry out the forward policy the Colonial Secretary was resolved to follow. A subordinate of a completely different metal was required at the scene of action.

It was in these circumstances that Sir Alfred Milner was invited to the Colonial Office and asked to take charge at Cape Town in Lord Rosmead's room.

II

Milner's appointment as High Commissioner of South Africa and Governor of the Cape Colony was announced to the public on 15th February 1897. Three days later Sir Alfred journeyed to Windsor in order to kiss hands. His commission, signed by Queen Victoria, was a formidable document; according to its terms he was the supreme Imperial authority in British South Africa, authorised to exercise all the powers and jurisdictions of the Crown, subject only to instructions from a Secretary of State. He was also charged with the transaction of all business with the Governments of the Orange Free State and the South African Republic.

At the end of March he was the guest of honour at a remarkable farewell banquet in London. The Chairman at the dinner was H. H. Asquith; among the guests were Arthur Balfour, Joseph and Austen Chamberlain, R. B. Haldane, and John Morley. Lord Rosebery and Sir William Harcourt were unable to attend, but they sent handsome letters of apology which were read out to the diners. These men, representing every faction of the two major parties in the State, were united in their desire to honour Milner on the eve of his departure.

There could be no better testimony to Chamberlain's political skill than this dinner; the selection of Sir Alfred was an appointment that brought to the Imperial cause national support and unanimity of a rare order. Milner's speech at the banquet was received with an approbation that was denied to Chamberlain when he addressed the company. The difference was symbolic of much that was to follow. Milner was already recognised as a man above party, remote from the strife of factions, concerned solely with the discharge of national and Imperial duties.

In his speech Sir Alfred pointed out that he possessed a "cross-bench mind". But he emphasised that "On one question . . . I have never been able to see the other side, and that is precisely this question of Imperial union".[1]

This was the great age of Imperialism and in it Milner was accepted as the chosen emissary of his country. It was recognised that his task was to solve a grave problem on a critical frontier of the Empire; his business was to assert the position of the Imperial Government in South Africa. By means of his intellectual, administrative and moral gifts he was expected to achieve results without offending the principles of either party in the State. For this reason, when he left England he was fortified by the knowledge that he enjoyed the goodwill and encouragement of the generality of his countrymen.

Sir Alfred arrived at Capetown in May. For almost a year

[1] From the account in *The Times*, 29th March 1897.

he made no vital move, and devoted himself to mastering the local situation. Since the Jameson Raid the principal issue between the two powers was the political condition of the Uitlanders[1] of the Transvaal. The Colonial Office pressed the Boers to grant the Uitlanders some measure of political rights, while President Kruger and his Government sought to avoid or delay any genuine concessions. Early in February 1898 Kruger won an overwhelming victory in the Transvaal elections. His absolute power was thus confirmed and reinforced. This development decided Milner's attitude. He reported to Chamberlain that: "There is no way out of the political troubles of S. Africa except reform in the Transvaal or war. And at present the chances of reform . . . are worse than ever".[2] From this moment he looked forward to "the great day of reckoning".

The High Commissioner was not content with reports. Early in March in a speech at Graaf-Reinet he lashed the Boer inhabitants of the Cape Colony who were, of course, British subjects. The local branch of the Afrikaner Bond had complained to him that ther loyalty had been called into question. "Well, gentlemen, of course you are loyal", was his cool reply, "It would be monstrous if you were not". He also turned upon Kruger in order to blame him for all the friction in South Africa. He warned the President that his Government was suffering from evils of its own creation, caused by its own "unprogressiveness". These were terms without precedent for a Governor of the Cape to address to the citizens of his Colony and to the head of a foreign State.[3]

Milner's report and the Graaf-Reinet speech had serious consequences in their respective spheres. The Boers now recognised him as their most dangerous opponent while

---

[1] The Uitlanders were the alien inhabitants of the Transvaal, mostly British, who worked the mines. They were denied political rights. See the figures about them in Marais, *op. cit.*, pp. 1–3.

[2] Headlam, vol. I, p. 221.

[3] See the analysis in E. Halevy, *Imperialism and The Rise of Labour* (London, 1951), p. 71.

the British in South Africa hailed him as the new leader of their party.

More important, however, was the effect in London. There, Chamberlain and others in authority observed that Milner's object was to "work up to a crisis".[1] Clearly, their new agent supplied all the force and vigour feeble Lord Rosmead had lacked.

It was also obvious that he had lost sight of the original nature of his mission. He had been picked for the South African post in the first place because he was a safe man, a man with a "cross-bench mind", who could be relied upon to act in such a way that the mass of English public opinion would remain united in its support of Chamberlain's policies at the Cape.

The Colonial Office now proceeded to apply a brake. Milner was warned by Chamberlain and Selborne that the Government was confronted by diplomatic complications with France, Russia and Germany which did not permit a forward policy in South Africa. Equally important was the fact that public opinion at home was not yet ready to countenance a radical change in the South African situation. It was on this occasion that Milner, for the first time, found himself reined in by his superiors because his policy threatened to damage that popular support of the Government on which all depended.[2]

We must mark it as a development of consequence to our story. From this time onward the High Commissioner's logical appreciation of the right course in South Africa was confronted by Chamberlain's resolve that nothing must be done to sacrifice the goodwill of the English electorate. The effect on Milner was significant. He came to despise the views of the generality of his countrymen, which counted for so much in the eyes of the politicians at home. The ordinary voter, ignorant and short-sighted, was not qualified, in his opinion, to have any share in the creation

---

[1] See Garvin, *Chamberlain*, vol. III, p. 364.
[2] See the account in Garvin, *Chamberlain*, vol. III. pp. 366 ff.

of Imperial policy. This conviction, which reinforced earlier experience, now became an important element of his political outlook.

III

Throughout the rest of the year and for a good part of 1899 the real burden of policy lay upon Chamberlain. He agreed with Milner's support of the Uitlander case against the South African Republic; but he had to consider the effect of the High Commissioner's strong opinions upon the attitude of Englishmen at home. In April 1899 he took a considerable step forward. He caused Lord Selborne to write to Milner in order to ask the High Commissioner to draw up, in a despatch, the details of his indictment of the Boers. The object was to prepare the country for future developments by publishing Milner's views, at an opportune time. The result was Milner's famous "Helot" despatch of 4th May 1899. This document set out in passionate terms the gravamen of the charges against the South African Republic.

Shortly before the despatch reached the Colonial Office, a petition from the British Uitlanders in the Transvaal arrived in London. The petitioners, following an ancient custom, appealed to the Queen to help them in their misfortunes. Fortified by the arguments of the "Helot" telegram, Chamberlain won over the Cabinet; with the approval of his colleagues he now drew up a despatch of his own, accepting the Uitlanders' appeal to the Crown. At the end of this document, he proposed a meeting between Milner and President Kruger. The object of the meeting was to achieve a solution of the problems that plagued South Africa. By these means, the Unionist Cabinet committed itself to a new policy. If they could not secure redress for the Uitlanders by means of negotiation, their only other course involved an ultimatum, and this might be followed by a war.

The Bloemfontein Conference between President and High Commissioner accomplished nothing, and ended in failure. Shortly after it, Milner's "Helot" telegram and Chamberlain's despatch accepting the Uitlander petition were published, in June 1899. The attitudes and postures of the chief actors were now made clear to the English public. These revelations had a crucial effect upon the further course of English politics.

Until this June Chamberlain had appealed, with some success, to the Liberal Party to stand by him in the trouble with the Transvaal. War could be avoided, the Colonial Secretary had argued, if the Boers were impressed by the fact that both British parties were united in support of the Government policy. Three days after the publication of the "Helot" telegram, however, Sir Henry Campbell-Bannerman, the leader of the Liberal Party, publicly warned the Government, in a speech at Ilford on 17th June, that nothing in the South African situation could justify a war. This was the first sign of the storm to come.[1] From this moment, the Liberals began to prepare an alternative policy. The savage struggle between parties that lasted until 1914 and after was about to begin. From the middle of June Chamberlain realised that he and his policy of Imperialism were now involved in a fight for life. And he resolved to hit back, without mercy.

After Bloemfontein, further efforts of negotiation were made by both sides for some months. They achieved no real solution. As hope for peace dwindled the Boers readied their Commandos for the field, determined to strike first. The British began to move troops. By 7th October, after other measures had been taken, Royal Proclamations were issued in London calling the reserves to the colours. War began when the Boers invaded British territory on 12th October.

[1] The vital significance of this speech is sometimes overlooked. See the emphasis placed upon it in Garvin, *Chamberlain*, vol. III, p. 412; and in J. A. Spender, *Life of Sir Henry Campbell-Bannerman*, vol. I, pp. 231 ff.

IV

The first stage of the war was marked out by an unbroken tale of British defeats and disasters. In the political sphere these developments served to unite the British people behind the Unionist Government. A frenzy of patriotism brought Chamberlain the popular support he desired.

In Milner's case, the public was now able to recognise a significant change in his status. His warnings at Graaf-Reinet, his cable of the 4th of May, his firm stand at Bloemfontein—were all looked upon in a new light. Sir Alfred was no longer a gifted civil servant, highly regarded at Whitehall; he had now become an Imperial statesman of the first rank. The Unionist Party, in particular, looked upon Milner as the man who had mastered the situation in South Africa, and had then struggled mightily in order to get his country ready in time. He was the new champion of the Imperial cause.

It is, however, a sad fact of politics that when an individual is treated as a hero by one of the parties in the State, he at once becomes the target of the other parties. This was now Sir Alfred's fate; as time passed Milner, the "cross-bench man", was dragged into the whirlpool of party politics.

The reason for this development lay in the condition of the Liberal Party. For years past the Liberals had been divided into quarrelling factions. As the war went on these divisions became more prominent. The party leader, Campbell-Bannerman, refused to commit himself to either side for a long time; his object was to prevent a definite split. On the left were the Pro-Boers, dominated by their unqualified opposition to the war and to the Government and the High Commissioner they held responsible for it. They included among their leaders Sir William Harcourt, John Morley, John Burns and a rising young Welshman named Lloyd George. On the other side was a group known as the Liberal Imperialists. Their leader was Lord Rosebery, but he only led on occasion; the real power of the Liberal Imperialists lay with Asquith, Sir Edward Grey, R. B. Haldane, and Sir Henry Fowler. This group confined its criticism to the inefficient conduct of the war, although they approved of the war itself. They despised Chamberlain but most of them admired Milner and tried to support him as the one Imperialist on the Unionist side worthy of national approval. Chamberlain struck back at both factions with that envenomed skill which marked him out as the most capable politician of his day.

As their differences increased passions rose in either camp; by the summer of 1901 the Liberals were assailing the Government and each other in public, especially at political dinners and banquets. This was the famous "war to the knife—and fork" which rent the Liberal Party in this period. In these mighty clashes no one in authority was spared from attack.

The best example of Milner's new position occurred a little earlier, in the spring of 1901. In May he came home for a rest from his massive labours at the seat of the war. The Pro-Boers who had been attacking him for some time spread a rumour that he was being summoned to London in order to be dismissed in disgrace. Chamberlain decided to seize upon this situation in order to strike a blow that would attract the attention of the whole Empire. He arranged a spectacular demonstration, a "Roman triumph", for the returning Proconsul. Milner was met at the station by the Prime Minister and other members of the Cabinet. He was at once taken to the presence of the King, and emerged from the interview as a Peer of the United Kingdom. Later on, he was created a Privy Councillor; finally, he was presented with the Freedom of the City. These striking developments had a profound effect upon contemporary opinion. The only civilian in living memory who had been afforded such a reception was Disraeli, when he returned in triumph from the Berlin Congress, decades before.

From this time Lord Milner could do no wrong in the

eyes of the Unionists, and nothing right in the opinion of the Liberals, although the Liberal Imperialists continued to support him.

Victory in South Africa came in the following year. A brilliant journalist of the day, H. W. Nevinson, who had known him at Balliol, visited Milner a few days before the treaty was signed. He has left us with a vivid picture of the exhausted High Commissioner:[1]

I found him looking older, nearly bald, and deeply wrinkled. . . He cannot pronounce "th" clearly, perhaps owing to his German education, and it gives him a tone of weakness. He was not so polished and "superior" as I remember in old days. . . He dwelt very much on the personal side of things, especially on his own career . . . and described what a terrible five years he had been through; how he had been fighting all the time—with Boers, English, Colonials, everyone; how he expected to be flung aside ("scuppered" was his repeated word) soon after the war was over, and on this he spoke bitterly . . .

. . . My general impression was of a perfectly honourable and very sensitive nature, rather inclined to introspection and examination of his own motives; perhaps inclined to exaggerate himself generally, like a man always on the defensive, without the calm assurance and unquestioning belief of a born conqueror in his cause. . .

V

After the peace treaty was signed Milner was advanced in the peerage and became Viscount Milner of St. James's and Cape Town. Long before, in February 1901, he had been asked to undertake the administration of the two Boer States, which were now annexed to the Empire as the Transvaal and the Orange River Colony. Although he retained the title of High Commissioner, Lord Milner gave up the Governorship of the Cape Colony and moved the seat of his authority to the Transvaal, in order to come to grips with the many problems that confronted him there.

The task of reconstructing the civil administration in the two colonies was a tremendous challenge. With farsighted

[1] H. W. Nevinson, *Changes and Chances* (London, 1923), pp. 318–20.

wisdom, Milner had begun his preparations long before the war was over. Within a month of the signing of the Treaty of Vereeniging he published, in June 1902, the Letters Patent which established a new system of Crown Colony Government in the conquered territories.

This was only a beginning. The business of reconstruction after such a long war was an enormous undertaking. Thousands of the enemy had to be resettled on their farms; they had to be provided with the necessities of existence because their homes had been burnt in the course of military actions during the guerilla; capital had to be provided for irrigation schemes and those other agricultural improvements which the Boers had always neglected. The gold-mining industry, the key to the prosperity of the whole area, had to be started up once more, and as quickly as possible. The railways were in urgent need of repair, and new lines were required. In the towns, new systems of municipal government were needed to replace the corrupt machines of the Boers, which, in any case, were no longer functioning. All these problems and many others fell under Lord Milner's hand. Every administrative task was made more complex by the ravages of the war.

In this new phase of his career, Lord Milner demonstrated administrative ability of the very highest order. Although the English Radicals continued in their bitter opposition to him, many others realised that no ordinary Imperial statesman could have done the job so well. It has been said, and correctly, that the reconstruction of South Africa after the Boer War remains one of the great achievements in the history of British Imperialism.[1]

One remarkable aspect of his administration was the corpus of brilliant young men from Oxford and from the Colonial Office which Milner gathered about him as assistants. He realised that the burden of his affairs made it necessary for him to delegate authority, in a variety of

[1] The remark is made in Julian Amery, *Life of Joseph Chamberlain* (London, 1951) vol. IV, p. 67.

directions. In the selection of his lieutenants, however, he struck out on an untraditional line, and for a good reason. In 1900, before his plans became known, he explained it to Sir Percy Fitzpatrick:[1]

". . . I mean to have young men. There will be a regular rumpus and a lot of talk about boys and Oxford and jobs and all that. . . Well I value brains and character more than experience. First class men of experience are not to be got. Nothing one could offer would tempt them to give up what they have. . . No! I shall not be here for very long but when I go I mean to leave behind me young men with plenty of work in them. . ."

This was the origin of the famous "Milner Kindergarten"; the nickname had been applied to Milner's group in the first place by Sir William Marriott, a former Judge Advocate-General, who did not like either the High Commissioner or his young friends. Although his object was derision, the group soon became proud of the title and regarded membership in the Kindergarten as a distinction of the first quality.

The reason was obvious. Lord Milner selected the members with care, and then put into their hands power and opportunity of the kind most young men can only dream about. His policy involved far more than the offer of interesting jobs; their task, under his direction, was to remake an entire country. Nor was this all; every member of the Kindergarten realised that his work in the two Boer Colonies, however important in itself, was only part of a larger scheme. Every aspect of their plans was designed to further the cause of a Union of all the South African Colonies, and behind this goal lay the greater idea for which all of them laboured, the idea of a Federation for the entire British Empire. It was their intention to achieve a Union of South Africa, and then to hold up their achievement as a signpost to guide the entire Imperial movement, in Britain and in all the other territories of the Crown.

The personality of their chief was another factor that

[1] These remarks are taken from Sir Percy Fitzpatrick, *Lord Milner and his Work* (Reprinted from the *Cape Times*), p. 4.

served to awaken the pride and enthusiasm of the group. Milner never became a popular man, but he was an incomparable leader for those who were allowed to come close to him. He roused in his lieutenants feelings of respect, devotion, and even awe. Any important statesman usually attracts to himself a group of secretaries and assistants who admire their chief and entertain feelings of loyalty for him; in Milner's case, however, something extra-ordinary occurred. He created a school of disciples that looked upon him as their master. These disciples—Geoffrey Robinson, Philip Kerr (later Lord Lothian), R. H. Brand, John Buchan, and others—were men destined to play significant and peculiar roles in the history of their country. We shall meet them again in the course of this study.

High opinions of Milner were not, of course, confined to the members of the Kindergarten. His conduct in South Africa gained for him the respect of Imperialists in all the British territories. By the end of his period of service there he was recognised as a man who would adorn any position in the service of the Crown, however exalted.

In 1903 he was offered the post of Secretary of State for the Colonies, and two years later he was asked to become Viceroy of India.

The first of these tremendous offers came at a moment of political crisis, in the autumn of 1903. Milner was on leave in Europe when Joseph Chamberlain resigned from the Government in order to begin his campaign for Tariff Reform and Imperial Preference. This development had an explosive effect upon the further course of English politics; it dominated the actions of both parties for nearly a decade.

The resignation was a challenge. By it, Chamberlain sought to defy Arthur Balfour, the Prime Minister. He meant to bend Balfour to his will by demonstrating to him the popularity of the Tariff Reform campaign in the country.

Faced with a first-class political problem, Balfour reacted with cool and ruthless skill. He instantly forced certain of his Ministerial colleagues to resign, and replaced them with lesser men. In this way he made certain of his own control over policy at the same time that a liaison was maintained with those who disagreed with him.

In an attempt to strengthen these arrangements even further the Prime Minister despatched a messenger to Milner at Carlsbad, where he was taking the cure in company with a number of friends. In his letter Balfour invited Milner to join the Government as Chamberlain's successor in the Colonial Department. Even before Milner could reply, Balfour increased the pressure upon him by writing again in order to convey the opinion of the King, who was anxious for Milner to accept.

Joseph Chamberlain was without doubt the greatest Colonial Secretary in history. Milner could not help but be honoured by these expressions of confidence from such high quarters; despite them, however, he refused the place. He explained to Balfour that it was his duty to remain in South Africa until his task of reconstruction was more nearly completed. He felt also, and its important for us to notice this opinion, that in case the Unionist Government was turned out of office, he would be "less powerless for good as a returned proconsul, free from party connections, than as a rejected Minister".[1]

The second of these tremendous offers was made in the summer of 1905, shortly after Milner's return to England. For a long time the Indian Viceroy, Lord Curzon, had been a source of irritation to the Government; his cavalier actions had caused unnecessary friction in India and at home on several occasions; the last of these disturbances involved him in a bitter quarrel with Lord Kitchener. Curzon, driven almost to despair by the tactics of his enemy, resigned his post in August 1905.

The position of Viceroy of India was "the greatest post under the Crown abroad". As soon as Balfour learned of the resignation he sent a telegram to his Private Secretary, J. S. Sandars. This telegram reveals the high

[1] Headlam, vol. II, p. 474.

position Milner occupied in the mind of the Prime Minister:[1]

TO SANDARS, 10 DOWNING STREET.   AUG. 14
I HEAR RESIGNATION FINAL PLEASE ENQUIRE WHETHER
I MAY OFFER TO MILNER MINTO JERSEY AMPTHILL
PROBABLY IN THAT ORDER . . .
                                                    BALFOUR.

When Lord Lansdowne, the Foreign Secretary, heard of
the resignation he too thought of Milner at once; in a letter
marked "Secret" he informed Balfour of his preferences;[2]

George Curzon, as most of us anticipated, resigned, and I do not
suppose you will press him to reconsider. . .

I do not know whether you have already made up your mind as
to a successor. . .

Milner would be admirable, but he is a bachelor which is a serious
drawback, and will he want to begin hard work again so soon?

Jersey I think would be excellent. . . Please consider whether
Minto might not do. . .

Meanwhile, St. John Brodrick, the Secretary of State for
India, now intervened. He knew that Milner was in urgent
need of a long rest but he begged Balfour for authority to press
Milner to accept the position. The Prime Minister's only comment was: "What a murrain there is among Viceroys! . . ."[3]

Despite the eagerness of the Cabinet Ministers, Milner
refused the place. He called at the India Office and told
Brodrick that if the offer were formally made, he would not
accept it. He was exhausted by his long period of service in
South Africa and was resolved to rest for a year before he
concerned himself with any new public work. The confidence of Ministers in his capacities, however gratifying, was
not enough to deflect him from his decision.

VII

Long before Lord Milner left South Africa he knew that

[1] B.M.Add.MSS.49763 (Balfour Papers) Balfour to Sandars, 14th August 1905.
[2] B.M.Add.MSS.49729 (Balfour Papers) Lansdowne to Balfour, 15th August 1905,
marked "Secret".
[3] B.M.Add.MSS.49763 (Balfour Papers) Balfour to Sandars, *n.d.*

no Liberal Government, whatever its complexion, would permit him to remain in a position of authority. As Balfour's Ministry tottered to its fall, the High Commissioner realised that his days in South Africa were numbered. In these circumstances he became a man with a problem; and it was a problem to which he could discover no easy solution.

He was still determined to do what he could to advance the cause of the Empire, but he was unable to decide upon the proper sphere of activity for his energy and devotion. Certainly he was a tired man, but his faith in the Imperial idea was not quenched by his physical exhaustion. He needed to rest and recuperate for a long time, but what could he do when the strain of South African affairs was removed? What course lay open to him at home when his flagging energies were revived? How could he obtain the power and authority that would permit him to guide the Imperial movement in any new crises that might arise to threaten the Empire?

In the ordinary way a man of his quality could expect to take his place among the leaders of the Imperial party in the House of Lords. But Lord Milner's condition at the end of his South African period of service was far from ordinary. It was, in fact, exceptional.

His experiences in South Africa served to convince him that the English system of government was inefficient and worthless. He felt only loathing for the way things were done in England, in the political sphere. This opinion was one that was shared by a small number of contemporary statesmen, but in Milner's case the feeling amounted to a conviction; it was in the degree and quality of his attitude that he stood out as one who was different from his fellows. In 1905, when he returned to England, he was reluctant to play any part in the ordinary political life of his country. He despised English politics.

He believed that the parliamentary system, based upon the necessities of party and the whims of a "rotten public opinion", was totally unfitted for the rule of a great Empire.

He especially loathed those compromises and arrangements, sometimes valid and sometimes not so valid, which make up the very stuff of politics.

It would be easy enough to reproduce his letters to a score of correspondents on this subject; however, his opinions as they were expressed in 1903 to a close friend, Lady Edward Cecil, will serve to establish the nature of his attitude, provided that we keep in mind that these documents are illustrations of his usual outlook upon affairs.

For some time, Milner had been anxious to suspend the Constitution of the Cape Colony, in order to rule it more efficiently. He had even threatened resignation, but Chamberlain refused to permit the suspension. In March 1903, Milner wrote to Lady Edward:[1]

> All the interferences from home are bad. . . No man can expect to have all his own way. But I will not be their agent for big mistakes . . . It is not very likely that they will press me for these. Joe, as dictator, never would . . . But Joe may, under certain circumstances, give way to the pressure of parliamentary necessities, of Party, of a rotten public opinion.
> . . . But the system is wrong . . . I set sail in a rotten ship. . . The day might come—who knows?—when I should have the opportunity of pointing out, *why* we make such a mess of things . . . *where* the system is wrong. But I should not attempt that for a long time . . . till personal bitterness had died out of me. . .

He wrote again a month later:

> . . . the system is hopeless. Only one man in a hundred dares give effect or utterance to the statesmanship that is in him. . . Perhaps a great *Charlatan*—political scallywag, buffoon, liar . . . and in other respects popular favourite—may some day arise, who is nevertheless a *statesman* . . . and who, having attained power by popular art, may use it for national ends. It is an off chance . . . If I am making sacrifices it is not for this effete and dislocated Body Politic. . .

These remarks were not the idle vapourings of a moment of frustration. Milner made them at a time when he had been engaged in a long struggle with Chamberlain over the suspension of the Constitution of the Cape Colony. He had a

[1] For these extracts from letters to Lady E. Cecil, see Headlam, vol. II, pp. 446–8.

powerful case. In strict logic, his was the correct course. He feared that despite the British victory in the war, the Boers of the Cape Colony, including many rebels, would seize power there in the ordinary course of parliamentary politics. It would be intolerable, he argued, to permit the Boers to nullify the result of the war merely because the British element in the Colony was not yet able to win a clear majority in the Cape Parliament.

Chamberlain, for his part, realised that the English public would be angered by so cavalier an action as the suspension of a Colonial Constitution. He knew also that the citizens of the other great Colonies, in every part of the Empire, were watching the development of affairs in South Africa. Their opinion of British Imperial policy would be affected, adversely, by so radical a solution to the problem. As an English politician, he believed in the democratic process, at home and in the Colonies. He realised that calculation about public opinion was part of the business of a British statesman. He refused to give way.

Chamberlain's biographer, Julian Amery, has pointed out the validity of Milner's opinion in the quarrel, but he has also observed of him that: "His genius was of the autocratic kind, and in his heart he never recognised with much good humour the right of the opposition . . . there were moments when he would have thought the suspension of the British constitution itself a wholesome step toward the more efficient development of the Empire".[1]

Now, as this quotation suggests, the English point, and in this case it is with justifiable pride, to the fact that their constitutional system is the greatest political work of man. They do not mean that their system is perfect; they do not imply that better and more efficient public and Imperial work could not be accomplished under some other system. But after centuries of experience the English like to believe that in an imperfect world their constitution provides them with a method of governing men that is better than any

[1] Julian Amery, *Life of Chamberlain*, vol. IV, p. 100.

other available alternative. John Buchan, one of Milner's disciples, once called his chief "Plato's philosopher-turned-king". This may be a fair description but it is certain that Milner was never able to understand the point of view of politicians like Chamberlain who believed in the consti-tutional arrangements of their country. Lord Milner could only see the tactics, and the evasions, and the faults of the system he loathed. These things were there, but Chamber-lain and others like him felt that their work involved them in much more; and they were not men prepared to abandon their authority to a philosopher. Their arena was the Cabinet and the House of Commons and the public platform, and they were proud of the work they could do in those places, even if it was open to valid criticism.

Lord Milner's problem in the political society of 1905 was recognised by friend and critic alike. One of his warmest admirers was Philip Kerr, later Lord Lothian, who served with him in South Africa, and also at Westminster. In 1925, when Milner died, Lord Lothian wrote an article about his old chief. In it, he fixed upon the difficult position of the returned Proconsul who disliked party politics but was eager to serve and guide the Empire. The reader who desires to understand Lord Milner after 1905 must pay some attention to Lothian's remarks. He devoted much of his article to Lord Milner's problem:[1]

... Lord Milner was really a Roman of the Augustan age... The absorbing passion of his life was the British Empire ... he saw in the preservation and development of its adminstrative ideals the principal hope for the progress of mankind.

The unsolved problem of Lord Milner's life was how to reconcile this great tradition of government with democracy ... he was unable to see how the democratic movement which was sweeping everything before it in his time was to be made compatible with that scientific unity and order which he perceived to be more than ever necessary in the complicated modern world. In every fibre of his being he loathed the slipshod com-promises, the optimistic "slogans", the vote- catching half-truths with which democracy seemed to compromise the majestic governing art...

[1] Philip Kerr, "Lord Milner" in *The Nation & the Athenaeum,* 23rd May 1925.

There was, as Lord Lothian suggests, an air of Roman gravity about Milner; but in the years between 1905 and 1916, in that long period after his return from South Africa and before he enjoyed power once again, there was something else that we will notice about him. It was the bitter feeling of a man who knows that he can rule the State well, but must sit by and watch lesser men fumble with the government of the country. This was the essence of Lord Milner's problem until the crisis of the World War returned him to a seat of authority in the War Cabinet.

PART II
OPPOSITION

III.   Chinese Slavery: The Background

The Proconsul's return – A battering blow – Hostility of
Sir Henry Campbell-Bannerman – The Liberal Imperialists
support Milner – The *religio Milneriana* – A naked clash over
the idea of Empire – The "Milner wedge" – Chinese
coolies on the Rand – The Economic aspect – The
Imperial factor – Asquith, Grey and Haldane support the
Chinese plan – Details of the Chinese Labour Ordinance
– An explosion of anger – The trio of Milner worshippers is
broken up – A cruel blow to Milner's hopes – Mrs. Asquith
and the Wallpaper for 10 Downing Street – Milner, the
tool of "parasites" – Lord Milner's blunder – "Extraordinary stupidity" of Milner – Reasons for Arthur
Balfour's anger – "Slavery under the British Flag" – The
triumph of Sir Henry Campbell-Bannerman – Milner
vulnerable to any attack.

I

IN the spring of 1905 Lord Milner resigned his offices in
South Africa and began to prepare for the next phase of
his life. His first task was to provide himself with an
income, since he refused to accept a pension from the State.
In order to earn his living he turned to the City where he
was at once appointed to a number of directorships. He
became associated as a director with the London Joint Stock
Bank, the Bank of British West Africa, the Rio Tinto Company, the Mortgage Company of Egypt, and other firms of
the kind. Shortly after his return to London he noted in a
diary that the capital value of his investments was slightly
more than £25,000.

Early in the first session of the Parliament elected in
January 1906 the Liberal Ministry made ready to introduce
its plan for the future government of South Africa. Lord

Milner at once intervened, for no one in England knew South Africa as he did. He entertained the curious notion that he would be allowed to bring his rich experience to bear upon the matter. As a result of this intervention he brought down upon himself an avalanche.

The January elections had provided the Liberal Ministry with an unprecedented majority in the Commons; so powerful was the tide which confirmed Sir Henry Campbell-Bannerman and his Government in office that the host of their supporters included in addition to the ordinary Liberal rank and file a large number of Radical extremists, partisans, and "cranks" who had never expected to win their seats in the first place.

On the morrow of the 1906 election these triumphant Radicals resembled Lord Milner in one thing only; they were men who knew they were right, and were dangerous in consequence. In their fervour they proposed to deal Milner a battering blow, and remove him once and for all from the British political scene. Their moral indignation at his activities in South Africa convinced them that they were justified in any course, however extreme, where he was concerned.

Milner came back from South Africa in the certain knowledge that the Liberals would soon be in power, and that they would do what they could to defeat his arrangements for the government of the Transvaal and the Orange River Colony. But the Radicals were not content with this solution; they were anxious to treat with the ex-High Commissioner on a more personal level. They now decided to follow a cardinal rule of low and high politics alike; this rule was— Never kick a man except when he is down.

The Radical attack upon Lord Milner in 1906 has never received the attention it deserves from students of English political history. The attack was not an isolated incident; it had profound effects upon the future relations between parties, as we shall see.

The action of the Radicals reflected an anger not often

observed in English public life; but the anger of ardent back-benchers seldom becomes effective in Parliament unless the leaders of their party accept its political validity. In this case, Lord Milner had aroused the formidable enmity of Sir Henry Campbell-Bannerman, the new Prime Minister. It was his attitude which provided the Radicals with their opportunity.

II

In 1899 Campbell-Bannerman became leader of the Liberal Party. At that time he was completely eclipsed by Sir William Harcourt and Lord Rosebery, brilliant statesmen who seemed to be much more qualified to lead. Their rivalry, however, gave Campbell-Bannerman his chance. He decided that his main business was to preserve intact the unity of his party until those better days when he could guide it back to the promised land. His position was far from easy; the party was divided into bitterly opposed factions. On the one hand, the Pro-Boers were suspicious of Imperial ideas and feared that the "infection of Jingoism" was attacking the Liberal creed; on the other, the Liberal Imperialists were caught up in the great movement of Imperialism; they sought to discard the Little England outlook of an earlier time and to put in its place more modern doctrines.

After a brief period as leader Campbell-Bannerman found that his difficult task was complicated by the influence Milner exerted upon one section of the Liberal Party. The Liberal Imperialists generally and Asquith, Grey and Haldane in particular became very angry whenever any member of their party criticised Milner. They looked upon him as a man who deserved their confidence; and they maintained a regular correspondence with him so that they could support his policies in the way that he desired Campbell-Bannerman soon came to regard Milner as an obstacle to the unity of the Liberal Party. He decided that Milner made his problems as leader more complex than they might have been; and he began to resent the prestige of the High Commissioner as yet another of his many burdens. His biographer put the matter concisely:[1]

> Rightly or wrongly, he attributed a large part of his difficulties with his colleagues and especially those of them who were Balliol men to what he characteristically called the *religio Milneriana* ... this blind belief in a Balliol hero he regarded as a psychological infirmity of the Oxford mind.

There was a second area of disagreement. Campbell-Bannerman was irritated by Milner's attitude to public life. Sir Henry was, in the old phrase, a great House of Commons man. This meant, in this case, that he believed that the business of the State was best discharged in Parliament. His rival, Lord Rosebery, was a man who abandoned party connections, who sought to strike out on his own whenever he chose, who avoided regular responsibilities only to clutch at power whenever opportunity offered. Campbell-Bannerman resented Rosebery's actions because he felt that a party leader should carry out his duties day in and day out, in good times and in bad. In this period, however, Rosebery found the party connection a tedious tie; he sought to influence events from a position above the parties in the State. Like Milner, he was now embarked upon the path that would lead him eventually to the status of a "cross-bench man". Campbell-Bannerman believed in the party system; experience soon taught him to suspect those like Milner who held it in contempt.

A third factor was equally important. By the summer of 1900 Campbell-Bannerman's hostility to Milner became even more intense. The reason for this development was a difference in outlook which brought their latent antagonism out of the realm of politics and on to the higher plane of Imperial statesmanship.

Campbell-Bannerman had a genuine interest in Imperial matters although his enemies sometimes sought to deny

[1] J. A. Spender, *Life of Sir Henry Campbell-Bannerman* (London, 1932), vol. I, p. 264, hereafter cited as Spender, *Campbell-Bannerman*.

this fact. He looked upon the Empire as a "commonwealth of free nations"[1] which depended for healthy existence upon the exercise of Liberal principles.

From the very beginning of the Boer War he decided that a British victory must mean the end of the dual system in South Africa, and the annexation of the two republics. The chief object of this policy was to make certain of the safety of the Imperial power; secondly, he desired to secure the harmonious co-operation of the two peoples, British and Dutch, in the new Colonies.

In the summer of 1900 it seemed that the war was almost over. In a speech of vital significance, at Glasgow on 7th June, Campbell-Bannerman explored the question of how the safety of the Empire and the harmony of British and Dutch could be achieved:

> Now, how is this to be done? Is that a question which I need ask any meeting of Liberals? We need have no doubt how it is to be done—by applying our Liberal principles from which the strength of the Empire has been derived and on which it depends... Let us restore as early as possible and let us maintain those rights of self-government which give not only life and vigour but contentment and loyalty to every colony which enjoys them.

His biographer rightly says that:[2] "No speech in the whole of his career deserves more careful attention". This Glasgow speech was typical of Campbell-Bannerman's

[1] Spender, *Campbell-Bannerman*, vol. II, p. 97. The phrase was used in 1903. Milner's disciples liked to say that they were the only ones who made popular the term "commonwealth".

[2] *Ibid.*, vol. I, p. 283. In this connection we ought to notice Edward Crankshaw, *The Forsaken Idea, A Study of Viscount Milner* (London, 1952), p. 107, hereafter cited as Crankshaw, *Forsaken Idea*, which states: "Campbell-Bannerman, Lloyd George, and the Little Englanders . . . were, of course, openly implacable and on principle against anything at all calculated to strengthen the British position in South Africa". This statement is made in connection with the question of Chinese labour in the Transvaal. It is obviously unfair to Campbell-Bannerman, who had definite ideas about strengthening the British position in South Africa, as we have shown above. The theme of Crankshaw's book seems to be that the Britain of the 1950s would be saved by recourse to Lord Milner's ideas. It is fair to say that in tone this book is hagiographical since Lord Milner, according to it, was always right and his opponents were almost always wrong. Crankshaw's brassy comments on Campbell-Bannerman should be compared with the acute analysis in Nicholas Mansergh, *South Africa 1906–61* (London, 1962), pp. 20 ff, pp. 92–9.

political bravery; the war was still being waged and British soldiers were still being killed by the enemy. Despite this, he was prepared to talk about self-government. The Pro-Boers of his own party refused, as yet, to accept the idea of annexation as a valid course; even Asquith, a Liberal Imperialist, had declared in an ardent moment that there must be no annexations in the event of victory. Nevertheless, Campbell-Bannerman took this early opportunity to reveal his Imperial purpose.

As he saw it, the requirements of the Empire made it necessary to annex the conquered republics; these same requirements also made it necessary to grant to the Boers, as quickly as possible, a system of Colonial self-government so that they would realise what it meant to be citizens of a Liberal Empire. The arguments of this speech became the principles which guided his course from this moment; and they remained with him until he put them into effect as Prime Minister.

It was central to Milner's Imperial statesmanship, however, that the Boer and British inhabitants of the new Colonies could not be granted self-government for a considerable period of time. To follow any other course would mean, in Milner's opinion, that the fruits of victory were to be thrown away in order to satisfy a ridiculous Liberal theory that ought not to be applied to a dangerous and resourceful enemy. Milner, and the Unionist Ministry, decided that self-government should be postponed for a time; they arranged to replace the military government of the Boer territories with a system of Crown Colony government, based on the principle that genuine authority was to be in the hands of nominated officials, and not in the control of the elected representatives of the people.

This difference in outlook was nothing less than a naked clash over the idea of Empire. Milner was disgusted by the Liberal attitude; he knew the Boers as no one else did, and his experience convinced him that time, more than anything else, was required for the proper settlement of affairs in

SIR HENRY CAMPBELL-BANNERMAN

"He knew how to bide his time".

South Africa. Campbell-Bannerman marked down the High Commissioner's opinion as yet another example of how Imperialists of his type were ready to destroy the Liberal basis of the Empire upon which all depended.

III

Sir Henry Campbell-Bannerman's enmity was something to avoid. He was not the man to forgive or forget those who wantonly toyed with the fate of Liberalism; and, as his private secretary said of him after his death, he was a good hater. He knew how to bide his time.

On the surface, he appeared to be a worthy man of the second rank, but this was an illusion he fostered for a definite purpose. In fact, the impression he sought to convey that he was merely a simple and genial fellow was an item of his political equipment. As a result, he was always underestimated by cleverer men.

Sir Henry was a man of parts, and not the rough Scotsman he pretended to be. He was a cosmopolitan who regularly visited Paris, Vienna, Brussels, and Marienbad. When a royal princess desired to improve the quality of her coffee, he was able to call her attention to a shop in Vienna that prepared the finest coffee in Europe; he was an epicure of the first rank and was even applied to by King Edward VII for his opinion in culinary matters.

He possessed a cynical and well-developed sense of humour. In his private correspondence Rosebery was often referred to as "the Lord"; Sir Charles Dilke, a leader of the Radical section of the party, was "Citizen Dilke"; Sir William Harcourt, a corpulent man who lived at Malwood, was "that bulky nymph, the fair Malwoodina"; Sir Edward Grey, who sometimes disagreed with him, opposed his designs with "Greyish obstinacy".

Unlike his predecessors in the leadership Campbell-Bannerman did not regard himself as an exalted figure; for this reason affronts to his dignity were never looked upon as crises or emergencies. Nevertheless, he believed in Liberalism and in the Liberal Party. From the moment he became leader he resolved to restore the party to its rightful place in national affairs. His honesty and integrity may not have been sparkling qualities but in the long run they gained for him a respect neither Harcourt nor Rosebery ever received. He was, in fine, better qualified than most to lead and control a divided party that had no chance to gain power for a long time.

In his innocence of English politics Lord Milner had made an enemy who was prepared to wait for a Liberal victory; but when he did at last achieve power, Campbell-Bannerman was resolved to revenge himself upon those who had tampered with the destiny of the Liberal Party and the country. Milner was marked down in his mind as a dangerous element in national life who would be dealt with when circumstances allowed.

Until 1902 Chamberlain regularly drove the "Milner wedge" into the Liberal ranks whenever opportunity offered. Campbell-Bannerman could do little to heal the divisions in his party in the face of these tactics. When the Radicals criticised the High Commissioner they were set upon by the Liberal Imperialists who denounced them and defended the actions of their friend—in the House, in private, and at public meetings in the country. Asquith put the matter bluntly: "To countenance an attack on Milner", he told Campbell-Bannerman, "would be to split the party at once into fragments".[1]

However, when the peace treaty with the Boers was signed in 1902 Imperial matters became less prominent in English politics. The Government's Education Bill of that year outraged the feelings of Nonconformists in both parties. At the same time the issue of protection began to loom up as the dominating political topic of the day. By 1903 when Chamberlain's campaign for Tariff Reform began in earnest, politicians devoted all their energies to

---

[1] Sir Charles Mallet, *Herbert Gladstone* (London, 1932), p. 179.

this vital controversy. It was at this time that Asquith was definitely marked out as a future Liberal Prime Minister for wherever Chamberlain went in the course of his crusade Asquith followed, in order to challenge and deny the validity of his arguments. "Wonderful speeches", murmured Sir Henry Campbell-Bannerman, "how can these fellows ever have gone wrong?"

It seemed that Lord Milner would be ignored as the Liberals rallied to attack the Unionist Government on these other issues. Early in 1904, however, the situation was completely changed. It was then learned that the High Commissioner proposed to introduce indentured Chinese coolies into the Transvaal to work in the Rand mines as unskilled labourers.

The decision to have recourse to the Chinese was not lightly taken. Chamberlain refused to consider the proposal because he instantly recognised the political danger in the plan. Lord Milner, however, regarded the presence of the Chinese workers in the mines as a political and economic necessity; and he forced the Unionist Cabinet to comply with his wishes.

Milner looked upon these Chinese labourers as the key to the success of his entire South African policy. The prosperity of South Africa depended upon the condition of the gold-mining industry, but the mines could not be worked to their full capacity at this time because of a shortage of unskilled labour. Milner had recourse to every kind of expedient before he fixed upon the Chinamen as the answer to his problem. Unskilled white men were allowed to work in one mine, but there were objections from their fellow workers and from the mine owners, who were worried about increased costs; native workers from other parts of South Africa were sought out, in vain; some Englishmen were brought to the Transvaal to do unskilled work, but the project was a failure. By 1903 the High Commissioner was convinced that his only chance to save the situation lay in bringing indentured Asiatic workers into the country. In

Milner's opinion the time factor was crucial; to delay the arrival of the Chinamen would be to jeopardise the economic foundation of his whole programme of reconstruction.

There was an even more vital aspect. Milner was convinced that the struggle between Briton and Boer would go on in South Africa, despite the issue of the war. How could he, as an Imperialist, make certain that the victory would not be lost in the years to come? The answer seemed simple to his logical mind; it was to increase the British population of the country until they outnumbered the Dutch. "If two years hence", he said, "there are three men of British race to two of Dutch, the country will be safe. . . If there are three of Dutch to two British, we shall have perpetual difficulty".[1]

The next question followed as a matter of course; what could he do in order to increase the British element? Immigrants would come to South Africa, he decided, if they had the opportunity to maintain themselves at a decent standard of life. This standard depended upon the economic condition of the country. If the mines prospered secondary industries would flourish, and social conditions would so improve that the "right type of Britons", as he called them, would be eager to settle in the Transvaal. It thus happened that his Imperial policy for South Africa, as well as his immediate economic plans, came to depend upon the Chinamen who would, at a stroke, supply the mines with the one element they lacked in the post-war period of reconstruction.

In the autumn of 1903 Milner came to England, determined to force the Ministry to a decision about Asiatic workers. Alfred Lyttelton, the new Colonial Secretary, was not a man of Chamberlain's political quality; his respect for Milner decided the issue; he agreed to support the High Commissioner's proposals.

A crucial factor at this stage was the attitude of the Liberal Imperialists who had helped Milner so much in the

[1] Quoted in E. A. Walker, *Lord Milner in South Africa* (London, 1942), p. 16.

past. Even before he confronted the Cabinet Milner sought out Asquith, Grey and Haldane in order to explain his plan and to sound them about it:[1]

> Milner was fully aware that a policy of this kind could not be carried through, if it were to be used as a political cry. But as the result of conversations with the more moderate section, he had been assured that those Liberals who had supported him during the war, would continue to do so in a measure which he showed them to be essential to a successful peace... On that understanding, and that understanding alone, he had decided to go on with ... (the) ... project...

IV

On 10th February 1904 a Chinese Labour Ordinance, sanctioned by the Colonial Office, was passed by the Transvaal Council. The details of this measure were responsible for the troubles that followed.

The Ordinance provided that the Chinese were to come to the Transvaal for a fixed term of years only; during their stay they were to reside in compounds which they were forbidden to leave, save on a permit limited to a period of forty-eight hours and restricted to the district around the mines; the Chinese were not allowed to own any real property or mineral rights, nor were they permitted to engage in any business; they were to work for the mine owners for ten hours of the day and for six days each week; they were granted no rights of access to the courts of law; fourteen particular offences were defined in the Ordinance and special penalties, different from those usually sanctioned by the law, were provided. Although the Chinese were not forbidden to bring their families with them, the conditions were such that it would be impossible for them to do so. At first, no minimum wage was guaranteed, but later on a minimum of 2s. per day was fixed, in their interest.

[1] Headlam, vol. II, p. 477 and n. (1) which states emphatically that Milner was promised the support of the Liberal Imperialists "Notably in long conversations after dinner-parties given by the Asquiths, on the 1st and 29th October, in which Sir Edward Grey (Lord Grey) and Mr. (Lord) Haldane took part". Headlam's statement is clear though he adduces no documents on this point.

The Ordinance produced an explosion of anger in Britain when its details became known. A hymn of hatred and rage against Milner and the Unionist Government swelled up in every section of the country. Trade Unionists were convinced that cheaply paid Chinamen were depriving them of jobs so that the Rand capitalists could increase their profits. Allied to this feeling was the anger of the Nonconformists who, on humanitarian grounds, objected to the conditions in which the Chinamen were to live. Those Radical and Nonconformist leaders who had suffered every kind of humiliation for years past because of their opposition to the Boer War now saw their worst prophecies fulfilled. They were resolved not to submit to this further degradation of British honour by a Unionist Ministry, prodded on by a ruthless High Commissioner.

At Westminster an agitation developed even more quickly than the feeling in the country. There, the politicians and those who concerned themselves with public matters had known of the plan for some time. On 8th February the Bishop of Worcester wrote to *The Times* in order to stress the moral dangers if the Chinamen were not accompanied by their families. He condemned their employment as an exploitation of mere "living tools" which fulfilled Aristotle's definition of slavery. On the 10th a large protest meeting was held in the Queen's Hall. The matter was then taken up in both Houses of Parliament. The most effective of these early attacks was made in the Commons by Herbert Samuel, the member for the Cleveland division of Yorkshire. His speech was not the isolated effort of a back-bench partisan; it was delivered at the suggestion of the Liberal leaders in the House.

On 19th February the controversy was continued in the Commons; in the division of that day Haldane was the only Liberal Imperialist leader to abstain from voting against the Chinese proposals. Three days later H. H. Asquith condemned the scheme because the House as the "trustee of the liberty of the subject throughout the Empire" had not yet seen the regulations. On 23rd February Sir Edward Grey reported to his wife that "There is a horrid set being made at Haldane because he abstained from the vote against Chinese labour. . . But he is the same dear old Haldane still".[1]

Sir Henry Campbell-Bannerman noticed with calm pleasure that the "trio of Milner worshippers" was at last broken up, even if the development was merely temporary.

The reaction of the Liberal Imperialists was a cruel blow to Lord Milner's hopes for the scheme. His friend, Leo Amery, then a staff member of *The Times*, sent him a report on these developments which reflected an expert's knowledge of affairs in England and in Parliament. His letter began with a general analysis of the opposition to Chinese labour:[2]

The last week or two has been giving us a splendid example of the impossibility of running the Empire by the British democracy in the House of Commons. If you had not had a Government already very shaky, and an Opposition thirsting for the spoils and still more for new cries on which to get in, you would never have heard anything about the Chinese Labour Ordinance. As it is, the thing has been worked with a vengeance. All the trade union leaders, who are much keener on being second-rate Liberal politicians than on really considering labour interests, are working the thing for all they are worth. Every little Bethel is an anti-Chinese assembly room . . .

And then he became more particular:

. . . I did think you had got Asquith straight on the point, but I am afraid the temptation, with office looming so near and wall paper for 10 Downing Street already selected by Mrs. A., was too much for him, and his performance was as bad as anybody else's, if not worse. Haldane won't speak, because he says he is too suspect with his own party. Lyttelton has fought excellently. . .

Amery then added a warning of vital significance:

However, there we are, and the storm may subside, but you may be sure that if you do get your Chinamen you will have enterprising people at work to try and "nose out" some scandal as to their treatment. . .

[1] Trevelyan, *Grey of Fallodon*, p. 87.
[2] Amery Papers, L. S. Amery to Milner, 26th February 1904.

On 21st March a vote of censure was moved against the Government by Campbell-Bannerman. By this time the agitation in the country was assuming tremendous proportions. The Unionists tried in vain to show that no British workmen were being deprived of employment because of the Chinese. They pointed out that similar Ordinances had been sanctioned in other Colonies by Liberal Governments. They emphasised that the Chinese were willing to go to South Africa because the wages there were many times greater than anything they could obtain in their own country. They denounced the Liberal and Radical agitation as a miserable attempt to gain votes by misleading an honest but ignorant population at home. The issue of Chinese Labour created so much heat that in some by-elections it received more prominence than did the great question of Tariff Reform and Imperial Preference on which the fate of the country seemed to depend.

Lord Milner was singled out as the villain most responsible for the introduction of "Chinese slavery" into South Africa; he was denounced as an agent of the mine owners who had betrayed his position of trust in order to satisfy the foreign capitalists of the Rand who cared only for profits and not at all for the Empire. After the first outbursts there was a lull in this storm of invective until further developments brought the issue into new prominence in 1905; but the hostility of the Radicals to Milner continued unabated despite the temporary pause in the Chinese agitation. An article in the *Daily News* of 13th October 1904 was not untypical of Radical opinion. On that day the paper said of Milner:

... The British Empire has never, perhaps, produced a ruler who has been so consistently wrong... He has never shown any width of outlook or breadth of sympathy. From first to last he has acted, not as the representative of the whole South African people, but as the tool of a set of parasites, whose presence is a curse to the country...

V

Despite their strong feelings about Chinese labour on the Rand the Liberals, so long as they remained in Opposition, were powerless to stop the arrival of the Chinamen. As soon as the coolies began to live in the compounds and to work in the mines, the cardinal issue about them became the nature of their treatment at the hands of their employers and those officials of the State who were appointed to look after their interests. Leo Amery had put his finger on this aspect of the matter at once; he warned Milner, as we have seen, that the treatment of the Chinese would be observed with very great care.

The original decision to import the Chinamen was dangerous enough. Lord Milner, despite Amery's warning, now proceeded to commit a blunder which gave the Radicals the chance they had been waiting for.

As early as 11th February 1904 the Chinese Minister, vigilant in the cause of his countrymen, suggested that a clause be inserted in the Ordinance providing that the employers should not be allowed to inflict corporal punishment on the Chinese workers, and that any violation of this provision should be punished by law.

The matter was referred directly to the High Commissioner. On 5th March 1904 his reply was sent to the Foreign Office by an official of the Colonial Department:[1]

No. 2. Colonial Office to Foreign Office.

Downing Street March 5, 1904.

Sir,

...I am directed by Mr. Secretary Lyttelton to state...that he has been in communication with the Governor of the Transvaal by telegraph on the subject of the Chinese Minister's note of the 11th February respecting the Transvaal Labour Importation Ordinance...

With regard to the...point raised by the Chinese Minister relating to corporal punishment, Lord Milner pointed out that any labourers

[1] Cd.2026. "Transvaal. Further Correspondence Relating to the Transvaal Labour Ordinance". May 1904.

imported would be amenable to the law of the land by which everybody, including whites, is liable to corporal punishment for certain offences. But no corporal punishment would be allowed except for such offences, and in these cases could only be inflicted after trial and sentence by a Magistrate or a Judge. . .

I am etc.

H. Bertram Cox.

This admirable document made the situation as clear as crystal; it served to allay the generous uneasiness of the Chinese Minister when the information it contained was conveyed to him by the Foreign Office.

From this time until the summer of 1905 Ministers were regularly interrogated in Parliament about the condition of the Chinamen in the compounds. On 16th and 17th May 1905, for example, Alfred Lyttelton, the Colonial Secretary, was asked in the House of Commons whether it was the case that some coolies had been tied by their pigtails "in such a way that their toes only just touch the ground"[1] because they had asked for wages of 2s. per day. The Minister denied that this had been done. Despite the denial extravagant rumours continued to circulate at Westminster and in the country.

As late as 27th July 1905 Lyttelton said in the course of a debate in the Commons that Chinamen were only flogged after conviction by a magistrate and on confirmation of the sentence by the Supreme Court. This was the answer he always gave in reply to a regular and protracted series of charges about illegal flogging. However, this statement of the 27th July was the last denial he was able to make.

At the end of August the Colonial Secretary was astounded to learn that the Chinamen were being flogged by their overseers without any recourse to the courts of law whatsoever. Upon enquiry he was even more surprised to discover that Lord Milner had given his sanction to this illegal state of affairs.

Lyttelton's explanation of this development was made in

[1] Cd.2786. "Transvaal. Further Correspondence Relating to the Labour in the Transvaal Mines". December 1905.

a very carefully worded telegram to Lord Selborne, who by that time had replaced Milner as the Governor of the Transvaal. This telegram, dated 24th October 1905, was published for all to see in December of that year so that it became a factor in the election campaign of January 1906: Lyttelton wrote to Selborne on 24th October:[1]

... At the end of August I received from you a statement as to an arrangement which Mr. Evans, the late Superintendent of Foreign Labour, had made on his own responsibility. There appears to be no record of this arrangement, and I accordingly referred to Mr. Evans for his account of it.

He states that, realising as he did the impossibility of personally inquiring into every trivial offence, and the desirability of allowing the compound manager some authority over the men for whose order he was responsible, he informed the mine managers that in cases of breach of discipline and trivial offences, for which it was not considered necessary to prosecute, he would not interfere if slight corporal punishment, limited in degree to punishment of such a nature as is permitted in schools in England, was administered after due enquiry, at which the offender should be present, before the Chinese-speaking compound manager...

He informed Lord Milner of his action, and the latter took no objection.

Subsequently, on his departure from the Transvaal, Mr. Evans informed Sir A. Lawley, the Lieutenant-Governor, who had recently returned from leave, to the same effect, and told him that the arrangement had received Lord Milner's sanction...

Although Lyttelton states that he learned about the illegal floggings in August, the information does not appear to have been conveyed to his fellow Ministers until late in September; the Blue-book (Cd.2786) which contains his explanation in its published form does not include any August statement from Lord Selborne dealing with the flogging, although reference is made to it. However, the news burst upon the distracted Unionist leaders at a particularly awkward time.

[1] *Ibid.*, "No. 36. Mr. Lyttelton to Governor the Earl of Selborne. Telegram, 24th October..."

VI

Throughout 1905, especially in the autumn of the year, Arthur Balfour was carefully calculating the advantages which would accrue to him in case he suddenly resigned office instead of following the more normal course of dissolving Parliament and arranging for a General Election. He sounded most of his colleagues on this important decision, but at this stage he had not yet definitely made up his mind. In any case, the idea of an election occupied a prominent place in the thoughts of all the Unionist leaders.

Balfour often found the business of ruling the State tedious, but he had long since schooled himself to accept the limitations and shortcomings of his principal colleagues and subordinates. He seldom allowed himself to become angry at their mistakes because he realised that few of his political friends, however earnest and sincere and hard-working they were, could attain his own perspicacity in public business. Since that was the case, he was fortified throughout his political career by a cool and philosophic calmness of outlook which enabled him to discharge his duties easily, without any of those crises of temper that so often mar the active statesman's life. Now, however, when he learned of Lord Milner's blunder, he burst out in a fit of irritation that deserves particular notice because it was so untypical.

He wrote first to Sir Alexander Acland-Hood, the Chief Whip of the Conservative Party, in order to tell him of the effect of Milner's action upon the party.[1]

Copy.	North Berwick.
Private.	Sep. 21st 1905.

My dear Alec,

I believe the arguments you advance against an Autumn Dissolution are practically unanswerable... But... I am full of misgivings... I think we may have renewed trouble over Chinese labour, owing to the extraordinary (and, at present, quite unexplained) stupidity of

[1] B.M.Add.MSS.49771 (Balfour Papers) Balfour to Acland-Hood, 21st September 1905.

Milner in permitting before he left Africa, the infliction of "light corporal punishment" on the coolies by the overseers. This gross illegality was stopped immediately by Selborne, but the Colonial Office got no information about it until the House was up. Alfred is boiling with rage, and declares it has completely spoiled his holiday. The public, however, so far do not seem to take *much* interest in it, and it may blow over. . .

Yours ever,
Arthur James Balfour.

On the same day the angry Prime Minister wrote to Lord Selborne about the matter. Selborne was one of Milner's warmest admirers but Balfour roundly declared to him that:[1]

. . . the worst rock ahead from a purely electioneering point of view is due to the quite inexplicable illegality of which Milner seems to have been guilty in permitting, before he left, overseers in the mines to inflict corporal punishment. I am anxiously waiting to see what excuse, if any, he can produce for this amazing blunder, which seems to violate every canon of international morality, of law, and of policy.

A month later Ministers were still occupied with the problem Lord Milner's mistake had thrust upon them. At the Colonial Office a deliberate attempt was made to exculpate Milner from some of the responsibility; he was, however, too honest a man to permit the authorities to carry out their plan. Bernard Holland, Alfred Lyttelton's private secretary at the Colonial Office, explained the details of the episode to Jack Sandars so that Balfour could be informed about them. On 20th October Sandars duly reported to the Prime Minister:[2]

. . . I sent you a telegram this morning which was the result of an interview I had with Bernard Holland on the subject of that blunder of Milner's about the treatment of the Chinese. Holland was very anxious that you should understand that Milner's had not been a cold assent to the paragraph relating to his responsibility. On the contrary, a paragraph designed to make it easier for him was rejected

---

[1] B.M.Add.MSS.49708 (Balfour Papers) Balfour to Selborne, 21st September 1905, copy marked "Private".

[2] B.M.Add.MSS.49764 (Balfour Papers) J. S. Sandars to Balfour, 20th October 1905, marked "Confidential".

71

by him, on the ground that he wished to take all the responsibility on his own shoulders. It is a horrid business. I told Holland that the papers ought not to be published...

It was in these circumstances that Alfred Lyttelton prepared his telegram of the 24th October, to which we have already made reference. Balfour took care to send the Colonial Secretary his own opinion of the case before the draft of the telegram was put into its final form: "... It is a bad business, and, in my opinion, we have great and just reason to complain of what has occurred in connection with Coolie labour... The more I consider the subject, the more amazed I am at Milner's carelessness!"[1]

The Lyttelton telegram of 24th October ended by denouncing the floggings in no uncertain terms:[2]

Your statement, which as I have already said reached me at the end of August, was the first intimation which I received from the Colony that official permission for any corporal punishment had been given...

But I profoundly regret that the corporal punishment, however slight, was authorised without the safeguards of the law, and that the matter was not brought to my notice as Secretary of State before it was authorised.

Mr. Evans appears to have held that it was possible to draw a distinction between slight corporal punishment for disciplinary purposes and flogging, for which the Government was bound to prosecute if brought to its notice. Such a distinction cannot be maintained.

VII

There were good reasons for Arthur Balfour's anger. Until this time only some of the secrets about the Chinese coolies had been published. The Prime Minister was certain that as soon as the Liberals came to power further revelations would be made. This is exactly what happened when Balfour resigned office in December 1905. The first

[1] B.M.Add.MSS.49775 (Balfour Papers) Balfour to Lyttelton, 20th October 1905, marked "Private".
[2] Cd. 2786. "Transvaal. Further Correspondence..." December 1905.

act of Lord Elgin, the new Colonial Secretary, was to lay open the archives of his Department.

In May 1904, as we have seen, the Conservative Government published the Blue-book (Cd.2026) which contained Lord Milner's reply to the Chinese Minister promising that no corporal punishment would be permitted, save after trial and sentence by a Magistrate or a Judge.

In December 1905, however, the Lyttelton telegram was also published; it revealed that the Chinese had been subjected to light corporal punishment "without the safeguards of the law". The telegram also made it clear that Lord Milner raised no objection to this illegal development, when it was explained to him. Exactly what Milner had done was still a mystery, but these other facts became known to the public before the election campaign of December-January 1906.

The Liberals and Radicals were thus in a position to maintain that Lord Milner had involved the Foreign Office in statements which were eventually falsified by developments in South Africa; they could point out that he had failed to inform the Colonial Secretary of his actions in the matter, and that he had allowed Lyttelton to deny that any illegal floggings had taken place; as a result, they said, he had helped to mislead the House of Commons and the British people. Above all, they were able to say that Lord Milner had broken the law at a time when he occupied a position of high authority and responsibility.

The phrase "Slavery under the British Flag" was also used by many Liberal speakers during the campaign. This statement outraged the Tories; in their opinion, such a description of the employment of indentured Chinese labourers was a contemptible falsehood that damaged the reputation of the country.

After the election the Liberals withdrew the offensive phrase. In consequence, contemporaries and later writers have laid stress upon the "shameless mendacity" and "deliberate cynicism" of their tactics. There can be no doubt that the Liberals took every political advantage of the issue of Chinese labour; but we ought to notice, at this stage of our analysis, that cynicism was not confined to one side. No one exceeded the political cynicism of Arthur Balfour when he defended the actions of Lord Milner in public, after he had laid stress upon their stupidity, illegality and immorality in his private correspondence with his colleagues.

Balfour's resignation had another serious effect upon Lord Milner's position. When Sir Henry Campbell-Bannerman became Prime Minister, Asquith, Grey and Haldane pressed him to go at once to the House of Lords. Their idea was that Asquith should lead the party in the Commons and that Sir Henry, after six trying years as leader, should instantly remove himself from his place at the moment of victory. The plan failed. Campbell-Bannerman remained in the Commons; Asquith became his Chancellor of the Exchequer, Grey went to the Foreign Office, and Haldane accepted the post of Secretary of State for War in the new Government.

The three Liberal Imperialists later maintained, very properly, that these transactions were a great triumph for them since they gained three very important offices; but the matter may also be looked upon in another light.

It has often been said that Campbell-Bannerman gained stature and confidence after he became Prime Minister and saw the tremendous number of his followers in the new House of Commons, elected in January 1906. The process began, however, during his struggle with Asquith, Grey and Haldane in the crisis of December 1905.

It was the culmination of a long series of battles and skirmishes. Campbell-Bannerman had always sought to keep these men inside the party, and had never tried to exclude them from positions of authority in it. In this crisis he managed to succeed with them all, for the first time.

The effect of the struggle upon Campbell-Bannerman deserves notice. Lord Morley tells us of the way in which he shouted out in "triumphant voice, with gesture to match" an exultant "No Surrender!" when the three were seeking to bend him to their will. Shortly after the crisis Campbell-Bannerman described the details to his crony Lord Shaw of Dunfermline, later Lord Craigmyle. He said:[1]

> Do you know it was the comicality of it that I could hardly get over... But Asquith was always uneasy... I let it go on for three days; and then I said to each and all of them, "Now look here I have been playing up till now... But let me just say—*that it is I who am head of the Government; it is I who have the King's command: I am on horseback*... I will not go to the House of Lords... I will not have any conditions imposed upon me... *Do you understand*..."

So far as Sir Henry Campbell-Bannerman was concerned, this was the end of waiting and the time for action. Things were going to be done in the new Parliament in the way that he, the Prime Minister, desired; and he knew that his South African policy was the first item on his political agenda.

Lord Milner was now vulnerable to any attack that his enemies might care to make upon him. Later on, as we shall see, it was noticed that not one of the Liberal Imperialists tried to help him at a time when the extremists of their party sought to bring about his public humiliation and disgrace. As a result of Sir Henry Campbell-Bannerman's patient skill, the *religio Milneriana* no longer existed in the Liberal Party.

---

[1] Lord Craigmyle, *Letters to Isabel* (London, 1936), pp. 258–9. Campbell-Bannerman may, perhaps, have told this story with advantages, but it certainly reflects an increase of confidence on his part after the crisis. Asquith in his *Memories and Reflections*, vol. II, p. 193, calls Lord Shaw's account "entertaining and picturesque", but his own story of the crisis is hardly a model of accuracy. In connection with the crisis of 1905 it is important to see a letter by Alfred Gardiner published in the *Nation* of 4th June 1921.

IV. Chinese Slavery: The Censure

The new political scene – A novel tone in politics – Milner
is closely watched – Lord Milner's maiden speech – The
Liberal trap is sprung – A manly answer – The Radicals
attack – The situation in the Commons – Winston
Churchill "rubs in" Milner's confession – A Resolution
and two amendments – The cautious support of Arthur
Balfour – "Lay on the lash" – "Bilious Byles" – Chamberlain's defence of the High Commissioner's conduct – The
reaction of the House of Lords to the censure – Sir Henry
Campbell-Bannerman's Cabinet Report to the King – A
conflict between the two Houses – The reaction of King
Edward – Society, the Establishment and the Ruling Class
– The selfless leader – A myth about Lord Milner – Significance of the Milner debates.

I

THE election of January 1906 followed hard upon the
formation of the Liberal Government. Although the
question of Tariff Reform was the main issue, the
Liberal agitation against "Chinese Slavery" played a
tremendous part in their victory. They were returned with a
total of 377 members. The Tories were crushed at the polls;
they managed to retain 157 seats, a mere handful. The
political scene was thus altered out of all recognition.

For a time men wondered what would happen in these
novel circumstances. Many Unionists allowed themselves
to believe that "those fellows" would never be permitted
to "run the State", and thus tamper with the nation's safety.
On the Radical side, in a transport of joy, their more ardent
members were convinced that they were now in a position
to do anything—and some of them meant to do it.

The new tone in politics was quickly established. Parliament met for the first time on 13th February; on the 19th Herbert Paul, the Radical Member for Northampton, declared that the policy of the late Government in South Africa "was engineered . . . by bloodthirsty money-grubbers, mostly of foreign extraction, without honour, without conscience, without country, without God".[1] Milner's friend, L. S. Amery, at once wrote a letter to *The Times,* which was printed on the 22nd: ". . . I do not complain of the great wave in our politics which has swept the Liberal Party into Power. But I do profoundly regret that it should have carried along so much noxious scum on the surface, and that it should have given a voice in the councils of the Imperial Parliament to men, such as this Mr. Paul . . ."

More serious skirmishing followed these pleasantries at once; on the 22nd an amendment to the Address was moved which expressed regret that ". . . Your Majesty's Ministers should have brought the reputation of this country into contempt by describing the employment of Chinese indentured labour as slavery. . ." Winston Churchill, the new Under-Secretary for the Colonies, outraged the Opposition by coolly withdrawing the offensive phrase as a "terminological inexactitude".

In these explosive circumstances Lord Milner decided to make his maiden speech in the House of Lords by beginning a debate there on the South African policy of the new Government. This decision, from a political point of view, was a serious mistake.

Although he may not have realised it, Milner was closely watched at this time. Lord Ripon, the Liberal leader in the Lords, at once flashed a warning to Sir Henry Campbell-Bannerman:[2]

Milner is going to raise the question of South Africa in the Lords on Monday. I am glad for we can then bring out our whole case. . .

[1] All quotations from Parliamentary speeches in this chapter are taken from the accounts published in *The Times,* unless otherwise specified.

[2] B.M.Add.MSS.41225 (Campbell-Bannerman Papers) Ripon to Campbell-Bannerman, 20th February 1906.

The case Lord Ripon referred to was not the Ministry's plan for South Africa, but the case against the former High Commissioner.

On 26th February Lord Milner rose in the Lords in order to call attention to the situation in South Africa, and to ask the Colonial Secretary if he could give the House any information about the proposed constitutions for the Transvaal and the Orange Free State. He spoke before a crowded and brilliant company who were as anxious to witness the returned High Commissioner's first parliamentary performance as they were to listen to his arguments. The occasion was looked upon as an opportunity to observe him at close quarters. Here was a chance to see the aloof Proconsul in action in the company of his Peers. Milner's tall figure, his commanding presence, his gravity of deportment, and his serene detachment from ordinary mortals were the characteristics of a Viceroy or of one accustomed to the exercise of the highest authority. Men were now eager to see them put to the test in the difficult atmosphere of the British Parliament.

II

In his speech Lord Milner ranged over the whole of his South African policy; he came to the conclusion that he could find nothing morally wrong with it. His arguments were lucid, and they impressed a critical audience. He spoke with that air of unbending firmness that usually attracted his friends and distressed his opponents. Something of the effect was lost, however, because he adhered too closely to the typewritten draft of his speech, and now and then he failed to pick up his place from the papers in his hand. On occasion, his bitter resentment of his critics made itself too apparent.[1]

On the next day, 27th February, the adjourned debate was resumed; and it was on that occasion that the Liberal trap was sprung.

[1] See Sir Almeric Fitzroy, *Memoirs* (London, n.d.), vol. I, pp. 283–4, who observed the scene.

Lord Portsmouth, the Parliamentary Under-Secretary for War, was a principal speaker on the Government side. His remarks were not concerned with the Government's South African policy. Instead, he read out to the House extracts from the Blue-book of December 1905 (Cd.2786, which we have already noticed) which established the fact that there had been illegal punishment of Chinese coolies in the mines. He placed particular emphasis upon the passages in the Blue-book which said: "Mr. Evans . . . the late Super-intendent of Foreign Labour . . . informed the mine managers that in cases of breaches of discipline and trivial offences . . . he would not interfere if slight corporal punishment was administered. . . Mr. Evans went on to say that he informed Lord Milner of his action, and the latter took no objection".

At this point in his discourse Lord Portsmouth turned round in his place and looking directly at Milner, he said: "I ask the noble viscount—is that true or not?"

The Lords leaned forward to listen to Milner's reply.[1] It was a straightforward and manly answer:

Viscount Milner said it was no doubt true that he was informed by the Superintendent of Foreign Labour . . . that he had found it necessary to allow the infliction of corporal punishment at the mines in certain cases. . . He fully recognised that he took upon himself the whole responsibility. He thought in the light of subsequent events that he was wrong. Shortly afterwards, the Lieutenant Governor, Sir Arthur Lawley, was informed that on one or two of the mines ill-treatment of the coolies had taken place, and he immediately forbade all corporal punishment whatever at any of the mines. If he himself had been there he should have done exactly the same.

With this reply, Lord Milner delivered himself into his enemies' hands. Until this moment, his position had not been made clear. The Blue-book merely contained an account of Evans's statements but Milner now admitted that this account was correct. Lord Portsmouth went on:

The Earl of Portsmouth said the noble viscount had admitted that

[1] From the description in the *Morning Leader* for 28th February 1906.

he sanctioned this illegal flogging... He would like to call their lordships' attention to a despatch from the Colonial Office to the Foreign Office under date March 5, 1904... In this it was said: "... Lord Milner pointed out that any labourers imported would be amenable to the law of the land by which everybody, including whites, is liable to corporal punishment for certain offences. But no corporal punishment would be allowed except for such offences, and in these cases could only be inflicted after trial and sentence by a magistrate or Judge." He maintained that it was a monstrous thing for a Lord High Commissioner first to make a statement of that kind and then to sanction illegal flogging... That was the kind of abuse which went on... illegal flogging which, they were now told, received the sanction of the Lord High Commissioner...

The Lord Chancellor, Lord Loreburn, made his own contribution to the debate:

...The noble viscount was asked whether he had sanctioned illegal flogging or corporal punishment, and he said he had given his sanction... I have no desire in the least to attack the noble viscount ... but it is the fact that it was illegal, and it must be owned that he knew it. When I had the honour of acting for this country in the Venezuela Arbitration I remember the President of the United States ... saying: "The greatness of England and her high estate in the world does not depend on Waterloo or Trafalgar, but on the adminstration of justice all the world over." Is this English justice when illegal punishments are sanctioned by the Chief Officer of the State?...

With the situation made clear by Milner's remarks in the Lords, the Radical Press sprang to the attack upon him: Headlines in the *Morning Leader* for 28th February announced: "THE FLOGGING OF CHINESE"; "LORD MILNER'S GRAVE ADMISSIONS"; "SANCTIONED ILLEGALITY". *The Speaker* for 3rd March asked: "Is it any wonder when an esssentially German mind drives English policy that the result is not exactly what the English public looked for?" A special article in *The Speaker* of that day was written by H. W. Massingham. It expressed the opinion of Radicals in no uncertain terms:

Persons and Politics
By H. W. Massingham.
It is good for a nation to see clearly who are the authors of its

misfortunes. It is better still for those men to show themselves for what they are. We have had this rather melancholy satisfaction over Lord Milner. After his speech in the House of Lords none of us who opposed him in South Africa need have any misgivings as to our judgment. Lord Milner has many gifts; he has no capacity of self-concealment. . .

What struck me chiefly about him was his essentially un-English character. He has hardly any English characteristic. He is not placable, he has no belief in any of our British prepossessions. . . He is a pure bureaucrat and a pure idealogue. Men with him are things to be compressed within formulae and to be hated and driven. if they won't be compressed. His theories are applied without any saving quality of humour, tact, knowledge of men, affectionate or reasonable insight. . .

Lord Milner is an extinct force in our politics; yesterday he spoke for authority, today he is in the wilderness, *bombinans in vacuo*. . .

The first leading article in the *Manchester Guardian* for 27th February contained the opinions of a more moderate section of the Liberal Party:

Lord Milner's speech. . . showed the difficulty that he finds in understanding expressions of public opinion. . . Lord Milner's speech is perhaps no evidence of a political relapse; it is rather one more proof that he cannot gauge popular opinion. . . An expression of difference of opinion with him he calls a "scream" or an "instant low growl of menace"; his opponents are "enemies of Great Britain". . . He empties the stale dregs of his war vocabulary on to his public, and never, apparently, suspects that what used to excite now merely disgusts. . .

Most significant of all, however, was an ominous comment in the *Daily News* of 28th February: "The Chinese debate has revealed the fact that the effective Conservative opposition has passed into the House of Lords".

III

In the House of Commons Joseph Chamberlain was now in temporary command of the Conservatives, because Balfour had lost his place in the elections. Chamberlain realised that Lord Milner's admission of responsibility forced the Unionist Party into a difficult parliamentary situation at the same time that it jeopardised everything that the late Government had tried to achieve in South Africa.

The tactics of the Liberals were quite clear to him. The Radicals in both Houses were concentrating their attacks upon Lord Milner's illegal action in permitting the coolies to be punished by their overseers in the mines. There could be no successful defence against these attacks because Milner had publicly assumed the responsibility; long before, Milner had explained to the Conservative leaders that his mistake was merely an oversight, the momentary lapse of a man too busy with more important affairs; "at the time", Milner had written to Selborne in October 1905, ". . . I really gave very little thought to the matter."[1]

While the Radicals emphasised Lord Milner's guilt, the Liberal Ministry was planning to seize this opportunity to condemn the entire South African policy of the Unionist Government. Milner's careless blunder furnished the Liberals with a situation in which they could disparage everything that the Imperialists had tried to achieve since 1899.

This aspect of the affair explained the fierce anger of the Conservatives. One error at the end of almost a decade of arduous service was to be exploited in order to ruin a policy of Empire for which thousands had died and millions had been spent. They regarded it as political opportunism in its meanest and lowest form, choosing to forget their own merciless tactics of the recent past.

The personality of Winston Churchill served to increase the resentment of the Conservatives. He had entered Parliament a few years before with their blessings, but his adherence to the principles of Free Trade caused trouble between him and Arthur Balfour. In Balfour's opinion Churchill was merely a playful, if belligerent, cub who was hardly worthy of serious notice. The Conservative leader made Churchill the butt of a series of private jokes and quips which finally exasperated the younger man. In 1904 he

[1] Headlam, vol. II, p. 559.

crossed the floor of the House in order to join the Liberals. He was welcomed by them as a colourful, dashing and aristocratic recruit; the Conservatives now looked upon him as a political renegade who had abandoned class and party in order to join the enemy at their moment of victory. In the *National Review* the stalwart Leo Maxse liked to refer to him as "this ridiculous jackanapes", "a violent and reckless political adventurer", and "the pot boy of Downing Street".

When the Liberal Ministry was formed Churchill was delighted to become the Under-Secretary for the Colonies because Lord Elgin, the Colonial Secretary, was far away in the House of Lords. Churchill realised that in this post he would be charged with the handling of a good deal of the Government's business in the new House of Commons. His exuberance and high spirits were now brought to bear upon the Tories in general and Lord Milner in particular, with deadly effect.

On 14th March, as the following exchanges in the Commons show, he "rubbed in" the impression created by Lord Milner's confession:

SIR J. JARDINE (ROXBURGHSHIRE) asked the Under-Secretary for the Colonies whether, in the year 1905, any Chinese coolies . . . were subjected to any flogging or corporal punishment otherwise than in accordance with Ordinances or enactments.

MR. CHURCHILL (MANCHESTER, N.W.)—The hon. member will find information to the effect that such corporal punishment took place in Mr. Lyttelton's telegram of October 24, printed on p.44 of Cd.2786. . . The sanction which Lord Milner is understood to have given . . . appears to have been oral. There is no information in the possession of the Secretary of State to show that Lord Milner consulted the Lieutenant-Governor or any Law officer.

MR. BELLOC (SALFORD, S.) asked the hon. gentleman whether there was any guarantee whatever that Lord Milner did anything at all illegal if they had no record.

MR. CHURCHILL—I think my hon. friend will see that there is no doubt whatever that in authorising illegal punishment of this character at the same time that his official superiors were denying that such punishment was being permitted Lord Milner committed a grave dereliction of public duty (cheers) and at the same time an undoubted infringement of the law. . .

MR. MACKARNESS (BERKS., NEWBURY)—Has any information been sought from Mr. Evans in this matter?

MR. CHURCHILL—No...the fact that Lord Milner has himself publicly assumed responsibility has placed Mr. Evans in a somewhat indirect position in regard to this matter.

At this point in the proceedings Chamberlain made a bold effort to retrieve the situation. Turning to the Prime Minister, and ignoring Churchill, he said: "I beg to ask the first Lord of the Treasury whether he will now advise His Majesty to appoint a Royal Commission, of a judicial character, to examine and report upon . . . the system of indentured labour in the Transvaal . . . and to enquire whether the accusations of general cruelty and torture inflicted by British subjects on Chinese coolies are true. . ."

Campbell-Bannerman's reply was instant: "No, Sir, we have no such intention"; it was not his purpose to remove the matter from the realm of partisan politics.

IV

The skirmishing between parties was now over. On 20th March issues were joined by both sides in the form of a resolution and two amendments to it. The resolution was the work of William Byles, the Radical Member for Salford. It declared:

That this House expresses its high disapproval of the conduct of Lord Milner, as High Commissioner of South Africa and Governor of the Transvaal, in authorising the flogging of Chinese labourers, in breach of the law, in violation of treaty obligations, and without the knowledge or sanction of his Majesty's Secretary of State for the Colonies.

The first of the amendments was that of Captain Kinkaid-Smith; it had behind it the support of the Unionist leadership. It said that any attack upon the conduct and policy of Lord Milner in South Africa was ill-advised because it would revive and accentuate racial animosity in the new Colonies. However, an official Government amendment in the name of Winston Churchill was also put down, and this enjoyed precedence over Kinkaid-Smith's. It stated:

> That this House, while recording its condemnation of the flogging of Chinese coolies in breach of the law, desires in the interests of peace and conciliation in South Africa to refrain from passing censure on individuals.

Meanwhile, Arthur Balfour had returned to the Commons, as the Member for the City of London. As soon as he came back he assumed the tactical control of the Opposition's forces. Although he and Chamberlain disagreed about many things in the post-election period, they were agreed upon the need to defend Lord Milner's South African administration. Balfour at once sent Jack Sandars to Chamberlain in order to work out with him the details of the Unionist course in the Commons. They realised that the Government was embarrassed by the extravagance of Byles' censure but they were not prepared to apply "whitewash" to Milner's actions because they were so indefensible in themselves. Sandars reported to Balfour on the 20th:[1]

Private   March 20, 1906.
. . . I have seen Joe about the Milner debate. I put the various arguments involved in the various aspects of the forthcoming discussion. I won't bore you with the recital.

It comes to this that Joe decides in favour of our supporting Kinkaid-Smith's amendment.

He did not like the full whitewash of a front bench amendment.

. . . I have taken it upon myself. . . to get out a strong whip for tomorrow & to telegraph for the "boys".

So much for this . . .

It is clear enough that Balfour and his secretary, who reflected his master's opinions, were not passionately involved in Milner's defence. Their attitude was marked out by a certain coolness, however carefully it was concealed from their followers in general and their ardent Imperialists in particular. For Balfour, the affair in its essence was a

[1] B.M.Add.MSS.49764 (Balfour Papers) Sandars to Balfour, 20th March 1906, marked "Private".

matter of tactics. He could not allow the Liberals to condemn Milner in the way that they proposed, but he was not
desperately concerned to defend one of the champions of
the Tariff Reform section of his party. The Tariff Reformers
blamed his lukewarm attitude toward their policy as the
cause of the electoral disaster; and, as we shall see in the
next chapter, some of them were already looking to Milner
to assume the leadership of their movement since Chamberlain was an old man who might not be able to carry on for
very much longer. In February Chamberlain had already
pressed Balfour, with some success, to accept the Tariff
policy as the master theme of their party; Balfour, in these
circumstances, was not disposed to fly to Milner's defence
in uncalculating enthusiasm.

Balfour's position was not easy. The mass of his party
was outraged by Byles's resolution and Churchill's amendment. On the same day that Sandars made his report, George
Wyndham, a bitter and disappointed man in politics, wrote
to the leader in order to express the general attitude of the
Unionists. Wyndham had already ruined his own career
because of his blunders as Irish Secretary in Balfour's
Government. The Tory leader could now look upon him
as one who gave voice to the extreme views of their party.[1]

Milner Debate   20. 3. 06.
My dear Arthur,
   The *Government* are going to move an amendment to Byles' Resolution to this effect: "Whilst *condemning* flogging in the interests of
peace and *conciliation* decline to censure individuals". Winston Churchill
will move the amendment; we can imagine in what manner & in
what taste. . .
   To condemn Milner's action & to spare him as one out of many
individuals in the interests of conciliation is the meanest thing proposed even by this Government. I can say no more. They ought to
be trounced.
   . . . they . . . not only condemn a man who worked for 8 years
without any acknowledgment from Parliament, but insult him into

[1] B.M.Add.MSS.49805 (Balfour Papers) Wyndham to Balfour, 20th March 1906.

the bargain & insult us by talking about conciliation. Lay on the lash.

Yours affectionately,
George Wyndham.

V

The clash between parties took place at the evening sitting of the House on 21st March. The debate began when Byles rose to move his resolution. He was a Radical stalwart of the old school who was sometimes derided in the Tory Press as "bilious Byles" and as "Parliament's Cuckoo". Despite these sophisticated witticisms he was recognised, even by his enemies, as a man of great moral courage, prepared to defend the causes he believed in with fierce determination. For years past he had owned the *Bradford Observer* and made it the vehicle for his views on social reform.

On this occasion, however, his speech was spoiled by Chamberlain's frequent interruptions. More effective were the remarks of F. C. Mackarness, the Liberal Member for the Newbury Division of Berkshire, who seconded the resolution. He summarised the history of the Chinese labourers and concluded by saying that "He hoped the House would make it clear that when it discovered that one of its servants had misused his powers, it would interfere and vindicate the principles of freedom, humanity and justice".

Then, amid cheers, Chamberlain was up. At first, he made no appeal to passion, but spoke with obvious sincerity, while the Radical and Labour men cheered and laughed. Chamberlain complained that the House was asked to inflict a public humiliation upon a "most distinguished member of our great Civil Service" because of a single error of judgment. Milner, he said, was accused in his absence; Ministers had not called him to the Bar of the House to answer their charge; the Byles resolution was retrospective and vindictive, and was moved solely for party reasons. He went on to deal with Winston Churchill's amendment:

... Sir, it is a cowardly amendment. It is an amendment which insults Lord Milner, and at the same time accepts the substantial part of the resolution of the hon. gentleman opposite. They think to gain votes by distinctly pointing at Lord Milner and at the same time withdrawing his name. (Hear, hear.) That is party tactics; Liberal policy ... it will be treated with contempt by everyone who has the honour to appreciate the services of Lord Milner. (Cheers.) You cannot condemn him in words of this kind without admittedly laying yourselves open to the charge that you do not believe what you say, for if you do believe it you would impeach him.

MR. CROOKS (WOOLWICH)—I will vote for it if you will move it (Cheers).

MR. CHAMBERLAIN—I see hon. gentlemen below the gangway appreciate the force of my argument. They would impeach him. They have the right to do it. They would repeat the experiment in the case of Warren Hastings... What I complain of is the policy of the Government ... a policy of contemptible weakness... Well, I do not think Lord Milner has lost much...

... During a great part of that time he was in a sense responsible to me, and as my colleague and friend a greater man I have never known (Cheers)... This man has given his life, he has risked his health...

... I rely upon the future Parliament to ... repair ... a great injustice and expunge from our record a resolution which, if it is ever placed there, would be a disgrace to it.

Chamberlain was followed by Winston Churchill. His object was two-fold. He wanted the Commons to accept his amendment; at the same time in order to mollify the Radicals he was ready to condemn Milner in the most forthright terms. He spoke in the high and cavalier terms of ardent youth:

... Lord Milner has gone from South Africa, probably for ever. The public service knows him no more. Having exercised great authority he now exerts no authority. Having held high employment he now has no employment. Having disposed of events which have shaped the course of history, he is now unable to deflect in the smallest degree the policy of the day ... he is today poor, and honourably poor. After 20 years of exhausting service under the Crown he is today a retired Civil Servant, without pension or gratuity of any kind whatever... But I do seriously say to my hon. friends, Is it worthwhile to pursue him any further... Lord Milner has ceased to be a factor in public life... As we have triumphed, so we may be merciful; as we are strong, so we can afford to be generous...

... It is for these reasons ... that His Majesty's Government have placed on the paper the amendment which I now have the honour to move...

After Balfour and others addressed the House, Churchill's amendment was passed with a majority of 220 votes.

The Press of the next day was wild in its partisan exclamations. Some Liberal newspapers were angry with the Government for side-tracking the Byles resolution. The first leading article in *The Times* for 22nd March was, perhaps, the most sober of all in its argument, although the conclusion was violent enough. *The Times*, brushing aside the clamour of the Radical Press, explained that a mistake had been made in South Africa, but the paper pointed out that the whole affair was comparatively trivial. Despite the triviality, however, the House of Commons had been asked to record the censure upon "one of the greatest and most devoted of England's public servants". The effect of such a step, *The Times* concluded, "can only be characterised as disastrous ... it will be taken as another indication of the fact that the destinies of the country and to a large extent of the Empire are at the present moment in the hands of a number of fanatics..."

There was also a pointed comment in the *Outlook* of that day:

The House of Commons has defaced its records... Not one Liberal Imperialist in the Government had ventured to speak... The debate served one great purpose. It showed that Liberal Imperialism is an exhausted imposture and that not one of Lord Rosebery's disciples in the Cabinet can be trusted to make a stand for any principle against the clamour of the pack. When we remember the professions of certain members of the Government during the war, and the personal associations which formerly existed between them and Lord Milner, we may doubt whether a more ignoble desertion has been known.

VI

The affair of Lord Milner and the vindictive Radicals was far from finished; it now entered a more serious phase that involved consequences of the gravest kind.

Lord Milner was a man who enjoyed the respect and friendship of those who moved in the most exalted circles of English life. They were not prepared to witness his humiliation at the hands of politicians who were experiencing an ephemeral power merely because they had won an election and controlled the support of a majority in the House of Commons. The decision was made that there must be a counter-blow to the partisan action of the lower House.

On 23rd March Lord Ripon once again sent a warning to the Prime Minister. He told him that Lord Halifax was preparing a resolution in Milner's support, and that it was to be moved in the House of Lords:[1]

> Halifax has given notice this afternoon that on Thursday he will move a Resolution in the House of Lords approving of Milner's South African Administration. I have not yet seen the exact terms of it but they will be in our hands tomorrow morning. I think that it will be advisable to discuss the mode of dealing with this Motion at the Cabinet tomorrow.

Lord Halifax's motion was discussed at two separate meetings of the Cabinet; it declared "That this House desires to place on record its high appreciation of the services rendered by Lord Milner in South Africa to the Crown and the Empire".

Campbell-Bannerman reacted to the challenge with unobtrusive skill. He knew that no Liberal Prime Minister could hope to affect the attitude of the Tory majority in the House of Lords. However, there was one authority who might influence decisions there; if King Edward chose, his wishes might play some part in deciding the actions of the Lords.

[1] B.M.Add.MSS.41225 (Campbell-Bannerman Papers) Ripon to Campbell-Bannerman, 23rd March 1906.

On the morning of 26th March Campbell-Bannerman chanced to meet King Edward's friend, Lord Esher. Whenever the King was concerned with military or naval matters, he paid close attention to Esher's opinions. On this occasion Sir Henry went out of his way to be "very pleasant" to Esher. He began the conversation by speaking "very freely" to him about the Army. He also mentioned to this grey eminence of Edwardian politics that he was in correspondence with Lord Lansdowne, the Conservative leader in the House of Lords; the correspondence, he said, concerned the Halifax motion. According to the Prime Minister, he and Lansdowne were agreed it would be a mistake to "bring the two Houses into collision upon a question of that kind".[1]

Having thus prepared his ground by sweetening one of the most influential courtiers of the day, Sir Henry wrote his report to the King in order to inform him of what had happened in the Cabinet:[2]

10 Downing Street,
Whitehall, S.W.

Sir Henry Campbell-Bannerman, with his humble duty, begs to inform Your Majesty that the Cabinet met on Saturday and again today.

The motion of which Lord Halifax has given notice for Thursday in the House of Lords in approval of Lord Milner's policy and conduct in South Africa was discussed, and the unanimous feeling was that it was most undesirable, just when we are on the eve of establishing a new constitution for the new Colonies, and when feeling in South Africa is running high, to revive the old controversy. We would on this ground decline (probably by moving the previous question) to discuss this acrimonious subject, harm having already been done by Lord Milner's intemperate speech in the House of Lords a short time ago, and it being pretty certain that if violent partisan speeches are made in that House, the House of Commons will not be slow to take up the challenge. A mischievous, and unseemly, and wholly unnecessary, conflict between the two Houses would thus arise, with the worst effect. It was therefore resolved on Saturday that communications should be opened with Lord Lansdowne in order to point

---

[1] Maurice Brett ed., *Journals and Letters of Viscount Esher* (London, 1934), vol. II, p. 153, hereafter cited as Esher, *Journals*.

[2] Royal Archives, R.27, No.41. Sir H. Campbell-Bannerman to the King, 26th March 1906.

out these reasons for the abandonment of the motion. Today, however, Lord Ripon reported that both Lord Halifax and Lord Lansdowne had been seen and that they intimated that the motion would be persisted in . . . 26 March . 06.

VII

The initiative was now in the hands of the Unionist leaders. Decades before, Benjamin Disraeli had personally warned Balfour that the future condition of their party depended upon their management of the House of Lords: "no conflict must be permitted between the two Houses", the great man had said, "unless something substantial is to be gained thereby".[1]

Now, in the first crisis between Lords and Commons since the January defeat of the Conservative Party, their leaders had to decide upon a course of action. Were they to allow a conflict to develop between the two Houses, or should they bide their time in order to exploit their majority in the Lords upon some more favourable occasion?

At this decisive moment in the history of their party it was felt that Lord Milner was the man to make the decision. When Lord Esher considered the matter he wrote: "The only person who can effectively intervene would be Milner himself".[2]

But Lord Milner had already given blunt and public expression to his opinion of the party. In the peroration to his maiden speech in the House of Lords on 26th February he had explained his bitter dislike of party and his objection to the evil effect of party spirit upon those national interests he desired to serve. On that occasion, he made it clear that, in his view, the motives of a party man were not those that could be entertained by a genuine servant of the State. Party, so far as he was concerned, was a vehicle for "extremists". His conclusion was: "I am not much of a party man".

[1] See A. J. Balfour, *Chapters of Autobiography* (London, 1930), p. 126.
[2] Esher, *Journals*, vol. II, p. 153.

Nevertheless, at a meeting of the Conservative leaders at Lansdowne House it was decided that the Halifax motion should receive the support of their party in the Lords. Although Arthur Balfour was among those present, it was Milner who determined the issue. He strongly urged the Conservatives to vote for the Halifax resolution "not upon any ground personal to himself" but in order to "give support to the Loyalists in South Africa".[1]

Meanwhile, outside Parliament an agitation was begun in the columns of *The Times* and the *Morning Post*; the object of this agitation was to demonstrate that public opinion in England and in the Empire disagreed with the recent vote in the House of Commons. Those behind the agitation declared that they were preparing for Lord Milner a public testimonial which would reveal the widespread sentiments of admiration and respect felt for him by people in every part of the British world.

By this time the Prime Minister's Cabinet Report of 26th March was in the hands of the King; the King's reaction to the problem of Lord Milner and the two Houses of Parliament was a disappointment to Campbell-Bannerman. In spite of his skilful handling of Lord Esher, Campbell-Bannerman failed to impress the King with the correctness of his policy in the House of Commons and in the Cabinet.

King Edward explained to the Prime Minister that in his opinion Lord Milner's speech in the Lords was not "intemperate"; he also informed Campbell-Bannerman that Winston Churchill's remarks in the House of Commons during the Milner debates had caused offence in royal circles.

Until this crisis, the King had been annoyed with Milner because he had refused to become Colonial Secretary in 1903. Now, however, their former intercourse was resumed, and Milner was invited to Windsor where he was told of the King's "impatience" with the House of Commons.

---

[1] This information is contained in Lord Esher's report to the King. See Esher, *Journals*, vol. II, p. 154.

Milner and the Conservatives in the Lords thus gained a powerful ally whose influence would be felt not only in political but also in social circles. The King, at this time, wrote to Lady Londonderry, the leading Conservative hostess, in order to say that Churchill's actions in the Commons were "simply scandalous".[1]

The way was now clear for the House of Lords to begin upon that path which led them to reject a Budget in 1909, and to pass the Parliament Act in 1911.

VIII

Lord Halifax moved his resolution in support of Milner in the House of Lords on the evening of 29th March. The efforts of the Liberal Colonial Secretary, Lord Elgin, to move the previous question were brushed aside by the excited peers. They spoke in cohorts in order to emphasise their confidence in Milner. After Halifax, Lord Ampthill, Earl Cawdor, Viscount Goschen, Lord Roberts the soldier hero, Lord Halsbury, the Marquess of Londonderry, and the Archbishop of Canterbury expressed their approval of Lord Milner and his conduct of affairs in South Africa. The resolution moved by Viscount Halifax was carried without a division.

The significance of the Lords' action was instantly recognised. The first leading article in the *Daily News* of 30th March declared: "Yesterday the House of Lords essayed its counter-move to the Chamber of Democracy. . . The motion was commended . . . as deprecating the decision of the House of Commons. . . It would be idle to deny that the House of Lords is still capable of much mischief. . . "

The *Daily Mail* for that day said: "The House of Lords has rarely yielded to the petty . . . and transient impulses which often render the House of Commons an indifferent interpreter of the real and deeper feelings of the nation. The

[1] For these developments see Sir Sidney Lee, *King Edward VII* (London, 1927), vol. II, pp. 480–1.

resolution proposed by Lord Halifax . . . translated into words the true sentiments of the race to Lord Milner. . ."

The first leader of *The Times* explained that: "The House of Lords performed yesterday one of those invaluable services which entitle it to the gratitude of the nation, and which, while it continues to perform them, will always justify its existence as an integral part of our Constitution. . ."

Observers noticed something else that was involved in the action of the Lords. They made reference to that eminent company which at the present day is sometimes called "the Establishment"; in those less complicated times men were content to say that Milner was the hero and darling of "society" but they meant more than the term implied.

H. W. Massingham, the Radical firebrand, aimed his attack upon the Archbishop when he sought to make clear the nature and condition of those who were supporting Lord Milner; Massingham wrote in the *Daily News* of 30th March;

> . . . Then came the Primate. His speech was in the line of the general expectation. Lord Milner is nothing if not the embodiment of the spirit of intolerant, unsympathetic . . . ascendancy. This is why Society has taken him up after the politicians deserted him. Let such a statesman plunge his country deep in the mire and mischief, and Society will forgive him, so long as he speaks the same smug language of this narrow creed. And the Church is never unwilling to pronounce its unctuous benison on such a type of Englishman. This was the Archbishop's object. . .

The *Daily Chronicle* and the *Daily Mail* were content to describe the "ladies of high degree" who thronged the galleries of the Lords to hear the debate. With that accuracy of detail which Lord Northcliffe required from his reporters, the correspondent of the *Daily Mail* presented his readers with a list of the "distinguished listeners . . . the Marchioness of Lansdowne, the Duchess of Marlborough, the Duchess of Norfolk, the Duchess of Northumberland, the Duchess of Buckingham, the Countess of Halsbury, the Countess Waldegrave, Viscountess Halifax, Viscountess Hood, Lady Ribblesdale, and Lady de Roos. . ."

A sour comment in the *Speaker* of 31st March echoed Massingham's opinions:

". . . Everybody knows that the House of Lords, which represents society and high finance, admires Lord Milner. . . The hero of the capitalists in South Africa could not fail to be the hero of the capitalists of the House of Lords".

Now, the Parliamentry aspect of the affair was over. Outside the legislature, however, the agitation in favour of Lord Milner continued to swell in volume for months. He was the guest of honour at dinners attended by the leading Imperialists of his time, and by public men unconnected with party politics. At a great banquet on Empire Day a representative company gathered to pay tribute to him; an account of this affair took up no less than five columns of *The Times*, and it was also the subject of the first leading article in that paper on 25th May. A Public Address to Lord Milner was prepared and the readers of *The Times* and the *Morning Post* were informed that this address could be signed by them at any of the bookshops of Messrs. W. H. Smith & Sons. In August the Address was presented to Milner at a private ceremony; it contained the signatures of more than 370,000 citizens who resented the slur cast upon him by the House of Commons; Lord Milner received it together with a letter from the Duke of Somerset, the Chairman of the Address Committee. In September in a ceremony at the Imperial South African Association Milner was given another Address, signed by more than 25,000 inhabitants of the Cape Colony. *The Times* declared that this presentation brought the episode to a "fitting and satisfactory conclusion".

These developments certainly constituted a powerful reaction to the cruel attack of the Radicals. Nevertheless, they could still congratulate themselves upon the political results of their clash with the returned High Commissioner. Lord Milner had come back from South Africa in the summer of 1905 determined to avoid partisan politics and to take that year-long rest from public affairs which his exhausted condition demanded. However, as a result of his maiden speech in the Lords, he precipitated the hostility and antagonism between the two Houses of Parliament which became a master theme of English politics for the next five years. He revealed himself as a man who despised the English party system, and he further offended the Liberals by condemning out of hand their plans for the future government of the South African Colonies, even though his supporters defended him as a great representative of the Civil Service.

IX

There was yet another aspect of Lord Milner's situation, which was almost unique.

Often enough, the English ruling class attaches to itself a champion—a great journalist, a brilliant lawyer-politician, even a statesman like Disraeli or Lloyd George, who, in a moment of crisis, may become as Prime Minister the chief officer of the State with the power and authority to determine the destiny of the country. In all these cases such men depend for their existence upon success; in the words of a contemporary historian they are "expendable"; and after they have performed what is required of them they are, as a matter of course, expended.

This was not the case with Lord Milner. At the very darkest hour of his fortunes "Society" or the "Establishment" or the "ruling class" or elements from each of these groups rallied to his support. How can we explain this extraordinary development?

The answer lies in the conditions of the time and in the mystery of his political personality. Lord Milner was still swathed in the glory of his South African achievements. He had already proven his quality during a period of strain and danger. In addition, his young disciples and certain other adherents had energetically done what they could to add to his massive reputation, especially in the highest circles of

English public life. As a result, he was looked upon as a man who deserved to occupy a position above the strife of parties. The vulgar assault of the Radicals was dismissed as an aberration of domestic politics that could take place only at a moment of national intoxication.

Unlike almost every other politician of his day, there was never any need for him to descend into the turmoil of active politics; it seemed that those mean and unseemly actions which are sometimes required from any political leader, however illustrious, were alien to his nature. Even Arthur Balfour who ruled England almost by right of inheritance found it necessary to deal with constituents and deputations and party organisations and those everyday problems that confront the man who is in charge of affairs. In South Africa, of course, Milner had been burdened by these details which accompany the exercise of power; but people in England were not familiar with the details of his South African administration. They only knew that at a time of crisis in South Africa he had acted as a strong man concerned with the interests of an Empire. The Army in South Africa had blundered; but from the beginning Milner had assessed the situation and had tried to prepare his country to meet it. People felt that Lord Milner was a man upon whom they could rely; his great intellect and his moral courage could be brought to bear upon national affairs for national purposes, unhampered by the calculations that inspired the leaders of parties.

The condition of Britain in the early years of the century certainly seemed to require the presence of a strong, far-seeing and selfless leader. Men were already beginning to worry about the menace of the German Empire while the election of January 1906, with the return of large numbers of Labour politicians, raised up the awful spectre of Socialism. Milner, in these circumstances, was not regarded as a mere agent of established interests, but as a man who could save the country from the dangers which threatened it. Unlike Disraeli or Lloyd George he brought with him no legacies

THE STAIN OF CENSURE.

History (to Lord Milner). "LEAVE YOUR SHIELD IN MY KEEPING. I SHALL MAKE IT
BRIGHT AGAIN."

from the past that might make the ruling classes uneasy when they contemplated placing power in his hands.

These feelings extended far beyond the ranks of the Imperialists, who were, in any case, devoted to Lord Milner. So intense was the admiration he aroused that a myth sprang up that the more responsible Liberal Ministers lived to regret the action of their Government in the House of Commons. For example, in a work written a quarter of a century after Milner's death we find the statement that "... disgusting as the Liberal Government's behaviour was and bitterly as the more responsible leaders came to regret it, some of the mud did stick in the popular mind. . ."[1]

This myth had no valid basis. The affair of the vote of censure upon Lord Milner was not an isolated and meaningless incident. It was the harbinger of that extreme bitterness in English politics which distinguished the years 1908–14. For it represented in the minds of contemporaries two different ways of dealing with the crisis of the nation and the Empire as they entered the twentieth century.

The Liberals continued to rely upon the more familiar policies of peace, world-wide Free Trade, domestic reform, and social improvement at home. The Imperialists felt that the salvation of Britain depended upon a radical change in national policy; they believed that their country could confront the great nation states of the time only by turning away from the older Liberal ideas and placing reliance upon an organised, integrated and unified Empire, powerful enough to defy all enemies. They fought over Lord Milner because he was looked upon as a symbol. When the Liberals

---

[1] Crankshaw, *Forsaken Ideal*, p. 117. Sir Evelyn Wrench in his *Milner* writes with much more care than Crankshaw. Wrench points out, at p. 261, that it was Mrs. Asquith who regretted the censure. Important as she was, we cannot look upon her as a responsible Liberal leader. Sir Edward Grey's biographer has emphasised that Grey realised that he had been wrong about Milner; see Trevelyan, *Grey of Fallodon*, p. 79. Grey, Haldane and Asquith all voted for Winston Churchill's amendment. More valid than Crankshaw's repetition of the myth were two wholly different complaints advanced by Lord Milner's friends. They pointed out that the Liberals did not abolish the system of Chinese indentures as soon as they came into office; and they demonstrated that the Byles resolution was incorrect when it declared that Milner's action was a violation of treaty obligations.

condemned him they condemned the Imperialism that Chamberlain and his followers advocated; when the Unionists supported him they upheld the Imperial idea which alone, in their opinion, could save the nation.

Seven years after the debates of 1906, on 30th June 1913, Oliver Locker-Lampson, the Conservative Member for North Huntingdonshire, asked the Prime Minister in the House of Commons if he would reconsider the vote of censure passed upon Milner. Asquith replied with a blunt refusal. In 1914, just before he died, Chamberlain said to his son: "My first act when the Unionists return to power will be to move that the Resolution be expurgated from the records of the House."[1]

It is clear enough that none of the partisans on either side came to regret their actions. Although it had not been his intention, Lord Milner's intervention in the House of Lords involved both parties in the State in a serious controversy that extended far beyond his personal position. He was at once caught up in a rush of tremendous forces that submerged the personal aspect of the affair. Despite the fact that he was at the centre of the disturbances it is important for us to notice that he was only one element in an uproar of profound consequence to the political life of the country.

---

[1] Wrench, *Milner*, p. 261.

V. Olympian Jove

Problems of a returned Proconsul – The gloomy position
at home – A "useful" party with the Webbs – Amery
becomes Milner's lieutenant – The Compatriots Club –
Revolutionary effect of Joseph Chamberlain's illness – One
must explain to these d—d fools – Milner's policy for the
country – Lord Milner's bid for leadership – The reaction
of Arthur Balfour – The threat to his position as leader –
Objects of the Tariff Reform Campaign – Chamberlain
enforces his will upon Balfour – The threat of Milner's
rivalry – Balfour's acute distress – Lord Milner's message
to Balfour – Amery's new plan – Plans for a new Milner
Kindergarten – Milner will not accept public funds –
Failure of the plan – Milner's curious position.

I

IN spite of its importance, the vote of censure affair was
peripheral to Lord Milner's central problem, the problem
of the returned Proconsul who loathed the political system
of Britain but still wanted to guide and determine the
Imperial destiny of his country.

After his experience at Harrow in the 1885 election Milner
recoiled from party politics and sought another means of
achieving the power he desired. As a civil servant and an
Imperial official he gained the kind of authority that he
craved; but he had come so far since those days that mere
official appointments could no longer provide him with the
scope and influence that were required for his purpose.

He recognised that the politicians and the party leaders
were the ones who decided matters but he was unable to
bring himself to work with them. Scores of friends in the
Press, in politics, and in other walks of life begged him to

lead the country after his return from South Africa; but he refused to associate himself with the "rotten" system that sacrificed so much that was valid in order to pander to the base appetites and transitory whims of an ignorant democracy.

Shortly after his return to England he wrote to Lionel Curtis, a member of his Kindergarten, in order to give expression to his feelings about the deplorable political situation he found at home:[1]

> ... The position at home is, I feel, rather gloomy. I don't refer so much to the impending misfortune of a Liberal & "Little England" administration. We shall be able to prevent them doing much *positive* mischief. My trouble is that I don't see who is going to do any positive good.
>
> There is a sort of blight on men of both parties, & indeed on public life generally. We are flogging dead horses, mumbling the formulae of the past. I can see no realisation of the facts of the present: there are certainly no big ideas—indeed I don't see ideas of any kind—with regard to the future. Not among politicians I mean. There are occasional spasms of vitality in the press and outside, wh. the party organisations on both sides seek to suppress.
>
> This may be all a distressing illusion. But I don't think so... I am certainly not the victim of any kind of personal disappointment. Why *should* I take a pessimistic view...

Since party politics were so dismal Lord Milner began to cast about for some other means or method of serving the causes in which he believed. For a time he considered the idea of establishing a non-party Government that would remove Imperial affairs from the political arena, but he realised that he was unable to bring about such a development in England. In the autumn of 1905 he explained his feelings to Beatrice Webb, who listened to him with sympathy. The Webbs had supported the Boer War; after the war, they hoped to bring about an arrangement between the Liberal Imperialists and the "progressive" wing of the Unionist Party; their plan was to create a new force in English politics which would have as its objects a programme of municipal socialism in Britain and a policy of enlightened Imperial-

[1] Lionel Curtis Papers, Milner to Curtis, 25th August 1905.

ism overseas. At a "useful" party in their home they brought together Milner, Sir Robert Morant, Lord Grey and Halford Mackinder; after dinner Beatrice Webb had a long talk with Milner and confided her impressions of him at that time to her diary:[1]

> ... I had a long talk with Milner... He has grown grim and (perhaps temporarily) bitter... obsessed too with a vision of a non-party Government without having invented any device for securing it... He would take colonial affairs "out of politics", but he does not suggest how. He is a strong man and an intensely public-spirited man—but he is harder and more intolerant, more distinctively the bureaucrat than when he left England. And he is sore, and bitter to opponents—not a good state of mind with which to enter politics. A little religion, or a purely intellectual pursuit, or perhaps some emotional companionship, is needed if he is to get back his sanity —his sense of proportion...

By degrees, Lord Milner came to the firm decision that he should restrict the scope of his political activities and leave aside the whole sweep of public affairs in favour of concentrating upon more limited aims and tasks. He decided that he could serve the State best if he avoided the ordinary course of politics and devoted himself to a few particular causes, which he believed to be vital to the well-being of the country.

II

In these circumstances he turned for help and advice to L. S. Amery, a young admirer who had known him in South Africa. At this time Amery was a member of the staff of *The Times* where he was looked upon as a man with a brilliant future in journalism. Despite this opinion, however, he was already anxious to begin a career in politics and had refused

---

[1] Beatrice Webb, *Our Partnership* (London, 1948), p. 312. Beatrice Webb was one of the founders of the "Coefficients", a small political club which sought to unite the "best brains" of the Liberal Imperialists and certain of the younger Tories. Milner was attracted to the group; its members include Haldane, Lord Grey, Halford Mackinder, Leo Maxse, H. G. Wells, Bernard Shaw and others. Wells has written a satirical account of the "Coefficients" in his novel, *The New Machiavelli*.

to accept the Editorship of *The Observer* when it was offered to him by Lord Northcliffe. Amery was desperately eager to do what he could to further the cause of Imperialism; he regarded Joseph Chamberlain and Milner as the two great leaders of the movement he desired to serve. In 1901 he had almost gone to South Africa as Milner's private secretary but he was then involved in preparing his history of the South African War for *The Times*, and was unable to leave London. As a result of this circumstance, he never became a member of the Kindergarten although his devotion to Milner was equal to that of any of the young men in South Africa. Unlike most of them, Amery longed to become a member of Parliament and thus play some part in the traditional political life of the country. At regular intervals he had kept Milner informed about political developments at home while the High Commissioner was still in South Africa. Now, his experience of domestic politics made him a valuable ally for the returned Proconsul; their relationship, already close, became even more intimate. Physically small, Leo Amery was pugnacious, likeable and well-liked by men in both the great parties. His patriotic ardour made men accept, with good humour, his occasional excesses. Once, he boxed the ears of a political opponent, but when the affair was brought to the attention of a magistrate the victim was pointedly asked why he had allowed a smaller man to act as Amery had, without exercising his rights of self-defence. Lord Milner knew that he could rely upon him as an energetic, loyal and extremely capable lieutenant.

As soon as Milner resigned his South African offices, Amery began to urge him to consider the part he should play in national affairs when he returned to England. Amery fully appreciated Milner's dislike of party politics; in an effort to avoid this obstacle he once suggested that Milner should accept a Professorship and use his academic position to further the Imperial idea and that reorganisation of English political machinery which seemed so necessary to them both if the Empire was to survive. Milner was far too

L. S. AMERY

wise a man to accept such a fate, and he refused to consider the suggestion.

Even before he retired from South Africa, Amery was energetically preparing the ground for his return. Early in 1904 Amery and a few friends formed the Compatriots Club, a body of keen Imperialists who wished to make certain that Joseph Chamberlain's campaign for Tariff Reform and Imperial Preference preserved its Imperial tone and flavour, and was not swamped by manufacturers concerned only with the narrow idea of industrial protection for their own businesses.

Amery at once informed Milner about his new Club and its aims because he knew that the objects of the Compatriots were just those Milner held to be so vitally important. On 26th February 1904 Amery wrote:[1]

> I have been engaged... lately in trying to get together a small League or Association of people who think constructively and Imperially... So far, though there has been plenty of revolt against Laissez-faire and Little Englandism, there has been no coherent general outcome to put in its place... At present, no doubt, we shall mainly think and worry about the economic side, but there are lots more in the background, from compulsory service and the demolition of the Treasury to the construction of an Imperial Council and the putting of the House of Commons in its proper place. If we get on at all, I hope you will join us when you come back... we are limiting ourselves to fifty... Fossils, even if "whole hog" Chamberlainites, protectionist manufacturers, Parliamentary place hunters, and all that clan, will be... kept out...

This was exactly the kind of small but influential group that appealed to Lord Milner's political tastes. The Compatriots were chosen for their ability by a select number of their friends. Political popularity and those qualities which appealed to the mass were no qualifications for membership. Milner soon became a member of this congenial company.

However, in the summer of 1906 Joseph Chamberlain, the great popular leader of the Imperial movement, was removed from the public scene when he suffered a crippling

[1] Amery Papers, Amery to Milner, 26th February 1904.

stroke that impaired his physical movements and his ability to speak. At once, Amery began to urge Milner to step forward and take the place of the stricken leader. Private clubs and select companies would no longer serve; Amery begged his friend to save the Imperial movement by assuming the public leadership of their cause.

III

In this new situation Lord Milner decided to act, within limits, but he refused to give way completely to Amery's pleadings. He agreed to deliver two public addresses, but he insisted that Amery must not think of them as political speeches. These public pronouncements were prepared in the autumn of 1906, with Amery's help.

It was agreed that Milner should speak at Manchester on 14th December, and at Wolverhampton, where Amery was the Conservative candidate, on the 17th. It was probably at this time that Amery fixed upon the curious word *agoraphobia*—a morbid dislike of public places—which, as we have seen earlier, he employed to describe Lord Milner's personality and character. Early in December the two speeches were ready, and Amery was asked to read them and make suggestions for their improvement. Milner wrote to his friend:[1]

My dear Amery   1 . 12 . 06
    ... The Manchester speech is already rather bulky—not to say flatulent. It is so hard to get off generalities. One must unfortunately explain to these d—d fools why we want and an Empire, it pinches one in dealing with the methods of maintaining it...

Yours ever
M.

This letter can help us to explain one of the mysteries about Lord Milner. Several of his younger disciples were always distressed by the fact that he could not "put himself across", as they put it, when he spoke in public. The

[1] Amery Papers, Milner to Amery, 1st December 1906.

delightful leader that always aroused their sympathy could seldom attract to himself any measure of public enthusiasm. It seems clear that his contempt for a mass audience was so strong that it at once chilled the ardour of the public at the same time that it hampered him in speaking freely and naturally to them.

The two speeches were models of their kind. In them, Lord Milner ranged over the most vital topics of the day, illuminating all by the clarity of his thought and the depth of his insight. He explained that he was not a party leader while he stressed that he did not even aspire to a place among the leaders of parties. He urged his audience to reject the shallow notion that there was a logical antagonism between social reform and Imperialism. The two were, in his opinion, inseparable. Britain's prosperity rested upon the fact that she was a world power; those who were concerned with social reform at home could never neglect this aspect of the national situation, on which all depended. The United Kingdom alone could not continue as a great power of the first rank but a Greater Britain, an organised Empire, could remain at the head of international affairs for ever. Sentiment by itself could not provide the bonds of Imperial Union which were required. Imperial Preference, on the other hand, might supply that economic basis from which more formal ties could easily develop. There was a desperate need for a valid organ of Imperial government; the machinery of Empire was lacking because the Imperial Parliament was not Imperial at all; the periodic Colonial Conferences were more representative but they sat only at intervals; during the intervening periods there was no opportunity for the various members of the Empire to consult with each other. The time had come, Lord Milner argued, for Englishmen to recognise that a policy of Imperialism combined with a programme of universal military training and naval preparedness were vital for the future safety of their country and the Empire.

Amery believed that these speeches "might well have

formed the starting point for a great campaign"; but he realised that this was not Milner's intention. Milner had confided in him alone when the speeches were being prepared, and he knew that they were an isolated excursion, and no starting point at all.

Others, however, besides the "d—d fools", paid close attention to Lord Milner's remarks. In the *Speaker* for 22nd December his speeches were described as "Lord Milner's bid for the future leadership of the Protectionist section . . ." The *Morning Post* of 15th December observed that: "Lord Milner is no longer considering Imperialism from the circumference . . . but he has proved by his great speech of last night that he is able to adjust himself to the new point of view which his future work at the centre of the Empire demands. . ." Even *The Times*, for which Amery worked, remarked: "Lord Milner . . . delivered a speech which is at once remarkable and welcome . . . it marks the re-entry of Lord Milner . . . upon a field of political labour in which workers are few, and from which the powerful personality of Mr. Chamberlain is for the present most unfortunately removed".

So far as the political Press could see, a new element had been introduced into national politics. Men began to wonder what Arthur Balfour's reaction would be. Everyone knew that the confidence of his party had been severely shaken after the disaster of January 1906. Would Lord Milner succeed where Joseph Chamberlain had failed, and win the Conservative leader to a wholehearted support of the campaign for Tariff Reform and Imperial Preference?

On 18th December Sir Robert Filmer, one of the defeated Unionist candidates, pressed this course upon the Conservative leader. Writing from the Carlton Club he explained to Balfour:[1]

. . . I read Lord Milner's speech at Manchester in The Times of Saturday. It struck me as a very fine declaration of the Imperial

[1] B.M.Add.MSS.49859 (Balfour Papers), R. Filmer to Balfour, 18th December 1906.

ideal combined with the very natural more local ideal of Social Reform, and I feel sure no Unionist who has at heart the good of this country & the Empire could refuse to follow the essence of such a policy. As I think that you thoroughly agree with Lord Milner & would endorse the speech after reading it, and as I am certain that you could sweep the country with such an official policy . . . whenever . . . the Radicals may . . . next appeal to the country, I hope you will be able to see your way in the course of a few weeks to publicly compliment Lord Milner on this speech. . . I feel sure you could reunite the whole party on such lines. . .

IV

The alarm which Lord Milner's sudden burst of activity caused was very real. Arthur Balfour, in particular, was touched upon a raw and sensitive spot. He felt, with reason, that his position as leader of the Unionist Party was threatened.

When Chamberlain was struck down the Tariff Reformers in Britain suffered a shattering blow; they lost their dynamic leader at the very moment that they were in a position to dominate the policy of the Conservative Party, for the first time. It was only natural for Balfour to assume that Lord Milner was now seeking to take over the vacant place Chamberlain had abandoned for the seclusion of an invalid's room.

Since 1903 Balfour's political life had been plagued by Chamberlain's activities. In that year Chamberlain began his famous campaign for Tariff Reform and Imperial Preference. The object of the campaign was to solve the problems of the Empire by bringing the United Kingdom and the Colonies into a closer economic and spiritual union. If Chamberlain could establish an "Imperial Zollverein", a unified Imperial power, Britain's paramount position in world affairs would be secured. There would be no need to fear the monolithic strength of nation states like Germany or the United States if British statesmen could rely upon the vast resources of a united and organised Empire.

In order to accomplish this grand Imperial design Chamberlain proposed to levy a protective tariff upon articles of food imported into the United Kingdom from foreign countries, while Colonial foodstuffs were to be admitted free of duty. By means of these devices he hoped to create, for the first time, a community of economic interests within the Empire. On this firm basis of material self-interest the various parts of the Empire could then advance in harmony to the conclusion of those military, naval and strategic arrangements and agreements that comprised Chamberlain's object in the first place.

It was clear that these Imperial Preferences which were designed to attract the Colonies would increase the cost of foodstuffs in the United Kingdom. In order to compensate the British worker for assuming this burden Chamberlain found it necessary to add yet another system of tariffs to his plan. He proposed to safeguard certain British industries from foreign competition by means of a separate system of protective duties upon manufactured articles.

This programme of protection at once aroused the passionate support of many Imperialists who regarded it as the only means of saving Britain and the Empire in the hard conditions of the new century. Unfortunately for Chamberlain's purpose, however, the old system of Free Trade was still revered in Britain as the source of the country's prosperity.

The unity of the Unionist Party was shattered into fragments as soon as his designs became known. A group known as the Unionist Free Traders dismissed his arguments as economic nonsense that would spell the ruin of the country if they were ever adopted. In an effort to keep his party together Balfour hurriedly produced a compromise plan of his own, but he was unable to convince either faction of its validity. From 1903 until 1906 the Conservative leader was daily threatened by the disintegration of his party. After the election, however, the situation inside the Unionist Party was completely altered.

In the new House of Commons there were 157 Unionists but this number was made up of 109 Tariff Reformers, 32 followers of Balfour and 11 Unionist Free Traders. Chamberlain, for the first time, was the master of the majority faction of the party in the Commons. Although he observed every canon of courtesy and loyalty he now proceeded to enforce his will upon the Conservative leader. By February of 1906 Balfour agreed to recognise fiscal reform as the "first constructive work of the party".

Miraculously, the party triumph of the Tariff Reformers was destroyed in an instant by Chamberlain's disappearance from the political scene. Although they were in a clear majority in the Commons there was no one in their ranks with the stature that was required to dominate Balfour. Austen Chamberlain never inspired the confidence and enthusiasm his father enjoyed and Bonar Law was hardly more than a promising newcomer at this time.

Balfour recognised that only Lord Milner, the Imperial hero, could fill the vacant place. For once, the Conservative leader was unable to maintain that air of cynical calm which was his ordinary political attitude. He could not believe that Milner was sincere when he insisted that he was not interested in becoming a party leader. For tactical purposes most politicians in England and elsewhere exhibit a certain coyness before they strike out in a confused political situation. It seemed to Arthur Balfour that Milner was at last ready to abandon his Olympian aloofness in order to guide the Imperial wing of their party to the victory Chamberlain had almost secured.

Balfour's acute distress at this period of his career has never been recognised, but it was this feeling that was responsible for his suspicions of Milner's intentions. When Chamberlain forced him to agree to his demands in February of 1906 Balfour believed that he was about to lose control of the policy of his party even though he would be allowed to remain as the titular leader.

Everything depended upon Chamberlain's physical condition; after his illness, his family sought to conceal the terrible effects of the disease so that his colleagues and the public would expect his return to an active course after a period of rest and recuperation. In the newspapers and periodicals of the time there were vulgar descriptions of the invalid's every action. Whenever Chamberlain left the seclusion of his home, the journalists described how his wife or a servant helped him to step into a carriage or how he was assisted to leave a railway car. Balfour was so anxious upon this point that he caused his own secretary to look into the matter in a most curious and untypical way. Jack Sandars reported the result of the investigation to Wilfred Short, Balfour's amanuensis:[1]

Tell Mr. Balfour that the doctor, whom I consulted a week or two ago as to the nature of Mr. Chamberlain's illness, brought me the enclosed yesterday from a last week's illustrated paper, pointing out that the photograph *absolutely* confirmed his conjecture that Mr. Chamberlain must have had severe hemuplegia—and that, having regard to the length of time which has elapsed since the stroke, recovery must be *very very* doubtful.

Mr. B. knows, I think, that Mr. C. had to be lifted into the railway carriage yesterday. . .

If Chamberlain were permanently disabled the threat of Lord Milner's rivalry became much more serious to the Conservative leader in his uneasy condition.

V

Lord Milner was perfectly aware of Balfour's attitude when he agreed to deliver his two speeches at the end of December 1906. Early in the new year he decided to allay Balfour's fears; he sought out E. B. Iwan-Müller, a journalist who worked for the *Daily Telegraph* and other newspapers, in order to explain his position. Iwan-Müller was practically Balfour's servant in political journalism; he had worked closely with Lord Salisbury and with Balfour for

[1] B.M.Add.MSS.49765 (Balfour Papers), Sandars to Short, 4th March 1907.

years past. Although he was not a journalist of the very first rank, when he died some time after this episode Balfour personally arranged with the proprietors of the *Daily Telegraph* for a pension to be paid to his dependants. Iwan-Müller had known Milner since his South African days and had secretly reported to Balfour the attitude of South Africans to Milner as early as 1899.

In January 1907 Iwan-Müller dined alone with Milner and then repeated the details of the conversation to Jack Sandars who, in his turn, conveyed Milner's message to Balfour:[1]

> I have been having a good deal of correspondence with Iwan Müller . . . but what I am minded to write to you in particular just now is an account he gives me of a tete a tete dinner he had last week with Alfred Milner.
>
> The language I use is practically that used by Milner, reported by Iwan in the first person. . .
>
> Milner describes himself as a Free Lance, anxious to impress upon public opinion (which in Imperial matters is quite rotten) certain strong views he has. . . He will continue to press these views on the country subject to this condition. He will lead no movements that will cut across the programme of a united Unionist party. There are those—to wit Maxse et. al.—who would use him as a tool to dismember the party. He will have nothing to do with them. . . He is devoted to you, and he thinks you like him. You have all the qualities requisite for carrying out the policy to which he is prepared to devote his life. He can see no other possible leader.

Having made his own position clear, Milner went on to give Balfour some advice based upon his own analysis of the situation. Sandars's report explained:

> What you want—he continues—is a Lieutenant such as Ld. Salisbury had in Randolph & Lord Derby in Dizzy. He can't suggest a Lieutenant to do the swashbuckling, but one is necessary. He thought Bonar Law wd. do—if (and it is a big if) he wd. be loyal. Asked if there were any conceivable conditions under which he, Milner, would take office, if asked to do so, he replied that at present there were no conceivable conditions, just as he has always said that there were no conditions under which he would marry. Yet it must not

[1] B.M.Add.MSS.49765 (Balfour Papers), Sandars to Balfour, 13th January 1907, marked "Confidential".

be argued that he has absolutely cut himself off from office or matrimony. He desires neither: but there is no such thing as the eternal negative. . . This is how Lord Milner stands in the political world and I thought it well that you should know it.

Balfour received this report with coolness, and for a good reason. He already knew that the Tariff Reformers were making desperate efforts to revive their movement in the country and that many of them looked upon Lord Milner as their new leader.

At exactly this time Leo Amery, in his enthusiasm, pressed a new plan upon Lord Milner. He urged him to accept the direction and control of the Tariff Reform League, an influential non-party organisation that had been established in 1903 to support the Chamberlain crusade. The Tariff Reform League was a powerful engine of propaganda and political influence which did great service for Chamberlain's policies for a decade. Amery believed that if Milner agreed to his proposal to take charge of the League's activities, the impact and force of the organisation would be increased tremendously. He suggested that he and Halford Mackinder, the only prominent Liberal to be won over to the cause of Tariff Reform, could serve as Milner's lieutenants. Amery reckoned that Milner, in this position, could create and inspire a new Kindergarten that would dominate British opinion and politics within a reasonable period of time.

At first, Milner was reluctant to consider the plan. However, on 20th January he wrote to Amery in order to tell him that he had changed his mind. A few days later a dinner with Austen Chamberlain was arranged in order to set the plan in motion. Milner's letter to Amery, marked "Confidential", declared:[1]

On reflection, I think I was mistaken in rejecting entirely the scheme we discussed. . .

My reason is that, thinking the thing over again, I see that, under certain conditions, it may not only be not inconsistent with my general scheme of life . . . but actually further my views. I have always

[1] Amery Papers, Milner to Amery, 20th January 1907, marked "Confidential".

felt convinced, & nothing shakes me in that, that my business was to help to shape opinion & not to do the hack-work of Opposition *or of office.* But I have always considered that I might do definite jobs—piece-work & it seems to me that this a definite job, wh. could be done, & perhaps done all the better at this stage, by one who was not of the regular band of political protagonists.

My view is, as you know, that *T.R.* by *itself* is not enough. On the other hand . . . if I had the direction of the T.R. campaign for a year or two, I might *broaden it,* in a way wh. would not only make T.R. a sounder plank in itself, but inevitably, in the long run, lead to other things.

. . . *Between us,* I think we might make a great difference to the movement.

And meanwhile the desired all round fighting leader might have been found. We should have something to give him worth fighting for, & he would have to do the rest.

This was exactly the kind of development that Arthur Balfour feared. It mattered little to him that Milner was anxious only to work outside the formal ranks of the party, and in the company of a few select friends and assistants. So far as Balfour could calculate, the result would be the same; the Tariff Reform section of his party would be greatly strengthened if Milner lent his powerful abilities to the business of the Tariff Reform League.

A second part of this letter revealed Lord Milner's truly remarkable notions about receiving public payment for his services. Although he was eager to decide the course of national and Imperial affairs he loathed the thought of accepting money from public funds. The realisation that some of his fellow citizens had objected to his official actions made him despise the very idea of being paid by the State. This attitude was certainly curious in one who had been a civil servant for most of his adult life; it can be explained only by reference to the extreme bitterness he felt as a result of the attacks made upon him during and after the period of his South African administration. He explained his position to Amery in his own forthright manner:

Lastly, as regards finance, again I think I was hasty. I have an unconquerable aversion to taking public money. This was why I begged Lyttelton before leaving S. A. *not to try* & get a pension for me, a pension for services, wh. half the nation think were no services. I don't want *their* money.

But the case is different if I take money from an individual, or individuals, who are in complete sympathy with what I am doing. We may all be wrong together, but they at least would get value in the promotion of their views. . .

I should be paid for a particular job, wh. we were all agreed about. . .

The plans of the Tariff Reformers were quickly reported to Balfour by Jack Sandars, whose business it was to keep his chief posted upon all those developments which affected their party. On 22nd January he wrote to Balfour to tell him that "There is a widespread belief that in the course of next month we shall see a forward move taken by the Tariff Reform party. Something has happened to give them a new lease of life . . ." Sandars continued:[1]

. . . The result of all this has been a general weakening of your authority throughout the country. To this weakening Austen and Lee and Bonar Law, Maxse & Amery among others have contributed and are contributing. I have written to you about Milner so I say nothing about him. George Curzon has designs of some kind. . .

Lord Milner's part in the "forward move" of the Tariff Reformers foundered, however, upon the issue of finance. He required the sum of £20,000 if he was to undertake the direction of the Tariff Reform campaign, assisted by Amery, Halford Mackinder and certain other selected lieutenants. After months of discussion with those who might have supported the plan, Milner explained the matter to Amery:[2]

I am sorry to tell you that I think the idea of the Private Secretariat must be abandoned. I have not met with any success worth mentioning in quarters, in which, if anywhere, an appeal from me on personal grounds was likely to meet with most support. . .

It is a blow to me to think that your & Mackinder's services cannot be wholly concentrated on those public affairs, wh. are the most important & the most neglected. But, as far as I am personally

---

[1] B.M.Add.MSS.49765 (Balfour Papers), Sandars to Balfour, 22nd January 1907, marked "Personal".

Amery Papers, Milner to Amery, 28th June 1907.

concerned, I own to a certain sense of relief. I don't feel absolutely
certain that my strength would have been equal to the direction of so
great an enterprise.

VII

These episodes illustrate Lord Milner's curious position
in English politics as a returned Proconsul with a record of
significant achievement behind him.

Here was a man who had attracted, as a result of his
accomplishments, the loyalty and constant devotion of a
small group of friends; in their company his personal
ascendancy awoke feelings of respect, and even veneration.
If he gave the signal they were prepared to rally a much
larger band of adherents to his standard. In the country, a
leaderless host was already waiting for the guidance and
direction he could supply.

Despite the ardour of these friends, Lord Milner refused
to act. They knew that he was a zealous man, and not the
cold and arrogant Proconsul of popular imagination; they
could see that he was warmed by a noble purpose, that he
desired to achieve great things for his country and the
Empire, that he longed to serve the State. But he recognised
what his friends and disciples refused to understand.

He realised that Chamberlain's movement was a crusade;
at the same time he knew that he, himself, was not fitted to
act as a crusader in a modern democratic State. He was not
the "fighting leader" the Imperialist movement required,
after Chamberlain fell ill. It was hardly his fault if contemporary politicians, be they friendly or hostile, were unable
to understand this aspect of his position. The very act of
public speaking was painful to him. On several occasions
he implored Leo Amery to help him in this connection:
"who was the voice specialist you once advised me to go to
. . . my voice is apt to give way . . . I think I tire myself
unnecessarily in public speaking".[1]

[1] Amery Papers, Milner to Amery, 11th September 1907.

Milner's devotion to Britain was equal to Chamberlain's, but his gifts were of a different order and quality. Neither by inclination nor experience was he equipped to rally a mass following in the country to the support of those Imperial policies he cherished. His genius lay elsewhere, in the sphere of administration. His political personality could find full expression in a position of power and authority, but his friends asked more than he could give when they begged him to follow in Chamberlain's footsteps as a popular leader of men.

This situation explains much of Milner's bitterness during these years. He believed that the Liberal Government was embarked upon a course that could end only in a national disaster; he was convinced that the safety of the country could be secured only if his plans for Empire unification were carried out. In order to implement these plans he required supreme power in the State, but in Britain possession of political authority depended upon the decisions of an electorate which he did not respect and which he refused to court. His bitterness was not the shallow acrimony of a man jealous of his contemporaries; it stemmed from his understanding and resentment of these facts.

Denied a proper outlet for his energies, he fell back upon an Olympian aloofness that sometimes puzzled his friends and always increased the suspicions of his enemies. The man who turned away from English party politics in 1885 made himself unfit for the role he desired to play in the period after his return from South Africa. Milner was prepared to sacrifice his life in the service of the State, but he was reluctant to squander his limited stock of strength in the interests of factions or parties. Only a Unionist victory at the polls, which he refused to organise, or a great national emergency could provide him with the opportunity to exercise his talents in a way that would satisfy his patriotic devotion. He knew the uses of power but he rejected the English method of winning it as the province of the "charlatan" and the "liar".

Something of the contradictions which plagued his course in this period was recognised by Beatrice Webb who visited him at Sturry Court, his little house in the country near Canterbury. In her diary she wrote of Milner:[1]

> As I listened to his feeble, forceful voice, watched his rigid face and wrinkled narrow brow, noted the emphasis on plentiful capital, cheap labour and mechanical ingenuity, I thought that perhaps, after all, there was some justification for Leonard Courtney's hard epithet "a lost mind". A God and a wife would have made Milner, with his faithfulness, persistency, courage, capacity and charm, into a great man: without either he has been a tragic combination of success and failure. . .

More masculine, and more precise, was the comment of one of Lord Milner's most devoted admirers. Years afterward, Lord Altrincham sought to analyse Milner's public career in an article in the *National and English Review*. In his analysis, Altrincham laid particular stress upon one aspect of Milner's political life: ". . . If his life is studied, it will be seen that he never acquired official power for himself . . . he wielded power because it had been conferred upon him by men who had themselves acquired it and wanted his assistance . . ."[2]

Lord Milner sought neither the sympathy nor the understanding of contemporary politicians in this period of his public career. Years afterward, he liked to call himself "an emergency man"; by his use of this phrase he meant to suggest that in a moment of crisis or national danger the party politicians were required to call upon him in order to save the situation. When party tactics and the narrow schemings of the "vote-catchers" and the "hacks" could no longer serve, then his great gifts were recognised by the popular leaders, and then they placed power in his hands so that the genuine business of the State could be discharged by one who was a master in the exercise of administrative and executive authority. Looking back, in later years, upon

[1] Beatrice Webb, *Our Partnership*, p. 352.
[2] Lord Altrincham, "Forgotten Patriot" in *The National and English Review*, December 1952, p. 363.

the entire length of his career Lord Milner could, and did, comfort himself with the reflection that the politicians had come to him in the great crisis of Empire in South Africa, and that they had sought him out at a dark hour in the World War. When deeds and actions were the requirements of the day no thought was wasted and no reliance placed upon the tawdry accomplishments of the facile and popular leaders whose abilities were limited to the winning of elections.

Between 1905 and 1915, during that bitter decade when their party was denied the fruits and prerogatives of office, the idea of such a figure, like the hero of one of those ancient sagas who slumbers in some remote and distant retreat until he is summoned as a saviour at the eleventh hour, was very attractive to many of the Tories who placed their faith in Lord Milner. They liked to believe that he would descend into the fray at the vital moment in order to restore, with a few powerful strokes, all that had been squandered by the Liberal and Radical demagogues of the Campbell-Bannerman–Asquith era.

But Lord Milner was not asleep at this time. His condition as an "emergency man" could never be easy because his very mastery of the nation's requirements made clear to him the shortcomings and the faults of the politicians who occupied the seats of authority, who had blundered into positions of power merely because they were adepts at attracting the attention of the electors. He was painfully aware of the dangers and the pitfalls of the day. Unlike Arthur Balfour, he was not fortified by the cynical aloofness of the philosopher; unlike Lloyd George, he could not bring himself to look upon the condition and fate of the country and the Empire as matters to be decided in a game played out by the politicians of either party. There was no comfort for him—during these years between emergencies.

The aspect of aloofness that he assumed was a mask and a shield. The era of Liberal power which witnessed the decline of the Imperial Party tried his patience, caused him genuine distress, increased his irritation with the English political system and fortified him in his dislike and suspicion of democracy. The time would come, as we shall see in this history, when all these factors in combination produced a situation in which Lord Milner became a genuine menace to the familiar and established order in England, when one of his disciples could describe him accurately as a man who might emerge as "the real leader of the resistance" in a civil war. When the English constitutional system was tested to breaking point during the Home Rule crisis in 1914, Lord Milner was prepared to consider recourse to actions of the most violent kind. He was dominated, at that time, by his desire to preserve the Union and to protect the Ulstermen of Northern Ireland, but these other factors, which we have discussed above, had so inflamed his temper that he was ready to look forward to a clash of arms in order to free the country of the "tyranny" imposed upon it by parliamentary Pharisees like Asquith, Lloyd George and Winston Churchill.

VI   The British Race Patriot

The 1907 Colonial Conference – The New Imperialism –
Organic unity and the Council of Empire – Opposition of
the Colonial Nationalists – Opposition of the Liberal
Government – Fury of Milner and his friends – One last
method – The policy of Imperial Preference – A third
factor – Milner's race patriotism – Lord Milner's "Credo" –
The bond of common blood – Reaction of the Aga Khan –
Importance of the racial bond – Milner and the 1907
Colonial Conference – A meeting with Haldane – The
dictum of Sherlock Holmes – Milner and Alfred Deakin –
Failure of Milner's Press campaign – Sir Wilfred Laurier
and British Imperialists – Significance of Chamberlain's
blunder – The French dancing master – Lord Milner's
Canadian tour – A warning from Lord Grey – The brain
carrier of Imperial policy – Lord Northcliffe, Milner and
Balfour.

I

MEANWHILE, the Imperialists on the Conservative
side were looking forward to the meeting of the
fifth Colonial Conference which was to take place
in London in the spring of 1907. Many of them turned to
Lord Milner to give their movement the leadership that was
required for the occasion. They knew that Campbell-
Bannerman, Lord Elgin and Winston Churchill, the men
who controlled the policy and attitude of the Colonial
Office at this time, were hostile to their desire to use the
Colonial Conference as a means of securing that Empire
unity and integration they held to be so necessary for the
future. Arthur Balfour was scarcely interested in the matter;
Chamberlain lay at Highbury, neglected and without the
influence or strength the moment demanded.

These Imperialists properly regarded Milner as the great author or exponent of what has been called "the New Imperialism"; contemporaries and later writers have emphasised the novelty of his outlook; on it, the Imperialists fixed their hopes and dreams for a powerful and "consolidated" Empire. *The Cambridge History of the British Empire* refers to Milner as: "The unsuccessful exponent of a militant imperialism which soon became old-fashioned, he was one of the chief architects of a pacific and constructive imperialism which held promise for the future". The *History of The Times* refers to one of his South African speeches as "the clearest definition of the New Imperialism that had been given; and it was the most authoritative". Parts of this speech were twice republished by Leo Amery, the devoted disciple, in his introduction to Professor Halperin's book on Milner, and also in his own autobiography.

What was it that Lord Milner said to inspire such enthusiasm and confidence? In his farewell speech to the citizens of Johannesburg in 1905 Lord Milner declared:

. . . The word Empire, the word Imperial, are, in some respects, unfortunate. They suggest domination, ascendancy, the rule of a superior state over vassal states. But as they are the only words available, all we can do is to make the best of them, and to raise them in the scale of language by a new significance. When we, who call ourselves Imperialists, talk of the British Empire, we think of a group of states, independent of one another in their local affairs, but bound together for the defence of their common interests and the development of a common civilisation, and so bound, not in an alliance—for alliances can be made and unmade, and are never more than merely nominally lasting—but in a permanent organic union. . . Our ideal is still distant, but we are firmly convinced that it is not visionary nor unattainable . . . think of the greatness of the reward—the high privilege of having in any way contributed to the fulfillment of one of the noblest conceptions which have ever dawned on the political imagination of mankind.

II

How can we possibly explain the determined and relentless opposition to Lord Milner's noble conception, for which he was prepared to devote his strength and his life?

The Imperialists of his day believed that two general factors combined to defeat their ideal of a United Empire. These factors were the attitude of certain Colonial statesmen and the malignant hostility of the Liberal Party, determined to gain party advantage from a situation which should have been treated in a spirit that was above party.

In this period Milner and some of his friends were convinced that there could be no permanent and effective Imperial Union unless a completely new organ of Empire Government was created for the purpose. They desired to establish an Imperial Council or a Council of Empire with sovereign powers to direct and control the purely Imperial business of the Empire. The foreign policy of the Empire, Imperial Defence and control over the affairs of the Dependent Empire were all matters that might be directed by this proposed organ of government, the Council of Empire. This is what Lord Milner meant in his speech at Johannesburg when he referred to a "permanent *organic* union".

However, the Imperialists of this persuasion were confronted by the hostility of Colonial leaders like Sir Wilfred Laurier of Canada and General Botha of South Africa, who were completely opposed to the plan of an Imperial Council. These men looked upon their countries as developing nations in the first instance, even though they recognised and cherished the Imperial connection. They were jealous or afraid of any development that might touch their sovereign authority in the smallest degree. In particular, they were opposed to the establishment of any Imperial institution that would involve or even imply a surrender of Dominion autonomy. If a permanent organic union of the Empire of the kind Milner advocated were to be established, men of this stamp were convinced that the great Colonies would lose something of that independence from British control they had already won or were still seeking to gain. We may call their attitude the opposition of the Colonial nationalists to Lord Milner's desires.

In the second place, the Liberal Government was completely hostile to the conception. The Liberal leaders believed that no valid reason existed for so radical an innovation as the proposed Imperial Council. They appreciated the Colonial desire for and insistence upon autonomy and self-government; in their opinion the Empire would be injured if the Government of the United Kingdom sought to impose the idea of an Imperial Council upon those Colonial Prime Ministers and statesmen who objected to it. The Liberals believed that the plan was not merely untraditional but that it violated a basic trend of Empire development, the trend toward self-government and representative institutions responsible to Colonial opinion and free from the interference of Whitehall. They dismissed the whole idea as a ldangerous menace to those spiritual ties and that common oyalty to the Crown which were the real basis of Imperial unity.

Lord Milner and his followers were savage in their denunciations of this attitude. They were, of course, in no position to criticise publicly the Colonial Prime Ministers who objected to their plan; for that reason they turned upon the Liberal leaders with redoubled fury.

The Liberals, they argued, were dominated by their archaic devotion to the idea of Free Trade; as a result they deliberately neglected the broad significance of Chamberlain's Empire Crusade in order to complain about its narrow details. These Imperialists pointed out that Chamberlain was not a selfish business man who advocated a policy of protection for the sake of inefficient British industries. The Liberals argued in this way merely in order to win votes for their party; they were prepared to damage the future of the entire Empire for the purpose of misleading an ignorant electorate. Milner, in particular, despised the Liberal leaders as mere politicians—votegetters—completely unqualified to discharge the duties of Imperial statesmen.

The truth was, the Imperialists maintained, that Chamberlain had risked his political life for the cause of the Empire.

His policy of Tariff Reform was only a means, a method designed to advance a part of the way toward a United Empire, and not a goal in itself. Lord Milner and the Imperialists who agreed with him supported Chamberlain as a "great fighting leader" for this reason; no one could suggest that Milner and his friends were protectionists seeking guaranteed profits for their industrial connections or their "lagging" industries. Chamberlain, they said, embarked upon the Tariff Reform policy as a result of his Imperial experience, experience that was longer and better informed than that of any other British statesman. At the Colonial Conference in 1902 he had proposed the idea of a political federation of the Empire; some of the Colonial Prime Ministers received his suggestions too coolly for them to be acted upon; he also proposed that the great Colonies should participate more fully in the Imperial Defence of the entire Empire; however, the generals and admirals raised technical difficulties which blocked this path toward closer Empire co-operation; there remained one last method, the idea of reciprocal trade Preferences within the Empire.

The most ardent of the Colonial nationalists, the men who wanted to see their Colonies as sovereign nations, were in favour of the idea of Imperial Preference. Chamberlain launched his campaign of 1903 only after he had been convinced that it was the best solution to the problems of a divided Empire. He cared nothing for protection in itself; he destroyed his health in his efforts to convince his countrymen that a policy of protection and Imperial Preference was the last practicable method available to begin upon the long and complicated business of creating a powerful and united Empire that could hold its own in the new century. Milner and his friends were outraged by the Liberal politicians who presumed to tamper with the fate of such a plan, for the sake of party.

If the attitude of some of the Colonial statesmen and the position taken up by the Liberal Government may be regarded as two of the external factors which explain why

Lord Milner failed in his object at this time, we have to notice a third factor which was not external to his attitude. This factor has been neglected by some who have written about his Imperial ideas, but it deserves a place in any discussion of them because it helps to make clear why his contemporaries were unable to accept his genuinely constructive proposals.

The key to Lord Milner's Imperialism, his master theme, was that all the "partner nations" of the United Empire he desired should be regarded as completely equal to each other in Imperial affairs. This third factor, however, weakened the impact and effect of his proposals.

Lord Milner's race patriotism—his racialism—made some of his contemporaries look upon his Imperial ideas as inadequate for the purposes of the modern British Empire.

III

This race patriotism was not the vulgar racialism that sought to conceal British Imperial self-interest behind those tedious neo-Darwinian slogans which claimed that the strongest were best fitted to survive and to dominate in world affairs; nor was it the dangerous creed of Houston Stewart Chamberlain, the English renegade who played such an important part in contemporary Germany where he explained the entire history of civilisation as a racial struggle between the forces of good and evil. Lord Milner's ideas about race were not even essential to his Imperial policies. Nevertheless, they were the motive force behind every one of his political and Imperial proposals. He was dominated by his desire to serve what he called the "British race".

As a realist Lord Milner observed that in the 20th century we are born in a world of nations; in this condition of affairs he was convinced that the most peaceful and the most harmonious world order would be achieved if Great Britain controlled the international condition of mankind. However, he always made it clear that he was not a cosmopolitan. His declared object in seeking to create a powerful Empire was to safeguard and advance the condition of the British race in the struggle between nations. It was for their sake and in their interest that he laboured.

In the period between the Boer War and 1914 men like Louis Botha, a South African Boer, and Sir Wilfred Laurier, a Canadian whose ancestors came to Canada from Normandy in the 17th century, were Imperial statesmen of the first consequence. As we have seen, they objected to some of Lord Milner's proposals because they were Colonial nationalists who feared that the sovereign authority of their countries would be diminished if those proposals were accepted. Lord Milner's race patriotism contributed to their suspicions of his ideas; his emphasis on race was an irritant which served to increase their hostility to his programme for a United Empire.

It has been said that Milner spoke "a good deal about race in his later years".[1] This statement is misleading for as far back as we have records of Alfred Milner's opinions, they are dominated by his ideas upon race.

The reason for the belief that Milner concerned himself with the issue of race in his later years lies in the fact that his most famous statement upon the subject was discovered in his private papers shortly after his death. This document, Lord Milner's "Credo", was published in *The Times* of 27th July 1925.

It declared:

CREDO—Key to my position.

I am a Nationalist and not a cosmopolitan. . .

A Nationalist is not a man who necessarily thinks his nation better than others, or is unwilling to learn from others. He does think his duty is to his own nation, and its development. He believes that this is the law of human progress, that the competition between

---

[1] Crankshaw, *Forsaken Ideal*, p. 121. This writer appears to believe that Liberals, the Labour Party, and the United States of America were responsible for Lord Milner's failure to achieve a united Empire of the kind he desired. His book contains almost no reference to that Dominion nationalism which played so great a part. See p. 147 where Liberals and Socialists are blamed and p. 152 where the Americans are treated as the successors to the Liberals, in the work of opposition.

nations, each seeking its maximum development, is the Divine Order of the world, the law of Life and Progress.

I am a British (indeed primarily an English) Nationalist. If I am also an Imperialist, it is because the destiny of the English race... has been to strike fresh roots in distant parts... My patriotism knows no geographical but only racial limits. I am an Imperialist and not a Little Englander, because I am a British Race Patriot... It is not the soil of England, dear as it is to me, which is essential to arouse my patriotism, but the speech, the tradition, the spiritual heritage, the principles, the aspirations of the British race...

The wider patriotism is no mere exalted sentiment. It is a practical necessity... England, nay more, Great Britain, nay more, the United Kingdom is no longer the power in the world which it once was... But the British Dominions as a whole are not only self supporting. They are more nearly self-sufficient than any other political entity... if they can be kept an entity...

This brings us to our first great principle—follow the race. The British State must follow the race... We cannot afford to part with so much of our best blood...

The "Credo" of Lord Milner was republished as a pamphlet by *The Times*, then under the editorship of Geoffrey Dawson, a former member of the Kindergarten; the pamphlet was widely distributed to schools and other public bodies; it was the subject of a number of leading articles in *The Times* which described Milner's ideas as the "conscious political faith of the best and most thoughtful patriots of the Empire".

The document also aroused another response that received less prominent treatment. It was a letter from a source that could not be dismissed easily in that period. The Aga Khan wrote to say that Lord Milner's ideas were "inadequate" and an "absurdity". His letter was published in *The Times* of 5th August 1925: it was the criticism of a partisan with a particular cause:

...I have been pondering over his "Credo"... and with great diffidence I offer the critism that his attitude of mind was in some respects inadequate to the many-sided needs of the British Empire as we know it today.

Taking the racial... view of Imperialism, Lord Milner wrote himself down "a British race patriot". Now, if the dominions of

his Majesty consisted only of the British Isles and the colonies . . .
mainly peopled by the British race this view might or might not be
best. But . . . the issue was settled by the acquisition of India, the home
of three-fourths of the subjects of the British Crown. . . To call
India a Dominion in an Empire based on British race patriotism would
be an absurdity. . . AGA KHAN

IV

It must not be thought that the ideas of this "Credo"
were peculiar to the latter portion of Milner's life. In a
speech at Willesden during his 1885 election campaign he
said exactly the same things, practically in the same words:[1]

. . . I am no cosmopolitan . . . let us always remember that in speaking
of our country we do not mean merely these islands. We mean every
land inhabited by men of English race living under English institutions. . . I think we can foresee a time when the great Anglo-
Saxon Confederation throughout the world, with its members
absolutely self-governing in their domestic concerns, but firmly
united for purposes of mutual protection, will not only be the most
splendid political union that the world has ever known, but also the
best security for universal peace.

From 1885 onward Milner took every opportunity to
stress the significance of his race patriotism. In South
Africa before, during and after the Boer War he sought to
stand before his contemporaries as the champion of the
British race in that area. In his speech at Wolverhampton in
December 1906 he emphasised that "I am not a cosmopolitan. The conception which haunts me is the conception of the
people of these islands as a great family, bound by indis-
soluble ties to kindred families in other parts of the
world . . ." In the introduction to a book of his speeches
published in 1913 as *The Nation and The Empire* he returned
again and again to his race patriotism:

Throughout the foregoing statement I have emphasised the importance of the racial bond. From my point of view this is fundamental. It is the British race which built the Empire and it is the

[1] The speech is extensively reproduced in W. B. Luke, *Lord Milner* (London,
1901), pp. 103–4, for these extracts. Luke points out that of all the speeches Milner
made in 1885, this was the only one he deemed worthy of revision and printing.
His book deserves the attention of those interested in Milner.

undivided British race which can alone uphold it . . . deeper, stronger, more primordial than . . . material ties is the bond of common blood, a common language, common history and traditions. But what do I mean by the British race? I mean all the peoples of the United Kingdom and their descendants in other countries under the British flag. . .

This lifelong insistence upon such a curious theme requires us to ask a number of questions about Lord Milner's motives in life. He called himself a nationalist; but nationalism, however ardent, need not harp upon the idea of race.

Was the intensity of Milner's race patriotism a legacy of his youth, a legacy of the time when he felt insecure in the company of his fellow Oxford men because of the differences which separated him from them? Did he try too fervently to identify himself with his fellow countrymen because he was uneasy about his German antecedents? Did he seek to cleave too closely to "the great family of Britons" because he was embarrassed by his origins?

If this were the case his very fervour contributed to his failure. His plans for a unified Empire and for an Imperial Council were valid propositions. His desire to create a more powerful Empire by binding the Dominions together deserved the attention of his contemporaries. These were aspirations worthy of a statesman.

To advocate a novel and daring programme for the Dominions was difficult enough; to restrict the work of Empire unification to a portion of the "citizens" of the Empire was to add to the difficulties.

Lord Milner had no wish to penalise, in any way, those "citizens" of the Empire who were not of British stock, but he took care to make it clear that, in his opinion, genuine reliance could only be placed upon the British element in the Colonies, whenever the strength and unity of the Empire were under consideration.[1]

---

[1] In this connection the opinion of a South African scholar, Professor Marais, is worthy of notice. In his *Fall of Kruger's Republic* (Oxford, 1961), p. 172, he writes of Milner: "The men of the Dominions on whom Britain must depend in the construction and maintenance of . . . closer union were, he believed, the colonists of British race".

This insistence upon race made his ideas exclusive. He at once rebuffed the Boers of South Africa and the French Canadians. He also antagonised a great mass of Britons, for many of them, in the Dominions and in the home islands, believed that racialism, however qualified, was so illiberal that it could have no place in the modern British Empire.[1]

In the years before the first World War Lord Milner was struggling toward a splendid object; he desired to achieve something new in Imperial relations—a complete equality of status between the member nations of the Empire. But this third factor, his continual emphasis of his race patriotism, served to add to the heavy weight of inertia and tradition, at home and in the Colonies, that he was required to push out of his path if he were to achieve the powerful Empire of his dreams.

V

Lord Milner began his preparations for the Colonial Conference of 1907 long before the Colonial statesmen arrived at Westminster. He realised that the Liberal Ministry was not inclined to act in the manner he desired at the Conference, but he hoped that he would be able to influence their policies by applying external pressure in the Press, in Parliament and in those other circles which sometimes decide the actions of Governments in London.

The first step in his campaign was taken at the end of 1906; in his speech at Manchester in December he remarked that the Prime Ministers of all the self-governing Colonies were to meet in London in a few months time: "What use", he asked his audience, "is going to be made of that momentous occasion?" He pointed out that despite its high importance the Colonial Conference was a transitory affair

---

[1] The reader should, perhaps, remind himself that in this period the "Racial Question" generally referred to the relations between European peoples. In South Africa, for example, the "Racial Question" meant relations between British and Boers; these remarks are limited to this aspect of the problem, and are not concerned with the peoples of the so-called Dependent Empire, a matter that was not especially prominent at the time.

sitting for brief periods at long intervals; it was typical of "our present happy-go-lucky system". The Imperialists, he said, felt with "intense anxiety" the need to make use of the fleeting opportunity provided by the Conference, and he hoped that the occasion would not be neglected.

Early in February 1907 Milner made his next move. There was one member of the Liberal Ministry who criticised the illogical methods of the State almost as fiercely as he did. This was R. B. Haldane, the Secretary of State for War, who, in this period, advocated a "scientific" reorganisation of the machinery of Government. Although Haldane had deserted Milner's cause in company with the other members of the "trio of Milner worshippers" he had remained faithful to the friendship after Grey and Asquith abandoned it. Lord Milner now sought Haldane out in order to discuss Empire affairs with him in private. He was bitterly disappointed by the conversation and wrote to Amery in order to tell him of the episode:[1]

Very Confidential

I listened to Haldane for nearly 20 minutes the other night on the subject of "Imperial organisation"—a private conversation, so that he might have said something if he had a mind to. It was all *blather*. If that is *the best* we can expect from these fellows, Heaven help us. M.

In these circumstances Lord Milner decided to rely upon the public Press in order to create an atmosphere that would embarrass the Government if it failed to exploit the opportunity of the Conference. Milner's influence over the newspaper Press of his day was remarkable. Unlike the Ministers of the Crown he was not a man who could reveal the secret plans of the Government to the journalists; unlike the chief opposition politicians he was not in a position to provide selected newspapermen with advance information about the policies of the Unionist Party because he refused to join its councils as a member of the Shadow Cabinet. The "inspired leak", that great weapon of the public man, was not the means he employed to deal with newspapers.

[1] Amery Papers, Milner to Amery, 11th February 1907.

Nevertheless, Lord Milner enjoyed a powerful following in the public Press. The editor of *The Times*, G. E. Buckle, was a personal friend; Amery and others on the staff of that paper were devoted admirers. J. L. Garvin and Edward Grigg, later Lord Altrincham, were at this time editor and assistant-editor of the *Outlook,* an influential weekly paper; they regarded Milner as the greatest figure on the Conservative side in politics, second only to Chamberlain who was no longer active. Fabian Ware and H. A. Gwynne of the *Morning Post* were men who hoped Milner would save the Empire by assuming supreme power in the State. Leo Maxse of the *National Review* looked upon Lord Milner as the great hope of the country. He was admired by Lord Northcliffe. These men controlled the most important Conservative journals of the day; although they disagreed about many things they were united in their opinion of Lord Milner as a man who was worthy of power and authority in the State. There was never any need for him to seek their help; they were always proud to associate their journals with his name. Lord Milner, in short, was one of those who could agree with the dictum of Sherlock Holmes: "The Press, Watson, is a most valuable institution, if you only know how to use it".

In order to explain his Imperial policies to the widest possible audience Lord Milner prepared an article for the *National Review* for April 1907; the article was concerned with the theme of the Colonial Conference and the New Imperialism; advance copies were sent to the editors of *The Times* and the *Morning Post*. Both these journals devoted a considerable portion of their space to discussion of Lord Milner's ideas and proposals; long extracts from his article were reproduced in each of these papers before the April edition of the *National Review* was published; other Conservative journals added their own words of praise. A chorus of approval of Lord Milner's views dominated the Unionist Press on the eve of the Conference. A radical weekly, *The Nation*, in its issue for 6th April, grumbled that: "The Empire is above party. So we all agree. . . Yet the coming of the Colonial Conference casts its shadow before it in the shape of a too-familiar Press campaign, in which the name of the Empire is to be used once again in the interests of party. . ."

VI

Among the Colonial statesmen who came to London for the Conference in April 1907 there were two who towered above their colleagues; these were Alfred Deakin of Australia and Sir W. Laurier of Canada. British Imperialists looked upon Deakin as the champion of their ideas at the Conference; they despised Laurier as the man who could be relied upon to block all their proposals for a more closely unified Empire.

Lord Milner was not content to confine his pre-Conference activities to the United Kingdom; he decided to undermine the position of the Liberal Government in advance of the meeting and he calculated that this could be done most efficiently by warning Deakin, before he left Australia, of the conditions that he would find in London. In February he explained the plan to Amery who was helping him with his pre-Conference preparations:[1]

As regards Deakin, I am waiting to write to him. . .
I think I shall write to him very fully and frankly, telling him what a desperate mess we are in and imploring him to come to terms with the reasonable people while over here, so that, when this tyranny is overpast, if ever it is, we may be in a position to do something promptly. It is perfectly horrible to think that this Conference is bound to be a total failure. . . The only chance is to make the Colonial Imperialists realise that the attitude of the present holders of power is *not* that of the country, or even the whole of their own party.

This action was typical of Lord Milner's attitude to public affairs. Whenever he disagreed with his political opponents

[1] Amery Papers, Milner to Amery, 11th February 1907.

he convinced himself that they were not the true representatives of the national will; they were merely usurpers who had misled an ignorant electorate.

When they were settled in London Deakin, Dr. Jameson the Prime Minister of Cape Colony, and a few other Colonial statesmen were invited to dine with the Compatriots Club. Amery reported to Milner that his letter had been received and that Deakin "was very delighted" with it. At the Conference Alfred Deakin revealed himself as a staunch champion of Colonial nationalism; he was also the leading advocate of the New Imperialism among the Colonial leaders; he urged the Conference to accept the idea that the Empire must become a partnership of free nations, all equal in status and organised for their common welfare. In order to make these propositions a political reality he asked the great Colonies to surrender some portion of their individual sovereignty to an Imperial Council; he hoped that a permanent secretariat would be established to maintain and preserve the influence of the Conference during the intervals when it was not sitting. The choice for the Empire, he said, was between a closer union and disintegration. His proposals were most strongly supported by Dr. Jameson, the late hero of the Raid.

Deakin implored the Colonial Secretary to open the meetings of the Conference to the public but Lord Elgin refused to comply with the request. In consequence, Deakin spoke frequently at public luncheons and banquets so that he could communicate his ideas to the people of Great Britain. At a meeting held in the Queen's Hall on 16th May Milner joined him on the platform; Milner revealed to the audience something of Deakin's defeats at the private sessions of the Conference: "Mr. Deakin", he said, "was commonly supposed during his visit here to have been treated with a certain amount of official cold water. He probably did not expect anything else. He was more than compensated for it in the warmth of the welcome he was certain to receive in any assembly of unofficial Britons. . ."

Lord Milner's revelations became the subject of the first leading article in *The Times* for the next day: Referring to Milner the paper declared; "If, as he says, official cold water was freely thrown upon Mr. Deakin in the Conference, there has been abundance of compensating warmth in the popular reception of his vigorous speeches. We are indeed indebted to these speeches for most of what we know about the actual aims and arguments of the Premiers in the Conference, since it has suited the Government to issue only meagre and unsatisfactory summaries of their utterances".

Alfred Deakin made so powerful an impression upon the British Imperialists that many of them hoped he would abandon Australian politics in order to lead their party at Westminster. It was felt in Imperialist circles that Chamberlain's successor as "fighting leader" had been found at last. Milner later said of Deakin that "he appealed to me more than any other statesman of my time, except perhaps Mr. Joseph Chamberlain. . ."[1]

Milner's admiration was fully reciprocated by the Australian leader. After his visit to London was over, he wrote to Milner in order to beg him to realise that he bore upon his shoulders the hopes of the Imperial party. From the ship that carried him back to Australia Deakin wrote:[2]

> In the one confidential chat I was privileged to have with you, the tone of your remarks was distinctly pessimistic. I should be sorry if this is your general mood. The hope of the Imperial Party in the United Kingdom appears to me to rest upon *you*. If you doubt who shall guide and inspire?
>
> ... You can rally the younger men... you can attract the large section of the British opinion which is waiting for a lead and an Empire policy... I can see no other man who will be so much trusted... *You* can turn the tide...

The great object of Milner's activity at this time was to advance the Imperial cause at the Conference despite the lukewarm attitude of the British Government. He desired, above all things, to lift his campaign for Empire unity out

[1] Walter Murdoch, *Alfred Deakin* (London, 1923), p. 265.
[2] Deakin's letter to Milner is printed in Wrench, *Milner*, pp. 381–2.

of the cockpit of partisan politics. His revelations certainly aroused the ardour of the Conservatives; but Liberals were rebuffed by an agitation which seemed to be little more than a vigorous attack upon the Government by those who were always ready to criticise it. In their opinion, the Tories were exploiting one of the oldest of party tricks; they were trying to identify their party with the interests of the Empire, at the same time that they sought to prove that the Liberal Government was only anxious to neglect Imperial affairs. In this way Lord Milner helped to defeat his own purpose; the progress of his campaign was hampered by the narrow bias of his tactics. The antagonism between parties was increased as a result of his speech of the 16th May and the support it was given in the Unionist Press.

VII

Sir Wilfred Laurier received less attention from the Imperialists in London. However, he was the Colonial Premier who mattered most in this period of Empire history.

Laurier had served as Prime Minister of Canada since 1896; he thus brought with him to the Conference an experience of these meetings which was unrivalled by any other statesman in the Empire. His handsome presence (he bore a striking resemblance to Lord Beaconsfield), his eloquence in the English language which was not his mother tongue, and his political courage had long since won him the respect of people in Britain, in Canada, in France and in other parts of the Empire.

In addition to these high personal qualifications, Laurier represented the most important of the great Colonies; in this period Canada was regarded, in the contemporary phrase, as "the greatest Dominion under the Crown". The wealth and future potential of Canada were particularly treasured by British Imperialists at this time because they feared that Canadians might abandon the Imperial connection in favour of closer economic and even political co-operation with the United States.

Chamberlain, in particular, had been excited by Canadian participation in the Boer War; as his biographer tells us "Had not the great Dominion rallied with the rest in the Boer War he would not have been brought to stake his life upon his last crusade for Imperial unity".[1]

At the Colonial Conference of 1902 Chamberlain's great task was to impress upon Laurier the validity of his plans to unite the Empire. Sir Wilfred was the man who could decide the future course of Imperial history, in one direction or another.

At that vital Conference, however, Chamberlain committed an unbelievable blunder, which has been ignored by most British writers despite the effect it had upon the development of the Imperial idea.

The Colonial Secretary, with good reason, has always been regarded as an expert in the delicate business of handling men; on this occasion, however, he revealed an incompetence which defies understanding.

During their discussions Laurier insisted that the secret of the Empire's strength lay in "local diversity and freedom", Chamberlain disagreed with that opinion. In his enthusiasm "He made no concealment of his belief that Sir Wilfred was a very imperfectly assimilated Englishman, and that his reluctance was due to his French blood".

This suspicion rankled. Laurier tried to convince Chamberlain that he spoke as a Canadian, and not as a partisan of the French community in Canada. He suggested that Chamberlain would appreciate his attitude if he had a private interview with four of Laurier's Canadian colleagues, none of whom were Frenchmen. Laurier arranged to absent himself from the meeting; and the Colonial Secretary stepped into the trap. "Mr. Chamberlain jumped at the proposal. . . To his surprise . . . these four men of the chosen race, Anglo-Saxons all . . . took substantially the

[1]Garvin, *Chamberlain*, vol. III, p. 532.

same stand as the son of Quebec. Mulock and Borden talked particularly straight from the shoulder. They were loyal to the King, they desired to retain Canada's connection with the Empire, but they were Canadians. Like Mr. Chamberlain himself, they believed that the Empire began at home".[1]

The result of this incident was significant not only for Chamberlain but also for Lord Milner; Laurier was convinced that the Imperial movement in Great Britain was merely a device to strengthen the position of the United Kingdom at the expense of the other parts of the Empire:[2]

> Canada was not left to work out its own conclusions... Practical statesmen from Joseph Chamberlain to Lord Milner, theoretic propagandists from the British Empire League to the Round Table group... did all in their power to bring the Colonies more closely within the Imperial orbit... The need was urgent. Britain was losing her supremacy...
>
> ... Wilfred Laurier ... held a unique place in the imperial counsel. As the representative of the non-English speaking peoples of the white Empire, he typified a problem which the racial Imperialist had to solve or abandon his endeavour...
>
> The conception of Canada's status which Sir Wilfred developed... was that of a nation within the Empire... As for the Empire, its strength and its only hope of permanence lay in the freedom of the component parts; centralisation would prove unwieldy and provoke revolt...

VIII

When the 1907 Conference met the Unionists were no longer in power. As a matter of course they were required to rely upon other than official means in their efforts to influence the decisions of the Colonial statesman. A dinner with the Compatriots, a private conversation in the dignified gloom of a West-end club, the splendour of a country house

---

[1] For this incident see O. D. Skelton, *Life and Letters of Sir Wilfred Laurier* (Toronto, 1921), pp. 298-9; the reader should notice that the Borden referred to was Sir Frederick Borden, Canadian Minister of Defence and Militia, and not Laurier's political opponent, Sir Robert Borden.

[2] *Ibid.*, pp. 287-91.

weekend, an intimate meeting of selected guests at the House—all the traditional methods of charming an important visitor were used to further the objects of the Imperial party. Unfortunately, these well-proven devices sometimes failed to work. Laurier once delivered his opinion of them:[1]

A visit... to England is in many ways a pleasure... Yet it is always a strain... Along with much genuine and spontaneous kindliness one felt the incessant and unrelenting organisation of an imperialist campaign... In this campaign, which no one could appreciate until he had been in the thick of it, social pressure is the subtlest and most effective force. In 1897 and 1902 it was Mr. Chamberlain's personal insistence that was strongest, but in 1907 and after, society pressure was the chief force. It is hard to stand up against the flattery of a gracious duchess... We were dined and wined by royalty and aristocracy and plutocracy and always the talk was of Empire, Empire, Empire. I said to Deakin in 1907, that this was one reason why we could not have a parliament or council in London... Fortunately, there were some good friends who seemed to like us for ourselves, not least the children...

Lest it be thought that Sir Wilfred was too sensitive or too bitter to appreciate the hospitality of those who received him in London we should notice the opinions of him held by some of the Imperialists at this time. In the ordinary course such opinions are concealed behind that façade of good manners which is a requirement of successful international or Imperial diplomacy. When Dr. Jameson, the hero of London society, met Sir Wilfred for the first time, at the 1907 Conference, he dismissed the Prime Minister of Canada in a phrase. He said to Leo Amery: "I don't care for your French dancing master".[2] In 1911 when Laurier's long term as Prime Minister came to an end after the defeat of his party at the polls, Rudyard Kipling at once wrote to Milner to tell him the significance of Sir Robert Borden's victory in the Canadian election:[3]

[1] *Ibid.,* pp. 299–300.
[2] Amery, *My Political Life,* vol. I, p. 313.
[3] Milner Papers, Kipling to Milner, 23rd September 1911. The Bryce mentioned in this letter was James Bryce, British Ambassador in Washington.

Batemans,

Dear Lord Milner,   Sep. 23rd 1911

Yesterday I was at Sir Max Aitken's place sitting in the sunshine while telegrams of the results of the Canadian elections were handed to me on a lordly dish. It's some few years—7 or 8—I think—since I have been happy, and knowing that you also must have rejoiced a little, I write to you, to remind you

(*a*) that this busts the Laurier-Botha liaison in what are called our Imperial councils.

(*b*) that it sickens Bryce which is always a work acceptable to God.

(*c*) that Fisher of Australia will now have leisure to modify his views on the limited liability of Colonies within the Empire, because Borden will explicitly repudiate Laurier's pronouncement on that subject.

(*d*) Australia will be deprived of Big Sister's example as an excuse for nibbling after American "protection" on her own behalf.

(*e*) I do believe it smashes the French power for good. . .

(*f*) It is the making of a new Canada because the U.S. will now . . . say rude things and that will stiffen Canada's national back. . .

These and many more points you know a hundred times better than I: but it's consoling to write them out in order. Seriously don't you think it's the best thing that's happened to us in ten years? I was so resigned to defeat that I didn't realise what victory meant . . . anyway it should give us five years of breathing space and one can do three-quarters of anything in that time.

Ever sincerely,
Rudyard Kipling.

P.S. Also we've worked *very* hard for it.

In view of this letter, the acid comment on Lord Milner and his followers by a recent writer deserves our notice: "The trouble with Milner, and the whole school of contemporary British Imperialists of which he was the intellectual leader, was that they were determined to force a large part of the world voluntarily to associate with them. And that is rather a difficult thing to do".[1]

IX

The Imperialists, despite their ardour, expected the Colonial Conference of 1907 to produce few valid results.

[1] John Strachey, *The End of Empire* (London, 1959), p. 94.

Some of the objects urged by Milner in his *National Review* article were achieved: it was decided that the Conference should be called "Imperial" and not "Colonial"; the British Prime Minister was to be its future president, *ex officio*; it was to meet regularly every four years as a permanent institution of Empire; from this time the great self-governing Colonies were to be styled Dominions or Self Governing Dominions.

So far as contemporaries could see, these developments were open to two separate interpretations. They might be looked upon as the first steps toward Imperial Federation; or, they could be regarded as an arrangement to provide an opportunity for consultations between the Premiers of independent nations within the Empire. The real decisions about the fate of the Empire were left to the future. The Conference of 1907 merely postponed the issue of Empire integration at a moment when the Imperialists believed that time was a vital factor, if Britain was to maintain itself in the 20th-century world of great nation states.

It was recognised by the Imperialists that the attitude of Canada was the key to this undefined future. As a result, many of them began to urge Lord Milner to carry his Imperial message to that vital frontier of Empire; Amery and his friends begged their chief to go to Canada, for the sake of the Empire. Their appeals were powerfully reinforced by the attitude of Lord Grey, the Governor General of Canada; he had known Milner since the 1880s when they were colleagues at the headquarters of the Liberal Unionist Organisation.

At this time Grey was one of those racial Imperialists who believed that Canada was in a position to become the dominating power in North America. He felt that the national authority of the United States was certain to decay because of the influx into that country of millions from southern and central Europe. He imagined that the "best people" in the United States were emigrating to Canada and leaving their country in the hands of a degenerate and corrupt population which would soon reveal itself as inadequate in international affairs. Grey urged Milner to come to Canada in order to explain to Canadians the mighty significance of the New Imperialism.

For a long time, Milner refused to consider the idea; he desired to husband his physical energies for political work in Britain. Eventually, however, he decided to give way to the exhortations of his friends, and a Canadian lecture tour was arranged. In these circumstances Milner was naturally anxious to meet as many Canadian leaders as possible, before he visited their country.

Among the Canadian guests in London in the spring of 1908 was W. L. Mackenzie King, already recognised in Britain as a "future Prime Minister of Canada". As a matter of course King was zealously entertained by the Unionists at Westminster and in London. His impressions of the scene at Westminster are especially valuable because he observed his hosts as an outsider; he could look upon them with that clarity of insight which the visitor to a foreign country often enjoys. King's biographer tells us that he liked the Unionist leaders but "he distrusted their political views, and he especially disliked their brand of Imperialism, with its corollary of central control. . . They . . . failed completely to grasp the strength of national feeling in the Dominions".[1] In his diary King wrote:

> There is in England a real *Governing* class, in the sense that it seeks to control and actually does control and guide the national interests both in England and in the Dominions beyond. The English mind has been so long trained to this way of looking at the world that I can see wherein it will be many years before it will ever come to fully appreciate what self-government means.

Mackenzie King was a guest at a Compatriots Club dinner. The chief speaker on that occasion was Lord Milner. He made a powerful impression upon the young Canadian who wrote in his Diary for 3rd April 1908:

> I could see his strength as he spoke, and became conscious that it

[1] For these quotations and extracts from Diaries see R. MacGregor Dawson, *William Lyon Mackenzie King* (London, 1958), pp. 167–70.

was the strength of one who believed that he was born to rule. His motives are, I think, above question. He would be guided by a sense of justice in everything, but believes with the inherent belief that many Englishmen have, that British power is the only means of asserting that justice. . . I am inclined to think that in the Tory camp are those who incline towards rule—in the Liberal camp those who have faith in the many and believe in them. . . What was borne in upon me particularly in listening to Lord Milner . . . was that it was not so much the welfare of human happiness irrespective of their race or creed, as the furtherance of the power and strength of the British race that constitutes the main purpose in their programme. . .

X

Lord Milner's task in Canada was extremely complicated; his object was to explain the New Imperialism to the Canadians while avoiding any offence to local opinion. He left England in company with Arthur Steel-Maitland in the autumn of 1908. After a fortnight of travel in the Dominion his Imperial speeches began, in Vancouver; he later said of this series of talks that it provided him with the rare opportunity to "develop my ideas in a more or less complete and systematic manner". At Vancouver, in the Canadian Club at Winnipeg, in Toronto, at the Board of Trade in Montreal, and in other important Canadian towns Lord Milner discharged his delicate task with skill. He avoided the strident tones of a partisan but he explained his own Imperial aspirations with that air of frankness which was typical of him. At Toronto he came to grips with the difficult question of closer Imperial union. He pointed out that some Imperialists believed that no progress in this direction could be made without the creation, as a first step, of an Imperial Parliament or a Council of Empire. He declared that he was one of those who believed in a Federal Empire; "I am unable to conceive the effective permanent all-round co-operation of the self-governing states of the Empire without a common organ, an executive belonging to all of them. . ." However, he laid emphasis upon his opinion that such a development was not the beginning of the process but its natural end and culmination; it was far more important for the nations of the Empire to begin to co-operate together in the everyday problems that confronted them; "While we keep the ideal in view, let us pay immediate attention to the one practical thing after another that arises and that can be dealt with here and now".

These speeches awoke the enthusiasm of the Imperialists in Canada and in the United Kingdom. However, the ardour of Milner's friends in Britain threatened to spoil the careful work of the tour. Lord Grey, writing from Government House in Ottawa, sent a warning to Milner:[1]

My dear Milner,   22nd January 1909
    I enclose an article from the "Victoria Daily Colonist" which is a sample of the articles appearing in other papers. You will note that your contribution to the crystalisation of Imperial sentiment in Canada is gratefully acknowledged; but the suggestion of the "Observer" the "Times" and the "Daily Mail" that imperial sentiment is weakening in Canada is violently resented, and a hint to this effect to Garvin, Maxse, Northcliffe & might be useful.
    I have written to Northcliffe privately. The idea which is being increasingly put forward by the Unionist Press at home . . . that unless the Unionists are returned to power for the purpose of establishing Protection in Great Britain, with a Tariff preference to Canada, the Canadian people will haul down the Canadian flag and run up the "Stars & Stripes", is regarded as an insult to Canada.

Yours ever,
Grey.

The article in the *Victoria Daily Colonist* of 14th January 1909, which Grey sent to Milner, deserves notice; it reveals the way in which some Canadian nationalists who were also Imperialists resented the cavalier tones and imputations of the Imperialists in Britain. The article declared:

A London paper says that Lord Milner found Imperial sentiment weakening in Canada, and arrested the decline. We do not believe that Lord Milner ever said anything of the sort. He has too much sense. He found nothing of the kind. He contributed to the crystallisation of imperial sentiment in Canada by laying stress upon the equality of the component parts of the Empire. This was very useful

[1] Milner Papers, Grey to Milner, 22nd January 1909.

work but such papers as the Observer... can undo a great deal of
good work by their efforts to speak oracularly upon a subject upon
which they are absolutely uninformed.

The people of Canada are growing very tired of such utterances...
The men responsible... are imbued with the notion that Great
Britain has a species of proprietorship in Canada, and that Canadians
owe a loyalty to them... If we endeavour to make a trade arrangement
with France, these wiseacres suggest that our loyalty is in some way
weakened... The British Press is doing its best to make the word
"loyalty" hateful to Canadians. It is being overworked... Another
expression that is being worked to death is "imperial sentiment".

Milner's Canadian tour also had its effect upon political
developments in Great Britain. By the beginning of 1909
Lord Northcliffe had renewed his allegiance to the policy of
Tariff Reform and Imperial Preference; this meant that *The
Times, The Observer,* the *Daily Mail,* the *Evening News* and
other newspapers were now committed to the support of
the Chamberlain programme; as a result the Tariff Reform
section of the Conservative Party was powerfully reinforced.
In the *Daily Mail* for 29th January 1909 an article by "A
Unionist" dealt with "The Future of Lord Milner":

... the whole Unionist party feels that Lord Milner... will be
the brain carrier of Imperial policy for the next twenty years...

Lord Milner cannot be less than second even in the next Unionist
Government. In any Unionist Government thereafter he will probably
be first, and this because Mr. Chamberlain's mantle has unmistakeably
fallen upon him...

... Lord Milner's speeches in Canada were a public education.
They revived the Imperial cause...

... And now he has the special support of the community holding
the casting vote in the whole Imperial problem—Canada... Lord
Milner as Secretary of the Colonies must hold a place no less commanding in the next Unionist Cabinet than Mr. Chamberlain held in the last.

This article was aimed directly at Arthur Balfour by a
marksman who always occupied a prominent place in his
calculations. From the very beginning of the Chamberlain
campaign in 1903, Lord Northcliffe always insisted that the
Tariff Reformers would never succeed in their design unless
they persuaded Canada, the wealthiest and most important

of the Dominions, to support their proposals. "Canada and the Preference Scheme" became a refrain in the Northcliffe Press, constantly repeated whenever the Tariff Reform campaign was analysed in all its aspects. Northcliffe now made it clear that, in his opinion, Milner had triumphed in that vital sphere where Chamberlain had always laboured in vain.

It was Arthur Balfour's little joke to pretend that he never paid any attention to the newspapers; in fact, no statesman watched the Press more vigilantly. It may well be that he spared himself the tedium of reading the journals of the day but his staff had strict orders to perform the task in his interest. He was instantly informed of the speeches of his fellow politicians and the editorial comments made upon them. This article in the *Daily Mail* was a sign, among others, that made the Conservative leader realise that he would shortly have to come to terms with his Tariff Reform extremists or else abandon the field to them. For years, as we have seen, his political life had been disturbed by Chamberlain's independent actions; he was not the man to contemplate with folded hands the appearance of a new rival for supreme power in their party. His great object after the 1906 election was to preserve the unity of the party, and he now knew that this could be done only by following the boldest course; he was coming to the decision that Milner, the Imperialists and the Tariff Reformers could be controlled only if he himself assumed the nominal leadership of their movement. Balfour, by the beginning of 1909, realised that he could not afford to wait for the appearance of an heir to Joseph Chamberlain's political authority.

VII. "Damn the Consequences" and The Round Table

A classic episode – Milner and Lloyd George – The themes of the struggle – Asquith convinced that a return to protection is a "moral certainty" – Milner advocates a policy of social reform – Unionism on its present lines "is hopeless" – Milner and the Licensing Bill – His objections to the 1909 Budget – "Damn the Consequences" – Results of the Glasgow speech – The Round Table – Origins of the group – Milner and the newspaper Press – Plans for an "Imperial Press Service" – The Return of the Kindergarten – Membership of the Round Table – An intimate fellowship – Objects and methods of the Round Table – Influence of the Round Table – Reasons for its failure – The desire for power without responsibility – Blunders of the Conservative Party – Milner's isolation.

I

IN the years between 1909 and 1911 there took place a classic episode of British political and constitutional history. When Lloyd George introduced his famous Budget of 1909, men in both parties recognised that a decisive battle had been joined. They were convinced that the result of their struggle would determine the fate of the country; and they were right in their conviction. The part Lord Milner played in this great crisis decided his political destiny.

Such is the piquant charm of English politics that it is fair to say that Milner's violent opposition to the Lloyd George Budget helped to win him a place in the Lloyd George War Cabinet of December 1916.

When Lloyd George formed his wartime Ministry in 1916 he needed the help of every section of the Tory Party in order to build up a secure majority in the House of Commons. Milner's conduct in the period 1909–11 convinced the die-hard element among the Conservatives that he was worthy of their support and allegiance. Men like George Wyndham and Lord Salisbury looked upon his actions at this time as a corroboration of his high achievements in South Africa. In consequence, Lloyd George chose Milner for the War Cabinet in order to rake in the fund of good will Milner possessed in those quarters normally hostile to himself.

Two tremendous themes were linked together in the series of political battles that began in 1909.

The first was constitutional; despite the Liberal majority in the Commons, Campbell-Bannerman's Government had been hamstrung by the partisan actions of the House of Lords. One Government Bill after another was regularly thrown out or amended by the Conservative majority in the Upper House. However shortsighted, the policy of the Lords was carried out with some measure of tactical skill and cunning. Care was taken to avoid offence to the Labour Party and the working men in the country; Bills concerned with matters of particular interest to them were allowed to pass. The object was to make the Government appear ridiculous and impotent; and this is exactly what happened. By the end of 1908 the distressed Liberals realised that a violent reaction was required of them if the political impasse created by the Lords was to be overcome.

In a speech at the National Liberal Club on 11th December 1908 Asquith, who had succeeded to Campbell-Bannerman's place, took up the challenge: "I invite the Liberal Party", he said, "to treat the veto of the House of Lords as the dominating issue in politics . . . the Budget of next year will stand in the very centre of our work. . . Finance is an instrument of great potency . . . and it may be found to be . . . a partial solvent of what, under our existing

Constitutional conditions, would otherwise be insoluble problems. . ."

The second theme of the struggle was even more significant for the future of the country. Since the battering of 1906 the Tariff Reformers had been thirsting for another trial of their policy. By the spring of 1908 it seemed that their hour had come.

At that time a severe depression in trade made a mockery of the Radical plans for social reform. Working men all over the country began to appreciate the value of Chamberlain's goal of industrial protection as something more concrete than the vague promise contained in Liberal schemes like Asquith's plan for old age pensions. If the Free Trade system failed to provide men with employment, the electorate was prepared to reconsider the programme of Tariff Reform and Imperial Preference as a valid alternative.

As early as January 1908 the Tariff Reformers won a startling victory in a by-election at Mid-Devon. The Radical *Daily News* of 23rd January reported with a hint of sadness that "On Friday the people of Mid-Devon gave Tariff Reform its first electoral success".

Mid-Devon, however, was only the beginning. During that year the Tariff Reformers carried one constituency after another in a prolonged series of by-election victories. They were convinced that the tide had turned and that the ill-luck which had plagued Chamberlain since 1903 was now a thing of the past.

The Liberals, for their part, were eager to accept battle on the issue of finance. Asquith's warning at the National Liberal Club was repeated by Lloyd George in a passionate speech at Liverpool on 21st December 1908. He deliberately linked together the constitutional and economic aspects of the situation: "You may depend upon it", he said, "those are the issues upon which you will be called upon to decide. . . Free institutions and Free Trade . . . on the other hand Privilege and Protection".

This theme was repeated by Winston Churchill when he

spoke at Birmingham on 13th January: "I should be quite content", he declared, "to see the battle joined . . . upon the plain and simple issue of aristocratic rule against representative government . . . between the reversion to Protection and the maintenance of Free Trade. . ."

One aspect of the situation has failed to impress itself upon students of the period. This was the tremendous impression made upon the Liberal leaders by Chamberlain's movement. In 1910 Lloyd George was prepared to consider Liberal support for a policy of Empire unification; in that year he proposed a National Government made up of leaders of both parties in the State; his idea was that the problems which confronted the country at that time were too ominous to be solved by the representatives of one party alone. Later on in his career, on more than one occasion, he seriously considered advocating a policy of protection. His plans have sometimes been dismissed as the calculations of a man without political scruples of any kind. However, we should notice that by 1908 Asquith himself was convinced that a return to protection was a "moral certainty" if the Free Trade system failed to provide the vast sums required for the military and social obligations of a modern State.

A few weeks after he became Prime Minister Asquith confided this opinion to St. Loe Strachey, the Free Trade editor of the *Spectator*. He took care to mark his letter "Strictly Private".[1]

		10 Downing Street,
Strictly Private	9 May 1908	Whitehall, S.W.

My dear Strachey,

I must send you a line to tell you what a disappointment & regret it causes me & most other Free Traders, to see the "Spectator" losing its way—I might add its head—in the whole domain of finance.

I have realised from the first that if it could not be proved that social reform (not Socialism) can be financed on Free Trade lines, a return to Protection is a moral certainty.

This has been one of the mainsprings of my policy at the Exchequer...

Yours sincerely,

H. H. Asquith.

[1] Strachey Papers, Asquith to Strachey, 9 May 1908.

Such an admission from a man who at that time owed his occupation of the first place in the Government in good part to his Free Trade attitude was a startling secret; it explains a great deal about the kind of thinking that occupied Ministers in the latter part of the year.

II

Lord Milner was dragged into this struggle almost against his will. Although the Liberals condemned him as the most reckless and violent of Tory partisans for the part he played in the crisis, at the beginning of this period he nearly broke away from the Conservative Party in order to advocate a policy of Socialism and Social Reform.

In the autumn of 1907 he arranged to deliver a number of speeches in various parts of the country. He hoped to achieve two separate objects as a result of these public appearances. Of first importance was his desire to further the cause of Empire Unity and Imperial Preference; secondly, he hoped to broaden the base of the Unionist Party so that it would have a wider appeal in the country. He undertook this brief campaign with reluctance, but he felt that duty required him to speak out.

On 25th September Milner explained the design behind his actions in a letter to Leo Amery; it was a declaration of war upon those narrow and selfish objects of the Conservative Party which disgusted Milner because they spoiled so much that was valid in the Unionist programme:[1]

> ... I am meditating a bold move, which is to cut myself quite adrift from "anti-Socialism". It means going into the wilderness, but I have come to the conclusion that Unionism on its present lines is hopeless, that the only chance—any way a poor one—is to have a new policy, root & branch, & trust to luck & the future to reform ... our present party, with perhaps a strong contingent of the saner workmen, on a broader basis than that of Conservative Mandarinism & middle-class timidity, lethargy & narrow mindedness.

[1] Amery Papers, Milner to Amery, 25th September 1907.

In a speech at Guildford Milner warned the Unionists to beware of an anti-Socialist crusade. If the Unionist Party sought to neglect those social evils which were a blot upon the national record it would be unfaithful to its best traditions, the traditions handed down by Disraeli in *Sybil* and in *Coningsby*. At Rugby on 19th November 1907 Milner returned to this theme. "Why", he asked, "should we not have Unionist Labour members as well as Radical Labour members? I think that the working classes of this country are misrepresented . . . I do not believe . . . the working classes are the unpatriotic, anti-national, down-with-the-army, up-with-the-foreigner, take-it-lying-down class of Little Englanders they are constantly represented to be". These fiery sentiments were hardly welcome in the circles which controlled Conservative policy; but Milner was reasonably content with the effect of his independent course. At the end of the year he wrote to Amery about this series of speeches:[1]

. . . I have done enough speaking to satisfy even you, &, if I have achieved no positive good, I hope I have at least prevented some mischief. The Unionist party, with the *Times,* I am sorry to say, at the head, were all "rushing violently down a steep place" into the bogey of a purely narrow middle-class & negative policy. I think I have helped to spoil that rotten game & kept the constructive & Imperial ideas to the front. . .

The game of politics in England, despite these remarks, seldom allows an individual to pursue an independent course of action. Although Milner made one or two more speeches like these, though he joined the Council of Toynbee Hall and eventually became its Chairman, this was the limit of his Socialist activity in this period. The hammer blows of the Radicals, as they developed their now policy in 1909, beat him back into the Tory fold and choked off almost at its inception the new course he began at Guildford.

In 1908 Milner was away from England for considerable periods; early in the year he travelled to Egypt, in the service

[1] Amery Papers, Milner to Amery, 27th December 1907.

of the Bank of Egypt; in the autumn, as we have seen, he went to Canada in order to explain the New Imperialism to Canadians. When he came back from Canada he was distressed to learn that the Lords were determined to throw out the Government's Licensing Bill of that year. He believed that such an action would be a tactical mistake because the Liberals were already losing so much ground in the country. The forward march of the Tariff Reformers in the constituencies foreshadowed the end of the Liberal Ministry; Milner felt, in these circumstances, that a policy of caution in the Lords would serve Unionist interests best. On 22nd November he explained his opinion about the Licensing Bill to Lord Lansdowne, the Conservative leader in the Upper House, in a letter marked "Confidential":[1]

> ... The very fact that I am so little of a party man brings me into touch with a great many of the neutral unpartizan people, whose wobbling to and fro turns elections. I do not think I can be mistaken in thinking that there are a large number of men, especially in the middle & better working-class, whose general political attitude is increasingly Unionist, but who being brought much into practical contact with the consequences of intemperance are keen ... to strike a blow at it...
>
> I think it will make a great difference ... if they can salve their consciences by attributing ... failure ... to the intractability or bad management of the Govt. & not to a wholly unsympathetic attitude on the part of the Lords...
>
> Forgive these humble lucubrations of a "man in the street"...

Milner was not to remain as a "man in the street" for very much longer. His differences with the Conservative leaders were banished in an instant when Lloyd George introduced his revolutionary Budget on 29th April 1909.

III

Lord Milner's objections to the Budget of 1909 were profound. His reaction to the counter-attack of the Liberals was

[1] Lansdowne Papers, Milner to Lansdowne, 22nd November 1908, marked "Confidential". Parts of this document are printed in Lord Newton, *Lord Lansdowne* (London, 1929), p. 370.

typical of his attitude to politics. As he studied the question, his convictions increased until he was prepared to advocate any course, however violent, in order to defy those with whom he disagreed. John Buchan, in a brilliant analysis, once described this aspect of Milner's character. He wrote of his old chief:[1]

... When he had satisfied himself about a particular course—and he took long to satisfy—his mind seemed to lock down on it, and after that there was no going back. Doubts were done with, faced and resolved... It was a dangerous gift for a statesman in a democracy where policy to the end must often be kept fluid...

The Budget of 1909 was a gargantuan measure, designed to solve at a stroke all the problems of the Government and the Liberal Party. Income taxes were increased, and a super-tax introduced; legacy and succession duties were raised; in the sphere of indirect taxation heavy imposts were levied upon spirits and tobacco. A third category of clauses—the famous land taxes—introduced a novel set of imposts upon landowners. Small in themselves, these charges could be increased at the discretion of the authorities until they effected a revolutionary change in English society. In his *Life of Gladstone,* the sage, John Morley, has pointed out that "if anything can be more odious than a living tax, it is a dead one"; no one has studied the Lloyd George Budget for its contents alone. With this single Bill, the Radical Chancellor revived his party in the country, pumped new life into the Free Traders, and began one of the most dramatic political campaigns of modern times.

Milner was astounded by the details of the Bill. As an Imperialist, he saw that the new programme threatened to destroy the arguments of the Tariff Reformers who insisted that the sums required for social reforms and armaments could be raised only by a return to protection; as a professional tax-gatherer, Milner believed that the new duties were unworkable in practice and dangerous in theory; there were, he said, distinct limits beyond which properly con-

[1] Buchan, *Memory Hold The Door*, p. 105.

ceived taxes ought not to go; "these enormous fines on capital", he declared, would stifle enterprise and diminish employment. Most vital of all were his objections to the unfairness of the Lloyd George scheme. The Radicals lumped all these measures together and defied the Lords to interfere with them since the traditions of the Constitution forbade the Peers to tamper with the financial provisions agreed upon in the Commons. If the Lords rejected the Bill, shouted the Radicals, it would be a breach of Constitutional practice. In Milner's opinion, however, the revolutionary details of the Finance Bill in themselves changed the nature of the Constitution. The object of the Radicals, he said, was to diminish the authority of the House of Lords in the entire sphere of legislation; it was their party, and not the Peers, who proposed to "knock the bottom out of the Constitution".

IV

Milner was dominated by a sense of indignation as the Radical campaign developed. The climax of his opposition took the form of a violent outburst in a speech at Glasgow on 26th November 1909. On that occasion he spoke in the forthright terms of a man wearied by the tactics of politicians; avoiding all side-issues, he concentrated his argument upon the duty of the House of Lords:

... We hold that this is a scheme of such exceptional magnitude, with such far-reaching consequences, that, believing these consequences to be evil, we cannot make ourselves responsible for the evil which will ensue... If we believe a thing to be bad, and if we have a right to prevent it, it is our duty to try to prevent it and to damn the consequences...

The results of the Glasgow speech were lasting, so far as Milner was concerned. Arthur Balfour was delighted with it. Months before, he had decided to order the Conservatives in the Lords to reject the Budget; his object in choosing so extreme a course was to rally the Tariff Reformers to the support of his leadership. His calculations

were now bearing political fruit of the most delectable
kind; the Imperialists in his party were, for the first time,
united behind him; Milner, the man he had looked upon as
a dangerous rival, now chose to forget his differences with
the official policy of the party and to join in the general
attack upon its opponents. Balfour congratulated himself
when he read the details of the Glasgow speech in his newspaper.

Lloyd George was also delighted. Here were the House of
Lords and the Conservative Party posing as the last bulwark
to revolution; and Milner shouted "Damn the Consequences!" This was exactly the line he hoped they would
follow. In speech after speech the Radical Chancellor
mocked his enemies as men who were prepared to advocate
anything, however reckless, in order to protect their narrow
class interests. On 3rd December he began the final phase of
his campaign in the country. He pointed out that many of
the Peers were opposed to a rejection of the Budget. He
said:

> There is Lord Balfour of Burleigh, who delivered one of the weight-
> iest speeches against rejection. . . There was Lord James, one of the
> greatest constitutional lawyers of the day. . . Lord Cromer, the
> biggest living pro-consul. . . Then there is Lord St. Aldwyn, the
> greatest of the Tory financiers. . .
> Who is really on the other side? Lord Curzon. . . For further
> particulars apply to Lord Kitchener. . .
> Then there is Lord Milner. . . His is a peculiar genius for running
> institutions and countries into destructive courses. There is the
> man who threw out the Budget. "D——the consequences" is his
> motto.

Lloyd George's attitude was reflected in the Radical Press
of the day. As we have seen, at the beginning of the crisis
Milner was exasperated with the Tories because of their
shallow class-consciousness. Nevertheless, he was now condemned as a bitter reactionary, concerned only with the
preservation of privilege. An open letter in the *Daily
Chronicle* for 7th January 1910 was typical of Liberal
opinion:

To Viscount Milner—My Lord, in your campaign for ducal dominion, for class privilege and pillage, there are men opposed to you who hail your advocacy with glee. Not once or twice . . . has it happened that blind reactionaries and obstructionists have unwittingly aided the cause of freedom . . . go on, my Lord, I beseech you, go on—and "damn the consequences".

This reputation stuck fast. Years later when Lord Hankey, then secretary of the Committee of Imperial Defence, met Milner for the first time he was surprised: "To me Milner was rather an unexpected man. I thought to find in him a man . . . with rather a tendency to rashness—'damn the consequences' Milner as the Radical newspapers used to call him. . . Actually his temperament was quite different". In the same way, Viscount Addison was astonished to discover that at close quarters Milner did not appear to be the violent creature of Radical legend. In the introduction to his published *Diary* Addison took care to write: "the views first expressed of Lord Milner . . . were based on . . . prejudices . . . to be corrected afterwards by knowledge gained from close personal work together. . ."[1]

Among the die-hard Tories, however, this image of Milner was cherished. Leo Maxse, George Wyndham, Amery and others of their group were still suspicious of Balfour, even though the mass of the Tariff Reformers were now prepared to support him. Amery and his friends could see that Balfour was guided by calculation, and that he was not the hot-blooded leader they required for the party. Milner, on the other hand, was a man prepared to act at the direction of his conscience; however harsh, the graphic plainness of his speech was more valid than Balfour's ingenious evasions. The feelings of this group were reflected in the Northcliffe Press, for at this time Lord Northcliffe was temporarily allied to the Tory extremists. In the *Daily Mail* of 10th January 1910, for example, one of his crack journalists, Charles Whibley, wrote:

[1] See Lord Hankey, *The Supreme Command* (London, 1961), vol. II, p. 578, and C. Addison, *Four and a Half Years* (London, 1934), vol. I, p. 5.

... Lord Milner is not a decorative orator. He did not learn his craft ... in Hyde Park. He possesses none of the sins of eloquence. His language is simple, as his argument is clear. .. He has lifted politics beyond the sphere of passion. His speeches are rare in the conflict of today. .. He aims at the triumph not of party but of England. ..

The General Election of January 1910 followed hard upon the Lords' rejection of the Budget. Only a triumph at the polls could justify and make valid the extreme course pursued by the Upper House, but the electors denied the Peers this satisfaction. Although Lord Milner hoped that the Conservatives would win, he was not particularly excited by the electoral campaign. Despite the image of him created by the Radicals he was always lukewarm in the matter of elections. In his opinion, the Budget policy was a threat to the safety of the country but mere politicians could not be expected to restore the situation, however many votes they received. Privately he informed his closest friends that he did not expect a Unionist victory in the election. Just before the final phase of the crisis, he explained his attitude to Geoffrey Dawson:[1]

My dear Robin,
    ... I don't feel very sure about a Unionist victory here next election. Large reduction of Govt. Majority is assured & general chaos probable. My own interest in what I call *Local* British politics is rather faint. It is only in their bearing on the bigger issues that they seem much to matter. Of course *good social legislation* in the U. K. is essential, but as regards that it is rather a case of Tweedle & Tweedle & both pretty bad.

Yours ever,
M.

V

Dislike of party politics was not the sole reason for Milner's lack of interest in the election. At this time he was busily engaged in building up yet another small circle of friends, unconnected with parties, but determined to influ-

---

[1] Geoffrey Dawson Papers, Milner to Dawson, 30th October 1909.

ence opinions and policies throughout the Empire. His new society was the famous *Round Table* group.

This curious band has yet to find its rhapsodist; but we may depend upon it that he will put in an appearance in the fullness of time. Meanwhile, certain fresh evidence contributes to our knowledge of the genesis of the company.

In the summer of 1909 an Empire Press Conference was held in London. Long before the Conference met, Milner and his disciples interested themselves in it.

At the end of December 1908 Geoffrey Dawson, at that time editor of the *Johannesburg Star*, warned Milner that the South African representatives to the Conference might not be Imperialist partisans of the kind they approved. Dawson was also distressed by the "perfectly appalling state of the newspaper correspondence from England *outwards*. . ." In these circumstances, he applied to Milner for help and advice; how could they make certain that their ideas dominated the Conference of newspapermen from every part of the Empire? What could they do to improve the quality of the news which was sent from Great Britain to the Dominions?[1]

In the ordinary course we might expect Milner to despise journalists and newspapers as a source of interference with the "majestic governing art"; but he had begun his career as a journalist, and throughout his life he sought to exploit the Press as a means of influencing public opinion. In South Africa he and his disciples always paid close attention to the periodical Press.

When he resigned as High Commissioner Milner turned to Lionel Phillips, a partner in the firm of Wernher, Beit and Company and at one time the President of the Transvaal Chamber of Mines, in order to recommend Geoffrey Dawson to his attention. Phillips, among other interests, controlled the *Johannesburg Star*; he agreed to appoint Dawson,

---

[1] Dawson's letter, dated 20th December 1908, marked "Private and Confidential" is preserved in the Amery Papers. Dawson changed his name in 1917; until that year his name was Geoffrey Robinson. The change was made in connection with a legacy.

Milner's Private Secretary, to the editorship of the paper. By this means, Milner hoped to make certain that his South African policies would continue to receive support in the country, after his departure.

In the same way, Philip Kerr (Lord Lothian) and Lionel Curtis were encouraged to interest themselves in the Press. Curtis, in particular, was anxious to secure control of a weekly paper in order to promote the two policies of South African Union and a federal plan for the whole Empire. In 1907 Kerr became the editor of a monthly magazine, *The State,* which advocated these programmes. In this case, the money required for the publication was guaranteed by Sir Abe Bailey, the South African mine owner.

When Milner received Dawson's appeal for help at the end of 1908, he recognised that his young friend had a valid case. News and articles sent from England to the Dominions did not always bear an Imperial tone and flavour. During his Canadian trip, Milner had been shocked by the "badness of the news from home". The Press Conference furnished the Imperialists with a splendid opportunity; if they could control the meetings, they might be able to work a radical change in the outlook of the journalists from overseas, and also in the quality of the stories despatched from England.

By the beginning of 1909 Dawson believed that he had discovered a solution to the problem. He hoped that an "Imperial Press Service" which "pooled" the news sent to the Dominions might be created. He explained the purpose behind his plan in the following terms: "it seems to me an excellent moment for establishing an organisation which might be . . . valuable in the days of a Government which made a serious effort to pull the Empire together". Milner at once agreed that such an engine of propaganda would be of value to the Imperial cause.[1]

---

[1] For the plans of Milner, Dawson and Amery see: Geoffrey Dawson Papers, Milner to Dawson, 19th February 1909, Dawson to Amery, 18th January 1909; Amery Papers, Milner to Amery, 25th January 1909. See also Amery, *My Political Life,* vol. I, p. 339.

In all matters concerned with the Press, Lord Northcliffe was the most powerful figure of his day; it was of vital importance to secure his interest and assistance in any project that involved newspapers and the transmission of news. Milner knew that he already enjoyed Northcliffe's respect and admiration; in addition, Leo Amery was one of Northcliffe's most valued employees, one of his "coming young men". Milner decided that Amery should tell Northcliffe something of the plan, so that he could help them with the scheme. Milner's idea was that Northcliffe should be consulted in the matter; but he warned Amery to take care; it was not his intention to allow Northcliffe to seize control of a project designed to influence public opinion in every part of the Empire.

By the time the Press Conference met in June of 1909, however, the situation had changed radically. Milner was now fired by another idea. During that summer several members of his Kindergarten returned from South Africa because their work in the Transvaal was finished. They were now free to turn to the next phase of their Imperial programme, and to employ in wider spheres those techniques which had succeeded so well in Johannesburg and at Capetown. Milner and his disciples, after a lapse of four years, were no longer separated by those vast distances which made co-operation in practical matters almost an impossibility. There was no need for them to rely upon Northcliffe, if they could work together in London as they had in the great days of the past. A first hint of this new development was contained in a letter Milner sent to Amery:[1]

... I am so glad you "knocked" Spender and Stead at the Press Conference.

I think we shall have to end by running a single Imperial Unionist party all over the Empire, which will cut itself adrift from all local parties & play the Irish game of impartially downing everybody everywhere who sells the pass.

[1] Amery Papers, Milner to Amery, 29th June 1909.

VI

During 1909 and 1910 the methods and purposes of Lord Milner's new group were worked out, by degrees. After a time they decided to call their symposium the Round Table.

In the early days, the membership of the Round Table fell into three separate categories. Milner, Lord Selborne and the members of the Kindergarten formed one element; a second section was made up of men like Amery and Sir Abe Bailey, who had known Milner for a long time but had never served under him in any official capacity; a third division consisted of newer adherents with no first-hand experience of South African affairs. F. S. Oliver, one of the brilliant wits of his day, and Waldorf Astor, the son of an American millionaire, were typical of these recruits. Oliver, a wealthy merchant-draper, was a welcome addition to the company. By means of his books and the letters he sent to highly placed political friends, he exercised a tremendous influence upon the politics of his day.

Many of these men made life-long friendships as a result of their association in the Round Table. Philip Kerr became the fast friend of Waldorf and Nancy Astor; R. H. Brand, one of the ablest of the old South African Kindergarten, established even closer ties when he married Nancy Astor's sister. The Round Table soon became an intimate fellowship. They looked upon each other with admiration; and they resolved to do great things together, in the national interest.

The object of the association was to win power and authority in national and Imperial affairs. Unlike most Englishmen concerned with such matters, however, the group scorned any connection with political parties.

The energies of the Round Tablers were directed into other channels. They intended to gain political influence by means of their conspicuous ability, by their social contacts and by the validity of their plans and proposals, which were to be decided on after long study and careful analysis.

Their programmes and projects were agreed upon at private meetings—or "moots"; on these occasions, the members met together and worked out in concert their own solutions to a variety of national and Imperial problems. They held their "moots" at Checkenden, Oliver's country home; at Hatfield, Lord Salisbury's seat in Hertfordshire; at Blickling, Lord Lothian's place in Norfolk; and at Cliveden.

In these congenial surroundings, the Round Tablers convinced themselves that their plans for the Empire deserved the attention of those in authority and of the public in general.

In order to acquaint the public with the fruit of their deliberations, they decided to publish books and articles on a wide variety of topics. Lionel Curtis, the most ardent of the Round Tablers, planned to establish a magazine for the purpose, in each of the Dominions. His enthusiasm, however, was received with some caution by Lord Milner who exercised a general authority over most of the projects of the Round Table. Always practical, Milner wondered where the funds for the scheme were to be raised, and where the men were to be found to carry out the plan. He told Amery at an early stage:[1]

About Curtis' plans . . . *Magazine.* I think one first rate Mag. in each Dominion would be of the greatest use. I don't see the use of one *here.*

Men. I also think One Man everywhere, *giving his whole time* to the direction, coordination etc. of efforts on our lines would be invaluable. For S. Africa that man might be Curtis. Here he *might* be Kerr. I don't know. Only I don't see, how if Kerr is to go into the House he could *give his whole time.* . . And he has nothing like the experience of you or Mackinder, even if he has the ability, which he *may* have, tho not certainly to my knowledge.

A considerable fund is required. . . My criticisms must not be treated as opposition, but more as contributions to working out a feasible plan. Perhaps you will bear these points in mind at Checkenden.

Eventually, it was decided to publish only one magazine, in London. This periodical, the *Round Table,* a "Quarterly

---

[1] Amery Papers, Milner to Amery, 3rd July 1909.

Review of the Politics of the British Empire", appeared for
the first time in November 1910. The editor was Philip
Kerr, but his name and those of the contributors were not
revealed. A note listed the offices where the *Round Table*
could be obtained in Canada, New Zealand, South Africa,
Australia and India. The aim of the magazine was to
"present a regular account of what is going on throughout
the King's dominions . . . entirely free from the bias of
local political issues". The promoters explained that they
did not seek "a large circulation"; their object was to
educate and influence a select public opinion. The funds
required for the paper were guaranteed by Sir Abe Bailey;
this point was not disclosed to the public, however.

In the years between 1910 and 1914 the *Round Table*
exerted a tremendous influence upon political thought in
every part of the Empire. When Leo Amery tried to explain
why the *Round Table* "failed to achieve any lasting effect" he
fixed upon the fact that "in order . . . to claim that it was
non-party, it deliberately kept the question of Empire
economic co-operation out of its programme. This was
staging *Hamlet* without the Prince of Denmark, and gave to
the whole movement an academic and unreal air".[1] Amery's
criticism is fair enough, but its emphasis is misplaced.

The Round Tablers were quite prepared to consider the
question of Empire economic co-operation. Like Milner,
however, most of them sought to obtain power and influence by "non-party" means; that is, they preferred to
exercise their great abilities elsewhere than in Parliament or
in the familiar controversies between parties.

Their chief had affected them with his dislike of the
ordinary methods of English political life. It was more congenial for them to achieve their aims by influencing the
Press; by acting behind-the-scenes; by demonstrating the
sagacity of their opinions in private conversations with the

---

[1] See his introduction to V. Halperin, *Lord Milner*, p. 14. For Austen Chamberlain's exasperated criticism of the Round Tablers see his *Politics from Inside* (London,
1936), p. 553.

statesmen, who possessed the visible trappings and the formal authority of office. They tried to act on a plane above that of the politicians.

Amery differed from most of these men because he was always vitally concerned with his parliamentary career. Philip Kerr never became a member of the House of Commons, although he was involved in political affairs throughout his life. R. H. Brand concentrated his efforts upon a career in finance; eventually, he became a director of Lazard Brothers, the merchant bankers; later on, as a director of *The Times* he was in a position to play a larger role in public life. When Geoffrey Dawson returned to England he was appointed editor of *The Times*, a post that consumed all his energies. Lionel Curtis chose the life of an academic; he sought to influence events with his books, lectures and pamphlets. F. S. Oliver disliked democracy and never attempted to win a seat in Parliament. The Round Tablers, like Milner, relied on these alternatives and avoided the routine of party politics when they sought to play their part in the political life of Great Britain.

In this peculiarity of the society lay a strong reason for its failure. The "moots" were usually private; the articles in the *Round Table* were always anonymous. As a result, an air of suspicion soon surrounded the Round Table set. Later on, this feeling became one of hostility because it was widely believed that Lothian, Astor, Dawson, Curtis and others were anxious, most of all, to exercise power without responsibility. This prerogative, so alien to the English way of life, is always resented in England.

VII

After their defeat in the Budget election of January 1910 the Conservative Party was involved in a series of protracted crises. They stumbled from one episode to the next, divided among themselves and without the effective leadership the situation demanded. The distracted Tories struggled for-

ward with hardship their garment, so confused that even
Arthur Balfour, one of the brilliant statesmen of recent times,
was unable to rally the Unionist mass to a coherent, organised and effective political Opposition.

The result of the January election was regarded as a
stalemate. For that reason, in the late summer of 1910,
Lloyd George advanced his proposal for the establishment
of a National Government, made up of the members of both
the great parties. The Liberal Chancellor believed, and many
Unionists agreed with him, that only a radical step like this
one could preserve and insure the security of the country
at a moment when the menace of Imperial Germany abroad,
and the rise of Socialism at home, threatened the established
institutions of Britain with novel and unprecedented
dangers. Arthur Balfour ruined the plan because of his Irish
prejudices; he refused to consider any compromise that
involved a valid measure of Home Rule for Ireland. As a
result the deadlock between parties which effectively stulti-
fied all positive action remained unbroken, and the country
was forced to hold another General Election, in December
1910.

On the eve of this election Balfour suddenly declared
that if the Tories won office his Government would submit
the principles of Tariff Reform, despite their victory at the
polls, to a Referendum, instead of at once enacting them into
law. Since Balfour was supported by Bonar Law and other
Tariff Reformers in this decision because they believed that
the policy of protection was a fatal incubus at elections in the
United Kingdom, his announcement not only split the
party but it also divided the Imperialists into quarrelling
factions. Many of them still adhered to the Chamberlain
policy of Imperial Preference. Austen Chamberlain and his
friends denounced Balfour's decision as a betrayal. Thus
divided, the Unionists failed to improve their position in the
elections.

In the summer of 1911 the unity of the party was smashed
to pieces once again. The die-hards refused to submit to

Balfour's decision to allow the Parliament Act of 1911 to pass into law. They believed that the Bill, which restricted the powers of the House of Lords, was a violation of the Constitution. They resolved to "die in the last ditch" before they permitted it to pass. They were outraged when Balfour and Lord Lansdowne agreed to accept the measure for tactical reasons, even though it involved revolutionary changes in the Constitution.

In November of that year a bored and weary Balfour at last resigned his post as leader of the party. He was replaced by Andrew Bonar Law, the most effective of the Tariff Reformers in the House of Commons. By the end of 1912, however, the new leader realised that the unity of the party could not be preserved unless the policy of Tariff Reform was abandoned. The Chamberlain plan, however valid for Imperial purposes, was a fatal handicap at elections in Britain. In consequence, Bonar Law ruthlessly scrapped the Tariff programme, to the dismay of the Chamberlainites.

Lord Milner observed these developments with feelings of disgust. Gradually, he withdrew from the political scene. He believed that the miasma which hung over the Imperial party would never be dispersed by politicians. On occasion he did speak out, especially in 1911, but his interventions were transitory complaints, lacking long-range purpose and design; although they were not without effect, and were sometimes of a sensational nature, Milner was tired out by the bickerings of the politicians and sought to separate himself from them and all their works. At the beginning of this period Amery and his friends begged Milner to rush forward and seize control. Amery wrote to him in tones of high and fevered excitement:[1]

. . . we are absolutely paralysed. . . What are you going to do about it? You are the one and only man who can give us life and coherence. . .

What we want is a Graaff Reinet speech, or rather a campaign to do for England what Graaff Reinet did for South Africa.

[1] Milner Papers, Amery to Milner, 9th November 1910.

...You won't have to do it alone: there are plenty of workers even among the politicians ... and lots of young men outside...

The moment you speak with real intention everybody will know it & sit up...

Milner made various replies to these entreaties, but he refused to act as his friends urged. Finally, he explained himself to Amery in unmistakeable terms.[1]

...I am not going to make any new commitments. Anything that is done or planned must be planned *as if I did not exist.* As long as I continue to exist, I *may*, at times, be useful, but that will be a windfall. I have got absolutely to paddle my own canoe. I say this now ... in order that there may be no vestige of a misunderstanding hereafter...

By the end of this period the Liberals were convinced that Lord Milner was a spent force in English politics. In the *Daily News* for 29th March 1913 Alfred Gardiner, the Radical editor of the paper, explained that:

When Lord Milner advised the Lords to throw out the Budget and "damn the consequences", he gave the world a character study of himself in a phrase... It was a phrase that explained the most dramatic failure of our time.

... Today he is the most solitary and negligible figure in our public life—a man whose name is synonymous with failure ... with harsh and provocative methods and reactionary views...

... He is merely an intellectual machine, and he is too honest to play the demagogue or assume virtues that his mind holds in contempt... Lord Milner has always left humanity out of his calculations...

... The fundamental fact about Lord Milner is that he is a German—born in Germany, the son of a German professor by an English mother, cradled in Germany, educated in German schools and German ideas... When this fact is fully realised, his entire divorce from the English spirit is readily understood. He stands for German, or rather Prussian ideas in English politics. In him we see the Bismarckian policy as well as the Bismarckian spirit in being... A drilled and disciplined proletariat is their hope against an insurgent democracy.

It is a vain hope. If Lord Milner's career proves anything it proves conclusively that Bismarckism cannot be successfully engrafted upon the tree of English liberty...

In attempting to transplant Bismarckism to British soil Lord Milner makes a mistake both of time and place. The creed is outworn even

[1] Amery Papers, Milner to Amery, 12th August 1911.

in Germany. In free England it never could and never will take root. The prison plant will not live in British air. . .

And so he stands, a forlorn, solitary figure in our midst, with no thinkable future. . .

Despite this article, it is clear enough that the Liberal impression of Lord Milner as a spent force was incorrect. The Liberals had allowed themselves to be misled by appearances. Milner stood alone for one reason only— because he refused to take an active part in the political life of his time.

Amery and the younger Tariff Reformers were continually appealing to him to seize control of their party, and the destinies of the country. The young men of the Round Table looked upon him as the wisest statesman of the period. The die-hard section of the Tory party thoroughly approved of his violent opposition to the Lloyd George Budget and the Parliament Bill of 1911; in September of 1911 George Wyndham, in despair at the futile bickerings among the Tories, asked Milner for an interview; afterwards he wrote to Milner to say "That talk meant a great deal to me. It saved the seed of all my political hope for this country".[1]

These different groups, together with their adherents in the country, comprised a formidable element in English politics. If Lord Milner ever decided to give the signal, his condition of isolation would be dissolved in an instant.

It was exactly at this time than an issue arose which impelled Milner to act. In his opinion, the Liberal plans for Home Rule in Ireland transcended the ordinary political business of the day. He was so hostile to this development that he resolved to do everything in his power to destroy the Ministry and its Home Rule Bill, which was already passing through the machinery of the legislature. He decided, at last, to forgo his isolation in order to emerge as a fighting leader.

[1] Wyndham's letter to Milner, dated 3rd September 1911, is preserved in the Amery Papers.

VIII. Jupiter Descends

I

THE problem of Ireland must be regarded as one
of the major failures of modern British statesmanship. The Irish crisis of 1912–14 was more terrible
than any other in recent English history, for, during those
years, the system of parliamentary democracy, so long accepted as the traditional method of politics in England, was
shaken to its foundations.

The reasons for this desperate situation lay far back in the
history of both countries; implacable hatreds, well-remem-
bered grievances, the conviction that justice and fair play
had been denied for too long—all these factors combined to
present the statesmen of 1912 with an affair that in its
essence was unlike any other that ever confronted them.

When John Morley in his biography of Gladstone sought
to describe Ireland in 1885 he wrote: "There lay Ireland—

squalid, dismal, sullen, dull, expectant, sunk deep in hostile intent". Since that time a few details had changed; the awful problem of land tenure in Ireland had been solved; but in essentials this was still the picture of Ireland that imposed itself upon the politicians of England.

There was one major difference. It made the issue even more critical than it had been in Gladstone's day. By 1912 the poisons which bubbled in the Irish cauldron threatened to spill over into the political life of England, with fearful results.

The politicians for a century past had failed to solve the Irish problem; but now the corrosive effects of the time factor had turned the affair into a matter of desperate moment. A solution, long delayed, was now vital, not merely for the well-being of Ireland but also for the tranquillity of England, at Westminster and also in the country. By 1912 Great Britain was face to face with dire emergency.

The extent of Lord Milner's part in the emergency has never been recognised, although some of the details have been revealed. We may look upon his activities in this period as a culmination of his hostility to the Liberal Government and to those methods of English parliamentary democracy he had learned to distrust during his career as an officer of the Empire. In 1914, as we shall see, one of his warmest supporters warned him that his plans for Ireland involved him in "crime" and "possible treason". Despite the warning, Lord Milner refused to abandon any of his designs. So great was his agitation at this time that he was prepared to advocate the most violent measures in order to achieve his objects. How often in human affairs is moral indignation a fruitful source of immoral action.

II

As a result of the deadlock election of December 1910 Ministers depended for their parliamentary existence upon the good will of the Irish Nationalist Party. The fate of the

Liberal Government hung upon Irish votes. John Redmond, the rotund and senatorial figure who led the Irishmen in the Commons, was at last in a position to exact from the Liberal politicians a measure that would satisfy the national demands of Ireland.

By 1912 he knew that the Tories were helpless in the face of any decision of the Liberal-Irish majority in the Commons. Since the passage of the Parliament Act in 1911 the House of Lords could delay, but it could not nullify legislation approved in the lower House. Despite this parliamentary situation Redmond's position was far from easy, for several vital reasons.

The Irish Nationalists sat in the House of Commons for one purpose only; their existence as a political party at Westminster served but one cause. Their object was to achieve Home Rule—to win for their country an Irish Parliament in Dublin, with an Irish executive dependent upon it for the exercise of authority. Exactly at this time, however, Redmond found that his position as leader of the Irish Nationalist movement was challenged by Irishmen resentful of his authority. These men were not convinced that independence could be achieved by parleying with English politicians at Westminster. They looked to direct action and even to violence for the fulfillment of their dream.

By 1912 Redmond and his colleagues were parliamentarians of long experience; although they represented Ireland's demand for Home Rule in the Imperial Parliament, they tended to do so as Westminster politicians. As the crisis developed, many of their followers became impatient. They began to question the policies and tactics of leaders who were willing to decide the destiny of Ireland by treating with Englishmen. By the time Redmond had closed his grip upon the parliamentary situation he began to lose the support of the Irish masses, the good will of certain influential trade union leaders, and the loyalty of a number of intellectuals in Ireland who now concerned themselves with the fate of their country. At first, their attitude was not particularly dangerous to Redmond's position, but it became increasingly more significant as time passed.

In order to understand the crisis of 1912–14 this aspect of Redmond's problems must be borne in mind. The situation on the eve of the introduction of a Home Rule Bill required the exercise of political and diplomatic skill of a high order. In the ordinary course Redmond was fully capable of guiding the negotiations with the Liberal leaders to the goal that he and his friends sought; but at this juncture he was hampered by the brittle demands of those in Ireland who suspected his determination and his ability to enforce his will upon Asquith, Lloyd George, Churchill and the other Ministers concerned with Irish affairs. The murmurings of this angry host confined him to a set course at a time when he needed room for manoeuvre in his negotiations.

III

Redmond's problems were not confined to difficulties with his own followers. The issue of Home Rule touched the English upper classes more nearly than most of the political questions of that day. The Irish Protestant landlords in the south of Ireland were their relations and connections. Both groups were terrified at the prospect of a Dublin parliament, dominated by Roman Catholics. This hostility to Irish nationalism had its effect upon their representatives in Parliament. Many Conservatives and Unionists at Westminster were prepared to sanction any course, however untraditional, in order to defeat Home Rule. For example, Lord Winterton, the Unionist Member for the Horsham Division, secretly established a small commando which was prepared to fight in Ireland in certain circumstances. By means of an advertisement in the newspapers he sought and found a small group of men "of courage and determination" who were ready to "undertake a desperate task". All these men had experience of war, either in South Africa or in

South American revolutions. Under Winterton's leadership, they expected to put their military accomplishments to use in Ireland.[1]

A third barrier that confronted Redmond was the most significant of all. The Irish Nationalists looked upon Ireland as a "seamless garment"; that is, they hoped to establish a state which encompassed all the provinces of Ireland in a single national unit. However, the Nationalists were violently opposed by the Ulstermen who dominated the north-east corner of Ireland. In order to maintain their independence of Dublin these Ulster Protestants were ready and willing to fight, against any odds.

The Liberals, for their part, chose to dismiss the attitude of the Ulstermen as bluff. Twenty years later, J. A. Spender still sought to ignore the realities of the situation in Ireland in 1912; in his *Life of Asquith* Spender remarks that "All sorts of causes have been held to justify rebellion— intolerable suffering, long-lasting oppression, the threats to life and liberty of an *instans tyrannus*—but the cause of Ulster fell into none of these categories".

The religious, social and economic differences between north and south in Ireland cannot be brushed aside so easily; to do so is to ignore the long history of Ireland and of Ulster. Although Redmond and the Liberals were reluctant to recognise it, the Ulster crisis was different from most of the political questions dealt with at Westminster; men were unwilling to accept a solution to it based upon a parliamentary majority in the House of Commons. This situation was pregnant with danger for Ireland, and for the British political system as a whole.

---

[1] This paragraph is based upon information sent to the present writer by the late Lord Winterton. See also Lord Winterton, *Orders of the Day* (London, 1953), p. 38. He and his friends, of course, planned to support Ulster, but their attitude reflects the general feeling of Conservatives about Ireland at this time.

[2] J. A. Spender and Cyril Asquith, *Life of Lord Oxford and Asquith* (London, 1932), vol. II, p. 39, hereafter cited as Spender, *Asquith*.

IV

The leadership of the Unionist movement at this time was in extremely capable hands. In February 1910 Sir Edward Carson was elected as the leader of the Irish Unionist Party in the House of Commons. In the autumn of the next year the Ulstermen instructed him to draw up a constitution for a "Provisional Government of Ulster" in case the Home Rule Bill eventually became a law. This was a grave challenge to the established order, but Carson accepted the commission. From this time, he bound himself, without reserve, to the Ulster cause.

In his new position as leader, Carson demonstrated a previously unrecognised ability to rouse and move masses of men from the public platform. Although he often suffered from ill-health he resolved to spare neither himself nor anyone else in his efforts to save the Protestant minority in Ulster from the domination of the Catholic South. His brilliant and effective personality was a factor of vital significance in the developing crisis. Tall and spare, dark and sardonic in appearance, a hypochondriac who always lamented his poor physical condition, he was, nevertheless, a peerless leader of men; he flamed with enthusiasm for the cause and was fully capable of inspiring his followers with his own zeal and passion. Behind his public presence lay the calculating shrewdness of the successful advocate. His colleagues could depend upon him to seize every tactical advantage that developed in the course of the struggle. John Redmond had good reason for distress when this man became the leader of his opponents in the House of Commons and in Ulster.

As the situation developed Carson worked in close collaboration with Andrew Bonar Law, the leader of the Conservative Party. The Irish crisis was Bonar Law's first major campaign as the new leader of the Conservatives. He has often been dismissed as a hard and ruthless business man in politics, concerned only with the fate of his party and indifferent to everything save political power and party advantage. His understanding of the Irish situation, however, was far sounder than that of any other contemporary politician. Blunt, tough and apparently insensitive, Bonar Law the Glasgow ironmaster of Canadian origin recognised that the Irish problem was different from most of the other business that occupied the attention of parliament. In 1912 he said to Lord Riddell of the Ulstermen: "It may seem strange to you and me but it is a religious question. These people are . . . prepared to die for their convictions". On another occasion he said: "These people look upon their being subject to an executive Government taken out of the Parliament in Dublin with as much horror, I believe with more horror, than the people of Poland ever regarded their being put under subjection by Russia; they say they will not submit except by force . . ."[1] Whatever else in life he failed to appreciate, Bonar Law knew his business when it came to dealing with Ulster and with Ireland.

Lord Milner's hostility to the Home Rule Bill was equally firm, and for several important reasons. The reader will recall his warm attachment to his mother, and the shock he felt at the time of her death. Her first husband had been shot and killed in Ireland in 1852, during a period of civil unrest. This personal disaster must have coloured his mother's outlook upon political affairs. There can be little doubt that she influenced her son's attitude to Ireland; his first successful excursion in politics occurred when he joined the Liberal Unionist Committee in 1886 in order to oppose Gladstone's Home Rule Bill. He was more familiar with the opposition to Home Rule than he was with most of the domestic issues of his day. The Irish issue had even dominated his ill-starred electoral campaign of 1885. For example, in his electoral address to the voters at Harrow, he had written (*Harrow Gazette,* 21st November 1885):

[1] For Bonar Law's remarks see Lord Riddell, *More Pages From My Diary* (London, 1934), p. 52, and Stephen Gwynn, *John Redmond's Last Years* (London, 1919), p. 65.

To The Electors of the Harrow Division of Middlesex

Gentlemen—. . . I appear before you as a supporter of Mr. Gladstone. . . The unity of the Empire is threatened by the coalition of Conservatives and Parnellites. By returning the Liberal Party to power you will secure a Government which will do justice to Ireland, but will not truckle to the Irish Separatists. . .

Alfred Milner.

A second factor of significance was his Imperial outlook. As we have seen, the great object of Milner's life was to unify the Empire; it was for that purpose that he joined forces with the Unionist Party. The Home Rule Bill, however, would mean a retreat from his goal, a step toward the disintegration of the Imperial system as he knew it, and for that reason a course he was bound to oppose with all his power.

Milner was also outraged by his interpretation of the political situation. He believed that Asquith and his fellow Ministers would do anything to remain in office; in order to secure the votes of Redmond's party in the Commons they were prepared, in his opinion, to pander to any or all of Redmond's demands. He was convinced that the Liberal politicians were ready to break up the United Kingdom itself, in order to prolong the life of their Government. This was exactly the kind of "rotten" politician's trick that made him despair of the British political system as a means of governing a great Empire.

A final factor that determined Milner's attitude was more serious than any other. When Sir Edward Carson and Bonar Law threatened violent and unconstitutional action during the course of the Irish crisis, they did so with genuine reluctance. They were parliamentarians of long experience; they cherished and respected the constitutional arrangements of the country; but they believed that the case of Ulster was exceptional and extraordinary—and that they were required to pursue unfamiliar methods in order to avoid a national disaster. They became advocates of extreme measures because of the singular and curious nature of the problem. Unlike them, however, Milner had little or no respect for the British constitution. When he emerged as one of the active Unionist leaders, he was less distressed than the others when it came to sanctioning plans that violated the constitutional customs and traditions of the country. As we shall see, in every phase of the crisis he always urged his friends to measures which were more extreme than those Carson and Bonar Law were prepared to sanction.

V

On 11th April 1912 the Prime Minister himself introduced the Government of Ireland Bill in the House of Commons. According to its terms, Ireland would have a separate parliament of two chambers—a senate of forty members nominated in the first instance by the Imperial Government—and a lower house of one hundred and sixty-four members, to be elected on the existing franchise. The financial powers of the senate were to be limited in the same way that the powers of the House of Lords were curtailed. The authority of the Irish parliament was restricted, however, in certain other important spheres.

No one could be favoured or penalised by it because of religious belief; furthermore, the parliament was not permitted to establish any denomination or provide any religion with sums of money drawn from public sources. The Irish parliament was also denied authority in other areas of government. These included the questions of succession to the throne, imperial defence, the composition of the peerage, and coinage. For a provisional period of six years control of the constabulary in Ireland remained the concern of the Imperial parliament. In the same way the Irishmen were also refused authority in the administration of all measures of social reform, and in the collection of taxes. Because of these restrictions, provision was made for the continued representation of Ireland at Westminster. Forty-two Irish members were to continue, according to the terms of the Government of Ireland Bill, to sit in the Imperial Parliament.

It will be seen that this was an essentially moderate Bill, drawn upon lines which determined the apparatus of government in several of the Colonies. This moderation, however, failed to affect in the slightest degree the passions which raged round the question of Home Rule. In addition, there were no separate provisions for Ulster with its population of about one million, with the concentrated wealth and industry that paid three-quarters of all Irish taxation.

The Unionists realised from the beginning that the Bill could not be fought by recourse to familiar methods. During the summer and autumn of 1912 they organised a series of meetings in every part of the country in order to give expression to their determination to refuse to accept Home Rule. By the end of the year, however, they saw that the device of the guillotine, grinding regularly in the hands of their opponents in the Commons, was cutting the life out of their parliamentary opposition to the Bill.

In these circumstances, Sir Edward Carson resolved upon a bold change of tactics. In December of 1912 he suggested to the Ulster Unionists that they should agree to a proposal to exclude Ulster from the terms of the Bill. His plan meant that the Irish Unionists in the south would be abandoned to their fate. After lengthy discussions the Ulstermen accepted the idea, and on New Year's Day, 1913, Carson moved a resolution in the Commons calling for the exclusion of Ulster.

Two objects lay behind the resolution. Since the Bill was originally framed to include Ulster, Carson's proposal could wreck the entire scheme and set back the regular progress of the measure in both houses of parliament. The Irish Nationalists perceived an even greater danger. Redmond's biographer has emphasised that the resolution "confronted Redmond with the most serious crisis he had yet encountered".[1]

---

[1] Denis Gwynn, *Life of John Redmond* (London, 1932), p. 219.

The reasons for his difficulty lay in the fact that the Irish leaders in the Commons were uncertain of the allegiance of the mass of their followers at home. Redmond fought the new resolution with all his might because no leader of the Irish Nationalists could accept, without qualification, a proposal that aimed at the permanent division of their country into two parts. For Redmond to attempt a solution of the Irish problem on such lines would be to forfeit at once the allegiance of his own supporters.

Nevertheless, a new element had been introduced into the situation. Despite its tactical purpose, Carson's resolution implied that a compromise was possible; that no Nationalist could consider the compromise was hardly Carson's affair. Moreover, English politicians would have no qualms about bargaining on such a basis; in the opinion of the Nationalists, they were always prepared to negotiate when the vital interests of others were at stake.

For a long time the idea of exclusion lay dormant and neglected. Unionists, throughout 1913, fixed their hopes upon two other methods of resistance. The Ulstermen had always threatened to defy the Home Rule Bill by force of arms. They now resolved to replace their wooden rifles, with which they had been drilling, with large numbers of modern serviceable weapons. In the second place, Unionists intensified their agitation among the officers of the regular army. Their object was to win the officer *corps* to their side so that Ministers and the people of England would be uncertain of the army in case of a crisis in Ulster.

In the autumn of 1913, however, Lord Loreburn, the former Liberal Lord Chancellor, astonished contemporaries by urging that some kind of "accommodation" for Ulster had to be found, if civil war in Ireland was to be averted. His proposal, in a letter to *The Times*, was put forward at an opportune moment. For months past, the King had been distressed by the deteriorating situation which threatened to involve his officers, his Government, and the monarchy itself. He now urged the politicians to meet in order to seek a compromise solution to the problem of Ireland. Between October and December 1913 Asquith, Bonar Law and Sir Max Aitken met several times; their parleys produced no valid result; and Bonar Law's suspicions of Asquith were increased as a result of the discussions. As 1914 approached the situation grew more and more ominous.

Until this time Lord Milner had played little or no part in the crisis. He was not interested in the parliamentary opposition to the Bill. He placed no faith in the meetings between party leaders; they were merely the tactical excursions of politicians. He dared not rely upon them to save Ulster.

Now, however, time was running out. Parliament was to reassemble in January 1914. The Home Rule Bill would pass the Commons for the third time; as a result of the Parliament Act the measure must become law, whatever the action of the Unionist Opposition in the House of Lords.

Exactly at this juncture Lord Milner decided to abandon his isolated position in order to act. Despite the parliamentary situation he resolved to emerge into the public arena in order to attack the moral authority and the material power of the Liberal Government. He wrote first to Sir Edward Carson, on 9th December 1913. The phrases of his letter, marked "very confidential", deserve the reader's most careful attention. Carson received the document shortly before Asquith summoned him to an interview to discuss a compromise solution to the Ulster problem:[1]

My dear Carson—. . . For all ordinary purposes, I have done with politics. But the business we have been brought face to face with goes far deeper than ordinary party struggles.

I am completely in accord with you about Ulster, and what I want to know is whether there is not something which men like myself, who disbelieve in mere talk . . . can do to help you.

I don't think the Government are serious in their advances. I think they are just passing the time. If they are not serious, there must very soon . . . be a "rebellion" in Ulster. It would be a disaster of

[1] The letter is published in Ian Colvin, *Life of Lord Carson* (London, 1934), vol. II, p. 241, hereafter cited as Colvin, *Carson*. It is reproduced in several other works, as well.

the first magnitude if that "rebellion"... of loyalty to the Empire
and the Flag—were to fail! But it must fail unless we can *paralyse the
arm* which might be raised to strike you. How are we to do it? That
requires forethought and organisation *over here*...

Milner also wrote to L. S. Amery to tell him that the time
for action had come at last:[1]

... What I want to say is

(1) That I am all for compromise to the very last possible moment
but

(2) that, in as much as the Govt seem determined to go through
with their scheme unaltered, we have no time to lose in
thinking how we are to implement our promise to "support"
Ulster in the last resort. We must be getting ready for that
detestable contingency, & it must be by doing something over
here... The thing is to weigh carefully... & to decide...
And then to divide the Labour... instead of "gassing round"
in a perfectly indefinite way...

VI

The first step in Lord Milner's campaign was taken at
once, in the public sphere. He planned to bring the weight
of public opinion to bear upon the Government, in order to
impress upon Liberals the hostility to Home Rule which was
latent in many parts of the country. The actions of the
Ulstermen furnished him with a model and guide for his new
course.

In 1912 Carson and his friends in Ulster, in order to make
patent the reality of their enterprise, prepared an oath to be
signed by the people of Ulster. This document, the Ulster
Covenant, was signed by Carson and a host of others on
Ulster Day, 28th September 1912, in the town hall of
Belfast. By means of that act the Ulstermen publicly dedicated themselves to defiance of Home Rule.

Milner now decided to prepare a British Covenant, to be

[1] Amery Papers, Milner to Amery, 8th January 1914. For Amery's account of his
part in Milner's new course, see L. S. Amery, *My Political Life*, vol. I, pp. 440 ff.
As so often happened after 1906 much of the initiative in their relationship came
from Amery. This is a significant aspect of their partnership, often neglected or
unnoticed by students. Amery often supplied the detailed plans, and even the ideas.

signed by citizens of the United Kingdom residing outside Ulster. This document, couched in the terms of a solemn protest, explained that the Home Rule Bill was contrary to the spirit of the constitution. Those who signed it declared that they held themselves justified "in taking any action" that might be effective in preventing the Home Rule Bill from becoming law. They also agreed to prevent the use of the armed forces of the Crown "to deprive the people of Ulster of their rights as citizens of the United Kingdom".

The master object of the British Covenanters was to force the Government to hold a General Election before the Home Rule Bill became law. Unknown to the mass of his followers, however, Milner privately hoped to establish a network of local units of active Covenanters in every part of the country. These small groups might become vitally important in case of a clash of arms in Ulster.

As an administrator of the first class, he realised that his movement would be ineffective without an efficient organisation to direct its activities. Since time was a factor of vital significance at this stage he saw that he would have to act quickly, and that he could not devote weeks to the creation of an administrative headquarters. Fortunately for his purpose, however, an organisation of the kind he required lay ready to his hand.

On 19th February 1914 he appeared before the Council of the Union Defence League, and explained his purpose to them. As a result of his remarks, the staff of the League was placed at his disposal, and a special sub-committee was appointed to help in the launching of his project.[1]

The Union Defence League had been established in 1907 in order to keep alive resistance to the idea of Home Rule. At that time, the Irish issue had faded into the background of politics but the Leaguers were determined to maintain a vigilant propaganda hostile to Redmond and all his works. In 1914 the President of the League was Walter Long, a

[1] For the best published account of the activity of the Union Defence League and the British Covenanters, see Viscount Long of Wraxall, *Memories* (London, 1923), pp. 193–207.

former Unionist Chief Secretary for Ireland, and a life-long enemy of Irish nationalism; the first Secretary of the Union Defence League was Ian Malcolm, the Conservative Member for Croydon; the members of the Executive Committee included the Earl of Harrowby, the Earl of Westmeath, Lord Oranmore and Brown, and Lord Balcarres. By 1914 the League had years of experience of propaganda and missionary work in the constituencies. It was exactly the instrument Lord Milner required.

Milner threw himself into the new movement with every ounce of his energy. In March he told his friend, Lady Edward Cecil, the future Lady Milner, that: "for the last 3 or 4 months *I have really worked hard*—at public things—for the first time since South Africa. . ."[1]

In concert with Leo Amery and a few other lieutenants preparations for a vast agitation were begun. In order to strengthen the impact of the British Covenant, they decided that a list of distinguished signatories should be collected, and that their names should be appended to the appeal of the Covenanters at its first appearance. Milner sought out his friends in the City to win their support; Amery, a Fellow of All Souls, was despatched to Oxford to awaken the interest of the most famous academic figures in the country; Arthur Steel-Maitland, at one time Milner's secretary and now the Chairman of the Unionist Party, was also approached. Milner, in addition, turned to his friends in the Press to beg them to support the British Covenant with as much publicity as possible; he wrote to Dawson of *The Times*, to Garvin of *The Observer*, to Strachey of the *Spectator,* to the editor of the *Morning Post,* and to the controllers of other Conservative and Unionist newspapers. As the preparatory agitation developed, Milner became suspicious of the politicians and their attempts at compromise. In February he informed Amery that "It will be a bore if Bonar Law tries to turn the thing down. But *I mean to go on with it*".[2]

---

[1] Milner Papers, Milner to Lady E. Cecil, 11th March 1914.
[2] Amery Papers, Milner to Amery, 18th February 1914.

On 3rd March 1914 the appeal of the British Covenanters appeared in the public Press. The original signatories of the declaration included in addition to Milner, Lord Roberts, Lord Balfour of Burleigh, Lord Desborough, Professor A. V. Dicey, Viscount Halifax, Rudyard Kipling, and Dr. Herbert Warren, President of Magdalen College, Oxford. Later on, a magazine called the *Covenanter,* with articles by Milner, Kipling, Amery, Carson and Walter Long, was published. The motto of the magazine was: "Put your trust in God and keep your powder dry".

The impact of this movement upon the British public has not been recognised by students of the period. The Union Defence League was assigned the task of collecting signatures to the Covenant in every part of the country. By July 1914, when the agitation was halted because of the imminence of war, it was estimated that nearly two million persons had signed the British Covenant.[1] Nor was this all; many people in public life preferred not to commit themselves to a public declaration in favour of the Covenant, although they agreed with its objects. For example, Viscount Goschen, the son of Milner's old chief, refused to sign; nevertheless, in a letter marked *"Confidential"*, he assured Milner that he agreed with him about Ireland, and promised that if an emergency came he would be found at Milner's side.[2]

Lord Milner's movement was not confined to the mere collection of signatures. He and his friends meant what they said when they declared that they proposed to aid and succour the Provisional Government of Ulster. In pursuit of this object, they turned to certain of their wealthy adherents in order to build up a vast fund of money.

Two undated documents in the Milner Papers reveal the extent of their success in this sphere; the first document, marked "Very Secret", contains a list of names together with an identifying letter; it reads, in part, as follows: "A.

---

[1] Viscount Long of Wraxall, *Memories,* p. 203.
[2] Milner Papers, Goschen to Milner, 10th March 1914, marked "Confidential".

Mr. Astor, B. Sir Samuel McCaughey, . . . D. Lord Roths-
child, E. Lord Iveagh, . . . G. Duke of Bedford. . ." The
second paper, also marked "Very Secret", contains the
identifying letter and the amount of money promised by the
person named in the list. These papers were clearly meant to
be kept separate. The second document reveals the following: "A—£30,000 subject to certain conditions. . . D—
£10,000. E—£10,000. G—£10,000 . . . and many contributions of £1,000".[1]

By the early spring of 1914 Lord Milner had cast himself
far out upon waters that were, for a British statesman, deep
and uncharted. Nevertheless, he was only warming to his
task; the British Covenant movement was merely one phase
of his opposition to the Home Rule Bill and its threat to
Ulster.

VII

A second aspect of Milner's activity was far more secret
than his public agitation for the Covenant. As we have seen,
when he first approached Sir Edward Carson he declared
that the object of Unionists must be to "paralyse the arm"
which might be raised against the Ulstermen. Milner was not
a man who indulged in literary flights or excursions. He was
resolved to render the British Government impotent by
nullifying its military authority in Ireland.

He was particularly well equipped to interfere with the
military arrangements of the country. Since his return from
South Africa he had devoted a good deal of his time and
energy to the National Service League, an organisation
which advocated military training and conscription in
peacetime. As a result of his association with Lord Roberts
and other leaders of the National Service League, Milner
made the acquaintance of many army officers including
General Sir Henry Wilson, the Director of Military Operations at the War Office, and Sir Charles Hunter, a former

[1] Based on two lists in the Milner Papers, undated, marked "Very Secret". These
lists were probably prepared a few months after the Covenant appeared, but the
canvassing for funds must have begun by March 1914.

officer in the Rifle Brigade, and in this period the Conservative Member for Bath. These soldiers were grateful to Milner because of the help he gave to the National Service League from the public platform and at the League's headquarters, where his administrative ability saved the organisation of the League on more than one occasion.

For years past, the Unionist leaders had been dallying with a military plan of the deepest gravity, one they had toyed with since 1910 but had not dared to touch. This was a proposal that the House of Lords should amend or refuse to pass the Army Annual Bill, the law which annually regulated the code of military discipline for the Army.

A chief object of the Unionists was to force a General Election upon Ministers before the Home Rule Bill became effective. Agitation in the country and a series of violent scenes in the Commons had failed to achieve their purpose. The parleys with Asquith and other Liberals had achieved nothing. Frustrated in these excursions Bonar Law and his friends now returned to their considerations of the Army Annual Bill.

They did so with very great reluctance. If the Act were refused a passage in the Lords, the Government would have no legal control over the military forces of the Crown, and they would be left with no alternative save an appeal to the country. In this case, the Parliament Act would be ineffective in curbing the powers of the Lords because the delay that they could impose would deprive Ministers of their military authority for at least two years, the years of crisis in Ireland. Bonar Law realised that recourse to such tactics violated a basic and ancient principle of the constitution. Since the seventeenth century the Army Act had been passed each year as a matter of form and custom; this practice was designed to make certain that Parliament would always be able to exercise control over the armed forces of the country, and that no Executive, however arbitrary, could use the Army for tyrannous purposes. It was one of the cornerstones of the constitution, an inheritance of the

"Glorious Revolution" of 1689. Nevertheless, Bonar Law and his colleagues felt themselves bound to consider the idea, for the sake of Ulster.

Lord Milner, despite Bonar Law's caution, was an ardent advocate of the plan, even though many of his friends were opposed to it. For example, on 18th March 1914 Geoffrey Dawson of *The Times* saw Ian Malcom of the Union Defence League in order to discuss with him the course their party should follow when the Army Annual Bill appeared in the House of Lords. Dawson was astonished to discover that Malcolm, a staunch Unionist, reacted with "unusual ferocity" to any mention of the plan. If the Lords touched the Act, said Malcolm, he would leave the Unionist Party. Dawson at once warned Milner of this attitude; his letter was tinged with contempt for Malcolm as a politician of no importance but he emphasised to Milner Malcolm's opinion that his views were shared by many Private Members on the Unionist side.[1]

These back-bench Unionists believed that the scheme was too violent and too revolutionary for it to be entertained by the Conservative Party. In the face of this warning, however, Milner dined that evening with Carson, Dr. Jameson, Sir Henry Wilson, and Sir Charles Hunter; they all agreed that the "Lords must amend the Army Annual Act".[2]

In addition to this bold action in the legislative sphere, Lord Milner also sought to influence the attitude of officers in the reserves. Ian Malcolm was assigned the task of collecting signatures to the British Covenant from officers in the Territorial Army. He reported to Milner that many of these men refused to sign, and he suggested that Milner and Lord Roberts should take counsel together in order to discover some way of overcoming their objections. The officers Malcom approached were anxious to sustain the cause of the Union, but they were uneasy about the situation in

[1] Milner Papers, Dawson to Milner, 18th March 1914, marked "Private".

[2] See Sir C. E. Callwell, *Field Marshal Sir Henry Wilson, His Life and Diaries* (London, 1927), vol. I, p. 139, hereafter cited as Wilson, *Diaries*. Amendment of the Bill was the first step in the challenge planned for the Lords.

general and the matter of their adherence to the Covenant in particular. Malcolm advised Milner to consult "some lawyers of eminence" in order to be able to resolve the doubts of officers and Members of Parliament who hesitated before committing themselves to the British Covenant.[1]

It seems clear that many keen Unionists and Conservatives were unable to maintain that singleness of purpose which was so characteristic of Milner in action. Their attitude to the question of Ulster and the military forces of the Crown was affected by several considerations which failed to deflect him from his chosen course.

In the first place, they objected to some of Lord Milner's plans because they were distressed by the idea of injuring the military and constitutional traditions of the country. In this period, also, a chief Tory complaint against the Government was that Liberals were unfit for high office because their party refused to make adequate preparations in the sphere of national defence. For years past, the Tories had been dominated by their fear of the German menace; in such circumstances many of them were unwilling to interfere with the Army at a season when they believed, with good reason, that the nation was in danger because of the attitude of Germany.

VIII

It is necessary to pause at this point in order to observe the singular nature of Milner's position at this stage of the controversy. We should notice that unlike most of the other statesmen engaged in the struggle over Ireland, Lord Milner regularly urged upon his adherents courses of action which many of them believed to be too extreme, too disruptive of national life, too fierce to be entertained by men who bore responsibility for the welfare of the State. His position in this respect was unique.

In Ireland, both Redmond and Carson were always

[1] Milner Papers, Ian Malcolm to Milner, n.d.

hampered by the pressure exerted upon them by the partisan enthusiasms of their followers, though neither of these leaders can be charged with weakness or vacillation. In England, the Liberal Ministers were often conscious of the fury and anger of the Radical masses in their party during periods of negotiation with the Opposition. In the same way, Bonar Law and Lord Lansdowne were sometimes confronted by the demands of the Unionist rank and file who were suspicious of compromise, who questioned the fixity of purpose of those who led them.

The effect of these subterranean pressures upon the responsible leaders has been analysed by one whose conclusions deserve the attention of everyone interested in British politics and British political history. In his *World Crisis,* Winston Churchill has declared:[1]

It is greatly to be hoped that British political leaders will never again allow themselves to be goaded and spurred and driven by each other or by their followers into the excesses of partisanship which on both sides disgraced the year 1914... No one who has not been involved in such contentions can understand the intensity of the pressures to which public men are subjected... The vehemence with which great masses of men yield themselves to partisanship and follow the struggle as if it were a prize fight, their ardent enthusiasm... their swift anger... the extortion and enforcement of pledges... the cries of "treachery" with which every proposal of compromise is hailed; the desire to keep good faith with those who follow... To fall behind is to be a laggard or a weakling, not sincere, not courageous; to get in front of the crowd... prompts often very violent action... Force, that final arbiter... may break upon the scene.

Whether because of his temperament or his experience or a combination of these factors, the roles of leader and followers which Churchill has described, were reversed in the case of Lord Milner and his friends during the Irish crisis of 1914.

Milner's devotion to the idea of the Union, his loyalty to the Ulstermen, his want of respect for some of the parlia-

[1] Winston Churchill, *The World Crisis* (London, 1938), vol. I, pp. 146–7.

mentary and constitutional traditions of the kingdom, his inability to take into consideration the difficulties of his political opponents, his conviction that he was right and that those who disagreed with him were wrong—all these things conspired to produce in him a curious result. They led him to contemplate Churchill's final arbiter without any of the qualms that afflicted the several leaders of the Ulstermen, Nationalists, Liberals, Unionists, and Conservatives.

This does not imply that he welcomed the prospect of civil war or that he was unmoved by the awful dangers of the situation. Nevertheless, we shall see that his actions during the Home Rule crisis reveal how different he was from almost every other statesman of his time.

Compared with all the other leaders of the first rank, he was the least anxious to seek a compromise solution to the Ulster problem. His suspicions of the Liberal Government were so intense that he was not prepared to bargain with them for any purpose. At one critical moment he wrote to a friend that this was the "gravest crisis but one, that I have known in sixty years". In his opinion he was back in the brave days of Graaff Reinet and Bloemfontein when there were worse things abroad in the world than the idea of a resort to force, when unbending firmness alone could save the day.

In these circumstances the rally round him of thousands of British Covenanters, the raising of vast funds of money and his own determination combined to create a situation in which he was prepared, and in a position, to do almost anything. We may conclude this phase of our analysis by reproducing Leo Amery's description of Lord Milner's attitude, written four decades after the events of 1914. Amery wrote in terms that could be applied to no other English politician:

... so long as the battle was fought on ordinary political lines he was prepared to leave its conduct mainly to others. A very different issue arose for him if the Government really contemplated to coerce Ulster by military force. Whether technically legal or not, that would in his eyes have been an act of revolutionary illegality which all good citizens were in duty bound to resist by every means in their power, not only in Ireland, but wherever the action of the Government could be frustrated. From that issue he was not prepared to shrink, and if the Government had been demented enough to precipitate civil war he would almost inevitably have found himself the real leader of the resistance.[1]

[1] See Amery's Foreword to Halperin, *Milner*, p. 17. We may observe in this connection that Walter Long was, perhaps, as ardent as Lord Milner in this period, but that statesman's qualities, however high, were not those men sought in a "real leader of the resistance". He had led the Irish Unionist Party in the Commons until 1910, but when Home Rule became a serious issue Carson took his place.

IX. Crime and Treason

Milner and the officers of the Regular Army – Domestic complications – Professor Dicey warns Milner – "I am certain that all members of the Army will obey orders" – A Guarantee Fund for officers who decide to resign – Asquith's compromise offer – Mutiny at the Curragh – Milner's anger with the Liberals – A comparison of the attitudes of Bonar Law and Milner – Strachey and Lord Curzon – Their concern over the Army Annual Bill – Angered by Milner's attitude – Milner criticises the British Unionists for their "cold feet" – Enter the *Round Tablers* – Their plan accepted by Lord Roberts – Rejected by Milner – Taken up by Churchill – Milner defeats the Federal Plan – Milner as a successful public orator – The plan for action in Ulster – A convention of Ulster Magistrates – A grammar of rebellion and anarchy – "This letter had better receive no answer" – Currency for Ulster – Milner and Sir Henry Wilson – Carson's disagreement with Milner's purpose – The black spot for Squiff.

I

WE must turn now to yet another phase of Lord Milner's plans for the support of Ulster. This phase is so important that it deserves and requires separate treatment. His agitation among the officer *corps* of the regular Army was a key element in his campaign. Although the Unionist efforts to win the regular officers to their side during the Irish crisis have often been described, certain significant details have remained secret.

Many regular officers were Ulstermen; more were supporters of the Conservative Party in politics. As early as November 1913 Sir Henry Wilson told Bonar Law that "if we were ordered to coerce Ulster there would be wholesale defections".[1] Shortly afterwards, the King himself warned the Prime Minister that if negotiations with the Opposition failed, "many army officers would resign their commissions rather than fight".[2]

On 14th November 1913, before he began to pursue the matter actively, Milner said to General Wilson that "the Unionists of England would soon have to pass from words to deeds. One of the first declarations to be made would be that, if any officers resigned, they would be reinstated when the Conservatives came into power".[3]

Although this unprecedented declaration was made in the cosy seclusion of Brooks's Club, Milner knew that Wilson was a notorious gossip who could be relied upon to spread the information broadcast at the War Office and also among officers serving in other parts of the kingdom. Milner's object was to make certain that the officers did not make up their minds about their duty in a political vacuum, isolated from the opinions of those who were anxious for them to disobey the orders of the Liberal Government.

The situation that depended upon the attitude of the regular officers could not be confined to Ireland, or even to Ulster. We have already noticed the tensions with Germany. There were also domestic complications. In recent years, the authorities had been confronted by a series of syndicalist strikes in various parts of the country. Winston Churchill and other Ministers felt themselves unable to rely upon the staves and batons of the police alone, during these industrial crises. In order to preserve order they had called out the military forces in aid of the civil power. The Army had responded to the call with perfect discipline, but agitators who sought to wean the men from their loyalty to the officers were already active, as preachers of class-solidarity and enemies of military discipline. Everyone concerned with these matters could be certain that the leaders of the working

---

[1] Wilson, *Diaries*, p. 131.

[2] Harold Nicolson, *King George The Fifth* (London, 1952), p. 233.

[3] Wilson, *Diaries*, p. 132.

classes who opposed the syndicalists would be outraged, if the officers now refused to obey the Government in the case of Ulster, an affair already tinged and tainted with class-feeling.

There can be no doubt that the Ulster crisis presented contemporaries with a terrible and unfamiliar conflict of loyalties. The case for the Ulstermen was clear enough; but the problem for Englishmen who desired to help Ulster was infinitely more complicated. How far could they reasonably go in violating cherished traditions and in interfering with the established institutions of their country? What weight should they place upon those diplomatic and domestic factors which were bound up in the matter? Where was the moral frontier beyond which they ought not to tread, however wrong the Liberal Government might be in its proposals for Ulster? So far as their own country was concerned, Englishmen had settled the moral and philosophic problems involved centuries before. Few tasks are more difficult for the historian than the attempt to ascertain with any measure of accuracy the moral values and standards of men who lived in the past, even a past so recent as the last half-century. Academic generalisations are easy enough; valid conclusions about concrete actions in a time of crisis are less easily made. The Milner Papers, however, contain contemporary material of genuine historical importance which bears upon these issues.

One of Milner's most pugnacious supporters was Professor Albert Venn Dicey, the celebrated author of *The Law of The Constitution* and other standard works, a former Vinerian Professor of English Law in the University of Oxford, and the acknowledged authority in his chosen field of constitutional history and law. Dicey was convinced that the Liberal Government had forfeited the respect of the country because of the Home Rule Bill. In this period he was in the grip of an agitation of a kind that occasionally seizes upon the academic mind and produces curious, extraordinary and even violent results. He wrote letters to the Press attacking the Home Rulers; he drew up legal plans and schemes in profusion and regularly brought them to the attention of Unionist politicians and editors; in 1913 he was one of a group of eminent jurists who put forward a solemn demand that the King should force a dissolution of parliament by dismissing Asquith from his post; in 1914 he was among the first to sign the British Covenant. On 3rd March 1914 he wrote to Lord Milner about the Covenant movement: "I am sure it is now or never for the Union. . . I should not have had the boldness to risk everything on the rally round us of thousands. I am glad that a bolder man than myself has staked everything upon this stroke. All I ask from each one of the signatories is to remember that everything is at stake".[1]

A few days later, however, the essential nature of Milner's agitation became more clear to Professor Dicey. In these circumstances he felt it his duty to send Milner a solemn warning. Writing with the terms of the Treason Felony Act in his mind, he said:[2]

Private   6th March 1914.
Dear Lord Milner,
    . . . I have not the least doubt that if the Home Rule Act is passed, defiance of it will be crime and probably treason. I can go a good way in defending this action on the part of the Ulstermen. About the part to be taken by Englishmen after the passing of the Home Rule Act, I have my doubts.

Dicey went on to explain the reasons for his doubts:

    . . . I am pretty certain that all members of the Army, officers or soldiers, will obey orders. My opinion is that it is their duty to do so. I am certain that the English public will never tolerate the dictation of the Army. I think the public in this are right. Two historical events have always greatly impressed me. All Cromwell's great services . . . never gave him that popular sanction which he earnestly strove to obtain. The reason is quite clear. The country would not acquiesce in the rule of the Army. When again the Nore Mutiny took place Burke. . . was consulted by the many admirers who treated him as a political

---

[1] Milner Papers, Dicey to Milner, 3rd March 1914, marked "Private".
[2] Milner Papers, Dicey to Milner, 6th March 1914, marked "Private".

prophet. It was admitted that the sailors suffered from terrible grievances. His advice was clear: Put down the mutiny first, and then, when this is done, remedy the grievances. This will always be the feeling of ordinary Englishmen if the armed forces refuse to obey lawful orders. I must add that I think Burke was emphatically right. And Carson agrees with me. . .

. . . I wish you and the other leaders whom I am following to know exactly where I stand.

Yours most sincerely,
A. V. Dicey.

Despite these grave and measured opinions, Lord Milner, as we shall see, continued to make preparations for the efficient defiance of the Home Rule Act by Ulstermen and Englishmen alike; he continued also to do what he could to influence the attitude of Army officers about Ireland.

II

From this time, the correspondence between Lord Milner and Sir Edward Carson became extremely guarded; they were dealing now not merely with political secrets but with schemes that were bound to bring them into collision with the law, if they were discovered.

One episode deserves particular notice. It has often been said that Sir Edward Carson never tried to interfere with the discipline of the Army. Ian Colvin, one of Carson's biographers, has written: "I can find no trace in his correspondence or his speeches of any design to interfere with discipline: he took the simple line that it was the part of the Army to obey, the part of Ulster to resist. . ."[1] Evidence in the Milner Papers makes it clear that Sir Edward Carson's attitude to the Army was not quite so straightforward as his biographer suggests.

On 18th March 1914 Carson wrote to Lord Milner in order to bring to his notice a suggestion that the British Covenanters should consider establishing a guarantee fund for "officers in the Army who decide to resign rather than

---

[1] Colvin, *Carson*, vol. II, p. 243.

violate their consciences".[1] Carson pointed out that the
Ulstermen had already raised a guarantee fund of more than
one million pounds for any working-class people in Ulster
who might suffer in case of fighting there. Carson's letter
was written in the cautious phrases of a lawyer; nevertheless he did urge Milner to think about a "guarantee fund for
purposes to be determined".[2]

Evidence has not been found to show whether Milner
acted upon Carson's suggestion. The very nature of the case
enforced secrecy of the most rigorous kind. We may
observe, however, that Milner had already suggested a
form of guarantee for the officers, when he told Sir Henry
Wilson that the Conservatives would reinstate those of their
number who resigned because of Ulster. He and his friends,
as we have seen, already possessed vast and secret funds
from Astors, Rothschilds and Bedfords, and they were in a
position to collect more money for their purposes as the
crisis became more intense. Now the essence of insurance
schemes of this kind is that those who are insured
must know about it; the object is to comfort men who
expose themselves to extraordinary inconvenience or
danger. If the scheme were to serve any purpose, the
officers had to be informed of the provisions made for
their welfare.

One of Lord Milner's chief objects was to make certain
that the officers of the regular Army came to no decisions
without realising that he and his friends, and many important members of the Conservative Party, were prepared to
reinstate them, in case they left the Army rather than act
against Ulster. Later on, when a crisis was at last caused by
certain officers who chose to resign, Milner hoped that their
"revolt" would not be confined to a few regiments, but

---

[1] This phrase is contained in a letter from R. King Stephens, a lawyer familiar with
insurance schemes, who was engaged in working out plans for officers. Carson
enclosed this letter, dated 17th March 1914, with his letter of the 18th to Milner.
The correspondence is preserved in the Milner Papers. R. King Stephens's letter was
addressed to Carson.

[2] Milner Papers, Carson to Milner, 18th March 1914.

that it would spread to other units in the Army. On 23rd
March 1914, he wrote to a friend:[1]

... My own hope is that the Revolt, having gone so far, will go
still further. We shall then be relieved from this horrible nightmare.

It seems possible, although there is no positive proof,
that Lord Milner took steps to inform officers in the Army
that plans were being made to reimburse them in case they
were forced to resign their commissions because of their
scruples about Ulster.

III

Meanwhile, however, the Opposition's intention to interfere with the passage of the Army Annual Bill had come to
the notice of the Government. In Asquith's opinion their
plans constituted a grave danger to his Ministry, and to the
State itself. After reflection, the Prime Minister decided
that it was essential that he should "make an offer to Ulster
of such a character that in the event of their refusal of it . . .
it would deprive them of all moral force".[2]

The offer which Ministers now decided to bring forward,
though generous, was not unaffected by tactical consideration. They proposed to permit each county in Ulster to
decide for itself whether or not it chose to remain outside
the provisions of the Home Rule Bill, for a period of six
years.

The generosity lay in the fact that before the expiration
of these six years two General Elections would have been
held in England, and if Unionists won either they would be
in a position to alter the entire arrangement to their satisfaction. The tactical aspect of the plan sprang from Lloyd
George's devious brain. His object was to reduce the
rebellious fevers which were raging in Ulster; as he pointed
out to his colleagues, "men could not possibly go to war to
prevent something which was not to occur for five years".[3]

[1] Milner Papers, Milner to Bertha Synge, 23rd March 1914.
[2] See Denis Gwynn, *Life of Redmond*, p. 251.
[3] *Ibid.*, p. 235.

Liberal historians have placed stress upon the generosity of Ministers, and Unionist writers have emphasised the calculation behind the stroke. When Asquith explained the Government's proposal in the House of Commons on 9th March, Sir Edward Carson brushed the whole scheme aside in one of those colourful phrases that are destined to live in the history of Ireland: "We do not want", said Carson, "sentence of death with a stay of execution for six years".

His attitude convinced certain members of the Government that the time for action in Ireland had come. They decided that it was necessary for the Ministry to make some show of asserting the authority of Parliament in Ulster. Sir Arthur Paget, the Commander-in-Chief in Ireland, was summoned to the War Office for consultations with J. E. B. Seely, the Secretary of State for War, Sir John French, Chief of the Imperial General Staff, and Winston Churchill, the most bellicose of the Liberal Ministers. Unfortunately, their conversations of 18th and 19th March were not recorded; for that reason, mystery must always surround the incident which was a consequence of the meetings at the War Office.

On the 20th, Paget was back in Ireland with instructions to advance into Ulster in order to protect military stores and establishments in the province. The selection of Sir Arthur to carry out the project was not especially happy, since he was a soldier of few and limited capacities. A statement about him in his obituary notice in *The Times* was curious, even for that newspaper: "Had he only devoted to military study a fraction of the time which he gave up to the observation of trees and shrubs, he might have ranked as a learned soldier".[1]

On this occasion, part of his task was to deliver an expository lecture to his officers, dealing with the intentions of the Government. As a result of his remarks, the officers at the Curragh camp were convinced that they were about to

---

[1] This singular reflection aroused the interest of A. P. Ryan, a distinguished member of the staff of *The Times*. See his *Mutiny at the Curragh* (London, 1956), p. 106.

take part in a general campaign to break the military power of the Ulstermen.

In addition, Paget presented his subordinates with an absolutely unprecedented opportunity to decide matters for themselves. Officers "domiciled" in Ulster would be allowed to absent themselves from duty during the forthcoming operations; Paget's exact words were that these officers "would be permitted to disappear"; afterwards, they could return to their posts as if nothing had happened. Those other officers who were not prepared to carry out their duties would be allowed to resign their commissions, but the resignations would not be accepted, and they would be dismissed from the Service at once. These orders, if Paget's efforts at arbitration merit the term, were a complete negation of military discipline, and a travesty of the directives soldiers might reasonably expect from their Commander-in-Chief. By the evening of that day, General Hubert Gough and fifty-seven officers of the 3rd Cavalry Brigade preferred to accept dismissal, rather than march north into Ulster; other officers in Ireland made a similar choice. This was the famous "mutiny" at the Curragh.

When the centre of the military storm moved from Ireland to the War Office, Sir Henry Wilson regularly informed Milner and other Conservative leaders of every detail of the Government's plans. The story of his conduct is well known, and need not detain us. However, an important result of the Curragh episode was that Bonar Law became convinced that there was no longer any need for the House of Lords to amend the Army Bill; it was clear enough that the Army was useless as an instrument of coercion in Ulster. This decision of the party leader was one that Lord Milner refused to accept. It reinforced his opinion that English politicians were not to be relied upon in a crisis. His attitude to his political opponents after the Curragh episode was explained to Lady Edward Cecil in the clearest terms:[1]

[1] Milner Papers, Copy of letter to Lady E. Cecil, 23rd March 1914.

... These people are capable of every treachery. They are *crawling* today, but unless we are wary and give them no chance, they may jump up again tomorrow.

IV

The manner in which Bonar Law carried himself in the explosive atmosphere which settled upon the Westminster scene after the Curragh incident is a matter of definite importance in the history of British political parties. It also provides us with a standard of comparison by which we may measure and gauge Lord Milner's actions at this stage of the Irish crisis.

As the leader of one of the great parties, Bonar Law could not permit himself the luxury of Milner's violent opinions. His biographer has pointed out that Bonar Law decided to reject the Army Act plan even before he learned of the Curragh mutiny; on 20th March, before the news from Ireland arrived in London, he wrote to the editor of the *Scotsman* in order to tell him that it was impossible to carry out the plan.[1] At first sight, this seems to be evidence of the flimsiest kind, based upon a change of course at the eleventh hour, but it is absolutely correct and accurate.

The exact moment of Bonar Law's decision cannot be defined, but his mind was probably made up as the result of an interview which took place on 19th March.

On that day, St. Loe Strachey, the influential editor of the *Spectator*, called on the Conservative leader in answer to a summons from him. Strachey was one of those in the Unionist ranks who deplored the proposal to tamper with the Army Bill. Bonar Law's object in seeing him was to ask him to refrain from writing about the matter in his newspaper.

At this time, the relations between Strachey and Bonar Law were particularly cordial even though Strachey was the leader of the Unionist Free Traders in the Press, and Bonar

---

[1] Robert Blake, *The Unknown Prime Minister, Life and Times of Andrew Bonar Law* (London, 1955), p. 181, hereafter cited as Blake, *Bonar Law*.

Law had risen to his present eminence because he was an ardent Tariff Reformer. When the Home Rule Bill became a measure of practical politics, Strachey voluntarily abandoned his opposition to the Tariff Reformers so that their party could present a united front to the Liberal-Irish coalition. His loyalty to Bonar Law in 1912 and 1913 was a source of strength which the leader welcomed and appreciated. By 1914 he was grateful to Strachey and prepared to listen to him on most matters concerned with the conduct of their party's affairs.

While the Unionists were endeavouring to make up their minds about the Army Act, Strachey enjoyed especially close relations with Lord Curzon, who opposed the plan with more consistency than he showed in the other political issues he took up in this period. On 17th March Strachey explained his attitude to Curzon in unmistakeable terms:[1]

I feel very unhappy about the drift of things, especially as regards the proposed alteration of the Army Bill, which I regard as disastrous. . .

I wonder whether the Unionist leaders realise how disastrous an appeal to the country not on the Irish issue but on the Army issue would be. I hear of Members of Parliament and of candidates saying that if things went that way it would be perfectly useless for them to stand, and that they should abandon their candidature, so convinced are they we should lose with the accusation of tampering with the army against us. The men I have heard this from are, oddly enough, not people of the moderate "Spectator" complexion, but vehement Tariff Reformers. It is rather a sign of the times that they should come to me, whom they detest, to get me to try and represent to the Unionist leaders the precipice over which they fear the coach is going to be driven.

On the same day, in a letter marked "Private", Lord Curzon told Strachey in reply that there was no cause for alarm. He assured him that as a result of his own representations among the Unionist leaders, the danger which Strachey feared was now past. They arranged to meet together on 18th March in order to discuss the problem.[2]

[1] Strachey Papers, Strachey to Lord Curzon, 17th March 1914.
[2] Strachey Papers, Curzon to Strachey, 17th March 1914, marked "Private", with docket stating "Most Confidential".

Meanwhile, Bonar Law, who knew nothing of this meeting, asked Strachey to call on him on the 19th. His object, as Strachey explained it to Lord Curzon, "was to induce me not to write. He put forth all his arguments . . . and though I cannot say I shook him, I at any rate made a certain impression". The impression which Strachey made upon Bonar Law at their meeting of the 19th March makes it clear that the leader, by that date, was not prepared to sanction the proposal that his party in the Lords should tamper with the Army Annual Bill. In a letter marked "Very confidential", dated 19th March, Strachey reported the details of his conversation with the party leader to Curzon. The letter is a document of very considerable importance:[1]

Very Confidential   Thursday. March 19th 14

My dear Curzon,

I think I ought to tell you the result of my conversation with Bonar Law. . . He was very frank. . .

Though we were very amicable, I had to point out to him that much as I should like to refrain from writing if he desired me to refrain, I should thereby abandon the only instrument I had for preventing what I regarded as a very great blunder. He then told me that I need not be anxious on that point because there was plenty of time and nothing would be decided at present. Further, he told me that though he was evidently disappointed, he could not honestly say he thought there was much chance of the Bill being amended because it would obviously be impossible to do so unless there was a completely united party, and as at present advised, he did not think it at all likely or possible that there could be an undivided party. On this I thought the best thing for me to do was to tell him that if he would give me a pledge or assure me that nothing would be done unless the party was united, I should then feel justified in not taking the opportunity to awaken the people in the party who agreed with me to the danger of the situation and get them to make their voices heard. On this understanding we parted. . . Your words, in fact, made it certain that Bonar Law's condition of unanimity could never arise, and gave me a perfect sense of security. . .

[1] Strachey Papers, Strachey to Curzon, 19th March 1914, marked "Very Confidential".

After the Curragh incident Bonar Law did not again consider the plan to amend the Army Act. It was obvious that the Government could not arrange a military operation in Ulster. Moreover, many of the Unionist leaders realised that it was essential for their cause that the action of the officers should appear to have been spontaneous and entirely unconnected with politics and politicians. As information from the constituencies poured into Westminster, they appreciated that the English people were not likely to tolerate either meddling with the Army for the purposes of party politics, or the dictation of the Army in political matters.[1]

Strachey and Curzon were, for these reasons, angered and astonished when the latter was approached once more, and asked to give his sanction to the scheme. In these circumstances, Strachey sought out Lord Milner, but he was distressed to learn that he still favoured action in the legislative sphere. On 25th March Strachey told Curzon of the interview:[2]

I think it advisable that I should tell you of a talk I had with Milner yesterday. I am sorry to say I found him very much on the wrong side and still quite anxious to amend the Army Act, and though perhaps I shook him a little, I did not really convince him. . .

It seems clear that Bonar Law was personally inclined to sanction this violent proposal, but he believed that he was required to consider the opinion of his party before he gave the signal to the Conservatives in the House of Lords. When he was advised that the party was not united behind the idea, he decided that his duty as leader was to abandon it, for a time at least; after the Curragh incident he was convinced that the plan had to be dropped altogether.

[1] For example, J. W. Hills, the brilliant Tariff Reform Member for Durham, who had a wide following in the North of England, reported to Strachey that: ". . . in the North . . . the cry that the Peers were tampering with the army would be most injurious to our cause..." Strachey Papers, Strachey to Curzon, 25th March 1914, marked "Confidential".

[2] Strachey Papers, Strachey to Curzon, 25th March 1914, marked "Confidential".

Lord Milner, on the other hand, refused to entertain the protests of his own followers, or the objections of other Conservatives and Unionists in England. From this time, although he continued in close association with the Unionist leaders in England, he occasionally allowed himself a jibe at their expense. For example, on 12th May 1914, he wrote to Sir Edward Carson to say: ". . . some of our British Unionists are bold enough when talking generalities, but always get 'cold feet' when confronted with any definite proposal".[1]

Although we may appreciate Milner's feeling of disappointment, it must be recognised that the responsible Unionist leaders of this period were not timid men. Bonar Law's most ardent admirers have pointed out that his conduct during the Home Rule crisis was brutal, tough and harsh; there was nothing flaccid about his efforts to protect the Union, and the Ulstermen. Lord Lansdowne and Balfour, by reason of their background and experience, were staunch enemies of Irish Nationalism. Lansdowne, who owned large estates in Ireland, was always an active and energetic spokesman for the Southern Irish Unionists in England; if anything marred Balfour's largeness of outlook as a statesman, it was his prejudice against Irishmen. For the sake of the Union and in order to help Ulster, these men were ready to entertain plans and proposals they would never consider in the ordinary course of politics.

Despite their concern, when the time for action came not one of these leaders was prepared to urge their party in the Lords to interfere with the Army Annual Bill. In their opinion, it was not a moment to "Damn the Consequences". Lord Milner's attitude to the subject shows how different he was from the other statesmen of his day, during this period of his career as a Proconsul in politics.

---

[1] Milner Papers, Milner to Carson, 14th May 1914.

V

For a month after the Curragh incident, the Unionists at Westminster regularly assailed the Government for planning a "pogrom" against Ulster; the effect of their bitter and violent attacks was reduced, however, by the events of the 24th April. On that date the Ulstermen, in a brilliant coup, seized the ports of Larne, Donaghadee and Bangor in order to land a huge cargo of rifles and ammunition, purchased in Germany. Their action revealed to everyone that they were well able to take care of themselves.

Asquith spoke in the Commons of this "grave and unprecedented outrage"; but men could not fail to notice that his only resort was to words, that his Government was powerless to interfere with the designs of the Ulstermen.

The Curragh mutiny and the gun-running at Larne produced results of vital consequence. In Southern Ireland there was a rush of men to join the Irish Volunteers, a semi-military organisation of patriots who proposed to emulate their neighbours in the north by placing reliance upon armed force, who were disinclined to listen any longer to John Redmond and his parliamentary colleagues. Redmond, in these circumstances, was forced to put himself at the head of these Volunteers, even though he deplored their tactics and objects. In England, the responsible leaders on both sides saw that the Government could not enforce its will upon the Ulstermen; for that reason they tried again, however reluctantly, to reach a settlement of the problem by means of a compromise.

Meanwhile, Lord Milner's young friends of the *Round Table* were particularly active. They believed that they could settle the matter, despite the patent failure of the politicians. For a long time they had been advocates of a Federal solution to the problem of Ireland. They argued that the establishment of a Federal system of government which would confer upon England, Scotland, Ireland, Ulster and Wales a measure of Home Rule of the kind demanded by the Southern Irishmen would solve the Irish crisis, and a host of other national and Imperial problems as well. If each of the regions of the United Kingdom received a measure of local power and autonomy, the Ulstermen would be satisfied, the Irishmen of the south would be mollified, and the Imperial Parliament relieved of all those local burdens which hampered it in the discharge of its Imperial tasks and duties.

In the ordinary course, Lord Milner agreed with the Federal proposals of his disciples, but at this time he was not prepared to listen to them.

The Federalists, however, managed to attract the interest of Lord Roberts who now became an adherent of their movement. Until this time Roberts was an ardent, active and partisan supporter of the Ulstermen. He provided them with military counsel and advice, and supplied them with the names of retired officers who were prepared to lend their military experience and skill to the cause. General Sir George Richardson, the Commander of the Ulster Volunteer Force, was Roberts' nominee. As the senior officer of the British Army Roberts had been distressed and outraged by the Government's policy which resulted in the Curragh incident; his public and private protests at the time had a serious effect upon popular opinion and upon the attitude of the leaders of the State. He was, with good reason, the most respected soldier of his day. His word carried great weight with the people of England, with the politicians at Westminster, and with the King and his advisers.

At the end of March Roberts happened to read an article in the *Round Table* written by Edward Grigg, later Lord Altrincham, a brilliant member of the Milner group. In his article Grigg pointed out that although the Unionists were desperately trying to force a General Election upon the Government, an election by itself could solve none of the problems that plagued Ulster, or Ireland as a whole. The situation, Grigg argued, required something more concrete and defined than mere recourse to an election.

Lord Roberts was so impressed by Grigg's views that he asked him to come to see him; at their meeting, on 1st April, Grigg drew up a paper which pointed out that the Liberals in Parliament and in the Press had at last recognised the dangers of the situation and had adopted, in consequence, a new and conciliatory tone. He suggested, and Roberts agreed with him, that the Home Rule Bill should be abandoned, on the understanding that a Federal solution would be taken up at once by all the parties.[1]

Grigg proposed that four representatives of the various factions should meet together in order to discuss the plan. The names he put forward for the purpose were Loreburn and Bryce as the spokesmen for the Liberals, and Milner and Roberts as the Unionist representatives. If they could agree, a joint declaration signed by each of them might have a powerful effect upon the country. It would result in a movement few of the politicians would dare to oppose. It would be a new and significant development.

The Federal idea would be launched with the sanction of a former Lord Chancellor, a distinguished Ambassador, the senior Field-Marshal of the Army, and the late High Commissioner for South Africa. It would be transformed from the panacea of a few journalists and intellectuals into a serious suggestion brought forward by elder statesmen of great experience who were no longer influenced by the ties and demands of party.

On 2nd April 1914 Roberts sent Grigg's paper to Milner, and asked him to consider it. Roberts explained that he agreed with Grigg's arguments and that he was prepared to act upon them. Lord Milner, however, refused to consider the plan.

His attention was fixed upon other aspects of the Irish situation. Exactly at this time he had arranged to establish the organisation of the British Covenanters upon a more formal basis. This was not, in his opinion, the moment for

[1] This account of the incident is based upon Roberts' letter to Milner, dated 2nd April 1914, preserved in the Milner Papers.

compromise. His arguments were accepted by Roberts at once; the Field-Marshal always looked upon himself as a simple soldier, less able than the politicians when it came to reckoning with the complexities of any political situation. On 3rd April at a great meeting in the Caxton Hall, Westminster, Lord Roberts was elected as the first President of the British Covenanters; Milner, Professor Dicey, F. E. Smith, Lord Halifax, Rudyard Kipling and Sir Edward Elgar were selected as members of the Executive Committee. They pledged themselves to support Carson and the Ulstermen by every means in their power.

In this way, the change of course Grigg sought to bring about was still-born. We should notice that the project was a typical example of the way Lord Milner usually urged the Round Tablers to act. The essence of the arrangement was to create a significant change in the situation while avoiding all connection with party politics; Grigg hoped to influence the actions of a few selected individuals who were eminent and powerful; his object was to win their interest by presenting them with a policy worked out by experts, and then to allow them to proceed with the matter in the public sphere. Despite this close adherence to Lord Milner's manual of tactics, he was responsible for the failure of the scheme.

On the day after the ceremonies at the Caxton Hall Milner, Balfour and others spoke at a great demonstration in Hyde Park, in order to protest against the policies of the Government. Shortly afterwards, Milner sent an entire series of letters to the Press, urging action upon the Covenanters. His letter to the editor of the *Daily Telegraph*, dated 18th April, was typical of his attitude:[1]

To the Editor:—
It is evident that the Government still hanker after the coercion of Ulster. . .

It is, therefore, absolutely necessary for British Covenanters to bestir themselves, and to reinforce the Hyde Park protest by meetings great and small, all over the country. . .

[1] Milner Papers, Milner to the editor of the *Daily Telegraph*, 18th April 1914. Similar letters were sent to *The Observer, Morning Post, Daily Express* and *Daily Mail.*

The formation of strong local committees ad hoc is the great need of the moment. . .

The headquarters organisation at 25 Victoria Street . . . is prepared to give every assistance. . .

Milner.

VI

We may only imagine the pain and distress of the Round Tablers, rebuffed by their chief, spurned at a moment of high promise. Nevertheless, secure in the knowledge that they were right, they persevered in their self-appointed task. At the end of April they managed to score a signal success.

During a cruise with Winston Churchill on board the Admiralty yacht *Enchantress*, Grigg and Lionel Curtis convinced him of the validity of their Federal proposals. On 28th April, in the House of Commons, Churchill appealed to Sir Edward Carson to help him in the establishment of a Federal system. Asquith gave his support to the scheme on the next day. The Unionist leaders in the Commons did not at once reject the idea. Early in May, as a result of these exchanges, a meeting between the Prime Minister, Carson and Bonar Law took place. Although no agreement was reached, Carson's remarks about the meeting were significant: "Only a fool would fight if there is a hope of accommodation. And what a great thing it would be if this long-standing controversy could be settled once and for all!"[1]

Lord Milner, however, was still one of those who refused to approve of these efforts at compromise. He was caught up in the grip of his Covenanter campaign. For the first time in years he was experiencing the powerful excitements and enthusiasms of the successful public orator. On 4th May he wrote to Lady Edward Cecil to tell her of his popular reception at Coventry, where he spoke in company with Balfour and others:[2]

[1] H. Montgomery Hyde, *Carson* (London, 1953), p. 367.
[2] From the typed copy in the Milner Papers, Milner to Lady E. Cecil, 4th May 1914.

... When I got up at 4. Balfour had spoken, well, if somewhat haltingly, for nearly an hour. I felt doubtful, whether I could hold them. A long low hall, 2,000 people seated, at least 2,000 more standing packed like herrings in a barrel and it was Saturday afternoon, the sunshine outside visible through every window, and the hall was intensely close. And yet I held them easily for 40 minutes. There was no coughing, no interruption, no shuffling of feet. They had *come to hear*... I am very sensitive to these things... I felt I had got under the skin. My belief is that with a dozen people of "guts" and go we could win this time easily...

The reasons for Milner's ardour were not based solely upon the public's appreciation of his speeches. By May of 1914, he and his closest friends believed that they had discovered a method which would permit the Ulstermen to act, at the same time that an immediate collision with the law would be avoided. Milner was convinced that he and his colleagues had at last hit upon a "forward move" that could bring success to their cause.

VII

On 12th May Asquith explained to the House of Commons that Ministers proposed to secure the third reading of the Home Rule Bill before the Whitsun recess; he also promised that an Amending Bill would be introduced, because he hoped that an agreed settlement could be achieved in the intervening period. This announcement spurred Lord Milner and his friends to action.

For some time they had been preparing a number of Memoranda dealing with the opportunities which lay before the Ulster Provisional Government; they now drew up a paper that suggested a method by which the Ulstermen could seize power in the province, and begin to exercise some of the prerogatives of a sovereign authority. This document, an undated and unsigned Memorandum, is preserved in the Milner Papers. It begins by explaining that :[1]

[1] Milner Papers, "Memorandum", undated. The author, in all probability, was L. S. Amery.

The policy which is now obviously contemplated by the Government is to get the Home Rule Bill on the Statute Book as it stands without delay on the understanding that there is to be a subsequent amending Bill dealing with Ulster . . . it is certain to offer less than Ulster is prepared to accept today. . .

The only way to prevent this policy being successfully carried out is for Ulster to take action as soon as possible, preferably before the Home Rule Bill leaves the Commons.

The object of the Ulstermen, the Memorandum went on to say, should be the destruction of the Home Rule Ministry:

Such action, if it confronts the Government directly with the alternative of taking steps to coerce Ulster or of confessing its impotence openly to its own supporters, might bring about the Government's collapse—at any rate nothing else can. . . The only way to break up the Liberal Party is to make the Government openly contemptible in the eyes of its followers.

At this point the Memorandum recognised a serious legal difficulty, but a solution to the problem was also brought forward:

The difficulty in taking immediate action is to make sure that the steps taken will not give too severe or sudden a shock to the British instinct of legality. . .

The question is whether any action can be taken which would in effect begin to bring the Provisional Government into existence with legal and constitutional justification, and to which the Government could only reply by aggressive measures which would put it in the wrong and afford a reasonable pretext for the Provisional Government to come out into the open and take over the administration. From this point of view it is essential, in the present conflict between the rights of the people and a tyrannous Parliamentary Executive, acting in the name of the Crown . . . to keep in mind those fundamental principles of our constitutional law which make the responsibility for the maintenance of the King's peace rest not upon the Crown and its ministers and officials, but upon the local magistrates, and in which respect of the duty of assisting the magistracy make no distinction between officials, military or civil, and ordinary citizens. . .

The suggestion now put forward is that acting upon these principles the lieutenants, deputy lieutenants and magistrates in Ulster, or as many of them as are trustworthy, should be convened to consider how best to fulfil their duty of maintaining the King's peace, and should decide on the appointment of a special Provisional Committee to assist them in this task and more particularly in the organising of a force of special constables...

By this means, the Memorandum argued, the Provisional Government would be brought into existence:

The publication of the resolutions of the magistrates' conference appointing this Committee and calling upon all good citizens, including of course the police and the military, to give every assistance and support to the Committee, and warning evilly-disposed persons against interfering with the Committee, would in effect call the Provisional Government into existence for the limited purpose of assisting the magistracy to keep the peace. It would not assume any general administrative functions...

The Memorandum then turned to the results which would follow upon the action of the magistrates:

The Government would then be placed in a considerable difficulty. If it did nothing, which is the most probable course, it would be seriously shaken in the House of Commons, and it could not prevent the Provisional Committee rapidly extending its authority and so making things much easier for the subsequent taking over of the administration by the Provisional Government. On the other hand it is not easy to see what it could do without putting itself in the wrong. To dismiss the lieutenants and magistrates who had issued the resolutions would be a gross act of tyranny... In England, it would arouse widespread indignation and might justify a general refusal of Lord-lieutenants to carry on their duties—more particularly in connexion with County Council administration and the Territorial Force—and possibly of Unionist magistrates generally.

In any case, by whatever method the Government provoked a conflict it would give the Provisional Government a reasonable justification for taking over the administration...

Affixed to this Memorandum was a Draft Form of a letter for the convening of a "special meeting" of lieutenants, deputy-lieutenants and magistrates in the province of Ulster. Although the object of the writer of the Memorandum was to make the actions of the Ulster magistrates appear to be spontaneous, little or no room for their initiative was allowed for in his plan. He attached to his paper, in draft form, the very Resolutions he hoped they would pass! Number (4) of these Resolutions is of particular interest:

(4) That the Provisional Committee be authorised on our behalf to call upon the assistance of the police and of the naval and military authorities, and that, in order to avoid confusion, no use to be made of the services of the naval and military authorities for the purpose of maintaining law and order in the province except on the direct request of the Provisional Committee.

This ingenious and remarkable document, a grammar of rebellion and anarchy, was accepted in its entirety by Lord Milner. Professor Dicey's warnings about crime and treason, though they were not forgotten, were completely ignored. Milner readily gave his sanction to the ruse whereby a scheme drawn up by Englishmen in London was to be foisted upon the Ulstermen; he never considered the terrible damage that would be done to the Ulster cause in case the true source of the plan were ever discovered; he also agreed that the English public should be fooled into the belief that the idea originated with the Ulster magistrates, anxious only to discharge their local responsibilities. His one fear was that British Unionists might draw back at the last moment. On 12th May, the very day that Asquith spoke in the Commons, Milner wrote to Sir Edward Carson in order to explain his position. The last sentence of his letter, for good reasons, was written in the cautious terms of the conspirator:[1]

47 Duke Street, S.W.

Confidential   12 . 5 . 14

My dear Carson,

Forgive my bothering you. I have heard of the plan to get the Ulster magistrates to set the ball rolling, and it seems to me such an excellent one, that I am only afraid that it may be "turned down" by people here without adequate consideration. You will know what I mean when I say that some of our British Unionists are bold enough, when talking generalities, but always get "cold feet" when confronted with any definite proposal. I expect you may have, in this as in other cases, to buck them up.

[1] Milner Papers, Milner to Carson, 12th May 1914, marked "Confidential".

Of course you know much better than I whether the scheme is feasible. If you thought it an impracticable one, I should not have a word to say. But I should be slow to let people here put it out of court if it smiled to the Ulstermen. Something has got to be done, and I cannot think of any forward move, which would be less open to objection.

Success no doubt depends upon keeping the thing so secret as to come upon the Govt., as an absolute surprise. Therefore I would not dream even of hinting at it to anyone not already "in the know" —And this letter requires, and had better receive, no answer.

Yours ever,

M.

VIII

During May and June Milner continually urged the Unionist Peers to organise themselves in order to defeat the Amending Bill, which was introduced into their House by Lord Crewe on 23rd June. His object was to block any development in the Lords that might ease the Government's difficult situation. Lansdowne, Salisbury, Crawford and other Peers were so impressed by his arguments that they asked him to join the Unionist "Shadow Cabinet" and thus enrol himself formally in the ranks of the Unionist leadership in the Upper House.

At the same time Asquith was making further casts at a compromise. Eventually, the assistance of the King was secured, and at his invitation the Liberal and Unionist leaders, together with the chief representatives of both Irish factions, met at Buckingham Palace on 21st July.

While their negotiations were going forward, Milner was involved in talks of a very different kind. He, and Walter Long, and Moreton Frewen, the former Unionist Member for North-East Cork, were engaged in a new scheme to strenghten the hand of the Ulster Provisional Government. They were working out, in strict secrecy, plans for the "currency that would be required for a 'rebel' Government in Ulster". Frewen, a financial expert with considerable experience of British and American banking procedures, was particularly valuable during their discussions. He submitted various specimens of paper currency for the approval of his colleagues in the plot.[1]

Milner joined in these preparations because he still deplored the idea of a compromise. He was now eager for action in Ulster. Once again, he sought out Sir Henry Wilson in order to influence the attitude and the actions of the Army. On 3rd July Wilson recorded in his diary:[2]

I went to see Lord Milner. He told me that unless Asquith agreed to the Lords' amendment, and he does not think that there is a chance of it as Redmond won't allow it, Carson will set up a Provisional Government and will take over such Government offices as he can without bloodshed. This will bring matters to a head. Milner, who is giving the whole of the time to the Ulstermen, is entirely in favour of this action. He is altogether against Ulster waiting any longer to suit Asquith's convenience, and is urgently in favour of a strong forward policy. . . It is undoubtedly a tremendous step to take, but I agree with Milner. Milner wanted to know what the army would do. I told him that so much depended on the way the picture was put to us. I thought that if Carson and his Government were sitting in the City Hall, and we were ordered down to close the hall, we would not go.

Later I talked the situation over with Douglas and Sclater, without, of course, saying anything about Milner. I was pleased with the result. They have no intention at all of moving, except in the ordinary way of quelling riots.

Sir Edward Carson was not yet ready to order a "strong forward policy" of the kind Milner was now urging upon Wilson. However reluctant he was to attend the Buckingham Palace Conference, Carson was determined to respect the wishes of the King and to try once more to work out an agreed settlement with Redmond and Asquith. His differences with Milner at this stage are reflected in a passage of Ian Colvin's biography; Colvin, an extreme partisan of the Ulster cause, was severely critical of Milner's "strong forward policy"; in his *Life of Carson* he explains "That the

[1] For the details of their plan see the present writer's *The Observer and J. L. Garvin, 1908–1914* (London, 1960), p. 421, hereafter cited as Gollin, *The Observer and J. L. Garvin.*

[2] Wilson, *Diaries,* vol. I, p. 148.

Ulster Loyalists intended to take over the Government, if they were put to it, is certain . . . but Milner was not in command, and both Carson and Craig, with cooler heads, must have seen the danger of premature action".[1]

Before the month was out, however, the fate of Ireland, and much else, was committed to the arbitrament of war. On 23rd July the failure of the Buckingham Palace Conference was recognised by all the participants. A few days later a terrible incident occurred at Howth, where the Irish Volunteers managed to land a cargo of rifles. When they tried to bring them into Dublin there was a collision with a body of British troops who, harassed by the crowd, opened fire. Three civilians were killed and a large number wounded; all prospects for a compromise now seemed hopeless. On 30th July, as the crisis in Europe swelled to ominous proportions, Bonar Law asked Asquith to call on him. At their meeting he and Carson told the Prime Minister that, in view of the international situation, it would be best if domestic differences were put on one side. It was agreed that the debate on the Amending Bill should be postponed. The issue of Home Rule was thus left to an uncertain future.

The political legacy of the Irish crisis could not be shaken off quite so easily, however. Milner and his friends had never liked the Liberal Ministers or their policies. As a result of the Home Rule controversy, their suspicion and hatred of Asquith became, in itself, a factor of consequence in the politics of their time. As we have seen at various stages in the long battle, Milner found himself opposed to the plans of Bonar Law, Lord Roberts, and even Sir Edward Carson because he felt that they were too prone to discuss an agreed settlement with the Prime Minister and his colleagues. It seems as if Milner forgot the aim and object of the brave people of Ulster; it was not their purpose to rebel, or even to defy the Liberal Government; their only goal was to remain a part of the United Kingdom, separate from the territories controlled by a Dublin Parliament. Physical resistance was

---

[1] Colvin, *Carson*, vol. II, p. 412.

their final and ultimate option, a choice which their responsible leaders prepared for, but only as a last resort. We have already suggested why Milner, in contrast with Carson, Bonar Law, and the others, seemed to look forward to a clash of arms. We should now add to this catalogue of reasons his curious and intense dislike of Asquith. By August of 1914 Milner's distrust of the Liberal Prime Minister dominated his outlook, decided his opinions, and influenced his subsequent conduct to a remarkable degree.

Two letters in the Milner Papers illustrate this feeling with exemplary clarity. Before the war began, in May, Professor Dicey wrote to Milner, to say:[1]

... Asquith as a political leader is thoroughly untrustworthy. I know nothing of him personally; he may in private life be as trustworthy as an ordinary English gentleman, but I have observed his public career with great care and I am certain that politics is to him a game on which his own reputation is staked, and which he plays with no great scrupulosity... Asquith... will not probably tell a direct lie, or escape from the effect of a promise unless he has already expressed it in language so ambiguous that he cannot be charged with indubitable breach of faith. His attitude is always that of a very wily advocate speaking from his brief, and not morally responsible for the statements contained therein. Hence the extreme danger of entering into anything like private negotiations with him...

On the day after the declaration of war F. S. Oliver wrote in the same sense:[2]

... The conduct of the war by a Government which has so messed and misconceived our domestic situation is not a thing in which one can have supreme confidence. Asquith is all right as long as he is on the path of least resistance; but what is now the path of least resistance will not of course continue to be so for long. And then?

When Britain entered the war in August 1914 she did so as a united nation. Nevertheless, Milner and his friends, surly, brooding, resentful, suspicious, kept a close watch upon the Prime Minister's every action. Above all else

[1] Milner Papers, Dicey to Milner, 9th May 1914, marked "Private".

[2] Printed in Wrench, *Milner*, pp. 294–5. It should be noted that the original letter in the Milner Papers refers to "Squiff" and not to Asquith; this was the nickname Milner and his friends applied to the Premier.

they hoped their country would be victorious in war. At the same time we ought to notice that, in Lord Beaverbrook's phrase, they were dominated by their desire to hand Asquith "the black spot".[1] The Prime Minister, adroit as ever, had managed to slip out of the Irish impasse; but even in the first stages of the war, before his conduct as War Minister could be measured or criticised, his enemies were already upon his track.

[1] Lord Beaverbrook, of course, has his own uses for the phrase, and uses it in other contexts, though it certainly applies in this case. For one example of his employment of the "black spot" see Beaverbrook, *Men and Power,* p. 163.

X.   Squiff and the System

The Expeditionary Force – The Stalemate of Trench
Warfare – Milner and Asquith represent two opposing
schools – The War Council – Criticised by Milner and his
friends – Squiff – Regulations for ensuring the defence of
the realm – Manpower – Compulsion – The financial backbone of the Entente – Free traders versus conscriptionists –
The opinions of Milner and Asquith – Milner's fitness to
lead in war demonstrated – Milner attracts the critics of
the Asquithian system – Sir Henry Wilson and Milner –
Henry "Rake-hell" Wilson – An army of Milnerites –
Milner hesitates to act – Asquith's fortunes decline as Lord
Milner's rise – Milner's first hint of public criticism – "The
chickens are coming home to roost" – Would Milner's
name be included?

I

WHEN war came the pacific people of Britain did
not at once spring to arms in order to rush upon
their enemies. In accordance with the carefully
nurtured plans of the Government, an Expeditionary Force
composed of four infantry divisions and one cavalry division
of the Regular Army was despatched to France where it
took up an assigned position upon the left of the French line
of battle. The immediate defence of the home island was
allotted to the Navy, and to the fourteen Territorial Divisions and the thirteen Mounted Brigades of the reserve.

For a fortnight in the middle of August this British
Expeditionary Force, amounting to about 90,000 men, was
carried safely across the Channel in complete secrecy, with
that swiftness and safety that R. B. Haldane and his officials
at the War Office had planned to achieve since the earliest
days of the Liberal Ministry. By 22nd August the bulk of

the crossing was completed and British soldiers, for the first time since the Crimea, braced themselves to meet the attack of a hostile Continental Army.

These regular troops carried with them the adulation and the confident hopes of their countrymen. Everyone in Britain believed that success would at once crown the efforts of the Regular Army. All, or nearly all, were certain that the war would be of short duration, that the fighting, in the contemporary phrase, would be over by Christmas.

However, by these pre-war designs the area of concentration assigned to the Expeditionary Force placed it directly in the path of the reinforced right wing of the German Army, the weighted sledgehammer of the famous Schlieffen Plan, the instrument that had been contrived by the German Staff to smash everything in its path, to crush and beat down the resistance of the French, and to bring the war in the West to a successful issue within the space of a few weeks.

The first crack and flash of the collision between these two armies took place at Mons on 23rd August. In this famous encounter battle the British Regulars fought brilliantly but they were engaged by an enemy host nearly three times as large as their own. A retreat that was to last for thirteen anxious days and to cover a distance of one hundred and sixty miles was thus begun.

The earliest news of these martial episodes, couched in the terms of disaster, fell upon the unsuspecting British public like a bombshell. Accounts in *The Times* of 30th August, a special Sunday edition, and in other newspapers spoke of: "bitter truths . . . a retreating and a broken army . . . a terrible fight . . . the broken bits of many regiments. . ."

The impression created in England by these first reports from the front has been captured in a brilliant phrase by H. G. Wells in his contemporary novel, *Mr. Britling Sees It Through*: "And then came the Sunday of *The Times* telegram. . . Mr. Britling was stunned. . . It was as if David had flung his pebble—and missed!"

H. H. ASQUITH

The Milnerites called him "Squiff".

The retreat from Mons was followed by a series of sanguinary attacks and counter-attacks. The Schlieffen Plan failed in its object; there was the great reversal of fortunes upon the Marne; the battle of the Aisne; the so-called "race to the sea"; the bloody German attempt to hack a way through to the Channel ports that was stopped in the first battle of Ypres. When none of these actions proved decisive the long period of trench warfare set in.

By degrees, there rose up a military deadlock in the West which none of the great professional soldiers was able to dissolve. By the autumn of 1914 the military art, so far as the great captains on either side were concerned, proved itself to be sterile and bankrupt.

Lord Kitchener has been praised as the first British soldier to perceive that the war would last for a long time, as the first officer to measure the dimensions of the conflict, the first to urge that millions must be recruited for a long campaign and a long war. But he was as baffled as the rest, in the sphere of high strategy. When the hostile armies were firmly entrenched in unbroken lines running from Switzerland to the sea, he explained more than once that "I don't know what is to be done . . . this isn't *war*".[1]

It was not the war that the military men had expected, but war it most certainly was. The failure of the generals, their inability to break the deadlock imposed by trench warfare, had very significant consequences.

II

The stalemate of trench warfare brought in its train problems of military and civil administration that were absolutely unprecedented, that had not been encountered in the lifetime of any British statesman then alive. It became clear that the war would not be over by Christmas, that the nations of Europe had involved themselves in a long conflict, that the end of the fighting could not be expected

---

[1] Viscount Grey of Fallodon, *Twenty-Five Years* (London, 1925), vol. II, p. 69.

for a considerable period of time. Nothing like it had been experienced since 1815. There were no precedents for so vast an enterprise. Ministers were required to learn their warlike tasks in the midst of the most bloody battles in history.

From the very beginning, Lord Milner observed their conduct with feelings of increasing tension and anxiety; uppermost in his mind was the cardinal fact that the Liberal Ministers were no longer dealing with politics but with the survival of Britain and the British Empire.

Unfortunately for the Liberal Government, a major strategic victory was denied to Allied arms for a very long period of time. Only victory upon such a scale could silence or assuage the disappointment, distress and baffled rage of the nation.

As the progress of the war absorbed the energies and consumed the life-blood of the country Asquith himself and the Asquithian method of conducting the war were subjected to extremely serious criticism.

As long as the boon of victory was denied to the Allied cause, criticism of the Asquithian system grew in intensity. In time, the political crises that resulted from this situation were destined to bring ruin to the Asquith Ministry, to the historic Liberal Party, and to the familiar social, political and fiscal order that had lasted for so long in Great Britain.

The task of creating a supreme directing agency for the conduct of the war was more complex for a British Government than for any other of the belligerent Powers. The military and civil problems of government were rendered more intricate by British traditions and by the peculiar and characteristic role Great Britain was required to discharge as the wealthiest member of the Alliance that opposed the Central Powers.

We ought to notice that the difficulties and trials of the statesmen of the 1914 era furnished the British authorities who directed the Second World War with a corpus of experience and precedent that proved to be invaluable.

Asquith, Lloyd George and their colleagues were pioneers in the business of war; their administrative ups and downs served as beacons to lighten the path of those who came after them a quarter of a century later.

Asquith's Government, however, were required to discharge their novel duties without any of these benefits. Their solutions to the problems of a wartime administration at once aroused the hostility and the opposition of Lord Milner and those who believed in him as the one British statesman who had successfully conducted a modern war, as the one Englishman with executive experience that included the direction of a civil administration in wartime.

It is fair to say that with the passage of time Milner's friends came to look upon him and upon the Prime Minister as the chief representatives of the two opposing schools of thought that grew up in wartime England.

Those who admired Lord Milner, and they were legion in the Army and among the civilians at Westminster, regarded him as an administrative master who could organise the nation for victory, while they raged against Asquith as an adroit *laissez-faire* politician of the old Liberal school whose manoeuvrings might be tolerable in peacetime, but were a dangerous incubus in war because they failed to provide the country with the positive direction, planning and rational co-ordination of effort that were the desperate requirements of the hour.

III

In the novel circumstances of world war it is not surprising that Ministers, at first, had resort to a strong man. This was Lord Kitchener, the brutal and impressive soldier who came as a "saviour" from the Eastern marches of the Empire at the moment of danger. In the beginning, he dominated his colleagues in the Cabinet when he was admitted to their company as Secretary of State for War.

If Lord Kitchener worked miracles for a time, the conduct

of such tremendous undertakings could not be discharged by one man for very long. A War Cabinet—a true Supreme Command—was needed to co-ordinate, to foresee, to prepare, to act—efficiently. Ministers were required to create a system for the waging of war.

It was not easy for the Prime Minister to fashion an efficient instrument for the central direction of the war. At first, the entire Cabinet concerned itself with the business of war-making, but it soon became clear that rapid decisions and their instant translation into action could not be achieved by this method. A smaller body of Ministers, charged with immediate direction and control, was needed in order to avoid the lengthy discussions and debates that were bound to take place whenever the *plenum* of the Cabinet met.

However, the creation of such a smaller organisation involved modifications of the rules, traditions and conventions encompassed by the idea of Cabinet responsibility. The Prime Minister was confronted by a serious constitutional problem. Cabinet Ministers were responsible to Parliament and to the nation for the discharge of their high tasks and duties; they were reluctant to delegate their powers, their authority or their responsibility to a committee of their colleagues.

By the autumn of 1914, however, Asquith established such a body, which was known as the War Council. In the beginning this War Council consisted of the Prime Minister, certain Ministers directly concerned with the running of the war, and their military and naval advisers. The War Council, although a step in the right direction, was in essence an Asquithian compromise, and not a genuine solution to the problem. It was not a true executive but merely a Committee of the Cabinet; as such, it was required, as a matter of course, to report its major decisions and actions to the larger body, which never relinquished a scrap of ultimate power or responsibility. The Cabinet could, and did, override the decisions of the War Council whenever it chose.

Debate and effort alike were thus duplicated, and efficiency was lost. The War Council was merely a supplement to the Cabinet and not the instrument for the vigorous prosecution of the war that was urgently required.

The faults and shortcomings of the Asquithian War Council were recognised by the Prime Minister's friends and enemies alike. It had been established in the first place in order to give authority and cohesion to a small group of War Ministers who were to act in concert as an effective executive, but it was observed that the numbers of the War Council continually multiplied at the same time that a few vigorous Ministers, isolated from their fellows, managed informally to keep the control of war policy in their own hands.

It was noticed by more than one critic that the War Council failed to meet at regular intervals, and that there were long periods when it did not meet at all.

It was generally realised that the Prime Minister recognised the vital importance of a small Council but it was seen that men were able to force their way into what should have been an Inner Cabinet of a selected few, because Asquith too often took into account the party and political claims of his colleagues, claims that seemed to have little or no bearing upon a more effective prosecution of the war.

These earliest attempts to combine rapid and effective executive action with the preservation of Cabinet control and responsibility as they were known in time of peace disgusted Lord Milner and the vigilant company of his friends who were intensely concerned with the progress of the war. It seemed obvious to them that a small Cabinet, sitting daily, and reinforced by the best expert advice, was a vital necessity if the military enterprises of the nation were to prosper. In particular, they condemned the War Council as a Committee of the Cabinet which was powerless to give effect to its own decisions. They deplored the waste of time and the duplication of labour that were inherent in the

Asquithian system for the conduct of the war in this early period.

Lord Milner and his friends were convinced that the Prime Minister's actions were typical of the peacetime politician who always seeks to postpone a crisis by resort to a patchwork compromise. In their opinion, Asquith was prepared to sacrifice the reality of administrative efficiency in order to achieve an appearance of national unity; it was characteristic of him, in their view, to balance party and political factors against the genuine demands of the war.

These convictions at first awoke their concern, then their anger, and finally feelings of disgust and loathing so powerful that they may be described as rare in the history of modern British politics. Their dislike of the Prime Minister, already robust in peacetime, was so nourished by his actions as War Minister that they regularly referred to him not as Asquith, but as "Squiff" or even "Squiffy", the contemptuous nicknames they had hit upon to concentrate their hatred, enmity and bitterness.

Very early in the war, as we shall see, these men were already casting about for some method to drag Asquith down from his place as Prime Minister.

IV

A second aspect of Asquith's direction of the State in wartime aroused even stronger feelings among Milner and the group that was now referred to as the Milnerites. Success or failure in this sphere, they believed, would decide the outcome of the war.

In August 1914 an extraordinary law, the Defence of the Realm Act, was passed by Parliament. This measure conferred wide, novel and absolutely undefined powers upon the Government to make regulations for ensuring "the public safety and the defence of the Realm".

In Lord Milner's opinion, the Act was symbolic of the

people's desire to place at the disposal of the Government all the human and material resources of the country. However, he was soon convinced that Asquith hesitated, for reasons that were not valid, to make use of the vast powers thus granted to him by a patriotic Parliament and nation.

In the beginning, there was no scheme or plan for the mobilisation of the manpower of the country for war. Some high-ranking soldiers and their civilian adherents desired to sweep the manhood of the kingdom into vast conscript armies, as soon as it became obvious that the war would be fought out upon a continental scale, over a long period of time.

It was clear, however, that the issue was not so simple for Britain as these ardent partisans believed. The Government had to balance and weigh a number of simultaneous requirements, all of which were bound to have vital effects upon Britain's war effort.

It was evident that the Government, in the first place, had to furnish the armed forces of the Crown with an adequate supply of men. As the fighting forces expanded in size, however, the number of men and women who were required to feed and equip them increased, and provision had to be made to secure an adequate army of workers on the home front, as it was called. In the third place, it was necessary to arrange for a labour force to engage in those vital export trades upon which the financial stability of the country depended. Finally, the necessities of the civilian population, however restricted and curtailed, had to be met by yet another group of labourers. No easy solutions to these problems were ever discovered by any Government during the war.

Although a measure of conscription might have passed in the very first period of the war, the straightforward formula of those who believed in compulsory National Service was not accepted, for a number of important reasons. As time passed the traditional British hostility to the very idea of compulsion reasserted itself. Labour unions were suspicious of the plan, working men in general were afraid of industrial as well as military conscription, and many Liberals and Radicals were against the proposal because it seemed, in their opinion, to violate the very liberties that were threatened by the German public enemy. Despite the evidence of the Defence of the Realm Act, the nation was not ready to submit to the unquestioning discipline of compulsory service unless valid cause could be shown for it.

In the opinion of the Prime Minister, who did not like the idea in the first place, such a measure might become a military and even an industrial necessity, but he believed that time was needed to prepare the country for so radical a change, that if compulsion should be required eventually, his Government had to advance upon the goal by a series of careful and easy stages.

At one point in the controversy which developed over National Service, the Chief Government Whip solemnly informed Asquith that reports from the country indicated that the introduction of conscription might cause a revolution.[1] The Prime Minister was convinced that the affair required delicate and cautious handling, if the unity of the nation was not to be ruptured by premature action in this sphere.

There were other compelling reasons for postponing a general scheme of conscription. At first, there were more volunteers for military service than weapons for arming them. Facilities for the equipment and training of the masses of recruits who hurried to join the colours were not available. Unlike the Germans, who always prepare for their wars in advance, the pacific people of Britain were simply not ready for this massive clash of arms that was deciding their fate and destiny.

Legislation for the purpose and the registration of the men would take time, and might, if put into effect too hastily, reduce the flow of voluntary recruits. There was, in short, no administrative machinery to deal with the matter.

[1] See Asquith, *Memories and Reflections,* vol. II, pp. 109–10.

In the early stages of the war the voluntary system seemed to be adequate for the military requirements of the country.

V

Compulsion raised other issues that could not be ignored, if the position of Great Britain in the Alliance against Germany was not to be injured beyond repair.

For nearly three years of war, before the entry of the United States, Britain's task was not simply military, in the narrowest sense. In that desperate period, Great Britain stood out as the financial backbone of the Entente, as the wealthiest member of the Coalition that opposed the Central Powers.

In this capacity the country was obliged to pay for the equipment of its own forces, and for that of its Allies. Upon Britain, almost alone, rested the massive financial obligations of the war; she provided the loans and subsidies that enabled the other Allied countries to fight on. No one, in those years, expected the United States to join in the conflict; if a mistake were made in this area of the British war effort how could it ever be retrieved in time? How, men began to ask, would National Service or industrial compulsion affect this vital aspect of Britain's position in the struggle with Germany?

The fate of the Allied military effort depended to a large degree upon the British export trade, especially the trade with North and South America. It was from these areas that the countries of the Entente drew much of the raw materials, weapons, ammunition, supplies of food and other necessities that enabled them to wage war. If Britain's ability to export to this part of the world were damaged in any way or for any reason, serious consequences would follow. The financial capacity of the country to pay for the purchase of these warlike stores would at once be reduced or destroyed, a result that must have a fearful effect upon the military power of the Entente.

233

The armies, navies and civilian populations of the Allied Powers were able to carry out their tasks in wartime because they were nourished by the goods and resources of the New World. What would happen to them if the British Government was unable, because of a breakdown in the American trade, to pay for these supplies?

The sums involved were enormous. Could the British export industry, or the other necessary trades for that matter, spare the men for the huge armies that were now being planned? Could Britain divert from her essential industries the labour army that would be required to maintain so vast a force in the field? Lord Kitchener had early resolved to raise an army of one million men to man the trenches of the stalemate war. How could such an army be staffed, provisioned and paid for by a country with a limited population and a limited financial capacity? These were matters that could be decided only by the wisest distribution of the manpower of the nation. By the autumn of 1914 the extension of Britain's military commitments and her subsidies to her Allies made the answers to these questions extremely doubtful.

The Free Trade economists in the Government were certain that Britain had to limit and define her obligations. In their opinion the burden was already heavy enough. To attempt to bear the further heavy costs of a conscript army would mean the economic ruin of the country. They saw the various Departments of State spending upon a scale that had never been dreamed of before. How, they asked, could Britain "pay for the war" if the demands of the generals were met without check or reservation?

These Liberal Ministers, despite their political traditions of Free Trade, individualism and *laissez-faire*, realised that the industries and manpower of the country had to be organised for war. However, there was no scheme to determine the nature or extent of the organisation that was required. In any case, they refused to believe that the proposals of the conscriptionists and those who desired

Government control of industry were anything more than the demands of unthinking and economically ignorant enthusiasts.

The Free Trade Liberals found a good deal of support in the country, where the working men and their employers agreed that the interference of the State was to be deprecated. The business men believed in the rights of property and in the merits of *laissez-faire*. In the opinion of many of them, if the State sought to direct or control their activities or those of their workmen, the result would be the substitution of an inefficient for an efficient industrial organisation, to the detriment of the war effort.

They were suspicious of State control and interference. They argued, and in this early period they were supported by politicians in both parties, that the traditional *laissez-faire* economy of the country was the most effective method for the home production of war material, most effective for the requirements of the export trade, and for the provision of those financial balances and reserves that were a further requirement of the situation. A prosperous state of trade, regular employment and high profits and wages would supply the Government, they said, with rich sources of taxation; and also make available the vast funds the Treasury now sought to borrow from the people of the country.

These opponents of State direction and control, in the Government and in the country, understood that the State was obliged to intervene and to guide the industries of the nation to a certain extent, but too much interference, either by means of conscription or by direction of industry, would, in their opinion, serve only to cripple the war effort on the home front. They argued that only by an "economic" exploitation of the industries and the manpower of the country could maximum production be achieved for military purposes, for the lucrative export trades, and for the domestic requirements of the day. Blind recourse to National Military Service and to too extensive a scheme of industrial direction would be, in their opinion, self-defeating and irretrievable blunders that would encompass the military and economic collapse of the country.

VI

What was the attitude of the Prime Minister? Where did he stand in the controversy that began to develop in the early days of the war? What conception did he have of his own position as the chief officer of the State in the emergency of the nation and Empire? Upon what system or method did he rely?

At the outbreak of war, Asquith had made a tremendous contribution to the stability of the country. Several of his most prominent Ministerial colleagues hesitated over the correct course during those awful days at the end of July and the beginning of August. There was, at that time, no unity of opinion in the Cabinet upon the vital question of peace or war. By his patience, firmness and tact, the Prime Minister had carried the members of the Government with him in the decision to enter the war, save for two or three unimportant exceptions. This lesson of August 1914 made a powerful impression upon his mind.

Since 1910, in fact, Asquith had ruled England with the parliamentary support of a Coalition consisting of the Liberal, Irish and Labour parties. During that period he had learned that in order to govern men it was often wise to avoid a crisis by resort to tactical delays, by the postponing of decisions, by determinedly seeking compromises whenever differences of opinion seemed to be irreconcilable. There were definite and tangible advantages to be gained, despite the opinions of enthusiasts or hotheads, by proceeding slowly in council when the counsellors were unable to agree upon a particular plan of action.

When the issues of conscription and State direction of industry began to convulse the minds of the politicians at Westminster, Asquith set himself one goal. His task, as he saw it, was the same one he had accomplished with such marvellous skill in August 1914—the preservation of national unity.

He was personally inclined to agree with the arguments of the *laissez-faire*, Free Trade opponents of compulsion, but there seemed to him to be something more important than a clear-cut victory for either side in the controversy. This was the maintenance of that delicate fabric of national unity which he, as Prime Minister, was resolved to preserve.

Let the critics and the carpers complain about his lack of resolution, about his want of driving force, about his failure as a positive leader; Asquith was satisfied that he could carry out the programme he had set himself. He was the King's First Minister; his was the power and his the authority; he was confident of his ability to arbitrate or mediate between the different factions until the time was ripe for a decision, until the march of events or the inclinations of public opinion weighed the balance in one direction or another.

If measures of direction or compulsion had to come in the fullness of time, the delays his critics complained of were not unaccompanied by compensating advantages. Public opinion was opposed to the interference of the State in what had previously been the private sphere. If, after a period of waiting, Asquith finally did permit a measure of State control, it would be clear to all that the step was a vital necessity of the war effort, and not the action of some militarist or planner unconcerned with the liberties and the rights of Englishmen.[1] In this way the Prime Minister proposed to demonstrate his appreciation and understanding of the wide powers granted to him by the Defence of the Realm Act, and to show also his fitness for his high office.

It was this attitude that awoke the fierce anger of Lord

---

[1] For the genuine validity and success of what we may well call Government by delay for the sake of national unity in this sphere, see the authoritative work of E. M. H. Lloyd, *Experiments in State Control* (London, 1924), p. 269, who lays stress upon the benefits which "a thorough psychological preparation for State interference brought about".

Milner and his disciples. It was this method which made Milner and his friends long for the hour of reckoning and retribution. In their view the times were too stern to permit Asquith's policy of drift, too stern to allow a man who seemed to shrink from decisions to remain as War Minister in a conflict that would decide the national and imperial future.

In Lord Milner's opinion these were grave and serious problems, but he believed they were capable of solution if the supreme directing authority was placed in the hands of men who were administrators and executives, men prepared to discharge their tasks without worrying about politicians, and party alignments, and the attitude of an uninformed public opinion.

In his view, the nation was in good spirit. The people of Britain, he believed, asked only for guidance, direction and firm leadership. Milner was convinced that Asquith's tactical course was a fatal error. The business of a War Minister was to get on with the war; so far as Lord Milner was concerned the grave issue of Freedom or Control was out of date in wartime.

Lord Milner was a leading advocate of the policy of National Military Service, but conscription for him was merely a talisman, the sign and symbol of the kind of control and direction that were required for the successful conduct of the war effort. As we shall see, when power was finally placed in his hands, he refused to allow the generals to make unlimited demands upon the manhood of the country. When he was one of those who controlled war policy, he decreed that men should be directed into certain vital industries, despite the cry and clamour of the generals for more and more soldiers. Nevertheless, he condemned the Asquithian system as a ridiculous and dangerous abdication of authority at a time when planning and State direction were more important than ever before.

The voluntary method, Milner argued, was haphazard at a time when order, system, control and foresight based upon exact knowledge were the crying needs of a people struggling for their very lives. When Asquith listened to the "vote-catchers" and the "hacks" and the "Mandarins" who claimed to speak for the people of Britain, he committed a grave blunder; Lord Milner was convinced that the people wanted one thing more than anything else—they wanted to win the war. And this could not be done under the voluntary system.

At a very early period, he satisfied himself that Britain could not achieve decisive victory as long as Asquith remained in his place as Prime Minister.

So far as Lord Milner could see, the first problem the nation had to overcome was the problem of how to remove Asquith from his post.

VII

In the very first hours of the emergency Lord Milner demonstrated, to the satisfaction of his friends, his fitness to occupy a place alongside those who were directing Great Britain's affairs in war.

For example, Austen Chamberlain later recalled that Milner was the first of his colleagues to demand the instant despatch of the Expeditionary Force to France. Although the Liberal Government was already putting the matter in train, there were one or two understandable hesitations and delays. Sir Henry Wilson, loyal as ever to his official superiors, at once informed Milner of these developments.

On the morning of the 4th of August Milner related the facts to Austen Chamberlain. He was "very anxious that the Opposition should put fresh pressure on the Government". He took Chamberlain to Lansdowne House and there, he convinced Lansdowne that a letter must be sent to Asquith urging the despatch of 100,000 men. At the same time, Chamberlain was sent off to warn Balfour of the delay, and to persuade him to write to Haldane about the need for the immediate departure of the force.

Lansdowne and Balfour were convinced by Milner's arguments that they were required to act. When Bonar Law was informed, he, also, was brought to the same conclusion. However, they discovered that the Cabinet would meet before their letters could have effect. Nevertheless, Chamberlain was impressed by Milner's promptness and resolution in the affair; he was convinced, once again, of Milner's qualifications to be one of the country's leaders, especially in time of war.[1]

In the same way, Leo Amery's admiration for Milner was reinforced by his conduct in an episode of some significance that took place in London at the start of the conflict.

At this time, Sir Henry Wilson informed Amery and Lord Lovat that Asquith proposed to appoint R. B. Haldane as Secretary of State for War; in the same interview Wilson revealed the Government's hesitations over the despatch of the Expeditionary Force. It seemed to Amery and Lovat that Lord Kitchener, who was then in London, was the best possible choice for the War Office. Kitchener, in those days, was looked upon as a martial demi-god, different and superior to other men, a brilliant soldier who could act as a national saviour in the effete councils of the Liberal politicians.

Amery and Lovat hastened to Milner with the news of Asquith's intentions. After some talk, Amery persuaded his two friends to see Kitchener. At their interview, they learned that Kitchener had been told that the Government "would be glad of his advice", but no specific post, at the War Office or anywhere else, had been promised him.

Milner and Lovat thereupon forced Kitchener to go to Downing Street in order to demand a definite appointment from the Prime Minister. Two days later, on 6th August, Lord Kitchener's selection as Secretary of State for War was announced.

Although Asquith later declared that he had chosen

---

[1] For the incident see Sir Austen Chamberlain, *Down The Years* (London, 1935), pp. 104–5.

Kitchener upon his own initiative, Amery and the Milnerites were certain that Lord Milner had played a very significant part in the matter. In the early period of the war, this appointment was looked upon as the master stroke of the Liberal Government. The public and the politicians, alike, were heartened and delighted by Lord Kitchener's elevation to a place of power. Amery was anxious that Lord Milner should reap the credit for what he had done. In a letter to Leo Maxse, written in 1917, Amery explained the significance of Milner's actions at the time. Referring to Kitchener, Amery said:[1]

. . . My impression is that he had not actually seen Asquith at all, because what I am quite clear about is that Milner, having elucidated from K. that he had no views at all about the Expeditionary Force, worked up K. on the other question to the point of putting him into a taxi there and then to go to Downing Street and tell Asquith that things in Egypt were serious and that he must go off at once, unless Asquith wanted him to stay for some more definite and important work. I don't think, however, that you can quote this, because it was told me by Milner at the time and of course he could be the only source of information, and that would embarrass him in his present position. But I put it down to confirm you in the view that up to that moment Asquith, whatever vague ideas he may have had as to utilising K. in some capacity . . . had certainly not decided to make him Secretary of State and had not in fact offered K. anything at all.

These incidents, involving Austen Chamberlain and Amery, were of very definite importance. They indicate that as early as August 1914 the process was begun, among the Milnerites at least, of demanding that Lord Milner should receive some active role in the Councils of the State in wartime because of his power of decision in a crisis, and because of his ability to pick the best men for posts of importance in the direction of the war.

[1] Amery Papers, Amery to Maxse, 14th May 1917, marked "Private". See also Amery, *My Political Life*, vol. II, pp.21–3. The reader should, perhaps, remind himself that Amery referred to Milner as "the only source of information" for this incident because Kitchener was dead in 1917.

VIII

In the early months of the war, Lord Milner became the focus of the opposition to Asquith's War Ministry; soldiers and politicians, whenever they desired to criticise the conduct of the war, wrote to Milner in order to inform him of the details of their complaints and grievances.

On 14th August General Sir Henry Wilson crossed to France as a member of Sir John French's General Head-quarters. Before he had been a week in the field he sent Milner the first of a series of complaints, condemning the "cowardly ignorance" of his superiors in London. In September Wilson blamed the retreat from Mons upon the "initial blunder" of keeping two divisions of the Expeditionary Force in England: "If we had the 4th and 6th Divs. at Mons on Aug. 23rd as we might easily have done, we would have been in a position to *attack* . . .", he wrote on the 10th of that month. In October, letters full of criticism were sent by General Wilson to Sir Charles Hunter and were relayed to Milner. In November, Geoffrey Dawson of *The Times* wrote to Milner to condemn the apathy of the Government. In that month, also, Lord Roberts informed Milner that the Army Commands in the United Kingdom were very "disjointed"; Roberts pointed out that there was no "head in the field" in this area of Britain's defences. Later on in November Leo Amery, who was already on active service in France, wrote to Milner in order to urge him to talk to the Unionist leaders so that they might press for the adoption of National Military Service. From all these sources Milner received information almost as good as that furnished to any member of the Government.[1]

The most important of these informants in this period was General Sir Henry Wilson. Although his military abilities have sometimes been questioned, there can be little doubt that Sir Henry was a capable soldier. At the time of

---

[1] The letters from these correspondents, in the period August–November 1914, are preserved in the Milner Papers.

the Agadir crisis in 1911, for example, his arrangements for the movements of troops were generally recognised as a brilliant demonstration of a staff officer's work. Lean, extremely tall, with a homely yet attractive face, Henry Wilson was, perhaps, the most accomplished intriguer produced by the British Army in recent times.

Unlike some of his fellow officers, his Irish charm and his easy fluency in conversation always attracted the politicians, even when they were suspicious of his motives. These qualities made him a very dangerous man. He was able to flit from the technical and professional sphere of the soldier to the completely different world of the politicians whenever he felt the inclination to do so, which was often. He became the spokesman of the Army in political circles. Lloyd George, who knew how to control men, used Wilson to great effect during the war, but even he was bruised by the association. In his *War Memoirs* he has remarked rather ruefully of Wilson that "one can understand the imputation of treachery which was associated with his name".[1]

Lord Milner first came to know Wilson, and many other serving officers, during the prolonged crisis over Ireland in the years just before the war. As we have seen, at the time of the Curragh episode Wilson revealed to the Opposition leaders all the secrets of the parleys and conversations that were then taking place in the War Office. The historian of the Curragh mutiny has remarked of Wilson in connection with the incident that "the legend that grew up around him magnified the effectiveness of his intriguing to far beyond its true proportions".[2]

Though accurate, this observation does less than justice to the General's high qualities. Men of his stamp, and they are a large and successful class, do not rely upon concrete achievements in order to gain a reputation. They are more concerned with the impression that they make upon their contemporaries. In this aspect of the Curragh affair lay

[1] D. Lloyd George, *War Memoirs,* vol. I, p. 1695.
[2] A. P. Ryan, *Mutiny at the Curragh,* p. 191.

much of its importance for a man of Wilson's calibre. As a result of his actions at that time, Lord Milner was convinced of Wilson's significance. He said then that "They talk a lot about Gough, but the man who saved the Empire is Henry Wilson".[1]

Sir Henry, not unnaturally, was quite content with this judgment upon his activities. He realised that Lord Milner was a man prepared to listen to him. There can be little doubt that Wilson was already placing some reliance upon Milner when he looked forward to the day, which was bound to come in the fullness of time, when the Unionists regained office. They would then be in a position to dispose of the highest places in the Army. As we shall see, long before the event General Wilson calculated that he would like to serve as Chief of the Imperial General Staff when Lord Milner became Secretary of State for War.

After the Curragh incident Asquith proposed to banish Wilson to some remote outpost of the Empire, there to serve out his course at a safe and convenient distance from the Westminster politicians. However, by a curious and unfortunate lapse, Asquith held his hand in the matter. He failed to put his idea into effect. The General was to exact a bitter payment from the Prime Minister for this indulgence.

It thus came about that upon the outbreak of war, Asquith had a resourceful enemy in a position of high authority at the headquarters of the Expeditionary Force in France. Wilson's qualities as a commander later made a powerful impression upon the Americans, and their opinion of him deserves the careful attention of an English reader. For example, when the biographers of General Douglas MacArthur sought to compare his "island-hopping" campaigns in the Pacific with the carnage that had raged in France, they turned to the case of Sir Henry Wilson in order to make the contrast as clear as possible:[2]

[1] Wilson, *Diaries,* vol. I, p. 144.
[2] C. A. Willoughby and John Chamberlain, *MacArthur: 1941–1951* (London, 1956), p. 10.

The incomparable virtue of the MacArthur strategy is that it resulted in large territorial conquests . . . without involving any butchery of American troops. . . War is a terrible book-keeping process . . . The most brutally outspoken discussion of the gruesome balance-sheet of war is to be found in Henry "Rake-hell" Wilson's . . . *Memoirs*. Wilson was . . . a cool professional who occupied highest positions. This cynical book-keeper of the dead and dying spoke casually of "intake" (i.e. recruits) and "outgo" (the killed and wounded). He recognised scientifically that the abattoir of Flanders was a deadly drain on British manpower. . . MacArthur knew all about Wilson's "intake-outgo" terminology—and was resolved to keep the "outgo" to a minimum. . .

A man of this quality would be ready to face the "frocks", as he called the politicians, without a qualm, so long as he knew that other politicians, genuine contenders for power, favoured his intrigues. He early fastened upon Lord Milner as one of the civilians who could give effect to his schemings, in the all-important political sphere.

In addition to sending Milner detailed criticisms and complaints about the Government, Wilson took care to inform him of the extent of his connections with publicists and politicians at home. On 24th September 1914 Wilson wrote to Milner in order to explain that he was already in contact with H. A. Gwynne of the *Morning Post*, with Leo Maxse of the *National Review*, with Leo Amery, and with General Callwell at the War Office. In the same letter he criticised Winston Churchill because Churchill was one of those most eager to raise new armies for the field, while Wilson and Milner, at this time, preferred to use the recruits as replacements for units already in being. Wilson could also be certain that Milner would not object to any complants about Churchill, his old enemy. Furthermore, to condemn Churchill was to condemn the Asquithian system, because in this period control of war policy, by Asquith's design, lay with himself as Prime Minister, with Kitchener as Secretary of State for War, and with Churchill as First Lord of the Admiralty. Wilson wrote:[1]

---

[1] Milner Papers, Sir Henry Wilson to Milner, 24th September 1914.

24.9.14

Dear Lord Milner,

How kind of you to write to me. I was greatly pleased to get your letter. . . I got a long letter from Gwynne enclosing a copy of a still longer letter written to Lord K. . . Gwynne's line of argument was quite sound. . .

I enclose a copy of my answer to Gwynne. . . I am sending my answer to Gwynne through General Callwell at the W.O. as I am just a little nervous of saying too much to Gwynne good fellow as he is. However I am sure you will see him. . . Otherwise I am taking no action . . . because I see by your letter how intensely alive you are to the danger of these "shadow" armies & also how you hope to get Lord K. to see the picture as it really is. . .

Leo Maxse writes to me also & Amery. . .

Winston was here yesterday . . . & I am sorry to say he was talking unadulterated rubbish about the immense armies he was going to send over next spring! Armies, so far as I can see, without officers, rifles, guns, ammunition or services . . .

Every sort of good wish in the great work you are engaged in.

Ever,

Henry Wilson.

It was not by accident that Wilson fixed his attention upon Lord Milner in this period of the war. They had already worked well together during the Irish crisis. Moreover, Bonar Law and most of the other Unionist leaders were dominated at this time by the feeling that it was their duty to act as a loyal Opposition; they believed that their primary task as Opposition politicians in wartime was to avoid factious criticism of the Government, however vigilantly they watched the actions of Ministers. This attitude, however, was one Lord Milner was unable and unwilling to adopt. Sir Henry Wilson chose well when he picked upon Milner in order to send him complaints about the way Liberal Ministers waged war.

IX

It was a natural and logical process for Lord Milner to progress from the status of one who attracted and focused the criticisms of the Asquithian system, to a condition where he was looked upon, by his friends at least, as the man who ought to do something to correct the situation, and thus save the country from failure in war. This change in Lord Milner's position took place in the late autumn of 1914 and in the early months of 1915.

As usual, the first call to action came from Leo Amery. In France, he saw something of the fighting on the Western Front, and was appalled by the terrible casualties sustained by British troops. On 11th November he implored Milner to act:[1]

> . . . we must *begin now*. And there is of course only one way in which we can begin. Decide on national service *now*, to come into force in March . . . and meanwhile . . . set up everywhere great training centres . . .
>
> Have you had any talks with the Unionist leaders about National Service in this emergency? I don't suppose any of them realise even dimly what wastage in war means or what numbers are required in present conditions. . . If a real political crisis should come this winter, as the result of reverses or otherwise, call me back, for I think I should be more use at home than out here.

From the *Round Table* office in Toronto, Milner's old friend M. G. Glazebrook wrote in more pointed terms:[2]

> I should feel very bitter at the thought of your powers being apparently lost to England but for just one thing, and that is the fact that there is in reality an army of "Milnerites" who depend on you for guidance . . .

An exhortation of a different kind came from F. S. Oliver, at the end of the year.[3]

> . . . Democracy is not going to win this war or any other—if we win it will be because the spirit of the small remnant who hate and despise democracy and all its works will save the country in spite of its democratic government. Wars are won by personal loyalty, discipline, self-sacrifice, pride of race and all the positive qualities which are the direct negation of democratic theories.

[1] Milner Papers, Amery to Milner, 11th November 1914.
[2] Milner Papers, Glazebrook to Milner, 21st December 1914.
[3] Milner Papers, "Copy letter" with docket stating "sent by F. S. Oliver", dated 26th December 1914. This letter was probably sent on to Milner by some mutual friend.

It is democracy which nearly betrayed France—if France is saved it will be by the personal loyalty of the Army . . . not by the spouting of all the Vivianis, Caillauxes, Asquiths and Lloyd Georges. . . Democracy has already in five months . . . proved its utter incapacity to prepare for and to conduct war. I hope someone will draw the attention of the Round Table young men to this elementary fact . . .

Early in 1915 Geoffrey Dawson of *The Times* explained the attitude of the Milnerites to Lord Esher, a man who still exercised a powerful influence in royal circles. On 19th January 1915 Esher recorded in his diary that:[1]

I lunched with Geoffrey Robinson today. . . Robinson although he recognises its hopelessness, thinks that his old friend and chief, Milner, would be the best man to conduct the war. Certainly it is a pity that the services of Milner should be lost to the state . . .

Milner's gifts of character have been obscured by clouds of factious and unfair criticism. If his policy in South Africa was unsound, he was not its protagonist. But he showed in the conduct of that policy and of the war precisely those qualities of moral courage and tenacity that will become more and more essential in those who have to conduct this great struggle to its unknowable end.

Lord Esher's comments can help us to understand why Lord Milner took no decisive action at this early stage of the war, even though he was already seething with distress and resentment against the Asquithian system. Milner realised that he was disliked in the country at large; at the same time he hesitated to embark upon the kind of public campaign that would be required to undermine the Prime Minister's position. His principal hope for the safety of the country lay in the policy of National Military Service, and all that it implied for him, but this solution was as unpopular to the generality of Englishmen as was his own personality.

Moreover, he naturally shrank from stepping forward into the glare of the public arena as a critic who, in a terrible hour, was ready to condemn out of hand the honest efforts of his fellow countrymen. The Unionist politicians, under the leadership of Bonar Law, who knew what he was doing at this time, were still pursuing the course of a loyal

[1] Esher, *Diaries,* vol. III, pp. 206–7.

Opposition, anxious most of all to preserve national unity in the face of a foreign enemy. How could Lord Milner, in these circumstances, rush forward in order to destroy the political truce that was still respected by most of the eminent men in both parties?

It seemed clear to him that the time was not yet ripe for action.

X

Nevertheless, significant changes were already beginning to take place in the political condition of the country. They were bound to have an effect upon the relative positions of the Prime Minister, Lord Milner, and others who aspired to power.

Asquith's biographers have wisely pointed out that he owed his authority to his mastery over the House of Commons. In describing his fall from power at the end of 1916 they wrote of him: "he was now to pay the penalty of being a great Parliamentarian when Parliament was on the wane".[1]

There can be little doubt that the authority of Parliament seemed, to contemporaries, to wane during the war, but the process began as early as August 1914. From the beginning, Ministers felt themselves dominated by the need for secrecy; in consequence, they seldom offered detailed explanations of their strategy to either House. Lord Kitchener occasionally made an Olympian pronouncement upon military policy, but he sat in the Lords and refused to permit his Under-Secretary to follow his example in the Commons.[2] In addition, after the outbreak of war, Parliament was often in recess, for considerable periods. This seeming decline in the power of Parliament had its effects upon the political fortunes of the Prime Minister long before 1916.

[1] Spender, *Asquith,* vol. II, p. 242.
[2] See in this connection a brilliant article, A. J. P. Taylor, "Politics in The First World War", in *Proceedings of the British Academy*, vol. XLV, 1959, p. 70.

In the same way, a second source of Asquith's authority was swept away with the commencement of hostilities. As leader of his party, Asquith enjoyed an uncontested control over the Liberal Party organisation in the country. In time of peace this relationship with the party machine in the constituencies was a powerful asset; in war, however, when there was a truce between parties, the activities of the Liberal agents and officials were non-political; they now arranged recruiting campaigns and spoke at non-partisan meetings and propaganda rallies, in the company of their Conservative and Unionist opposite numbers. Their influence upon public opinion no longer served the cause of the Prime Minister and his party, but the cause of the nation; and however much the nation gained, it was the Prime Minister who suffered a serious loss as a result of these developments.

A vacuum was thus created in the political life of the country. It was filled almost at once by the newspaper Press; the influence of the newspapers now grew by unprecedented leaps and bounds, because Parliament and the public platform no longer served as counter-attractions to the campaigns of the journalists. Nor were the politicians slow to recognise and respond to these altered conditions. Deprived of their familiar opportunities for partisan oratory, they made certain of their arrangements with selected advocates and adherents in the Press. Confidential information was freely given upon the one hand, in return for support, adulation and praise upon the other. Although Asquith's connections with the Press were stronger than his biographers admit, the new situation placed him at a definite disadvantage in comparison with certain of his Ministerial colleagues and other rivals.

Lord Milner, for his part, could never rely upon the goodwill of the House of Commons, after his return from South Africa. He depended for support and political power upon the activities of his young, energetic and influential friends who were dominated by his personality, who sang his praises in the ears of those who enjoyed status and position in the England of those days. In addition, the controllers of the Conservative Press were almost unanimous in their adulation of him; Dawson of *The Times*, Garvin and Waldorf Astor of *The Observer*, Maxse of the *National Review*, Gwynne of the *Morning Post*, Northcliffe himself, all agreed that Milner was worthy of power in the crisis of the war. And all these journalists found that their influence grew immensely, as the debates in the House of Commons and party speeches in the country gradually lost all force of impact upon the popular mind.

There was yet another development of some significance. Since the Irish crisis, Liberals in general and the Prime Minister in particular were not liked by the men who led the British Army. Asquith's later association with certain generals in 1918 was a purely artificial arrangement, an unholy alliance based upon nothing save mutual impotence and defeat. Lord Milner, however, was the hero of the regular officers, one of the politicians they particularly respected. As the authority of the military men increased in national affairs, their attitude was bound to have a serious and favourable effect upon his position.

More significant than anything else, however, was the inescapable fact that the Asquith Government had been unable to achieve a decisive victory, on any front. In these circumstances, despite Bonar Law's attitude, Ministers lay wide open to attack as soon as the party truce, a fragile thing at best, began to wear away in the heat and friction of war.

XI

By the early spring of 1915, the moment to strike at Asquith had not yet arrived. Lord Milner, in the national interest, was anxious to replace the Asquithian system for the conduct of the war with some more vigorous method. He was certain that the Asquith policy of delay, compromise, and mediation between political rivals for the sake of harmony and national unity could never produce decisive results. He believed that more urgent and completely untraditional methods were required.

However, there was little that he could do until the course of events furnished him with political allies of such power that their collective demands must result in definite changes in the situation at the top. So long as he remained isolated from the other politicians, in his desire for more effective measures, he was required to act with the very greatest vigilance. Should he move too quickly, he would expose himself to the charge that he was merely a factious critic, jealous of those who were weighed down by the responsibilities of the war.

In March he permitted himself a hint of criticism. He reasonably chose the sphere which he looked upon as his own, the sphere of imperial relations.

When war was declared upon the advice of the Imperial Government in London, the entire British Empire found itself in a state of war with Germany. Beyond this major fact, however, the autonomy of the Dominions was rigidly respected. Although their military, naval and financial contributions to the common effort were welcomed, no genuine attempt was made to co-ordinate these activities with those of the Imperial Government. By the beginning of 1915 people in London began to urge the summoning of a Conference of all the Dominion Governments; for a variety of reasons, these suggestions met with no success in official quarters; on 3rd February it was announced in the Commons that no such meeting would be held.

On 24th March 1915 Lord Milner spoke at a meeting of the Royal Colonial Institute; in guarded terms he touched upon the general subject of Empire co-operation. He remarked, with reference to the peace settlement after the war, that: ". . . those who had the destinies of the country in their hands must look ahead. They must take counsel betimes with men who occupied a similar position in the

Oversea Empire. . ."[1] Beyond this point Lord Milner did not venture, in his speech of the 24th March.

The Milnerites, however, at once recognised the purpose of his remarks. By this time, Leo Amery was in the Middle East, at Lemnos, the base which had been chosen as a staging area for the troops engaged in the assault upon Gallipoli. On 27th April he wrote to Lord Milner that:[2]

> Off Lemnos,
> April 27th 1915
>
> . . . I have not seen the papers regularly but I see Robin on the 20th had a leader saying that the only result of the last six months' war was a growing loss of confidence in the Government. Does this really mean that they are getting shaky and that if things go wrong this spring a sudden storm will arise and sweep them away? . . . I think the storm will come, and even the splendid Kitchener Umbrella (which you were largely instrumental in forcing into Asquith's reluctant hand) will not save them. But hardly before the autumn . . .
>
> I am very glad you raised the question of consulting the Dominions again. I see the Canadians lost heavily at Steenstraate last week, and all they knew at Lemnos was that the brunt of the losses in the landing had been borne by the Australians.

Meanwhile, in France, preparations were being made for a great British attack. This offensive, the battle of Festubert, began on the 9th May. The British effort failed at once, with fearful casualties, largely because of a shortage of high-explosive shells. Colonel Repington, the military correspondent of *The Times*, revealed the extent of the disaster and its cause, in a famous article published by his paper on the 14th May. Three days earlier, however, he had reported the details of the Festubert catastrophe to Geoffrey Dawson; his letter bore the curious message "This . . . is marked 'passed by the censor' but he will not have seen it".[3]

It seems probable that Dawson revealed the contents of Repington's letter to Milner before any public announcement was made in *The Times*. On 13th May 1915 Milner wrote to his lifelong friend, Sir Harry Birchenough, in

[1] From the account in *The Times*, 25th March 1915.
[2] Milner Papers, Amery to Milner, 27th April 1915.
[3] *History of The Times*, vol. IV, p. 274, n. 1.

very grave terms; his letter combined his resentment of the Asquithian system with a resolve to see the war fought out to a successful issue:[1]

> 17 Great College Street,
> 13th May 1915.

My dear Friend,

... Yes. The chickens are indeed coming home to roost, and it is mighty little comfort though, to be honest, it is just *some*—to think that one has been battling all one's life, however ineffectively, against all the tomfoolery of politicians—quacks—for which we are now paying such a heavy price!

But, as Spenser Wilkinson says "the last word in war is *Never say die*."

And we are very far from finished yet, though we have not much more time to use in fumbling.

> Yours ever affectionately,
>
> A. M.

It was clear enough that in Leo Amery's phrase "things had gone wrong". Would the "sudden storm" now arise and sweep away Asquith and his ineffective Government? On 18th May Lord Milner wrote a few lines in his diary. They contain a mere hint of his interest and concern; "the air is full of rumours of a Cabinet Crisis. There is likely to be a Coalition Government including a number of Unionists and a member of the labour party".[2]

In this period of his career Lord Milner did not take care to warn his young friends to look to others for political guidance and leadership, as he did in the years after his return from South Africa. This was a great national emergency. He was desperately eager to play his part. Would his name be included in the number of Unionists that were invited to join the Coalition Government? After nearly a year of war would a measure of power at last be placed in his hands? The answers to these questions would decide his next course of action.

---

[1] Milner Papers, Milner to Birchenough, 13th May 1915.
[2] Milner Papers, extract copy from Milner's Diary for 18th May 1915.

XI. Freedom or Control

The Coalition of May 1915 – Lord Milner's reaction to it –
Asquith's ability as a politician – The events of the 17th of
May – The Coalition of vital consequence to our history –
Asquith's solution – The key offices – The Asquithian
balance – Lord Milner does not count in the crisis of May
1915 – He is left out – Milner as a critic in war – *The Times*
of 27th May – The politicians look at the Coalition –
"Squiff" slips out again – Milner and the National Service
League – Milner and Northcliffe – Lord Milner's Manifesto
– The attitude of King George – Milner is summoned to
Windsor Castle – The King speaks out – Lord Stamford-
ham intervenes – Milner's Memorandum on National
Service – The campaign goes on – Industrial Conscription.

I

WHEN the Prime Minister selected the members of
his Coalition Government in May 1915 he realised
that the essence of his task was to meet a challenge,
the first formal challenge to his position as War Minister.
Although we may find in his solution to the problem the
causes of his final defeat and ruin, we should notice that his
actions at this time were those of a strong man, and not the
fumblings of a weak one.

He believed that by reason of the arrangements he made,
he could remain in perfect control of the situation.

The Coalition of May 1915, as we shall see, was Asquith's
answer to the awful problem of Freedom or Control. It
was his answer to the problem of how Britain was to fight
the war—under the voluntary system or under the rival
system of military conscription and State direction of
industry. Serene and confident in his own powers, the

Prime Minister believed that the solution to his difficulty lay not in measures, but in the proper selection of men for certain key posts in his administration.

If the great offices of State were parcelled out with a knowing and judicious hand, the adherents of the two competing policies, by their very fervour, would cancel out the arguments of their opponents. It would remain for the Prime Minister to arbitrate between the two groups, conferring an advantage now upon the one side, and now upon the other. In this way and by these designs Asquith believed that he could remain above the clash of factions in his Ministry, at the same time that he continued to discharge his most important duty, the preservation of national unity.

Despite the high hopes of the Milnerites, there could be no place for their chief in such an arrangement. As a result, Lord Milner condemned the reorganisation as the adroit scheme of a few party leaders. It seemed so much at fault to him that he determined to take his first step as a public critic of the administration, even though the country was at war.

Nevertheless, the Minister, after the business of forming his Government was over, sat back, content in his opinion that the country looked upon him as the only man to carry on its business. He believed that by a wise and timely reorganisation, he had harnessed to his will those turbulent forces which were then raging in England. So far as Asquith was concerned, the Coalition of May 1915 was a further demonstration of his skill in the conduct of the nation's affairs.

In spite of the arguments of certain apologists, we must realise that Asquith was a man of strength and political resource, fortified by years of hard experience in Downing Street. He was not the plaster saint of a spurious Liberal legend that has been created round his memory.

The Prime Minister was a tough and capable politician. When the political occasion required it, he could, and did, act with ruthless harshness. This quality is part of the equipment of any man who deals with great affairs. To suggest that Asquith lacked it, is to imply that he was unfit for the high offices he adorned for so many years. It was not the case. Whatever else he was, the Prime Minister was not a weakling, for no weakling could discharge the grave responsibilities of the post for the best part of a decade.

Unless we realise the extent of Asquith's powers as a politician, there can be no genuine appreciation of the mortal conflict that was shortly to take place between him and the Milnerites and their allies, after the formation of the Coalition of May 1915. The massive skill and composure of the Prime Minister, so valuable to a British statesman in ordinary circumstances, now began to serve as a goad to outrage those who were dissatisfied by what they regarded as his lethargy and indifference to the vital affairs over which he presided.

II

By the early spring of 1915 certain factious Tories in the Commons were becoming restive. They knew that the Government had been unable to produce an adequate supply of shells and ammunition. Colonel Repington's article in *The Times* of 14th May came as no surprise to them.

By 13th May they had prepared a motion critical of the Government for its failures in this sphere. Despite their purpose, however, Bonar Law, who was determined to preserve the truce between parties, effectively quelled their movement.

Suddenly, this situation was completely altered by a grave development in another quarter. Admiral Fisher resigned his post as First Sea Lord. Fisher's object was to register and make patent his severe disapproval of the Dardanelles campaign, which had been begun earlier in the year. His blow was struck at Winston Churchill, his First Lord, the advocate of the Dardanelles plan in the Cabinet. The Admiral believed that no possibility of success existed in this theatre of operations, that vital units of the fleet were exposed to unnecessary dangers by being stationed there, and that no lesser action on his part could deter Churchill from pursuing to a bitter end his misguided Turkish projects.

When Bonar Law learned of Fisher's action his attitude changed, for two reasons. In the first place, the Admiral was the darling of the Tories in the House and in the country. They relied upon him to preserve the Navy and all that depended upon it in time of war. At the same time the Tories disliked Churchill. They looked upon him as a renegade in politics, and an amateur in war. Bonar Law recognised that he could never keep his party in line if Churchill remained in his place while Fisher was banished from all responsibility. Secondly, Bonar Law agreed with his followers on this issue. He believed in Fisher, and suspected Churchill. He resolved to act before the news of Fisher's resignation was made public.

On 17th May he called upon Lloyd George. He explained the rebellious attitude of his party, and his own feelings. He was received with open arms. Lloyd George appreciated his difficulties. He suggested that a national Coalition Government should be formed in order to solve the problem. The two men at once placed their plan before Asquith.

The Prime Minister accepted their proposal on the spot. He welcomed the suggestion. Why did he do so? What was the inner motive that moved him to agree to the instant dissolution of his Ministry, which had served the country for so long? Why did he not take alarm at the formidable combination of the second Minister in his Government acting in concert with the leader of the Opposition?

Few political episodes have been subjected to so many different interpretations. It has been said that Asquith's motives must remain a matter for surmise. His actions, in any case, decided Lord Milner's course.

The formation of the Coalition of May 1915 and the manner in which the politicians looked upon it are matters of vital consequence to our history. The Asquithian Coalition determined the political position at Westminster throughout 1915 and 1916. The fate of all the leading politicians was bound up in its fortunes. Although Lord Milner was isolated from many of them, he could not act with any effect in isolation. Their conduct and their response to the Coalition exerted a powerful influence upon him.

We have now to examine these several issues with very great care if we are to grasp the meaning of Milner's activities in this phase of his political career.

III

Asquith realised at once that the Tory concern over Fisher was merely the outward sign of a deeper discontent. In the event, Fisher was forgotten, even by the Tories. His resignation achieved only one of his objects, the dismissal of Churchill from the Admiralty. For the rest, the affair ended in the Admiral's complete and utter ruin.

Much more was involved in the crisis of May 1915. Asquith knew that Bonar Law and the Tories in general were advocates of the policy of universal military service. He knew that Lloyd George had flirted with the idea as long ago as 1910, and had never lost interest in it. He knew also that since the earliest period of the war Lloyd George had been passionately eager to organise the peacetime industries of the country for the production of munitions. Lloyd George's disputes with Kitchener in this sphere had already threatened to tear the Government to pieces. In March 1915 Lloyd George introduced a new Defence of the Realm Bill in the Commons. Its object was the mobilisation by the Government of the industrial resources of the country. It was observed at the time that the powers demanded by the Bill were more drastic than any that had ever been asked of a House of Commons. Nevertheless, in the debate Bonar Law remarked that if the Government had asked for such authority six months earlier, the House would have granted it. Asquith knew, as well, that the factious Tories of the Unionist Business Committee, the rebels of the 13th of May, already looked to Lloyd George as the man who could lead the nation by co-operating with their party.[1] On that fateful 17th of May Lloyd George warned him that he would resign unless a Coalition was formed,[2] while Bonar Law threatened a debate in the House unless there was a change in the constitution of the Ministry.

What was the nature of the problem as Asquith saw it? What solution did he fix upon in order to solve the crisis? The Coalition he formed decided affairs in Britain for a further eighteen months of war. It determined Lord Milner's actions and attitude. The essential nature of Asquith's reply to Lloyd George and Bonar Law has been neglected by historians. We have to pay close attention to it for the purposes of our story, because the Asquithian solution turned Lord Milner into one of the bitterest public critics of any Government in recent political history, as we shall see.

The Prime Minister realised that he was being confronted once again by the old problem of Freedom or Control, the great underlying political conflict of the war.[3] He believed that he was strong enough to deal with the emergency.

He would permit the Tories to join him in a new Government, but he would make certain, by his distribution of offices, that neither side gained any advantage. He would preside over both factions—over those who believed in the voluntary system, and over those who placed reliance upon the policy of compulsion and State direction of industry. In judging their arguments, his casting vote would determine on which side the balance fell. He alone would decide the pace at which the State was to break into the private sphere, for the purposes of the war. Power would remain

---

[1] For the attitude of the Tory rebels see W. A. S. Hewins, *Apologia of an Imperialist* (London, 1929), vol. II, p. 21.

[2] Churchill, *World Crisis,* vol. II, p. 798; Spender, *Asquith,* vol. II, p. 166.

[3] This phrase is A. J. P. Taylor's. See his "Politics in The First World War", p. 76.

in his hands. Discord would be confined to his Coalition Cabinet, where he would control it. And national unity, his cardinal object as the King's First Minister, would be preserved, at the very moment that a public debate upon the policies of the Government had been threatened by a cave of uncontrollable rebels in the Commons.

We must be clear that this analysis and these decisions were those of a man convinced of his own power. In a letter of record which he wrote on the 17th of May Asquith made his attitude plain for all to see: "Neither I nor any of my colleagues have anything to regret or to be ashamed of in the steps . . . we have taken . . . since the War began. I am proud to think that we have a record which, when it is impartially appraised by history, will stand the most exacting scrutiny, and be always gratefully and approvingly remembered".[1]

Asquith's appreciation of his powerful position was correct. Lord Beaverbrook, writing of this period, has explained that ". . . Mr. Asquith still possessed prestige and power enough to quell disputants. . . He was then strong enough to face even Lloyd George's resignation".[2]

Having come to these decisions, the Prime Minister proceeded to the formation of his new Government.

IV

The key to Asquith's plan lay in his selection of the men for certain offices. For this reason, he revealed an unbending firmness in the distribution of places, at least in the places that mattered for his purpose.

It has been said that the Prime Minister favoured the Free Trade exponents of the policy of *laissez-faire* in the reconstruction of his Government. His personal feelings certainly inclined him to their side. Like them, he was distinguished by what was called "the Treasury mind". But

---

[1] Asquith, *Memories and Reflections*, vol. II, p. 96.
[2] Beaverbrook, *Politicians and The War*, p. 145.

more important for his purpose was the creation of a Ministry which balanced the arguments of the two groups.

When the Coalition was being formed the leading Free Traders were not at all certain of their position. They resented the change. Walter Runciman wrote to McKenna, the foremost of the Free Traders: "If we are honoured with invitations to come in I feel that we must first know with whom we are asked to associate and then be told what demands were made or assurances given on policy to Bonar and his colleagues: in particular if they were told that we had an open mind on compulsory service or taxation or trade policy. . . I am to breakfast with Grey".[1] These are not the remarks of a man who knows that his side is being favoured by the dispositions of the First Minister. On the contrary, they reveal the uneasiness of the Free Traders in the face of the new departure. They did not like it.

Asquith took care to mollify them almost at once: "I let it be publicly understood from the first—lest there should be any suspicion that there was to be a new departure in policy—that the three principal offices would remain unchanged: those of Prime Minister, of Foreign Secretary, and of Secretary of State for War".[2]

These high offices were vitally important. But others were of equal significance in the battle for Freedom or Control. The Ministers selected for these other offices would decide the contest. Between them, they would determine the pace of developments in this sphere. They would be required, and empowered, to direct and animate the whole of the manpower of the nation.

Of first importance in the new scheme was the Ministry of Munitions, which went to Lloyd George. The accession of the Tories was a tremendous reinforcement of his position. In any case, he could be relied upon to press his

[1] For this quotation and the general hostility of the Liberals to the change, see a brilliant biography by Stephen McKenna, *Reginald McKenna*, p. 223, hereafter cited as McKenna.

[2] Asquith, *Memories and Reflections*, vol. II, p. 100.

colleagues without mercy in order to force them to surrender to him unprecedented powers for the direction of
labour and for the compulsory organisation by the State
of large areas of the nation's industries. He had already
launched a vicious campaign in the Press to make certain
of a powerful Ministry of Munitions.

In order to balance his tremendous and fearful energy,
formidable dispositions would have to be made. The
Exchequer was a post of overmastering significance because
of the general authority and influence of the Chancellor
over the whole field of policy. Bonar Law could reasonably
claim it as his own. His colleagues pressed him to do so.
Asquith refused to comply with their wishes. He outraged
the Tories and offended the feelings of their leader. He made
it clear that the Coalition was to be his instrument. He
selected Reginald McKenna, the leading Free Trade
opponent of compulsory service and State direction, as his
new Chancellor.

He took equal care over the other offices that directed the
manpower of the country. Lloyd George and the Tories
were denied any control over them.

In the pre-war organisation of the Government the Board
of Trade enjoyed close and important relations with industry and labour. It was heavily involved in industrial matters.
It was the department responsible for the arbitration of
labour disputes. Its marine department was responsible
for the treatment of merchant seamen. It worked closely
with the management of the railway companies. Its Department of Labour Statistics collected vital information upon
which policy in this sphere was based. This post went to
Walter Runciman, McKenna's closest ally.

The Home Office, in this period, administered the
Factory Acts. For this reason it was recognised as a depart-
ment of consequence in industrial matters. Home Office
inspectors regularly visited all the factories of the kingdom.
They could be looked upon as the trained agents of the
State, already stationed in the industrial sphere. Sir John

Simon was selected as the new Home Secretary. He was the foremost enemy of compulsion in the Government.

Yet a third department, by pre-war practice, was involved in industrial affairs. This was the Local Government Board which administered the Poor Law. The Local Government Board was responsible for the care of those workers who required the help of the State, because of illness, unemployment or some other misfortune. The man who was given the post of President of the Local Government Board was Walter Long. He was the head of the Unionist Business Committee, the group of Tory rebels in the Commons who precipitated the crisis in the first place. He was also notorious for his jealousy of the titular leaders of his party. He had been Bonar Law's rival for the leadership of the Conservatives in 1911. And he never forgot it. A skilful politician would not find it difficult to tamper with his allegiance to Bonar Law. In a crisis he might be induced to follow some other course than that advocated by the leader of his party.

By these arrangements the Prime Minister hoped to curb and control the onrush of Lloyd George and the Tories. Asquith has been too often dismissed as a weak man, unfit to lead. For him, the central problem was a question of team management. Who could manage affairs better? As he saw it, if either side won a clear-cut victory at this stage of the war, there would be serious discontent in the country. Time was required to permit the development of public opinion. He alone, rising above the factions, could gain it.

Bonar Law grasped the nature of Asquith's position at this time. He later explained to the House of Commons that the Coalition of May 1915 saved the country from disunion and internal strife. That was the reason which impelled him to join it. He said of May 1915: "I will tell the House exactly what I think would have happened. I feel perfectly certain . . . that within a few months the Government of another party, and that the party to which I belong, would have been responsible for the conduct of the war. . . If that had happened we should at once have been faced with the question of compulsion. We as a party would have tried to carry it immediately, but we could only have done it by dividing the country from top to bottom at that time, and we should have . . . had . . . far more disunion in the nation, and the result would have been worse for this country in the struggle in which we are engaged . . ."[1]

Despite his hopes and those of his followers, despite his fitness to play a part, despite his patriotic ardour, despite his unrivalled experience, Lord Milner could not be given a place in the new Government. He was an unyielding partisan. He would never consent to serve as one of the forces to be weighed in the Asquithian balance. Moreover, he had no organised following in the House, and no mass of supporters in the country. So far as Asquith was concerned, Lord Milner did not count in the crisis. Austen Chamberlain offered to serve as Milner's Under-Secretary if a place could be found for him. On 21st May before all was settled Austen wrote to Bonar Law: "Now, judged simply by the test of personal capacity—brains, character, earnestness, courage, organizing power—I set Milner absolutely in the first rank . . . few appointments would bring more confidence and strength than his. I feel this so strongly that I urge you again and much more forcibly than I have yet done to put his name forward. . . In particular I offer to you and Asquith that, if it will facilitate Milner's inclusion—I will gladly serve as Under-Secretary to him in any office. . . I write this very seriously and after full reflection. . . I am confident that the inclusion of his name would give confidence both to the country and the Army that this was a *national* Govt. and not merely a two-party or three-party Govt. and that it meant business".[2]

In Asquith's opinion, however, Lord Milner could be ignored with complete safety even though a dozen other

[1] *Parliamentary Debates,* vol. XCII, 4th April 1917, col. 1392.
[2] Sir Charles Petrie, *Life of Austen Chamberlain* (London, 1940), vol. II, pp. 27–8.

Unionists were given office. He was left out. No position was found for him.

V

Ministers were engaged in the distribution of offices for a week. When that week was over Lord Milner struck his blow.

He was confronted by a complicated and difficult situation. Asquith had made it clear that the policy of the Government was not to be changed. But in Lord Milner's opinion this was exactly what was required, if calamity were to be avoided. The matter was urgent. It was ridiculous to hazard the national position upon the lax, illogical and unorganised methods of the voluntary system. But what was to be done? The shifting of Ministerial places was no answer. This was the old politician's trick that he had despised since South African days and before.

How could he speak out as a critic in war? The new arrangement was accepted by the leaders of all the parties. To attack it would be to expose himself at once to the cruel charge that he was a disappointed seeker after office. Harsh and bitter in opposition, Lord Milner lacked that thickness of skin which enables the politician to receive and deal out the buffets and blows that are a part of public life in Britain. He was sensitive. Surrounded by his young friends or in the company of these who knew him, he could convince his listeners of the validity and worth of his ideas. Such intimate exchanges were congenial to his nature. His natural charm and courtesy were most effective at close range. He could deal with men in the restricted atmosphere of the salon, the club, the study, the office. This was not the case when he advanced into wider spheres. It was painful for him to seek the limelight. How could he instruct the public, so unprepared to deal with the realities of any situation? How could he be certain that his motives would be understood? How could he guard himself from their deliberate misinterpretation by those shallow but adroit enemies who had hounded him so often in the past?

Should he then withdraw from an active course, and leave matters to the politicians, as he did in the years between 1906 and 1913? It was impossible for him to do so. He could never sulk in his tent, whatever the personal provocation, when the nation cried out for help in the emergency of the war.

He resolved to take action of some kind because he was convinced that someone had to act. He knew that the politicians who were willing to allow the voluntary system to continue were in error. As a patriot he felt bound to interfere, whatever the personal consequences.

By the early spring of 1915 the gross blunders of the voluntary system were clear to those who could see behind the exhortations of the recruiting posters and the propaganda meetings. The first rush of volunteers had produced recruits in plenty but at a fearful cost. At a time when small arms and rifles were in short supply, large numbers of men engaged in the manufacture of these weapons had been allowed to join the Army. At a time when there was a grave shortage of high explosives, nearly twenty-five per cent of the men who produced them had left their places of employment for military service. The engineering trade, responsible for the manufacture of shells, fuses and other warlike instruments, lost more than twelve per cent of its workers in the first unthinking response of the country's manhood. These were skilled men, not easily replaced. At the very moment the War Office began to order ammunition in tremendous and unprecedented quantities, the armament firms were losing their men at a rate never known before.

Lord Milner believed that these were matters that could be controlled by the intervention of the State. He wanted official surveys made to determine the requirements of the war and the resources available to meet these requirements. In his opinion, individuals were not qualified to decide where or how they should serve. Ardour might sway one man and the desire to avoid duty another. In any case, it was impossible for the individual to decide logically. The situation demanded more stringency than the half-measures so far applied. The Government alone had the power to discover needs, and to meet them. To abandon the task to the caprices of the voluntary system was a gross and criminal neglect of authority and responsibility.

How could all this be urged in wartime by a man who shrank from public controversy, who could act in the popular arena only after he overcame the most painful doubts and hesitations? Lord Milner resolved upon two steps. One was a long-range programme, which we will examine below. The other was a more immediate protest. The preliminary move was designed to awaken the country to the fact that the Coalition of May 1915 was no answer to its problems.

As he had so often done in the past, Lord Milner turned to Geoffrey Dawson. A column on the leader page of *The Times* was given over to him for his purpose. Headlines in *The Times* of 27th May proclaimed:

UNFAIR METHODS
Lord Milner's Call for Leadership
To the Editor of *The Times*

Sir,—The change of Ministry will not bring us victory without a change of method. We have now got the best men of all political parties working together. . . But even the best Government cannot do the impossible. . . You might as well expect an army using the old Brown Bess to beat one equipped with quick-firing rifles, as a country that still clings to the voluntary system to be a match for one which is organised throughout on the principle of national service. The handicap is too enormous. It hampers us everywhere, in the provision of ammunition no less than in the provision of men. It is the root cause of nine-tenths of the hitches, delays, and blunders, and of the widespread and justified uneasiness and discontent. . .

What has been achieved so far . . . has been achieved largely by the aid of a number of exceptional measures, drastically interfering with our famous "rights of property" and "liberty of the subject". Yet nobody complains. . . The spirit of the nation is excellent. It simply needs firm leadership. . .

The State ought not to be obliged to tout for fighting men. It ought to be in a position to call out the number it wants . . . and to call them in the right order. . . To do this systematically and fairly requires a census and proper classification. It is a big work of national organisation. It will take time. That is why it is so terrible to see day after day passing without its being begun. . .

. . . It is high time that the whole of our able-bodied manhood . . . should be enrolled . . . except those who can render the more efficient aid in other ways. And the nation is ready to obey the order. It only needs the captain on the bridge to give the signal.

> Your obedient servant,
> MILNER.

In this way Lord Milner avoided the nagging tones of the critic. At the same time he pronounced his judgment upon the Coalition. He demanded positive direction and leadership at the very moment that Asquith chose to fall back upon the arts and tactics of the politician who negotiates, mediates and compromises between the conflicting opinions of his colleagues.

However much it might be delayed, an explosion was bound to come between the advocates of these two policies. And if one explosion failed to settle matters, a whole series of convulsions might be expected until one side or the other was battered into silence.

VI

Lord Milner was not the only one to look upon the Coalition as a blunder. Others watched the development of the affair with critical interest. Winston Churchill disagreed with the Asquithian analysis, upon which the Coalition was based. He believed that the arrangement of May 1915 was "one of the greatest disasters which happened in the whole course of the War".[1]

No one had been more eager for Coalition than Churchill. From the earliest days of the war he had sought to bring about such a development. But he was convinced that when

[1] For Churchill's opinions see *Parliamentary Debates*, vol. XCII, 4th April 1917, cols. 1383–6, and *World Crisis*, vol. II, pp. 804 ff.

Asquith accepted the demand of Lloyd George and Bonar
Law, he committed an irretrievable mistake and lost an
opportunity that would never recur. Although Churchill's
own place at the Admiralty was forfeited in the reorganisation, it is clear enough that he rose above personal concerns
when he advised Asquith to defy his visitors of the 17th of
May. The opinions of the man who later became the most
successful War Minister in modern British history deserve
our attention. They merit a place in our story of Lord
Milner's hostility to the Asquithian Coalition.

Since the outbreak of war, as we have seen, the authority
of Parliament had steadily declined. Debates were few in
number and lacking in significance. As the influence of the
Press upon the public mind increased in these circumstances,
the status of the Prime Minister was steadily undermined by
the hostility of certain newspaper proprietors and their
agents in journalism. However, the crisis of the 17th of
May presented Asquith with the opportunity to revive the
waning authority of Parliament and to bolster up his own
deteriorating position.

Churchill urged him to summon a Secret Session of both
Houses in order to explain and defend the record and policy
of the Government. Churchill was convinced that the Prime
Minister would have received the support of "large majori-
ties" at such a Secret Session. By this single and significant
stroke Asquith could have reversed the trend which sapped
the very source of his power: "I am certain", wrote Churchill, "that had he fought, he would have won; and had he
won, he could then with dignity and with real authority
have invited the Opposition to come not to his rescue but
to his aid. On such a basis . . . a true national Coalition
could have been formed . . ."[1] Asquith rejected this advice.
The consequences were fatal for himself, and for the party
he led.

Bonar Law was also critical of the new arrangement. He
was certain that he had come to the aid of a moribund

[1] Churchill, *World Crisis*, vol. II, p. 805.

Ministry, for Asquith had not fought back on the 17th of May. The Unionist leader was prepared to co-operate with Asquith for the sake of national unity and the party truce; he believed, as we have seen, that conscription could be gained most easily under Asquith's Premiership. But he found himself denied high office in the Coalition. He was refused the Chancellorship and the Ministry of Munitions. He was fobbed off with the Colonial Office, a minor post in war. Although he wanted to work with Asquith as an equal partner, he found that this was not the Prime Minister's purpose at all. Despite Asquith's cavalier actions over offices, however, Bonar Law had seen on the 17th of May that the Prime Minister could be pushed when he was confronted by resolute men who demanded action. The lesson was not lost upon him.

Reginald McKenna, the Free Trade leader, came to a similar conclusion. He resented the sacrifice of Haldane and his other Liberal colleagues. They were forced to retire as a result of Asquith's harsh decision. At the same time McKenna was resolved to preserve the Free Trade *laissez-faire* position of the country in the face of the impossible military and economic programmes of the conscriptionists. Their proposals, in his opinion, would bankrupt the nation by destroying the balance between its military and financial obligations. In his view, Lloyd George and the Tories planned to ask more of Britain than her capabilities could bear. To give way to them would be to ruin the country's ability to wage war. He realised that Bonar Law and the Tories looked upon Asquith as "indispensable"—for their purposes. But what would happen when conscription was at last carried by an Asquithian Government? What would then be the fate of Liberal Ministers and the Liberal Party? How could Asquith assert himself when that fateful hour struck? He had already given way in much more favourable circumstances. The Prime Minister had taught his opponents the awful lesson that if they applied enough pressure, he would yield. He would put up with anything, for the sake of national unity. If Lloyd George and his Tory friends managed to carry conscription under Asquith's leadership, would they still regard him as the indispensable man? McKenna did not believe it. He made ready to fight the battle of Freedom or Control from the beginning—for the sake of his colleagues, his party, and the country's war effort.[1]

Lloyd George, burning with ambition and zeal in equal measure, was already dissatisfied with the measures taken and the energy shown in the conduct of the war. He watched the formation of the Coalition with the sharpest eyes. He saw that at the first blast of a hostile trumpet the Asquithian fortress had fallen. He may have known, even at this early stage, that his co-operation with Bonar Law on the 17th of May was symbolic of much that was to follow.

Yet another man observed the new arrangement with keen interest. He was much feared by the politicians of all parties, and with reason. Sir Edward Carson, the newly appointed Attorney-General, believed that he had taken Asquith's measure years before. Dr. Addison later wrote of Carson's opinion of Asquith, formed during the pre-war Irish crisis: "A friend of mine who knew his mind (and I think his judgment was right) told me that Carson, having observed Asquith carefully . . . in the House of Commons, went on with his preparations openly, having deliberately come to the conclusion that he could afford to risk it, and that Asquith would not step in and stop him".[2] The events of May 1915 served as a further proof to reinforce Sir Edward in his low opinion of the Prime Minister. Carson was not the man to sit by with folded hands if he once believed that firm leadership and direction were absent at the top. Unlike the other party leaders, he could be depended upon to do something in such circumstances.

Finally, the events of the 17th of May and after were

---

[1] For McKenna's views, see McKenna, *passim,* especially pp. 230 ff., 255 ff., 306 ff.
[2] Christopher Addision, *Politics From Within 1911–1918* (London, 1924), vol. I, p. 36.

measured by the keenest analyst of them all. Lord Beaver-brook, ever vigilant in the service of Bonar Law, brooded upon the new arrangement for a time and then came to a characteristically decisive conclusion: "Of all the actors . . . the role assumed by the Prime Minister was the most amazing. He watched the feud develop . . . with a kind of mild interest. . . He showed no sign of realising that his own fortunes and those of his Ministry were at stake. . . Obviously, it was a matter of vital concern to him that he should either bring about a reconciliation between the opponents, or that he should utterly crush one or the other. Instead of this, he did nothing . . . favoured McKenna just enough to irritate the Minister of Munitions, and took no steps whatever to ensure that the irritated Minister should be rendered harmless".[1]

It is thus clear that despite Asquith's confidence and serenity, the Coalition was not the brilliant stroke he believed it to be. Nevertheless, the Milnerites were angered by his escape. In the immediate opinion of Milner and his friends, "Squiff" had slipped out of the trap once again. He had swallowed the Opposition by means of his Coalition. He had denied Lord Milner any place in the central direction of the war. Their feelings of baffled rage were well expressed in a letter from F. S. Oliver to Amery:[2]

I agree that Squiff & Squiffery . . . must go. "Liberalism" in the worst sense of that vile word—which they most worthily represent—is *dead—dead—dead*. It is a dead foetus in the womb of Government & more dangerous being dead & putriescent than it would be were it still alive.

Nor can you wait philosophically . . . Squiff was due to be . . . buried under quicklime (along with all his horrid sort) . . .

. . . Look you out for a Perceval or a Castlereagh. . .

The failure to include Lord Milner in the Government, and his instant response in *The Times*, brought messages of support from his army of Milnerites. Rudyard Kipling wrote to bless him for his letter to *The Times*. Kipling

[1] Beaverbrook, *Politicians and The War*, p. 145.
[2] Amery Papers, Oliver to Amery, 23rd July 1915.

believed that the new Ministry was merely a return of the Old Gang. He was convinced that they could make no serious contribution to the progress of the war. Austen Chamberlain explained that he had done his best to win Milner a place; his failure, he said, was the nation's misfortune. Leo Amery wrote to condemn the Coalition as a purely Parliamentary proceeding which could never alter the terrible political situation at Whitehall. Henry Wilson, writing from France, declared that: "I don't think you can have any idea how disgusted & disheartened I am that you are not in the new Cabinet. . . You know well all I mean".[1]

Thus fortified by the bellicose goodwill of his friends, Lord Milner resolved to take a second and more decisive step in his new role as the public critic of the administration. He decided to launch a public campaign against the policies of the Coalition Ministry.

VII

In the middle of July Lord Milner called upon Admiral Fisher, a man capable of the most desperate intrigues. Fisher had plagued the pre-war Asquithian Government without mercy, by means of his astounding revelations to journalists and others, in his efforts to enforce his will upon Ministers. Although Milner often conspired with soldiers, his papers reveal that his private intercourse with the leading admirals was very rare. Nevertheless, on 14th July he visited Lord Fisher in order to talk to him about the submarine menace. Was this an issue that could be used to beat Ministers into some more active course? Despite Milner's hopes in this direction, the Admiral did not believe that the danger from submarines was vital, in 1915. He was unable to help Milner with his plan.[2]

---

[1] These letters in the period 26th May to 2nd June are preserved in the Milner Papers.
[2] Milner Papers, Fisher to Milner, 15th July 1915.

Meanwhile, however, Lord Milner was making more progress in another direction. On 8th June he was invited to become chairman of the National Service League. Here was the opportunity he had been waiting for. On the next day he dined with R. H. Brand, Philip Kerr, F. S. Oliver, Lionel Hichens, and Valentine Chirol of *The Times*. On that occasion they discussed the policy of National Military Service, and the best means of promoting it.[1] After this dinner, Milner resolved to urge this policy upon the public by means of a great national campaign.

A distinguished authority has observed of the question of conscription that "the attitudes taken by public men at various times, the compromises, the disputes, constitute a chapter in English history to which no doubt in years to come dull history professors will direct their duller research students". It may, perhaps, be observed in this connection that dullness, like beauty, resides in the eye of the beholder. When conscription, with its corollary of industrial direction, are considered together, we deal with the overmastering political conflict of the war. A. J. P. Taylor has acutely observed that the rank and file of the Unionists who pressed for compulsory military service "did so from simple impulse. They were after all simple men. . . More clear-sighted Unionists . . . were content either way. If compulsion produced millions of fresh soldiers, then their needs would overwhelm the 'free' economic system. Alternatively, if it produced only claims for reservation, industrial conscription was being attained by the back door".[2]

On 16th June Lord Milner spoke at the annual meeting of the National Service League. His speech was the first tentative step of his new course. It was reported upon the leader page of *The Times* on the next day. Lord Milner said:

[1] Milner Papers, Diary Extract.

[2] The distinguished authority is Robert Blake. See his *Bonar Law*, p. 282. For Taylor's comment see "Politics in The First World War, pp. 77–8. The origins of Blake's comment seem to lie with some remarks of Lord Beaverbrook. For Beaverbrook's firmer grasp of the matter, however, see A. J. P. Taylor's lecture, at p. 68 and n. 4.

. . . We all want the same thing, which is to make an end of fighting with . . . only half our strength . . . We must have organised effort and that means regulations. . . How are you to get orderly cooperation among millions upon millions of people without rules . . . and yet . . . you get this absurd outcry against compulsion. We are fighting today. . . for dear life, against a most formidable enemy. There is a strong ally of that enemy in our midst. It is the power of catchwords, of phrases. . . This nation has always a fatal proneness to be led astray by clap-trap. The present pother about compulsion is a case in point. All law, all order, all discipline, involves . . . compulsion. Does any sane man on that account object to law, order and discipline?

. . . The question was how to get the maximum of service out of a willing people with the minimum of friction and inequality and waste. . . Something better than the present haphazard system was needed. . .

. . . Universal service was finer, fairer, more conducive to national solidarity . . . than our present way of going on. . .

On 29th July Lord Milner's selection as chairman of the General Council of the National Service League was announced in the Press. Leo Amery, ardent as ever, was not convinced that Milner planned to do enough from his new point of vantage. On 2nd August he urged upon his chief the need for action of a more extensive kind. He begged Lord Milner to prepare himself to become Prime Minister:[1]

. . . National Service if we could get it established at once would be only a step in the tremendous effort required—and required almost at once—if we are to have any hope of raising our forces to the strength that can strike a decisive blow & save us from stalemate.

But there can be no question of such an effort while we still have Asquith; and things wouldn't be better under Lloyd George. If it is possible to do it at all, you are the only man who can do it—the only person who has in these last few years been facing realities, the only one with knowledge and courage. Austen, Curzon, Lloyd George, even Carson, who is the best of the lot . . . are only good lieutenants. . . I believe you must do it. And you have got to do it yourself—I mean you can't wait like Cincinnatus till they remember your existence & come to find you. Somehow or other you have in the next few weeks got to assert yourself, to declare to the public what your policy for this war is, so that when the moment for getting rid of Asquith & Co. comes they may know where to turn. To urge N.S. alone is too

[1] Milner Papers, Amery to Milner, 2nd August 1915.

276

abstract. You want to proclaim the outlines of a complete policy, in which N.S. fits in as an essential lever, but which also deals with all the other problems, munitions, finance, food & so on. . . The Milner policy or National policy as distinct from the Party or Mandarin Policies, must be something clear & definite in the public mind.

The real question is . . . how and where to launch it? Should it be a speech in Birmingham . . . our old Covenant Council[1] might make a nucleus. . . Austen is always hampered by Front-Bench loyalty . . . but Carson would I feel almost certain cooperate. So *will* Lloyd George, if he once felt certain that he has no chance of becoming Prime Minister . . . Robin will help. . . Gwynne might be useful. . . But there must be an effective board of conspirators for you to lead. . . Henry Wilson could do a lot. . .

It's got to be done somehow & *you've* got to do it . . . the rudder has got to be seized from the nerveless hand that now holds it.

Despite these exhortations, Milner was convinced that the launching of an agitation for National Service would occupy all his time and all his energies. The Coalition of May 1915 had effectively captured the politicians, for months to come. None of them would dare to break away from Asquith, so shortly after joining his new Government. Milner was isolated from them. For these reasons he paid more attention to a letter from F. S. Oliver, who was able to report to him the discussions that were taking place in the Cabinet.[2]

Saw C. at lunch today. A long Cabinet & apparently a strong push for N. Service—Curzon, Ll. G. & Winston all pushing hard. . . K. even went so far as to say he thought we should have to resort to N.S. before an end with this war! But Squiff will probably get at him alone and frighten him with logic. It is K. that must be battered down. . .

VIII

The conscription issue was already the subject of a violent controversy in the Press. In general, the Liberal newspapers were strongly hostile to the proposal. They

[1] Amery refers here to the British Covenant of Irish crisis days.

[2] Milner Papers, Oliver to Milner, 11th August 1915. Asquith found it necessary to appoint a Cabinet Committee in August 1915 to investigate conscription, man-power and resources.

were opposed most fiercely by *The Times*, the *Daily Mail*, and the other journals owned by Lord Northcliffe. Milner was doubtful of the value of Northcliffe's support in the struggle. On 19th August he explained his plans to Lady Roberts, whose husband had been the patron of the National Service League for so many years before the war:[1]

> ... I was just going to a meeting—the second—of the Council of the N.S.L. as it was decided we could no longer sit still. The embargo on further propaganda was therefore taken off, and we shall do all we can to help, without trying to "boss", the movement which has sprung up independently of us. It is unfortunate that it should have originated with Northcliffe—he excites justly, or unjustly, so many animosities—but I think the feeling is now too strong and widespread for even this evil god-fathership to hamper it materially. . . The real difficulty, of course, is Kitchener. . . He has no doubt been got at by clever people. . .

Despite this letter, Lord Northcliffe could not be ignored. Asquith's failure to summon a Secret Session of Parliament, as Winston Churchill advised, had left the newspapers in unchallenged control of the field abandoned by Parliament. On the very day that Milner complained about Northcliffe to Lady Roberts, he received a letter from the Press Lord who promised him full support in the campaign for National Service. For the moment, the politicians could not act. They were all Coalition Ministers. However much he disliked it, Milner was compelled to proceed in concert with Northcliffe. If none of the politicians would speak out in public, Milner could not permit his new movement to perish for lack of publicity. He was required to accept Northcliffe's help, however distasteful it might be. Geoffrey Dawson acted as the go-between in the new arrangement. On 19th August Northcliffe wrote to Milner:[2]

> Robinson and I are extremely glad that you have decided to join your forces to our little manifesto, and arouse the country to the fact that we shall be faced with a separate peace on the part of Russia or

---

[1] Milner Papers, Milner to Lady Roberts, 19th August 1915.
[2] Northcliffe Papers, Northcliffe to Milner, 19th August 1915.

France with Germany unless National Service is adopted in this country. . .

My newspapers will do all in their power to help the National Service League. . .

On 20th August, in consequence of these several arrangements there came a second and more powerful blow in Milner's campaign for National Service. The Press on that day published a Manifesto, over his signature. He explained in this declaration that at the beginning of the war the National Service League had decided to suspend its propaganda in order to place its whole organisation at the disposal of the Government. However, the situation had changed since those early days. The policy of the League had been reconsidered, for the existence of the Empire was now at stake, and in jeopardy. Half-measures could no longer serve. "The National Service League", Lord Milner wrote, "has decided to take an active share in the movement in favour of National Service. . . The time has come for the League to resume its propaganda. . . In changed circumstances the League has changed its policy. It now advocates not merely National Service for home defence, but universal and compulsory military service for the duration of the war. . ." The Manifesto was signed by Milner in his capacity as Chairman of the Council of the National Service League.

The Manifesto of the 20th August was the signal for a spirited public agitation to begin. It followed hard upon the publication of Lord Milner's declaration. *The Times*, the *Daily Mail*, and other Unionist journals continued to cry out for the new policy. Subscriptions were collected at public meetings in London and in the country. A fund was built up to finance the new movement. The Liberal journals shrieked back at the brazen militarists who presumed to tamper with the freedom of the individual and the rights of Englishmen. There was little or no discussion of the subject in the commons. Since the formation of the Coalition, in fact, the Press had completely overshadowed the Parliament in dealing with this tremendous issue. The *Daily News*, the *Daily Chronicle*, the *New Statesman*, and the *Nation*, were especially prominent as advocates of the voluntary system.

Despite the political truce, Lord Milner had succeeded in seriously disturbing the even course of the Ministry. His new movement caused genuine distress and even alarm in the very highest circles, as we shall see.

On the day that his Manifesto appeared in the Press Lord Milner confided his private opinions of the affair and its implications to his old friend, Philip Gell. He expected, he said, to see a "bad peace" concluded before the autumn of 1916 "unless there were to be a moral miracle and the character of our rulers were to be suddenly completely changed". He went on:[1]

The situation could still be saved, but only by the consistent display of qualities, which are the absolute antithesis of what we know of Asquith, McKenna, Simon, *et hoc genus omne*, and I fear I must add of A. J. B., Lansdowne, and most of their Unionist colleagues. Of course Kitchener might save the situation, and I think he would have supporters in Carson, Curzon and Lloyd George. Selborne and Austen are also all right. . .

Of course I am thinking of National Service. We have now arrived at the eleventh hour, and unless we do something instantly we shall lose the game. . . Of course there is a great deal else needed besides National Service . . . all need to be tackled with vigour and insight . . . the position is perfectly infuriating because the spirit of the country is so good, and our undeveloped resources still so enormous. But there is a degree of muddle and incompetence which would ruin anything.

On 26th August Lord Curzon, Lord Privy Seal in the Coalition Government, visited Lord Milner. Curzon, Milner wrote in his diary, "brought me some Cabinet papers about the economic aspect of National Service. I was busily writing a Memorandum for Curzon's information all evening".[2] Later, Milner met Amery, Carson, and R. H. Brand, the banker. It is clear enough that Lord Milner, in company with these men, was concerned with the issue of National Service as an aspect of the larger struggle for

[1] Milner Papers, Milner to Philip Gell, 20th August 1915, marked "Confidential"
[2] Milner Papers, Diary Extract.

Freedom or Control. He was not one of those "simple men" in the Unionist ranks who urged the policy of conscription "from simple impulse", however keenly he was attracted by it.

On 25th August Henry Wilson sent a message of support from France:[1]

25.8.15   Gen. Headquarters.

My dear Lord Milner,

You know with what pleasure & what hope I follow your campaign in favour of compulsion.

I shall never be quite happy until I see you War Minister. I hear, often, of your doings from Leo Amery, Gwynne . . . Fred Oliver & others. . .

Ever yours,
Henry Wilson.

IX

Meanwhile, the King, brooding upon the disasters which befell Allied arms in the black month of August 1915, was further distressed by the agitation for National Service. It threatened to endanger the unity of the country. The King liked Asquith and respected Lord Kitchener. He failed to sympathise with Lord Milner's new movement in general, and he was particularly concerned because it was launched at one of the blackest moments of the war. The King hoped that his Prime Minister and his Secretary of State for War, in whom he felt the highest confidence, would be allowed to discharge their difficult tasks without the added burden of a political onslaught which fell upon them from behind.

The causes of the King's concern were very real. Early in August, new landings had been made at Suvla Bay in the north of the Gallipoli peninsula. This bold stroke promised well in the first hours, but the conception was ruined by the senile lethargy of the commanders of the assaulting troops. A great opportunity was cast away. By the end of the month the men were suffering from disappointment, disease, and a

[1] Milner Papers, Wilson to Milner, 25th August 1915.

desperate shortage of water. The attack was a failure and the fate of the whole expedition dismal. On the Russian front, grave reverses were suffered during the month of August. On the 4th, Warsaw fell to the advancing German Army; a few weeks later the Russians were thrown out of the fortress town of Brest-Litovsk. August saw the Russians engaged in a desperate retreat. The news was equally grim from Italy. Much had been hoped of the Italian intervention in the war. It was one of the reasons that decided the politicians in London to join the Asquith Coalition. They hesitated to reveal internal dissension at a time when Italy was preparing to join the Allies. However, by the end of August it was clear that the Italian forces could make no progress against the Austrians on the Isonzo front, where they suffered fearful casualties. The outlook for the Allies was black.

In these circumstances, the King was upset by the growing division of opinion in Britain over the issue of compulsion. On 24th August an informal conference to discuss the matter was held at Buckingham Palace. In addition to the King, the Prime Minister, Lord Kitchener, Balfour and Sir Edward Grey were in the company. Asquith had recently discussed the matter with Walter Runciman. As President of the Board of Trade, Runciman had been in close touch with the trade union leaders. He reported to the Prime Minister that without any exceptions, the trade unionists were very hostile to compulsion and were prepared to fight against it with all their power.[1]

Four days after this conference, on 28th August, Lord Milner was summoned to the King at Windsor. Since the vote of censure debate in 1906 he had enjoyed the goodwill of the Royal House. His intercourse with King Edward and with King George was cordial. On this occasion, however, the King was unable to approve of Lord Milner's political policies.

[1] See Asquith, *Memories and Reflections*, vol. II, p. 109; Nicolson, *King George V*, p. 270. For the disputes inside the Cabinet over conscription from midsummer 1915 until the spring of 1916, see below, ch. XIII.

After dinner on 28th August King George took Milner aside in order to explain his views on National Service. The King's attitude, according to Lord Milner's diary, amounted "to a laudation of Asquith and Kitchener and a strong expression of opinion against the agitation for National Service".[1]

On the next day Lord Stamfordham, the King's Private Secretary and an experienced royal counsellor, called upon Milner in order to discuss the matter again. "Stamfordham", Milner wrote, "came to see me in my room, and talked at length on the N.S. question. I put to him pretty frankly my view of the case . . ."[2]

In consequence of these representations Milner prepared, while he was still at Windsor, a long memorandum on the subject of National Service. Dated Sunday, 29th August 1915, the paper deserves our careful attention. It reveals the powerful influence of the Press on the conduct of national affairs in this period, and its importance in the eyes of the leading men of the time. Asquith had sacrificed a great deal when he refused to accept Winston Churchill's suggestion for the summoning of a Secret Session, in order to revive the authority of Parliament in the public mind. Lord Milner's memorandum was most probably written for the information of the King:[3]

A great deal of fuss has been made about the "Northcliffe" agitation. This is, as a matter of fact, a thing of the last 3 weeks. Personally I discouraged it for all I was worth, foreseeing that, as Northcliffe is a "red rag to a bull" not only to the Liberal but to a large section of the Unionist Press, the fact of his making himself prominent in the agitation for National Service would create a reaction against it.

As a matter-of-fact this is just what has happened. Almost the whole Press—the *Morning Post* is almost the only exception—has joined in the hue and cry against Northcliffe.

But with a difference.

1. A great many of the papers, while denouncing Northcliffe & declining to press the Govt., yet make it clear that they would support National Service, if the Govt. & especially Lord Kitchener wanted it.

[1] Milner Papers, Diary Extract.   [2] Ibid.
[3] It is preserved in the Milner Papers, dated 29th August 1915.

These, I believe represent the feeling of a quite overwhelming majority of the nation.

2. On the other hand some papers like the Daily News, the Daily Chronicle, the Nation, & the Star have thrown themselves furiously into the anti-Northcliffe agitation with the obvious intention of using the unpopularity of Northcliffe to damage the cause of National Service. . . An attempt is being made to commit the Trade Union leaders—& this is very important in view of the forthcoming Congress— to a declaration condemning National Service in principle. . .

Under these circumstances it becomes impossible for those who honestly believe that the adoption of National Service, *with all that it entails*, is essential to avert Defeat, to sit still and do nothing. Above all things it is necessary to prevent National Service—which everybody admits we *may* have to resort to—from being heavily damned in advance by being represented as degrading, un-British, & fatal to the maintenance of our essential industries. . . Should we be justified in allowing this to be preached without attempting an answer?

In any case, as it seems to me, controversy cannot be avoided. The subject is uppermost in all men's minds. . . I strongly deprecate the idea that the advocates of National Service have any wish to attack the Govt. We all know that no other Govt. is possible. . .

. . . If it is ever any use advocating it, the time is now. Six or even three months hence it will be too late.

Here was the complete case for the compulsionists. The reasons were marshalled in regular order. The Press was vitally important because the politicians were not speaking out; the Press represented the feelings of the nation in this matter. Moreover, the Liberal Free Trade opponents of National Service were seeking to influence and seduce the trade union leaders, for their own objects. In this connection, National Service could not be considered in isolation; it had to be looked upon as a part of the struggle for Freedom or Control. The policy—"with all that it entails"—was necessary in order to avoid defeat in the war. It was not un-British, and if it were administered properly the export and arms trades, upon which so much depended, would not suffer. Beyond these facts, everyone agreed that compulsion might become a necessity of the future. It was merely a question of pace and timing. Those who believed in it could not remain silent and allow it to be condemned in advance. Despite the wishes of the King, it was necessary for the agitation to go on.

Three days later, on 1st September, as a result of his experiences at Windsor, Milner went to the War Office, in order to call upon Lord Kitchener. He implored him to accept the policy of compulsion and National Service. After an hour's talk, Milner gave up the struggle. He could not convince Kitchener of the need for action.[1]

X

Despite Lord Milner's conversations with the King and with Lord Stamfordham, he resolved to press forward with his campaign. The agitation went on. On 1st September extracts from an article he wrote for the *Empire Review*, dealing with compulsion, were published prominently in *The Times* and in the *Daily Mail*. Later on in the year, Milner sought to make public repayment to Northcliffe. He summoned a correspondent of the *Sunday Times* to his home, granted him an exclusive interview, and remarked to the journalist that in his opinion Northcliffe and his newspapers "have done good service in the country". (*Sunday Times,* 5th December.)

Although he explained his attitude to the King with exemplary clarity, Lord Milner's activity in the public sphere was less happy. The British public was suspicious of the idea of compulsion. It was feared that it might lead to the industrial conscription of labour. Milner was required to adduce his public arguments in defensive tones, which were ill-suited to his purpose of rousing the country. He always found it necessary to explain that those who advocated National Military Service were not militarists scheming to fasten upon the country in time of war the schemes they had nurtured in peace. Late in September, for example, he replied to an article by Arnold Bennett, in the *Daily News*. His answers to Bennett's criticisms of National Service were

[1] Milner Papers, Diary Extract.

lacking in vigour, because the long explanations he had to make crippled the force of his exposition. By the early autumn of 1915 he realised that a great deal remained to be done before his objects could be achieved.

In particular, he had to conceal from the public his ideas about industrial conscription. Lord Milner was one of a small company who believed in that policy, not only for the immediate purposes of the war, but also as a means of strengthening Britain and the Empire at all times. Years before, in 1912, he had explained to Leo Amery his impressive plans for social reform, industrial conscription and military service:[1]

... I have often thought myself of industrial conscription, & it would work in with the needs of military defence. The worst of thinking about any of these things seriously is that one is led further and further, till one is brought to contemplate so huge a measure of social reconstruction that one gets frightened. . .

The big thing would work, I do believe. But it is very difficult to see how any small slices of it would work by *themselves*. And the big thing is so enormously beyond anybody's power to lift.

One great difficulty of conscription, whether on the vast ideal scale, wh. would combine industrial with military training, or even on our small N.S.L. scale, is the break it makes in a man's *earning* life. If it came between his education and the beginning of his earning life, it would fit in with our whole system. . . Also it would be better in itself to continue education—*everybody's* education—up to 18 at least. . . Economically it is not impossible. . . Here we are making quite young boys, often children, work, to the detriment of their future *efficiency*, & turning men adrift long before they are, or ought to be, or would be, if they had not begun too early, worked out.

But if education lasted till 18, you could conscript till 21! You could then make your military training really complete. . .

All this seems to me really feasible, but how to do it, *when to begin*—these are the real stumpers.

If these ideas were political impossibilities in 1912, it also seemed clear that not even a portion of them could be achieved easily in 1915. Lord Milner realised that his agitation for military conscription, with all that it entailed, lacked the essential support of those politicians who controlled

[1] Amery Papers, Milner to Amery, 24th May 1912.

the votes of their fellows in the House of Commons. If Parliamentary influence and status had declined, if speeches in Parliament no longer moulded opinion as they had in earlier days, Members alone were still the only ones able to force a change of policy upon the Government. It seemed clear that his next task was to form an alliance of some kind with one or other of those political leaders who seemed, to the public at least, to have been smothered by the enveloping cloak of the Asquithian Coalition.

The public campaign for National Service had carried him only a part of the way to his goal. Would private intrigue help him to complete the process, and achieve his object? This was an area of political activity that now merited exploration.

XII. A Tiger is Let Loose

I

AMONG the many Unionists who joined the Asquithian Coalition was the Earl of Selborne, one of Lord Milner's staunchest and most devoted admirers. Like Austen Chamberlain, Lord Selborne was genuinely disappointed when a place was not found for Milner in the new administration. Nevertheless, he resolved to make use of his friend's great powers and capacities.

Lord Selborne's post in the Government was that of President of the Board of Agriculture. One of the wartime tasks of his department was to do what it could to increase the production of food in the country. On 17th June he appointed a Departmental Committee to consider what steps should be taken for this purpose. Selborne selected Lord Milner as chairman of this body, which included among its members Sir Harry Verney, R. E. Prothero, F. D. Acland and others.

Lord Milner's Committee set to work with despatch. By July, it was ready to make the first of its two reports. The Committee decided that the only way to increase the production of food in England and Wales was to restore to arable cultivation some of the poorer grassland that had been laid down since the 1870s. In order to achieve this goal, several decisive recommendations were made. They urged the Government to promise the farmers a minimum price for wheat over a period of four years, subject to certain guarantees. The farmer, in order to take advantage of the minimum price, would be required to increase his arable land by one-fifth over the area tilled in 1913; or, if this were not done, he should be required to grow wheat upon at least one-fifth of the total land he kept under grass and annual crops.

The Committee also expressed the opinion that there should be an increase in wages for agricultural workers. In addition, the Committee suggested a scheme to guide and direct the farmers in their wartime activities. This scheme was based upon the idea that compulsory powers would be provided. The creation of an organisation under the President of the Board of Agriculture was proposed. His department, according to their plan, would be in direct touch with each of the County Councils. In their turn the County Councils were to appoint small committees of experts for each rural district. These district committees were to consider the capacity of the farms in their areas, and fix the increased quantity of tillage for each farm. At the same time, the committees would inform the Board of Agriculture of the labour needs in their localities, and their requirements in fertiliser, labour-saving machinery, and other necessities.

These far-reaching proposals were not acceptable to the Asquith Government in 1915. They were looked upon as too rigorous, and they involved too much regulation. To Milner's disappointment, the plan of his Committee was turned down.

Despite this disappointment, Lord Milner and every

other politician in the country could see that one Minister was driving forward at an unprecedented speed in organising and regulating that portion of the nation's business assigned to his charge. Lloyd George at the Ministry of Munitions had successfully embarked upon a revolutionary programme of compulsion, interference, and State direction of both management and labour. Nothing was allowed to stand in his way. By the autumn of 1915 Lord Milner could see that Lloyd George, in his own sphere of munitions production, was imposing upon the nation those very policies of industrial conscription and State regulation which had always been so dear to his own heart.

The process had begun even before the Ministry of Munitions came into being, but it developed most rapidly in the spring and summer of 1915. In Lloyd George's own phrase his Ministry was cut from the living flesh of the War Office. This drastic and painful operation had been performed for one purpose only, to make certain that the munitions of war were produced in adequate supply.

The new organisation throbbed with energy. Lloyd George had never allowed himself to be hampered by the ancient traditions of his party. His National Insurance Bill of 1911 was a violation of much that the old school of Liberals held dear. Now, in 1915, he cared even less for the formulae of the past.

Already at this stage, his dynamic posture contrasted starkly with the attitude of the Prime Minister. While Lloyd George contrived to turn out the materials of war, Asquith was engaged in those delicate political adjustments which were necessary to maintain the equilibrium and balance of his Ministry.

II

In order to understand the next phase of Lord Milner's activities, it is necessary to examine, however briefly, the revolutionary framework of control Lloyd George pressed down upon the munitions industry. He has himself admitted that he never worked harder than in this period. And many qualified witnesses believed that in his long career, Lloyd George never made more vital contributions to the life of the country than in this phase. Lord Milner, by degrees, was forced to admit the skill and value of his old enemy's contribution. Once such an admission was made, further steps were bound to follow, in spite of the experiences and attitudes of the past.

From the very beginning, the Ministry of Munitions assumed functions previously exercised by the War Office and the Admiralty. At Lloyd George's command, his Ministry embarked upon the first attempt to establish a single authority to deal with all the workers engaged in the production of munitions. His department issued badges to these workers to protect them alike from the criticisms of the public who asked why these men were not in uniform, and also from the claims of the military and naval authorities. The badging department of the Ministry of Munitions was so successful that the War Office, desperate for recruits by this period, began to enquire if the process had not gone too far. This was not Lloyd George's affair. His business was to secure the supply of ammunition. Overall direction of the war was not his province, at this stage. He was not the originator of the badging plan, but he used it as it had never been used before in order to make certain of his labour force.

More decisive were the provisions of the famous Munitions of War Act, 1915. Introduced in the Commons by Lloyd George on 23rd June, it was passed into law by 2nd July despite the hostility of certain Liberal and Labour Members. This Bill laid the foundations of labour regulation in Britain for the entire period of the war. Fundamental to it was the idea that the worker employed in the munition industry remained a civilian who enjoyed all the rights, dignities and privileges of the ordinary Englishman. However, his industrial rights were sharply and severely controlled and curtailed.

Certain innovations were introduced by this law in order to remove those obstacles to production which had hampered the cause in the past. The ancient privileges, practices and customs of the trade unions were suspended—for the duration of the war. Stoppages of work, the hostility to the dilution of skilled with unskilled workers, the traditional methods of production, the limitations upon the hours of work, the restricted class of men or women admissible to certain types of work—all these things were swept away by the Act.

But the whole problem was approached with a marvellous ingenuity. The Act made an attempt to balance the sacrifices of labour and capital. If strikes were rendered illegal in the munitions trade, so were lockouts. Heavy penalties were provided for violations of these provisions. The Act provided for the compulsory settlement of differences between employers and employed. They were required to submit their disputes to arbitration.

Certain factories were designated, under the Act, as Controlled Establishments. In these firms, any excess profits were paid back to the State. At the same time, any proposal to alter the rates of wages of those employed in the Controlled Establishments had to be submitted to the Minister of Munitions. This provision was not aimed at the workers alone. Since the beginning of the war employers had used the promise of high wages as a lure to win the men to their factories. By means of this portion of the Act, a strict control over the manpower of the industry was achieved. The men were confined to those factories where they were already employed. They could no longer be induced to move to another factory, in order to earn a higher wage.

The worker in the munitions trade was compelled to go where he was required, he was prohibited from leaving his job without his employer's consent, and he was forced to abandon the trade union practices he had won in the struggles of the past. Special Courts or Tribunals, staffed by representatives of the unions, management and the State, were established and empowered to deal with offences under the Act. The consequences, for the munitions trade, were revolutionary. Furthermore, this industry did not exist in isolation. Developments there were bound to work their effects upon other areas of Britain's effort in the war.

If much languished in wartime Britain in 1915, Lord Milner could see that this was not the case where Lloyd George held sway. Lloyd George was fearless in his resort to untraditional and un-English methods. By the autumn of the year Milner realised that the Minister of Munitions had to be taken into his calculations as a factor of vital importance.

The agitation for National Military Service had shaken Asquith in his complacency; but he had managed to deal with the arguments of his colleagues. The King himself had decided, or had been induced, to take a hand. Milner had been called to Windsor and pressed by the monarch, face to face, to abandon his plan. Would Lloyd George respond to an approach made by those like himself, who were anxious most of all to "get on with the war"? Could Lord Milner bring himself to traffic with "Jack Cade", his enemy for two decades of bitter political strife?

III

In the sophisticated terminology of the Milnerites if Asquith was called "Squiff", Lloyd George was often referred to as "the Goat". The Prime Minister's nickname was employed in order to reflect contempt and loathing; Lloyd George's implied that he was rank, unpleasant and incapable of admission to decent society—like that adorned by Lord Milner and his friends.

Nevertheless, their exclusive circle was required to deal in realities. However much they enjoyed and appreciated the high quality of their own company, however pleasant and congenial it was to condemn the responsible statesmen of their time, they could obtain neither power nor influence if they confined themselves to their own intimate group. In order to allow their superior talents to have any effect, they had to descend into the sordid world of the politicians. They had to traffic with the men who exercised power, if the politicians were to be dominated, influenced and led. It was necessary to deal with them. It was now decided that contact must be established between Milner and Lloyd George.

The issue of conscription provided a link. While Lloyd George organised his Ministry, the Milner campaign in the country went on. Although it was known that Lloyd George was an ardent advocate of military conscription, some of the Milnerites were not yet able to appreciate the new conditions of the time. They did not, as yet, include the Minister of Munitions in their plans. For example, Sir Henry Wilson, writing from France to Leo Amery, considered some very bold proposals, but Lloyd George was not involved in them. On 2nd September Wilson wrote:[1]

My dear Leo,

. . . It is amazing to me why K. won't face compulsion. The arguments against it are puerile, & for it overwhelming. . .

I don't think you can make K. a C. in C. of all the Armies . . . his ideas of strategy simply *terrify* me. . .

K. as P.M. and Milner at W.O. would do, but I suppose it is not practical politics to kick out Squiff altho' I honestly believe that unless we do we run a serious chance of losing the war. . .

Henry.

By Jove I would love to be C.I.G.S. to Milner.

The boyish and innocent enthusiasm of this letter was already out of date. Geoffrey Dawson of *The Times*, closer to affairs at Westminster, had a much firmer grasp of the situation. He believed that he could serve as a go-between in order to arrange a meeting between Milner and Lloyd George. Dawson knew that Milner liked and trusted him as one of his own. He also had the power to attract Lloyd George. As editor of *The Times*, he was a great force in the land; beyond this, if Lloyd George established genuinely firm relations with Dawson, his connection with Lord

[1] Amery Papers, Wilson to Amery, 2nd September 1915.

Northcliffe would be strengthened and reinforced. Northcliffe had already provided Lloyd George with the tremendous support of his newspapers in his struggles to launch the new Ministry of Munitions, against a host of critics. Dawson realised that both men, in spite of the past, would be prepared and even willing to listen to him.

On 16th September Dawson called upon Lloyd George. He found the Minister very ready to talk to him. Lloyd George gave the editor a concise summary of the state of the war as he saw it; the Russians were defeated, the Germans were free to attack wherever they chose, and Lord Kitchener, the man who controlled British strategy, was seriously misreading the situation at the same time that he resented the opinions of anyone who dared to challenge his views. When he was asked how he would correct matters, Lloyd George replied: "Conscription tomorrow".[1]

This reply gave Dawson his opening. Everyone knew who the leading advocate of conscription was. On 30th September, after a fair amount of scheming, a luncheon was arranged at Milner's house, 17 Great College Street. Dawson had first proposed that Milner and Lloyd George should meet at his home, but when the Minister learned that Reginald McKenna lived opposite, he refused to go there. With good reason, Lloyd George did not wish to be observed, by his principal enemy, upon the doorstep of the editor of *The Times*.[2]

The three men met at a particularly serious moment of the war. Joffre, the French commander, believed that his hour had come, because the Germans were heavily engaged in the East. On 25th September he launched a great attack in Champagne. Although his troops suffered terrible casualties, no strategic gains were made. The British part in this attack, known as the battle of Loos, was equally bloody, and equally inconclusive. Sir Douglas Haig, in charge of

[1] J. E. Wrench, *Geoffrey Dawson and Our Times* (London, 1955), p. 122, hereafter cited as Wrench, *Dawson*.

[2] The account of the meeting is preserved in Geoffrey Dawson's papers, and published in full in Wrench, *Dawson,* p. 123.

the attacking forces, found himself seriously hampered by the fact that Sir John French kept the reserves under his own hand until it was too late for them to intervene with any hope of success. The effect of the British advance, which marked out the first stages of the attack, was quickly nullified. Despite the hopelessness of the situation, Sir John refused to break off the action. His casualties were allowed to rise, to no purpose.

In London, Milner, Lloyd George and Dawson agreed at their meeting that this offensive made the need for more men urgent. Conscription was the only way to get them. But Lloyd George was not optimistic. How could they find out if a genuine victory was being won in France? The generals always refused to halt their operations when it became clear that there was no chance for a decisive result. The civilians, however highly placed, were not supplied with the information to enable them to gauge the course of events upon the battlefield. In conclusion, Lloyd George explained that he believed that Britain could not win the war without resort to conscription, but he was also convinced of the need for a small Cabinet armed with full powers of direction. In his talk, he reserved his highest praise for his Conservative colleagues in the Coalition. Later on, Lord Milner's home was used by Lloyd George as a rendezvous in order to meet Northcliffe. They selected Milner's house as a meeting place because "they were being watched", and it was felt that they could come together there, unobserved.

It seemed now that Lord Milner's relationship with Lloyd George was to become a factor of significance in the politics of 1915. The reasons for an alliance were clear enough. The Minister enjoyed the allegiance of scores of Members in both parties; his reputation in the country as a dynamic leader in war was firmly established; but he recognised that Lord Milner could furnish him with further sources of strength. For his part, Milner realised that the complacency of the Prime Minister could never be shaken to any effect by an agitation outside of Parliament. He could bring Lloyd George the close support of Dawson of *The Times,* and other Unionist journalists. Northcliffe had already backed the Minister of Munitions, but his temperament was mercurial; Lloyd George grasped that the political friendship of Milner and Dawson could help him to make certain of Northcliffe's co-operation, in case he decided to force a crisis or show-down at this time.

Despite these meetings, the march of events now intervened to provide Lord Milner with a new and more congenial collaborator. However critical he was of Asquith, however eager for more vigorous methods, Lloyd George refused to resign his post in order to declare war upon the Ministry.

This was not the case with Sir Edward Carson. By the autumn of 1915 he decided to leave the Coalition as a protest against its inept handling of affairs. Sir Edward's decision meant that his old alliance with Milner was instantly re-established. The combination that had worked so well in the last year of the Irish crisis was now to be revived.

So far as Lord Milner was concerned, Carson's determination to resign from the Government meant that the first crack in Asquith's specious mask of national unity had come at last.

Until this time Milner was practically helpless because the Asquithian Coalition, by design, had destroyed all semblance of an effective Opposition. All the potential leaders of the Opposition had been embraced or engulfed in the arrangement of May 1915. But now the farce of national unity was over. This development was bound to have a profound effect upon English politics in the months that followed. Sir Edward Carson was determined that the day of reckoning with Asquith would not be postponed again. And Carson was a man to be reckoned with.

IV

Carson's resignation was the visible sign of certain profound differences of opinion which split the Asquith Government in the autumn and winter of 1915. Ministers were unable to agree upon the strategic direction of the war. Since defeat or victory seemed to depend upon their decisions, tempers flared and explosions threatened. The Prime Minister had his hands full in trying to keep his Ministry from disintegrating.

In these circumstances, and at this juncture, Lord Milner threw off all restraints. He attacked the Government as it had never been attacked before. His hesitations were cast aside. He emerged as the open and avowed enemy of the Asquithian régime. He hoped that his public onslaughts would so arouse opinion that the dissident Ministers would feel compelled to resign their posts.

The failure of the generals to break the deadlock in the West was responsible for the fact that the politicians began to concern themselves with high strategy. In Lloyd George's opinion, by the end of 1914 it was clear, even to the rawest amateur, that the generals were mere fumblers in their chosen sphere. Lloyd George did not propose to stand by and permit the military bunglers to destroy the manhood of his country, to no purpose.

From that time he and certain of his colleagues began to question the decisions of their military advisers, and to adduce alternative proposals. When the Tories joined the Ministry in 1915, they brought with them another group of politicians interested in military and strategic affairs. The differences between Ministers over strategy cut across party lines, but this aspect of the matter failed to blunt the fierce anger of the various factions.

In general terms, the Prime Minister believed that the responsible statesmen should select the commanders for the field with very great care; after that, their duty was done and the soldiers, in his opinion, should have been left with a free hand to carry out their tasks. This was not the view of Lloyd George or Winston Churchill.

They looked upon the war as a single great conflict, but they soon saw that a comprehensive Allied strategy did not exist. In particular, they were aroused by the fact that the Russian masses were being beaten to their knees because of a lack of equipment, while in the West millions of shells, guns and rifles were simply cast away in the futile and bloody attacks of the stalemate war. Both these Ministers were early convinced that the deadlock in the West could never be solved by the frontal attacks proposed by the professional soldiers.

Lloyd George and Winston Churchill regarded the war as a single great battle. They believed that British sea power should be employed in order to turn the flank of the enemy in the East, and thus bring the Russians into direct contact with the Western Allies. In their opinion, the ramshackle Turkish Empire, flaccid and far-flung, lay naked to the attack of Britain's amphibious forces.

When Turkey declared war upon Great Britain she bit the hand that had sustained her throughout the 19th century; she also opened up a gap in the defences of Britain's enemies. A well-found attack upon the Turk could lead to a great Balkan Alliance that would adhere to the Allied side; from that development it was but a step to the attack upon Austria. The East beckoned to these statesmen as the area in which the war could be won.

The generals, however, in France and in Britain, were convinced that victory could be gained only in the decisive theatre. They were scornful of, and outraged by, the babblings of these amateurs. Their eyes were riveted upon the German trenches in France. Destroy the enemy there, where he was most powerful, and all would be over. Eastern operations were mere sideshows which could have little effect upon the issue of the war, save that they weakened Allied power in the West, the only place where a genuine decision could be reached.

The high strategy of the British Government was further complicated by the fact that Churchill and Lloyd George disagreed over the area to be selected for their Eastern attack. They both saw that something must be done to avoid the blood test of the war of attrition proposed by the generals. But where should the blow upon the Turk fall?

Churchill and his friends argued for the Dardanelles and a direct thrust at Constantinople. Lloyd George urged an Allied landing at Salonica in order to furnish the Serbs with the reinforcements and supplies needed to sustain them in the war. If the Serbs were nourished, through communications between Germany and Turkey would remain broken, while the other Balkan states would adhere to their pre-war treaties and present a solid front of opposition to the Central Powers. In the event, Churchill's ardour carried the day. Early in 1915 the Gallipoli attack was launched. Although Lloyd George acquiesced in it for a time, he never abandoned his own plan, and he returned to it with vigour when the affair at Gallipoli began to falter.

This was the general condition of affairs when the Unionists joined the Government. In August 1915 Sir Edward Carson became a member of the Dardanelles Committee, the inner group of Ministers who were now directing the war. He soon came to certain decisive conclusions of his own.

Already at this early stage, Carson's strategic views coincided with those of Lord Milner who watched affairs as an outsider, but who was furnished with the most secret details by a host of his friends in the Government. By the end of August Carson's mind was made up. He believed that the Dardanelles operation held no prospect of success. Therefore he decided that the expedition should be abandoned, and the Allied forces withdrawn. The Cabinet could not come to a decision. Two factions struggled against each other for the fate of the Gallipoli attack, inconclusively. As early as 6th September Bonar Law was imploring Carson not to leave the Government. For the moment he gave way to the wishes of his leader. By 25th September Lloyd George took care to inform Carson that "I always opposed this Gallipoli enterprise, and so have you. I opposed it at the start, and you have opposed it since you joined the Ministry".[1]

V

In addition to this specific grievance, Carson was irritated by the Prime Minister's general conduct of affairs. Carson longed for decision, for decisive and bold action, while Asquith still concentrated his powers upon balancing the views and opinions of his colleagues. Although Bonar Law's intervention induced Carson to hold his hand for a time, the disaster which now fell upon Serbia caused him to break with his colleagues and resign from the Government.

The Allied military and diplomatic handling of the situation in Serbia and the Balkans was one of the least happy episodes of the war. The Serbs had brilliantly turned back the first Austrian offensives against them. By the beginning of 1915, however, it was universally recognised that they were in dire straits.

On 21st January 1915 Asquith analysed the situation with crystal clarity. He wrote: "The main point at the moment is to do something really effective for Serbia, which is threatened by an overwhelming inrush from the Austrians, reinforced by some 80,000 Germans. If she is allowed to go down things will look very black for us, and the prestige of the Allies with the wavering and hesitating States will be seriously impaired . . ."[2]

Despite the exhortations of Lloyd George in the following months, little or nothing was achieved by Sir Edward Grey in the diplomatic sphere, or by the generals who were ordered to concern themselves with the military condition of Serbia. As the Serbian calls for help increased in intensity, various proposals were made in London and in Paris, to no genuine effect.

[1] Colvin, *Carson,* vol. III, p. 87.   [2] Asquith, *Memories and Reflections,* p. 57.

By September of 1915 the possibility of a German attack upon Serbia was openly discussed in Parliament and in the newspapers. Although no definite arrangements had been made, Sir Edward Grey rose in the Commons on 28th September and declared: "we are prepared to give to our friends in the Balkans all the support in our power, in the manner that would be most welcome to them, in concert with our Allies, without reserve and without qualification . . ."[1]

In the opinion of Carson and Lord Milner, this was the eleventh hour. Now was the time when the Asquith Government should have acted. Military and diplomatic arrangements, in their opinion, should have been concluded with the Greeks, in order to win their help for the Serbs. Decisions should now have been reached about the more general conduct of the war. Either the Eastern theatre should have been abandoned; or troops should have been withdrawn from the Dardanelles to Salonica, where they could advance to the aid of the Serbs; or a final massive effort to force a decision at Gallipoli should have been made. There were advocates of each of these mutually exclusive policies in the Government.

On the 7th October, before the Allies were ready, the storm burst upon the Serbs. General Mackensen's German-Austrian forces fell upon them from the north, in overwhelming strength. A few days later the Bulgarians, unconvinced by the efforts of Allied diplomacy, attacked their neighbours from the east. Thus assailed, the position of the Serbs was hopeless from the very start of the campaign. They were soon broken and dispersed.

In London, after consulting the French authorities and their own military advisers the Dardanelles Committee came to a conclusion characteristic of the Asquithian régime. They decided to send reinforcements to the Mediterranean theatre. The next problem to solve was the destination of the troops. One powerful faction urged that

[1] Quoted in Colvin, *Carson,* vol. III, p. 93.

302

they be sent to Gallipoli; another group of Ministers demanded that they reinforce the handful of Allied troops recently landed at Salonica. A compromise solution was adopted. It was settled that the six divisions withdrawn from France should go to Egypt, and their ultimate destination be fixed at some later and more politically convenient time.

Winston Churchill's comment upon this decision merits our attention: "The Prime Minister felt himself constrained to agree to this arrangement. . . A more vigorous course would probably have broken up the Government. I was, and am, strongly of opinion that it would have been much better to break up the Cabinet, and let one section or the other carry out their view in its integrity, than to preserve what was called 'the national unity' at the expense of vital executive action . . ."[1]

If Asquith could agree to such an arrangement, Sir Edward Carson could not. He was outraged by a decision which left the Serbs to their fate despite Sir E. Grey's statement in the Commons on the 28th September. It was a culminating point in his hostility to the Asquithian method of directing the war.

The Times of 11th October suddenly reported a rumour that Carson had resigned. Sir Edward at once denied the rumour, but Lord Milner knew that Carson was in daily and even hourly contact with Geoffrey Dawson at this time. It was the signal Milner had been waiting for.

VI

Even before the announcement of the 11th October, the Milnerites already smelled blood. On the 9th Sir Henry Wilson sent Amery a report on the result of the offensive in France, together with his views of the situation on the home front. Though the military outlook remained bleak, he was more hopeful about developments at Westminster:[2]

[1] Churchill, *World Crisis,* vol. II, p. 897.
[2] Amery Papers, Wilson to Amery, 9th October 1915.

. . . at home the position is much more hopeful and you are much nearer breaking the line of Squiff—K.—Grey—Lulu—Runciman etc. . . .

One more good kick & the whole gigantic fraud of the last 9 years is tumbled & lies in the mud. So now is your chance, & I was never more confident . . . that unfortunate England will very soon be governed by the stout hearted (like Milner) instead of the craven fools like ——!

Write me your gossip again. I love to hear what passes.

On the 12th October Carson sent the Prime Minister a formal letter of resignation. And on that day Sir Edward was told by Lloyd George that "You are doing absolutely the right thing, and I hope you will not think me a coward because I don't do the same".[1]

The Prime Minister at once recognised the gravity of his situation. He knew that Lloyd George, Bonar Law and other Ministers agreed with Carson that the Dardanelles project should be abandoned, and that Salonica should be reinforced. He knew, also, that several of his most important colleagues were thoroughly dissatisfied with his general administration of affairs. The edifice of his Government was tottering.

On that day he launched a massive counter-attack. He earnestly begged Carson to reconsider his resignation. At the same time Bonar Law called upon Carson in order to express his distress at the latter's course. On the 13th Asquith was making valiant efforts to restore the situation. The Foreign Office now offered Greece and Roumania a military convention. The Cabinet began to debate conscription.

On the 14th Carson asked the Prime Minister, in a letter, to announce his resignation. But this letter was not sent. Carson was persuaded to hold it back by the entreaties of Bonar Law, who pointed out that the Cabinet was meeting next day. Asquith, meanwhile, wrote to Carson again, on the 14th, urging him not to make his resignation definite

[1] Colvin, *Carson*, vol. III, p. 96. This is also the source for the details of the crisis which follows.

until the Cabinet met. Walter Long was also hurried up to this breach in the Government's defences, as a reserve. He implored Carson to await the Cabinet discussions of the 15th: "Your resignation", he explained, "will be a fatal blow to the Government".[1]

Exposed to such powerful pressures, Carson hesitated. Usually resolute and determined, he now paused to consider the appeals of his friends and colleagues. On the 14th he failed to attend the House, or the meeting of the Dardanelles Committee. He made no definite move of any kind. At this moment, Lord Milner struck his blow. He was determined to force Carson to act.

On 14th October 1915 Lord Milner rose in his place in the House of Lords in order to deliver one of the most savage speeches of the war. He turned upon the Government with fierce energy. He discussed, to the shocked surprise of his audience, the question of whether or not the Dardanelles should be abandoned. Although he sought to excuse this grave breach of security and decorum by pointing out that he possessed no official information on the subject everyone knew that half a dozen admirers in the Government were in close and intimate contact with him. He explained that he and his friends had been silent for too long. He spoke out now in the hope that he could persuade the Government to take a "decided line", in one direction or another. He said:[2]

... The war has lasted for 14 months... I want to know what we meet here for... We do not meet here for legislation. If there is any object in our meeting at all it must be one of two things, either information or counsel...

... How about the enterprise ... at the Dardanelles? ... To speak quite frankly, I should have thought that whatever evils had resulted from the disastrous developments in the Balkans there was at least this advantage, that it might give us an opportunity which may never recur for withdrawing from an enterprise the successful completion of

---

[1] *Ibid.*, p. 99.
[2] From the account in *The Times*, 15th October 1915. Unless otherwise specified, all speeches reproduced in this chapter are taken from this source.

which is now hopeless. . . I cannot help asking myself whether it will not have a worse effect if we persist in the enterprise and it ends in complete disaster. These are considerations which really ought to be urged at a time like this. . . I must say, my lords, that I do not think any harm is done by frankly facing a situation of that kind, even in a public speech, especially when the discussion is raised by a person in my position, not occupying any official position . . . a mere "wild man" in politics . . . a fearful responsibility rests upon us now—upon those who have been silent for months, though often doubting whether they were justified in being absolutely silent—if there is anything we can say which may lead to the Government taking a decided line while there is yet time. . .

Milner then turned to attack the Balkan policy of the Government. Carson's position was clearly in his mind when he explained that:

> . . . it is really very difficult not to feel some disappointment in the result when we consider what the cards were which the two parties which had been struggling in the Balkans respectively held. After all . . . if you take the independent States of the Balkans . . . they all had reason to fear our enemies, every one of them. Germany, Austria, Turkey alike were states . . . the evil intentions of which towards the independence of one or all of the Balkan States were calculated to make their advances be regarded with suspicion.
> . . . we had this immense advantage. . . We had got a clean sheet, a clean record. . . We had befriended them. We could not be suspected . . . it does seem disappointing . . . we should find that one after another of these States are falling away from the Power which of all the others had the best character from their point of view. . . We cannot discuss the details of this unfortunate development. We do not know them. We can only judge by results. The results are profoundly disappointing.

Lord Lansdowne, the leader of the Conservatives in the House of Lords and Minister without Portfolio in the Coalition, at once replied. He expressed the astonishment of the House that Milner should have spoken as he did about the Dardanelles, a military operation that was still in progress. "It was remarkable", said Lord Lansdowne, "that his noble friend . . . had made to the Government this notable suggestion, that they should abandon the Gallipoli peninsula. . . . He dared say he could find a good deal to say on that subject, but . . . it would be out of the question for him or anyone else sitting on that bench to get up . . . to announce that His Majesty's Government had taken the resolve either for or against the proposal of his noble friend".

VII

Lord Milner's speech produced instant results. It was reported prominently in all the newspapers, on the next day. Particularly extravagant was the reaction of the *Daily Express* for 15th October. A headline on the front page of the paper stretched across the entire page: "LORD MILNER'S SERIOUS SPEECH ON THE DARDANELLES". A second headline in the *Daily Express* exclaimed: "LORD MILNER'S GRAVE STATEMENT IN PARLIAMENT". A third said: "LORD MILNER SUGGESTS A WITHDRAWAL".

On that day Arthur Steel-Maitland, Milner's former private secretary, wrote to his old chief in order to tell him that he was ready to leave the Government, because of its drifting and its cowardice. His resignation would be a heavier blow to the Government than that of most junior Ministers. His Ministerial chief was Bonar Law, the Tory leader in the Coalition. If Carson and Steel-Maitland resigned together, Bonar Law would be seriously embarrassed.[1]

Lord Sydenham also wrote to Milner, on the 16th October. Sydenham had been a member of the famous Esher Committee which had reorganised the War Office during Balfour's Premiership. He had served as the Secretary of the Committee of Imperial Defence, from 1904 to 1907. He was one of those non-political experts whose opinions carried very great weight in a crisis of this kind. Milner was confirmed in his attitude by Lord Sydenham's general criticisms of the Ministry:[2]

---

[1] Milner Papers, Steel-Maitland to Milner, 15th October 1915, marked "Private".
[2] Milner Papers, Sydenham to Milner, 16th October 1915, marked "Private".

Private   16.10.15
Dear Lord Milner,

I am very sorry I could not come to the House . . . and missed your speech. The terrible mistakes we have made in the conduct of the war are coming home to us & I am very anxious. . .

We must & at once have a complete change of methods. Could not the H. of L. press this. When the Coalition was formed, I wrote to Lord Lansdowne proposing a War Council of 5 or at most 6 with full and complete charge of all matters relating to the conduct of the War. . .

. . . It was precisely to ensure this direct contact that I proposed the establishment of the Defence Committee years before I was able to help in bringing it into existence. But the action of the Committee was intended to turn upon the Prime Minister, whose hands it would strengthen by securing his personal contact with facts and opinions. The ragged discussion of the Cabinet . . . lies at the root of our misfortunes. . .

Yours sincerely,
Sydenham.

On the next day came Sir Henry Wilson's opinion of the speech, in a letter from France. Wilson played with skill upon Milner's feelings:[1]

Just one line to say how pleased I was with your speech in the House of Lords. *Do* come and help us. What we want are the following.
1. Conscription.
2. Ammunition.
3. Withdrawal from Dardanelles.

It seems to me another very small push and we shall get conscription. Even the Westminster and that awful Spender see it coming.

As regards Gallipoli, I understand the great strategists at home now see that they can't remain there. . . But 'wait & see' won't work there . . . we want the Gallipoli garrison in *Salonica*. We must save Serbia if we can . . . so please, transfer the Gallipoli garrison to Salonica. . . *Do* come and take charge of us.

Confronted by a crisis of this magnitude, and still anxious to retain Carson as a member of the Government, Asquith struck back at Milner as quickly as he could. His counter-blow fell on the 15th October. On that day Lord Milner received two documents from Sir Maurice Hankey, the

---

[1] Milner Papers, Wilson to Milner, 17th October 1915.

Secretary of the Committee of Imperial Defence. Together, they comprised Asquith's reply to Milner's thrusts at the Government.

The first of these papers was a covering letter; it explained that Hankey was sending Milner, at the direct command of the Prime Minister, an extract from a Minute Hankey had submitted that morning. The extract, marked "Secret", declared that Milner's speech and its presentation in the *Daily Express* were calculated to have an unfortunate effect upon the enemy, upon neutrals, and upon the future of the British troops in Gallipoli.

The Minute revealed that intelligence reports indicated the Turks were in terrible difficulties in the peninsula; and that the Germans were trying to bolster up their courage. In such circumstances, nothing could be better calculated to assist the Germans than Lord Milner's speech.

In addition, according to this document, the speech was bound to have a disastrous effect upon British relations with Roumania, then at a critical and delicate stage. In Hankey's opinion, Milner's remarks were certain to be of very great assistance to the country's enemies.

Finally, with regard to the military operation itself, all the high officers involved, and their names were listed in the Minute, were convinced that the only method of reducing losses in a withdrawal was to make certain of absolute surprise. If surprise were lost owing to speeches like that made by Milner, disaster to the troops was bound to follow. According to the Minute, the speech of the 14th October made a British withdrawal from Gallipoli tactically impossible.[1]

---

[1] These paragraphs are based upon Hankey's letter, dated 15th October, and the Extract. Both are preserved in the Milner Papers. Fortunately, the Germans made a characteristic mistake. They attributed some of their own guile to the British politicians. The speeches of Milner and others who discussed evacuation from this time were looked upon as propaganda, designed to conceal further landings of reinforcements at Gallipoli. See in this connection, Alan Moorehead, *Gallipoli* (London, 1956), p. 341, and Taylor, "Politics in The First World War", p. 70, n. 2.

VIII

Inside the Cabinet, Carson's position remained unchanged. Sir Edward now believed that half the Ministry
might resign with him if he proceeded with caution. On
the 16th Asquith urged that the resignation be suspended
for the moment. On the 17th Walter Long sent a letter
of seven typed pages begging Carson to hold his hand.
On the 18th the Prime Minister asked Carson to see
the King in order to explain his position, before any public
announcement was made.

On that day Milner confided to his diary that "Carson
came to explain the reasons for his resignation". Asquith,
Bonar Law and Long had all failed in their efforts to bind
Carson to the Government. On the 19th October his
resignation was announced.[1]

Ministers had striven hard to keep Sir Edward Carson for
very good reasons. His resignation was a terrible blow to the
Asquithian system. He was the most feared man in British
politics. Asquith was afraid of his general hostility, while
Bonar Law was frightened by his tremendous popularity
with the Tory party.

Men in all parties respected Carson as an honest patriot
who could be depended upon to urge and ensure the
efficient conduct of the war, unhampered by any consideration save that of victory. His political skill and his ability
to attract the rank and file in the House of Commons were
also recognised as factors of very vital significance. Men
could see at once that a tiger had been let loose in the
political jungle at Westminster. From now on he would lie
in wait, ready to pounce on Ministers at a favourable
opportunity. Lord Milner's position of political isolation
was now a thing of the past.

On 26th October Lord Milner made certain of the new

[1] For these details see Colvin, *Carson,* pp. 100 ff. Milner's comment is preserved
in the Milner Papers.

arrangement when he wrote to Carson in order to condemn Asquith's flaccid conduct:[1]

Confidential.   17 Great College St.
                                                          26.10.15

My dear Carson,

I send you a French paper containing an article by Clemenceau on your retirement. . .

It is fair to say that Clemenceau, who is violently opposed to the Salonika enterprise at all, probably thinks that you are too, and that out going there at all, not our going feebly, inadquately, and irreso-lutely, was the cause of your resignation.

That does not touch the main point, which is the need *of a policy*. I mean of making up one's mind. . . Clemenceau may be right in thinking that Serbia must simply be left to her fate. You and I may be right in thinking that we should strain every nerve to help her and Greece. What cannot be right is to proclaim *urbi et orbi* that we are going to help Serbia and then to send a ridiculously inadequate force to Salonica, and leave them there without orders while we "wait and see".

Don't trouble to answer.

                                                          Yours,
                                                          Milner.

Reinforced by Carson's resignation, Lord Milner now proceeded to an even more vigorous assault upon the Government. The effort of Asquith and Hankey to cow him into silence was clearly in his mind when he spoke at Canterbury on the 30th October:

. . . it is said that to speak openly of what has gone amiss . . . is to encourage the enemy. The way to encourage the enemy is to make him think we are afraid of the truth. . .

. . . we are told, if we dwell on some of the blunders, heinous as they are, which have been committed on our side, that we are "carping" . . . if the very worst of our laches and failures, like the delay in providing shells and the brazen-faced attempt to conceal it, or the way we piled blunder upon blunder in the Dardanelles, or the really phenomenal failure of our policy in the Balkans—if these things are to be glazed over . . . if the nation can be induced to regard them as just ordinary incidents of war . . . then it can never expect, and it will not deserve, to see its affairs better managed in the future. . .

[1] Milner Papers, Milner to Carson, 26th October 1915, marked "Confidential".

Milner was so anxious about the effect of this speech that he asked Geoffrey Dawson to reproduce it at length in *The Times*. The speech had been reported in the *Weekly Dispatch* and in *The Observer*, but Milner did not like their brief accounts. "If the *Times* could do it", he wrote to Dawson, "it would be a very great help & probably forestall the damaging & unjust criticisms to which I am otherwise exposed". Dawson duly complied with the request.[1]

IX

Meanwhile, the Cabinet was being rocked by a further crisis. General Monro had been ordered to the Dardanelles to report upon the situation there. After an examination of the scene, he strongly urged evacuation of the peninsula. Asquith now proposed to send Lord Kitchener to Gallipoli, to do again what Monro had already done.

The Prime Minister's purpose was twofold; he would, by this tactic, conciliate Churchill and those Ministers who still advocated the Dardanelles plan, while he rid the Government of Kitchener, who had, by this time, lost the respect and confidence of his colleagues. Upon reflection, Bonar Law was unable to stomach these proposals. General Monro's opinion, that of the military expert, was clear enough.

On 5th November Bonar Law explained his misgivings to the Prime Minister. Three days later he actually sent him a letter of resignation. Eventually, however, Asquith managed to appease his colleague by agreeing to the proposal that the Dardanelles should be evacuated.

In these circumstances Lord Milner hoped to repeat his coup of the 14th October. On the 5th November he noted in his diary "the town is full of rumours today about a Cabinet crisis . . . we are approaching a general smash . . ."[2] On the 8th he delivered a telling speech in the House of

[1] Geoffrey Dawson's Papers, Milner to Dawson, 31st October 1915, and Dawson's reply of the same date.
[2] Milner Papers, Diary Extract.

Lords. It was made up of a series of solid shots aimed at the Government. He began upon the Prime Minister and the case of Serbia. His object was to so aggravate the situation that Bonar Law would find himself compelled to break with the Government:

> . . . Patience, which the Prime Minister so greatly admires, is all very well, and so is a courageous and confident air in the face of disasters of your own creation. But these virtues alone are not sufficient. Take the case of Serbia. That is the most heartrending tragedy of all in this awful war. . .

Three further hits followed in rapid order. They dealt with the Dardanelles, with the hesitations of Ministers, and with the resignations from the Government. Bonar Law was the target of this heavy artillery:

> . . . If the military considerations are against it, do not let us persist in that enterprise. . . If our prestige has suffered in the Dardanelles, then the way to recover it is by doing better somewhere else.
>
> Above all I do pray the Government not to lose any more time in making up their minds. Delay and indecision have been their besetting sin all along. . .
>
> What alarms me about the Cabinet is its tendency to shed its elements of strength instead of shedding its elements of weakness. It has lost Sir E. Carson, a very great loss, and it has lost at least temporarily Lord Kitchener. . . I was glad to hear that his absence is to be brief. . . I venture to predict that it may be very considerably prolonged. . .

Although *The Times* of 9th November called the speech "one of the most impressive and unanswerable made since the outbreak of the war", Bonar Law remained in the Government. He refused to tread the path taken by Sir E. Carson. Milner's attempt to hasten his resignation was a failure. Instead, Milner was forced to fall back upon prophecy and complaint.

At this time he was lecturing Lionel Curtis upon the need for a closer organisation of the Empire. He blamed the failure of their group in Imperial politics upon the fact that the men who controlled affairs were party politicians. Bonar Law, the leader of their party, had chosen to remain

at Asquith's side. Milner's distress at this development was
well reflected in a letter to Curtis, dated 27th November
1915. He explained that the basic fault of Great Britain as a
warring nation lay in her system of democracy which threw
up unqualified men to take charge of the supreme direction
of the country. Milner's hostility to British democracy
was qualified by one or two saving-clauses, but it is clear
enough that he and some of his friends did not believe in the
democratic system for either Imperial or military purposes.
He wrote to Curtis:[1]

. . . We are putting all our money on *Democracy*. Well, Democracy
is going to fail, & the British Empire with it, unless we can emancipate
ourselves . . . from machine-made caucus-ridden politics, & give men
of independence & character more of a chance or, to put it better,
encourage the development of independence & character instead of
encouraging nothing except sophistry & skilful manipulation.

It is time to stop burning incense on the altar of Democracy & try
to think how we can save it from destruction. Here we have the two
great European Democracies in the midst of the biggest struggle in
history without a single really eminent leader! The reason is not far to
seek. As Kipling brutally says . . . "A lifetime in watching the cat
jump does not breed lion-tamers".

Some of our "Moot", I think, like Oliver, really have an aversion for
Democracy. . . I myself am perfectly indifferent. I regard it, like any
other form of Govt., as a necessary evil. Democracy happens to be the
inevitable form for my country & the Empire at the present time.
Therefore I accept it, without enthusiasm, but with absolute loyalty . . .
to make the best of it. . .

Something is radically wrong about the method, by which Democracy in this country tries, and fails, to get its vital interests attended
to. . . Our Imperial Constitutions have got to be something better
than a copy . . . of the Augean stable at Westminster.

X

The decision of Bonar Law to remain in the Government
provided the Asquithian Ministry with a further lease of
life. Although Bonar Law, Lloyd George, Curzon, several

---

[1] Lionel Curtis Papers, Milner to Curtis, 27th November 1915, marked "personal
and not for circulation".

lesser Ministers and even the Free Trade Liberals were dissatisfied, Asquith was still looked upon as the indispensable man. Lord Milner, for this reason, now found it necessary to renew his attacks. The drama of Sir Edward Carson's resignation, however exciting, had not been enough to tumble "Squiff" from his Ministerial throne. Lord Milner now began to cast about for other chinks in the Asquithian armour. Later in November he began to probe for weak spots.

Whom else could he win to his side? Where or how could he find some means or method of exposing Ministers? How could he come to final grips with Asquith and his evil system? He was convinced that his problem was complicated by the effects of the party system, by the lack of candour and honesty displayed by the politicians who controlled the great parties, by the irresolution of men who were unable to concentrate upon their warlike affairs because they were always gauging and calculating the political consequences of their actions. Conscience and bias alike compelled him to act.

Until Sir Edward Carson readjusted himself to his new position, the House of Lords seemed to Milner to be the obvious sphere for his activity. He began to consult with his fellow Peers.

At the beginning of November, in an effort to re-establish the situation, Asquith reorganised the War Committee. The British Supreme Command was recast. Its numbers were reduced to five. But it continued to function as a Committee of the Cabinet. The new body was not a true executive, for it lacked the power to enforce its decisions. These had still to be referred back to the Cabinet, in the most important instances.

Before the names of the new Committee were announced, Milner and several other Peers sent the Prime Minister a stiff letter of warning. They cautioned him that if the new Supreme Command were composed exclusively of those Ministers who were responsible for the Dardanelles expedition, "it would certainly be challenged in public debate". In addition to Milner, Lords Cromer, Midleton, Morley of Blackburn, St. Aldwyn and Sydenham signed the document. They represented men of nearly every political complexion at Westminster.[1]

By this time, the ruin of the Allied cause in the Balkans seemed patent to all. For that reason, Milner selected this subject as his next topic. On 5th December 1915 he wrote to Lord Lansdowne in order to tell him that he proposed to ask a question about the Balkans in the House. The letter was a summary and a defence of his actions since the coup of the 14th October. It ended with a blunt warning that Milner would act again in the public sphere unless he was furnished with definite information about the Balkan policy of the Government. It was a direct challenge to Ministers:[2]

17 Great College Street.

My dear Lansdowne

. . . I have been strongly pressed . . . to try by a question in the Lords to obtain some further light upon the situation in the Balkans, which is the cause of such deep anxiety to all thinking people.

. . . I must frankly say it leaves my conscience no rest—whether one is justified in doing nothing in a situation so critical & with disaster . . . in sight, *without any assurance* that there is somewhere a supreme authority (be it War Council, Cabinet, Kitchener or Prime Minister: I don't so much care what it is, as long as there is one) & that this authority has now a definite & clear plan for . . . the North East Mediterranean. . .

. . . On October 14th I ventured . . . in the Lords to urge the necessity of a prompt decision. I was told . . . that the moment . . . was one which made any statement impossible. Well and good. Twelve days later . . . you told the Lords that Sir C. Monro had been sent . . . "to report *as soon as possible* on all the aspects of the case" . . . he must have reported *something* . . . but . . . on November 4th Lord Kitchener went out, to see for himself. No doubt he also reported. . . Seven weeks have been spent in elucidating the situation, which to some of us seemed pretty clear even on October 14th . . . the simple question is, *does the Government now know what it wants to be at?* Has it

---

[1] Asquith Papers, undated letter to "the Rt. Hon. H. H. Asquith, K.C., M.P."
[2] Lansdowne Papers, Milner to Lansdowne, 5th December 1915.

got a definite plan. . . ? If you are able to tell me privately, that this was the case . . . I should feel that I was justified in taking the course, most in conformity with my personal inclination, & keeping quiet. . .

If, on the other hand, you are unable, or do not, for whatever reason, think it 'right', to give such assurance, private or public, then I must settle with my own judgement and conscience, *entirely without guidance*, what is the proper course to pursue.

Yours ever,
Milner.

This was a hard letter. It meant trouble for the Government. Lansdowne replied by proposing a private interview. Their talk took place in the House of Lords on 7th December. Lansdowne could say very little on this occasion because the Cabinet was still fighting to come to a decision about the Dardanelles.

A fortnight later the British troops were withdrawn from Gallipoli. Their evacuation was one of the terrible gambles of the war. Ministers were weighed down by the fearful prospect of a slaughter of their men upon the open beaches. Although the retreat was carried out brilliantly, the tension of those responsible was almost unbearable, in the period before the action. So far as they were concerned, Milner's attitude was merely another of their many burdens.

After the meeting with Lansdowne, Milner, on 9th December, went to the House of Lords in order to talk to a group of Peers "who feel strongly about the mismanagement of the war". On the 15th he was selected as the leader of this "Forward Party", which included Midleton, Sydenham, Loreburn, Peel, Ancaster and others. Although there was much discussion, there was little that these men could do.[1]

Lord Milner could use the House of Lords as the public scene for his attacks upon the Government. He could urge the Lords to tamper with the Army Act or similar legislation, as he did in the Irish crisis. They could be induced to violate the Constitution, as they did in 1909. But it was ridiculous to believe that the Peers could force the

[1] Milner Papers, Diary Extracts.

resignation of a Ministry. Such power lay elsewhere, in the House of Commons.

On 11th December Milner went to Austen Chamberlain's home in order to leave a letter. In it, he begged Chamberlain to resign from the Government, and thus help to bring about the downfall of the Ministry. Chamberlain refused to comply with the request.

He explained that, in his opinion, Carson had committed a serious error when he abandoned his colleagues. If Unionists brought the Government down, they would be confronted by an Opposition like that in the Boer War. The nation would be torn by the strife of factions. Only the enemy would benefit. Politicians, Chamberlain argued, had to concern themselves with alternatives, and not with ideal courses. The present Ministry, he said, was not perfect, but there were definite national advantages to be gained by preserving it.[1]

The opinion of Chamberlain's reply to Milner exactly reflected Bonar Law's attitude. For reasons like these, most Ministers were prepared to remain in the Government, though not all were content with the Asquithian system. Despite Milner's efforts, Chamberlain and the others refused to act as he desired.

By 13th December, however, Sir Edward Carson had come to a definite decision. On that day he invited Milner to dine with him. He explained that he felt the need for Milner's advice, and that he greatly desired to see him more often.[2] This development promised fireworks for the future.

XI

Ministers and their friends had now suffered from Milner's public attacks for nearly three months. While disputes in the Cabinet shook the framework of the Government, Milner's blows rained upon it from outside. These

[1] Milner Papers, A. Chamberlain to Milner, 12th December 1915, marked "Personal".

[2] Milner Papers, Carson to Milner, 13th December 1915.

actions aroused the resentment of those who sought to preserve Asquith in his place.

In the House of Lords on 20th December Lord Milner provided his enemies with an opportunity to strike back at him. In the course of a debate in the Lords on that day Milner allowed himself, by implication, to make a very serious charge against the Government. He called the attention of the House to certain rumours "of the existence of some occult German influence in the very heart of our administration". Although he made it clear that he did not believe in such hints and whispers, he proceeded to say "that the policy of the Government was largely responsible. The constant halting between irreconcilable opinions, bold professions followed by irresolute action . . . were sufficient to account for the hold this pernicious belief had on the public mind. . ."

The Marquess of Crewe, the Lord President of the Council, and Asquith's close friend, at once rose in anger, to reply. He attacked Lord Milner in language used rarely in the Upper House. Lord Crewe said:

> . . . It was with surprise that I heard the noble lord below the gangway (Viscount Milner) allude to a belief which he said was prevalent in the mind of the man in the street that there was some 'occult German influence' which was brought to bear on the minds of members of the Government. I am inclined to ask the noble viscount to state precisely what he means by that statement, which is one, in my judgement, he ought not to have made, and, I am sorry to say it, in my experience of this House, now extending over 20 years, I have never heard a less creditable innuendo made by any noble lord against those who sit with him in that House. I will not pursue the subject further, except to express my regret that the noble viscount lent something like the shadow of his name . . . to monstrous calumnies of this kind directed against his Majesty's Government. (Cheers.)

Lord Milner's enemies of the Irish Nationalist Party now intervened. They had old scores to pay off. Milner had, by implication at least, suggested that people believed there was German influence in the Government. In December and January several Irish Nationalists in the House of

Commons enquired about Lord Milner's own German connections. They reminded the House of his German birth. And they asked the Home Secretary if Lord Milner was a British or a German citizen. It was an ugly thrust, aimed below the belt. It was particularly painful to Milner, the British race patriot.

The best example of the Irishmen's attack, which was supported in several Radical and Liberal newspapers like the *Star* and the *Daily Chronicle,* occurred in the Commons on 23rd December 1915:[1]

> Mr. Lundon asked the Home Secretary whether Lord Milner had taken out naturalisation papers; if so, upon what date did he do so; and, if no such papers had been taken out by him, will he be treated as an alien and be interned?
>
> Sir J. Simon: No, Sir, there is no occasion for Lord Milner to take out naturalisation papers, since he is already, I believe, a British subject. By virtue of the Statute of 1773, the grandson born abroad of a grandfather who was a British subject born in this country was declared to be a British subject and the repeal of the Statute of 1773 by the British Nationality Act, 1914, does not affect the status of any person born before the commencement of the Act.

XII

It is thus clear that the political alignments blurred by the Coalition of May 1915 were becoming more clearly defined. Although the formal truce between parties continued, men could now see that Sir Edward Carson in the Commons, and Lord Milner in the House of Lords, were the open and avowed enemies of the Asquith Government. The Prime Minister's attempts to clutch at national unity, for the purposes of the war, were only partially successful by December of 1915. The monolith was beginning to crack.

The measure of the success or failure of Asquith's opponents would be determined by three separate factors. A major strategic victory in the field would silence and disperse them at once. But if victory continued to elude

[1] Parliamentary Debates, vol. LXXVII, 23rd December 1915, cols. 592–3.

Ministers, the public attacks of Carson and Milner, supported by the most influential Conservative newspapers, were certain to have serious effects. Finally, inside the Government were a number of very important Ministers who watched and waited upon events. Lloyd George, for example, chafed at the delays of the Asquithian system. He had already established a measure of understanding with Milner, and with Dawson of *The Times*. He had taken care to inform Carson that he agreed with him in his decision to resign. Restrained by a native prudence which prohibited rash or even premature action, he was, nevertheless, spurred forward by ambition and by patriotic ardour. These are formidable sentiments. In combination they are often irresistible. Lloyd George was poised to strike, but he meant to bide his time. His future course would only be decided after calculation.

There was one further aspect of the situation which was bound to exert some influence. The generals, waxing stronger and more powerful with each day of the war, were interesting themselves in politics. Some of them looked to Carson and Milner to set the ship of State aright.

On 3rd December Sir Henry Wilson wrote three separate letters to Sir Edward Carson. In the first letter of that day he asked: "Can't you and Milner get a crowd round you and force Squiff to act or go?" In the third he said: "Now what I suggest to you is that you and Milner come out with the truth". On 13th December General Pole Carew wrote to Carson: ". . . if you approve of him, get Milner as your Lieutenant in the Lords. Lansdowne is no good. He was at Eton with me, and he has never been able to make up his mind".[1]

By the end of 1915 Lord Milner could not be satisfied with the results of his recent agitation. But he was determined to go on with it. However bleak the situation seemed, from his point of view it had improved since the arrangement of the previous May. There were a number of new

[1] Colvin, *Carson*, vol. III, pp. 122–5, for the opinions of the generals.

political factors which could be exploited in order to weaken and damage Asquith, for the sake of the war. This was the course he set for himself in the new year.

At the end of December he saw Sir Henry Wilson in London. In the train that was taking him back to France, Wilson scribbled a hasty note to Leo Amery. It was a concise and accurate summary of Milner's feelings:[1]

18.12.15

My dear Leo,

. . . I saw Milner yesterday. The outlook is certainly not bright, & the darkest part is the difficulty of getting rid of Squiff. And yet it *must* be done if we are to win the war. We can't win if we have to carry him.

Squiff—Grey—K.—even the Bosh could not carry that load. . .

Henry.

[1] Amery Papers, Wilson to Amery, 18th December 1915.

XIII.   The Monday Night Cabal

I

WHENEVER his political course seemed precarious or unclear, Lord Milner liked to turn
away from the hubbub of public life in order to
take counsel with his closest friends and disciples. He
furnished them with guidance while they provided him with
suggestions, and with that measure of respect an ignorant
public too often withheld.

In the middle of January 1916 yet another small group of
his intimates was formed into a circle for the discussion of
those political problems which loomed largest in their day.
In this case, as so often, the original impetus came from
Leo Amery. He looked to three men for the salvation of

Britain. Milner, Carson and Lloyd George were his heroes, in this period. The Minister was not a regular member of the new group, but Milner, Carson, Dawson of *The Times*, F. S. Oliver, and Waldorf Astor, owner of *The Observer*, began to meet regularly each Monday evening for dinners and talks. Occasionally, Lloyd George, Sir Henry Wilson, Philip Kerr or Dr. Jameson would join them in their deliberations.

The clique has usually been referred to as a "Ginger Group"; but their object was not merely to enliven the opposition to Asquith. They meant to throw over his Government in order to rule in his stead, or, at least, to deliver his power into the hands of those who had won their approval.

This kind of association, as we have already seen, was congenial to Milner's temperament. It was made up of men he respected, and did not include those party hacks and Mandarins who were lacking in character and honesty. Together, these men formed a very powerful fellowship.

Sir Edward Carson was the most dangerous politician of the time. The rebellious Tories in the House of Commons were looking to him for a lead; and certain dissatisfied Liberals, attracted by his incisive personality, were preparing to support him as the man who could help the country to win the war. Dawson of *The Times* enjoyed the most influential position of any journalist in the Empire. F. S. Oliver, a magnificent wit, had galvanised politics for a decade past by means of his biting, sarcastic letters to the politicians. Milner was the acknowledged leader of most of these men.

We have to pause to examine the qualifications of only one member of the group. Why was Waldorf Astor included in the company? What qualities equipped him to move in this circle of Olympians? The answers to these questions will help us to understand the nature and the aims of this Monday night cabal, which met for the first time in Lord Milner's house on the 17th January 1916.

Waldorf Astor was an able and pleasant man, married to a wife of quite extraordinary charm, and possessed of very great wealth. But other wealthy men, similarly equipped, flocked to Westminster in the hope that they could play a high part in the political life of the country. In 1912, Lady Edward Cecil, the future Lady Milner, wrote to Milner: "I had a good bit of talk with Waldorf who is one of the very dearest good fellows I know, and not at all stupid, as he has every right to be if he chooses".[1]

This was praise of a kind, but it cannot suffice to explain Astor's inclusion in a group which met for the very serious purpose of dragging a Prime Minister down from his place. The Monday night cabal was the general staff of the Opposition. The good fellows who supported Carson and Lord Milner in Parliament received their orders, after they had been agreed upon at the dinners of the smaller association. Rank and filers were never invited to these gatherings. Only the select were asked to attend.

It is clear enough that the key reason for Astor's membership of the cabal lay in the fact that he was proprietor of *The Observer*, a newspaper which exerted a very considerable influence upon affairs during the first world war. J. L. Garvin, the great editor of the paper, had conducted his journal brilliantly in the period 1908-11. In the latter year his impact and influence suffered a decline. When Lord Northcliffe sold *The Observer* to the Astor family at that time, some of the politicians lost interest in Garvin because he was no longer connected with the vast Northcliffe newspaper empire. In addition, Garvin's relationship with Arthur Balfour was always closer than his association with Bonar Law. When Bonar Law became leader of the Conservative Party in 1911, Garvin's position as "adviser in chief" to the Tories disappeared. The new leader looked to others for counsel, advice and suggestions.

However, when the war began Garvin's power was instantly revived. Not only were people desperately

[1] Quoted in Gollin, *The Observer* and J. L. Garvin, p. 366.

interested in news and in informed comment, but the editor now engaged in a very close association with Winston Churchill, and with Lloyd George. His co-operation with these prominent members of the Cabinet raised his paper to new heights of influence and power. When Milner and Carson began to cast about for sources of strength for their new group, the proprietor of *The Observer* at once occupied a prominent place in their calculations.

It was exactly in this period that Waldorf Astor fixed his grip upon the paper. Until 1915, he was not the owner of *The Observer*. His father, W. W. Astor, was the sole proprietor; and his remarkable personality sometimes made Waldorf's position insecure and uncertain.

W. W. Astor was a man of curious and splenetic humours. He had a viciousness and vindictiveness of temper that has been noticed in others of his tribe. When aroused he conceived the determination to vex not only his public critics, but also those members of his family who irritated him.

When he left the United States in order to live in Britain, the American Press subjected him to terrible criticisms. These were scores Astor meant to pay off. He was a man who could bear a grudge:

> The fact was that he made little effort to conceal contempt for his native land. It was doubtful if hatred could have been more bitterly expressed than by his gift of the battle flag of the U.S. frigate *Chesapeake* to the Royal United Service Museum. The *Chesapeake* had been taken . . . in a battle off Boston in the War of 1812 made memorable by Captain Lawrence's command: "Don't give up the ship!" . . . "Astor took no interest in the flag until he heard there was a plan afoot to buy it for America." . . . Henry Cabot Lodge reported to President Roosevelt: "I had a long talk with Balfour in London . . . he resented Astor's conduct about the flag as much as we, and has the same opinion".[1]

Peevishness of this general order sometimes marred the relationship between Waldorf Astor and his father. Although everyone knew that Waldorf's political position

---

[1] See Harvey O'Connor, *The Astors* (New York, 1941), pp. 374–5.

depended upon the fact that he exercised the rights of a proprietor of *The Observer*, W. W. Astor determined to sell the paper in the summer of 1914. It was a spiteful decision, designed to cripple Waldorf's career in politics.

On 25th July 1914 *The Times* announced that *The Observer* had been sold to Gardiner Sinclair, a prominent business man of the day. The announcement, however, was premature. Sinclair had paid a desposit upon the paper, but early in 1915 he became so ill that he was unable to attend to business of any kind. He was required to forfeit his deposit. When the fate of *The Observer* became so uncertain, Lord Rothermere and Sir W. M. Aitken, later Lord Beaverbrook, at once interested themselves in an attempt to purchase it. They dealt with J. L. Garvin. Waldorf Astor was permitted no part in these transactions because his father was angry with him at the time.[1]

Meanwhile, however, W. W. Astor became bored with the tedious business of trying to sell the paper. In February 1915 he wrote to Waldorf in order to inform him that he proposed to give him *The Observer*, the *Pall Mall Gazette*, the newspaper office in Newton Street and all the documents relating to those properties as a birthday present. One condition only was attached to the gift. It was that every connection between the journals and the Astor Estate Office should cease. It thus came about that at an early period in the war Waldorf Astor became the sole owner of *The Observer*, and cemented his already cordial and intimate relations with J. L. Garvin.

This was a development of some consequence for Lord Milner. He always relied upon the Press, in all his political activities. The support of Geoffrey Dawson of *The Times* was most important for him, but he knew that Garvin could strike out more dramatically than Dawson when occasion offered. The political guns of *The Times* were certainly heavier than those of *The Observer*, but sometimes

[1] This paragraph and the one following are based upon documents in the Astor Papers and upon private information from Nancy, Viscountess Astor.

the lighter artillery of the Sunday paper could be used to more deadly effect. In a later chapter we shall see how Milner exploited his friendship with Astor, in order to crush a troublesome political foe by means of an article in *The Observer*.

J. L. Garvin, for his part, admired and respected Milner as one of the great men of their time. But he realised that Milner lacked some of those attributes which in combination produce a successful British politician. Nor did he fit into the kind of intimate circle Milner liked to have about him. He was not one of the elect.

Waldorf Astor's loyalty to Milner was less complicated. He believed, as we shall see, that Lord Milner's proper place in the political order was to serve as Prime Minister of Great Britain. He was included in the Monday night cabal because of his pleasant personality, because he was a hard-working Member of Parliament, and most of all because he could bring the powerful authority of J. L. Garvin and *The Observer* to bear upon the Asquith Ministry in the way that Milner desired.

Sir Edward Carson controlled a powerful group in the Commons; Milner led the Forward Party in the House of Lords; Dawson decided much of the attitude and outlook of *The Times*; Astor supplemented these formidable elements by bringing *The Observer* into line as a support. With this mighty armoury, Lord Milner made ready for the political campaign of 1916. He was no longer isolated in his battle with the Asquith Coalition.

II

The activities of Milner's group have often been referred to in vague terms. We must now try to see exactly how they occupied themselves on those Monday evenings in the winter of 1916. They did not come together merely for the sake of good talk, nor were their meetings conducted in any haphazard fashion.

If it is too much to say that they worked to a formal agenda, their conduct was often guided by something very like an agenda. In the Amery Papers there is preserved a document, written by F. S. Oliver, which tells us a great deal about the meetings of the Monday night cabal. Entitled "Notes for Monday's Meeting", it is dated 19th February 1916. It clearly explains the purposes and methods of the group. It also reveals their hostility to Bonar Law, the leader of the Tories. He had refused to follow Sir Edward Carson. He preferred to preserve the unity of the country by remaining at Asquith's side. These decisions were marked down, and held against him by the Milnerites. Oliver's paper reads as follows:[1]

Notes for Monday's Meeting

Private

19.2.16

1. Can we clear our minds a little as to what we want (a) to do to win the war; (b) to pull down; (c) to set up?
2. Do we agree on these three propositions? . . .
    (a) We shan't begin to win the war under the present regime.
    (b) The chief obstacle to change in this regime is not the inherent strength of the government; nor the party partnership; nor the confidence of the H. of C. in Asquith and Bonar Law; nor the admiration of the country for them; but an altogether irrational though very widely spread belief—fostered hitherto by the whole of the Press—that there is no alternative to the combination of A. and B. L.
    (c) There *is* of course an alternative government. . .
What line do we want to take (a) in the Press, (b) in the H. of C. and (c) in the H. of L.?
        Suggested answer: To insist in season and out of season—
    (i) that the Asquith-Bonar Law influence on Cabinet, Parliament, country, the Allies, and the conduct of the war is *paralytic*, and
    (ii) that it is absurd to say that there is no alternative government or alternative spirit.

This document furnished a basis for the discussions that followed. While Lord Milner and his friends, in this

[1] Amery Papers, "Notes for Monday's Meeting", 19th February 1916.

period, were united in their hostility to Bonar Law and Asquith, they were unable to agree upon the men who were worthy of leading the country in war. Save for the fact that they approved of each other as qualified leaders, there was no unity of opinion in their small circle.

Sir Edward Carson and F. S. Oliver believed that Winston Churchill's fierce energy should be exploited by any valid War Government; but Lord Milner was unable to forgive his old opponent of the censure debates of 1906. Lord Milner hoped to work together with certain selected leaders of the Labour Party; but Oliver distrusted and despised the Labour leaders. Carson, Amery, Dawson, Milner and Astor were all prepared to consider an alliance with Lloyd George; but Oliver was dubious about the Minister of Munitions at this time.

Oliver's "Notes", which he liked to call his "Introduction" to the problem of destroying Asquith, provoked a good deal of controversy. In March he prepared a draft letter of nineteen typed foolscap pages, and sent it to the members of the cabal. In this letter he attacked the spirit of Liberalism as the reason for the nation's failure in the war; he condemned Bonar Law as inadequate; and he suggested that Lord Milner and his friends should take over the Government of the country.

In casting about for a candidate for the Premiership, Oliver nominated Balfour, Curzon and Austen Chamberlain as suitable aspirants. Nothing, we may observe, could be more fatuous than to suggest these names for the post, at this stage of the war. If Asquith were to be successfully thrown aside, his successor was required to be a man who could unite all the political elements of the country— Liberal, Labour, and Conservative. None of these rather time-worn Tory leaders was qualified to discharge such an almighty task.

The arrogance of the Milnerites, invincible though it was, could not bridge this yawning gap in their proposals. Unless they could fix upon an alternative Premier of out-

GEOFFREY DAWSON
The go-between.

WALDORF ASTOR
He depended on J. L. Garvin.

SIR HENRY WILSON
The book-keeper of the dead
and dying.

He said: "no mercy, please".

standing quality, their plans, however spirited, were doomed to failure. Already at this stage, Geoffrey Dawson was considering a triple alliance between Lloyd George, Carson and Milner; but Oliver was not yet prepared to agree to such a suggestion.

His draft letter of March 1916 reveals the attitude of the Milnerites, with crystal clarity. It merits the careful attention of the reader who desires to understand these men, in this period of the war:[1]

March 1916

Dear ——,

You are not the only person who has criticised my Introduction on the ground that, although I have very emphatically declared an alternative government to be possible, I have not clearly indicated its composition. . .

. . . the country is thoroughly shaken . . . in its respect for . . . Liberalism . . . the country . . . holds Liberalism largely responsible for the outbreak of the war, and mainly responsible for the unfortunate way in which it has hitherto been conducted. . .

. . . It would be desirable . . . to include Milner, Carson, Derby and Churchill. . . There are also many available who have never yet held office, viz: Mark Sykes, Amery, George Lloyd . . . Edward Wood . . . Astor etc. . . R. H. Brand (Financial Secretary to the Treasury), Philip Kerr (Under Secretary for the Colonies) occur to one's mind.

It is clearly of the highest importance that we should not kill Charles to make James King. We have got the wrong Prime Minister at present, and unfortunately we have not got the right leader of the Unionists to succeed him. . . Mr. Bonar Law has many conspicuous public virtues, but it must be apparent even to his warmest admirer that he has not been cast in a large mould; that as Cromwell put it, "he has not the real root of the matter in him"; . . . A man may fairly be judged . . . by the company he keeps; by the friends in whose society he takes pleasure, and who take pleasure in his. Measured by this test Mr. Bonar Law is not the superior of Mr. Asquith. . .

. . . the question who is to be Prime Minister seems to be one rather for his own chief colleagues, than for public opinion, or even for his Majesty. . . The three names which occur to me are those of Mr. Balfour, Lord Curzon and Mr. Chamberlain. . .

Lord Milner seems to be naturally marked out for the War Office. No appointment would be more popular with the Army, and he is

---

[1] This document is preserved in the Amery Papers.

one of the very few people . . . of whom it can be truly said that he has proved himself a very great administrator. . .

The great need is to get rid of shams . . . of these . . . shams the Asquith sham is the greatest. He is sham all through. . .

The Way Out

The matter may be put briefly thus—"How to get in? . . . Get out!" It is fatal to wait for the appropriate occasion. It will never come. . . The only way is to force the situation and go out. And the "just men" must go out on the true plea . . . that the head of the Administration is wrong; that the spirit of the Administration is wrong; that things are going all wrong in consequence. . .

III

Although Lord Milner could not agree with all of these remarks, he was as incensed as Oliver by the failures of the Asquith-Bonar Law régime. On 12th March he drew up some "Notes on the Present War Situation". These Notes, preserved in the Milner Papers at New College, reflect yet again his hatred of the party system, and his dislike of Asquith and Bonar Law. They also reveal his absolute bankruptcy as a politician.

He desired to gain office for himself, and for his friends. He believed intensely that the warlike effort of the country was hamstrung by the ineffective leadership of the party chieftains. They owed their high places to their low skill as political tacticians. Yet the only way out that he could now conceive was to form a new party to carry those political objects which he had in mind. He was himself distressed by this paradox. He had raged against parties and the party system since his earliest days in politics. Nevertheless, he now wrote as follows in his Notes:

It is rather ironical that the only way to get rid of an INCUBUS, the curse of which is due more than anything else to the Party system, which has prevailed in the past, and which, thanks to the Coalition, still throttles us, should be the formation of a new Party. Yet it is hard to see how anything can be done without organisation. And organisation does mean something like a Party, if it be only an *ad hoc* Party, aiming at nothing more than *energy and forethought* in the conduct of the war. . . This object, call it what you will, an Organised Opposition, a National Party, or by any other name, seems . . . worth striving for. . . The moral seems to be that our first duty is to prepare for a General Election, so that the result may be a true expression of the New Spirit. . . This is not verbiage . . . the New Spirit is capable of Victory. . .

It is thus clear that, for the moment at least, Lord Milner's political outlook was wholly changed. He perceived, perhaps for the first time, that great political objects could not always be achieved by a small group of close friends, however active they might be behind the scenes. In order to accomplish things in Britain, tedious as it might be for the elect, political parties, and political organisations, and General Elections, and the spirit of the country, had to be taken into account. The need for this kind of outlook was obvious to any fledgling in English politics; to Lord Milner it was an irony, a perverse necessity that even the most qualified national leaders were required to face and master. For him, it was the curse of British public life.

Nevertheless, this was the new course that he and Sir Edward Carson set for themselves in March of 1916. In the Commons, Sir Edward was already recognised as the leader of the Unionist War Committee, a group of Tory dissidents who objected to the Asquithian method of conducting the war, and to Bonar Law's loyal support of the Prime Minister. These men were in contact with a smaller number of Liberals who agreed with them upon these matters. Carson hoped to secure Winston Churchill as the leader of a Radical War Committee, for Churchill had been cast aside by the Prime Minister and was, at this time, serving as an officer in the trenches in France. Lloyd George allowed Carson to learn, exactly at this stage, that he was anxious for a meeting.

While Carson's organisation of an Opposition in the Commons proceeded, Lord Milner's task was to develop the hostility felt for the Government in the House of Lords, and in the Army. In consequence of these designs, he spoke to several Peers, and wrote to General Sir Henry Wilson. Wilson's reply to his letter was encouraging:[1]

> Your letter . . . reached me this morning. . . You know my opinion of Squiff; he is a callous cynical blackguard—and a liar—who is physically & mentally incapable of action—an extinct volcano . . . under his nerveless and incompetent lead we shall drift into chaos, poverty, internal strife, exterior weakness, an inconclusive peace. . . This is what Squiff will do for us if he can. Since the war began—and before it—he has been worth Corps un-numbered to the Boche. He has never gone to war, he is not at war now, and he never intends to go to war, nor has he the slightest intention of allowing any one else to go to war. . .
>
> . . . Yes, we must get rid of Squiff first as a preliminary to any sort of action, and action we *must* have if we are desirous of winning the war. . .

Meanwhile, F. S. Oliver continued to pursue his own line. He believed that if a few important Ministers, his "just men", resigned from the Government, the whole Asquithian edifice would collapse. Like Milner before him, he fixed his sights upon Austen Chamberlain; and he believed that Milner was the only man who could convince Chamberlain that his loyalty to Asquith and Bonar Law was misplaced, that his duty was to abandon the Coalition in order to pave the way for a more vigorous War Administration. Oliver felt, however, that Milner might approach Austen too directly. He therefore wrote, on 6th April, in order to urge Milner to act, but he included in his letter certain words of advice about the nature and quality of the action he proposed. His letter suggests that the Milnerites, while they admired their chief, sometimes felt that his bluntness and frankness were qualities ill-suited to delicate political enterprises:[2]

> I wonder if and when you are going to see Austen. I feel more & more the urging of this, as you are really the only one I know to whom he is likely to listen with respect. . .

[1] Milner Papers, Wilson to Milner, 22nd March 1916.
[2] Milner Papers, Oliver to Milner, 6th April 1916.

. . . You apparently took Arthur Lee's breath away for a minute or two by proclaiming that you were frankly "a wrecker". Now if you had put it to Austen like this he would probably have had such a shock that he would never have recovered from it at all. Moreover, it is not true, as a statement of your faith, but only as a paradox & as paradoxes are Dangerous with ordinary men they are better avoided; they put all proportions wrong—& create a wrong atmosphere.

You are not a 'wrecker': You want to win the war: the present Government under Asquith and Bonar Law influence will lose the war: therefore it must be destroyed, for it can never be converted in heart. That is a different pair of shoes. . .

By mid April 1916 the political situation seemed to be approaching another crisis. In these circumstances Sir Henry Wilson adduced the names of the men he hoped would form an alternative Government. He believed, with some reason, that Asquith was about to fall from power, and he wrote to Milner to assure him of the support of the Army:[1]

. . . As regards the situation at home, I can't think Squiff can last much longer. It seems to me that, if things are properly managed now, he can be cornered. I want to see a foundation of yourself, L. G. and Carson with one Labor man added & possibly one other as our Cabinet. And nothing will persuade me that this is impossible. . .

There will be an absolute howl & yell of delight throughout the whole Army the day Squiff falls, and an amazing warmth and belief in those I have mentioned when they take over and *govern*. . .

IV

There was good and valid cause for Sir Henry's enthusiasm, for at this moment the Asquith Government was so torn by disagreement that its dissolution seemed inevitable. Ministers were quarrelling among themselves, with fierce anger, over the issue of compulsory military service. A decisive stage had been reached; Lloyd George threatened to resign unless the policy of universal conscription were at once adopted. Spurred on by General Wilson and by their own desires, the members of the Monday night cabal were about to act with effect, in the public

[1] Milner Papers, Wilson to Milner, 11th April 1916.

sphere. Their organised influence in the House of Commons, in the House of Lords and in the Press was now brought to bear, with deadly effect.

The problem of the proper disposition of the manpower of the country had plagued the Coalition Government from its earliest days. One of its first acts had been the introduction of a Bill for a National Register. Introduced in the Commons by Walter Long, President of the Local Government Board, the object of the National Registration Bill was to discover the exact number of men who were available to serve in the Army and in the munitions industry. The Bill was fiercely contested by certain Liberal and Labour members who were afraid that it was a prelude to industrial conscription. The returns made under this Act revealed that there were about five million men of military age in Britain who were not serving in the armed forces of the Crown.

In August 1915 a Cabinet Committee on national resources in men and money carried out an investigation. It was at this time that Lord Milner's campaign for National Military Service harried the Ministers in their deliberations, and the King acted in an effort to halt Milner's propaganda. So intense was the dispute in the early autumn of that year, that it was feared the Government might break up at any moment.

Walter Runciman, the President of the Board of Trade, used the figures of his Department of Labour Statistics to prove that there were not enough men in the country to staff an Army of seventy or one hundred divisions, the force Lord Kitchener then demanded. Reginald McKenna argued that the financial resources of the country could not stand up under the burdens of such a military organisation. After the battle of Loos, however, when the need for men became glaring, other Ministers demanded that the voluntary system be abandoned as inadequate. The struggle for Freedom or Control, extending far beyond the mere issue of military conscription, was thus joined once again.

Asquith met the situation with skill and cunning. His position was seriously weakened when Lord Kitchener at last admitted that the voluntary system was failing in its purpose of providing men. In order to mollify both sides in the Cabinet, the Prime Minister called in Lord Derby, a popular figure in those days, and appointed him Director General of Recruiting. He was charged with making a last canvass under the voluntary system. The Ministers who urged conscription were outraged by this tactic, for in their opinion it could serve only to delay the inexorable march of the country towards conscription. The Derby scheme, although it was pressed with vigour for several months in the winter of 1915, failed to rake in an adequate number of volunteers. Nearly one million unmarried men refused to come forward in order to attest their willingness to serve in the armed forces, despite Lord Derby's exertions.

After terrible arguments in the Cabinet when Grey, Runciman and McKenna threatened to resign from the Ministry, a measure of conscription was introduced by the Prime Minister on 5th January 1916. This Bill was passed into law on 27th January. It compelled unattested single men and childless widowers in the age group eighteen to forty-one to attest their willingness to serve. Under the terms of the Act these men were treated as though they had attested under Lord Derby's voluntary scheme. It may be fairly said that the new law was employed to compel men to volunteer their services.

It soon became clear, however, that the Act was yet another unsatisfactory compromise. Not only did it fail to furnish sufficient numbers of recruits, but its unfairness to those who were already serving roused the advocates of compulsion to fresh efforts. By the early spring of 1916 it became clear to the Cabinet that the older groups of married men were needed, to feed the maw of the stalemate fighting in France. In these circumstances Lloyd George warned the Prime Minister that he would leave the Government unless definite action were taken, without further delay or parley.

His was not an isolated threat, for at this stage of the

Cabinet controversy Lord Milner and Sir Edward Carson acted, in their separate spheres. Their demands for universal military conscription were warmly supported in the Unionist Press as a whole, and in *The Times* in particular. Every detail of the squabble in the Cabinet was "leaked" to the newspapers at once, by certain interested parties. The public was informed of the story of the struggle hour by hour, exactly as it occurred in the councils of His Majesty's Ministers.

V

On 11th April 1916 the public learned, such was the conduct of Ministers, that the Army Council had furnished the Government with a statement of their requirements of men, and that these requirements could not be met by the voluntary system. On the next day the Unionist War Committee in the House of Commons passed a resolution requesting Sir Edward Carson to bring forward a motion embodying the policy of compulsory military service. On the day following Lord Milner put down a similar motion in the Lords.

Meanwhile, a Committee of the Cabinet composed of the Prime Minister himself, McKenna, Lansdowne and Austen Chamberlain reported upon the problem. In the opinion of this Committee, no case had been established for the extension of the Military Service Act of January 1916 to all men of military age. The Committee made a few paltry suggestions, designed to glean further handfuls of men for the Army.

The Cabinet, at boiling point, refused point-blank to accept their report. They referred it back to the Committee. The matter was thus still undecided. The Cabinet was gripped by an inability to decide. Explosions threatened the Asquithian system.

Now the Milnerites acted. The first serious blow in the public campaign of the Monday night cabal was struck on 14th April 1916. The first leading article in *The Times* explained the situation. The article was a preliminary for what was to follow:

> . . . We seem to be in sight of a definite decision on recruiting. . . On Wednesday Sir Edward Carson gave notice of a motion in the House of Commons which embodies the principle of "equal sacrifice from all men of military age". Yesterday Lord Milner put down a motion to the same effect in the House of Lords. . .

> Let there be no mistake about it. What the country wants is leaders who are not afraid to go all lengths or to undergo all sacrifices. . . We believe that they possess such a man in Sir Edward Carson. . . We believe that in Lord Milner they possess yet another leader whose courage and character are needed in a national crisis. It is a most damning indictment of the Coalition, and especially of those Unionist leaders who had a free hand to strengthen its composition, that such a man should be out of harness at such a times. . .

These hammer blows, the reader will observe, fell equally upon the Prime Minister and upon Bonar Law, the Unionist leader. Behind the scenes, Lord Milner launched an attack of his own upon Lord Lansdowne, the Tory Coalition leader in the Lords. He insisted that his motion should be debated at the earliest opportunity. Lansdowne and Lord Crewe begged him to postpone his speech because Asquith had promised to make a statement in the House of Commons on 18th April. However, so serious were the differences in the Cabinet that on the 18th Asquith was compelled to rise in the Commons and ask that the matter be delayed a further twenty-four hours. In such circumstances Milner demanded that Lansdowne arrange for an immediate debate in the Lords.

No valid reply could be made to this new request. Crewe and Lansdowne were obviously embarrassed by the Government's evident lack of purpose. Lansdowne was required to bow to Milner's pressure; but he explained to him that no member of the Government in the Lords could possibly reply to him, since no decision had yet been taken in the Cabinet.[1]

On 18th April Lord Milner rose from his place on the

[1] For Lansdowne's dealings with Milner at this time, see the Milner Papers, Lansdowne to Milner, 17th and 18th April 1916.

Front Opposition Bench in the House of Lords in order to move his resolution. In his immediate neighbourhood sat a vigilant company of his supporters, clear evidence of the effect of his recent organising activities among the Peers. Lord Salisbury, a leader of the Diehard section of the Conservatives, Lord Derby, the latest recruiting agent of the Government, Lord Morley, an independent critic and former colleague of Liberal Ministers, and Lords Beresford, Peel, Portsmouth, Lovat, Ampthill and Willoughby de Broke all demonstrated their support of Lord Milner's arguments.

In his speech, Lord Milner recalled, for the Peers, the various expedients by which the Coalition had delayed a vital issue. He took particular care to praise Lord Northcliffe, for his part in urging a policy of conscription upon Ministers. He implored the Government to act, however tardily. "I am told", he said, "that in pressing these efforts we are imperilling the unity of the nation. . . I believe that, boldly faced, these internal difficulties . . . will disappear . . . you will find a ready . . . response to any demands that you feel bound to make". He then moved his resolution which said that "an Act should be passed without further delay rendering all men of military age to be called upon for military service during the continuance of the war".

It remained for Lord Crewe to reply for the Government. There was little that he could do or say, for Ministers were still unable to agree. He proposed that the debate should not be continued because the Government were "still thinking" about the matter. It was a lame and ineffective answer, in the circumstances of a terrible war.

VI

The Times of the following day, 19th April, carried the assault of the Milnerites to its next phase. The Political Notes of the paper remarked that "It was by common consent the best speech Lord Milner has ever delivered in the House of Lords. . . " More vigorous was the comment in the first leader of *The Times*: "The decision of the Government to leave everything undecided for another twenty-four hours is too typical to excite surprise . . . Lord Milner, with excellent reason, refused to be muzzled, and his speech . . . will stand in the days that are still to come as the complete case for an honest measure of National Service. . . He approaches the subject with the mind of a patriotic statesman, whose one and only object is to end the war in victory. . . He brushes all other considerations aside. . . The nation realises with Lord Milner that the time has come, and more than come, for action. . ." Geoffrey Dawson, it will be seen, was playing his part brilliantly.

These criticisms were rendered doubly effective because Asquith was forced yet again to postpone his statement to the Commons, on that day. The divisions among Ministers were thus made patent to all. The prestige of the Prime Minister was severely shaken by this evidence of his inability to control the deliberations of his colleagues.

The Milnerites had made extensive preparations to deal with Asquith in the Commons. The alerting of the Unionist War Commitee was only one part of their plan. Leo Amery, a serving officer, had been assigned to the Staff of General Callwell, the Director of Military Operations in the War Office. Callwell was the successor to Sir Henry Wilson in this post, and one of that soldier's least critical admirers. He later wrote Wilson's biography, and astonished the literary world of his day by the frankness of his published disclosures about his hero. In this period, General Callwell employed Amery upon a number of delicate quasi-military missions. In July of 1915 he assigned Amery the task of "working up the case for conscription";[1] as a "cover" for these activities, Amery was employed in the Balkan Section of Callwell's Staff. In order to make his secret and clandestine efforts more effective, Amery was put in touch with

[1] Amery, *Political Life*, vol. II, p. 63.

several of the Army Commanders in France. The result of his activities became apparent at this time.

On 17th April 1916 General Sir Henry Rawlinson, the General Officer Commanding the IVth British Army in France, wrote to Amery. His letter reveals the extent of the influence of the Milnerites in the Army, and something of the effect of that influence upon British politics. Rawlinson promised Amery that those Members of Parliament who were serving under his command would be granted leave in order to vote against Asquith on the issue of conscription.[1]

> Army Headquarters,
> IV Army,
> B.E.F.
> April 17, 16

My dear Amery,

I have already sent round to all my M.P.s to say they may have leave to go and vote for you in the House of Commons on Tuesday and Wednesday next week. I know a lot of them are going over so I hope you will make Squiff sit up even if you don't turn him out neck and crop which would be the best thing. Then you could introduce your Cabinet of five with Carson and Milner in it. But Squiff is a devil to wriggle out of a tight place. . .

> Yours ever,
> H. Rawlinson.

Meanwhile, there were further reactions to Milner's speech in the House of Lords. Lord Charles Beresford wrote to Milner to tell him that his remarks had achieved a tremendous amount of good in the country. Sir Henry Wilson wrote, on 20th April, that he and all his officers were delighted with the speech. Wilson deplored Asquith's delaying tactics: "If ever a man deserved to be tried and shot", he wrote of the King's first Minister, "that man is the P.M." He ended his letter on a characteristic note: "We hope that you and Carson and L.G. have, at last, got him by the throat. No mercy please".[2]

Finally, on the 20th April, an official statement was issued. It revealed that the Cabinet had at last reached an agreement.

---

[1] Amery Papers, Rawlinson to Amery, 17th April 1916.
[2] Milner Papers, Beresford to Milner, and Wilson to Milner, 20th April 1916.

The statement promised that the Government's new proposals on recruiting would be explained to a Secret Session of the Commons, the first Secret Session of the war.

This memorable event took place on the 25th April. Two days later, in an ordinary session of the Commons, Walter Long asked leave to introduce the new Government Bill. Sir Edward Carson's turn had now come. He at once attacked the Ministerial measure as inadequate. The feelings of the House were so violent and hostile, that Asquith arose in order to explain that the Government no longer felt justified in proceeding any further with the plan.

The compulsionists, by the vigour of their criticisms, had forced the Government to abandon its Bill. They had finally, and for the first time, triumphed over Asquith's predilection for half-measures. They had imposed their will upon him in open session. They were wild with delight.

A climax came five days later. On 30th April Asquith described to the Commons the details of a new Government Bill for the establishment of universal compulsory service. This Bill was introduced in the House on 3rd May. According to its provisions, all males between the ages of eighteen and forty-one were subject to compulsory enlistment in the Army. Ireland was not encompassed by its terms. On 25th May this measure of National Military Service received the royal assent.

So far as Lord Milner was concerned the battle he began in the summer of the previous year was now at last brought to a successful issue. The singular gyrations of the Prime Minister had delayed matters, but in the end he had been required to bow to the demands of his enemies. The arrangements of the Monday night cabal had worked perfectly. Having achieved so much, was there any reason why they could not, by recourse to the same tactics, go on to further victories?

VII

In the opinion of the Milnerites, two aspects of the situation now dominated the political condition of the country. We must examine these themes separately. On the one hand, they looked upon the achievement of universal military service as a triumph of their own, and of their friends, acting in concert in the Lords and in the Commons. In their more ardent moments they chose to ignore or neglect the fact that Lloyd George, Bonar Law and other Ministers had pressed Asquith very hard during the April crisis.

Their confidence in their own powers was reflected by the events of the 4th of May. On that day the members of the Unionist War Committee in the House of Commons entertained Sir Edward Carson at a luncheon. Lord Milner presided at the celebration; and he proposed the health of the guest. About one hundred Members of the Commons attended. Their presence served as an ominous warning to Andrew Bonar Law, for they all belonged to his party.

Sir Edward's speech, prominently reported in the *Morning Post,* a high-Tory organ that was devoted to him, laid stress upon the fact that his Committee had seriously damaged Asquith's prestige. They had forced the Prime Minister to abandon a Government Bill on the very floor of the House of Commons. Sir Edward spoke in the high and boastful tones of the successful leader of an organised party. He said, after one or two graceful compliments to Milner, that (*Morning Post* 5th May 1916):

> . . . The Unionist War Committee was the outcome of the dissatisfaction that was felt by many, and of what we conceived to be . . . the studied contempt by the Government of the House of Commons. We grew tired of eloquence and of perorations. We grew tired of self-complacency . . . we wanted action, immediate and decisive. Our policy, as I laid it down . . . was that we should support the Coalition Government . . . and that we should not hesitate to put forward . . . any proposal that our judgment and our patriotism thought necessary. . . . I think I may say that the constitution and the existence of our

Unionist War Committee has been fully justified. I am not going into the question of the Military Service Act. We have got it . . . we do not want to brag about it . . . we want to claim no victory; but we feel in our hearts . . . satisfied. . .

We must turn now to the second aspect of the situation that excited Lord Milner's friends. Their triumph in the House of Commons, they hoped, would stimulate Lloyd George to act. Unless he and certain other Ministers resigned their places, the Prime Minister could continue to nourish himself upon their association with him. So long as they participated in Asquith's Ministerial minuet, his nimble whirlings involving one step forward and two back would continue, to the detriment of the national effort in war. The Milnerites hoped for some kind of definite arrangement with Lloyd George.

At this time and for this reason Waldorf Astor called upon Dr. Addison, Lloyd George's principal parliamentary henchman. Astor had met Addison years before, during the early days of the National Insurance Act, when they both worked together under Sir Robert Morant, the first chairman of the Insurance Commission. Astor became involved in the administration of the Act after his name had been urged upon Lloyd George and Morant by J. L. Garvin. Morant, in particular, required the support of *The Observer* in the earliest days of the new Insurance Commission; at Garvin's urging he appointed Astor chairman of a Departmental Committee on Tuberculosis.

On 1st May 1916 Astor spoke to Dr. Addison about an alliance between Lloyd George and Milner. He was so excited by the recent triumph of the Unionist War Committee that he actually proposed an arrangement whereby Lord Milner should become Prime Minister, with Lloyd George as his second-in-command. Addison was astonished by what seemed to him to be a particularly ridiculous and even a bizarre suggestion. He wrote in his diary: "Astor paid me a long visit this morning . . . urging L.G. to clear out. He asked me what I thought of Milner as a leader and, if necessary, as P.M. with L.G. as second. I said that both proposals were absurd. Rightly or wrongly, few men in the country were more distrusted than Milner, and in my opinion it was stupid of his party to put forward such a suggestion".[1]

The reader will hardly need to be told that the proposal did not catch Lloyd George by surprise. He was busy with certain arrangements of his own. As early as this month, Dr. Addison began to prepare a highly secret list of those Liberals in Parliament "who were in favour of a more active policy and who would be willing to give support to Lloyd George . . ."[2]

Despite the eagerness of the Milnerites, the Minister of Munitions was not yet ready to take decisive action. The situation, in his expert opinion, was not yet ripe for so extreme a course. Much work remained to be done.

VIII

Suddenly, on the 5th of June there came a tremendous and terrible development. The cruiser *Hampshire* was sunk; when the ship went down, Lord Kitchener, who was on board, perished. The highly important post of the War Office now lay vacant, a prize of the first quality for the politicians to clutch at, in their patriotic ardour.

Although Kitchener had been shorn of many of the powers usually exercised by a Secretary of State for War, the position was still looked upon as one of immense importance. The new Secretary of State was bound to exercise a decisive influence upon war policy, unless a mere hack were chosen for the post. Beyond this, as certain of the interested parties calculated, if the Secretary of State for War should ever resign from Asquith's Government, his defection would be a very serious blow, more damaging than if the head of some other Department left the Ministry.

[1] Addison, *Four and A Half Years*, vol. I, p. 201.
[2] Addison, *Politics From Within,* vol. I, p. 252.

Bonar Law and Lloyd George at once became rivals for the place. In the *Morning Post* and in *The Times* the name of Lord Milner was mentioned prominently as the most suitable candidate. Much depended upon the answer to the question which was now asked in the lobbies and in the clubs—"Who is to be Secretary of State for War?"

Geoffrey Dawson's task was extremely complicated at this juncture. He desired to press Lord Milner's general claims to some part in the war administration; at the same time he had to avoid offence to Lloyd George. For Dawson was now convinced that Milner and Lloyd George, in combination, were the only ones who could save the country. He had sent Waldorf Astor on his futile mission to Dr. Addison. In a memorandum prepared at this time, Dawson wrote: "It seems to me essential to get Lloyd George bracketed with someone. . . He and Carson in conjunction would be immeasurably stronger than either of them single-handed. The only alternative that I see is to get Lord Milner associated with Lloyd George inside the Government. . . The two of them would either control affairs in the Cabinet, or would bring it down with a run if they were to resign together. . ."[1]

In *The Times* of 8th June 1916 Dawson discharged his difficult task with skill. The first leader for that day explained that Milner would probably make the best War Minister, but the paper doubted if he could be induced to serve. *The Times* said:

> . . . the prophets are at present canvassing the names of Mr. Lloyd George and Lord Milner. . . As for Lord Milner, who would probably make the best War Minister of all, we confess that we can hardly picture his inclusion in the present Cabinet of party men. It would be a sign of grace if Mr. Asquith were to turn to him, and of wisdom too. . . But frankly we cannot imagine any man of Lord Milner's strong character joining the Cabinet in these days. . .

The Monday night cabal now became very active. F. S. Oliver, who had expressed one or two doubts about Lloyd

[1] Quoted in Wrench, *Milner*, pp. 307-8.

George, wrote to Carson on the 9th June: "He (Milner) with Lloyd George would form a hard core in the . . . Cabinet—attracting to them good but weaker men—and together they could either mend the administration—or— if *there were* no other way—end it by coming out together". So much depended upon Lloyd George that Oliver wrote to Carson a few days later that there would not be "much good putting Milner in unless the Goat saw an advantage in having him there".[1]

On 13th June Geoffrey Dawson saw Sir William Robertson, the Chief of the Imperial General Staff. He asked him whom he would like to have at the War Office. Robertson replied that Lord Milner was his choice for the place. On the next day Dawson lunched with Lloyd George and Arthur Lee. It became clear to the editor that Lloyd George meant to have the War Office, with all its powers revived, as his own. As the "War Minister", Lloyd George's position would be enhanced in the eyes of foreign Powers, and he would be able to co-ordinate the efforts of the Allies. With regard to Lord Milner, Lloyd George made it clear that Asquith was not keen to have him, and that the Unionist members of the Cabinet were certain to oppose his joining the Government.[2]

On 29th June Oliver was still entranced by the prospect of Lord Milner's admission to the Ministry. On that day he wrote to Sir Edward Carson, urging that he should return to the Government: ". . . *you could take Milner in with you*. Then at least there would be other persons in the Cabinet—Lloyd George, Milner, and you—who know that there is a war going on. This would be a nucleus, or spear head, or whatever you might like to call it".[3]

These exchanges make it clear that a pattern had now emerged. Lloyd George succeeded in winning the War Office from Bonar Law. It was evident enough that certain

[1] Quoted in Colvin, *Carson,* vol. III, pp. 186–7.
[2] See the *History of The Times,* vol. IV, p. 287,
[3] Colvin, *Carson,* vol. III, p. 187.

Unionists wanted to see him co-operating with Carson and with Lord Milner. This proposed triumvirate menaced not only the Prime Minister but also Bonar Law, the Conservative leader. The Milnerites disliked him. He was, in their opinion, unworthy of their support. Unlike them, he was an ordinary man. Nevertheless, he was not so helpless as they supposed. He had sources of strength and power of his own. Sir W. M. Aitken, later Lord Beaverbrook, was watching the situation very carefully. In the shifting scenes of contemporary British politics his loyalty to Bonar Law was a fixed and stable element. The alarm signals were now beginning to sound in his brain. Bonar Law was in danger. Actions would soon be required to save his position.

IX

Now came a lull in the political struggles at Westminster. After the Easter Rebellion, Asquith sought to divert Lloyd George by involving him in an attempt to settle the thorny problems of Ireland. For his part, Lloyd George was delighted to immerse himself in Irish affairs. His recent actions during the crisis over conscription had alienated his Radical followers. Ireland afforded him an opportunity to regain their allegiance.

Shortly afterward, the Prime Minister agreed to a number of committees of enquiry into certain British campaigns which had failed in the field. By these means, the Prime Minister hoped to interest the House of Commons in the study of the recent past. It might be, he calculated, that such labours would distract Members from criticism of the present. On 20th July it was decided to inquire into the campaign in Mesopotamia. A few days later Bonar Law wrote to Lord Milner with another proposition. He wrote, at the Prime Minister's request, in order to ask Milner if he would agree to become chairman of the Committee appointed to examine the Dardanelles operation.

Here was the party Coalition in action. The Liberal and

349

Conservative leaders of the Coalition were proposing, together, that their severest critic should immerse himself in a non-political commission of inquiry. It was an adroit move:[1]

Colonial Office   25 July 1916
My Dear Milner,

   The Prime Minister, who has had to go to the Palace, has asked me to invite you to be Chairman of the Committee appointed to examine the Dardanelles operations. It would be desirable to announce the names this afternoon if it is possible for you to accept at once.

   I need not say how much I personally hope that you will accept & indeed you doing so will be regarded as a great public service by us all. The other members proposed are Fisher and Mackenzie, the Australian & New Zealand High Commissioners, Sir Frederick Crawley, a Liberal M.P. & Clyde, the Scottish Unionist M.P., and in addition Redmond if he will accept. . .

Yours sincerely,
A. Bonar Law.

Lord Milner at once declined. Bonar Law, however, did not easily abandon the matter. He sent a message asking Milner to call upon him at the House. After a talk with Austen Chamberlain and later with Carson, Milner definitely refused the offer, at his interview with the Colonial Secretary.

Aside from the political considerations, Lord Milner had good reason to regard this request as curious. He was already engaged upon an important public task of the very highest significance. On the 4th of July 1916 Lord Robert Cecil, the Parliamentary Under-Secretary at the Foreign Office, had asked him to supervise the supply and distribution of coal for Britain, and for foreign countries. By that time the need for the co-ordination of the various bodies involved had become a matter of some urgency. It was causing the Government anxiety; and an administrator of the first quality was required to deal with the question.[2]

---

[1] Milner Papers, Bonar Law to Milner. The document is partly printed in Wrench, *Milner,* p. 311.

[2] The following account of Lord Milner's activities is based upon documents in the Milner Papers.

At this time three committees dealt with the supply and distribution of coal. The problem of coal production was supervised by a committee responsible to the Home Office. The extraordinary demands made upon the industry in wartime, combined with the indiscriminate recruiting of miners for the Army, had resulted in a serious shortage of labour in the mines. A Coal Mining Organization Committee had been set up, and was responsible to Herbert Samuel, the Home Secretary.

A second aspect of the matter involved the export of coal to Britain's Allies. A large part of France's coal-mining areas were in the grip of the enemy. There was a vigorous rivalry among the Allied countries to obtain British coal. In this case, a Coal Exports Committee, responsible to the Board of Trade, had been established. Since Walter Runciman was ill, "Lulu" Harcourt, the Acting President of the Board of Trade, overlooked the work of this committee. Lord Robert Cecil, at the Foreign Office, was also concerned in its functioning.

A third problem involved the distribution of coal upon the home market. In this area, a Central Coal and Coke Supplies Committee, responsible to the Board of Trade, did its best to satisfy the domestic requirements of the country.

By the summer of 1916 a supervisor of these several committees was required, so that they would work in harmony, and not as mutually independent authorities. A person of some skill and eminence was needed. Lord Milner was asked to fashion these bodies into the departments of one centralised organisation. He accepted the invitation, upon conditions.

He asked and required that the three Ministers should make the appointment "definite and clear in writing", furnishing him with a valid set of "credentials". These conditions were instantly accepted by Herbert Samuel, the senior Minister involved; he, Cecil and Harcourt sent Milner a document, signed by each one of them, authorising him to supervise and co-ordinate the work of the coal committees, in consultation with their respective chairmen.

Lord Milner's conduct in this position deserves the attention of those interested in his political outlook. He believed that he now enjoyed an opportunity to accomplish much more than a reorganisation of the coal trade.

He began his task by consulting the colliery owners and the representatives of the miners. He was most impressed by Lord Rhondda in the one camp, and by Robert Smillie, President of the Miners' Federation, in the other. In the autumn of 1916 he arranged that discussions should take place between the two groups.

Lord Milner's ideas dominated their meetings. His object was to establish in the industry rates of wages that would remain unaltered during the period of the war; conversely, the price of coal was to be fixed. But Lord Milner's plan went far beyond these details.

He desired to render the cost of living in the country stationary, so that his arrangements for the coal-mining industry would not be jeopardised. He looked upon his immediate task as a lever, whereby he could stabilise the economic condition of the entire country. He hoped to fix wages in all other industries, and also the prices of commodities. "Fixation of wages, fixation of the cost of living and consequential subsidation of industries was the scheme in brief".[1]

These ambitious programmes, and his more immediate plans for the coal-mining industry, were rejected. The opposition came from the representatives of the colliery owners, and from the permanent officials at the Board of Trade. Although some of Milner's ideas were later put into effect during Lloyd George's administration, the opportunity for the stabilisation of the cost of living in the country was lost. Regulations were made under the Defence of the Realm Act whereby the Government exercised

[1] Milner Papers, "Lord Milner's Connection with Mining", by Sir Robert Redmayne,

control over the coal mines in Wales and in other areas, but the larger aspect of Milner's plan was stillborn.

By the end of November 1916, shortly after these defeats, the political scene at Westminster was no longer quiescent. In these circumstances Asquith tried twice to get Milner to associate himself with the Government. On 28th November the Prime Minister invited Lord Milner to lunch in Downing Street on the next day. He asked him to become Food Controller. The offer was promptly refused:[1]

17 Great College Street,
1.12.16

Confidential

My dear Asquith,

I saw Runciman, as you suggested, and he gave me further information about the functions of the Food Controller.

After thinking the matter over most carefully, I have come to the conclusion, that the position is not one, which I could fill with any benefit to the country. The duties, which the Controller will have to discharge, are not such as I feel myself well qualified to undertake.

Believe me
Yours sincerely
Milner.

The Prime Minister instantly replied with another request. He urged Milner to "tackle" the coal question. It is clear enough that this offer was tempting; while Milner did not refuse it, he declined to accept, and contented himself with making clear a number of conditions:[2]

2.12.16.
17 Great College Street.

Confidential

My dear Asquith,

I do not reject the idea of trying to tackle the Coal Question, although, as you know, it is a most thorny one. But if I am to approach it with any hope of success, my powers must be very clearly defined & I must also know, before I begin to deal either with owners or men exactly what degree of backing I can count upon from the Govt. in certain eventualities. . .

Yours sincerely,
Milner.

[1] Asquith Papers, Milner to Asquith, 1st December 1916, marked "Confidential".
[2] Asquith Papers, Milner to Asquith, 2nd December 1916, marked "Confidential".

The reasons for this hesitating attitude did not stem from Lord Milner's previous experience with the coal industry. He desired to serve the State in some way; but by this time Lloyd George had decided to act. The question was now to be put to the test whether or not Asquith would continue to direct the country's efforts in war. Already on the 27th November, the Monday night cabal had agreed that Carson should approach Lloyd George and press him to resign. On the 30th Milner lunched with Arthur Lee in order to meet Lloyd George and Sir Edward Carson. Lord Derby, the "genial Judas" of those days, also joined the company. Another political crisis was at hand. If Asquith emerged from it as the victor, Lord Milner seemed prepared to serve him, on conditions; if he lost the battle Milner would be required to make other arrangements with the new rulers of the State. In the circumstances, when the issue hung in the balance, it seemed prudent to delay in furnishing Asquith with any definite answer.

X

The life and death struggle of Asquith's Government was begun by Lloyd George on 16th November 1916. At that time Lloyd George was in Paris. He had just witnessed the defeat of all his strategic plans at the hands of the generals. In a rage of frustration, he decided to act in the political sphere. Here, he knew his business. He was no amateur in that precinct, whatever his limitations in military matters.

Once his decision was made, Lloyd George telegraphed to Sir Max Aitken to arrange a meeting with Bonar Law. Lloyd George had threatened to resign times without number, but now he would not turn back until vital decisions were forced. When he called in Aitken he was playing with fire, and he knew it. Their separate attitudes must now be examined, for the purposes of our story.

The reasons for Lloyd George's anger were fundamental

to the further conduct of the war. On 15th and 16th November a great Conference was held in Paris, to discuss Allied strategy. Lloyd George had prepared for this meeting with very great care.

On 3rd November at a sitting of the British War Committee he had stated his considered views in detail. Three campaigns had been fought up to this time, he said. At the end of the first, Belgium and much of Northern France lay in the grip of the enemy; at the end of the second, in 1915, Serbia had been knocked out of the war; at the end of the third Roumania, which had joined the Allies, lay broken, occupied by the Germans. The road to Constantinople was open, while huge supplies of corn, oil and foodstuffs had been seized in Roumania by a triumphant enemy. France, after Verdun, was gasping for life. The British Armies on the Somme had suffered appalling casualties, to no purpose.

All was not yet lost, however. Lloyd George believed that the Allies could strike with effect if they rearranged their strategic outlook. Their powers had been misapplied so far. This mistake could be corrected.

The peace-loving people of Britain had not been ready for a war of this kind. But after two years of struggle, the British had caught up with their enemies. Munitions and materials for war were now, at last, being produced in adequate and even ample quantities. How should these warlike instruments be employed?

If the Allies were to fight on, Lloyd George argued, it must be done in such a way that they had a reasonable chance for victory. What changes, then, were required in Allied strategy?

Lloyd George believed that he knew the answers. He urged upon his British colleagues a conference between the Western leaders and the Russians. Abandon, he said, the war of attrition in the West. It was a negation of the military art, a senseless waste of men and equipment. Instead, furnish the Russians with the accoutrements of war. Wage the struggle as a single great battle. Use the varied resources of the Allies, their men and their materials, in a rational way. Co-ordinate Allied policy by providing Russia with a very substantial measure of help. In the East lay the hope of the Allied cause. Contain the enemy on the Western front; revive the Russians in the East, and employ their hordes, well armed, to crush the foe. This was the programme he explained to his colleagues, and this the plan he carried with him to Paris.

He was out-foxed completely by the generals. While the politicians prepared to meet in Paris, Joffre held a military conference of his own at Chantilly. Here, he and the other generals decided upon a series of offensives in the West, as the plan for 1917. On the 16th November the generals came to Paris. They were capable of victory on this kind of field. Their conclusions were pressed upon the political leaders. The statesmen had been talking to no purpose. The generals had decided matters alone, and they now won over the civilians to their point of view. Lloyd George was caught off-balance. He later called the Paris Conference "a complete farce".

He seethed with anger. He was not prepared to tolerate such conduct. The statesmen were the principal leaders of their countries, responsible at the last for victory or defeat. The generals should have been their advisers, the technicians to be consulted, and not the men to make the supreme decisions. There was something wrong with the Allied war direction when it allowed a development of this kind.

Lloyd George at first proposed to resign. He was restrained by Colonel Hankey. They agreed upon a new plan. Lloyd George would now insist upon the creation of a small War Council, to direct Britain's conduct in the war. The chairman of this body had to be tough, resilient and energetic. The Prime Minister was ineligible for the post. He had plenty to do in his own sphere, and he was exhausted after nearly a decade of service in the first place under the Crown. It was decided to put this proposition

LLOYD GEORGE

The Milnerites called him "The Goat".

before Asquith. In these circumstances, Lloyd George wired to Beaverbrook to arrange a meeting with Bonar Law. It was the first step.

The telegram of the 16th of November spurred Sir Max Aitken to action. He had been uneasy for some time past because he feared for Bonar Law's position as leader of the Conservative Party. His fears were based upon those considerations which dominated the outlook of the Milner-ites. They hoped for an active alliance against Asquith composed of Lloyd George, Carson, Milner and their various followers, in Parliament, in the Press, in society and in the Army. Such an arrangement would leave Bonar Law isolated, out in the cold. Aitken was determined to prevent this from happening.

Lloyd George has explained for posterity, with exemplary clarity, that one rule guided his conduct in politics. It was brought home to him as a young man that in high politics there are "no friendships at the top". He certainly conducted his own affairs in strict conformity with this hard principle. However much we may be distressed by it, the painful admission must be made that politicians in every age usually conform to Lloyd George's precept. One exception stands out in recent English political history. Lord Beaverbrook's loyalty to Bonar Law never wavered; while his friend lived, and after his death, Beaverbrook was always vigilant on Bonar Law's behalf. He has, himself, deprecated the extent of his influence over Bonar Law. In one limited sense, he did not dominate the Tory leader as much as some of their critics supposed. But if we examine the relationship during the crises of Bonar Law's career, during the testing periods, a different picture of the two men emerges. In 1911 when Bonar Law sought the leadership of the Conservatives, it was Beaverbrook's hand that guided him to the place. In 1913, when Bonar Law made the radical decision to throw over the policy of Tariff Reform in order to preserve the unity of the party, Beaverbrook was largely responsible for the decision. This was one of the best kept

secrets of recent political history.[1] Now, Beaverbrook
stepped forward once again, in order to act for his friend
at a moment of supreme crisis. Milner, Dawson and Oliver
meant to act with Lloyd George and with Carson, and to
leave Bonar Law alone. This, Lord Beaverbrook was not
prepared to permit. The telegram indicated that Lloyd
George was of the same mind.

XI

In the late autumn of 1916 it seemed, to the casual
observer, that no instrument could be designed to overthrow the Ministry. Despite the opinion of men like Milner,
Asquith was still generally regarded as the indispensable
man. So long as Bonar Law continued to cleave to him, the
Ministry appeared to be safe.

But Sir Max Aitken's keen eyes perceived a flaw in this
reasoning. Bonar Law, when he joined the Government in
May 1915, promised to resign if ever his Conservative
followers disapproved of his membership in the Coalition
Ministry. When Carson joined the Milnerian Opposition,
the Diehards in the Tory party were powerfully reinforced.
Now, Tory turned upon Tory in bitter dispute. The relations between Bonar Law and Carson were no longer
cordial. The famous Nigerian debate of the 8th of November
1916 brought these matters to a head.

We need not concern ourselves with the details. The
point Aitken noticed, and it is of moment for our account,
was that Carson's attack upon the Government, and upon
Bonar Law, was supported by a large number of Conservatives, in the voting that followed this debate. Sixty-five
Unionists voted for Carson, and only seventy-three for
Bonar Law, their official leader. Aitken realised that Carson
was free to continue his attacks whenever opportunity
offered. Bonar Law, for his part, could do nothing to silence
Carson and his friends, in the House or in the Press.

[1] The secret is revealed in Gollin, *The Observer and J. L. Garvin*, ch. XI. "The
Victory of The Hermit Crab".

Aitken noticed something else. Lloyd George was not present in the House on the night of the Nigerian debate. Where was he? Aitken knew. "Lloyd George was dining that night with Lord Lee of Fareham at his house in Abbey Garden where several meetings had already taken place between Lloyd George, Carson and Milner. All three had met that evening to discuss the . . . possibilities of co-operation".[1]

Now Aitken took serious alarm. He actually urged Bonar Law to resign from the Government, in order to save himself from the jaws of the trap. Carson was attacking the Ministry in public, on the one hand. Lloyd George was treating with the Opposition on the sly, on the other. "If he stayed in", Beaverbrook has written of Bonar Law, "he would be, in my opinion, infallibly destroyed".[2]

All would be well, Aitken reasoned, if an agreement could be reached between Carson and Bonar Law. But how could this be done? Unless definite action were taken, the two men must inevitably drift further apart.

Under the influence of Milner, and his other friends of the Monday night cabal, Carson was regularly exposed to very serious criticisms of the Conservative leader. Milner, Dawson and Oliver hoped that Bonar Law would also fall in any crash that tumbled Asquith down from his place. Matters could not, in Aitken's view, be allowed to follow this course. The Milnerites must not be left as the sole influence upon Sir Edward Carson's mind. Furthermore, though this was peripheral, Aitken did not like Lord Milner and his friends. He has described Milner as being "impres-

---

[1] Beaverbrook, *Politicians and The War*, p. 301. Lest an innocent reader believe that the fires have gone out of this controversy, he should note that Sir Evelyn Wrench in his *Life of Dawson* has succeeded in telling the story of the December crisis without mentioning Lord Beaverbrook's name, a singular achievement. In addition, Lord Hankey's two volumes on *The Supreme Command* (London, 1961), contain a short bibliography in which Lord Beaverbrook's books are not mentioned. This is especially noteworthy since Lord Hankey stresses the political aspects of his subject; and Beaverbrook's books are without doubt the best analyses of the British politicians in the war.

[2] *Ibid.*, p. 296.

sive but not attractive".[1] Conversely, the Milnerites did not care for him. In their opinion, he was not one of the elect. He was hardly disturbed by this opinion of the Olympians. His business was to protect Bonar Law's position.

On the weekend of 11th–12th November Aitken gathered Churchill, F. E. Smith and Bonar Law together in his country home. His brilliant account of the crisis, *Politicians and The War,* takes fire from this point. Churchill's attacks upon the Government in Aitken's house outraged Bonar Law. He retorted savagely: "Very well, if that's what the critics of the Government think of it—we will have a General Election".[2]

Churchill, an opponent of the Ministry, was staggered by the threat. If the leaders of the two great parties combined to fight an election in wartime, they must destroy their critics. But Churchill was not so upset as Aitken; the latter has set out the issues as he saw them very clearly. We must pay close attention to his views. In the end, they decided the issue:[3]

Churchill had been greatly startled by Bonar Law's threat of a dissolution—but I doubt if he was as perturbed as I was by the suggestion. . .

. . . If the Diehard Conservatives persisted in their course and forced Bonar Law to resign, Asquith, backed by Bonar Law and these Tory Ministers, who were notoriously under Asquith's influence, would appeal to the country against the followers of Carson.

. . . the recalcitrant Tory members would have been opposed in their constituencies by Bonar Law Conservative candidates. These candidates would undoubtedly have swept the Diehards out of existence. . .

[1] Beaverbrook, *Men and Power,* p. xxi. Lord Beaverbrook was unable to discover a cause for Milner's disapproval: "I don't know why he disapproved, perhaps on account of my self-confidence . . . he did not think well of me" (pp. 276–7). The reason is clear. Beaverbrook could not fit into the select company of Milner's friends, the élite company he chose to have about him.

[2] Beaverbrook, *Politicians and The War,* p. 308.

[3] *Ibid.,* pp. 309–11. A. J. P. Taylor in his *"Politics in The First World War"* makes the ingenious suggestion, pp. 82–3, that the Unionist rebels would have been returned in greater numbers, after an election. He supposes that Beaverbrook, Bonar Law and Churchill were all wrong in their appreciation of the situation. It hardly matters. The only way to save Bonar Law's position, in either case, was to avoid the election. This was Aitken's sole object.

George. There was good reason for this development. Once, when Lloyd George sought to sum Milner up, he wrote of him that "He had no political nostril".[1] Milner was not equipped, either by training or inclination, to take part in the deft but murderous sword-play that now engaged the Ministers. Political lives were at stake. Lloyd George would permit Milner no part in this mortal game.

This fact has misled certain observers of the political scene. It has been suggested that Milner's appointment to Lloyd George's War Cabinet came as a stunning surprise. It was not the case. Lloyd George, as we shall see, reckoned upon definite and concrete political advantages when he chose to include Milner in his Government, even though he realised that Milner could do very little in the Cabinet crisis that led to Asquith's destruction.

The Milner Papers contain a daily, and even hourly, account of Milner's position in the first week of December 1916. Certain typed copies of his letters to Lady Edward Cecil are preserved. Some of them are marked "Burn". On 3rd December Milner wrote to Lady Edward:

. . . The rumpus here is simply awful. . . About 2:15 yesterday my telephone suddenly went mad and it has not completely recovered sanity yet.

. . . L. G. is really making a Gigantic Effort to get rid of H. H. A., bring Carson back and form a small real War Govt. All the perfectly useless members of the Govt.—some 16 or 18 out of the 23—are clinging round H. H. A.'s knees and beseeching him not to give in. No thought of what is happening to the country—you may observe. It is just *their* positions.

H. H. A. returned to Walmer last night, almost beat, but . . . he is returning today and wants to see L. G. this evening. Thereon much depends. . .

My fear is—there will be another compromise and a patch up. Two to one on the patch up, but there is the odd chance of a smash.

What I say to everyone is "*You come out*—of Sodom and Gomorrah. There is plenty of room and air outside". . .

What I dread is a Patch-up. . .

On 5th December Milner wrote to Lady Edward again:

[1] D. Lloyd George, *The Truth About The Peace Treaties* (London, 1938), vol. I, p. 262.

. . . No fresh news of the crisis. Asquith having succeeded in gaining time—his own supreme art—procrastination—will, I believe, succeed in mixing things up again. . .

I cannot see what L. G. is waiting for. He has absolutely everything in his hands—*and it is his last chance.* . .

B. L. is surprisingly sound *considering.* . .

On the 8th came a further report to Lady Edward. This letter reveals, among other things, Lord Milner's definite hostility to Bonar Law:

. . . I was absolutely right in insisting, as I did ceaselessly and almost with too much vehemence, that a clean cut was essential, and I rejoiced at the prospect of L. G. and Carson being left almost alone . . . and getting rid of the whole truckload of Mandarins. . . Unfortunately, as I think, the *unexpected firmness* of Bonar Law, while it certainly gave the *coup de grace* to Squiff, has resulted in the return of the old Unionist tail—A. J. B.—and all the rest of them—so that the new Govt. is really old Unionist hordes, L. G. and *some* new men. . . So we have not, after all, completely sloughed off the old party skin. . .

Whether I am to be in it or not, I have not as yet the least idea. . . Tonight I have received two several mysterious summons to a "War Committee"—whatever that may be. . . I shall then no doubt know what their plan is, if there be a plan.

My own disposition is strongly against being in the Govt. at all, most strongly against being in it unless I am part of the Supreme Direction". . .

When Lord Milner responded to his mysterious summons, he discovered that he was to be a part of the "Supreme Direction". The bitter decade which had begun with his return from South Africa was over at last. In his opinion, the politicians and the hacks had been swept into second place. The administrators, statesmen and governors of men were now to assume their rightful positions, and so dispose of the resources of their country that the war would be won after months of bungling. Now, in his sixty-third year the nation had summoned him back to a place of authority and power, at a moment of desperate crisis. A new phase of his long career was about to begin. He appreciated the weight of the burden, but he was resolved to do his duty. The emergency man had at last come into his own.

PART III
POWER

XIV.   The Threshold of Power

A Milner myth – Why Milner was selected for the War
Cabinet – The Attitude of the Tory Diehards – Rivalry
of Carson and Milner – The attitude of the King – The
opinion of Lord Northcliffe – Lloyd George's object in
selecting Milner – The struggle for places in the new
Government – Lord Milner's young men in office –
Amery, Kerr, Curtis and Buchan gain places – The
solitary condition of Waldorf Astor – The New Bureaucracy – Lord Milner's Monster – Lloyd George's opinion
of Milner – Gratitude as a factor in politics – Lord Milner's
new chief – Lord Milner and the charlatan who is also a
statesman.

I

THERE can be little doubt that Lord Milner's elevation to the War Cabinet was a transition remarkable
in the annals of British political history. For more
than a decade, with trifling exceptions, he had enjoyed or
adorned no official post. Now he was part of that small
Supreme Direction which would decide the fate of the
country in the most terrible war that had ever convulsed
the British nation.

Nevertheless, we must pause at the very beginning of
our analysis of his new condition in order to examine a
curious yet typical comment about his appointment.

During his lifetime and after his death as well, the influence of Lord Milner's personality was nowhere more
powerful than in the cloistered regions of the Printing
House Square. Northcliffe, Dawson, Lord Brand and others
who controlled *The Times* in these years were all, for shorter
or longer periods, devoted Milnerites. Lord Milner, while

he lived, and after his death also, such was his power, often dominated the outlook of the great newspaper. It is for these reasons that we find a remarkable and incorrect statement about him in the official *History of The Times*. It must engage our attention, however briefly.

The statement is typical of much that was written by the Milnerites in praise of their chief, after death had removed him from the political scene. It is a part of the Milner myth or legend, created by his loyal disciples in the period when they exercised tremendous influence upon the minds of their contemporaries.

In the *History of The Times* we find the following remark about Lord Milner and the Government of December 1916: ". . . Once Lord Milner had attained office, passing in a fashion unprecedented except by the younger Pitt straight to the second position under the Crown, he had much less time to write or to read letters. . ."[1]

It is no denigration of Lord Milner to point out that this comparison with the younger Pitt is unhappy and inaccurate. Our history will show in detail his marvellous achievements as a member of Lloyd George's wartime administration; but we must take care to avoid adding incorrect information to the corpus of that *religio Milneriana* which has been successfully revived by his disciples in recent years.

The reader will recall that Sir Henry Campbell-Bannerman stamped the effects of the *religio Milneriana* out of his party in 1905, after a series of grim battles with Haldane, Grey and Asquith. They were the worshippers at the shrine in that period.

More recently, however, strenuous efforts have been made to present accounts of Lord Milner's career—in the Press, in books, and in articles—which sacrifice accuracy of statement in order to swell the volume of praise for him. Ardour has taken the place of authenticity, where Lord Milner is concerned. This revival of the *religio Milneriana*,

---

[1] *History of The Times*, vol. IV, part II, p. 1068.

LORD MILNER IN DOWNING STREET

with its spurious aspects, will be dealt with in the final chapter of our history.

Meanwhile, we have to notice that the high claim for second place in Lloyd George's Government, if such distinctions must be made, can belong only to Andrew Bonar Law. At no time was Milner second in the Government.

Lloyd George has himself pointed out with reference to December 1916 that: "I had to take into account the fundamental fact that I was working under a Parliamentary system, and that it was essential for the Government to secure the support of Parliament..."[1]

In this sphere, he depended to a very great extent upon the goodwill, loyalty and co-operation of Bonar Law. The relationship has been well described by Bonar Law's biographer: "... Bonar Law stood at the very centre of events. He was, in effect, a second Prime Minister... he occupied a position of power second only to Lloyd George himself. As leader of the Conservative Party, which constituted the great majority of the new Coalition's supporters, he was responsible for the political machine, whose smooth running was ... essential even in time of war for the stability of the Government".[2]

Lord Hankey, who was in a position to observe the new administration very carefully, reinforces this opinion: "... as Leader of the House of Commons... Bonar Law held the vice-presidency of the War Cabinet... Bonar Law was his loyal and devoted supporter... This loyalty... gave Bonar Law an influence on Lloyd George which was wisely exercised and exceeded that of any other member of the Government... The intimacy between the Prime Minister and his first lieutenant was a real asset to the Government and the country".[3]

---

[1] Lloyd George, *War Memoirs,* vol. I, p. 620.
[2] Blake, *Bonar Law*, p.342.
[3] Hankey, *The Supreme Command,* pp. 577–8.

II

We must now ask why Lloyd George selected Milner for the War Cabinet, in the first place. Lord Beaverbrook has referred to Milner's surprise at his inclusion. Randolph Churchill has emphasised how restricted was Milner's influence: "Milner ... enjoyed a preternatural prestige in the limited but active circles which found their inspiration in Printing House Square and the Cliveden and Round Table sets, but politically he mounted very few guns".[1]

We have to observe that Lord Milner's political artillery could fire with effect in exactly those areas where Lloyd George was weakest.

The construction of the Government of December 1916 was Lloyd George's master work as a politician. If we leave aside his accomplishments as a statesman, this was a supreme triumph of his public career. We may depend upon it that, from the political point of view, he knew what he was doing when he selected the members of his small War Cabinet.

Lloyd George counted upon definite political advantages when he included Milner in his Government. In his *War Memoirs* he points out:[2] "I was satisfied that I would receive the active co-operation of Mr. Bonar Law and Sir Edward Carson (much the most influential leaders in the Conservative Party ...) and Lord Milner—who carried great weight with the Tory intelligentsia and Diehards (not by any means identical groups)".

Lloyd George's appreciation of Milner's position, it is clear, is different from that presented by Randolph Churchill.

It is obvious enough that Lloyd George, in selecting Lord Milner, sought to win support among those exclusive regiments of the Tory party in which Milner was highly respected. The Prime Minister's political sagacity is borne

[1] Randolph Churchill, *Lord Derby* (London, 1959), p. 242, hereafter cited as Churchill, *Derby*.
[2] Lloyd George, *War Memoirs*, vol. II, p. 596.

out by a letter which Lord Salisbury wrote to Milner at this time. Salisbury was a leader of the Tory Diehards; he exercised considerable influence in the House of Lords, and also among the rebellious members of the Unionist War Committee who now saw Carson and Milner, their titular leaders, disappearing into the upper regions of the new administration.

On 11th December 1916 Lord Salisbury wrote to Milner in order to congratulate him upon his appointment. He pointed out that he did not approve of the new Prime Minister, nor was he excited by the inclusion of Arthur Henderson, the Labour leader. Henderson, in Lord Salisbury's opinion, would prove of little value to the Government. The inclusion of Bonar Law in the War Cabinet was not a source of strength, Lord Salisbury believed. However, he relied upon the two other members, Milner and Lord Curzon, to do the genuine work of the administration. When they had worked out the plans of the new Government, Lloyd George could drive them through to completion. After one or two criticisms of Curzon, Lord Salisbury emphasised that he relied upon Milner, with his skill and experience, to set the right course for the administration. Since Milner was a member, Lord Salisbury, despite his doubts about the others, was prepared to support the Ministry.[1]

This was exactly the development Lloyd George had worked for. By admitting Lord Milner into the Government, a formidable critic had been won over. The hostility of an important leader of the right wing of the Tory party had been converted into an attitude of friendly support. It was a significant political achievement.

Lloyd George revealed a considerable measure of skill if we look at the appointment from another point of view. In one sense, Lord Milner and Sir Edward Carson were rivals for a place in the War Cabinet.

[1] Salisbury's attitude as described above is based upon his letter to Milner, dated 11th December 1916, preserved in the Milner Papers, marked "Confidential".

They were both the recognised champions of the extreme Tories. Both had plagued Asquith and Bonar Law in full measure, in the period before December 1916. For a time it seemed that Sir Edward Carson would win the day. The original plan was to include him in the War Cabinet, while Lord Milner was sent to take charge of the Admiralty. Lloyd George, however, was afraid of the Irishman, and with good reason.

Sir Edward was too powerful and too dangerous to be given one of the first places. He was always ready to resign. If he ever did separate himself from the Government, he would tear too great a hole in the Ministry when he left. As Lloyd George put it in his *War Memoirs*: "Carson . . . Whether in or out of office . . . was always 'agin the Government' for the time being".

On the other hand, Milner was far more amenable. His soul had been parched in the deserts of Opposition. He would not readily give up office after a decade in the wilderness.

If he were given Carson's place the very forces which adored Sir Edward would be mollified, since they trusted Milner more than any other man. They relied upon him to provide the new régime with the qualities of soundness, steadiness tempered by experience, and administrative skill of the highest quality. Lloyd George's course, in these circumstances, was quite clear. There was no need for anyone to be surprised when he awarded the palm of office to Lord Milner.

The selection carried other political advantages in its train. Lord Esher, a man who was always close to the King in these years, thoroughly approved of it. Lloyd George realised from the first that King George preferred Asquith to himself. The King made no secret of his preference. By selecting Milner, the Prime Minister could reckon that the King would be pleased, however much he deplored the departure of Asquith. Esher's letter of congratulation to Milner is worthy of our notice. It reveals exactly where

Milner stood, in the opinion of his contemporaries:[1]

You can imagine how heartily glad I am that at last you have come to your own, in spite of the terrible slum of democracy through which your way has lain and lies.

In addition, Austen and Neville Chamberlain, and those Midland cohorts they led, were gratified by Milner's selection. Of the very greatest importance for Lloyd George was the attitude of Lord Northcliffe. The Press always occupied a prominent place in the new Prime Minister's calculations.

Although Northcliffe was delighted by the fall of Asquith, he at first showed a serious measure of hostility to the new combination. Lloyd George understood that Northcliffe respected Milner as one of the leading statesmen of their time. He could be induced to give the Government his support, if Lord Milner were included in the administration.

According to the *History of The Times*, Northcliffe was not especially pleased by Milner's appointment. That history declares: "it is not obvious that Northcliffe was enthusiastic over the appointment"[2] of Lord Milner.

We must regard this statement as yet another baleful example of the *religio Milneriana*. If the statement has any validity at all, it is only comparative. Northcliffe, obviously, could never be as enthusiastic as Geoffrey Dawson, where Milner was concerned. But this does not mean that he was lukewarm in his appreciation of Milner's qualities. Dawson believed that Milner's proper sphere was the Premiership itself. If others could not share in Dawson's exaltation and rapture, it does not mean that they were unable to notice or mark Lord Milner's gifts as a statesman.

Northcliffe and Milner eventually quarrelled, in the autumn of 1918. Before that time, however, Northcliffe always respected Lord Milner. As an Imperialist, he regularly supported Milner's policies in his newspapers in the period

---

[1] Esher, *Journals and Letters,* vol. III, p. 80.
[2] *History of The Times*, vol. IV, part I, p. 308.

1905–14, as we have seen. Both men agreed upon the need for National Military Service in the early years of the war, and collaborated in the campaign to win it for the country. In this period Northcliffe placed his greatest faith in the generals, to whom he was prepared to give almost unlimited power, in order to win the war. Milner was the political hero of the Army at the time that he joined the Government. As late as the spring of 1918 Northcliffe sought Milner's advice upon political, military and business matters, including Geoffrey Dawson's position as editor of *The Times*. To suggest that Northcliffe was in any way cool to Milner in December 1916 is to compress the march of events so much that reality is distorted, and historical accuracy abandoned. When Milner's appointment was announced, Northcliffe sent him a letter of congratulation. The document has not been preserved, but Milner's reply begins: "Many thanks for your very kind letter".[1]

An example of Northcliffe's high regard for Milner occurred in January 1918. In that month Northcliffe was advanced in the peerage to the rank and dignity of a Viscount. He asked Milner to act as his sponsor for the ceremony in the House of Lords:[2]

My dear Lord Milner,
  Would you be one of my sponsors in the Lords on my elevation to a viscount. . .
  I shall be much honoured if you would accompany me in that mediaeval ceremony.

In December 1916 Lloyd George was certain that the appointment of Milner as Minister Without Portfolio in the War Cabinet could only help him in his relations with Northcliffe, and with the Northcliffe Press as a whole.

It seems clear that Lord Milner was included in the Lloyd George Government because of the political benefits that would follow upon his selection. The right wing of the Tories who were uneasy under Bonar Law's leadership,

[1] Northcliffe Papers, Milner to Northcliffe, 12th December 1916.
[2] Northcliffe Papers, Northcliffe to Milner, 11th January 1918.

the supporters of the generals, the bulk of the Conservative Press, Imperialists generally, the King and his friends, the enthusiasts of the *Round Table,* were all reassured when they learned that Milner was to be a director of the new combination.

Lloyd George certainly expected to benefit from Milner's great ability as an administrator. He was aware of the brooding power and the masterly grasp of his new colleague, in administrative affairs. But these advantages made themselves clear only after Milner had begun to discharge his duties. At first, he owed his place to the political support he could bring to a shaky, untried and suspect administration.

III

As soon as the fall of Asquith was accomplished, a kind of incuriousness descended upon Sir Edward Carson. He acted as a man does who believes that his work is done. He made no claims for office for himself, and failed to urge the Prime Minister to reward any of his particular friends with those fruits of victory which lie within the gift of any first Minister. Carson played the part of the disinterested patriot. He reported to his post at the Admiralty where he did everything in his power to bolster up the high sailors who were conducting the naval war against Germany. For the moment, he confined himself to his administrative task. He seemed to abandon politics completely.

This was not the case with Lord Milner. He and his friends acted as if their hour had struck, as indeed it had. They were like hounds round a kill, after a long chase. They struggled to seize places, high or low. Serene in their conviction that they were better equipped than their fellows to serve the State, they rushed forward in order to offer their services.

When an ordinary politician rewarded his lieutenants with positions in an administration, the Milnerites, for so long above the dust and strife of politics, were always the first to talk about "jobs", and that low level of morality among English politicians who were unfit to discharge the duties of statesmen. From the very first moment that he won office, Milner began to urge his friends upon Lloyd George. The object was to permeate the new Government with Milnerites, from top to bottom, and on all sides as well. The members of the Monday night cabal were determined to have their friends and themselves in certain key posts of the Lloyd George régime.

F. S. Oliver was quickly off the mark in this sphere. When he wrote to congratulate Milner on 10th December 1916 he took care not to confine his letter to mere platitudes. He urged Milner to exploit, in the national interest, the youthful talent of their young friends:[1]

I expect you are about the most miserable man in England. If so you had better remember that ten days ago you were *quite* the most miserable man in England. . .

Judged by his own standards The Squiff was as good a fox as ever ran; only it wasn't fox hunting days: he should have been trapped long ago.

. . . good stuff should not be wasted. So I sent Carson a list the other day of what from my advanced standpoint appears as youthful talent.

Class I. Edward Wood.

Class II. Amery, Astor, George Lloyd, J. W. Hills, Mark Sykes. . .

Class III. Brand and Philip Kerr (the latter Undersecretary for Colonies).

. . . A. J. B. of course is a blot & a bad blot; and W. Log or Long is just damnable, but as you managed to work with him over Ulster you may perhaps manage to work with him on this.

I think now that England will be saved—my only dread is Squiff getting back. Oh! that he had eaten the fatal bread of enchantment the Chancellorship, belted himself an Earl and. . .

This singular, curious and immodest list was taken very seriously by Lord Milner. His first step was to place Leo Amery upon the staff of the new War Cabinet Secretariat. Sir Maurice Hankey, the Secretary, was at first suspicious of the appointment: "Amery, at Milner's behest, was brought home from Salonica and attached to the War

[1] Milner Papers, Oliver to Milner, 10th December 1916.

Cabinet. At first I was not quite happy about it, as I had a suspicion that he might be intended to replace me, a suspicion that was strengthened, when a short time after his arrival and in my absence with Lloyd George abroad, I read in a newspaper that in future Mark Sykes, Amery and I were to be joint secretaries of the War Cabinet... Lloyd George assured me there was no foundation for the story... Amery proved to be a most loyal colleague... Probably Milner, in bringing him home was 'insuring' against a failure on my part to fill the bill ... "[1]

Next, Lord Milner called the Prime Minister's attention to Philip Kerr, later Lord Lothian. Milner urged Lloyd George to appoint Kerr as his Private Secretary. When Lloyd George accepted this advice, Kerr left the *Round Table* where he was still engaged, in order to join a group of Lloyd George's personal secretaries in the so-called Garden Suburb at No. 10 Downing Street.

This Garden Suburb consisted of a number of wooden huts erected during the war to house Lloyd George's private staff; they stood outside the Prime Minister's official residence, and soon became a target for the quips and jokes of Lloyd George's critics. "No man", Lloyd George wrote of Kerr in later years, "more completely justified his recommendation". Lionel Curtis, another eager disciple of Lord Milner, also became a member of the Prime Minister's personal staff in the Garden Suburb.

The very first letter Lord Milner wrote to Lloyd George was concerned with appointments. On 14th December Milner urged Amery and Arthur Steel-Maitland, his former Private Secretary, upon the Prime Minister's attention:[2]

... To be short: You will remember that you asked us all to think of men for the Civil Side of the Staff of the War Cabinet. Well, after many discussions, the 3 members of the Cabinet present this morning, *consulting with Hankey,* came to the unanimous conclusion that the *Immediate* starting of the civil side is of the greatest necessity. We were also unanimous in recommending that Steel Maitland at present Under

[1] Hankey, *Supreme Command,* vol. II, p. 590.
[2] Lloyd George Papers, Milner to Lloyd George, 14th December 1916.

Secretary for the Colonies, who would be willing to come, should be offered the Civil Secretaryship as an equal colleague of Hankey. . . We were all agreed as to 2 men, whom we should like to get, viz.— Young, at present on Henderson's staff as Labour adviser, & Captain Amery (M.P.) at present a staff captain in Salonica but just coming home on leave. . .

. . . the great thing is to make a start. The congestion here will be awful if we don't, & then we should be back in the old discredit of delay in execution. . .

In the event, Hankey's position was not reduced to the extent that Milner intended. Steel-Maitland went to the Foreign Office, and not to the Secretariat of the War Cabinet.

In the middle of January 1917 Lord Milner recommended yet another of his young men to Lloyd George. His letter reveals something of his persistence in this important sphere:[1]

17 Great College Street,
S.W.

Private

My dear Prime Minister,

Don't think me too insistent!

I wish you would not "turn down" John Buchan, without seeing him yourself.

If you had a talk with him, & were not favourably impressed, I should have nothing more to say.

But I am not satisfied to have him rejected on hear-say, & ill-informed hear-say at that.

Yours very sincerely,
Milner.

Eventually, the hostile critics were overcome. John Buchan, one of Milner's Private Secretaries in South Africa, later Lord Tweedsmuir, was appointed to Lloyd George's staff as Director of Information.

Alone among the chosen people Waldorf Astor lay at Cliveden, brooding upon his sorry condition. All the members of the Monday night cabal who were available for office, save for himself, had been awarded one post or

---

[1] Lloyd George Papers, Milner to Lloyd George, 17th January 1917. marked "Private".

another. By a curious oversight none of the spoils fell to him. Lord Milner had taken good care of most of his young friends, but Waldorf Astor was left out. His political career was grinding to a halt in the very hour of victory.

Fortunately, J. L. Garvin came to Astor's rescue. Astor depended upon Garvin to save him in these crucial circumstances. Lloyd George was always prepared to listen to the editor's suggestions and advice.

On 18th December Garvin wrote to the Prime Minister: " . . . poor Waldorf is sore, discouraged even more than I expected. I beg you to put him on your new Secretariat".[1] There is no record of any similar action taken by Lord Milner, on Astor's behalf.

The time would come when Garvin grew old in his harness; when his political influence and his business acumen were alike diminished; when his bickerings over his own position became too irritating; when his loyalty to Winston Churchill annoyed Lord Astor; when Astor desired an editor's job for a younger son; and then, after three decades his relationship with Waldorf Astor was dissolved in an instant, and he was summarily dismissed from the journal he had fashioned into one of the world's great newspapers. But this was not yet. Despite Lord Milner's neglect, as a result of Garvin's intervention the last of the Milnerites found a place in the new administration. Waldorf Astor became a secretary in the Garden Suburb—"the yard", to employ Lord Beaverbrook's phrase, "where huts were set up for the overflow of secretaries".[2]

[1] Lloyd George Papers, Garvin to Lloyd George, 18th December 1916.

[2] Like Milner himself, mystery and falsehood surrounds the careers of the Milnerites. This applies to Astor's relationship with J. L. Garvin. In Lord Astor's obituary notice in *The Times* we find the following statement about his relationship with J. L. Garvin: ". . . the partnership ended for reasons which (in spite of rumour to the contrary) had nothing to do with the leadership of the nation in war. . ." This statement is incorrect. In a document which the late Lord Astor personally prepared for the information of the present writer, he explained that when Garvin publicly advocated the return of Lord Beaverbrook to the Cabinet in 1942, he refused to continue with Garvin as editor of *The Observer*. This document is preserved. The incident illustrates the extreme care which is required when the student attempts to analyse the careers of the Milnerites. Their actions in British politics have been obscured by diligent apologists.

Lord Milner's close connection with the Garden Suburb was instantly recognised by the Asquithian enemies of the administration. Although Asquith's biographers have suggested that he was prepared to go when he was no longer wanted, this was not the case. It has been well said of Asquith that he lay like a crocodile in the shallows, ready to pounce upon Ministers at the first opportunity.

An early Asquithian attack upon the new régime was launched by H. W. Massingham in the *Nation* of 24th February 1917.

Massingham pointed out in his article that a new bureaucracy had been established in Whitehall, under Lloyd George's régime. The object of this "Monster", as he called it, was to stifle British freedom and democracy. According to Massingham, the "Monster" had been fashioned by Lord Milner. His purpose was to use his young men to secure the triumph of reactionary Imperialism in Great Britain. The article declared:

The New Bureaucracy

. . . A new double screen of bureaucrats is interposed between the War Directorate and the heads of Departments, whose responsibility to Parliament has hitherto been direct. . . The first is the so-called Cabinet Secretariat. . . The second is a little body of *illuminati,* whose residence is in the Prime Minister's garden. . . These gentlemen stand in no sense for a Civil Service Cabinet. They are rather of the class of travelling empirics in Empire, who came in with Lord Milner, and whose "spiritual home" is fixed somewhere between Balliol and Heidleburg. . .

Reactionary Imperialism has thus seized the whole body of Liberal and democratic doctrine. . . The governing ideas are not those of Mr. Lloyd George . . . but of Lord Milner. . . Mr. George has used Toryism to destroy Liberal ideas; but he has created a Monster which, for the moment, dominates both. This is the New Bureaucracy, which threatens to master England, unless England decides in time to master it.

IV

Lloyd George had no objection to the swarm of Milnerites who now fastened themselves upon his new Government. His long experience of men and affairs had made him a master in gauging the aspirations, qualities and motives of those who sought to play a part in the high politics of the country. He knew that he could dominate Lord Milner and every one of Milner's young allies. He welcomed the Milnerites as extremely capable subordinates. The only man among his allies who caused him uneasiness in the early days of his Premiership was Sir Edward Carson. For that reason Carson was kept out of the War Cabinet.

Lord Salisbury in his letter of the 11th December 1916, which we have noticed above, explained to Milner that it seemed to him that the Premiership had been put in commission for the duration of the war. Salisbury was prepared to support the new arrangements because he looked upon Lord Milner as one of the commissioners. This was not the case. Lord Salisbury misread the situation. He made a mistake when he looked upon the small War Cabinet of five members in this light. Lloyd George proposed to dominate his colleagues. And he knew that he could do it. He was to be master. If Salisbury and the high Tories chose to regard the administration differently, that was their own affair and none of Lloyd George's business. Provided that his Government received their support, Lloyd George was content. He dealt in realities, and not in the illusion of power.

Bonar Law recognised that his national duty was to support the new Prime Minister with the votes of the Tory legions in the House of Commons. He was always loyal to Lloyd George. Arthur Henderson, the leader of the Labour Party, was a vital asset to the Government. His membership in the War Cabinet made it certain that industrial strife in the country would be reduced to a minimum. He also carried with him the votes of a majority of the Labour Members in the House of Commons. But he could never be a rival for Lloyd George's position. Lord Curzon, a third member of the War Cabinet, may have entertained designs upon the first place, in his more ardent moments. However, he was mistrusted by nearly everyone who knew him. Even though his high talents as an administrator were everywhere recognised, men were suspicious of Curzon's political reliability. In the years before the war he often advocated certain definite policies, only to change his mind at the last moment and reverse his course. These political somersaults were observed and marked down against him, especially by those Tories upon whom he depended for his political power and authority. Lloyd George knew that Curzon, in the grip of high ambition, would do anything to retain his hold upon office. For that reason the cynical Prime Minister sometimes treated Curzon with a cool contempt that could have been tolerated by no other man. Lloyd George amused himself on several occasions by humiliating Curzon. Each incident was swallowed by his colleague. To offer defiance and a show of spirit would mean resignation from office. Lord Curzon was not a man prepared to remove himself from the seats of power.

It seemed to some contemporaries that Lord Milner was, in one sense, Lloyd George's most formidable colleague. His temper was stern and unbending. He was not a man to be trifled with. Office, for the sake of narrow political advantage, held no attractions for him. However, the Prime Minister understood Milner's position more clearly than anyone else did. He knew that he had nothing to fear from Milner's membership of the Government.

As a youth, David Lloyd George had made a journey to Westminster in order to visit the House of Commons of the day. He listened to the speeches. He came away convinced that he could master every one of the politicians he heard, that he had it in him to dominate the House, and Westminster itself. Years of experience had served only to fortify his youthful convictions. When he met Lord Milner on those various occasions in 1915 and 1916 he accurately gauged the older man's political character.

Although both men had been political enemies in the

days before the war, their largeness of outlook enabled them to put past differences upon one side in the hour of dire emergency.

Lloyd George was always prepared to work with anyone willing to co-operate with him. A partisan capable of dealing severely with his opponents, he never allowed himself to be shackled by the ties of party. In this case he observed that Milner's patriotism was his dominant quality. Milner longed to serve his country. He suffered agonies of spirit during the seventeen months of Asquith's war administration. This distress was obvious to Lloyd George, the master of men. Both understood that Lord Milner was not equipped to win power for himself under the British system of democracy.

Lloyd George seized upon an important fact. He realised that if he gave Milner a place in his Government, if he brought Milner's decade of tedious Opposition to an end, he would win for himself the Proconsul's gratitude, however aloof he seemed to contemporaries.

In the ordinary course, the idea of gratitude is a bizarre element to introduce into political calculations, as more than one politician has discovered to his disadvantage. Such was Lloyd George's genius in dealing with men, however, that he understood Lord Milner's quality. He was unlike the other politicians. The man who gave him a second chance at power would engage Milner's loyalty, a quality not readily given, but not easily abandoned. Lloyd George saw that to appoint Milner to the War Cabinet would win him a resolute, dauntless and immensely capable colleague.

This analysis of their relationship is borne out by a letter Milner wrote to the Prime Minister shortly after the war ended. The struggle had been long. Tempers had flared in the heat of action. Relations had been strained. They had sometimes disagreed. Nevertheless, Lord Milner wrote to Lloyd George:[1]

[1] Lloyd George Papers, Milner to Lloyd George, 7th December 1918. The envelope is marked "Strictly Personal".

. . . I shall always be grateful to you for having given me the opportunity of doing such important work.

I am sure no one else in your position would have given me that chance, and I have sought to repay you by strenuous and loyal service.

Lloyd George knew all this from the beginning. It explains, together with the political calculations set out above, why his choice fell upon Milner in the crucial days of December 1916.

V

Lord Milner's new chief was an interloper in the highest realms of British politics. He did not fit into the customary order of things. With two notable exceptions, he was unlike any of the men who have served as Prime Ministers of Great Britain. Only Disraeli and Ramsay MacDonald may be classed together with Lloyd George as outsiders who managed to swarm to the top of the "greasy pole".

Each of these men reached the highest office only because the political circumstances of his time were curious, singular and untypical. Suspicion and mistrust have always been connected with their names. The reason is clear. They were unable to play the political game in conformity with the familiar rules. Had they tried to do so, defeat would have been their portion.

The man who became Prime Minister in December 1916 was as devious and crafty as any politician of any generation. He was an expert in every device of the intriguer's art. Contemporaries often condemned him as a rabble-rouser. Even his closest colleagues could never be certain of him. Asquith spoke only the truth when he once said that Lloyd George did not inspire trust. Yet, at the supreme crisis of the war he became the King's first Minister. And, in the opinion of many, not one of his contemporaries was so well equipped to discharge the duties of that high office. We must now examine his political personality in order to discover the qualities which enabled him to seize and to keep Lord Milner's devotion and loyalty.

In 1916 Lloyd George was in his fifty-fourth year. He had begun his political course as a Welsh Nationalist, as the champion of his people against the political and religious intolerance of their English neighbours. During the Boer War he enlarged his reputation. In that period he demonstrated moral courage and oratorical ability of such magnitude that he became a national figure. He was accepted by the Radical masses in Great Britain as their hero.

After Asquith became Prime Minister in 1908 he was recognised as his first lieutenant. He carried forward the Radical banner which had languished in defeat for nearly a decade. At the Board of Trade, and later at the Exchequer, he revealed administrative powers of the first class. He could get things done. In the sphere of social reform he stood alone, even in a reforming Ministry. His National Insurance Act of 1911 carried the nation and the people whose lives were affected by it into the modern age. His speeches in the House and in the country roused the ardour of his friends, and the frenzied hostility of his enemies.

Unlike Winston Churchill or Asquith, however, Lloyd George contrived to maintain and even promote friendly personal relationships with a large number of Tories at Westminster during the high summer of the Asquithian Government. He was always prepared to discuss matters with his opponents. He could charm anyone and everyone. His public attacks were balanced by his private courtesies.

In 1910 he urged upon the Conservatives the formation of a National Government so that the major objects of Liberals and Tories alike could be achieved, unhampered by the narrow restrictions of party tradition. Although his plan failed, many of the younger Conservatives never forgot the proposal and the broad outlook of its author.

He could be relied upon to place nation before party whenever a genuine crisis came. In 1911 at the time of the Agadir episode he astonished the Germans by publicly warning them that there were limits to the pacifism of Liberal England.

The coming of war tested Lloyd George more severely than any of the peacetime crises he had surmounted. For a moment, in August 1914, he hesitated. Should he seek to lead and guide the pacifists of Britain, or should he join the great mass of the nation in its desire to aid Belgium and France?

Once his mind was made up, Lloyd George never looked back. He threw himself into the struggle with every ounce of his strength. He soon saw that he was qualified to meet the test. He proved to be a better war leader than any other of his colleagues.

Moreover, at an early stage he realised that the generals, despite a lifetime of training, possessed no secrets that might equip them to control the supreme direction of the State in time of war. His great personal triumph as Minister of Munitions served to fortify him in his belief that he was fitted for the first place in the Government. The Radical orator disappeared from the political scene. In his place there now stood the man who was determined to win the war. Lord Milner observed the change, and acted accordingly.

Can we discover a red thread that links the aspects of Lloyd George's career together, that turns a series of episodes into a unity?

Lloyd George fed upon power. His qualities swelled in the exercise of it. He was a man who dealt in power. As a leader of the Welsh Nationalists, he fought his way to Westminster. As a reforming Minister he established himself upon an eminence in Whitehall. When he became Premier, he dominated the hopes and aspirations of an Empire. Essentially, he was not a Nationalist, or a Radical, or even a reformer. These were the phases of his course. He was a governor of men; one of those who is fitted to direct the lives and energies of his fellows.

Small of stature, Lloyd George throbbed with physical and intellectual energy. He was seldom at rest. Unlike Arthur Balfour, for example, he could never observe the political scene with the weary eye of the satiated aristocrat.

In order to maintain his position he found it necessary to be in action constantly. At all times he felt obliged to prove himself.

He was inordinately proud of his large head. Such are the foibles of great men that he always measured his contemporaries by the size of their heads. Neville Chamberlain, for example, was dismised as a "pinhead" who would never amount to anything in the political world of Westminster. Lloyd George never abandoned this curious opinion, although he was to live to regret it after Chamberlain became the master of the Conservative Party. A handsome shock of hair, worn in a flowing mane that descended below his collar, was another curious source of pride. He wore a fairly full moustache for a different reason. Once, when he shaved it off, he was astonished by the aspect of the thin line of his mouth. The moustache was restored as quickly as nature allowed. Too much that was better hidden from the eyes of men was revealed by the absence of this facial adornment.

Although he took pride in these minor details of his physical appearance, no man was more of a realist than the new Prime Minister. The weaknesses, ambitions and idiosyncrasies of other men were qualities to be fastened upon for his own purposes. Flattery might work with one colleague, an air of honest purpose with another, the harsh demands of the man of power with a third. Lloyd George was a master of all these roles. He seldom made a mistake in dealing with men.

Loyalty was a political concept that he never understood. When a subordinate had served his purpose, he was jettisoned with ruthless speed. In the same way, if a political object could not be attained frontal assault, there was always another way round.

This was the man who now attracted Lord Milner's loyalty. One admirer has offered posterity this striking picture of Lloyd George as Prime Minister:[1]

[1] Lord Beaverbrook, *Men and Power*, p. 344.

Perhaps we are too near the masterpiece to see the real worth of the picture. We can say, however, that in the day of our dire need, when the blast of the terrible one was against the wall, a strange figure sprang into the arena to do battle.

It was clad in a jewelled breastplate set in a vesture of rags and tatters. It faltered in its walk, and yet leapt with a wonderful swiftness. The sword looked as fragile as a rapier and yet smote with the impact of a battle-axe. As it was held on high, so was the hope of Britain. And when the swordsman stumbled, anxiety filled the breasts of the multitude.

Lord Milner's appreciation, though less exotic, was similar to this one. The reader will recall his distress at one period of his service in South Africa, when he was upset by the interference of the politicians at home. Then, he had cried out for a real leader. "Perhaps", he had written to Lady Edward Cecil, "perhaps a great *Charlatan*—political scallywag, buffoon, stump orator and in other respects popular favourite—may some day arise, who is nevertheless a *statesman*—the combination is not impossible—and who, having attained . . . power by popular art, may use it for national ends". Lord Milner believed that this was the case with the new Prime Minister. In his opinion, everything depended upon Lloyd George.

We shall see in the further course of our narrative that where Lloyd George led, Lord Milner was prepared to follow. On several critical occasions he supported the Prime Minister with a bravery and steadfastness that outmatched Lloyd George's own consistency of purpose. Milner was convinced that the hopes of the country lay with Lloyd George. For this reason he willingly took up service as his lieutenant. The Lloyd George Government has been described as a "Dictatorship in Commission"; the same authority has also referred to his War Cabinet as a "band of brothers". For Lord Milner, these were accurate descriptions. When he took office as Minister Without Portfolio in December 1916 he resolved to serve Lloyd George to the limit of his physical and mental capacities. By doing so, he believed that he would be serving the best interests of Britain and the Empire. As a politician, he was grateful to the man who now placed power and authority in his hands. Asquith had refused to do so. When the Tory leaders joined the Coalition in May 1915, he had been neglected by the men who professed to admire his unrivalled qualities. Now, the political sham was over. As a patriot, Lord Milner was prepared to set aside the prejudices of the past in order to work with the charlatan who proposed to use his power for one purpose only, the highest national object, the defeat of the public enemy.

XV. The Milner-Lloyd George Alliance

The new system – Lord Milner's outstanding quality as an administrator – How the Milnerites served Lloyd George – The Imperial War Cabinet – Milner urges a Federal scheme upon the Prime Minister – Milner's plan invalid – Lord Milner's Imperial legacy – The mission to Russia – The Rome Conference – Lloyd George and the Milner report – Lord Milner's Committee on Manpower and Recruiting – The way in which the business of the War Cabinet was carried on – Menace of the submarines – Milner's supreme efficiency – The effect of the sunshine of office – Lord Hankey and the Milnerian myths – The Corn Production Bill of 1917 – A revolutionary change – The Opinion of Lloyd George – Lord Milner's contribution.

I

THE new Government was dedicated to a more effective prosecution of the war. It came into existence for that purpose. It would survive only if contemporaries believed it was discharging that paramount duty. It was beset by a host of enemies—in all parties. They lay in wait to strike, whenever opportunity offered.

Lloyd George had severed his established ties with the Liberals. Lord Milner enjoyed no regular or acknowledged position in any party. They were more vulnerable than their colleagues in the War Cabinet, in case failure doomed the efforts of the new combination.

Their colleagues were relatively secure. Bonar Law was still the formal leader of the Tories. Arthur Henderson's grasp upon the Labour Party was firm. Lord Curzon continued to enjoy the support of the Conservatives. For

Lloyd George and Milner, however, there would be no place in any further arrangements between the political leaders, in case the Government of December 1916 were to be replaced. In these circumstances, Ministers set to work at once.

The essence of the new system lay in the small War Cabinet of five members. This body enjoyed supreme power in the State. Unlike the Asquithian War Committees of 1914–16, the Lloyd George Cabinet exercised the authority of an effective supreme command. The whole machinery of Government was engaged in order to put its decisions and directives into instant effect. Power was surrendered into the hands of Lloyd George, Curzon, Milner, Henderson and Bonar Law so that the war might be won as speedily as possible. In combination, as members of the War Cabinet, they became a central organ for the direction of the war.

A chief object of the new Government was to avoid the mistakes that had ruined Asquith. His Ministry had been unable to reply with any effect to the charge that there was a lack of central control over war policy. Men lost faith in Asquith's war management because it seemed to lack grip and energy. It was necessary to erect something new upon the wreckage of the Asquithian system.

For the sake of efficiency, it was decided that the traditional idea of collective responsibility should apply only to the five members of the War Cabinet. No other Ministers were involved in the obligations and liabilities of the Government, as a corporate entity. Not even the Foreign Minister, usually a key member of any administration, was touched by the collective responsibility of the War Cabinet. These five men alone were responsible as the supreme governors of the State. Their power was not divided among their Ministerial colleagues.

It followed that the compromises and concessions required of Ministers in peacetime, in order to satisfy the scruples of their associates, did not apply. The urgent requirements of war took first place. It was no longer necessary, as it had been in Asquith's time, to refer the decisions of the War Committee to the consideration of a Cabinet of twenty-odd members. Business could be discharged more quickly and more effectively under the new system.

With the exception of Bonar Law who was Chancellor of the Exchequer and Leader in the House of Commons, the members of the War Cabinet were unencumbered by Departmental duties. They were spared all connection with the routine of administration. Instead, they met daily in order to control administration and decide policy. Experts and Ministers were only summoned to their meetings for a particular purpose. They were not regular members of the war Government.

The members of the War Cabinet presided over inter-departmental committees. They co-ordinated the work of several allied Departments as overseers, unburdened by everyday routine. In this sphere of Government, Lord Milner's qualities were outstanding. In time, he became the fireman of the War Cabinet. Whenever an administrative problem threatened to flare out of control, he was sent to put out the flames.

While Lloyd George leaned upon Bonar Law for political support, he came to rely upon Lord Milner in the administrative sphere. Milner's position has been accurately described by Dr. Addison, who observed the new system from within:[1]

> . . . it is the custom to refer questions affecting big problems belonging to a number of different Departments to individual members of the War Cabinet. . . With a man of Milner's capacity it works excellently, but for some time past extra work has been packed onto him because of his splendid efficiency. Henderson is really not his best at a job like this. . . Curzon does his share but is very slow, and Bonar, of course, is full with House of Commons work and the Exchequer, so that there is really only Milner of good administrative capacity to do this kind of thing. . .

A second important feature of the new system was the Secretariat of the War Cabinet. Under the command of Sir

[1] Addison, *Four and a Half Years*, vol. II, p. 392.

Maurice Hankey, the principal task of this Secretariat was to make certain that the new Government worked efficiently.

Hankey's Secretariat was charged with a great variety of duties. They drew up an Agenda paper for the meetings of the War Cabinet. Each official or Minister who was summoned to the Cabinet received a copy of the Agenda, and he was informed of the time when his business would be dealt with. At the meetings of the War Cabinet, Hankey and his staff took notes of the discussions, and later summarised them as Cabinet Minutes which were circulated to those members of the administration who were involved. Definite decisions were thus recorded in writing, and made patent to all. Ministerial or Departmental delays or evasions were no longer possible under this system. It was difficult to evade the wrath of the Prime Minister in the face of these recorded directions and decisions. In addition, the secretaries were also charged with making certain that the Departments acted in good time, after the War Cabinet had determined upon some action or line of policy.

The third aspect of Lloyd George's Government was his personal Secretariat in the Garden Suburb. Their task was to deal with the immediate requirements of the Prime Minister, and to provide him with ideas, suggestions, and proposals for the more efficient conduct of his business.

The new system was early described by Leo Amery, in a letter to "Billy" Hughes, the Prime Minister of Australia. Amery's comments are a valuable contemporary account of the working of the Lloyd George Government from its earliest days. They make clear the differences between Lloyd George's system and that of Asquith. On 8th January 1917 he wrote to Hughes:[1]

... We have ... swept away altogether the old system ... of twenty-three gentlemen assembling without any purpose and without any idea of what they were going to talk about, and eventually dispersing for lunch without any idea of what they had really discussed or decided, and certainly without any recollection on either point three

[1] Amery Papers, Amery to Hughes, 8th January 1917.

months later. Under the new system the Cabinet has definite agenda; there are no speeches but only short, business-like discussions between the four or five Cabinet Ministers and the Departmental Ministers or professional experts brought in for the discussion; full Minutes are taken, more particularly of the actual decisions arrived at; these are circulated the same day . . . and the Secretariat assumes that the decisions hold good and makes it its business to see that the Departments are informed of the decisions and carry them out.

There is of course a little trace of touchiness here and there among Departmental Ministers who are not in the Cabinet that their status has been lowered. . .

Lloyd George is of course wonderfully quick and active. . . But it is invaluable having Milner, with his steadiness and strength of mind alongside him. . .

In fairness to Asquith, it must be noticed that his Government had done much to pave the way for these developments. His latest reforms had made his War Committee more efficient than it had been. An Agenda was issued before each of its meetings. Records of its discussions were kept in manuscript. The War Cabinet Secretariat was developed from the Secretariat of the Asquithian War Council.

Nevertheless, and this is the important point, contemporaries were convinced that the new system was infinitely more effective. Amery's letter, however accurate, was the report of a partisan. But we should notice that partisan accounts like this one were an essential aspect of Lloyd George's tenure of power.

Here, the Milnerites served him with brilliant skill. Lord Milner and his friends had important acquaintances in London, in Westminster, in the country, and in the furthest reaches of the Empire. They spread broadcast the news of the new and more efficient system created by the coup of December 1916. They were responsible, in good part, for the way in which men now looked upon the Government, and how they contrasted it with what had gone before.

II

As soon as Lord Milner became a member of the Government, he resolved to bring the Dominions into closer co-operation with the Cabinet in London. It was upon his initiative that the Prime Ministers of the Dominions were invited to London in the middle of December 1916. His success in this area of Empire relations worked a profound if unexpected change in his Imperial outlook.

When war was declared in 1914 the decision was made by the Imperial Government, acting upon its own initiative. Nevertheless, a state of war was at once created between the whole of the British Empire and Germany. Despite this consequence of the declaration of war, no demands were made by the Cabinet in London upon the Dominions for naval, military or financial assistance.

The autonomy of the Dominions was respected with scrupulous rigidity. Their offers of help were gratefully received; but the Dominions were never pressed to play a co-ordinated part in the war activities of the Empire.

In the period 1914–16, the Imperial Government was so careful in this sphere that its active co-operation with the Dominions languished, to the detriment of the war effort. Early in 1915 Lord Milner and others urged the Asquith Government to summon an Imperial Conference, to be held in London. Their appeals met with no success.

On 15th July, 1915, Lord Milner, in a speech at the United Empire Club, took up the matter in its widest connotation. He expressed the hope that an "Imperial Cabinet" might be established: "We should have", he said, "a single British State embodying all the scattered portions of our race throughout the world . . . free and independent in their local concerns, but standing as one State among the nations. . ."

Until Lloyd George came to power, Lord Milner was disappointed by the attitude of the British Government. However, at an early meeting of the War Cabinet Lloyd George agreed that the Prime Ministers of the Dominions should come to London for a series of meetings. The object of these meetings was to consider more efficient methods for the prosecution of the war, and those terms of peace which might prove acceptable to the Empire as a whole.

The Prime Minister of Australia was unable to attend the London Conference because of a political crisis at home. In consequence, Leo Amery, who did much of the secretarial work in connection with these meetings, wrote to him in order to make clear the purpose of the Imperial Government's invitation. Amery explained that the Dominion Prime Ministers would sit together with the members of the Lloyd George Cabinet, as an Imperial War Cabinet. They would deal with the issues of the war, and the terms of the peace. At the same time another series of meetings would be held, known as the Imperial War Conference, at which the overseas representatives including the colleagues of the Dominion Prime Ministers would discuss those Imperial problems unconnected with the war. Amery wrote to Hughes:[1]

> As regards the invitation to the Conference, the main idea which decided the Cabinet to make it a Meeting of the War Cabinet and not of the Conference in the ordinary sense, was to lay emphasis on the full equality of status between the Dominion Prime Ministers and the Ministers here, and the right of the Dominion Ministers to have the fullest say, and to have it in good time, on the question of the terms of Peace . . . what is really happening . . . is that the Imperial Government is being carried on by a small Committee of Public Safety, which, though it has not been called into being by a vote either of the Electorate or the House of Commons, does command general confidence; and that Committee of Public Safety will be temporarily enlarged to include men who represent the public confidence of the rest of the Empire . . . the urgent thing is to get the half dozen or so strongest men in the Empire together to make sure, first, of winning the war, and then of not allowing that victory to be thrown away in the Peace negotiations. . .

Lord Milner was excited by the vistas opened up by the prospect of an Imperial War Cabinet. It seemed to him that here at last was the opportunity to establish that organ of

[1] Amery Papers, Amery to Hughes, 8th January 1917. Amery did the secretaria work for the Conferences at the insistence of Lord Milner.

Empire Government he had urged upon his fellow Britons for years past.

His ardour was reflected in a report which Leo Amery sent to the Australian Prime Minister. On 9th May 1917 Amery wrote to Hughes:[1]

> . . . The experiment of an Imperial Cabinet was felt to be so satisfactory by everyone that the question of its perpetuation was mooted privately. . . There was a good deal said in favour of trying to preserve direct continuity for the rest of the war by letting each Dominion appoint a confidential Minister here in London with a view either to a meeting of the Imperial War Cabinet being summoned say once a week, or at any rate to their being invited to all meetings of the British War Cabinet where matters of general Imperial concern were discussed. Apparently, however, neither the Colonial Office nor Borden nor Smuts liked the idea, their feeling being that the Imperial Cabinet should essentially consist of Prime Ministers or actual right-hand men, and in the end the suggestion of making the Imperial Cabinet annual, which I understand was originally Borden's prevailed. . .

In this case, it is clear that Amery's enthusiasm for Empire coloured his description of developments at the Imperial War Cabinet. Like Lord Milner, he was so anxious to see the creation of a genuine Imperial Government that he misread the situation. The Imperial Cabinet, though it met again in 1918, did not become an annual event. Subsequent meetings of the leaders of the Empire were not regularised; they were regarded as *ad hoc* reunions. Furthermore, although the participants looked upon the meetings of the Imperial War Cabinet as beneficial, disturbances marred the proceedings of the delegates. Lord Milner, in particular, threatened to "break-up" the Conference if his views were rejected.

At this time, Walter Long was Secretary of State for the Colonies. He was not a member of Lloyd George's War Cabinet. However, he was always jealous of his rights and prerogatives. When the Dominion Prime Ministers sat together with the members of the War Cabinet, Long insisted that he should be present at every meeting of the

[1] Amery Papers, Amery to Hughes, 9th May 1917.

Imperial War Cabinet. He argued that the office of Colonial Secretary would be diminished if he were left out. His arguments were so strong that Ministers agreed to include him as a member of the Imperial War Cabinet.

Although he was a member of the Government, Long still enjoyed close connections with the Unionist Business Committee in the House of Commons. Early in April 1917 when the Imperial Conference had being going on for nearly a month, Long told Professor Hewins of the Unionist Business Committee that: "Milner was trying to get the Premiers into a Federal scheme, but he did not think he would succeed".[1]

According to Walter Long, Lord Milner pressed the Dominion Prime Ministers to accept a Federal arrangement for the Government of the Empire. When they refused to do so, Milner threatened to destroy the Conference. Professor Hewins wrote in his diary that Walter Long told him: "Things were not improved by the attempt of Milner and his friends to stampede the Premiers into Federation and then, according to W. L., to break up the Conference".[2]

III

The Imperial War Cabinet of British Ministers, Dominion Premiers and the representatives of India met on fourteen separate occasions between 20th March and 2nd May 1917. They did valuable work for the prosecution of the war. They resolved that an Imperial Cabinet should be held annually, or even at times of crisis, but this resolution was stillborn, in its largest aspects. A unanimous resolution was passed in favour of Imperial Preference. Lord Milner presided over a subcommittee that dealt with the non-territorial terms of peace that could be accepted by the Empire.

Nevertheless, his chief object, his goal for years past, the establishment of some form of Imperial Federalism, was

---

[1] Hewins, *Apologia of an Imperialist,* vol. II, p. 134.
[2] *Ibid.*, p. 144.

not accepted by the Dominion Prime Ministers. He was bitterly disappointed by his failure to convince them of the value of his scheme.

This harsh experience as a member of the Government forced Lord Milner to realise for the first time that the plan he had urged for more than a decade was not a measure of practical Imperial politics. As we have seen in an earlier chapter, Milner believed that the unity of the Empire could be achieved if a new instrument of Government, a Council of Empire, were created for the purpose of dealing with the purely Imperial business of Britain and the Dominions.

He and his friends had savagely criticised Campbell-Bannerman, Asquith and the Liberals in general because they had refused to accept this idea in the years between 1905 and 1916. Now, at last, Lord Milner saw that his proposal could not be put into effect.

His great plan for a Council of Empire was invalid. The Dominion Prime Ministers refused to accept it. They were unwilling to surrender any of their sovereign authority, in the way that Lord Milner desired.

On this occasion the Liberals had nothing to do with the rejection of the Milner plan. They had been dispersed as a result of the events of December 1916. The plan was without validity because it was not acceptable in the Empire as a whole.

However attractive to the Imperialists in Great Britain, the entire conception was based upon a fallacy. Lord Milner had failed to take into account the strength of national feeling in the Dominions. Dominion Nationalism, and not the hostility of the "Liberal enemies of Empire", was responsible for the ruin of the dream he had cherished since the end of the South African War.

Leo Amery, writing years later, explained this significant change in Lord Milner's outlook:[1]

Up to the First World War he certainly hoped for the embodiment of Imperial unity in some formal constitutional machinery . . . some

[1] See his introduction to Halperin, *Milner and the Empire*, p. 15.

Council of Empire definitely entrusted with the general control of foreign policy and defence, and, if possible, also of the Dependent Empire. But I believe that the success of the Imperial Cabinet system in that war . . . convinced him that the method of intimate consultation would serve his purpose. . . At any rate, I do not remember his ever recurring to his earlier conception in the years during which we worked together afterwards.

Amery has further explained in this commentary that Lord Milner, in these circumstances, fell back upon one fundamental principle which "in his mind . . . overrode all others . . . that of the complete equality of the partner nations of the Commonwealth. . ."

We have to observe that this conception did not seem very different from the ideas adduced by Sir Henry Campbell-Bannerman, as early as 1903. The reader may recall how in the third chapter of this history we saw that Sir Henry, in that year, explained that he looked upon the Empire as a "commonwealth of free nations", which depended for existence upon the exercise of Liberal principles.

Does this mean that Lord Milner at last recognised the value of his old opponent's Imperial outlook? This was not the case.

Lord Milner, in his heart, still hoped for the kind of formalised unity he had advocated for so many years. When he realised that it could not be achieved easily, he turned to another of his old concepts, one he had always cherished, since the earliest days of his political life. This was that British Race Patriotism that he had urged in his electoral campaign of 1885, and in all the years that followed.

No experience of practical politics ever weakened this aspect of his thought. For him, the unity of the British Race always remained as *the* practical necessity. Although Amery never placed any prominence upon this strand of Lord Milner's Imperial aspirations, it always dominated Milner's outlook.

Constitutional schemes and plans might be accepted or rejected, according to the caprices of the times. For Lord Milner, the unity of the British Race, however it might be achieved, always stood out as the cardinal object of any British Imperialist. He never concerned himself with the question of whether or not a united Commonwealth could be created upon such a basis in the twentieth century. So far as he could reckon, it was the only valid foundation of Empire. If he abandoned the idea of a Council of Empire, if he gave up his Federal proposals, he remained a British Race Patriot to the end. Formalised machinery of government was peripheral to his thought. He laboured as a politician and a statesman for the sake of the British Race. He was convinced that the Empire could prosper only as a result of the co-operation of the members of that Race.

These concepts had nothing in common with those of Sir Henry Campbell-Bannerman. He was interested in a Commonwealth made up of a community of many nations. Lord Milner, for his part, was dedicated to a *British* Empire. That was the essence of the Imperial legacy he left behind him. No experience, either in opposition or in power, ever affected this fundamental doctrine. His Race Patriotism was the mainspring and the motive force in all that he sought to accomplish, in every phase of his life.

IV

Even before the invitations were despatched to the Dominion Prime Ministers, Lloyd George decided to send Lord Milner on a mission to Russia. The Prime Minister always believed that neglect of the Eastern Front was the fatal blunder of Allied strategy.

The man he now selected as head of the delegation to the Russians had to be one who enjoyed his confidence. For Lloyd George, the matter was vital and urgent. Victory in the war seemed to him to depend upon a revival of Russia's military capacities.

Although several candidates were considered, as early as 10th December 1916 Lloyd George fixed upon Lord Milner as the Minister to be charged with this high task. He had already observed Milner with very great care, and was pleased with what he had seen. On the evening of that day Lloyd George remarked to his crony, Lord Riddell: "Milner strikes me as very able. I watched him very carefully today. He picked out the important points at once".[1]

As soon as Lloyd George seized power, he determined to revive his opposition to the strategic plans of the Allied military leaders. As we have seen, in November 1916 he had been completely out manoeuvred by the generals at the Paris Conference. In his anger, he had then decided to strike down the Asquith Government in order to reassert the authority of the civilians who were ultimately responsible for defeat or victory. Now, as Prime Minister, he hoped to be in a position to change the strategic arrangements that had already been agreed upon for the year 1917. The mission to Russia was an integral part of his new plan.

In December the Government Departments were required to prepare detailed memoranda for his purpose. Sir Maurice Hankey and his staff, under the Prime Minister's direction, drew up a paper which set out Lloyd George's policies and strategy. Thus armed, he made ready to attend the Rome Conference of Allied civilian and military leaders. He selected Lord Milner as his principal colleague for this conference. His idea was that the Allied discussions at Rome should be continued and brought to a conclusion when their missions arrived in Russia.

At the Rome Conference, which met in the first days of January 1917, Lloyd George argued that the Russian masses had to be armed adequately, if they were to continue to play any part in the war. He pointed out that the Russians could not be helped by attacks on the Western Front. This method, he said, had been tried throughout 1916. It had failed miserably, whatever the generals might think or say.

The Prime Minister begged the generals to reconsider their policy for 1917. He suggested an Allied attack upon

[1] Riddell, *War Diary*, p. 232.

the Italian Front, in order to avoid the impregnable defences of the enemy in France. He insisted that Russia was the weak spot of the Grand Alliance, and he argued that closer co-operation with the Russian leaders was indispensable for the Allied cause, in every theatre of the war.

Lloyd George failed in his principal objects at the Rome Conference. The plans drawn up by the generals at Chantilly were not discarded. The blood test of attrition was to be tried out again, as the Allied programme for 1917. However, it was agreed that detailed discussions must be held with the Russian leaders in order to discover their exact needs and requirements.

It was in these circumstances that Lord Milner and his staff, together with emissaries of the French and Italian Governments, sailed from Oban for Russia on the 21st January 1917. They were bound for the first formal Allied meeting of the war on the Eastern Front.

Lord Esher and others had warned Milner not to go. Missions to the East had been employed before to rid Whitehall of some eminent personality who had outlasted his welcome in Government circles. The bitter fate of Lord Kitchener was in everyone's mind. Journeys to Russia were not dangerous merely in a political sense. Lives might be lost upon such excursions.

Nevertheless, Lord Milner gauged the situation more accurately than his friends. If Lloyd George had begun to appreciate his quality, he already understood the Prime Minister. He realised how important was the Russian mission as a part of Lloyd George's entire strategic outlook.

One incident of this Russian mission deserves our immediate attention. In 1917 R. H. Bruce Lockhart was serving as a diplomatist in Russia. He acted as Lord Milner's interpreter upon several occasions. Milner's charm captured his loyalty at once. He has given the clearest proof of Lord Milner's ability to win the devotion of his subordinates:[1]

---

[1] R. H. Bruce Lockhart, *Memoirs of a British Agent*, (London, 1932) p. 208.

I find it hard to write of Lord Milner in anything but superlatives. . . His nobleness of mind, his entirely natural charm of manner, his lofty idealism, the complete absence of ambitious scheming or of anything approaching self-conceit in his character and his broad and vigorous patriotism made him the ideal inspirer of youth. With young men, he was at his best. . . I must have been one of the last young men to worship at his feet and there I have remained . . . he stands out as an example to the country of the ideal public servant . . . among all the so-called great men of the world whom I have met there has been none who in this respect is fit to hold a candle to Milner. . .

Although this Russian journey involved Lord Milner in the first of his great missions to the seats of the war, his activities in Russia were of little value. The revolution broke out less than a fortnight after he left the country. The new masters of Russia who eventually assumed power entertained other objects than an Allied victory.

When Lord Milner returned to London he allowed it to be known that, in his opinion, there would be no revolution in the country until after the war. He also reported to the War Cabinet that the talk about a revolution in Russia was greatly exaggerated.

These impressions later provided Lloyd George with an opportunity to exercise his capacity for sarcasm, derision and irony, congenial qualities in which he excelled. In his *War Memoirs* he wrote:[1]

The Head of the British Delegation, Lord Milner, was by training and temperament a bureaucrat. He knew nothing of the populace that trod the streets outside the bureau. He did not despise them. He just left them out of his calculations. . . Henry Wilson was . . . a professional soldier. The soldiers were not supposed to take cognisance of the people, except the specimens who joined the Army. . . So he quite independently and from another angle supported Milner in the conclusion that there was no danger of any upheaval in the immediate future. The chief missioners therefore were unanimously of opinion that although revolution was inevitable, it would be postponed till after the War. . .

Having regard to the warnings which were blaring at them in every direction, it is incomprehensible that they should have been so deaf and blind. It is one more proof of the way in which the most intelligent

[1] Lloyd George, *War Memoirs*, vol. I, pp. 942–3.

human judgment has always been misled by the tapestries of an established order without paying sufficient regard to the condition of the walls they hide and on which they hang. . .

It has been said that Lloyd George never forgave Lord Milner for this Russian report.[1] This was not the case. The passages reproduced above were written in the leisure of retirement when indulgence was the order of the day, when the issues were no longer of immediate importance. At the time, Lloyd George drew a very different conclusion from the report Lord Milner submitted to authority. It was a conclusion that excited his hopes and inclined him to place much of his faith in the alliance that was developing between Milner and himself.

In this report Lord Milner wrote: "It might be good policy to sacrifice some addition of strength on the Western Front for the purpose of supplying Russia's urgent needs. For it is at least possible that an amount of material which would not make any vital difference . . . on the Western Front might make the whole difference between success and failure on the Eastern Front".

Here was Lord Milner, the champion of the Army, the hero of the generals, urging strategic suggestions of an order which the soldiers had always dismissed as the nonsense of civilian amateurs. Lloyd George seized instantly upon this passage of the Milner report. It gave him much ground for speculation.

Despite Milner's friendship with the generals, it now seemed possible that his largeness of outlook in strategic matters might permit him to appreciate the Prime Minister's case. Lloyd George was excited by the prospect. In his *War Memoirs* he wrote of the Milner report:[2]

These quotations show how firmly Lord Milner had come to support the view which . . . had long been urged by me, that if a share of the ammunition blazed away in France on senseless and sanguinary attacks

---

[1] For a recent statement of this opinion see the *Irish Independent* for 30th August 1958.

[2] Lloyd George, *War Memoirs*, vol, I, p. 934.

... had been given to the Russians, Serbians and Roumanians, it would have enabled them to roll back the foe and produce decisions.

Lloyd George knew that a bitter struggle with the generals lay ahead of him. A collision was bound to come. When the fatal hour arrived, he would need all the political support he could get.

He had beaten Asquith. The generals still remained. Their defences were as impregnable as the enemy fortifications in the West. Lord Milner had not yet abandoned their camp for that of the Prime Minister. But his Russian report revealed that he could think for himself, a rare quality that Lloyd George appreciated in his colleagues. Milner was prepared to learn. He was ready to accept new suggestions and new ideas. Lloyd George could hardly ask for more in the first months of his Premiership. And he was a man who knew how to suggest things to a colleague.

This report convinced Lloyd George that he had chosen well when he selected Milner for the mission to the East. Perhaps the generals had won at Paris in 1916, and at the Rome Conference in January 1917. The game was not yet over. The Prime Minister was determined to try yet another fall with the military leaders.

If he abandoned his opposition to their strategy, it could only mean the slaughter of Britain's manhood, to no valid purpose. Lloyd George had not become Prime Minister for such an object. He was ready to defy them at every opportunity. In order to make this defiance effective, it would be necessary to gather his political reserves for an attack upon their plans. The adherence of Lord Milner would be a massive addition to his forces. This development, as a result of the mission to Russia, now seemed a possibility of British politics in 1917.

This was one immediate result of the Milner mission to Russia. Others were of such consequence, to himself and to the country, that we must postpone analysis of them to a later chapter of our study.

V

When Lord Milner returned from his Eastern excursion, he took up those administrative burdens he could bear better than any other member of the War Cabinet.

The task of Ministers was to make the entire nation more efficient as an instrument of war. Lord Hankey has accurately described the functions of Lloyd George's colleagues in this tremendous undertaking.[1]

Bonar Law was the first lieutenant whose political authority enabled the Government to exist, in the first place. His advice was more important to the Prime Minister than that of any other counsellor.

Lord Curzon's energy and industry were matched only by his eloquence. However, "what he lacked was resource in finding solutions to the problems he stated so well".

---

[1] For these comments on the members of the War Cabinet, see Hankey, *The Supreme Command*, vol. II, pp. 578–9. His sober analysis completely refutes the hagiography of the *Religio Milneriana*. For example, Professor Halperin in his *Lord Milner and the Empire*, p. 158, writes: "It is no exaggeration to say that with the exception of Lloyd George, from the end of 1916 until 1918, Milner was the most important personality in the Government". Lord Milner's great achievements do not require the extravagant, and sometimes inaccurate, praise that dominates every page of this book. No service is rendered to Milner's memory by the adoration heaped upon him by Professor Halperin, who attempts the canonization of his subject with a fervour that exceeds that of the British Milnerites. By contrast, Lord Hankey's comments furnish the student with that kind of careful analysis that helps in the difficult business of understanding the past. Professor Halperin at p. 158 writes: ". . . Lloyd George emphasised Milner's predominant role in the War Cabinet. In the preface to . . . his *War Memoirs* are the names of the very few . . . leaders to whom he considered the victory of the Allies was really due; that of Milner heads the list". This statement is incorrect. In his preface Lloyd George wrote as follows: "I have gladly recognised the service rendered by Bonar Law, Milner, Balfour, Smuts, Borden, Hughes, Geddes, Maclay, Arthur Henderson, Barnes, Clemenceau and many others". Milner's name does not head this "list"; and there is no suggestion that Lloyd George had worked out any priority of service in adducing these names in the order that he did. We should also notice the following: Sir Evelyn Wrench in his *Milner*, p. 351, states that Amery and Lloyd George, at the end of the war, drew up separate lists of "those who had made the most difference in winning the war . . ." The lists, when compared, were identical: Lloyd George, Milner, Henry Wilson, Hankey. But Amery in his *Political Life*, vol. II, p. 172, makes it clear that the lists were drawn up by himself, Austen Chamberlain, F. S. Oliver, and Dawson. Lloyd George was not involved at all, in this "list-making". The opinions of the others are certainly valid and worthy of attention, but we should be clear about the authorship of these lists.

Arthur Henderson, in Lord Hankey's opinion, was without the glitter of his formidable colleagues. His presence in the War Cabinet made certain that the "façade" of national unity was preserved.

Lord Milner was slow but sure in dealing with the problems that confronted the Government: "Lloyd George used him, as he used Curzon, for many purposes, including the chairmanship of many committees that were set up by the War Cabinet to inquire into matters involving intricate detail".

The nature of Lloyd George's co-operation with Lord Milner is well illustrated by their work in dealing with the vital issue of manpower. The new Government desired to conscript men for industry, as well as for military service. It was recognised, however, that the British worker would not readily submit to industrial compulsion.

In order to deal with the problem Lloyd George established a new Department of National Service, in the first days of his Ministry. Neville Chamberlain was selected to take charge of the Department. He was required from the first to work very closely with the representatives of organised Labour. His task was to create a machine to control and direct, in the most efficient manner, the whole manpower of the country. At first, the voluntary system would be tried; but if it failed, the Government was ready to furnish Chamberlain with additional powers to compel compliance with his decisions.

On 12th January 1917 a conference was held for Chamberlain's benefit. At this conference, the Prime Minister, Lord Milner, Arthur Henderson, the Minister of Labour, and other authorities discussed with Chamberlain the nature of the organisation he was required to establish, the measures he should adopt, and the powers he would need for his purpose.

In Lloyd George's opinion, the Ministry of National Service was a disappointment and a failure. When Chamberlain was unable to produce instant and effective results, the

Prime Minister became bitterly critical. He plagued Chamberlain's course with Lloyd Georgian malice. In August, as a result of these attentions, Neville Chamberlain resigned. He retired to the more congenial atmosphere of his native Birmingham. Thus was born a bitter feud between the two men that was destined to have serious consequences in a later period of English history.

In these circumstances, Sir Auckland Geddes was asked to take Chamberlain's place. The definition of the exact nature of his task was a vital matter, if the mistakes of the past were not to be repeated. In August Lord Milner was appointed as chairman of a Committee on Manpower and Recruiting. The business of this committee was to set out the functions and duties of the Ministry of National Service.

On 4th August 1917 Lord Milner wrote to Lloyd George about the problem. His letter furnishes us with a clear and exact example of the manner in which the business of the War Cabinet was discharged, on the highest levels. It confirms the opinions of Lord Hankey, to which we have referred above. It reveals that Lloyd George was the master of the system; and that Lord Milner looked upon himself as his administrative handmaiden. This does not imply that Milner, Bonar Law or Curzon did not determine policy, that they did not furnish their chief with advice and ideas; but it does mean that Lloyd George was the overseer of the business of his Government.

If Lloyd George did not dominate his Cabinet colleagues to the extent that Winston Churchill did in the second World War, they, nevertheless, did not embark upon administrative schemes without his entire approval. If Lloyd George's Cabinet was more of a team than Churchill's, there was never any doubt about who was Captain. On the 4th August Lord Milner wrote to the Prime Minister:[1]

My dear Prime Minister,   17 Great College Street.
    I hate adding to your load, but I *do want* ½ hour's talk with you about Recruiting and the Man-Power Question generally. . .

[1] Lloyd George Papers, Milner to Lloyd George, 4th August 1917.

It is a heavy job, but I don't despair of it. I have got ideas about it and know how I should like to proceed. But I don't want to plunge into the jungle without being sure that I am working *on lines which you approve*.

If once we are agreed about the general direction, I am confident that the details can be worked out, & that we can save you & the Cabinet any amount of time and future trouble.

But I am anxious to avoid a false start.

Yours very sincerely,
Milner.

The discussion between Milner and the Prime Minister took place. Lloyd George accepted the ideas his colleague adduced. The functions of the Ministry of National Service were carefully defined. On 12th September 1917 the War Cabinet approved and confirmed the new arrangement. From this time, the new Ministry worked smoothly and efficiently. Despite a false start, the situation was retrieved by the work of Milner, the members of his Committee, including Arthur Henderson, the officials of the Ministry of Labour and those of the Ministry of National Service, all working under the eye of the Prime Minister. It was the Lloyd Georgian system in action.

VI

On 1st February 1917 the German Government embarked upon a policy of unrestricted submarine warfare. This deadly blow was designed to destroy Great Britain's ability to wage war. For much of the year the menace of the submarine was the chief preoccupation of the War Cabinet. Lord Milner played a vital part in re-establishing the British position, gravely weakened by this new assault.

The achievements of the War Cabinet in this sphere must be measured against those of their predecessors in office. During the latter part of 1916 as the sinkings caused by submarines grew in number, the Asquithian Government took an increasingly dismal view of the situation. At a meeting of the War Committee on 9th November 1916

Walter Runciman, the President of the Board of Trade, expressed his opinion that "a complete breakdown in shipping would come before June 1917". He believed that the Allies would be unable to carry on in these desperate circumstances. The policy of unrestricted submarine warfare was designed to make this situation even more critical.

In order to combat the effect of the submarines, the War Cabinet decided upon a number of far-reaching measures. The Navy was pressed to carry the fight to the enemy at sea. It was determined to increase the shipping tonnage available, by a number of expedients. Ships were chartered from neutrals. Tonnage was further increased by a programme of ship construction that drew upon men who in other circumstances would have been assigned to the Army for military service. Vessels were purchased abroad, with little or no thought of the cost in money. In addition, a programme for the restriction of imports was worked out, in order to lighten the burden of the Navy and the merchant marine.

Each of these several policies could be made effective only after the most careful study and investigation. The resources available to the nation had to be measured, weighed and allocated. If even small mistakes were made in this balancing process, disaster was bound to follow as the grip of the submarines tightened upon the flow of imports.

Committees of the War Cabinet were created in order to master the problems involved. Lord Milner and Lord Curzon presided over these committees, which were assigned the task of deciding between the rival claims of the Army, industry and the various Departments of State for tonnage, and for the manpower they required to carry out their functions. Lord Milner's first task was to fix the number of men that were needed by the shipbuilding industry. Dr. Addison has testified to Milner's supreme efficiency in this high and delicate matter:[1]

Lord Milner, after his return from Russia, was the War Cabinet

[1] Addison, *Politics from Within*, vol. II, pp. 33–4.

Minister to whom the difficult and thankless task was allotted of
dealing with the many inter-departmental conflicts that ensued, and the
most tantalising among them was the conflicting claims of the shipyards
for labour and the Army for men. It was a favourite device of the War
Cabinet to saddle Milner with tasks of this sort, but the reason was that
he was so grandly efficient and had such well-balanced constructive
faculties that he stood out as the man for the work.

Of even greater significance was the need to restrict imports. A system of priorities was required in order to exploit,
in the most efficient manner, the tonnage that was available.
In April 1917 British shipping losses amounted to well over
500,000 gross tons. If the limited number of ships plying
between Britain and her sources of raw material brought the
wrong supplies to the ports, they would be contributing
as much to the defeat of the country as the submarines of the
enemy. A vital programme of shipping priorities was
worked out by Lord Milner. Dr. Addison described
Milner's work in this sphere, as follows:[1]

Some time before April the machinery for the restriction of imports
had been got into working order, but the growing danger . . . and the
number of departments involved . . . called for single oversight . . .
and it provided another task for Milner. He continued until 1918 to be
the collecting centre and War Cabinet Minister with oversight of
questions relating to food stocks, to conflicting claims for shipping,
and to additional import restrictions.

Milner never came into the limelight. He disliked it. . . All through
1917 he did heroic work. . .

. . . but there was immensely less shipping to do the work. . .
It was this that made rationing essential for 1918. . . Milner, therefore,
was called upon to prepare a scheme for enabling us, during 1918, to
do with nearly 8,000,000 tons less than we had received in 1917. . .
He felt justified . . . to begin with . . . (a) . . . lower figure. . . The
sequel showed that his forecast was justified. His scheme provided for
reducing munitions imports by 1,500,000 tons, food by 2,500,000 tons,
and timber by 1,000,000 tons. . .

The meaning of these activities was profound. As a
result of his decisions relating to imports, Lord Milner took
under his charge the final solution of the problem of Freedom or Control. The priorities he now established decided,

[1] Addison, *Politics from Within*, vol. II, pp. 57–63.

in good part, which industries would continue to function in the country; they decided the volume of food that was imported; and the amounts of military stores available for the armed forces.

After the United States joined the Allies, the economic situation was completely altered. Unlimited dollar credits now relieved the pressure upon Britain's export industries. There was no longer any need to pay at once for the imports from America. The maintenance of the export trades, for which the Free Traders had fought so hard, became a matter of secondary importance in the British system of war economy.

The limited amount of tonnage available to carry the goods was now the determining factor. Lord Milner decided, in good part, the way in which this tonnage was exploited.

There was never anything like an Economic General Staff in the war organisation of the British Government. Lord Milner's system of import priorities which determined the rival claims of the Departments of State, industry and the armed forces performed some of the functions of such a General Staff. His system, the decisions of the Ministry of Shipping and those of the Allied Maritime Transport Council became the final arbiters in this sphere of the British and Allied war effort.

In this phase of Lord Milner's work reside some of his most important contributions as a member of the War Cabinet. The task demanded the qualities of an exceptionally capable administrator. Milner met the challenge brilliantly. Lloyd George was delighted, and relieved, to have a lieutenant of this high calibre in the company of those who served him in the discharge of his business as Prime Minister.

VII

It is generally recognised that it is more difficult for a politician to act in Opposition than in power. This was the case with Lord Milner. Before he became a member of the War Cabinet, he enjoyed friendly and intimate association with a very small group. Few were those who were permitted to come close to him. However, as the range of his official contacts increased, a larger company of men began to appreciate the true nature of his quality.

Lord Milner was a rigid man who did not make new friends easily. The glib and facile capacity of the politician who could charm each casual acquaintance was completely alien to his nature. Nevertheless, the members of the administration who now began to work with him soon learned that his public image reflected only an aspect of his complicated personality. Men who despised his politics came to recognise and appreciate his natural charm and courtesy. At close quarters they saw that he was totally devoid of personal ambition, that he desired to help his colleagues in their common tasks, that he cared for none of the petty personal triumphs that too often determine the actions of men.

Lord Milner worked well as a member of the team. In a position of power and authority, when he enjoyed the right to put his ideas into effect, the bitterness which distinguished him as a leader of the Opposition disappeared. The sunshine of office thawed his reserve, and allowed his more attractive qualities to predominate.

No one was more hostile to Milner than Dr. Addison, in the years before 1916. Nevertheless, after they had worked together for a time Addison fell under the Milnerian spell. In his memoirs, on several occasions, the doctor expressed regret for his earliest opinions of Milner. In fact, such was the extent of the conversion that it is fair to say that Addison became, in time, a devoted Milnerite. By 1918 he was convinced that: "Except for Bonar and Milner, there is nobody who can give real assistance in the War Cabinet".[1]

Lord Hankey experienced a similar transformation of feeling. His high praise of Milner, however, never degener-

[1] Addison, *Four and a Half Years,* vol. II, p. 484.

ated into the unthinking adulation of the genuine Milnerite. In his *Supreme Command* Hankey always took care to dispel the myths that seemed to grow up about Milner's name. In this connection he mentioned that: "Mark Sykes . . . once drew a delightful cartoon in which Lloyd George was depicted as a 'rogue elephant' chained between two staid old elephants. One of these bore the features of Milner, the other of Curzon. . . Prance and dance as he might, the 'rogue elephant' was firmly held. This cartoon, however, did more justice to Sykes's imagination that to his accuracy, for, in fact, neither Curzon nor Milner ever exercised as much influence over Lloyd George as Bonar Law".[1]

So great was the change produced by office that Lord Milner found that he could associate, upon friendly terms, with men whom he would never have recognised in the years of his Proconsular aloofness. In his diary for August 1917 Lord Riddell, Lloyd George's crony, recorded, after a few hours spent in Milner's company, that: "Milner is a very pleasant, courtly person". This impression was formed by Lord Riddell after a discussion with Milner upon the literature of the ancient Greeks. Here was a remarkable change. Nothing is more indicative of the alterations in Lord Milner's personality, after he won office, than this fact that he could enjoy such cordial relations with the man who was proprietor of the *News of the World*. Gone were the days when Lord Milner confined himself to the select company of his disciples, and a few chosen friends. He had emerged from his shell. After December 1916 he found that he could deal easily with all sorts and qualities of men.

VIII

Lloyd George was particularly impressed by Lord Milner's massive labours in connection with the Corn Production Bill of 1917. This was a revolutionary measure of the very greatest importance. Its immediate effects, in

[1] Hankey, *Supreme Command*, vol. II, p. 578.

wartime, were of profound significance, while its principles have since become a basic part of British economic policy in the twentieth century.

In December 1916 when Lloyd George came to power there was only fourteen weeks' supply of grain in the country. As the submarines increased their pressure upon the flow of imports into Britain, the food situation became increasingly more serious. By mid-April 1917 the amount of wheat in the country was reduced to a nine weeks' supply. As early as 20th March an appeal was issued by the Government which asked the wealthier classes to abstain altogether from eating potatoes, and to consume instead the more expensive cereals, and other vegetables. But such palliatives were of little real value. The shortage of wheat became the most menacing feature of the situation.

As we have seen, Lord Milner was asked by the War Cabinet to investigate and to determine the shipping priorities that would enable the country to meet this challenge to its existence. But the problem naturally lent itself to two general solutions. If a more rational and intelligent exploitation of the shipping resources available could ensure a larger supply of food imports, an increase in the domestic production of wheat and other cereals could also contribute to the relief of the shortage. Lord Milner attacked the problem in both these spheres.

The Asquith Government had refused to accept the recommendations of his Departmental Committee in 1915; at that time his agricultural proposals were dismissed because they involved too great a measure of State intervention in the private sphere. The condition of the country was now far too serious to permit such ancient shibboleths to continue to bar the way to a solution of the food shortage. Lord Milner was given free rein to make any proposals that seemed best calculated to increase the domestic production of wheat, oats and cereals.

His first step was to make certain that the supply of agricultural labourers was not reduced by the demands of the Army for more and more conscripts. In this aspect of his work, he was at once challenged by the generals. Their need for recruits was unlimited. The maw of the stalemate fighting in France could never be filled adequately. In this case, however, the generals encountered a resolution as formidable as their own.

Lord Milner was convinced that the agricultural workers could serve their country best upon the farms, and not in the trenches. He refused to give way. As an administrator, the issue was clear to him. The War Office was required to accept his decisions. Despite his intimate relations with the Army, the soldiers were now given a taste of his unbending firmness in action. In a memorandum dated 31st May 1917, the Army Council complained to the War Cabinet that: "the Army was . . . being supplied with men only after all other national needs had been satisfied".[1] Later, Sir William Robertson, Chief of the Imperial General Staff, complained that: "Milner was all for men for agriculture and we were . . . giving him 80,000 whom he said he could not do without".[2]

The securing of an adequate labour supply was only one phase of Lord Milner's programme. The great requirement was to stimulate production. He proposed to achieve this object by means of the Corn Production Bill of 1917. By the terms of this Bill, a minimum price for wheat and oats was established in the country as a whole. Whenever the average market price fell below this minimum, the occupier of any land upon which wheat or oats had been produced would be entitled to receive a quarterly sum from the State equal to the difference between the minimum price and the average price. In that period this was a revolutionary step. It astonished contemporaries. The Bill struck a murderous blow at the established system of Free Trade. Not since the days of Sir Robert Peel, when protection had been abandoned as a national policy because it favoured landowners

---

[1] Robertson, *Soldiers and Statesmen*, vol. I, p. 312.
[2] Repington, *The First World War*, vol. II, p. 29.

at the expense of the rest of the population, had bounties been paid to agriculturalists.

In the eyes of the Free Traders, led by Reginald McKenna, the State had no right to tamper with the free functioning of the agricultural market. McKenna, in the Commons, led the Liberals in an attack upon the Bill because it re-introduced protection, the very negation of everything Liberal England stood for. The concern of contemporaries over this radical innovation was well reflected in the comment of the *Annual Register* for 1917: "The Corn Production Bill represented . . . the most complete break with the Victorian system of free imports. . . It was by far and away the most important business to which Parliament had put its hand in the first part of the session of 1917".

Nevertheless, this was only a portion of the Milnerian reform. A second part of the Bill provided for the establishment of an Agricultural Wages Board; the purpose of this Board was to introduce a minimum wage for agricultural workmen in every part of the country. A third section of the Bill limited the rights of landowners to raise rents. A fourth part was equally untraditional. In order to make certain of the proper exploitation of the land, in cases where it was not used to its fullest capacities, the Board of Agriculture was empowered to authorise the landlord to remove the inefficient farmer from his tenancy. In case the landlord failed to act, the Board of Agriculture was given authority to end such a tenancy by its own order. The Board was also empowered to take possession of any land not in the occupation of a tenant.

The Corn Production Bill was hotly opposed by the Liberals. Nevertheless, it received the Royal assent on 22nd August. It was one of the major reforms of Lloyd George's wartime administration.

Lloyd George was delighted by Milner's energy in this sphere of his work as a member of the War Cabinet. The Prime Minister was convinced that he had chosen well in selecting Milner as one of his principal colleagues. Amuse-

ment and pride are both reflected in his summing up of
Milner, in *The Truth About The Peace Treaties*. The passage
refers to a high-point in the Milner-Lloyd George alliance:[1]

. . . Milner was much the best all-round brain that the Conservative
Party contributed to our Councils. He had none of Curzon's brilliancy
or Carson's dramatic oratory—he was a poor, dull speaker. He had no
flow of words. He had no colour, his voice had no resonance, his
delivery was halting. . . But in constructive power and fertility of
suggestion he surpassed them all. . . Up till the spring of 1918 it is
difficult to exaggerate his value as a counsellor. . . . He was at his best
when I invited him, as I often did, to a quiet talk in the Cabinet room on
the perplexing questions which constantly arose during the War. He
was dauntless; he never shrank from making or concurring in a proposal because it was original. . . When we came to deal with food
production, his suggestions were revolutionary. When they came up
for discussion in the Cabinet I remember Balfour gaping with
astonishment. Looking at the clock, he turned to his neighbour and
said: "As near as I can reckon we have had one revolution for every
half hour".

If, as has been shown in this chapter, the true nature of
his position has been exaggerated by the fanciful accounts
of the Milnerites, it is nevertheless clear that Lord Milner's
contributions to the efficient functioning of the War
Cabinet were of the highest significance. His supreme skill
as an administrator made itself felt in almost every department of the higher direction of the war. His achievements
vindicated his vicious criticisms of the haphazard methods
pursued under the voluntary system during the years of
Asquith's wartime Premiership. His constructive faculties
mastered the details of the War Cabinet's schemes, and
turned them into effective measures for the successful
prosecution of the war. If he was not Lloyd George's most
"predominant" colleague, the quality of his massive
accomplishments is not diminished by that fact. The Prime
Minister and everyone else concerned with the war direction
of the country recognised his supreme value to the Government. In 1916 and 1917 he proved himself to be an almost
indispensable member of the Lloyd Georgian team.

[1] Lloyd George, *The Truth About The Peace Treaties*, vol. I, p. 261.

XVI.   The Staunch Colleague

The two problems of the Navy and Ireland – Convoys –
Reasons for action over Ireland – Sir John Jellicoe's report
– Lord Milner is involved – Technical arguments – Lloyd
George plans to visit the Admiralty – The convoy plan is
adopted – The comment of Admiral Sims – "Prime
Minister, it may be a fierce attack. Get ready" – Carson fuses
the Irish and Naval problems – The intervention of Sir
Douglas Haig – Lord Milner reveals his hand – Lord Midle-
ton's clarion call – Lord Milner's note of the 5th of June –
A remarkable change of attitude – Lloyd George turns to
the Army – The Milner Plan – A messenger is despatched to
Birchington – Lord Milner's intervention – The Prime
Minister flounders in irresolution – Milner decides the
issue.

I

THE Milner-Lloyd George alliance was not confined
to co-operation in the administrative sphere. The
first half of 1917 witnessed their association in a
political affair that might have spelt ruin for them both.

Sir Edward Carson was always a factor to be reckoned
with in the politics of the first World War. Lloyd George
was afraid of Carson's power, and Carson was often suspicious of Lloyd George. No bond of trust existed between
the two men.

Early in 1917 the Prime Minister became uneasy over the
way in which the Admiralty was conducting its business.
At the same time, he began to seek yet another solution to
the Irish problem, which always vexed the even course of
English politics. Both these issues involved him in a direct
clash with Sir Edward Carson.

As First Lord of the Admiralty, Carson resented the

urgent prodding of the Prime Minister into the affairs of his department. As leader of the Ulstermen, he was instantly aroused by Lloyd George's determination to settle the Home Rule controversy. Lloyd George felt himself bound to take action in both these high matters. Carson was equally resolute in his inclination to defy the Prime Minister in case he proposed to go too far.

This situation, by the late winter of 1917, was fraught with danger for the Government. Lloyd George discovered that Lord Milner was his staunchest ally in the series of crises that followed.

As the submarine attacks increased, Lloyd George became convinced that the Admiralty should try to overcome the danger by resort to convoys of merchant ships, escorted by vessels of the Royal Navy. However, the admirals were not at all certain that convoys were the answer to the problem. Furthermore, they knew that the Navy lacked the resources in destroyers and sloops that would be required to make the convoy system a success.

On 23rd February 1917 the whole matter was "thrashed out" at a meeting at the Admiralty. It was decided then that the convoy plan should not be adopted.[1]

On 8th March in a speech at the Aldwych Club Carson took up the matter in his own decisive fashion. He said: ". . . as long as I am at the Admiralty, the sailors will have full scope. They will not be interfered with by me, and I will allow no one else to interfere with them".

This was a public declaration of his support for the admirals. It was a clear warning to Lloyd George to draw back. It was a signal that wise statesman was not prepared to ignore.

Nevertheless, the Prime Minister's relationship with Carson was now strained in another direction. Lloyd George's Government was sometimes accused of being Sir Edward Carson's tool. Men like Carson and Milner, the critics argued, were using Lloyd George and his Ministry

---

[1] See W. S. Sims, *The Victory at Sea* (London, 1920), pp. 89f.

for their own narrow purposes. For that reason, it was said, the terrible situation in Ireland would remain frozen, though it cried out for a solution of some kind. This was a damaging argument which Lloyd George was required to meet.

His own closest followers were anxious to satisfy the demands of the Irishmen for Home Rule. The Labour Party, an important segment of his Coalition, believed in some amelioration of the condition of Ireland. The votes of the Irish Nationalist Party in the House of Commons were a factor that had always to be considered. In the Dominions, there was grave concern over Ireland in a war fought for the self-determination of peoples. In the United States many politicians and vast sections of the population resented the British handling of Irish affairs. For these cogent reasons, Lloyd George deemed it prudent to take action of some kind. He was prepared to move slowly but the problem, in his opinion, demanded and required exploration.

On 2nd March he had an interview with Sir Edward Carson. They discussed Irish affairs. Lloyd George urged an expedient upon his colleague. Perhaps something could be contrived to deal with the situation. A Royal Commission, the Prime Minister suggested, might be appointed to examine the problem of Ireland.

Lloyd George also presented Carson with a memorandum which had been drawn up by Professor W. G. S. Adams, a leading member of his Private Secretariat, a prominent inhabitant of that Garden Suburb at Downing Street which contributed so much to the stock of the Prime Minister's ideas. In this document, the professor proposed that an Irish Convention should be convened so that the authorities might learn what the Irishmen from North and South could agree upon. If the Irish Convention could adduce a plan, the British Government might then be able to work out an arrangement acceptable to both sides and to themselves.

Carson's advice to the Prime Minister upon this occasion was succinct. On the next day, in a letter to Lloyd

George, he advised the Prime Minister to "leave matters alone".[1]

Their differences of opinion over the work of the Admiralty and over the Irish situation remained unresolved. The two matters marched hand in hand, though they still might be dealt with separately.

Lloyd George paused for a moment. What would be the reaction of his colleagues? He depended upon the support of Tories and Unionists for the existence of his Government. How would Bonar Law react in case a crisis with Carson took place? Even if he could rely upon Bonar Law, he would be injured seriously if Lord Milner chose to adhere to Carson in the event of a showdown. Lord Milner had worked closely with Carson for years past. As allies, they had hammered the Asquith régime without mercy. They were close friends and staunch Unionists, ready enough to sacrifice place and office for principle. How could Lloyd George hope to discharge his heavy tasks in such a precarious condition? He was not the man to abandon his objects easily, even if time were required for him to win out.

II

As the losses from submarines increased to frightful proportions, the Prime Minister determined to take action. He was not satisfied with the attitude of the Admiralty. He later described the condition of the high admirals as one of "crouching nervousness". Too much was at stake for him to allow the terrible losses at sea to continue. If Sir Edward Carson resented his interference with the Navy, then the crisis with Carson would have to come.

In April 1917, Sir John Jellicoe, the First Sea Lord, submitted a memorandum to authority. This paper, entitled "The Submarine Menace and the Food Supply", was a disappointing document to Lloyd George, who burned for positive action. In it, Jellicoe expressed his opinion that the

[1] Colvin, *Carson*, vol. III, p. 240.

maritime condition of the country was very serious. He refused to look upon the convoy system as the final answer to the problem. Instead, he argued that the situation must be met by conserving the food supplies that existed in the country, and by increasing the pressure upon the submarines at sea.

The Jellicoe memorandum at once involved Lord Milner in the problems of the Navy. He was the War Cabinet Minister most directly concerned with the increase of food production at home, and with those shipping priorities which fixed the amount and kind of imports that were brought into the country. He was not satisfied by the Admiralty's proposals to deal with the menace of the submarines.

If Sir Edward Carson and his technical advisers refused to establish the convoy system, they were bound to incur Milner's hostility. So far as he was concerned the matter was not one of personalities, but of administration. If the Navy was not succeeding in its tasks, however novel and difficult they might be, changes would be required in order to produce more beneficial results. Lord Milner was prepared to listen to the technical arguments of the admirals, which were impressive, but if he were once convinced that they were at fault he would not hesitate to act. Those personal and political considerations which weighed so heavily upon Lloyd George were allowed almost no significance in Lord Milner's consideration of the problem.

The Prime Minister was convinced that convoys were the answer to the danger. The admirals argued that there were not enough destroyers to act as escorts. In reply, Lloyd George pointed out that the Grand Fleet, immured in its bases, was protected by a lavish complement of destroyers. To the Admiralty and to Sir John Jellicoe, in particular, this argument was the ridiculous babbling of an amateur strategist, the comment of an ignorant civilian Minister who was not equipped by training or experience to make technical suggestions in time of war. The very fate of the Empire rested upon the Grand Fleet. If the great battleships were reduced in numbers by a series of successful submarine attacks, the Grand Fleet might be unable to meet the challenge of a full-scale engagement with the German Navy. Jellicoe and his admirals were the only people in Britain who could lose the war in an afternoon. If their fleets were beaten at sea by the Germans, the country would be open to invasion, and all would be lost.

There were other technical arguments against the convoy plan. It was feared that the merchant ships would be unable to keep station at sea in large convoys. Accidents and collisions might cause more losses than those inflicted by the enemy. Furthermore, it was doubted if the ports could sustain the burdens of the convoy system. Under that plan, said the Admiralty, the ports would be empty at one moment, and glutted with assembling ships at the next. Time would be lost in loading and unloading cargoes. The convoy plan might be valid, the admirals argued, but the resources of the Navy were still not adequate to put it into effect. As the experts involved in the problem, they were required to deal in practicalities, whatever the Prime Minister urged upon them in his fervour.

On 26th April Lloyd George decided to force the issue. He would wait no longer. He informed the War Cabinet that he proposed to visit the Admiralty himself, in order to establish there those conditions that would relieve the country from the menace that was clutching at its source of life. He meant to force the admirals to accept the convoy plan.

This was a radical step. Lloyd George planned to invade Sir Edward Carson's official preserve, and to take decisions in his room. Carson was not the man to permit anyone to tamper with his prerogatives as a Minister, or to interfere with him in any way. Beyond this personal aspect, Sir Edward placed his complete confidence in Jellicoe and the other serving officers at the Admiralty. He would allow no amateur to tamper with their vital decisions. He had already hoisted the danger signals. In the clash that was now to come, there were bound to be sparks in a restricted area where political gunpowder lay about in profusion.

Lloyd George recognised the danger. He wanted one of his Conservative colleagues to accompany him upon his raid. Bonar Law promptly refused to act as escort. He explained that he had already encountered difficulties with Carson, over the Irish situation.[1] Bonar Law's prudence was wise. Some newspapers already argued that an attack upon the Admiralty was really aimed at Carson, and at the Union with Ireland. Bonar Law remained firm in his decision to stay at home. He would take no part in the forthcoming action.

By 30th April, the fateful day, Lord Curzon had agreed to act as the Prime Minister's Conservative companion, upon the occasion of his visit to the Admiralty. On that day he submitted to Lloyd George a catalogue of subjects which might be raised at the meeting, while he expressed the hope that his list would be of use when the interview took place.[2]

Now the preliminary arrangements were complete. However, Lloyd George knew something of Lord Curzon's record in political affairs. He had, in the past, sometimes urged the most extreme courses upon his Conservative colleagues, only to draw back at the eleventh hour. A discreet distance from the scenes of action often became desirable to Curzon, when issues were forced to their final conclusions. For this reason Lloyd George cast about for a reserve. He wanted a second Conservative string to his bow. Lord Milner was asked to hold himself in readiness on that 30th of April. He was not one who hesitated to follow the extreme course, once he was convinced of its necessity.

---

[1] See Beaverbrook, *Men and Power,* p. 154.
[2] *Ibid,* p. 155.

III

Thus fortified, the Prime Minister repaired to the Admiralty. In his opinion, the meeting justified him in the extreme course he had pursued. When the admirals re-examined the returns of entrances and clearances of ships, it was discovered that a mistake had been made in the figures upon which Naval strategy had been based. Lloyd George believed that the sailors had blundered in their calculations about the number of ships arriving in and leaving British ports. The apologists of the Navy and Carson's biographer have argued that these figures were never taken seriously by the Board of Admiralty. In any case, it was decided to put the convoy plan into effect, upon an experimental basis.

The disputed figures were not the sole cause for this change of policy. On the 6th April 1917 the United States entered the war upon the Allied side. When Admiral Sims, the American officer who was sent to co-ordinate matters, arrived in London, he was at once told the details of the situation by Sir John Jellicoe. On 24th April a squadron of American destroyers was dispatched to Queenstown, to take part in the submarine war. These reinforcements, and the promise of more of the same kind, eased the strained condition of the Royal Navy. They materially altered the Admiralty's attitude towards convoys.

On 30th April Admiral Sims was summoned to the Admiralty, and told by Jellicoe that an experimental convoy would be sent to Gibraltar. The convoy plan was to be given a trial, in the hard conditions of the sea-war. Later that day, Sims dined with Lloyd George, Carson and Lord Milner in order to discuss convoys. His comment upon this meeting is suggestive:[1]

... at dinner I met Mr. Lloyd George, Sir Edward Carson, and Lord Milner, and once more discussed with them the whole convoy idea. I found the Prime Minister especially favourable to the plan and,

[1] Sims, *The Victory at Sea*, p. 95.

in fact, civilians in general were more kindly disposed toward the convoy then seamen, because they were less familiar with the nautical and shipping difficulties which it involved.

Within a month, on 20th May 1917, the first convoy reached England, in perfect safety. This date marked one of the turning points of the war, for a solution to the submarine menace was now at hand. On the day following, 21st May, the British Admiralty decided to adopt the convoy system for all merchant shipping. They had now the resources in destroyers to enable them to supply an adequate number of escorts; it was discovered that the merchant mariners could keep station accurately enough for the purpose; and the port authorities were required to deal with the cargoes whenever the convoys arrived.

Despite this happy issue, the political passions which had been aroused in February, March and April were not soothed by these further developments. The effects of the convoy system were not felt at once. Lloyd George no longer placed any reliance upon Jellicoe, Carson or their Board of Admiralty. He determined, as he put it later, "to effect a change at the top in the Admiralty". At the same time, Carson and his friends prepared to strike back at the Prime Minister, for several valid reasons.

Once the United States came into the war, President Wilson began to urge his Ambassador in London to press the Prime Minister for a settlement of the Irish problem. With that bland arrogance which enabled him to interfere in the most private affairs of other countries, the President now required his Ambassador to speak out in London about Ireland.

The American Ambassador at the Court of St. James in this period was Walter Hines Page, a shrewd Southerner, who was well equipped to deal with affairs in London. Although Page was a sincere friend of Great Britain, his affection never blinded him to the realities of the English situation. He was not one of those Americans who are overcome by paroxysms of vicarious patriotism as soon as they land upon the British shore. He observed his hosts with a penetrating, if friendly, eye.

Late in April or early in May, Lloyd George dined with the American Ambassador. In a corner of the room, Page delivered to him the President's message about Ireland. Lloyd George assured Page that he was trying to do something about the Irish problem, but he broke out: " 'Madmen, madmen—I never saw such a task', and he pointed across the room to Sir Edward Carson, his First Lord of the Admiralty". Carson and Jellicoe now joined Page and Lloyd George, and the Prime Minister said: "I've been telling the Ambassador, Carson, that we've got to settle the Irish question now—in spite of you".[1]

Carson's reply was instantaneous. He never hesitated for an answer. He said to Lloyd George, in Page's presence:

> I'll tell you something else we've got to settle now. . . Else it'll settle us. That's the submarines. The press and public are working up a calculated and concerted attack on Jellicoe and me, and, if they get us, they'll get you. It's an attack on the Government . . . Prime Minister . . . it may be a fierce attack. Get ready for it. . .

Carson had deliberately fused the Irish and Naval problems of the Government into a single issue, by means of this reply. He warned Lloyd George to get ready for a fierce attack. He accepted the challenge of the Prime Minister, over the conduct of Naval affairs, and over the future handling of the Irish situation. He was prepared to fight, and he wanted Lloyd George to be certain of his attitude.

Shortly afterwards, on 17th May, Carson carried his hostility to Lloyd George's plans into the public sphere. He selected the occasion with some care. At a luncheon in honour of the American Navy, he said: "I can divide my critics into various categories. There are my political critics. I despise them in the middle of war. . . Whenever you read criticisms of my colleague Sir John Jellicoe, try

[1] For these quotations from Page's report to the President, see B. J. Hendrick, *Life and Letters of Walter H. Page* (London, 1924), vol. II, pp. 259–60.

to find out what is the origin of them. But after all it does not really matter. . . Let them grumble and growl and let us get on with our work".

Now the gauntlet was thrown down. How was Lloyd George to meet the challenge? Was he to determine the policy of the British Government, or was Sir Edward Carson to impose his will upon the deliberations of the War Cabinet?

The first explosion over convoys had been successfully avoided. It now could be looked upon as a mere skirmish of outposts. Ireland and the general conduct of Naval affairs loomed up as issues which might cause a convulsion inside the Lloyd George administration. Nothing was settled, but the main engagement could no longer be postponed.

Lord Milner's position at this stage was still undefined. He had recently become the particular target of the Liberals. For example, on 12th May 1917, A. G. Gardiner published an open letter to him in the *Daily News*. It was a ruthless and savage attack. It read as follows:

A LETTER TO LORD MILNER
By A. G. G.

. . . You are one of the three autocrats of this country, and the most powerful of the three. You are our master. You are the last person to wish us to be conscious of this fact. We shall greatly misunderstand you . . . if we do not remember that you prefer to be forgotten. . . You have no vanity. You are not hungry for popular applause. . . You are a solitary, alien figure in our midst, not so much a man with feelings like ourselves as an embodied idea, a philosophy in a frock coat. . . You are the Prussian ideal. . .

. . . You have cast-iron convictions. . . And the power you exercise is notorious in inner circles. . . You are surrounded by the bright young men—known as the Kindergarten—whom you have trained . . . and whom you have got judiciously planted out in influential positions. . .

And this power is exercised in absolute isolation from the nation. . . You have never succeeded in an electoral contest. . . You represent no one. You are the negation of democracy. You are the symbol that Parliament and the constitution have been set aside. . . You were appointed by Lord Northcliffe and the "Morning Post". Mr. Lloyd George was the humble instrument of the miracle. His coup *d'état* hinged upon you. He could not have deposed Mr Asquith without making the idol of the "Times" and the "Morning Post" the Mayor of the Palace. . .

Yours, A. G. G.

Despite this fierce evidence of Liberal hostility, Lord Milner refused to be deflected from the course he had decided upon. As the crisis between Carson and the Prime Minister approached its climax, the prudent politicians of the War Cabinet hesitated to commit themselves openly to either side. But Milner's mind was now made up. It was in these circumstances that he stepped forward in order to show himself as Lloyd George's staunchest political colleague.

IV

If Sir Edward Carson was a ruthless political antagonist, the Prime Minister was not without resource in the battle that now began. They were worthy adversaries; hard, skilful, devious, without mercy, determined.

As a first step, for the initiative lay with him, Lloyd George had a conversation with Sir Douglas Haig, the Commander-in-Chief of the British Army in France. Haig's status and position at this time were extremely powerful. He was trusted by the King, and respected by the public. He explained to Lloyd George that he thought Admiral Jellicoe too rigid and conservative in his ideas, and that he thought little of Carson's abilities as an administrator. Here was a useful ally. Lloyd George at once pressed Haig to act, in those spheres where his opinions carried weight and influence.

In June Sir Douglas spent several busy days in London, undermining the position of Sir Edward Carson and the Board of Admiralty. He visited Buckingham Palace. He had a word with Arthur Balfour. He spoke to Lord Curzon about the inefficiency of the Admiralty. He interviewed Sir

Eric Geddes, whom Lloyd George had already selected as Carson's successor. He produced substantial results in the attitudes of those who might determine the political balance.

Lloyd George, however, realised that he could not rely upon Haig. His help was of great value, but further support was required to bring the affair with Carson to a successful issue. Sir Douglas Haig, though he always pretended to be a simple, straightforward, politically innocent soldier, was devious and inconstant in his loyalties. He believed in himself, but in very few other of the King's servants. He had no affection for Lloyd George. The Prime Minister could calculate that his campaign against Sir Edward Carson had begun well, but he could do so only because of the attitude shown by Lord Milner. Haig was a valuable auxiliary, but only if he knew that he had joined the winning side.

Even before Sir Douglas intervened Lord Milner had already made it clear that he placed his entire faith, and support, in the Prime Minister. The manner in which Lord Milner revealed his hand was curious, and deserves our special attention. It was a method he chose to follow upon several vital occasions.

Late in May and early in June 1917 the preparations for the Irish Convention were going forward. The Irishmen, of every faction, approached the Convention with feelings of suspicion. They were all impressed by the dangers involved. The extremists in Ireland refused to associate with the Convention. John Redmond, and the Irish Nationalist politicians, realised that they had to exercise very great skill and care, if they were not to alienate the support and the goodwill of their people at home. The Ulstermen hesitated, but Carson persuaded them to attend the Convention, where he warned them to be on their guard. The Southern Irish Unionists played a devious game of their own.

The composition of the Convention, and the selection of

a chairman, were matters that were soon in dispute. Lloyd
George at first thought that General Smuts might serve as
the chairman of the Irish Convention. Sir James Craig, the
Ulster leader, persuaded Smuts that he would be wise to
decline the appointment.

It was also suggested that the Speaker of the House of
Commons could discharge the tasks of the chairman. This
proposal caused Lord Midleton, the leader of the Southern
Irish Unionists, to write an angry letter to Lord Milner.
Midleton had known Milner since his days at Balliol. He
knew that Milner was the most fierce friend of the Irish
Unionists in the War Cabinet, barring only Carson himself.
On 2nd June 1917 Midleton wrote to him:[1]

My dear Milner,   June 2nd, 1917.
   . . . You will run serious risk if you go beyond Lloyd George's
term of reference "For the future Government of Ireland within the
Empire".

You spoke of the Chairmanship. The appointment of the Speaker
would cause much heart searching. He has made it clear what his views
are and is impregnated with the House of Commons standpoint, based
on the presence there of 80 Nationalist M.P.s for 30 years and the
passage of the 1914 Act.

As the solution on which Ireland can be united depends on realising
that new forces have arisen, that the Nationalists can never be set over
the Unionists but must co-operate with all Loyal men and that the
Act of 1914 must be scrapped, he would have everything to unlearn.
Do let us have Simon or some unpledged judge.

Here was the kind of clarion call that had brought Lord
Milner rushing into action in years past. In 1914, as we have
seen, he sometimes differed with the English Unionists, the
men who suffered from "cold feet" at the threat of positive
action, and with Carson himself, because they hesitated to
follow the most partisan courses in their conduct of Irish
affairs. Would he now insist that Lloyd George pay attention
to Lord Midleton's opinion? Would he align himself with
Carson in the developing crisis over Ireland and the Navy?
He might look upon the Naval situation with the cool eye

[1] A copy of this document is preserved in the Lloyd George Papers.

of an administrator, but how would he act when the Union with Ireland became the subject of disagreement between the Prime Minister and Sir Edward Carson?

On 5th June 1917 Lord Milner sent the Midleton letter to the Prime Minister. The document was accompanied by a brief covering note. This note was a very significant paper. In it, Lord Milner said:[1]

5. 6. 17

My dear Prime Minister,   17 Great College Street, S.W.

I forward this letter from Midleton *for your information*, not because I want to press his point of view, although personally I sympathise with the underlined position of it & hope that in nominating . . . we shall manage to go somewhat outside all the old gangs. . .

Yours very sincerely,
Milner.

This was a remarkable development. Lord Milner took the opportunity of the Midleton letter to inform the Prime Minister that he was behind him in his handling of Irish affairs. He stressed in the first line of his brief note that he sent Midleton's partisan request, for Lloyd George's "information only". He underlined these words. He explained that from the personal point of view, he was in sympathy with Midleton's attitude. But he made it clear that as a member of the War Cabinet, his personal feelings took second place. However much Midleton's opinion coincided with Milner's own, he was not prepared to press Midleton's arguments upon Lloyd George.

Furthermore, he took care to place these views upon the record. However brief, his covering note was a document that could be preserved. In case a crisis came over Irish affairs, Lord Milner would be unable to retract the statements contained in his note of the 5th of June. Lloyd George could now be certain of his attitude, whenever the clash with Sir Edward Carson took place. The note was not the handiwork of a politician who seeks to prepare himself for any eventuality. It could be interpreted, instead, as a

[1] Lloyd George Papers, Milner to Lloyd George, 5th June 1917.

clear-cut declaration of support, even though it was not written in that form or style. If Lloyd George proposed some genuine solution of the Irish problem, Lord Milner would not be among those who would condemn his efforts from the very beginning.

How do we explain this significant change of attitude? Until this period no one was more zealous in adducing the claims and desires of the Irish Unionists than Lord Milner. Why should he entrust the very fate of the Union to the man he had despised during the Home Rule crisis of 1914? Sir Edward Carson was not prepared to do so. He agreed that the Ulstermen should attend the Irish Conference, but they were required to be upon their guard. He never qualified his opinions by saying that they were "personal", or intended merely for the "information" of the Prime Minister, when Irish matters were the subject at issue.

The answer is clear enough. After he became a member of the War Cabinet, several of his friends often asked Lord Milner how he could work with so devious a fellow as Lloyd George. Milner always replied that the Premier was not without his faults, but he insisted that there was no better candidate for the first place to be found anywhere in the Empire. Lloyd George was the "charlatan" who could also act as a statesman, the man for whom Lord Milner had longed since the days of the South African War. In this instance, Irish matters were required to take second place in Lord Milner's thinking because Lloyd George, as Minister, was discharging duties and tasks upon which Britain and the entire Empire depended for survival. In such circumstances, Lord Milner was wholeheartedly loyal to his chief. Nothing could tamper with this loyalty so long as Lloyd George set about the business of winning the war.

So far as Lloyd George was concerned, he was now in a position to move forward in his campaign against Sir Edward Carson and the admirals. The Irish flank was relatively secure. The danger had been that Carson, in defending himself and his Board of Admiralty, would so rouse the Unionists over Irish affairs that a serious menace to the administration would develop from their hostility.

Now, however, the Prime Minister was certain of Milner's support. The very men who would be most prone to listen to Carson, the Unionist rebels in the Commons, were those who respected Milner more than any other Minister. The threat of a Unionist revolt was no longer quite so menacing to Lloyd George, after he received the Milner note of the 5th of June.

He could now proceed with his plans for a reorganisation at the Admiralty. He knew that Bonar Law was in general agreement with him. When Milner joined their group, Carson's power to create a genuine crack in the Tory support of the Ministry was very seriously diminished. The cards were falling into Lloyd George's hand.

V

On 26th June Lloyd George took the next step in his campaign against Carson. He entertained Sir Eric Geddes and Haig at one of those breakfasts in Downing Street which he often employed for significant political business. Together they discussed the situation at the Admiralty. Before they came to any decisions, Lord Milner was sent for in order to join in their deliberations.

It was necessary for Lloyd George's purpose that Haig should realise that Milner agreed with the decision to force a change at the Admiralty. Haig, as a matter of course, was familiar with the extent of Milner's popularity in Army circles, and in those right wing political groups that usually looked to Sir Edward Carson for leadership and guidance. Like most of the generals, Sir Douglas had a very high opinion of Milner's qualities. In May, for example, he had explained to Lady Haig that: "Milner . . . is the strongest member of the War Cabinet as well as being the best informed".[1]

[1] Robert Blake ed., *Private Papers of Douglas Haig* (London, 1952), p. 229.

Such was the Prime Minister's flair that he entertained the curious and dramatic notion that the Army might be brought in to redress those Naval shortcomings which plagued him in his conduct of the war. At the breakfast meeting Haig was persuaded to go to the War Office in order to ask Sir William Robertson, Chief of the Imperial General Staff, to accept Carson's position as First Lord of the Admiralty. Robertson, when interviewed by Haig, at once refused. This was a ridiculous move in a game that had been played thus far with the adroit skill usually associated with Lloyd George's name.

It was Lord Milner who finally hit upon a solution. His attitude to the problem was quite clear. As an administrator, he had come to the conclusion that Sir Edward Carson's conduct of the Admiralty was inefficient. For that reason, Carson would have to be removed from his place. It seemed to Milner that Lloyd George was over-reaching himself when he sought to involve General Robertson in the change at the Admiralty. Lloyd George disliked the Chief of the Imperial General Staff and placed no reliance upon his military advice. Had Robertson accepted the Admiralty offer, the Prime Minister would have killed the two birds with one stone—a proceeding he always relished. He would, by the same stroke, banish both Carson and Robertson from those places where they could offer effective opposition to him. Lord Milner could not, upon reflection, agree to this ambitious proposal, for he respected Robertson and wished him to remain in his proper place. Despite Lloyd George, Milner desired a wholly different solution.

After the breakfast meeting on 26th June Milner returned to his office in Whitehall Gardens and worked out a plan of his own. He wrote to Lloyd George in order to suggest that Carson should be invited to join the War Cabinet, "where he would be excellent". Such an invitation might soothe Carson's feelings because it was a promotion, even though it involved the loss of the Admiralty. As part of this bargain, Milner suggested that Carson should be

437

asked to agree to help Bonar Law in leading the House of Commons.[1]

Lloyd George was delighted by these proposals. If Carson agreed to them, not only could the reorganisation of the Admiralty take place, but Carson's political energies would be harnessed to the Government's car. It was a brilliant scheme, worthy of Lloyd George himself. The Prime Minister decided to act upon it.

It now remained for Lloyd George to sound his political colleagues. Bonar Law agreed to the idea, but he insisted that the change should be carried out without annoying Carson. Bonar Law had no wish to face the prospect of a rebellion inside his own party, led by the angry Ulster leader. Lord Curzon, in his turn, accepted the Milner scheme. Early in July Lloyd George revealed his hand to the King. He explained to Lord Stamfordham that he proposed to invite Sir Edward Carson to join the War Cabinet where he "would be very useful and especially in making speeches in the country".[2]

On 6th July 1917 Lloyd George put the issue to the test. That evening he wrote to Carson at his home at Birchington in order to ask him to become a member of the War Cabinet, and thus "strengthen" the Government in its central direction of the war. Lloyd George had at last advanced into the open. He waited with some anxiety to see the nature of Carson's reaction.

Would an explosion now come, or would the Ulster leader accept a proposal that would leave Sir John Jellicoe and the Board of Admiralty naked to the onslaught that was certain to be made when he was no longer First Lord? It was a most dangerous situation. Lloyd George must have been grateful to Lord Milner for his conduct at this stage of the crisis. On the morning of 7th July, Milner wrote to him as follows:[3]

---

[1] See Beaverbrook, *Men and Power*, pp. 168–9.
[2] *Ibid.*, p. 171.
[3] Lloyd George Papers, Milner to Lloyd George, 7th July 1917.

7. 7. 17

My dear Prime Minister,   17 Great College Street, S.W.

I sent a messenger down to Birchington today with a letter to Carson. He and I are such old friends, that I thought it might influence him to some extent to know that I felt strongly—as I really do—that he could be of most use to the Govt. and the country in the Cabinet. Anyway it can do no harm.

Yours most sincerely,
Milner.

It is thus clear that while Bonar Law and the members of the War Cabinet preserved a discreet silence in the battle between the Titans, Lord Milner stepped forward in order to deal frankly with Sir Edward Carson. Unlike the other Ministers, Milner did not hesitate, whatever the political dangers, when the moment of decision arrived.

By means of his letter to Carson, Milner made patent his support of Lloyd George. Furthermore, Carson was required to understand that if he proposed to resist the Prime Minister, he would have to reckon with Milner's disapproval and hostility.

Lord Milner's letter could be effective in one of two ways. On the one hand, Carson might choose to receive it as the timely advice of an old friend. If he did so, there would be no crisis. On the other hand, it could serve as a warning to Carson that if a battle were to be joined, Milner would be found at Lloyd George's side in the struggle.

This was the kind of unqualified support that politicians receive only too rarely. Lloyd George, the man who lived by his political wits, balancing one colleague's aspirations against those of another, must have been deeply impressed by Lord Milner's action. The menace of Sir Edward Carson's anger was very genuine in 1917. Nevertheless, Milner believed that a change should be made in the higher direction of the Admiralty. Therefore, he pressed Carson to accept the Prime Minister's proposal. No other considerations were allowed to affect his course of action.

It only remained for the Prime Minister to receive Sir Edward's reply. A messenger had already been despatched to Birchington. What news would he carry back on his return to Downing Street?

VI

Lloyd George's invitation to leave the Admiralty in order to join the War Cabinet arrived at Carson's home late at night, and the Ulster leader was roused from his bed to receive it. He delayed his reply until the following morning, but then fell back upon a typical and familiar tactic. He explained to the Prime Minister that he could give him no considered answer upon that day because he was suffering from a severe attack of neuralgia.[1]

The affair was still undecided. Carson had refused to commit himself to any course, but chose to preserve his freedom of action. He did not agree to join the War Cabinet, nor did he at once turn upon Lloyd George in order to launch an immediate counter-attack. He held his hand.

In Downing Street the Prime Minister had been waiting for a reply in a fever of excitement. He had screwed up his courage to press Carson to leave the Admiralty in order that the Board might be reorganised for the purpose of conducting the naval war against the submarines more effectively. By confronting Carson in this way, however valid the object might be, Lloyd George had jeopardised the safety of the Government.

We may obtain some measure of the dangers involved in this course of action if we refer to Lord Hankey's appreciation of the situation, made at the time. In casting about for an alternative First Lord at an early stage of the crisis, Lloyd George at one moment suggested to Hankey that he might agree to take up the post. To this proposition, the astute Colonel made a spirited and pointed reply:[2]

I pointed out that, while I believed that I could improve matters as regards anti-submarine warfare . . . I should be quite hopeless as

---

[1] Beaverbrook, *Men and Power,* pp. 173–4.
[2] Hankey, *The Supreme Command,* vol. II, pp. 654–5.

regards parliamentary matters. . . To enter a rather rocky Ministry in the most criticised post . . . to take on the most responsible office . . . these are risks which I would only exchange for my present post . . . under pressure of a very high sense of national duty, and under persuasion of the whole Cabinet. . .

Now, all these valid fears and hesitations came flooding back upon the Prime Minister. He abandoned his resolve. On 7th July he made haste to write to Carson to explain that his invitation had been misunderstood. The members of the War Cabinet, he said, would be delighted if Carson agreed to join them, but if he preferred to remain at the Admiralty, then "the suggestion falls to the ground".[1]

For ten days Lloyd George floundered in irresolution. He discussed the matter with his principal colleagues. He invited their suggestions. Not one of them dared to urge him forward. Alone in the War Cabinet, Lord Milner remained convinced that action must be taken. As so often in the past, "his mind had closed like a trap" upon the matter. So long as Carson continued to act as First Lord, efficiency was being lost and the Naval resources of the country were squandered. On 16th July Lord Milner wrote to Lloyd George in order to press him to implement their plan. His letter must be reproduced in order to show the quality of his steadfast courage, and his determination:[2]

Very Confidential   16. 7. 17
My dear Prime Minister,

Forgive my worrying. I am very anxious about the Admiralty. It is more than a fortnight now since I think you recognised there must be a change and every week is precious. Besides, the longer we wait, the more likely it is that something will get out, and then the papers will begin gossiping and criticising and the whole thing will be blown upon.

It would be best to make all Ministerial changes at once, but if this is not practicable, cannot the Carson-Geddes business in any case be settled right away? It is very urgent.

Yours very sincerely,
Milner.

[1] Beaverbrook, *Men and Power*, p. 174.
[2] The document is printed in Beaverbrook, *Men and Power*, p. 175.

Within twenty-four hours the changes Lord Milner urged were decided upon, and announced to the newspapers. Winston Churchill was brought into the Government as Minister of Munitions, Sir Eric Geddes became First Lord, and Sir E. Carson was advanced in rank to membership of the War Cabinet where he was assigned the oversight of the Government's propaganda activities. Lord Milner's resolution had determined the issue. Where Lloyd George, Bonar Law, Curzon and the others had refused to proceed, he caused decisions to be taken.

The Prime Minister, who was an able judge of men, would not soon forget Lord Milner's conduct in this crisis of the Government. On this occasion, the Carsonian volcano had rumbled ominously, but it had failed to erupt. Lloyd George's path was obstructed by other dangerous peaks at this stage of his Premiership. He knew now where to look for the companion to accompany him in any further ascents that might have to be made.

XVII. The Conversion of Lord Milner

I

DURING Asquith's Premiership Lloyd George had
threatened to resign on many vital occasions, but
only after the Paris Conference of November 1916
had he been incensed enough to take definite and positive
action. The fixity of purpose of the generals who insisted
that victory could only come as the result of a frontal
attack upon the enemy in the West so outraged him that he
finally decided to hazard all in order to change the British
leadership in the war, and the rigid strategy that was allowed
to flourish under that leadership.

However, after he became Prime Minister Lloyd George
found, despite his every effort, that he was unable to move
the generals in their determination to continue to batter
upon the German fortifications in France. The high
military leaders, devoid of genius or even flair, were stub-
born, inflexible, incapable of accepting another point of
view, supremely confident in their own professional

competence, contemptuous of the advice of those civilian Ministers they dismissed as mere amateurs in the art of war.

Beyond this, the professional soldiers of high rank were often in the grip of what we may call a gambler's exaltation. Occasionally, when some small advance was achieved, when a minor raid was successful, when an insignificant trench line was snatched from the enemy, the generals became flushed with optimism, confidence and fervour. They convinced themselves times without number that one more push, one extra effort, one more attack, would prove them right and drive a beaten enemy in confusion from the field.

Even on those occasions when reality banished the reckless mood of the gambler, the generals still insisted upon attack after attack in the West. They deluded themselves into the belief that they were "wearing down" the enemy in France. When their every military stratagem was exhausted, they resolved to wage a war of attrition, the very negation of the military art. Let every one of their plans miscarry; it could have no effect upon their purpose or their method; they were "wearing down" the manpower of the Germans.

Winston Churchill, although a partisan in the struggle with the generals, has written truly that: "Two, and even three, British or French lives were repeatedly paid for the killing of one enemy and grim calculations were made to prove that in the end the Allies would still have a balance of a few millions to spare. It will appear not only horrible but incredible to future generations that such doctrines should have been imposed by the military profession upon the ardent and heroic populations who yielded themselves to their orders".

In the late summer and autumn of 1917 Lloyd George was compelled to witness the dreadful series of events which are generally referred to as the Passchendaele offensive. Sir Douglas Haig, burning with zeal, hurled his Armies upon the enemy in Flanders for a period of nearly four months, in a series of murderous frontal assaults. When a hamlet was taken here or a trench there, he believed that the "crack" in the German defences was at last beginning.

By November, the authorities were in a position to reckon up the figures provided for them by these operations in the Flanders slaughter-house. The British Armies suffered the appalling total of 399,000 casualties, and they had gained less than four miles of useless mud and slime in a salient overlooked by the German guns upon three sides.

When the German counter-attack of March 1918 was made, the gains won during the Passchendaele offensive were instantly abandoned because the area was indefensible, from the British point of view. Moreover, the troops who lived through the carnage, the men who escaped the mincing effect of the Flanders "meat-grinder", were exhausted by the nervous strain imposed upon them by the fighting, and also by the terrain itself, a reeking swamp in which men floundered and drowned in the mud.

It is doubtful if any Western troops except the British would have tolerated such conditions for such a length of time.

Sir Douglas Haig, the Commander-in-Chief, was unmoved by these developments, and ignorant of the facts of life in the forward areas of his command. He and his chief staff officers often seemed to act upon the principle that it would be a grave dereliction of duty if they ever visited the trenches. They waged their war from a remote headquarters.

When Sir Douglas glanced up from his maps or when he stepped outside for his morning ride his eye fell upon scenes of order, precision and military tidiness. His world was not the world of the front line infantry soldier. This must, in the unpleasant nature of things, often be the case, but Haig and his staff never really appreciated the battlefield conditions of the Passchendaele fighting. He was prepared, and even resolved, to try the same methods in the spring. When the plans were being made for the 1918 campaign Sir Maurice Hankey recorded in his diary for 4th November that: "Haig seems as cocksure as ever that he is going to bring off a big *coup* this year".[1]

In Lloyd George's mind, the solution to his problem was clear enough. He believed that if he dismissed his principal military advisers, Sir Douglas Haig and Sir William Robertson, Chief of the Imperial General Staff, a new strategy might be devised.

However, so far as he was concerned the problem was a political one. The generals and the military party as a whole enjoyed the support of many politically powerful groups in the country. The people of Britain, unused to war, believed in their innocence that the generals were technical experts who ought not to be interfered with in their delicate tasks by ignorant civilian Ministers, fit only to direct affairs in time of peace. Politicians of both major parties trusted the military and suspected the administration. Several important members of his own Government seemed prepared to resign if Haig or Robertson were dismissed from office. A powerful section of the newspaper Press, independent of party affiliation, was devoted to the cause of the generals. Behind all these adherents of the military men was the King, who placed his trust in Haig, an old friend, and disliked the bustling, crafty, devious Prime Minister, spokesman of much that was alien to the royal circles in which he moved and lived.

In calculating his resources, Lloyd George could reckon upon the firm support of Bonar Law and those sections of the Tory party who were loyal to their official leader. George Barnes, the Labour representative in the War Cabinet, did not count for much in case of a crisis over the generals. Lord Curzon's position was doubtful, masked in lofty and flowing phrases. He could be depended upon to choose the winning side.

There remained Lord Milner, the political hero of the Army, the man who had helped so much in the difficulty with Sir Edward Carson and the high admirals. Where would

[1] Hankey, *Supreme Command*, vol. II, p. 719.

he take his stand if Lloyd George proposed to move against Haig, Robertson and the military clique firmly entrenched in the War Office?

II

When Lord Milner joined the administration he was one of those who placed their reliance in the soldiers for the achievement of victory. Lloyd George, as we have seen, included him in the Government because, among other reasons, he was so popular with the highest elements in the Army.

At one of his earliest public appearances as a member of the War Cabinet, Lord Milner made his position perfectly clear. On 1st January 1917 he took part in a New Year's party for wounded soldiers, held at the Caxton Hall. So seriously did Lord Milner regard his new duties that *The Times* was able to report the curious and remarkable facts that the programme consisted of ". . . music, conjuring and hat-trimming and dressing-up competitions. Lord Milner acted as judge in the latter contests. . ."

The assembly at the Caxton Hall was agreeably surprised when the Chief of the Imperial General Staff, Sir William Robertson, came to visit the scene of their festivities. Lord Milner interrupted himself in his judging of the "dressing-up competitions" in order to say (*The Times*, 2nd January 1917):

The men we look to these days . . . are men of the stamp of Sir William Robertson; and the best thing that men like myself and others in a similar position can do is to put our backs into the work that lies before us, and give them all the help we possibly can. We must look to their wisdom, experience and judgement to show us the right way. . .

This ideal relationship between the generals and the civilian Ministers did not long survive the heat and friction of administration in war. Lord Milner, in disposing of the manpower of the country and in discharging the other tasks assigned to him by the War Cabinet, sometimes found himself in disagreement with the authorities at the War

Office. The soldiers were often required to give way to his demands and requirements.

By August 1917 Sir William Robertson, who once hoped that Milner would become Secretary of State for War, had changed his mind. He wrote to Sir Douglas Haig: "Lloyd George . . . is a real bad 'un. Milner is a tired, dyspeptic old man. Curzon a gas-bag. Bonar Law equals Bonar Law . . ."[1]

Although Sir William included Lord Milner in these happily phrased descriptions of the civilian Ministers, it does not mean that Milner was no longer a staunch friend of the Army inside the War Cabinet. Experience had tempered his enthusiasm for the soldiers but he was not at all inclined to agree with the Prime Minister in his low estimation of Haig and Robertson.

A significant change occurred in September 1917. Early in the month Lloyd George retired to his home at Criccieth because he was suffering from neuralgia and nervous tension. After a few days he summoned Colonel Hankey to his side and complained to him about the narrow outlook of the General Staff and the timidity of his colleagues in the War Cabinet who were afraid to overrule the generals in their bungling conduct of the war. The Prime Minister was despondent and filled with disgust by a situation which tied his hands and prevented him from taking any positive action. Lloyd George hoped that the Allies would go over to the defensive in France so that troops and resources might be released for a smashing blow at the Turk. Only by means of an attack in the East, the Prime Minister believed, was there any chance for a victory in 1918.

On 17th September Lord Milner arrived at Criccieth and these discussions were repeated in his presence. Although Milner continued to rely upon the generals he was not a Westerner, one of those who believed with them that France was the only theatre of war where decisive results might be obtained. His wide Imperial experience helped

[1] Blake ed., *The Private Papers of Douglas Haig*, pp. 251-2.

LOYD GEORGE, MILNER AND PHILLIP KERR ON HOLIDAY IN WALES

him to realise with Lloyd George that a successful action against Turkey would have repercussions in the Balkans, in Austria, and in Germany itself.

By 18th September Lord Milner was convinced that there was no chance for a genuine decision in France, and for that reason he was now prepared to support the Prime Minister's Eastern policy. However, he insisted that the Turkish campaign could be launched only if the generals agreed to support it. In his opinion if the military were forced to undertake such an attack against their will, the result would be a disaster. He had seen how the generals had successfully crippled the offensive in the Dardanelles and he was not anxious to be a member of a War Administration saddled with such a fiasco. Colonel Hankey recorded Milner's conversion in his diary, as follows:[1]

> Milner seems to have come completely round to Lloyd George's view that the Western Front affords no opportunity . . . and that it is necessary to devote our main efforts against Turkey. He agrees fully with me, however—having reached his decision quite independently— that success in the Turkish theatre can only be achieved if the soldiers are in it whole-heartedly.

Here was the political support Lloyd George had been waiting for. If Milner did not agree with him completely, definite advances had been made at the Criccieth conversations. Instantly, Lloyd George sprang into action. A Press campaign in praise of Lord Milner was launched in the latter part of September. On the 21st, for example, an article by J. Saxon Mills in the *Daily Chronicle* praised Milner as a friend of the working classes. The article deplored those caricatures of Milner which sought to portray him as a ruthless autocrat, without feelings of any kind. It recalled his friendship with Arnold Toynbee, his efforts to "socialise" the pre-war policy of the Unionist Party, and his speeches in favour of Old Age Pensions. It explained that ". . . of his value as a public servant there can be no question among those who can see straight and think fairly, and if there had

[1] Hankey, *The Supreme Command*, vol. II, pp. 697-8.

been no seat for him in these days in our most responsible Council of wise and tried statesmen, our standards of choice must have been sadly at fault".

The Asquithian newspapers were at once alerted by these developments. They realised that something lay behind such public acclamations. A counter-blow was struck in *The Star* for 24th September. An article in that paper entitled "Lord Milner, Democrat!" declared:

> The weekend has been marked by a strange outburst of praise of Lord Milner. First a Liberal morning newspaper published a long eulogy, signed by a well-known Tory journalist; an influential Sunday paper followed with a leading article extolling the same subject; and the picture papers joined in with photographs of him walking about Criccieth in company with Mr. Lloyd George. The phenomenon suggests that the War Cabinet, being about to give Lord Milner some new job, feels that a little bell-ringing in his interests would not be amiss. . .

III

The next step in Lord Milner's conversion came early in November 1917. Once he agreed with Lloyd George upon the validity of an Eastern operation, he began to study the matter with that habitual attention to detail which marked him out as a successful administrator.

On 3rd November Lord Milner sent to the Prime Minister a Memorandum on "The Balkan Situation". This document, marked "SECRET", explored the conditions in the Balkans with painstaking care. We need not concern ourselves with its details. Of far greater political significance was the covering letter which accompanied the Memorandum.

In this letter, for the first time, Lord Milner expressed a certain dissatisfaction with the attitude of the high soldiers. By means of this covering letter Lloyd George was informed that Lord Milner not only agreed with him about the need for a forward policy in the East, but also that Milner was now inclined to press the generals to conform with the ideas and outlook of the Prime Minister. Lord Milner wrote:[1]

[1] Lloyd George Papers, Milner to Lloyd George, 3rd November 1917.

3 . 11 . 17

My dear Prime Minister,   17 Great College Street, S.W.

... The more I think of it, the more dangerous appears to me the idea of our tying ourselves up more than ever in France. The soldiers will like it because it keeps their army together. But it means that *for the whole of 1918* our Army will be condemned to a merely defensive role, while our more distant expeditions will also be smitten with paralysis, if not with failure.

... The great point is that if, next year at any rate, we cannot make the force strong enough to break through, it is waste to keep it stronger than is necessary for a lively defensive. The force we could afford to withdraw from France *should be the mobile force of the alliance*—the strategic reserve, which we have never had and without which we can never win. It, or some of it, is wanted now in Italy, but that does not mean we should immobilise it permanently in Italy. It goes there for a temporary purpose ... not for ever and a day to hold a slice of Italian frontier...

Yours ever,
Milner.

Here was a decisive change of outlook. It came at the exact moment Lloyd George was proposing to take a forward step in his delicate campaign to set upon one side the short-sighted strategic policies of the generals. Lord Milner had been won over to his side. Milner now looked upon the plans of the generals to lock up massive forces in France as "waste". As an administrator Milner would never tolerate such a policy. Typically, he now adopted an attitude of firmness and even hostility, where the generals were concerned. He was convinced that their strategy was invalid. They would be required to change it, or suffer the consequences of their defiance of the Government.

A few days later Lord Derby, the Secretary of State for War, and a firm adherent of the generals, found cause to complain of Milner's attitude, in a letter to Lord Esher. Derby's comments reveal that Lord Milner's conversion was now complete. He wrote to Esher:[1]

Milner is intolerable, I should like to put him in the ranks for six months and teach him what soldiers are like, that perhaps would stop

[1] Randolph Churchill, *Derby*, p. 293.

451

his continual sneering at soldiers as if they were all damned fools. If he only knew how the country generally, and the Labour party in particular, hate and distrust him, he might learn a little wisdom. I believe he is to remain in Paris with Wilson; I very much distrust the combination.

Lord Derby, in this letter, has put his finger upon the next phase of Lloyd George's plan to deal with Haig, Robertson and the General Staff.

IV

The Prime Minister was determined to sweep away the command structure that had been responsible for the failures of 1915, 1916 and 1917. But he had to avoid an open rupture with the generals because of their strength in the political sphere. Lloyd George could not risk a frontal assault upon men like Haig or Robertson. They were powerful enough to threaten the very existence of his Government. He had to find a way round the obstinacy of the General Staff. Early in the autumn he began to make a series of probing attacks upon their position.

Lloyd George believed that the Allies had failed up to this time because they lacked a unified and genuinely co-ordinated strategy. Lip-service was often paid to the idea of a unified strategy, but it had never been achieved in reality. The Allies had frittered away their strength and resources in piecemeal campaigns which had been success-fully parried by the enemy.

The Prime Minister came to the conclusion that an Inter-Allied body with its own Staff and its own Intelligence Department should be created. This new organisation, according to his ideas, would be required to examine and overlook the various seats of the war as parts of one single great Front. Its task would be to dispose of the manpower and the resources of the Allies in a rational and co-ordinated manner. It would be composed of civilian Ministers and high-ranking military and naval officers who would aid the Ministers in their deliberations by supplying expert technical advice. As early as August 1917 General Sir Henry Wilson had suggested such an Inter-Allied Staff. Now, in the early autumn, Lloyd George adopted the plan as his own.

Would the idea be accepted? In the first place the Prime Minister explained his purpose to President Wilson, early in September 1917. He invited the President to send American representatives to the Councils of the Allied Powers whenever strategy was under discussion.[1]

As a next step, he asked Sir Douglas Haig to state his opinions of the new plan. Haig explained that the only correct course was to maintain the attack in Flanders and thus destroy the manpower of the enemy in the West.

In the third place, Lloyd George applied to Sir William Robertson for a technical appreciation. The Chief of the Imperial General Staff informed the War Cabinet that it was necessary for Britain to concentrate her military energies in France, in the main theatre of the war. The idea of a "single great Front" was, according to Robertson, attractive in theory but less valid in actual practice. He insisted, with Haig, that the War Cabinet should try to predominate in the Councils of the Allies rather than seek to share decisions with the French, Belgians, Italians and Americans.

Lloyd George had come up against a blank wall. The Haig-Robertson combination was not prepared to accept or even entertain his new scheme.

Now the Prime Minister resolved upon a bolder course. He understood that the British people were certain to resent civilian interference with the soldiers. However, if he could discover generals of high rank who were prepared to agree with him, the difficulty might be overcome. No one could condemn him as an ignorant meddler if he found military support for his plan. In any case, the resolve of Haig and Robertson might be shaken if they realised that

[1] For Lloyd George's course and the reactions to it at this time, described below, see Lloyd George, *War Memoirs*, vol. II, pp. 1405ff.

other generals did not look upon the military situation in the same way that they did. Lloyd George would be content if he created quarrelling factions among the military chiefs.

On 10th October, after careful soundings had been made, General Sir John French and General Sir Henry Wilson were invited to a meeting of the War Cabinet. Sir W. Robertson was also in attendance. Lloyd George's cunning had never been exercised with greater skill. Sir John French, a choleric cavalryman, had been replaced as Commander-in-Chief in France by Haig, at the end of 1915. He had been relegated to the relatively unimportant command of the Home Forces. He seethed with resentment. He was jealous of the man who had taken his place. Sir Henry Wilson, for his part, was a soldier who understood the politicians. He knew what was required of him at the War Cabinet meeting.

Both these officers condemned the military appreciations adduced by Haig and Robertson while they gave their support to the idea of an Inter-Allied Council

Now Sir William Robertson rebelled. He would not tolerate such unprecedented and cavalier actions. He was the constitutional adviser of the Government, the Chief of the Imperial General Staff, who was not required to compete with other serving officers for the ear of authority. He looked upon Lloyd George's action as a grave personal and professional affront. He offered his resignation to the Secretary of State for War. The crisis had come.

On the evening of 10th October Lord Curzon intervened. He called upon Colonel Hankey in order to tell him that if the Prime Minister forced Robertson to relinquish his post, Balfour, Derby, Carson and Curzon himself were prepared to resign.

Lloyd George refused to give way. He sought to conciliate Robertson but he insisted that a Central Allied Council with its own staff of generals should be created. He fortified himself by asking French and Wilson to set out their views in formal Memoranda. By 22nd October Lord

Milner believed "that the Government would very likely come down over it . . ."[1]

Finally, in order to appease Robertson Lloyd George suggested that the Central Allied Council might be set up in London, rather than in Paris, so that Robertson, whose place was in the War Office, could be in a position to control the British Military Representative at the Council. For the moment, the strained relations between Prime Minister and General Staff were eased.

Lloyd George's opportunity came when the disaster of Caporetto burst open the Italian Front at the end of October 1917. The French and British Governments were required to furnish the Italians with military aid, without a moment's delay. It became necessary for the Allies to hold a high level Conference in Italy in order to stabilise the situation.

After consultations with Paul Painlevé, the French Minister of War, Lloyd George decided to make this Conference the occasion for the creation of a Supreme War Council for the Allies. Caporetto revealed that they had no reliable system for providing each other with mutual support and assistance when it was required at very short notice. They were fighting a series of separate wars instead of pursuing an Allied policy against the enemy.

On 2nd November Lloyd George called a meeting of the British War Cabinet in order to inform them that the French Government had accepted the plan for an Inter-Allied Council and General Staff. Sir Henry Wilson was appointed, at this meeting, as the British Military Representative at the Supreme War Council. It was also decided that the Prime Minister should leave at once for Rapallo in order to confer with the other Allies about the Italian situation, and also to establish in concert with them the constitution of the new Supreme War Council.

As late as the 9th October Sir William Robertson wrote to Haig that: "He (Lloyd George) is out for my blood. . . Milner, Carson, Curzon, Cecil, Balfour have each in turn

[1] Hankey, *Supreme Command*, vol. II, p. 715.

expressly spoken to me separately about his intolerable conduct . . . and have said they are behind us".[1]

Now, however, on the very eve of the Rapallo Conference Lord Milner sent his letter of the 3rd of November informing Lloyd George that the strategic plans of the generals involved "waste", that he was no longer divided in his loyalties, that his conversion to the Prime Minister's point of view was at last complete. Despite the hostility of Haig and Robertson, when Lloyd George left for the Rapallo Conference in order to set up the new Supreme War Council he knew that he could rely upon the political support of both Bonar Law and Lord Milner. The German stroke at Caporetto was not a severe blow to the Italians only; it also had very serious effects upon the fortunes of the Military Party in Great Britain.

V

At the Rapallo Conference of 6th–7th November 1917 a Supreme War Council was constituted "with a view to the better co-ordination of action on the Western Front". Since no representatives of the Russian Government were present, nothing could be done to link the Russians to the new organisation.

The Supreme War Council was composed of the Prime Minister and a member of the Government of each of the Allied Powers fighting upon the Western Front. Its task, aided by the Permanent Military Representatives, was to prepare recommendations for the decisions of the Governments. The Council had no executive authority; decisions in matters of strategy would continue to be taken by the several Governments of the Allies. However, there was now set up a central body charged with the duty of continually surveying the entire field of operations, a body, moreover, that would be in a position to collect and collate information from all the fronts and from all the different Governments

---

[1] Blake ed., *Private Papers of Douglas Haig*, p. 259.

and Staffs. While the military authorities in each country were to continue to act independently, their general war plans were to be submitted to the Supreme War Council which was empowered to suggest changes in such plans.

It was significant from the British point of view, and especially that of Sir William Robertson, that Lloyd George had abandoned his notion that the Council was to sit in London. The Permanent Military Representatives, together with their Staffs who watched the situation day by day, were to be stationed permanently at Versailles, which would be the regular meeting place of the Supreme War Council as a whole. The Council, according to the Rapallo arrangement, was to meet at least once each month.

Lloyd George, despite Haig and Robertson, had worked his will upon the entire field of Allied strategy. He was now required to face the British Parliament in order to answer for his high and cavalier actions.

In London, both sides began to prepare. Lloyd George, on 13th November, arranged that Lord Milner, the accepted political hero of the Army, should go over to Versailles for the first meeting of the Supreme War Council to be held in its permanent headquarters. The choice of Milner was designed to reveal to the soldiers and their friends that certain political alignments inside the War Cabinet had changed, to their disadvantage. It was a hint they failed to take.

The Prime Minister also sought out Colonel House, the representative of President Wilson, and tried to convince him of the value of the new arrangement. If Lloyd George could explain to the House of Commons that the Americans agreed with his plan, the suspicions of the House would be mollified, and his own path made more easy.

The Military Party, for their part, were engaged in extensive preparations to defeat the project. They did not propose to relinquish a scrap of their control over high strategy.

Sir William Robertson had a powerful case. When the

details of the Rapallo Agreement were conveyed to the War Office, the Army Council replied with a formal Memorandum, critical of the entire arrangement. The Army Council pointed out to the Prime Minister and the War Cabinet that they, by Letters Patent, exercised the powers and authority of a Commander-in-Chief with respect to all questions involving the Military Forces of the Crown. For that reason they assumed, in their Memorandum, that the technical advice given by the Permanent British Military Representative at Versailles would be advice tendered upon their behalf, and at their orders.

This was exactly what Lloyd George wanted to avoid. He refused to accept the arguments and assumptions of the Army Council.

Sir William Robertson's counter-attack was not confined to Memoranda. On the morning of 15th November he saw Asquith in order to prepare the ground upon his British Front, and Colonel House in order to win the Americans to his point of view.[1]

The political Press in London stirred uneasily. Members of the Commons began to take sides. In the clubs it was believed that a trial of strength was at last at hand. Was it Lloyd George's purpose, men asked, to rid himself of Sir William Robertson and the group of professionals who controlled British strategy in the War Office?

On the 19th November the debate took place in the House of Commons. Fortunately for Lloyd George, President Wilson's approval of the Rapallo plan was made public upon that day. Moreover, the President formally instructed General Tasker H. Bliss, the American Chief of Staff, and Colonel House to be present at the first meeting of the Supreme War Council at Versailles. In the debate Asquith led the opponents of the Government but he confined his attack to criticism of details. Lloyd George vindicated his actions at Rapallo brilliantly. The House approved of the new Supreme War Council.

[1] This information is contained in Hankey, *Supreme Command*, vol. II, p. 728.

Meanwhile, behind the scenes Lloyd George patiently continued with his preparations. He knew that his victory over the generals and their political associates was not decisive, that his position was still far from secure. It was his habit, whenever a colleague was doubtful about a proposed course of action, to involve that colleague in the details of the scheme, and thus win his interest and approval of it. This was the policy he now pursued with Lord Milner. As early as 13th November he suggested that Milner should attend the first Versailles meeting of the Supreme War Council. Like other converts before him, Lord Milner's enthusiasm for the new course of defying the Haig-Robertson combination increased as time passed.

Shortly after the Permanent Military Representatives at the Supreme War Council were installed at Versailles, Lord Milner was despatched upon a visit to France. He reported to the Prime Minister in glowing terms:[1]

My dear Prime Minister,   *Personal.*   23 . 12 . 17
    Cecil and I got over here last night. . . Conversations on the whole very satisfactory. . .
    I am staying on for a few days in order to attend to several other things, some of which you asked me to see about, & some of which have cropped up here & which I want to get to the bottom of for your information. . .
    I am staying at Versailles with Wilson and the others. . . On the whole I think the Versailles business is going well. They are doing a tremendous lot of work and will very shortly, I think, have collected an amount of information on the most important aspects of the war such as we have never yet had. Wilson is going strong, and as full of ideas as an egg is full of meat. One may not always agree with him, but I always feel personally, that I get more help from him in considering any of our big war problems than from any other "expert". . .
                                        Yours very sincerely,
                                                    Milner.

Milner was secure. The Prime Minister was now in a position to take his next forward step against the generals. He proceeded immediately to do so.

[1] Lloyd George Papers, Milner to Lloyd George, 23rd December 1917, marked "Personal".

VI

Early in December 1917 Lloyd George had asked Lord Derby, the Secretary of State for War, to replace both Haig and Robertson. He refused to do so. For the first time, Lord Derby revealed that he was prepared to support the generals to the hilt, and resign with them if ever they were forced from office. This was a new complication.

Edward Stanley, seventeenth Earl of Derby, was a political relic from a by-gone age of English history. He was one of the last of those great territorial magnates who exercised political authority because of their ownership of land, and the regional influence that accompanied such ownership. When he came into his inheritance in 1908 he succeeded to possessions and a fortune which had been built up by his family over a period of eight hundred years. His rent rolls brought in, at that time, the sum of three hundred thousand pounds per year. It was only in the nature of things that Derby should look upon himself as different, and superior, to other men. He was rightly proud of his singular inheritance and never sought to deprecate it, however incongruous it might be in the modern age. Once, during the depression of the 1930s, a retainer suggested that it was an extravagance to keep up Derby House, one of his costly London mansions. "Well", was Lord Derby's reply, "Lady Derby must have somewhere to change when she comes up . . . to go to the play".

When Lloyd George formed his Government in December 1916, Derby was one of the Tory leaders of the second rank he was required to place in office in order to win the support of their party for his new Ministry. Lord Derby was the man who controlled Lancashire for the Conservatives; he was generally liked in the party, and he enjoyed a popular reputation in the country as a genial and open-handed aristocrat who could associate with all classes. Like Sir Douglas Haig, Derby was a close friend of the King.

In recognition of these qualifications, Lloyd George invited him to become Secretary of State for War.

The Prime Minister, at that time, never dreamed that Derby would presume to stand in his way at a vital stage of his direction of the war strategy of the country. If Derby were forced to resign in December 1917, the King, people in the country generally and many in the Tory ranks would be outraged by the Prime Minister's conduct.

In order to neutralise Lord Derby's position, Lloyd George began, at this time, to confront him with the attitude and the arguments of Lord Milner. Derby supported the generals. Lord Milner was critical of the strategy advocated by Haig and Robertson. As we shall see, Lloyd George so contrived matters that when the crisis came it took the form, in part at least, of an altercation between Milner and Derby, a difference of view between two Conservative members of his Government.

In mid-January 1918 Lloyd George tried again. He proposed to get rid of Lord Derby by offering him the post of Ambassador in Paris. Derby declined the invitation because it involved his abandoning the generals to the tender mercies of the Prime Minister. He refused to go to Paris.

Lloyd George's energies were inexhaustible. Frustrated, but not yet worn out, he returned to the charge for the third time. He now hoped to bring about the dismissal of the Chief of the Imperial General Staff.

Late in January the Prime Minister declared that Robertson and his colleagues of the General Staff were communicating official secrets to the newspaper Press. In particular, Lloyd George accused them of trafficking with Colonel Repington of the *Morning Post*, previously the Military Correspondent of *The Times*.

The Prime Minister complained to Lord Derby of a "grave breach of discipline" and a "gross breach of Army regulations". He pressed his Secretary of State to put the affairs of his Department in order by taking drastic action.

461

These "knock-out blows" were deftly turned aside. Lord Derby explained to Lloyd George that after investigation he learned that the figures and statements in Repington's articles were wrong and inaccurate. Moreover, Repington was an experienced military writer who frequently came into contact with many official persons in London and with Clemenceau and other high authorities in France. It would be impossible, Derby explained, to single out the General Staff as the source of Repington's information.

Although his nickname was "Genial Judas", Lord Derby remained firm in protecting Robertson and the General Staff from the wrath of the Prime Minister.

VII

If Derby now stood out as the protector of the generals, Lord Milner chose this period to step forward as Lloyd George's adherent and champion. He began to skirmish far out upon the political flanks of the Prime Minister's position.

At the end of December 1917 he visited Sir Douglas Haig at his headquarters, and stayed the night. He sought to convince the Commander-in-Chief of Lloyd George's high abilities and driving power. Haig recorded in his diary:[1]

Lord Milner arrived from Versailles. . . He seems to me a most honest and level headed man, and he does very valuable work in steadying Lloyd George. M. told me that he is more than ever impressed with the latter's ability and power of work. This no doubt is true and I assured M. that I, as C. in C. in France, considered it my duty to assist the Prime Minister to the fullest extent of my power and not to countenance any criticism of the P.M.'s actions. . .

Lord Milner also involved himself in the Press controversy between the Prime Minister and the General Staff. Milner always paid close attention to the newspaper Press. We may be certain that so long as Colonel Repington

[1] Blake ed., *Private Papers of Douglas Haig*, p. 274.

remained as Military Correspondent of *The Times*, Milner complained about him to Geoffrey Dawson. As early as 18th January Lord Milner reported to the Prime Minister that:[1]

18 . 1 . 18

My dear Prime Minister,   17 Great College Street, S.W.

You may be interested to know that Geoffrey Dawson has got rid of Repington. The latter has been, as you know, very mischievous lately, and it seems that he tried to pick a quarrel, because the *Times* was not taking a sufficiently strong line—against the Government. . . He has, of course, lately been disposed to run the extreme military view, that all the Army does is right, and that the whole mischief lies in a *fainéant* Government which won't take the necessary steps to provide it with sufficient "cannon fodder".

R. will, no doubt, now, be up to some devilry in other quarters.

Dawson also tells me that the lobbies last night and journalistic circles today are full of strong and persistent rumours, that Haig is to be superseded. There will, it appears, be a strong attack upon the Army . . . and it has been put about that this is secretly encouraged by the Government. Dawson himself entirely disbelieved this, and I confirmed him in that impression. . .

Yours ever,

M.

Meanwhile, there came ominous rumblings from another quarter. Sir Edward Carson proposed, exactly at this juncture, to resign from the War Cabinet. The tiger was trying once again to break out of the cage of office. Lord Milner was hurried forward to persuade Carson to go quietly.

After he left the Admiralty in order to join the War Cabinet Carson paid a visit to Sir Douglas Haig, in France. There, he advised Haig to speak freely about his problems to Asquith, while he took care to tell Sir Douglas that the War Cabinet would not be allowed to interfere with the Commander-in-Chief's military arrangements.

Carson, to put it mildly, was pursuing an independent course. On 20th November, at the time of the Rapallo Conference debate, in a speech at the Constitutional Club,

[1] Lloyd George Papers, Milner to Lloyd George, 18th January 1918.

ostensibly in support of the Government, Sir Edward remarked that: "I know of no advisers on military matters except the Imperial General Staff, who attend the meetings of the War Cabinet. . . I have met in the course of my work . . . three great men . . . Field-Marshal Haig, Sir William Robertson and Sir John Jellicoe. They have my absolute confidence". On that day Robertson at once wrote to Carson in order to tell him that he had not approved of the Rapallo Agreement, and that his opinion had not been asked with regard to the establishment of the Supreme War Council. In fact, Robertson explained, he had withdrawn from the sitting of the Rapallo Conference because he could not agree with the policy adopted by the British Government at Rapallo.[1]

By the end of the year Admiral Jellicoe was dismissed from his post as First Sea Lord. Carson was angered by the step. His patience was also worn thin by Lloyd George's handling of Irish affairs. He made up his mind to resign from the Government in order to regain his freedom of action.

So far as Lloyd George was concerned, he looked upon Carson's decision as a factor that might be of influence in the struggle with the generals. The Military Party, at the War Office and in the House of Commons, was now in a position to gain the formal support and allegiance of the Prime Minister's most dangerous antagonist. Lloyd George turned to Lord Milner to smooth Sir Edward's departure from the War Cabinet. Milner instantly came forward to help.

On 22nd January Milner wrote to Lloyd George about Carson's last hours in office. In order to make certain that Carson resigned quietly, and not in the guise of an enemy of the Administration, Milner remained at his elbow while he prepared a letter of resignation. Milner also advised Lloyd George to publish the correspondence at once so that the public would be convinced, as Carson stated in his letter,

[1] Colvin, *Carson*, vol. III, pp. 284–5.

that Irish affairs were the sole reason for his decision to leave the War Cabinet. Milner was anxious to avoid the suggestion that was certain to be made, that Carson was resigning because of the military policies of the Government. He wrote to Lloyd George:[1]

> Carson is now drafting his letter in its final form. He comes to see you with it in *half-an-hour*. It is, I think, essential that both the letters should be handed to the Press before dinner-time, as Geoffrey Dawson tells me the thing is already beginning to leak and that it must be put properly before the public tomorrow morning.

On the next day, 23rd January, Milner was able to report that: "I have seen Carson. He has evidently no idea other than that he is giving it up. . . His one solicitude in the matter is that . . . his Secretary . . . should not be turned out".[2]

Lloyd George was relieved by this outcome to the affair. At the same time Carson was grateful for Milner's intervention. A friend of his family wrote at the time: "Sir Edward is very unhappy . . . Lord Milner has been very nice and understanding . . . the only man who *really* seems to understand. . ."[3]

In these circumstances Lloyd George proposed to move forward against Sir William Robertson once again. Bonar Law was staunchly loyal. Lord Milner was dealing with those generals who were prepared to listen to him, with the newspaper Press, and with dangerous politicians like Sir Edward Carson. In this combination of Bonar Law and Lord Milner lay the key to the Prime Minister's parliamentary power and authority. Bonar Law controlled the regular legions of the Tory party. Lord Milner was respected by those Unionist rebels who were uneasy in following their official leader. Together, these men made certain that the mass of the Unionists would cleave to the Prime Minister in the hour of crisis.

[1] Lloyd George Papers, Milner to Lloyd George, 22nd January 1918.
[2] Lloyd George Papers, Milner to Lloyd George, 23rd January 1918.
[3] Colvin, *Carson,* vol. III, p. 311.

The way ahead was still beset with dangers, but Lloyd George refused to hesitate any longer. He could not allow the generals by themselves to decide the high strategy for the 1918 campaign. It was necessary for him to settle matters with the General Staff, or relinquish his responsibility for the fate of the country into their hands.

XVIII.   The Strongest Man in the War Cabinet

A subtle solution – Lord Milner summons General Wilson to London – His plan – A General Reserve – Sir Henry Wilson reports to Milner – His Versailles plan – The counter-attack of the Military Party – Lord Milner outraged by the defiance of the generals – He advises the dismissal of Haig and Robertson – Lloyd George's caution – His "brain wave" of the 9th February – Milner attacks Sir W. Robertson – Lord Derby changes his mind – An astounding state of affairs – Lloyd George at breakfast – Milner threatens to resign – Military dictation – Milner, a Vice Regent of the Prime Minister – The strongest man in the War Cabinet.

I

IN the final phases of his assault upon the General Staff, Lloyd George turned to Lord Milner and Sir Henry Wilson, the British Permanent Military Representative at Versailles. Wilson provided the technical military advice, while Milner sustained the Prime Minister in the political sphere.

In the debate of the 19th November Lloyd George had assured the House of Commons that the Supreme War Council would enjoy no "executive authority". He was required to give this assurance in order to avoid the defeat of his entire plan. By this promise, however, he had delivered himself into the hands of the soldiers. If the Supreme War Council and the Military Representatives at Versailles had no "executive authority", the generals had little to fear from them as an alternative source for the production of Allied war strategy.

Lloyd George now set about the difficult task of effectively slipping out of his promise. He meant to avail himself of strategic plans that came elsewhere than from the British War Office. Eventually, he hit upon what he later called a "subtle solution". The original suggestions for this new course came from Sir Henry Wilson, a man accustomed at all times to the provision of subtle solutions.

From the very beginning of the Versailles arrangement, the War Office sought to control Wilson's activities as British Permanent Military Representative to the Supreme War Council. In his diary for 9th December Wilson wrote: "Another bid by the Army Council to keep a hold of me, by an order to submit to them any advice that I was going to give to the Supreme Council. I wrote at once . . . pointing out that I did not advise the Supreme Council but was only one of four, and that all our advice was collective, and therefore could not be sent to the War Office of any one country".[1]

Some weeks later Wilson was suddenly summoned back to London by an urgent telegram from Lord Milner. In London, Lloyd George proposed to dismiss Robertson and replace him as Chief of the Imperial General Staff by appointing Wilson to the post. Sir Henry's reply to the suggestion contained the germ of the new course that was eventually acted upon. Instead of such a drastic step, he advised Lloyd George and Milner to give him more power at Versailles and thus, without ostentation, reduce the extent of Robertson's authority:[2]

> . . . Milner told me that Lloyd George is so angry with Robertson that he proposes to kick him out and put me in. As I said to Milner again—I am opposed to this, though all in favour of Lloyd George giving me more power at Versailles, and reducing Robertson from the position of a master to that of a servant.

In January a further advance upon these lines was made Lloyd George had often thought about a Generalissimo, a

[1] Wilson, *Diaries*, vol. II, p. 39.
[2] Wilson, *Diaries*, vol. II, p. 47.

general who would be appointed to direct and co-ordinate the activities of the Franco-British Forces. He realised that from the political point of view this solution to the problem of creating a unified strategic outlook was impossible. National and professional jealousies in the 1914-18 era would never permit complete Allied unity of command, the placing of the Army of one nationality under the orders of a foreign Commander-in-Chief. In those days such a solution to the problems of the Grand Alliance of the Allied Powers was looked upon as an impossibility.

However, Milner and Lloyd George now took up the idea of what Milner called a "limited Generalissimo, disposing of the *general reserve* only".[1]

This suggestion was conveyed to Sir Henry Wilson for his comments by L. S. Amery. At that time Amery was in charge of the political branch of the British Staff at Versailles. At Lord Milner's direction, he wrote to Wilson to solicit his opinion about a "limited Generalissimo" who might control the General Reserves of the Allied Forces. On 14th January 1918 Wilson reported to Lord Milner about the proposal. His letter falls into two separate parts:[2]

My dear Milner,   14.1.18
   The P.M. wants to know my views on a proposal to appoint Joffre as C-in-C and me as his Chief of Staff?
   My views are these:—
   I have always been in favour of one C. in C. in theory and opposed to it in practice and for the following reasons:—
   (a) no great and proud nation would agree that its *main* armies should be commanded by a foreigner. (This does not apply to detachments such as Salonica, Gallipoli, Egypt, etc.).
   (b) It is impossible to give a man the power of C. in C. unless you also give him the power to dégommer.
   (c) It is impossible to give a foreigner the power to dégommer for such a power *if* exercised would break the Alliance.
   Imagine Joffre dismissing Haig or Byng or Pershing or Diaz!

Having disposed of the Generalissimo, Wilson then turned

---

[1] The phrase is used in a letter from Milner to the Prime Minister, preserved in the Lloyd George Papers, undated, but written in the middle of January 1918.
[2] Lloyd George Papers, Wilson to Milner, 14th January 1918.

to his own solution of the problem. His letter of the 14th
January went on:

... No, believe me a Generalissimo is impossible, nor is such an
appointment rendered more practicable by giving him a foreigner as
Chief of Staff. In my opinion the real solution of all our difficulties lies
in the further development of Versailles which the P.M. himself set up
... I suggest that a central Reserve be placed *under* Versailles. I believe
by this means we shall gain most of the advantages of a Generalissimo
and suffer few of the disadvantages.

When I first thought of this plan and laid it before Robertson ... I
told him I thought this Reserve might ... be under him & Foch.
I have had time since then to think the matter right out, and that
alternative would *not* do. I am clear now that this Reserve must be
under Versailles.

Heigh ho. What a long letter.

H. W.

The suggestion contained in Sir Henry Wilson's letter
was now adopted by Lloyd George and Milner. They
resolved that the solution to their problem with the
General Staff lay in the creation of an Allied Reserve Army,
commanded by the Permanent Military Representatives at
Versailles.

Lloyd George determined to force this decision upon the
generals, despite all opposition from the War Office and the
Military Party. As early as the beginning of February he
contemplated appointing Lord Milner as Secretary of State
for War and relegating Derby to the Ambassadorial post in
Paris.

II

In the last week of January 1918 Sir Henry Wilson mentioned the new plan to Clemenceau. He reported secretly to
Lord Milner that the French leader was pleased with the
idea.[1] After these preliminary preparations were completed
to their satisfaction, Lloyd George and Milner set out for
the meeting of the Supreme War Council which began on
the 30th January.

[1] Wilson's letter is preserved in the Lloyd George Papers.

At the Supreme War Council it was decided to furnish the Military Representatives at Versailles with executive as well as advisory powers.

Since Russia was now out of the war, everyone realised that a massive German attack was bound to fall upon the Allies in the spring. In order to meet this attack, it was agreed to set up a General Reserve of British and French divisions which could be thrown into the fighting in case the Germans threatened to break the line, either in the British or in the French sector.

This Reserve Army, according to the arrangements of the Supreme War Council, was to come under the command of the Allied Military Representatives at Versailles.

The decision meant that Sir Henry Wilson and Marshal Foch, the most important soldiers at Versailles, would be empowered to order British troops into action without referring to Sir William Robertson in London, or Field-Marshal Haig at the British Headquarters in France.

Lloyd George was now in a position to ignore or neglect Sir William Robertson's advice. He could, whenever he desired, turn to Sir Henry Wilson for technical assistance and suggestion.

Now, the soldiers were required to act. If they did nothing all would be lost to them. General Sir William Robertson could not be expected to accept a rebuff of this kind quietly.

The General was a remarkable man. His career in the British Army was unique. The son of a village tailor, he had enlisted as a trooper in 1877, at the age of seventeen. He had advanced from the ranks, step by step, until he gained the first place in the profession of arms when he was appointed Chief of the Imperial General Staff, at the end of 1915.

This upward course had been pursued without the help of highly placed friends or relatives. It was a fantastic achievement, based solely upon ability and determination. How could a soldier of this quality abandon his responsibility for the safety of the Army to men like Lloyd George and Henry Wilson? In the eyes of professional soldiers like Robertson, the Prime Minister was an ignorant civilian politician while Wilson was a colleague who had gained, and deserved, the deep distrust of his brother officers.

On 1st February Robertson prepared a minute which he despatched at once to Lloyd George. In this paper he argued that only a member of the Army Council in London could have the information about troops, supplies, munitions and other matters that was essential for the effective control of military operations. His minute implied that Sir Henry Wilson, stationed in France, was not in a position to secure information of this kind.

As a matter of high principle he urged that the Secretary of State and the Army Council must be consulted before British troops were engaged against the enemy.

There were, in addition, constitutional questions to be considered. In Robertson's opinion, a British Commander-in-Chief could not be required to obey the orders of any authority save the Army Council or the Secretary of State for War.

He suggested that these difficulties might be overcome if the Chief of the Imperial General Staff were made a member of the Versailles military organisation. In effect, he proposed that he should supersede Sir Henry Wilson as one of the commanders of the Reserve Army.[1]

At Versailles, Lloyd George ignored these opinions and suggestions. He paid no attention to them. It remained for the Military Party to take action in other areas. They were not slow to accept the Prime Minister's challenge.

Robertson's first step was to send a report of the Versailles proceedings to Lord Derby. His account, though exaggerated, was designed to have an effect in the political sphere. He informed Derby, in a letter dated 2nd February 1918, that:[2]

[1] For Robertson's views see his *Soldiers and Statesmen*, vol. I, pp. 226ff.
[2] Churchill, *Derby*, p. 306.

. . . The real question was one of command, and for all practical purposes we now have a French Generalissimo. I do not know how . . . powers are to be delegated to an officer, not on the Army Council and not directly under you, to issue orders to a Commander-in-Chief . . . It is folly . . . to imagine that anyone can issue orders about what is called General Reserves and stop there. The officer to issue orders about reserves must issue orders about many other things as well. . . Are you prepared to be Wilson's Minister and yet have no control over him?

III

Six days later, the counter-attack of the generals was launched in the public Press. On 8th February Colonel Repington of the *Morning Post* sent a telegram to his newspaper which declared that the recent decisions at Versailles were of so strange a character that "Parliament should demand the fullest details and a Parliamentary Committee should examine them at once and take the opinions of our General Staff and of our Commanders in the field concerning the new arrangements".

It has sometimes been said that this telegram caused the explosions which followed. It was not the case. On that evening the *Globe* newspaper reprinted the Repington telegram, dated 5th February, and added certain comments of its own, which Lloyd George later described as "full of significance having regard to what happened subsequently".

When Lord Milner opened his copy of the *Globe* on the evening of 8th February he was outraged by the leakage of highly secret information, and by the defiance of the generals. He sent the *Globe* article to the Prime Minister and told him that if the opposition to the idea of a General Reserve were maintained, it would be better to dismiss both Haig and Robertson rather than abandon the Versailles scheme.

Unlike the Prime Minister, who was always a careful man, Milner now threw all cautions aside. He insisted upon immediate and drastic action. So far as Lord Milner was concerned, the generals must obey without further demur or be broken and dismissed upon the spot.

The article in the *Globe* of 8th February read as follows:

WHAT HAPPENED AT VERSAILLES?
DISQUIETING RUMOURS FROM PARIS REGARDING THE HIGHER COMMAND.
DEMAND FOR HOUSE OF COMMONS INTERVENTION.

The veil of mystery with which His Majesty's Ministers have sought to involve the proceedings of the Supreme War Council at Versailles is lifted this morning by a disquieting telegram from the Military Correspondent of the "Morning Post" who is in Paris, and evidently knows the facts that have been so jealously withheld from the House of Commons. . .

It may be hoped that, as Mr. Asquith was responsible for entrusting the Higher Command to Sir Douglas Haig . . . and Sir William Robertson . . . who both to a peculiar degree enjoy the confidence of the British Army and the British nation—he will not stand by and allow this arrangement to be broken up. . .

It may also be hoped that the House of Commons, which claims to be the seat of power, will refuse to allow itself to be elbowed out of its proper functions, and that at least we may be allowed to know what is going on behind the scenes. . .

Is there or is there not a Generalissimo?

Milner's covering letter to the Prime Minister, which accompanied the *Globe* article, was the logical conclusion to the course he had adopted in the previous November when he became a convert to Lloyd George's strategic outlook. The political hero of the Army now took up a position as the most uncompromising enemy of the generals. Lord Milner was convinced that he and Lloyd George were right, and since that was the case, it followed in his opinion that the generals had to be wrong. Fiercely, he wrote:[1]

Confidential.   8 . 2 . 18
My dear Prime Minister,   17 Great College Street, S.W.
    You have no doubt seen the enclosed from the *Globe*.

---

[1] Lloyd George Papers. The letter is printed in full in Lloyd George, *War Memoirs*, vol. II, pp. 1671-2.

I think the sooner we make a move the better. This kind of thing cannot be allowed to go on.

About Haig, I greatly doubt whether he would make common cause with any W.O. people against the Government. . .

On the other hand, I do think that he is likely to offer a resistance of his own to the proposal, that he should allow any of his divisions to be placed in a General Reserve . . . he is incapable of seeing any point of view but his own. . .

Now the creation of a General Reserve is the key to the whole business. It is not only clearly right in strategy but it is the basis of our whole good understanding with the French.

It is no use having a great rumpus and getting rid of Robertson, if the policy is to be side-tracked, for quite different reasons, by Haig.

. . . it would be better to lose both Haig & Robertson than to continue at the mercy of both or either of them. The situation is much too critical for that. . . The Army will be quite happy, if the worst comes to the worst, with Plumer and Harrington vice Haig and Bertie Lawrence. . .

I don't *want* this . . . my only point is that, *if* Haig were intractable, I believe we could still deal with the situation. The one vital thing is, since there must be a change, that we should be able once for all to do what we know to be right.

> Yours v. sincerely,
> Milner.

Lord Milner had now advanced beyond Lloyd George's own position. The Prime Minister was still busy with his political calculations. But Milner was not prepared to accept a compromise of any kind. Within a few days he threatened to resign from the War Cabinet unless Robertson was instantly removed from his place.

IV

The problem that now confronted Lloyd George was the reduction of Sir William Robertson. Lord Milner was pressing him forward upon the boldest of courses. As a politician, however, the Prime Minister was not in a position to accept the forthright advice of his colleague. He was required to deliberate upon his actions with very great care. Although this episode of political history has often been described by skilful analysts, it is doubtful if Lloyd George's exact course of manoeuvre will ever be explained with complete accuracy of detail.

So far as we are concerned, it is clear that Lord Milner's recalcitrant attitude played a significant part in the events that followed.

On the 9th February Lloyd George had an interview with Ian Macpherson of the War Office and with Lord Derby and Sir Douglas Haig, who had been summoned home from France for the purpose. The interview was complicated, tortuous and thoroughly devious. Lloyd George believed that he had found a solution to his problem.

At this meeting Lloyd George suddenly explained that he "had had a brainwave to the effect that as Sir William Robertson evidently thought that Versailles was going to have a great deal of power that he should have the option of taking that place in preference to that of C.I.G.S. In that case Sir Henry Wilson should become C.I.G.S.".[1]

According to a document Lloyd George had drawn up in preparation for the meeting, it had been proposed to call the British Military Representative at Versailles a Deputy Chief of the Imperial General Staff. However, it was felt by Macpherson, Derby and Haig that this would be a humiliation of Robertson in case he chose the Versailles post. These words, as a result of their objections, were removed from Lloyd George's paper.

Late on the 9th February the Prime Minister reported these developments to Lord Milner while he explained that Haig had been "quite reasonable". According to his account, Haig agreed that Wilson might be selected as Chief of the Imperial General Staff although he did not like the idea, and pointed out that the Army would be "shocked" by the appointment. Lloyd George made it clear in his letter that Robertson was not to be called a Deputy Chief of the Imperial General Staff when Wilson replaced him at the War Office.[2]

[1] see Churchill, *Derby*, p. 310.
[2] see Lloyd George, *War Memoirs*, vol. II, p. 1673.

Although one authority has stated that the events of the 9th February meant that the crisis was over and that Lloyd George had won,[1] this was not the case at all. Haig and Derby were men who often changed their minds, if it seemed in their interest to do so. Nothing had yet been settled. The game was not played out. Robertson had not yet made his choice.

On the 11th February the Military Party struck another hard blow at the Prime Minister. Sir William Robertson and his friends were still full of fight. They meant to challenge Lloyd George to open battle. Nothing less than the fate of the Government was now at stake. Robertson and those who agreed with him believed that they were in a position to defy the decisions of the War Cabinet.

On that day an article by Colonel Repington was published in the *Morning Post*. It revealed to "friend and foe alike" the entire plan of an Allied Reserve Army under the command of General Foch at Versailles. Lord Milner and the Prime Minister were especially denounced in this article, which expressed the hope that the Army Council would make a "firm and united stand" against the new arrangement. Lloyd George, who remembered the effect of this thrust later, wrote of the article in his *War Memoirs* that: "I know nothing comparable to this betrayal in the whole of our history. It was immediately appreciated in Germany".[2]

Lord Milner was certain that the crisis was not yet over. On the 11th he wrote to the Prime Minister in order to impress upon Lloyd George his own opinion of the proposals which had been discussed with Derby and Haig, on the 9th February.

According to that arrangement Robertson was to be offered a choice between the Versailles place and the post of Chief of the Imperial General Staff. The object of Lloyd George's "brain wave" in presenting such an alternative was

[1] The authority is Randolph Churchill, see his *Derby*, p. 314. His chapter on the fall of Robertson is the fullest published account of the matter, based on several important sources.
[2] Lloyd George, *War Memoirs*, vol. II, p. 1676.

clear enough to Milner. If Robertson chose Versailles, the Prime Minister would be in a position to throw his support behind Wilson as Chief of the Imperial General Staff, while the Versailles Committee, including Sir W. Robertson, would be allowed to languish.

For these reasons, Milner now sought to depress the status and authority of the British Military Representative at Versailles.

It was not a complete reversal of course, on his part. Milner believed in the Reserve Army as that strategic mass of manoeuvre which the Allies had never had before. He was also convinced that the chief military adviser of the Government had to be a man in whom the politicians placed their faith and reliance. If Robertson were removed to Versailles, he believed that the Government's objects could be attained. He wrote to Lloyd George:[1]

Confidential   11.2.18
My dear Prime Minister,   17 Great College Street, S.W.
    I am still rather anxious about the W.O. situation.

    I hope the paper you drew up and showed to me on Saturday afternoon *still holds good*. Except in so far as it makes the Versailles man a Deputy Chief of the Imperial General Staff and a member of the Army Council, which is unnecessary and had better be abandoned.

    But if there is any question of Robertson having something more than the Versailles job, as defined in that paper, and retaining some over-riding or even concurrent authority at the War Office, then I am sure we are heading for disaster. The whole object of the change is to make the Chief Military Adviser of the Government a man with whom we can get on.

    Unless that is clear, and we are free from interference between him and us, all the fuss and commotion will have been worse than useless.

    . . . If there is to be a fight . . . we can win. But let us at least make sure that at the end of the fight we are free men and not still saddled with our Old Man of the See! [*sic*]

    If, to smooth matters over, we leave any ambiguity in the situation, we are done.

Yours very sincerely,
Milner.

[1] Lloyd George Papers, Milner to Lloyd George, 11th February 1918, marked "Confidential".

Lord Milner's attitude was much more straightforward than that of the Prime Minister. He had three aims in view, throughout the crisis. He wanted Robertson to be relegated to an unimportant post. He desired to see an effective Reserve Army created in the field. He hoped that the Government would at last secure the services of a high officer in whom it could place its trust. He was so afraid that Lloyd George might jeopardise these objects because of the political pressures to which he was being subjected that on 12th February he threatened to resign. Colonel Hankey recorded in his diary that: "Milner . . . hinted at resignation . . . he would not remain in office if Robertson stayed on. . ."[1]

On the 11th February the affair entered a new phase. On that day the Prime Minister's proposals defining the relations between the Chief of the Imperial General Staff and the Versailles Representative, the document discussed on the 9th February, were placed before Robertson by Lord Derby, for the first time.

The General's reply was clear and definite. He told Derby: "It seems to me absolutely necessary that the General Staff Officer who is to give orders regarding the reserves . . . must be in constant and direct touch with the various departments of the War Office. . . Only the C.I.G.S., residing normally at the War Office, can be in this position. . ."[2]

Robertson's opinion was at once adopted by the Army Council. On the afternoon of the 11th February the Army Council met and ". . . the Military members . . . suggested that the C.I.G.S. should also be our representative at Versailles".[3]

Lord Derby, on that day, brought this resolution to the attention of the War Cabinet. They refused absolutely to accept it. They would not entertain the suggestion of the

---

[1] Hankey, *The Supreme Command*, vol. II, p. 776.
[2] Robertson, *Soldiers and Statesmen*, vol. I, p. 234.
[3] Churchill, *Derby*, p. 316.

Army Council that the two posts of Chief of the Imperial General Staff and Military Representative at Versailles could be combined.

Now Lord Derby changed his mind. Although he had accepted the Prime Minister's suggestion that Robertson might go to Versailles, in the period between the 11th and the 13th February he began to back Robertson in his desire to remain on as Chief of the Imperial General Staff. However, he did not agree with Robertson in his claim that the two posts could be held by the same officer.

In these circumstances the Military Party adduced a new plan of their own. It has been well described by Sir W. Robertson: ". . . Lord Derby showed that he was now desirous I should remain C.I.G.S., and on February 13 he handed me a copy of a note which he had addressed to the Prime Minister proposing that this should be done. Sir Henry Wilson was to continue to act as the British Representative on the Executive Committee, and the position between myself and him was to be 'practically the same as between General Foch and General Weygand'. On being asked whether these arrangements were agreeable to me, I at once accepted them without qualification of any kind. As in the case of France, they left in the hands of the C.I.G.S. unquestioned authority over the employment of the Army, and did not divide it between two officers as was done in the Prime Minister's Note".[1]

What did this new proposal of the General Staff imply? It had one meaning only. It meant that Robertson should remain as Chief of the Imperial General Staff and that Wilson should only serve at Versailles as his subordinate or deputy, acting under his orders.

On the 13th February Derby was bold enough to take this suggestion to the Prime Minister. He actually suggested to Lloyd George that Wilson should become a Deputy Chief of the Staff while he continued to serve as British Military Representative. He proposed to the Prime Minister

[1] Robertson, *Soldiers and Statesmen*, vol. I, p. 235.

that Wilson should be looked upon as Robertson's deputy at Versailles. Lloyd George refused to consider this suggestion. One can understand his exasperation with the Secretary of State for War.

The proposal that Wilson should be considered as the deputy of the Chief of the Imperial General Staff outraged Lord Milner, and brought him back into the controversy. On 13th February he wrote to Lloyd George in order to warn him that such a course would bring on a "fresh series of squabbles and misunderstandings".

Lord Milner's letter reveals an astounding state of affairs.

We have seen that on the 9th February Lloyd George saw Haig and Derby in order to define with them the relationship between the Chief of the Imperial General Staff and the British Military Representative. When they suggested certain amendments to the Prime Minister's plan, when they said that if Robertson accepted the Versailles post he should not be referred to as a Deputy Chief of the Staff because he would be humiliated by the title, Lloyd George agreed to their proposed alterations in his paper.

It seems reasonable to believe that it might have taken the Prime Minister a day or two to circulate the amended paper to his colleagues in the War Cabinet. However, Lord Milner's letter of the 13th February reveals that as late as that day, four days after the Prime Minister's interview with Haig and Derby, two separate documents dealing with the matter were still in the hands of his colleagues.

One of these versions had been printed.[1] It contains no suggestion that the Versailles Representative should be regarded as a deputy of the Chief of the Imperial General Staff.

The other version of the document is completely different, in certain significant aspects. Point three of the second version declares:[2]

---

[1] In Robertson, *Soldiers and Statesmen*, vol. I, pp. 232–3; and in Churchill, *Derby*, pp. 315–16.

[2] The document is preserved in the Lloyd George Papers.

3. The C.I.G.S. to have two deputies, one at the War Office and the other at Versailles. The D.C.I.G.S. at Versailles to be a member of the Army Council

No historian can hope to plumb this mystery. Was it an oversight? It hardly seems possible. Was the Prime Minister presenting one group of his colleagues with one document and another faction with a completely different paper? It is impossible to say. Did Lloyd George deliberately create a confused situation inside his own Government or did he merely look upon each of the two papers as "another version of the same"? More simply, it may be that several drafts were prepared at various stages of the controversy.

In any case, Lord Milner and Sir Henry Wilson took strong objection to the second document. Since it now seemed possible that Robertson might remain at the War Office after all, Lord Milner, in these circumstances, sought to fortify and bolster up the independence of the British Military Representative at Versailles. He wrote to Lloyd George:[1]

13 . 2 . 18

My dear Prime Minister, 17 Great College Street, S.W.

Wilson has just been to see me at your request.

There seems to be two versions of the document defining the relations between the C.I.G.S. and Versailles. . .

Wilson makes a sound point I think in contending that he ought not to sit on the Versailles Board as any man's deputy. It is an independent appointment, like that of the other members of the Board, and the supreme control of the Government and the position of the C.I.G.S. as the chief adviser of the Government is amply safeguarded. . .

If you put your foot down . . . I am sure you will be on strong and unassailable ground and the thing will work, otherwise I foresee a fresh series of squabbles and misunderstandings.

Yours very sincerely,
Milner.

We should observe that by this stage of the controversy Lloyd George had so contrived things that his position now seemed to be that of a mediator or arbitrator between Milner

---

[1] Lloyd George Papers, Milner to Lloyd George, 13th February 1918.

upon the one hand and Lord Derby and the Military Party upon the other. The Prime Minister's happy position as an arbitrator beween two Conservative members of his Government is well revealed by an extract from a Memorandum prepared by Lord Derby:[1]

... The matter came before the War Cabinet (on February 13) and there was a very sharp division of opinion. . . I suggested that Sir William Robertson should be asked to continue his work as C.I.G.S. ... Lord Milner, Mr. Barnes, and Mr. Bonar Law were against this and were of the opinion that as Sir William Robertson had refused Versailles his employment should cease. Lord Curzon and Mr. Balfour supported me and it was left for the Prime Minister to give the deciding vote.

... next morning he invited Lord Milner and myself to breakfast. Lord Milner and I were absolutely opposed to each other and it was quite evident that whilst I wanted to keep Sir William Robertson and was indifferent to the fate of Sir Henry Wilson a precisely opposite view was taken by Lord Milner.

VI

After the breakfast meeting of the 14th February Lloyd George told Lord Derby that he had decided in his favour, and against Lord Milner. Sir William Robertson was to be asked once again to choose between the two posts. Lloyd George was seeking to appear before his colleagues, and before the King who was following the matter closely, as a fair man concerned only with the correct solution of the problem.

The Prime Minister realised, however, that he was offering Robertson nothing at all. If Robertson chose Versailles the Board of Military Representatives would be ignored by the British Government. If he decided to remain at the War Office the authority of the Versailles Council would be enhanced. The old soldier had been jockeyed into a hopeless position.

Unlike Lord Milner, the Prime Minister was prepared to

[1] Churchill, *Derby*, p. 322.

wait for a few days. He understood that his "brain wave" of the 9th February had delivered the General into his hands. Although Milner was dissatisfied by this course and was threatening to resign, Lloyd George would not be hurried forward. He was required to keep the politics of the affair firmly in his mind. He would not take the initiative. There was no need for him to do so. There was no reason for him to have recourse to the harsh step of dismissing Robertson. He would leave the initiative in the affair to the General. He would allow Robertson to make his selection between the two posts, and thus commit official suicide all by himself.

Sir William Robertson's understanding of the matter forced him to insist that he should remain on as Chief of the Imperial General Staff, and that the Versailles Representative should be looked upon as his deputy and subordinate. Robertson explained to all who would listen to him that only one man could give orders to the Army while he pointed out that under the Prime Minister's plan there would be two high officers in such a position.

The War Cabinet, however, insisted that he must make a choice. This situation explains the General's recalcitrance. His unhappy position has been perfectly described by Lord Beaverbrook: "What a dilemma for Robertson! What a desperate confusion of all his hopes and aspirations. Either way he was done".[1]

On 14th February the Prime Minister allowed Arthur Balfour to visit Robertson on behalf of the War Cabinet, and invite him to make his choice. Balfour, until this time, had been inclined to support Robertson and Lord Derby. However, the General's iron resolution to defy the Government by refusing to choose between the two posts convinced Balfour that it was now his duty to support the Prime Minister. Balfour could not agree that a soldier should attempt to force his opinion upon the British Government. "It was now a question", Lloyd George later

[1] Beaverbrook, *Men and Power*, p. 197.

484

wrote, "whether the Government of the day should submit to military dictation on a matter where they were by every constitutional precedent the supreme authority".[1]

By the 15th February Lloyd George had thus reached the political position he had sought to gain from an early stage of the crisis. He was well content with an analysis of the affair which Lord Stamfordham had prepared for the information of the King a day or two earlier. Lord Stamfordham wrote:[2]

Lord Derby . . . knew that if the Prime Minister agreed to Sir W. R.'s terms . . . that he should be both C.I.G.S. in London, and a Member of the Executive Committee, with a Deputy to act for him . . . Lord Milner and Mr. Barnes would resign; if on the other hand Sir William Robertson were to resign, Lord Curzon, and he (Lord Derby) would leave the Government, and if this resulted in the fall of the Government there was a serious danger of its fate being attributed to the work of the Army and might be a very disagreeable cry with which to go to the country.

By the 15th February Lloyd George was at last prepared to act. He could rely upon Bonar Law and Milner, whenever he moved against Sir William Robertson. George Barnes of the Labour Party was also on his side. Lord Curzon, though trafficking with both factions, could generally be depended upon to make a wise selection in the hour of crisis. Arthur Balfour had been won over as a result of his talk with Robertson.

The Military Party could still rely upon Lord Derby. Walter Long, Secretary of State for the Colonies, was another of their adherents. Lord Robert Cecil at the Foreign Office was wholly suspicious of the Prime Minister and a supporter of the General Staff. These men could count upon the assistance of a powerful section of the newspaper Press. In the House of Commons, many Members were looking for a lead.

[1] Lloyd George, *War Memoirs*, vol. II, p. 1687.
[2] The Stamfordham Memorandum is printed in Beaverbrook, *Men and Power* pp. 408ff., and in Churchill, *Derby*, especially p. 325.

On balance, Lloyd George decided to risk it. Sir Henry Wilson had been summoned to London by Lord Milner, as early as the 9th February. He and Milner had both chafed at the Prime Minister's delays. They were unable to understand the delicate course he had pursued. However, on the 15th Wilson recorded in his diary: "At last I found Lloyd George in real fighting trim".[1]

VII

It was arranged that Lloyd George should visit Buckingham Palace on the 16th February. He would see Lord Stamfordham and the King and tell them that if they objected to the dismissal of Sir William Robertson, the Government would resign. Ministers were not prepared to tolerate the "dictation of the Army". The final phase of the crisis was beginning.

On that day, probably before the visit was made, Lord Milner wrote to the Prime Minister. Since Lloyd George was now moving forward once again, Milner was eager to assist him in every way that he could.

Milner sent the Prime Minister a letter which he had just received from F. S. Oliver. In this letter Oliver urged that Lord Derby should be dismissed from the War Office in order to break the resistance of the high soldiers, and that he should be replaced by Milner as Secretary of State for War.

When Milner forwarded this letter to Lloyd George he was, in effect, renewing his allegiance to the Prime Minister at the very moment when the final decisions were being taken. He employed this method to reveal to Lloyd George that even if Derby resigned in order to support Robertson, the loss would not be too damaging to the Government.

Certain sections of the Tory party would certainly be angry if Derby left the Ministry. If he were replaced by

---

[1] Wilson, *Diaries*, vol. II, p. 61.

Lord Milner, however, large and significant numbers of Conservatives would be mollified. Lloyd George would still be secure, even if Robertson and Derby were banished together. Oliver's letter to Milner, which was sent on to Lloyd George, read as follows:[1]

. . . It seems to me that there is only one thing to do. . . I have always urged you to *begin* by getting the head right, and to leave the rest to look after themselves.

So long as you have Derby as Secretary of State . . . you will have misunderstanding, friction, chaos. . .

Six weeks ago when we dined with the P.M. a competent man like Simon Lovat might have filled the Bill. But now you want something a good deal bigger. Not only the Army but *the people are seriously disturbed*. Something equivalent to Squiff's move is needed—when he went to the W.O. after the Curragh crisis to restore confidence. Confidence must be restored. That is the prime necessity. The questions of "Henry" and "Wullie"[2] are really in the region of Tweedledum and Tweedledee. Confidence is the desideratum. And therefore I fear you must go to the W.O. . . . but not giving up your War Cabinet Ministership. . . . you are to clean up a mess as quickly as possible . . . *you are sent in an emergency as the Vice Regent of the P.M.*

If this is done, the questions of C.I.G.S. and Versailles, their mutual relations, and all the classical aphorisms of war—in which there seems to me to be a damned lot of pedantry—will certainly tend to evaporate very speedily. . .

This is the sense and you are at liberty to show this note to the P.M. or to send it to "John Bull" if you like. But *you* have got to move in the matter. . .

Thus fortified, Lloyd George faced the weekend of 16th–17th February with considerable confidence. At his interview in Buckingham Palace, he was assured by Lord Stamfordham that the King would not insist upon the retention of Sir W. Robertson. Later on that day Robertson's retirement from the post of Chief of the Imperial General Staff was announced to the Press.

All was not yet over, however. Derby, Haig and Robertson, the three champions of the Military Party, the

[1] The document, dated 15th February 1918, is preserved in the Lloyd George Papers in the form of a typewritten copy which Milner caused to be prepared.
[2] This was Sir William Robertson's nickname.

triumvirate on whom they had relied when they presumed to challenge the Government in the House of Commons and in the Press, still possessed one last chance. Haig had been summoned from France to be present in London upon this fateful weekend.

On Sunday, 17th February, Haig and Derby repaired to Lloyd George's house at Walton Heath. What would they say to the Prime Minister when they delivered their opinion upon the fate of their friend, the Chief of the Imperial General Staff?

VIII

Robertson had made it clear that he depended upon the support of Lord Derby, throughout the controversy. During the Passchendaele offensive, although his confidence in the attack had been shaken, the General had never flinched in his support of Sir Douglas Haig. He had always backed up the Commander-in-Chief in the presence of the politicians, despite his own doubts about the military validity of the Flanders operation.

How would this loyalty be repaid in the hour of decision?

At Walton Heath Haig refused to say a word in support of Sir William Robertson. When Lloyd George suggested that Robertson might be given the command of an Army in France, Haig refused to accept the proposal.[1] As a result of the Walton Heath meeting Lord Derby was isolated, for Haig derided him in the presence of the Prime Minister. Sir Douglas allowed Lloyd George to become aware of his low opinion of the Secretary of State for War.

For his part, Derby submitted his resignation. He had consulted the King on the point and had been advised that his retirement from the Ministry seemed to be his only valid course. He explained his difficult position to the Prime Minister. He was not in disagreement with the policy of the War Cabinet, but he had to remove himself from the administration out of loyalty to the men with whom he had

[1] Beaverbrook, *Men and Power*, p. 211.

488

served at the War Office. The Prime Minister could only bow to this straightforward interpretation of the situation. He arranged to secure the services of another Secretary of State for War. However, before the new arrangement could be completed, Lord Derby changed his mind. He desired to withdraw his resignation. And he promised to defend the Government's scheme in public, and to carry out the plans of the Cabinet in the War Office: "You may rest assured", he wrote to Bonar Law, "I should loyally work and defend the scheme".[1]

On Tuesday, 19th February, Lloyd George faced the House of Commons in order to defend the actions of the Government. On that day Lord Derby was in his place at the War Office, loyally working the new scheme; Sir Douglas Haig was back at his post in France, defying the public enemy in the field. There was no case for the Prime Minister to answer in the House. The attack of the Military Party failed to materialise. The crisis was over.

How different was the course pursued by Lord Milner, when compared with the actions of Haig and Derby. He had as much to lose as any of the participants in the crisis. As a patriot he was grateful to be in a position to serve his country as a member of the War Cabinet. Loss of office would have been a shattering blow to him, in February 1918. Had the Military Party succeeded, there can be no doubt that he, in company with Lloyd George, would have been swept to one side. Sir William Robertson had already dismissed him as a "tired, dyspeptic old man".

Despite these personal dangers, he never flinched from what he believed to be the right course. In November 1917, after studying the matter, he decided, as we have seen, that the strategic policies of the General Staff were invalid. From that moment he determined to change them. His iron will and his limited political insight prevented him from appreciating all of Lloyd George's devious writhings during the crisis. But the Prime Minister knew that he could

[1] Churchill, *Derby*, p. 332.

always depend upon his loyalty. It is no wonder that Lord Hankey, in his analysis of the struggle with the generals, wrote that: "Robertson's views were shared by Haig, Plumer and other Army commanders, while Lloyd George had the firm support of Milner, the strongest man in the War Cabinet".[1]

[1] Hankey, *The Supreme Command,* vol. II, p. 775.

XIX. The Secretary of State

Haig and the Versailles Plan – The Field-Marshal Com-
mander-in-chief – Pétain, Haig and Clemenceau – Lord
Milner cruelly disappointed – Ludendorff and the hour of
decision – Germany Hammer or Anvil – The 21st of
March – Lord Milner is sent to the Front – Milner visits
Clemenceau – The Doullens Conference – Milner explains
to Haig – Lord Milner breathes fire and defiance – Lord
Milner appointed Secretary of State – Lloyd George
furious with Milner – Colonel Repington attacks Milner –
His article in the *Morning Post* – Milner speaks to Waldorf
Astor – Five columns in *The Observer* – The crushing of
Colonel Repington – The Maurice Debate – An ancient
Persian proverb – A classic picture.

SIR WILLIAM ROBERTSON had been crushed with-
out mercy. He was required to pay in full for his defiance
of the War Cabinet. Of course, he was too eminent to
be banished completely, but he was relegated to the Eastern
Command, a post that could not compare with the one he
had lost.

Sir Douglas Haig, meanwhile, returned to France to
take up his duties at General-Headquarters. He had refused
to stand by Robertson when the issues between the
generals and the politicians had been put to the test.

Does this mean that the plans of Lloyd George, Lord
Milner and their colleagues in the War Cabinet to create
an Allied Reserve Army were now fulfilled? Did the
Executive War Board of Allied Military Representatives at
Versailles now take control of certain British, French, and
Italian Divisions assigned to them as a reserve?

This was not the case. Although Haig told Sir Henry
Wilson that "all these quarrels had nothing to do with him

and that he was prepared to accept whatever was decided by the Cabinet, and he would then play up all he could",[1] he had no intention whatsoever of being deflected from his course by the Whitehall politicians. His statements to Sir Henry Wilson were completely false.

Lloyd George later expressed surprise at the fact that Haig was unwilling to carry out the details of the Versailles scheme. We should notice, however, that the Prime Minister had no cause to be surprised by Haig's actions.

On 18th February, the very day after Haig forsook Sir W. Robertson, he was interviewed by Andrew Bonar Law. He told the Conservative leader that he would rather be relieved of his Command than "earmark" certain of his Divisions for the General Reserve. Bonar Law, who might have been required to make a statement upon the subject in the Commons, applied to Haig for his advice. The straight-forward and simple soldier, unaccustomed to the hair-splitting phraseology of the politicians, was thus forced to explain his abandonment of Robertson; and also his intention to refuse to accept the scheme Robertson had opposed to the point of resignation. He told Bonar Law: ". . . I thought it a bad scheme and unsound. . . 'He must not say that I thought the scheme workable but that I will do my best to work under it' ".[2]

This curious attitude to the problem was typical of Haig. It might seem to the public, from these words, that he was prepared to bow to the Cabinet's decisions; and to co-operate with the Government on the eve of the German attack in the West. Sir Douglas Haig, however, was not a man accustomed to setting aside his own convictions.

II

The dominant characteristic of the Field-Marshal Commander-in-Chief was his belief in himself. He was imper-

[1] Wilson, *Diaries*, vol. II, p. 62.
[2] Blake ed., *Private Papers of Douglas Haig*, p. 287.

vious to criticism. He possessed an invincible self-esteem. In the Somme battle in 1916, for example, he lost 60,000 men in the first day's fighting and gained no genuine objectives in his attack. He was neither shaken nor even disturbed by a development that might have cracked the nerve of a lesser man. The horror of Passchendaele worked no practical effect upon him, whatsoever.

The sources of Sir Douglas Haig's inner strength were twofold. In the first place, he knew that he belonged at the apex of English society. Unlike Robertson, he was not a man who had struggled up from the lowest ranks of the Army. He came from a wealthy Scots family of great antiquity. The Haigs of Bemersyde could trace their line back to the twelfth century, and were proud of the fact that they were the oldest family on the Scottish border. After a pleasant but undistinguished period of study at Oxford, Haig decided to make the Army his career. After Sandhurst, he received his commission in the 7th Hussars. His friendship with the Prince of Wales, later King Edward VII, was a source of help in the earliest days of his military life. In 1905, at the age of forty-four, he married the Hon. Dorothy Vivian, one of the Queen's maids of honour. By this time he had attained the rank of Major-General and, not unreasonably, was known in the Army as "Lucky Haig". Sir Douglas, by reason of his birth, his family connections, his wealth, and his marriage, was a secure and accepted member of the highest circles of British society.

In the second place, Sir Douglas was an extremely religious man. He was always buoyed up and sustained by his faith. He was convinced that he had been chosen by God as a man of destiny, while he knew that he could rely upon "Divine help" in all his enterprises.

In combination, these factors produced a personality that provides the student with much ground for speculation. The sturdy figure in the tight-fitting tunic belonged to a man who knew that he was right, and that whenever anyone disagreed with him that they were wrong.

No one who takes part in great affairs can expect the co-operation of those with whom he must work, at all times and in all circumstances. Differences of view are bound to arise, upon occasion. Whenever Haig disagreed with his colleagues or superiors or subordinates, he gave expression[1] to the most forthright and uncompromising opinions about these misguided men who hampered him in his pursuit of the right course. From his Diary we learn, at various times, that Lloyd George was a "cur"; that Foch was "selfish and obstinate"; that Generals Wilson and Rawlinson were both "humbugs"; that Lord Derby, Secretary of State, was a "very weakminded fellow . . . and, like the feather pillow, bears the mark of the last person who has sat on him".

As a professional officer Haig always laid strong emphasis upon the two qualities of loyalty and gentlemanly behaviour. He saw to it that he was surrounded by officers who were loyal gentlemen. For his own part, however, from the first days of his career in the Army, he had always been prone to secret criticism of his superiors. As early as the Sudan campaign, he had condemned his commander, Sir Herbert Kitchener, in private letters to the Prince of Wales. In 1914 and 1915 his complaints in high quarters about Lord French led to French's dismissal, and Haig's appointment to his place.

Whenever he met an officer for the first time, Haig observed his bearing and deportment with very great care. Foch, the great French commander, was dismissed by him upon one occasion as a soldier of little account because Foch gesticulated and waved his hands in conversation, in a manner alien to that of an English gentleman. Haig's gentlemanly qualities, if the scholar may advance into such a rarefied atmosphere, were themselves called into question by the 2nd Earl of Birkenhead:[2]

[1] In his Diary.
[2] Lord Birkenhead, *Life of F. E. Smith* (London, 1960), p. 287.

494

It may be observed that one of Haig's less attractive qualities was counting the glasses of brandy drunk by his guests. A reference to Asquith's consumption appeared in the *Private Papers of Douglas Haig* . . . Shortly after this book appeared, I happened to be lunching with Sir Winston Churchill who, pressing on me a second glass of brandy, said, "Have another glass, my dear boy. I shan't write it down in my diary!"

Unlike many of his brother cavalry officers, Haig, as a young man, devoted himself to serious study of the military art. In time, he became a Staff Officer of the first quality. When R. B. Haldane set about reforming the Army during the Campbell-Bannerman Ministry, Haig was one of his closest collaborators. Under that penetrating and critical eye he demonstrated military capacities of a high order; and won the approval of his official chief during a very important period in the history of the War Office.

It has often been said that Haig and Robertson were handicapped in their quarrels with the politicians because they were less fluent than the statesmen, less glib, less able to argue a case when confronted by the facile civilians. No one who has even glanced at Haig's military writings could ever accept the charge that he was unable to express himself. Often, he and Robertson deliberately chose to find refuge in the fact that they were blunt and simple soldiers, unable to explain the valid mysteries of their profession to an ignorant civilian audience. In fact, Sir Douglas Haig seldom wanted for words—either in conversation or in writing.

The Commander-in-Chief was a man of high, if rigid, capacities. Now, in February 1918, upon the eve of the German attack, he took up from Sir William Robertson's stricken hand, the opposition to the plans of Lloyd George and Lord Milner for the creation of an Allied Reserve Army.

III

Although the Versailles arrangement seemed to have been accepted, the attitude of the French authorities provided

Haig with his opportunity. Pétain, the French Commander, was anxious to keep all his Divisions under his own control. He was unwilling to surrender any of his troops to the Versailles Board. He was secretly encouraged by Clemenceau, who mistrusted Foch, the most eminent of the Versailles soldiers. In addition to his dislike of Foch, Clemenceau entertained certain vague military ambitions of his own, which inclined him to the thwarting of Versailles and the scheme of a Reserve Army.

In these circumstances, the ruin of the Versailles plan was speedily accomplished. On 6th February the Executive War Board at Versailles decided that the Reserve Army should be made up of thirty Divisions, drawn from British, French and Italian sources.

On 24th February, however, the French Premier visited British General-Headquarters. Sir Douglas Haig explained to him that: ". . . I had told my P.M. . . . that I could not earmark any Divisions at the present time as an Inter-Allied Reserve without upsetting my plans for defence. . . And that rather than change my plans . . . I would prefer to resign . . . M. Clemenceau at once said my statement indicated his line of action. He would arrange to 'écarter' (set aside) Foch gradually. He personally looked upon a close agreement between Pétain and myself as the surest guarantee of success."[1]

On 6th March Haig officially informed the War Cabinet that an enemy attack upon his Front was imminent. In such circumstances, he said, it would be impossible for him to send away any of his Divisions since all his troops were already assigned places in the British defence plan. He added that he was completing certain arrangements with Pétain, whereby they would rush to each other's aid in case of any emergency caused by the German attack.

[1] Blake ed., *Private Papers of Douglas Haig*, p. 289. According to Lloyd George, in his *War Memoirs*, p. 1714, he was not aware of Haig's attitude: "Had I been aware of his attitude", Lloyd George writes, ". . . I certainly would have imparted it to Milner. . ."

Lloyd George has explained that Haig's opposition to the Versailles plan might have been overcome. The new combination of Pétain, Clemenceau, and Haig, however raised immense difficulties. Moreover, Intelligence reports indicated that the enemy attack was coming soon. There was no time left to re-arrange matters.

On 14th March the Supreme War Council met in London. Before it sat, however, the fate of the General Reserve was sealed. All the advocates of the plan, distressed though they were, realised that there was no time for yet another major crisis in the Allied camp.

Lord Milner, in particular, was cruelly disappointed. He was the British civilian representative at Versailles. He had been the foremost opponent of Sir William Robertson and Lord Derby. He had convinced himself that the plan of a Reserve Army was the only correct strategic course for the Allies to adopt.

Nevertheless, so great was Haig's power and authority, Lord Milner was at last forced to admit defeat. For once, he abandoned his principles and looked at the matter from the politician's point of view. He was now concerned with "appearances", and not with the realities of the situation. This was a rare occasion in his career as a servant of the State. It deserves our close attention. On 14th March, before the meeting of the Supreme War Council, he wrote to the Prime Minister in the following curious and untypical terms:[1]

Confidential   14.3.18
My dear Prime Minister,   17 Great College Street, S.W.
    I hear that Haig is quite obdurate about the Reserve. He will have none of it.
    Desperately stupid and very awkward for us. The fact that *after all the fuss* there is no Reserve, when we have announced to all the world, that it was so vital and that all statesmen and generals and chiefs of staff were agreed about it, will look very bad indeed . . . hostile critics here will have us in the unanswerable dilemma: "Either what you said about this great new system was all humbug invented to

[1] Lloyd George Papers, Milner to Lloyd George, 14th March 1918, marked "Confidential".

serve an immediate purpose of personal intrigue, or, *if you really meant it,* you are risking disaster by your incapacity to carry it out".

My one hope is that you may yet succeed in inducing Haig to agree to the principles if we are content for the time being with a smaller reserve. That might not mean much *militarily,* though it would be of some use, but it would save our faces and preserve an important principle. . . But if Haig (or Haig and Pétain?) kill it now, I doubt if it will ever revive. And we shall have once more have passed under the yoke of the Generals.

. . . I hope the 3 Prime Ministers will agree among themselves how to get out of the mess and announce it to the meeting as *their* decision right away. Of course, that will only save appearances, but it will be better than having to listen to a rambling, incoherent, and totally illogical statement from Haig and then pretend to be convinced by it.

Of course, if Pétain has already got round Clemenceau, it might be best to let the French kill the thing and give the reason. But any discussion at the meeting would be regretable.

Yours very sincerely,
Milner.

Guile and bad faith were not confined to one side in this fateful period. Since the late winter of 1917 the Prime Minister and the War Cabinet had deliberately curtailed the number of reinforcements sent to Haig. They wished to make certain that he would not be in a position to renew the Passchendaele attack, that he would remain upon the defensive. He was also required to extend his front in order to relieve the French of a part of their burden. This decision of the Government, which Haig obeyed, was based largely upon political and diplomatic, rather than upon military factors.

In these circumstances, without a General Reserve, deprived of a full complement of reinforcements, and without an adequate trench system in their newly occupied areas, the British Armies made ready to meet the most stupendous German attack of the entire war.

IV

Meanwhile, in France, Ludendorff, the all powerful Quartermaster-General, brooding upon the difficult con-

498

dition of his own forces, realised that the hour of decision had come. He was confronted by a series of alternatives. Firstly, while the German Armies still held powerful positions in enemy territory, they might accept a limited defeat of their entire purpose in order to secure moderate terms of peace. In the second place, the Germans might shorten their lines by a retreat to their own frontiers, rallying their people to a defence of the homeland. In either of these cases, the Allies, themselves almost at the last gasp, would have been confronted by terrible problems.

However, Ludendorff fixed upon a third course of action. He would hazard all upon a series of tremendous strokes in order to achieve complete victory. He knew that his own Allies were at the point of collapse and that in Germany itself the signs of disintegration were beginning to appear. He decided, after calculation, to launch a series of massive offensives against the enemy in the early spring of 1918 in order to smash their powers of resistance before the reinforcements from America could have any effect in France.

Years before, Bülow, the German chancellor of the day, had explained that in the new century Germany would be Hammer or Anvil. She would accept no middle course. This *Hammer oder Amboss* philosophy still dominated the German mind. The Quartermaster-General, reinforced by Divisions sent to him from Russia, believed that ultimate victory lay in his grasp if his attacks could be made powerful enough to shatter the Franco-British forces within a reasonably short period of time. In order to accomplish his purpose, such is the stuff of great men, he was prepared to suffer one million casualties in the course of his spring offensives.

For a variety of reasons, it was decided that the first blow should fall upon the British Front. The arrangements were put in train; and shortly after dawn on the 21st of March the massed units of no less than thirty-seven German Divisions hurled themselves forward upon the British lines. Specially trained bodies of storm troopers led the way.

499

Their purpose was to "infiltrate" the British positions. The most significant advances were made upon the front of the British Fifth Army. Outposts were beaten in, or by-passed. The arrangements of the defenders were everywhere thrown into confusion. The British began to retreat, in disorder.

By the 23rd of March, General Gough, the Commander of the Fifth Army, ordered a general retirement of his entire force to positions behind the Somme River. Hundreds of guns and thousands of prisoners had already been lost by his Army.

It seemed, for a moment, that Ludendorff's supreme gamble was about to succeed. The enemy front had been broken in. The war of manoeuvre, with all that it entailed, the war that had eluded every Commander in the West since 1914, now seemed to lie in his hand. The stalemate fighting appeared to be over. Victory for Germany glittered upon the horizon of the military scene.

The immediate object of these hammer blows was fully understood at British General-Headquarters. If the Germans could take the rail and road junction of Amiens, they would be in a position to split the British and French apart, driving the British back upon the Channel ports in the north-west, and the French upon Paris in the south.

On 24th March, Pétain, the French Commander, informed Haig that if the enemy continued to drive forward he would fall back in order to cover Paris; and thus abandon all contact with his Allies. Pétain proposed to allow the enemy to penetrate between the two defending Armies. He believed that a further German onslaught was about to fall upon his own lines, and for that reason he was unwilling to commit his reserves to the support of the British.

Sir D. Haig reacted to this disastrous proposal at once. He instantly telegraphed to London asking that the Chief of the Imperial General Staff and the Secretary of State for War should come out to France, without delay. Haig realised that the very existence of his Army was now at stake.

Meanwhile, in London, the Prime Minister decided, even

before Haig's message arrived, that either he or Lord Milner must go over to France to discover why "the arrangements for mutual help had failed to materialise". They had been assured that Haig and Pétain had worked these matters out some time before the attack began. On the evening of 23rd March, Lloyd George and Milner agreed that the Prime Minister should remain at his post in London, and that Milner should leave at once for Paris.[1] The situation at the front seemed desperate. A strong man was needed to restore it.

We should notice that the Secretary of State for War was not sent on this mission. Although most accounts state that the Chief of the Imperial General Staff and the "War Minister" were sent out, this was not the case. Lord Derby was still the Secretary of State for War. Lord Milner did not succeed to that post until the middle of the next month, in April 1918. Lloyd George would not allow Derby to go. The Prime Minister wanted Derby anywhere but at the scene of action, in such fearful circumstances.[2]

This was the condition of affairs upon the 24th of March when Lord Milner left London in order to carry out his most important mission of the war. He carried with him the Prime Minister's authority to "do what he could to restore the broken Versailles Front by conferring upon Foch the necessary authority to organise a reserve and to control its disposition."[3]

V

Perhaps the fullest and best account of the famous Doullens Conference and the events leading to the appointment of General Foch as Allied "co-ordinator" is contained in

---

[1] Lloyd George, *War Memoirs*, vol. II, pp. 1730-1.

[2] It is curious that Haig's *Diary* for 24th March states that he asked ". . . the C.I.G.S. and the Secretary of State for War . . . to come to France," while his *Diary* for 25th March states that the request was for Wilson and Lord Milner to come. See Blake ed., *Private Papers of Douglas Haig*, p. 297.

[3] Lloyd George, *War Memoirs*, p. 1731.

a Memorandum prepared by Lord Milner on the 27th March 1918. This document, or parts of it, has been published in several books and articles, in both England and France. Extracts from Lord Milner's paper deserve a place in our study.[1]

Lord Milner's first problem in France was to discover the fate and condition of the British Fifth Army. The War Cabinet was uncertain about the condition of that force. It was clear, however, that it seemed to have disappeared, leaving a gap in the Allied line between the right of the British Third Army in the North, and the French in the South. Milner was not, at this time, concerned with the reasons that led to the Fifth Army's collapse, but with the more immediate problem of the yawning gap in the Allied line. He wrote in his Memorandum:

> The great mystery was the breakdown of the Fifth Army, which so far was not explained. . . Broadly speaking, however, there was no doubt that this Army was shattered and a breach effected in the Allied line. . . The retreating troops . . . were . . . still fighting . . . but were no longer anything like an organised barrier to the German advance. . . It was clearly useless to speculate with our present knowledge about the causes or the exact course of events . . . but the effect . . . on the general situation was, of course, perfectly clear and did not need to be dwelt upon.

Milner, after a day of travel, spent the night of March 24th at Versailles. On the next day Clemenceau sent him a message, asking for an interview. When they met, at the Ministry of War in Paris, the French leader declared that ". . . it was necessary at all costs to maintain the connection between the French and British Armies, and that both Haig and Pétain must at once throw in their reserves to stop the

---

[1] The following Extracts are taken from the *New Statesman* for 23rd April 1921, which published the Milner Memorandum in full, as a Special Supplement. *The Times* and the *Daily Telegraph* also published detailed accounts of Milner's activities at the time of the Doullens Conference. See, for example, D. Chapman-Huston, *The Lost Historian* (London, 1936), pp. 308 ff; and B. Worsfold, "March 26, 1918" in *The Times* for 26th March 1926. For a published account of Milner at Doullens, see also B. Worsfold's articles in *United Empire,* the journal of the Royal Empire Society, for May and June 1929.

breach. . ." This was a significant development, in view
of Pétain's declarations to Haig, made on the 24th March.
Clemenceau, according to Lord Milner's account, "said
among other things, it would be necessary to bring pressure
to bear upon Pétain to do more in that direction".

Later on that day, Lord Milner met with the French
leaders at Compiègne. There, they were joined by Pétain
who explained that he was sending reinforcements to the
aid of the Fifth Army. However, he "took a very pessimistic
view" of the situation, and pointed out that he could not
neglect the danger of a German attack upon his own positions. For that reason, he was not prepared to employ
all his reserves in the Amiens region.

His attitude was challenged by General Foch. About
Foch, Milner wrote:

> . . . General Foch evidently took a somewhat different view . . .
> He thought the danger of the great German push to break in between
> the French and British in the direction of Amiens was so formidable
> that risks must be taken in other directions. Even more divisions
> must if possible be thrown in, and . . . this might be done more
> quickly than Pétain thought possible. . . Poincare and Clemenceau
> were evidently in sympathy with Foch's view. . .

After this meeting at Compiègne ended, Lord Milner
had a private word with Clemenceau:

> . . . I had a few minutes' private conversation with Clemenceau,
> in which I impressed upon him that . . . I had some misgivings
> whether Pétain on his side was prepared to take sufficient risks in order
> to bring up all possible French reserves, on which, as it seemed to me,
> everything depended. He said that he agreed. . . He also agreed with
> me in sympathising with the attitude of Foch.

It was now necessary to meet with the British Commander-in-Chief, in order to discover his plans. Haig sent
a message to Lord Milner proposing that the meeting
should take place at Doullens, which lay behind the front
of the British Third Army, between Arras and Amiens.
The date of this meeting was fixed for the 26th March.

Lord Milner was accompanied by Sir Henry Wilson when he drove from Versailles to Doullens, on the 26th March. That wise counsellor took this opportunity to act as Foch's spokesman. During the journey, he urged that "the supreme direction" should be "virtually in the hands of Foch". Wilson told Lord Milner that all Foch wanted was "to have the express authority of the two Governments to bring about the maximum co-operation between the two Commanders-in-Chief". Lord Milner was convinced by Wilson's arguments. He explained in his Memorandum that:

> . . . it was, under the circumstances, the best solution. It was, in fact, something like a return to the original idea of the Council at Versailles directing a general reserve, with Foch in the chair, only with the substitution of a single man for the Council. . . There was also this in favour of it—that we knew that the British reserves had already been put in, and that the real question now was how much in the way of reserves could be got out of the French. . .

At Doullens, tanks were stationed at the Eastern entrances of the town, in case of an incursion by German cavalry. Clemenceau at once seized Lord Milner in order to tell him that Haig was proposing to uncover Amiens, and fall back upon the Channel ports. Milner was certain that the Field-Marshal had been misunderstood; and this proved to be the case. When Milner spoke to Haig and his Army Commanders he learned that Haig had no intention of abandoning the place, though Haig did fear that he would be outflanked unless the French came to his assistance.

As we have seen, it was Lord Milner's purpose, in order to retrieve the situation, to deliver a substantial measure of authority into the hands of General Foch. His Memorandum explains how he proceeded to the achievement of his object. Before the formal Conference at Doullens began, Lord Milner spoke to Sir D. Haig in private:

> I next had a few words with the Field-Marshal alone about Foch, and was delighted to find that, so far from resenting—as I had been led to believe he might do—the thought of Foch's interference, he

rather welcomed the idea of working with the latter, about whom his tone was altogether friendly.

With this much already accomplished, the Doullens Conference began. The French representatives were Clemenceau, Louis Loucher, the Minister of Armament and Aviation, Foch, and Pétain. Great Britain was represented by Lord Milner, Haig, and Sir H. Wilson. Poincaré was in the chair. It was at once agreed that every effort should be made to save Amiens.

Later, Pétain began to explain his difficulties, and the great effort he was making to help. Lord Milner observed that: "None of his listeners seemed very happy or convinced". Therefore, Milner decided to intervene:

At this juncture I asked whether I might have a word with Clemenceau alone. I then told him quite frankly of the conviction which had been growing in my mind since the previous day, and had been confirmed by my conversations with Wilson and Haig, that Foch appeared to me to be the man who had the greatest grasp of the situation. . . Could not he be placed by both the Governments in a position of general control, and given the sort of authority which he (Foch) had himself suggested to Wilson? Clemenceau, whose own mind I am sure, had been steadily moving in the same direction, at once agreed, but he asked for a few minutes to speak to Pétain. While he took Pétain aside, I did the same thing with Haig. When I explained to the latter what was contemplated, he seemed not only quite willing but really pleased. . .

Clemenceau then wrote out a formula to define Foch's status. After a minor alteration, the amended formula was read out. It declared:

General Foch is charged by the British and French Governments to co-ordinate the action of the Allied Armies on the Western Front. He will work to this end with the Generals-in-Chief who are asked to furnish him with all necessary information.

Lord Milner took particular care, in his Memorandum, to report to the War Cabinet upon Sir Douglas Haig's attitude: "Haig I was glad to see", Milner wrote, ". . . looked distinctly relieved and much happier than he had seemed earlier in the morning".

After the Conference, Milner and Wilson motored to Haig's Headquarters. There, Lord Milner noted that Haig ". . . certainly looked much less tired and in much better spirits than he had done earlier in the day. He told me again that he felt sure the new arrangement would work, as he would have to do with 'a man and not a committee'."

Thus ended Lord Milner's mission to the seat of the war in the hour of crisis and danger. Where previously there had been friction and suspicion, now all was harmony and mutual accord, for a time at least.

It seems clear from Lord Milner's account, prepared in those measured and careful tones he sometimes employed in his official writings, that the initiative in the appointment of General Foch lay with him. As we have seen above, several paragraphs of his report to the War Cabinet were devoted to establishing the fact that he approached the Field-Marshal in order to convince him that Foch should be appointed to a position of authority and power. Lord Milner took care to reveal the fact that Haig welcomed the idea, when it was "explained" to him.

Despite Lord Milner's clear account, Lord Haig's biographer, and the editor of his *Diaries,* have insisted that the plan to appoint Foch originated in the mind of Sir Douglas Haig. In describing Haig's attitude before the Doullens Conference, his biographer has written:[1]

> . . . At all costs the two armies must be kept together. Haig's simple and direct brain saw the only way in which it could be accomplished. Let both armies be put under one general. . .

It may be that Lord Milner was mis-informed about Haig's attitude by that devious creature, Sir Henry Wilson. In his *Diary*, Wilson claimed that on the 25th of March

[1] Duff Cooper, *Haig* (London, 1935) vol. II, p. 253.

he suggested to Haig that Foch should co-ordinate the action of both Commanders-in-Chief: "I suggested that Foch should co-ordinate ... In the end Douglas Haig agreed. I could not help reminding him that it was he (Douglas Haig) with Clemenceau's assistance, who killed my plan of a General Reserve. . ."[1]

In this matter of conflicting claims, which deserve to be recorded, perhaps the best conclusion was that reached by Haig's biographer:[2]

When many minds are travelling in the same direction and ultimately arrive at one conclusion, genuine doubt must always exist as to when, where and with whom the idea originated. . . It is to Milner's credit that he took upon himself the responsibility of committing the British Government to so important a step which was endorsed by the War Cabinet two days later.

. . . But wherever the idea originated . . . it can hardly be denied that its realisation at that time and in that way was due more to Haig than to any individual. . .

In any case, the Allied Governments had taken a very important step at Doullens. Although further conferences were required, in which Lord Milner played a part, Unity of Command in the Allied Armies was materially attained at Doullens. It was under this command arrangement, with its subsequent modifications, that victory, after further severe trials, was eventually achieved.

VI

Despite Doullens, and every other Allied arrangement, the weeks after the 21st of March witnessed the flood tide of the German offensive. It seemed to contemporaries that Ludendorff was about to force a decision upon the Western Front.

[1] Wilson, *Diaries,* vol. II, p. 77.
[2] Duff Cooper, *Haig,* vol. II, pp. 259-60. By contrast, the *History of the Times,* vol. IV, Part L, p. 355, states: "The Doullens policy, for which Milner deserves the chief credit. . ." etc.

In these grave conditions Lord Milner breathed fire and defiance. Often full of pessimism, he now told the Prime Minister that if a bad peace had to be made, he preferred to "let someone else make it". For his part, he urged Lloyd George forward, in order to retrieve the victory. On the very day of his return from Doullens, he wrote to the Prime Minister:[1]

27.3.18

My dear Prime Minister,　　　　　17 Great College Street, S.W.

... If there is a great disaster, we are as a Government "down and out" whatever we do, and we may as well fall gloriously over a big effort to relieve the situation.

If, on the other hand, "the plague is stayed", we are in for a long and dragging fight. It must be a year at least before the Americans can make their weight felt. We and the French can at the best *hold* the Germans. We are not strong enough to do more, and we shall not do that, unless we can prevent our army dwindling away. . . It is simply deluding ourselves to think that the Germans, after such success as they have had, in Italy and in France . . . *will not continue to press us for all they are worth.* They are certain to keep on pushing, and if they do not break us now, they will break us later. . .

Unless we can hold out another year, and that depends on what we do *now*—when people are thoroughly frightened and prepared for anything, a bad peace is a certainty.

I should prefer to let someone else make it. . .

Yours very sincerely,

Milner.

In such circumstances, when every national nerve and sinew had to be strained for a maximum effort, there was no longer any valid reason for Lord Derby to remain in his place as Secretary of State for War. Derby was not prominent in the councils of the Administration as a high strategist. His political position had been damaged beyond repair when he abandoned Sir William Robertson, in the previous February. By withdrawing his resignation at that time, he removed with his own hands the sting of his power. Since he refused to defy the Prime Minister, despite his stated

[1] Lloyd George Papers, Milner to Lloyd George, 27th March 1918.

intention to do so, who could stand forth as his champion? No one was prepared to defend Lord Derby after he, himself, refused to uphold the validity of his own actions and opinions.

Lord Derby had forfeited the respect of his associates. Robertson believed that Derby had betrayed him; Haig was full of contempt; and the Prime Minister later wrote brutally of him that: "He was not at his best in a crisis. In an emergency leaders who sweat despondency are a source of weakness".

A change had been contemplated for a considerable period of time. By mid-April 1918, no political dangers were involved in such a Ministerial reorganisation. Lord Milner was eager to take charge at the War Office. He believed that the soldiers would welcome his appointment. Several candidates were considered for the place. On 13th April Milner wrote to Lord George:[1]

13.4.18

My dear Prime Minister,   17 Great College Street, S.W.

Just off. A last word about the W.O.

Hankey or I. There is a good deal to say for both. . . H. has, of course, in some respects far greater qualifications. On the other hand, I should, I think, be more generally acceptable to the Army, could, if necessary, take drastic action with greater resolution and authority, and would be more easy to move, if the present push being over, I was wanted back in the Cabinet or not wanted at all. H. would not, I think, be a good man in the Commons, and he might not care to be forced into the Lords *nor would he be as acceptable there as I might be.*

Personally I have absolutely no feeling one way or the other. I only want the best thing done.

But if you decide to have Hankey, I strongly urge you to have a word with Wilson first. I don't think he would object, but clearly it might be a bit of a shock to him and to others. . . On the other hand there *may* be some real difficulty, which does not occur to you or me and might occur to him. . .

Yours very sincerely,
Milner.

[1] Lloyd George Papers, Milner to Lloyd George, 13th April 1918. The italics at the end of the second paragraph in this letter represent words which Lord Milner crossed out, but they remain legible.

By these skilfully phrased arguments, Lord Milner convinced the Prime Minister. On the 18th April it was announced that Lord Derby was to go to Paris as Ambassador; two days later he surrendered his seals of office to the King, and Milner took over in his room.

Thus, Lord Milner achieved the high distinction of becoming a Secretary of State.[1] It was a mark of Lloyd George's confidence in his powers and abilities. Even the *Morning Post*, the organ of the Military Party, gave a kind of tepid praise to the appointment. Its first leading article for 19th April explained:

> When Sir William Robertson fell we asked how it was that Lord Derby, who had publicly sworn that he would never desert him, reconciled it with his honour to remain in office. We remarked . . . "It might have been better, even from Lord Derby's point of view, to have played the man". We were wrong . . . for he has now been made his Majesty's Ambassador in Paris. . .
>
> If we cannot congratulate the Foreign Office upon this appointment we may at least congratulate the War Office, which is doubly fortunate in losing Lord Derby and gaining Lord Milner. It is true that Lord Milner has never shown any military capacity. . . However that may be, the soldiers will now have a man to whose intelligence they may appeal and on whose good faith they may rely. . .

When Lord Milner became Secretary of State for War he gave up his position as a Member of the War Cabinet. However, he continued to enjoy a very close association with the Prime Minister. It became their custom to meet each morning, before the Cabinet, in the company of the Chief of the Imperial General Staff. In this way, Lord Milner's opinions and advice were always readily available, whenever Lloyd George desired to avail himself of them.

The tasks of the Secretary of State in the midst of so terrible a war were extremely heavy. In fact, the history of the War Office in peace and in war was one of the least happy of all the great Government Departments. Lord

[1] It is curious that the *History of The Times*, vol. IV, part I, pp. 308-9 refers to Milner as the "Secretary for War" in its analysis of the formation of Lloyd George's Government, in December 1916. Milner, however, was not a Secretary of State at that time.

Milner's abilities as an administrator were certainly required in this new sphere. We should notice, however, that although Milner was responsible for a number of administrative improvements, his immediate burdens during his tenure of the post prevented him from carrying out any system of reform upon a large scale.

It is fair to say that the high point in the relationship between Lord Milner and Lloyd George had now been reached. Within a few days of the appointment, their alliance suffered an almost shattering blow, from which it never fully recovered.

VII

The defeat of the 21st of March was bound to be followed by political repercussions in London. Someone was certain to be blamed. And no one was more aware of this than the Prime Minister. He decided that his wisest course was to attack, to strike at his enemies before they had organised an assault of their own.

On the 9th April 1918, in consequence of these designs, Lloyd George rose in the Commons in order to say that despite the heavy losses of Passchendaele, the Army in France was stronger on 1st January 1918 that it had been on 1st January 1917. He also explained that there was only a relatively small number of British troops serving in Egypt and in Palestine.

These statements, taken together, could have but one meaning. It was that the troops in the West were there in adequate numbers; and that the line had been broken only as a result of the faulty dispositions of British General Headquarters. No blame could be attached to a Government which had furnished the Generals with an ample supply of men.

On the 10th April further figures were supplied to the War Cabinet by the General Staff. They confirmed the fact that the Allies enjoyed a superiority in infantry over the enemy, on the Western Front. On 18th April the Chief of the Imperial General Staff reported that the British and French had three more divisions in reserve than the Germans.

Suddenly, and without any warning, this picture changed completely. The War Office now reported that the German infantry outnumbered that of the Allies by a total of 330,000 men. Lloyd George was outraged by the production of these new figures. His entire Parliamentary case, and the very safety of his Government, rested upon the comparisons he had made in his speech of 9th April.

He was caught off balance. He later wrote: "Alas! All of a sudden our superiority disappeared in a weekend! I woke up on Monday, the 22nd of April, to read in the Weekly Summary prepared by the General Staff that an Allied superiority of 86,000 rifles had been converted into a German superiority of 330,000! Had some catastrophe befallen the Allies unawares, like the pestilence that destroyed Sennacherib's Army in a single night?... The disaster that tore such a yawning chasm in the Allied battalions occurred not on the blood-stained fields of France but in a carpeted chamber of the War Office. The devastation of our ranks was not wrought by German artillery but by a British fountain pen."[1]

Lloyd George at once recognised the purpose that lay behind the production of these new figures. The General Staff was striking back: "I realised," he wrote, "that the battle had been transferred to the Home Front."

In this battle the Prime Minister could permit no weakness upon his own side. His wrath and anger were directed against Lord Milner, the Secretary of State for War, who had allowed the new figures to be brought forward by his Department.

Already, in the public press, the supporters of the Generals were questioning the details of Lloyd George's speech of the 9th April. How came Lord Milner to make

[1] Lloyd George, *War Memoirs,* vol. II, p. 1781.

such a mistake? Was it a blunder on his part? Was it merely
the lapse of an old and tiring man? Was it an oversight?
Was it the result of some new intrigue, some shifting of
alliances, with deep and secret intent? No matter. The
Prime Minister, with so much at stake, was roused to a
passion of fury.

On the 22nd of April he sent Lord Milner a Memorandum, challenging the new figures supplied by the War
Office. It was couched in the hectoring terms of an irate
under-manager, furious at the inefficiencies of some obscure
junior clerk. It was not the kind of document a Secretary
of State usually received from the head of the Government.
Lloyd George wrote to Milner:[1]

Secretary of State for War.

I am entirely at a loss to understand the figures of Allied and enemy
rifle strength printed in last week's summary of the military situation.
Before I made my statement on the introduction of the Man Power Bill
in the House of Commons I asked the Staff to supply me with information as to the strength of the opposing forces on the Western Front
at the commencement of the battle. These figures showed a slight
allied superiority in infantry, a $3\frac{1}{2}$ to 1 superiority in cavalry, a considerable superiority in artillery. . . Now I am told that after four
weeks of the fighting, the enemy rifle strength is greater by 333,000
than that of the allies. What possible explanation can there be of this?
The attempted explanation is surely an inadequate one. . .

From any point of view this document is extraordinarily slipshod,
and I suggest that a thorough investigation be made as to how it came
to be prepared and who is responsible for the editing and issuing of it.

To these fierce charges about his Department Lord Milner
could make no valid reply. He remained silent, conscious
of the fact that he was responsible for the creation of a very
serious political situation. He sent no formal answer to the
Prime Minister's Memorandum of the 22nd April. It is no
wonder that Lloyd George later wrote of Milner:[2]

. . . Up till the spring of 1918 it is difficult to exaggerate his value
as a counsellor. . .

[1] *Ibid.,* pp. 1782-3. The paper is preserved in the Lloyd George Papers; and these
extracts are taken from it.
[2] Lloyd George, *Truth About the Peace Treaties,* vol. I, pp. 261-2.

When Lord Derby left the War Office Milner insisted on the succession. Neither Bonar Law nor I could dissuade him from undertaking so arduous a task. Physically he was not a strong man, and the interminable variety of bothering detail . . . soon wore out his limited reserves. The result was a tragic change in his quality. His nervous power was exhausted. His contributions henceforth were those of an exhausted man. His powers waned and his usefulness in the consideration of great issues gradually disappeared. Now and then we had a flash of his old powers . . . but the lamp was flickering for the oil was running out. . . The War Office literally killed him.

However exaggerated, we may assign the Prime Minister's change of outlook, and this diatribe, in part at least, to the matters touched upon in the Memorandum of the 22nd April.

VIII

The affair was far from finished. An agitation began in Whitehall, in the clubs, and in the Press. Charges were made in these quarters that the British Army had been forced back by an enemy considerably larger in numbers, in reinforcements, and in reserves. Furthermore, the veracity of the Prime Minister's figures, adduced upon the 9th of April, was challenged by several well-informed persons.

Foremost among these champions of the Generals was Colonel Repington, the Military Correspondent of the *Morning Post*. That paper, and those who read it, were usually looked upon as supporters of Lord Milner. The *Morning Post*, a high Tory organ, respected Lord Milner more than any other member of the Administration. Colonel Repington now decided to attack Milner in order to strengthen the case of the Military Party in the developing clash with the Government. It was a mistake on his part and, as we shall see, he was later required to pay in full for the error.

On the 26th April an article on the leader page of the *Morning Post*, written by Colonel Repington, condemned Milner and the War Cabinet in the most decisive terms. The blame for the 21st of March was placed squarely upon the shoulders of Lloyd George and Milner. Colonel Repington wrote:

Lord Milner's appointment as Secretary for War would, in normal circumstances, be welcomed by the Army. His capacity and application are acknowledged. . . But he is deeply involved in the past errors and miscalculations of the War Cabinet of Mr. Lloyd George, whose henchman he has been. . . Next only to the Prime Minister, it is to Lord Milner that we owe the cutting down of our infantry by one-quarter for the campaign of 1918, the want of drafts, and the defeats and losses of the past month. . .

In any future arraignment of the Ministry for its culpable misconduct of the higher direction of the war during the past fifteen months, Lord Milner must take his place on the bench of the accused alongside the Prime Minister. The infatuation and the ignorance of the War Cabinet and its contempt of the best military advice . . . are the sole and only causes of the present crisis on the Western Front. . . It is certainly astonishing that one so fully responsible as Lord Milner . . . should be placed in charge of the Army which, by these decision, has been brought into deadly peril. . . Bankrupt indeed must be an Administration . . . to place at its head, under the Crown, one of the two men most responsible for having brought things to their present pass. . .

By penning these words Colonel Repington sealed his own fate. He blamed the War Cabinet for the defeat of the Army in the field. He charged the Prime Minister and his Government with culpable misconduct.

Now, in the regular and ordinary course of British politics the Government of the day and the Prime Minister are often subjected to very severe criticism. A politician like Lloyd George must always expect to be attacked by his public enemies, in the most virulent terms, Colonel Repington was not ruined because of what he wrote about the Prime Minister.

The case of Lord Milner, however, was different. In the eyes of his friends he was sacrosanct, inviolable, secured by the sanctions of fair-play and the canons of good taste. Of course an extreme Liberal or Radical journalist might condemn Milner in the most extravagant terms, but conduct of that kind was only to be expected from bitter and narrow partisans of their calibre. The matter was completely different when the pages of the *Morning Post* were exploited in order to make public so base an outburst as this, upon so exalted a figure. Colonel Repington placed himself beyond the pale when he sought to fix upon Lord Milner the responsibility for the defeat of a British Army in the field.

On the 29th April Milner asked Waldorf Astor, owner of *The Observer*, to see to it that Repington's conduct did not go unpunished. In his turn Astor told J. L. Garvin that Repington had to be exposed—"thoroughly and ruthlessly".

In consequence of these high commands, the editor devoted almost a fortnight of his time to the preparation of a long article about the Military Correspondent of the *Morning Post*. Before the article was published Astor mentioned the matter to John Buchan, another of Lord Milner's disciples, at that time Director of Information in the Government. It was decided that Buchan should make certain that Garvin's article received the very widest publicity. In particular, Buchan promised to arrange that the article would be cabled to America, because Repington's military writings were very popular in that country.

On Sunday, 12th May, the mine was exploded. An editorial of five columns extending over two pages of *The Observer* was devoted to the "exposure" of Colonel Repington. He was reviled as an irresponsible and devious trouble-maker who urged one line of policy in one newspaper and a completely different set of opinions in another. Extracts from his articles were published in order to demonstrate and prove the validity of these charges. The colonel was dismissed as a man unworthy of trust or respect, as one who suffered from "weakness of character, defects of temperament, a fatal strain of hysterical instability". Often flamboyant in tone, and upon this occasion secured by the august support of Milner, Astor, and Buchan, Garvin was especially vehement in this article.

"There must be", he wrote, "an end to Colonel Repington's campaign of calumny . . . The scandal we have exposed has become a cancer of public life in war-time. We say that is must be cut right out . . . Mr. Lloyd George and Lord Milner are the men to make an end of this mutinous nuisance. . ."

Of Repington, Waldorf Astor later said: "The Garvin article finished him". And this conclusion, however blunt, was quite correct. Although the Colonel continued to write in the *Morning Post,* his reputation was destroyed.

When he criticised Lord Milner, Colonel Repington engaged the entire host of the Milnerites. No ordinary individual could hope to stand up to the counter-attack of that powerful company. With one notable exception Repington's name has been condemned absolutely in the literature that deals with this entire period of British political history. And this result was achieved, despite Repington's genuine contributions to the corpus of British military thought in the years between the end of the Boer War and 1918.[1]

It was a perfect Establishment "job". No risks in the affair were taken by Milner, Buchan, or Astor, the politicians most deeply concerned. Garvin, their agent in journalism, did their work for them, and disposed of the man who had presumed to annoy their chief.

IX

The crushing of Colonel Repington, however complete, was merely a skirmish of outposts. He was not the only one to question the veracity of Lloyd George's statements, made upon the 9th April.

More important were the actions of Sir Frederick Maurice, a General Staff Officer recently transferred from

[1] These paragraphs are based upon material in the Garvin Papers, and upon private nformation from the late Viscount Astor. The exception referred to is Randolph Churchill who, recalling his father's association with Repington in the Boer War period, offers a spirited defence of the Colonel in his *Life of Lord Derby,* pp. 311 ff.

the War Office. On the 7th May a letter from Maurice was published in several morning newspapers. The General accused Lloyd George of imparting incorrect information to the House of Commons in his speech of the 9th April. He also declared that Bonar Law had made false and inaccurate statements in the House.

These grave charges, if proven, could only result in the fall of the Ministry. In consequence of the General's letter, the issues between the Government and the Military Party were formally joined—in the famous Maurice Debate of the 9th of May. Despite the efforts of Asquith who led the Opposition, Lloyd George defended his Administration in a brilliant and telling speech. The House endorsed his Government with an overwhelming majority. The Military Party, as a result of the Maurice Debate, were broken and dispersed. They had tried conclusions with the Prime Minister in the House, and they had failed. This debate, such were the passions that it roused, also marked the final rupture between the Lloyd Georgian Liberals and those who followed Asquith. The future of their party was ruined by the events of the 9th of May.

Lord Milner was not involved in this clash in the House of Commons, save for the fact that the Prime Minister rehearsed his speech in his company on the day before the debate. However, as Secretary of State for War, Milner was concerned in an episode of some interest that was closely connected with the Maurice affair.

Among the many charges that were bandied about in the Press at the time, there was one that annoyed Sir William Robertson, who watched the affair from his headquarters in the Eastern Command. Several newspapers printed a story that Robertson had met with Asquith, General Trenchard, and Admiral Jellicoe, before the Maurice letter was published, in order to conspire with them against the Government. The object of these newspaper articles was to prove the existence of a military conspiracy.

On the 17th May General Robertson wrote to the Secretary of State for War in order to dismiss the story as a complete fabrication. The General explained that he supported no political party, and that he always avoided anything that smacked of politics.[1]

There is an ancient Persian proverb that says: "When the cat has eaten a thousand mice he goes on a pilgrimage to Mecca". This, or something very like it, was now Lord Milner's course. Having thoroughly smashed Colonel Repington by means of an article in *The Observer* which he had caused to be written, Lord Milner now deprecated all newspaper interference in the affairs of the State. He wrote to Robertson:[2]

Private   17 Great College Street, S.W.
My dear General,   19 May 1918

Thank you for your letter. I am glad you wrote it . . . personally I have attached no credence whatever to these tales. I am glad, however, to be in a position to give them an absolute denial, on your authority. . .

As you say, there is "much mischief and intrigue in the air." I am doing all I can to put a stop to a most poisonous controversy, which threatens not only to sow distrust of the civil authorities in the Army, but, on the other hand, to excite public opinion against some of our leading soldiers. . . Whether it is the *Morning Post* abusing the Government, or the *Daily Mail* abusing what it calls "the old gang"—it is all *equally detestable*. And with the enemy at our gates we simply must close our ranks and put an end to this internal discord.

                          Believe me,
                          Yours very truly,
                              Milner.

X

Lord Milner's first month as Secretary of State for War thus ended with the complete defeat of the Military Party. The Lloyd George Government, as a result of its triumph in the Maurice Debate, had vanquished its principal enemies in a formal debate. The strength of the Government was demonstrated for all to see. Its power and authority could no longer be called into question.

[1] His letter is preserved in the Lloyd George Papers.
[2] Lloyd George Papers, Milner to Robertson, 19th May 1918, marked "Private".

At about this time, Lord Milner entertained a visitor at his home in Great College Street. This was General Sir Hubert Gough, late Commander of the Fifth Army in France. Sir Hubert had been removed from his post because of the disaster of the 21st of March. The purpose of his visit was to beg Lord Milner to help him in his difficult circumstances.

Several high authorities, including Haig and Lord Derby, had promised Gough that a formal enquiry would be held into the circumstances of the defeat of his Army. The General, who had been subjected to very severe criticism, was eager to defend his own conduct and that of the soldiers who had been under his command. For him, the enquiry would provide an opportunity to vindicate his own actions and those of his beloved Fifth Army. Despite the promises, however, no enquiry had been held.

Gough had almost decided to abandon the matter when Lady Roberts, the widow of the Field-Marshal, intervened. She told Gough that it was his duty to make every effort to vindicate the honour of the Fifth Army. She urged him to ask the Secretary of State, Lord Milner, for an interview.

When General Gough visited Great College Street his object was to implore Lord Milner to arrange for an investigation into the actions and conduct of the Fifth Army during the early part of the Ludendorff offensive. The honour of his soldiers and his own honour as a professional officer were at stake.

This was the same Hubert Gough who had played a principal part in the mutiny at the Curragh in 1914. At that time Lord Milner had been one of his warmest admirers. Now, however, the situation was completely different. In describing the occasion of their interview General Gough has presented us with a classic picture of Milner in the guise of a high officer of the State who is confronted by an official visitor he is required to see; but one he is not prepared to help, in any way. It is a picture of obstinate and unbending firmness. It will serve to conclude this chapter upon Lord Milner as Secretary of State:[1]

Lord Milner had been in the habit of collecting round him certain bright young men whom he placed in important positions. . . He was still a very influential person and much in the confidence of Lloyd George. He then lived in a small but very comfortable house in Great College Street, Westminster.

On arrival I was shown into his study and found him seated at a big desk in the middle of the room. He asked me to sit down facing him. He was a distinguished-looking man who just missed being handsome. He had a long face and a pale complexion and his grey eyes looked rather coldly at me. He gave me the impression of reserve, lack of sympathy, perhaps just a hint of callousness.

I made my request briefly. An enquiry was promised and now the authorities went back on their promise. Could Lord Milner kindly help me by using his influence to insist that an enquiry should be held. . .

Milner straight away said that he was not prepared to do anything. . .

He actually said: "You must admit, General Gough, that your troops sometimes left their positions before they should have".

I admitted nothing of the sort. I said: "I do not know of a single case where the troops left their positions without orders".

He said nothing. Milner's remark was an outrageous mis-statement. . . It was evident that he was not even vaguely interested in my defence.

[1] Sir Hubert Gough, *Soldiering On* (London, 1954), pp. 179-180.

XX. The Appeaser

Milner considers a negotiated peace – At Russian expense –
Milner and the terms of peace – The effect of his Russian
Mission – Milner ready to consider peace because the
Germans cannot be beaten – The Russian Revolution –
A plan to bribe Lenin – The Imperial War Cabinet – Lord
Milner advocates a moderate peace – Lord Milner uneasy
about the effect of the March Revolution in Britain –
Labour, a "mad dog" – The Union of Democratic Control –
E. D. Morel – Milner urges action against "mischief
makers" – The Leeds Conference – Milner and Kornilov –
Milner and a tolerable peace – His attitude to the East –
Milner is thinking of peace at the expense of Russia –
His plans for a new war – Interview in *The Evening
Standard* – Milner and Northcliffe – The age of "appease-
ment".

I

THE members of the Monday night cabal continued
to meet after the fall of Asquith's Government. They
would not deprive the State of the benefit of their
considered counsel even though their friends were now in
power. They were, as a matter of course, delighted by Lord
Milner's assignment to the War Office, an appointment
they had urged for a very considerable period of time.

However, they were not pleased by the fact that Lord
Milner, after he became Secretary of State for War, gave
up his position as a member of the War Cabinet. They were
anxious for Milner to continue to concern himself with the
general direction of the war, in addition to his new Departmental duties.

It will be recalled that when F. S. Oliver urged Milner to
take over Lord Derby's place at the War Office in order to

restore confidence, he made it clear that Milner should accept the post as the "Vice Regent of the Prime Minister"; Oliver insisted at that time that if Milner went to the War Office, he should take care to remain a Member of the War Cabinet. F. S. Oliver's attitude was reflected by Geoffrey Dawson. On 19th April, the day after Milner's new appointment, Dawson wrote the first leader for *The Times* of that day. In it, he declared: ". . . It seemed in many ways an ideal combination that Mr. Lloyd George . . . should be . . . steadied by Lord Milner's clear brain . . . But the War Office is an all-absorbing problem. We doubt very much whether Lord Milner's transfer may not be dearly bought at the price of his absence from the central council of the Government . . . his presence at the centre of things has been so vital a factor in this Government that his appointment to the War Office should be definitely combined with continued responsibility for all the main decisions of the war. . ."

Although Lord Milner's limited stock of energy was consumed by his duties as Secretary of State, he continued to deal with the great affairs of the war.

Suddenly, on 13th June 1918, the serenity of Printing House Square was rudely disturbed by a startling letter. Clifford Sharp, editor of the *New Statesman,* wrote to Wickham Steed of *The Times* in order to tell him that Lord Milner was considering a negotiated peace with Germany at the expense of Russia. This plan certainly went far beyond the technical concerns of the War Office.

Sharp's information was bound to have a very great effect upon Lord Northcliffe, the powerful Chief Proprietor of *The Times*, a man always suspicious of those in Britain who even hinted at coming to terms with the German enemy.

Why did Clifford Sharp send this letter? What was his purpose? What were the qualifications and credentials that enabled him to make the charge?

Clifford Sharp has been editor of the *New Statesman* since

its foundation in 1913. In this post, as a matter of course, he worked in close connection with many of the leaders of the Labour Party, and particularly with Sidney and Beatrice Webb, the "policy-providers" of the Labour movement in Britain. In 1917 he was called up for military service, and began his training as an artillery officer. However, within a few weeks the War Office removed him from the Artillery in order to send him to Stockholm as an agent of the "Ministry of Intelligence". His task was to "pick up" information from foreign socialists.[1] Sharp, despite his altered circumstances, continued his close association with the Webbs. His experiences in Sweden and information furnished by the Webbs provided him with the facts he now sent to *The Times*. He wrote to Wickham Steed on 13th June 1918:[2]

> ... The matter seems to me vastly important and very disturbing ...
> It appears that the chief exponent of the idea of a negotiated peace with Germany at Russia's expense is *Milner* who has gradually converted two or three of his colleagues to the idea. When, about 8 or 10 weeks ago L.G. wanted the Webbs to dine with him and they refused, he arranged to meet them at the Haldane's house. The idea of course was to get, through them, at the Labour Party. . . When he found that he could not convert them he suggested that they should come and talk to Milner about it. This however they declined to do and they have not, in fact, met Milner. . .
> ... Our rulers . . . seem rotten, to have lost all their pluck, if they had any . . . Milner is perhaps an exception, as far as keeping his head is concerned, but then in his heart he is more of a believer in German culture than Haldane even. . .
> ... I have never been a Northcliffe enthusiast but I certainly am leaving England with the feeling that amongst those in high places here he more than any deserves the confidence of those of us who mean to see the thing through. Of course, we *shall* see it through, but heaven knows *how*, with such a crew in Whitehall. . .

Lord Northcliffe, a man to be reckoned with in the summer of 1918, was outraged by what he looked upon as Milner's perfidy. Until this time he had respected Milner

[1] See Margaret Cole ed., *Beatrice Webb's Diaries* 1912-1924 (London, 1952), p. 90, hereafter cited as B. Webb, *Diaries*.
[2] *History of The Times*, vol IV, pp. 360-1.

and the Prime Minister, and always contrasted their high qualities with those of their more mediocre colleagues. Northcliffe believed, and with good reason, that if Germany were given a "free hand" in Russia, she would become so powerful that she could menace the very existence of Britain.

What are we to make of Clifford Sharp's charge, so far as Lord Milner is concerned? These are deep waters. They are made murky by the fact that Lord Milner's papers, as the History of *The Times* puts it, "have been returned to the inaccessibility of the Cabinet office's files."[1]

However, we need not rely upon conjecture alone to determine Lord Milner's attitude to the idea of a negotiated peace with Germany. If we do not yet know all, certain factors may be adduced in order to help us in an analysis of the matter.

II

Lord Milner began to concern himself with the terms of

[1] *History of The Times*, vol. IV, p. 323, n. 3. See also the excellent work of Richard Ullman, *Intervention and The War* (London, 1960), who has examined a mass of previously inaccessible material concerned with British policy toward Russia in 1917 and 1918. At p. 83 Ullman complains that aspects of his story are "difficult to document without full access to the minutes of the Cabinet. . ." Unfortunately, Ullman's fine book falls down on this very point of a negotiated peace with Germany at Russia's expense. At p. 66, n. 31, he writes: "I have come across only two pieces of evidence which indicate that the idea of compensating Germany with Russian territory was ever given any consideration in British Government circles. . ." These two "pieces of evidence" according to Ullman, are to be found in J. L. Hammond, *C. P. Scott of the Manchester Guardian* (London, 1934), p. 232; and in Sir Henry Wilson's *Diaries*, vol. II, p. 49. Ullman makes no reference to Clifford Sharp's letter in the *History of The Times*; nor does he refer to this letter which is also printed in R. Pound and G. Harmsworth, *Northcliffe* (London, 1959), p. 645. Ullman also neglects the vital accounts on this matter of peace at Russian expense in B. Webb's *Diaries*, pp. 112-114. Despite these lapses, it is highly significant that Ullman's exhaustive researches turned up no other information upon the subject of peace with Germany at the expense of Russia. However, Ullman's conclusion must be balanced by the powerful analysis and summary of a brilliant American study—Arno J. Mayer, *Political Origins of the New Diplomacy, 1917-18* (New Haven, 1959), *passim.*, and especially p. 325 and n. 28 and p. 375, n. 20. There is also a summary of evidence upon the point in E. H. Carr, *The Bolshevik Revolution 1917-1923* (London, 1953), pp. 23-25, n. 6, who argues that there is strong "empirical" support for the Russian belief that Germany and the Allies could come to terms at the expense of Russia. Carr stresses that Milner was the most active advocate in the War Cabinet of a compromise peace.

peace long before the convulsion of December 1916 carried him to office in the Lloyd George Administration.

For example, as early as May 1915 Milner helped Geoffrey Dawson to work out the attitude to be adopted by *The Times* toward the general question of peace with the Central Powers.

At that time Wickham Steed, the foreign editor of *The Times* and for long its correspondent in Vienna, was distressed to learn certain of the details of the secret treaties concluded between the British and French Governments and Italy and Russia. These treaties were desperate war-time measures. They were designed by the British and French as measures to increase the military power of the Allies against the public enemy. Their object was to confirm the Italian and Russian Governments in their conduct of the war against Germany, Austria, and Turkey by the promise of territorial rewards. By the terms of these treaties of the spring of 1915 Italy and Russia would, at the eventual peace settlement, gain territory at the expense of the Central Powers and Turkey.

For his part, however, Steed argued that since the treaties secretly abandoned the principle of nationality, the Western Allies had sacrificed their moral and ethical position. They had, by agreeing to these awards of territory in order to make certain of the Italians and Russians, fallen back upon the principle of "strategic necessity", the very idea to which Germany had already appealed as a justification of her ruthless actions against her neighbour states.

In Steed's opinion there was another aspect to the matter, in addition to the moral one. He believed that the treaties, from the military point of view, were a blunder.

As an expert upon Balkan affairs Steed was concerned about the fate of the various Slav peoples in Eastern and Central Europe. Their national aspirations were affected adversely by these secret arrangements. Steed knew that the Slavs would be terribly upset whenever they discovered the details of the secret treaties. The Dalmatian and Tyrolese sections of the treaty signed with Italy, for example, affected the Serbs in particular. Steed, in a message to Dawson, argued that: "The disappointment of the Southern Slav world, and in particular of the Serbians, may have serious effects upon the military situation. (Serbia has) rendered greater service to the Allied cause . . . than those rendered even by Belgium."[1]

Geoffrey Dawson was required to reply to his foreign editor's criticisms of the secret arrangements of the Allied Powers. It was his task to set out for Steed's information the policy to be followed by *The Times*.

According to the *History of The Times* his answer to Steed was "probably composed under the inspiration, or even at the dictation, of Lord Milner". Dawson told Steed with regard to the secret treaties of the Spring of 1915 that:[2]

> The practical consideration . . . is that the thing has been done. Russia, France, and ourselves are all committed to it, and the extent to which each Power was active in the matter is only of academic interest. In these circumstances to encourage any agitation likely to inflame Serbia, or to cool off the Italians, seems to me both useless and mischievous. I cannot see why we in England should be more pro-Slav than the Russians. If we are to win this war . . . we shall want all the help we can get. . . So far as *The Times* is concerned, I think the only *possible* service we can render at this stage is to praise the Serbians. . . I am *against* any continued ventilation of the rights of small nationalities now that the Convention is signed. . .

We may conclude from this exchange with Wickham Steed that Lord Milner was not, when he considered British war-aims at this early stage, especially concerned with the aspirations of the Slavs in Central and Eastern Europe.

In the terrible circumstances of the war he believed that the Allies were required to seek and even purchase the aid of any power that might help them to stave off defeat at the hands of the common enemy. The agreement signed with Italy in April 1915 certainly violated the principle of

[1] *History of The Times,* vol. IV, p. 313.
[2] *Ibid.,* p. 314, and n. 1.

nationalities since Istria and portions of the Dalmatian coast were ceded to that country, even though the population was predominantly Slav. In Lord Milner's opinion "any agitation likely to inflame Serbia, or to cool off the Italians. . ." was both ". . . useless and mischievous".

III

Lord Milner's experiences during and after his Mission to Russia in January and February 1917 had a profound effect upon his outlook in this sphere. It will be recalled that he left for Russia on 21st January 1917, as the head of a British Delegation to an Allied Conference in that country. The purpose of the Conference was to establish closer contacts with the Russians for the more effective conduct of the war, upon all fronts. In particular, the Allied delegates proposed to do what they could to ensure adequate supplies for the Russians; and to make certain that the material sent to Russia was exploited to the best advantage.

Lord Milner's impressions of the Russian scene were gloomy. He recognised they they were discouraged by the course of the war, and appalled by the frightful casualties they had suffered. He worked out, in detail, a scheme for the supply of war material for the Eastern Front. Although he realised that this plan was valid he was, nevertheless, worried and depressed by what he saw in the country. On the 18th February he took the extreme step of paying a visit to the Tsar at Tsarkoe-Selo, where he urged a more active course upon the Emperor. Despite the boldness of his tactics, he told Sir Henry Wilson, his military colleague on the Mission, that "he had not been able to rub it in. . ."[1]

On the journey back to Britain Milner explained to Wilson that, in his opinion, the Germans could not be defeated in the field. For that reason, he was prepared to consider terms of peace with the enemy. Exactly what these terms were to be, he did not say.

[1] Wilson, *Diaries,* vol. I, p. 320.

Moreover, in more general terms, Milner questioned the value of Continental Alliances for the British Empire. Such alliances, in his view, needlessly involved Britain and the Empire in the complications and difficulties of European diplomacy. Why should the British Empire, he asked, concern itself with the quarrels of Europe? In Lord Milner's opinion, if Britain would only forge closer and stronger links with the Dominions she would be strong enough to defy any opponent.

These reflections, thrown out on the sea-voyage from Russia, soon occupied a dominant place in Milner's thought, and eventually in the thought of his young men. It is necessary for us to refer to Sir Henry Wilson's Diary at some length, because of the high significance of Milner's remarks. Wilson wrote on 1st March 1917:[1]

. . . Milner considers the defeat of the Boches in the field as impossible, and therefore he is prepared to consider terms of peace, which I think quite impossible. . .
Milner and I also discussed the question of the Dominions. He had a sort of vague hope that, in future, we might be able to keep out of European complications, saying that the Dominions have vast potentialities and that if we link up closely we should be strong enough to defy all comers. Here, too, I don't agree. We shall never be strong enough to stand alone, until the population is vastly increased. . . And this will take 100 years if we confine ourselves to English breeding. Meanwhile what is to be done? It seems to me that we must have alliances in Europe. But if we have alliances in Europe how are we to keep out of complications?

IV

When Lord Milner returned to London he prepared a report of his Russian experiences for the War Cabinet. In this document he expressed the opinion that: "there is a great deal of exaggeration in the talk about revolution in Russia". In company with most of the other British

[1] *Ibid.*, pp. 322-3.

delegates he believed that "there would be no revolution till after the War".[1]

Unfortunately for this prediction, the Russian Revolution of March 1917[2] broke out a few days after the report was written. As a result, Milner became the target for Lloyd George's scathing criticisms, which increased in their intensity with the passage of time.

Of far greater significance was the effect of the March Revolution upon the attitude of men in all the belligerent countries. The overthrow of the Tsar and the establishment of a democratic regime in Russia were matters of profound consequence to the governments and peoples of Britain, France, and Germany. The international importance of the Russian Revolution was instantly recognised, everywhere.

Men were not simply concerned with the military developments that might result from the change of Government in Russia, though such developments were certainly of desperate moment. Lord Milner, as we shall see, at once interested himself in certain other effects of the March Revolution in Great Britain.

When war was declared in August 1914 the mass of the British nation united behind the Prime Minister in the decision to take up arms. The few pacifists and dissenters who opposed the war at that time were unpopular and without much influence in the country. However, by 1917 the terrible casualties at the front and privations at home had resulted in a genuine war-weariness that gave the pacifists and those who disagreed with the policy of the Government a new opportunity. The March Revolution also played into their hands, with dramatic effect. Until this time they and their adherents had been uneasy about the alliance with autocratic Russia. Now, however, the example of the Russian democracy encouraged them in their desire to press upon the British Government certain new policies,

---

[1] Lloyd George, *War Memoirs,* vol. I, p. 942.
[2] This March Revolution was not, of course, a Bolshevik or even a Socialist Revolution.

policies which aimed at a "progressive" or a "liberal" peace. Those in Britain who questioned the secret diplomacy of the Government, the system of competitive armaments which they believed had led to the war, the pre-war colonial rivalries, and the refusal of Ministers to state their war-aims in the clearest terms began to acquire genuine authority, particularly among the working men. Although Lord Milner was already prepared to consider coming to terms with the German enemy, he looked upon the March Revolution with completely different eyes than did these Radicals of the Independent Labour Party and the Union of Democratic Control. The terms of peace that he envisaged had little or nothing to do with the programmes they entertained, as we shall see.

Although the press of other duties prevented Milner from developing any elaborate Russian policy, he watched with more vigilance than any other Minister certain effects of the Russian Revolution, both at home and abroad. For example, on 15th May 1917 he wrote to the British Ambassador in Petrograd that: "... I follow your proceedings and thoughts every day in the F.O. telegrams ... I am afraid there is nothing now to prevent Russia passing through the usual stages of the revolutionary fever ... This naturally knocks the bottom out of all our plans. The work which our Mission tried to do at Petrograd ... is all as dead as Queen Anne. We must for the present continue to carry out our part of the bargain, but it cannot, I fear, be long before the futility of continuing to send arms and munitions to Russia—when we know they will not be used against the enemy—must lead to a break-down of the whole thing."[1]

The British Government at this time considered some singular proposals in its efforts to re-establish its influences in Russia. Although Lenin was not yet in power in Petrograd, the Prime Minister and Lord Milner took some notice, slight though it was, of a proposal to bribe the revolutionary leader. On 31st May 1917 Milner sent Lloyd George certain

[1] Milner's letter is printed in the *History of The Times*, vol. IV, p. 250, n. 1.

recommendations which had been presented to him; the general object of these recommendations was to point out ways in which British influence in Russia might be increased. One method suggested in the paper was bribery. According to the document "even Lenin could be got by bribery . . . anything could be done in Russia, Turkey or Greece by bribery!" Milner's comment on these remarks, in his covering letter to the Prime Minister, was: "the enclosed brief note is well worth your *personal* perusal."[1]

Gloom continued to dominate Milner's outlook for some months after the March Revolution in Russia. His conclusions about the effect of that Revolution upon the Allied cause were well stated in a letter to a member of the staff of *The Times* in August: "The collapse of Russia upsets all our calculations. But for this great blow I felt sure of finishing the war this autumn. Now everything is more uncertain . . . I still feel . . . we certainly ought to win. But the prolongation of the war exposes us for an indefinite time to the chapter of accidents."[2]

It is thus clear that months before the Russians sought an armistice, Lord Milner had already despaired of them as an active Ally.

V

Meanwhile, the representatives of the Dominions and India had assembled in London for the meetings of the Imperial War Cabinet and the Imperial War Conference. These high officers of the Empire had been summoned to deal with three separate though related problems. They were to decide, as we have seen in an earlier chapter, upon ways to wage the war more efficiently; they were to examine the terms of peace that might prove acceptable to the Empire as a whole; and they were to discuss the post-war

[1] Lloyd George Papers, Milner to Lloyd George, 31st May 1917, and enclosure (undated).
[2] *History of The Times,* vol. IV, p. 252.

problems of the Empire. The meetings began on the 20th March 1917, immediately after the Revolution in Russia.

During the period of these meetings Lord Milner took certain steps to make clear to the public his own views about the terms of peace that might be accepted by the British Empire. The extent of the Prime Minister's concurrence in Milner's opinions upon the subject must remain a matter for conjecture, so far as the available evidence is concerned.

We should notice that the decision to summon a meeting of the representatives of the Empire was made at Lord Milner's suggestion, in the very first days of the Lloyd George Government. In the autumn of 1916, as Lloyd George has put it in a striking phrase, "the highest political circles were sibilant with peace whispers". In December of that year the German Chancellor, Bethmann Hollweg, approached the Allied Powers with a proposal that talks should be begun between the belligerents upon the terms of peace. Bethmann's suggestion was, in part at least, a tactical move. It was instantly rejected by the Russian and French Governments, though certain of their leaders were prepared to consider discussions with the enemy. Lloyd George, the adherent of the "Knock-Out Blow", spoke in the Commons on the 19th December. He gave his "clear and definite" support to the decision of the French and Russians. The situation was complicated at this time by the interventions of the American President who was urging upon the belligerents a policy of "Peace Without Victory".

In the opinion of the British Prime Minister the time had come to formulate the war-aims of the Empire so that the Allied peoples would know why they were being asked to continue the murderous struggle. In order to do so, it was necessary for the British Government to meet with the leaders of the Empire from overseas. It was in these circumstances that the Imperial War Cabinet was summoned. Lloyd George has given his explanation of the position in his *Truth About The Peace Treaties*. It deserves the reader's careful attention:[1]

When I undertook the formation of a Government early in December 1916, the War had been raging for nearly two and a half years. . . The contending nations were bleeding from every artery. It was the blind and insensate fury of a struggle to the death. Germany had thrown out certain signals . . . that her rulers were willing to confer. . . It was merely a manoeuvre designed to propitiate . . . powerful Neutrals, including America. . .

When I became Prime Minister I was strongly of opinion that, whilst not neglecting any legitimate means for prosecuting the War efficiently . . . we should simultaneously devote some time to working out . . . in concrete terms, the kind of peace for which these sacrifices were to be made. Terrible losses . . . had spread a general sense of disillusionment and war weariness throughout the nation. There was a growing demand that the Allied peoples . . . should be told . . . what we were fighting for and the terms upon which we were prepared to settle. But no such conditions could be defined and determined without calling into consultation the Dominions and India. . . I therefore thought it was essential that an Imperial Cabinet should immediately be constituted and convened to exercise control . . . over the direction of the War and to formulate the terms of peace which the Empire as a whole would regard as . . . equitable. . . This was the first Imperial Cabinet ever held in the British Empire.

Lord Milner, as we have seen, presided over a Committee concerned with the economic terms of the peace. However, he did not confine his activity to this official body. On the 28th March 1917 he sought out Sidney Low, a distinguished publicist of the day, and granted him an interview. That interview has been described as the "first comprehensive . . . statement of the conditions of a peace acceptable to Britain. . ."[2]

We must at once ask, in this connection, why Lord Milner did not approach his great friend and disciple Geoffrey Dawson, editor of *The Times,* if he desired to make his views public property. As we have so often seen in this study, Milner never hesitated to call upon Dawson

[1] Lloyd George, *Truth About The Peace Treaties*, vol. I, pp. 51–52.
[2] *History of The Times*, vol. IV, p. 330.

whenever he felt he had something of interest to say. It cannot be argued that a series of articles by Sidney Low would attract more attention than an editorial in *The Times*.

The answer is clear and obvious. Milner's views about peace in March 1917 would not have been printed in *The Times* by Dawson, or by anyone else connected with the paper at that time. Dawson might have been willing to consider the publication of Lord Milner's proposals but he knew that Wickham Steed and Lord Northcliffe would have been outraged had he done so. The terms of peace which seemed adequate to Lord Milner were very different, in certain significant particulars, from those which had been already entertained by the British Government.

VI

Lord Milner looked at the terms of peace that might prove acceptable to the British Empire with the eyes of an Imperial statesman. It seemed to him that the representatives of the Dominions could not be expected to consider prolonging the war for the sake of the oppressed minorities of Eastern Europe. We have seen already, in his conversations with Sir Henry Wilson, that Milner was suspicious of the validity of all Continental alliances, so far as the Empire was concerned. In this connection we should recall Lord Beaverbrook's acute summary of Milner's outlook; "The unity of the Empire, political and economic, was his goal. That Britain was no part of Europe was his conviction."[1]

In his interview with Sidney Low Lord Milner made it clear that the Allies were not powerful enough to insist upon those conditions of peace which dominated the minds of unthinking enthusiasts in Britain and France. He explained that he was "in favour of trying to detach Germany's allies by offer, in due course, of *moderate terms of*

[1] See above Chapter I, section VI; also the powerful argument about Milner in *The History of The Times*, vol. IV, p. 327.

peace". Lord Milner told Low that it was "useless" to insist upon the break-up of Austria and the expulsion of the Turk from Europe. Such a policy, he said, only compelled these countries to "go on to the last extremity with Germany; whereas if they felt their actual existence not endangered, they might make peace".[1]

Even in the case of Germany Milner contemplated a less fierce purpose than that expressed by others in Britain and France. Low recorded Milner's opinion that:

> Even with Germany it was undesirable to make her people feel they were fighting for sheer existence.
>
> If we continue this policy we may so stiffen their resistance that in the end we shall not beat them, and have to agree after all to a negotiated and unfavourable peace. He clearly does not believe that we can inflict such a defeat on the central Alliance as will enable us to impose peace. . .

In the same way, Milner's views about the Balkans and Turkey were very different from the plans of those in Britain and France who were determined upon decisive changes in Eastern and Central Europe:

> Regards the creation—as part of the war settlement—of Czecho-slovakia, Jugoslavia, enlarged Rumania, as impracticable. Very doubtful if these changes are in themselves desirable; but if they are, should be left for a post-war settlement. So with regard to Constantinople. Should be left with Turks for the present—with agreement to free the Straits. Thinks Russia might accept this.

Low next made a note of the conditions upon which Lord Milner would be prepared to end the war. He added to it certain diplomatic goals and objects which Milner believed to be invalid and incorrect, so far as the vital interests and the honour of the Empire were concerned.

> His view is that as to conditions for terminating the war we should insist only on our *irreducible minimum*: i.e. those things for which we went to war. . . These are:
>
> (1) Liberation of Belgium with reparation.

[1] The account of the interview is printed in D. Chapman-Huston. *The Lost Historian, A Memoir of Sir Sidney Low* (London, 1936), pp. 267ff; it is fully reproduced in the *History of The Times*, vol IV, pp. 328ff.

(2) Evacuation of Serbia, and occupied Russian and Rumanian territory.

(3) Cession of *some* Austrian territory . . . to Italy.

(4) Restoration of (some part of) Lorraine to France.

We did not go to war for Czechoslovakia, Jugoslavia or Rumanians, or Poles. We ought to try to make arrangements for their autonomy, etc.; but we ought not to insist that we shall go on fighting till their aspirations are satisfied. . .

Lord Milner then turned to the question of the condition of Germany, a matter that became more and more important for him, as we shall see later. Low recorded that:

As for "destruction of Prussian militarism" Milner does not see what direct steps we could take. He thinks that if Germany comes out of the war with no gain of territory in Europe, and her colonies lost, the people themselves will see that militarism is a failure.

Finally, in summing up his interview with Lord Milner, Low wrote: "I gather that this is *Milner's personal view; but that he has not yet got his colleagues to agree to it.* That is why he wants "independent" writers to air it in the Press."

When Low proposed to Lord Burnham, the proprietor of the *Daily Telegraph*, that he should write a series of articles for that paper embodying Milner's ideas, he was told that Burnham "was not going to pull Ministers' chestnuts out of the fire". In consequence, Low wrote to Milner on the 30th March in order to suggest that President Wilson might "do some chestnut pulling by suggesting that the primary and the secondary issues of the peace settlement should be divided and the latter (Czechoslovaks, Yugoslavs, etc.) discussed in a special post-war conference. . ." Milner replied to this letter on the 8th April:[1]

My Dear Low,

. . . Of course great care must be exercised in planting these ideas, as the soil of public opinion is not yet well prepared for them. But I think it can only do good to ventilate them prudently and the *Atlantic Monthly* seems to me a good medium.

Yours ever,
M.

[1] For these points see Chapman-Huston, *The Lost Historian,* pp. 268–270.

It seems clear that in the early spring of 1917 Lord Milner did not believe that the Allies were strong enough to impose terms of peace upon Germany. Moreover, he did not look with favour upon the policies of certain members of the Foreign Office, and the *New Europe* group, including Steed, R. W. Seton-Watson, G. P. Gooch, H. M. Hyndman and their friends, who believed in the destruction of the Hapsburg Monarchy and the liberation of the Czechs, Slavs, and other minorities of Central and Eastern Europe. It seemed to Milner that peace might be secured on those "moderate terms" he had mentioned to Low; and it was Milner's purpose at this stage of the war to "plant" his ideas in the "soil of public opinion", as a preliminary stage in the realisation of them.

VII

Although the Bolshevik Revolution with its call for a proletarian Revolution in Europe and an immediate peace did not occur until November 1917, Lord Milner was convinced that the example of the democratic March Revolution in Russia already menaced the safety of Britain. He suspected the loyalty of certain leaders of the Labour movement in this country who were excited by developments in Russia in the spring of 1917; and he determined to do what he could to counter their influence in the country.

Milner always believed that British working men were misled by the formal leaders of their movement. As we have seen in Chapter VII of this history, Lord Milner, in 1907, declared in a speech at Guildford that: "I think the working classes of this country are misrepresented . . . I do not believe . . . the working classes are the unpatriotic, antinational, down-with-the-army, up-with-the-foreigner, take-it-lying-down class of Little Englanders, they are constantly represented to be". In that pre-war period Leo Amery, Milner's lieutenant, was already trying to organise a

Unionist Labour Party. His plan was dismissed at that time by certain Trade Union leaders, who looked upon it as one of a number of spurious and "fake organisations" created by the Tories for their own purposes.[1]

When the war began Lord Milner tried again to establish some kind of patriotic organisation for the working classes. On 25th February 1916 he described his activities in this sphere in a letter to Lady Roberts:[2]

> I am at present trying very hard, but quietly to further a purely working class movement, which I hope will knock out the "Independent Labour Party" and start a "Workers League" among the Trade Unionists, which will make Imperial Unity and Citizen Service "planks" on its platform. This is confidential.

When the Monday night cabal appeared upon the scene, its members naturally concerned themselves with the attitude of Labour, as a part of the national effort in war. The views of F. S. Oliver were more extreme upon this subject than those of any member of that company. However, we must take some notice of them since they indicate the kind of thinking engaged in by Milner and his friends. While Milner and the others were certainly not so violent as F. S. Oliver, they were regularly exposed to his opinions upon the subject of Labour and the war.

In April 1916 the members of the Monday night cabal were eager to win Austen Chamberlain to their side. On 15th April F. S. Oliver wrote to Austen in order to warn him about the attitude of Labour. Oliver took care to send Milner a copy of this letter, marked "Very Private, Copy Letter". In this paper Oliver referred to Labour as a mad "dog", quite ready to "fix his teeth in his master's throat". Oliver explained to Austen Chamberlain in those picturesque terms of which he was a master that:[3]

---

[1] For Amery's efforts in this direction and the hostility of Ben Tillett, see Gollin, *The Observer and J. L. Garvin*, p. 329.

[2] Milner Papers, Milner to Lady Roberts, 25th February, 1916.

[3] Milner Papers, Oliver to Austen Chamberlain, 15th April 1916, marked "Very Private, Copy Letter".

. . . The nation . . . has been (as I see it) like a man engaged in
defending his house against thieves. Behind him is a dog of his own
household—an ill-tempered brute, who cannot be trusted, who growls
at his heels and is quite ready to fix his teeth in his master's throat . . .
The master, so far, has been pretending that the dog is a good dog;
and has spoken to him in very soothing accents, and has thrown him
bits of biscuit and bones galore. Well the dog growls all the more. . .
Perhaps he thinks . . . his master is afraid of him . . .

. . . I am for turning sharply on the dog, daring him to fly at my
throat, and beating his bones to a jelly if he does. . . Believe me,
you will have to have it out with that Dog sooner or later. . .

By the dog of course I mean Labour, not Ireland. And of course
only a minority of Labour—a really miserable and execrable minority
of Labour. . .

The effect of the March Revolution in Russia served to
increase and intensify Lord Milner's fears about some of the
leaders of the Labour movement in Britain. Unlike Oliver,
however, he believed that the problem could be dealt with
by creating a patriotic organisation for the working men in
order to counter-act the agitation of "mischief makers".

Lord Milner was not prepared to beat the dog's bones to a
"jelly"; but he was determined to do something about the
situation in the Labour world, for the sake of the national
effort in the war.

VIII

In order to understand his purpose at this time, we must
now look at the activities of those Radical and Labour
leaders in Britain whom Lord Milner regarded as "mischief
makers".

When war came in 1914 most people in the country believed in the validity of the decision taken by the Asquith
Government. A small group of Radical dissenters, however, did not. On the day after the declaration of war the
first leading article in the *Daily News* (5th August) declared
in uncompromising terms:

. . . We place on record our conviction that it was possible, and
that it would have been just and prudent and statesmanlike, for England

to have remained neutral. We shall record that a mistaken course of foreign policy pursued over ten years . . . has led us to the terrible conflict. . . We believe that the conviction that that policy was an error will steadily conquer the minds of the English people, and that they will one day come to the resolution that it is an error which must never be repeated. . .

The Radicals, whose views were reflected by this bold article, were not disloyal to their country, nor were they all pacifists. They were men who feared that as the war fever in Britain increased, Liberal principles would be forgotten or destroyed and all hopes for a reasonable peace that might prevent the outbreak of future wars crushed. They were, in the words of the historian of their movement, men who would not "let the case for Reason go by default".[1]

These Radicals were at once joined by those members of the Labour movement who refused to agree with the great majority of their colleagues in unquestioning support of the Government and the war. These dissenters, mostly from the Independent Labour Party, soon formed an alliance with the Radicals in order to work out a common programme for what has been called "loyal dissent".

The result was the formation of a group known as the Union of Democratic Control. The object of this organisation was to campaign in the country against those traditional policies which, in their opinion, had led to the war. They condemned secret diplomacy, the international rivalry in armaments, restrictive tariffs and other devices designed to hamper free trade between nations, the familiar pre-war colonial rivalries, and all those time-honoured activities of the diplomatists that they looked upon as the causes of war.

Above all else they argued that while public opinion in the modern age had been able to influence the course of domestic legislation, it had been allowed little or no part in

[1] H. M. Swanwick, *Builders of Peace* (London, 1924), p. 30. For two more recent and powerful accounts see Arno J. Mayer, *op cit.,* pp. 40 ff., and A. J. P. Taylor *The Trouble Makers* (London, 1957), pp. 133 ff.

the formation of foreign policy. The result of this denial of democratic control was the war; and unless something were done in this connection, the conflict between nations was certain to be followed by a vindictive peace that would sow the seeds of future wars.

The organising genius of the Union of Democratic Control was E. D. Morel, a curious but intensely able member of the Liberal Party. Morel was the son of Edmond Morel-de-Ville, an official of the French Ministry of War who died as a result of an illness contracted during his period of service in the Franco-Prussian war. Morel's mother came from an East Anglian family of Quakers. In 1896 he became a naturalised British citizen and for the sake of convenience he shortened his name to Morel. Together with Charles Trevelyan, Ramsay MacDonald, Arthur Ponsonby and Norman Angell, he helped to found the Union of Democratic Control. Under his direction the Union soon became a powerful engine of propaganda, in every part of the country.

In May 1915, after branches had been formed in Manchester, Newcastle, Glasgow, and Birmingham, the Executive Committee of the Union of Democratic Control appointed a "Special Commissioner" whose task was to "permeate" the labour world with the views of the group. In this campaign the chief targets of the Union were Trades Councils, local Labour Parties, co-operative societies, and branches of the Independent Labour Party. Although some of the pamphlets prepared by the Union were aimed at the middle-classes, large numbers of leaflets were addressed directly to the workers. In 1916, at the request of the Executive Committee, Ramsay MacDonald agreed to send a circular letter to the Trades Union Councils, describing and explaining the policies of the Union of Democratic Control. Furthermore, a periodical, the *Labour Leader*, edited by Fenner Brockway, was exploited as a more regular channel of communication between the Union and the workers. In every part of the country the leaders and the rank and file of the Independent Labour Party and other Labour groups who were uneasy about the war, seized upon the clear and logical arguments provided for them by Morel and his colleagues.

From 1914 to 1917, as might be expected, the Union of Democratic Control was regularly attacked by politicians and journalists who feared the effect of its propaganda upon the minds of working men, and upon the war effort. These critics deplored the Union's activities in the hour of the nation's danger.

However, the March Revolution in Russia re-invigorated the movement and provided it and its adherents with a wider appeal than ever before. At about the same time, a number of extremely serious strikes began in different parts of the country. These strikes resulted in good part from a revival of political activity on the part of left-wing groups, and from the effect of the Russian example upon the British worker. War-weariness, the "dilution" of labour in the factories, and more vigorous measures of conscription also played a part in contributing to the unrest that spread to several areas in the country.

In order to deal with these problems the Prime Minister appointed nine Commissions of Industrial Unrest, in the early summer of 1917. The tasks of the Commissioners were to investigate the grievances of the workers, and to recommend a policy that would prevent future strife.

Exactly at this time, however, Lord Milner decided to press his own plan upon Lloyd George. He believed that something more drastic was required to offset the effect of the Russian Revolution and the actions of "mischief makers" like E. D. Morel and Ramsay MacDonald.

IX

On 26th May 1917 Lord Milner despatched a long letter to the Prime Minister in which he explained that the plan of the Industrial Commissions was excellent, in so far as "justifiable" unrest in the country was concerned. He pointed out, however, that something had to be done about the "mischief makers":[1]

Confidential   May 26 1917
My dear Prime Minister,
   I am very sorry to keep on bombarding you with letters when I know that you are overwhelmed with them. . . But I don't like to remain in possession of important information . . . without passing it on; and I cannot always be sure of having an opportunity of doing so by word of mouth.
   The subject to which I want to refer now is that question of Labour unrest, which I know occupies so much of your attention. . .
   I think the new scheme of Industrial Commissions is an excellent one, and will go far to remove justifiable reasons for unrest.
   But there remains the problem of counteracting the deliberate agitation of mischief-makers, who sow discontent among the workmen, which will not be stopped, though it will no doubt lose some of its opportunities, by the removal of real grounds of complaint. The following is an extract from a letter, which I have received from a man . . . whose information about the state of feeling in the Labour world I have always found very reliable. It is a long and alarming letter. . .

The extract read as follows:

"During the last few weeks the Independent Labour Party in conjuction with the Union of Democratic Control, have made a very big stride forward. . .
   . . . their immediate object has been to bring about a strike, followed by rioting of such a nature that troops would be obliged to fire, and from this they hoped to evolve a general strike which would bring the whole War up with a jerk here, in much the same manner as the Revolution has stopped all military proceedings in Russia. . .
   In addition, there has been a very dangerous move started all over the country for the alliance between Civilian Committees formed by either the I.L.P. or the U.D.C. and discharged soldiers.
   . . . I look on the internal Labour political situation as more serious than it has ever been before. *The combination between the U.D.C., Quaker money, the I.L.P., the vast number of shirkers, together with the discharged and dissatisfied soldiers is a very ugly one. . .*[2]

   [1] Lloyd George Papers, Milner to Lloyd George, 26th May 1917, marked " Confidential."
   [2] The words in italics were underlined by Milner.

I have thought for a long time now that there is a master brain behind both the U.D.C. and the I.L.P., and I have been quite sure that it was not Ramsay MacDonald. I find that it is Morrell (De Ville). This man, *as you probably know*,[1] has been challenged again and again as a German Agent, and will not take any action . . . in spite of the fact that everybody knows he is a German agent, he very nearly succeeded at the end of last week in bringing about a complete Labour revolt in this country".

Lord Milner's comment upon this report, in his letter to the Prime Minister, was typical of his outlook. He explained to Lloyd George that:

Making every allowance, as I do, for possible exaggeration, I think there is a great deal of truth in all this, though I cannot say whether my informant is right about Morrell (sic). Anyway I don't believe much in the prosecution of individuals.

What I do believe in is systematic work by Labour men, who are on our side, to counteract the very systematic and active propaganda of the Pacifists, and to prevent their capturing the Trades Councils and other bodies, who profess to represent though they often misrepresent the working classes.

Milner went on to explain the way in which he believed the situation should be dealt with. He informed Lloyd George that he was already in contact with a loyal working men's association, the British Workers League, and that the secretary of this body, Victor Fisher, was the informant whose report explained the relationship between MacDonald, Morel, the Independent Labour Party, and the Union of Democratic Control. He stressed in his letter his wish that the Prime Minister should see Victor Fisher so that he might become familiar with him: If Fisher could win Lloyd George's confidence, the Government could provide his League with "encouragement" and "guidance". Milner also told the Prime Minister that Geoffrey Dawson was doing what he could to help the British Workers League by means of favourable publicity in *The Times*. The letter of the 26th May went on:

[1] These words are underlined by Milner and in the margin he writes: "I don't know anything about this. M." In spite of the spelling it is clear that the man referred to is E. D. Morel, born, as we have seen, E. D. Morel-de-Ville.

This process of counter mining has been carried on for some little time past . . . by a comparatively new organisation called the "British Workers League". I enclose a cutting from today's "Times" relative to some of their present doings . . .

This League is not, like some previous organisations of the kind, a bogus thing. It consists of genuine Labour men . . . but being at the same time patriotic and national . . . Their secretary is a very capable fellow—Victor Fisher—not himself a workman but a middle class man of good education . . . who knows as much as any man I have come across about the various Labour and Socialist movements. . . I very much wish you could yourself see Fisher . . . and size him up . . . he . . . with his League, might, with a little encouragement and guidance, do a great deal more useful work than he is already doing in the direction I have indicated.

I hope you won't think I have got hold of a mare's nest. I am sure I have not. I have followed this particular matter pretty closely for some time. . .

> Yours very sincerely,
> Milner.

Frederick Victor Fisher, Lord Milner's agent in this new enterprise, had been associated with the Socialist movement in Britain for a long time. In 1899 he joined the Fabian Society, and a few years later he became a member of H. M. Hyndman's Social Democratic Federation. In 1914 he resigned from the British Socialist Party because he abhorred the pacifism of that body. From that time he often attacked Ramsay MacDonald and also Arthur Henderson because of what he looked upon as their "lukewarm" attitude to the war.

Later on in 1917 Victor Fisher began to dine at Waldorf Astor's table. Dr. Addison in his diary records: "A most interesting evening at Astor's; the company being Lloyd George, Milner, Victor Fisher, and myself".[1] Victor Fisher had arrived.

X

Meanwhile, the pace of developments in the Labour world in Britain began to increase. In Lord Milner's opinion

[1] Addison, *Four and A Half Years*, vol. II, p. 458.

these new developments constituted a definite menace and danger to the State in time of war. Unlike the members of the Union of Democratic Control, Milner did not believe in the value of public opinion when foreign policy was being decided. In fact, as we know, he was always critical of the effect and the influence of "rotten" public opinion. Secondly, Milner deplored developments in Russia because he was convinced that the Revolution there, however democratic, was bound to destroy Russia's position as an effective Ally against the common enemy. He was also afraid of the effect of the Russian example upon working men in Britain.

On 9th May 1917 the Petrograd Soviet, suspicious of the foreign policies of the Provisional Government in Russia, issued a "preliminary" call for the holding of an International Socialist Conference in some neutral country. The object of this Conference was to provide Socialists of all countries with an opportunity to discuss methods for bringing the war to an end. By 15th May the Petrograd Soviet made known its own formula for peace. It urged upon the world "peace without annexations or indemnities, on the basis of the self determination of peoples". This formula at once attracted the enthusiasm of Socialists, everywhere.

Before the International Socialist Conference met, the Executive of the Petrograd Soviet, in pursuit of its own objects, invited the Socialists of Britain, France and Italy to an "exploratory" Conference at Petrograd. This invitation had an almost intoxicating effect upon Labour circles in Britain. Socialists of every complexion were at once eager to go to Petrograd in order to take part in the discussions. Lord Milner observed with some distress that those who were invited were not merely Labour representatives who approved of the war but also the so-called "minority" Socialists who were hostile to the British Government in its conduct of the war and also in its plans for the peace.

In order to strengthen their own position, these "minority" Socialists summoned a Conference to meet in the Albert Hall in Leeds, on the 3rd of June. Although every Socialist faction was to be represented at Leeds, the publicity of the more advanced groups astonished Lord Milner. On 1st June he sent the Prime Minister two articles which had been published in Fenner Brockway's *Labour Leader* for the 31st May. The first of these articles, entitled "Follow Russia", printed a letter signed by F. W. Jowett, George Lansbury, Robert Smillie, Philip Snowden, J. R. MacDonald, and others. This letter said of the Leeds Conference that:

> It will begin to do for this country what the Russian Revolution has accomplished in Russia. . . It will be a Democratic Conference to establish Democracy in Great Britain. . .

The article also printed the resolutions that were to be submitted to the Leeds Conference. Lord Milner marked certain passages in this part of the article, which read as follows:

> . . . This Conference calls upon the Government of Great Britain to place itself in accord with the democracy of Russia. . .
> This Conference calls upon the constituent bodies at once to establish in every town, urban and rural district, Councils of Workmen and Soldiers' Delegates for initiating and co-ordinating working-class activity. . . Such Councils shall . . . watch diligently for and resist every encroachment upon industrial and civil liberty. . .

The second article was signed by Philip Snowden. Lord Milner underlined some of the sentences Snowden had written, when he sent the cutting to Lloyd George. The underlined sentences declared of the Leeds Convention that:

> This Convention on Sunday is to be the beginning of doing things in this country.
> The war itself . . . and the unbridled swindling and profiteering which have accompanied it, as well as the evident incapacity of the Governments at war to settle the conflagration they have set blazing, call to the democracy of this and all the other belligerent countries to take matters into their own hands as the people of Russia have already done. . .

It has often been pointed out that despite the Leeds resolutions and despite articles like Philip Snowden's, the Leeds Convention had no sequel. No British Soviets were ever established, nor did the Provisional Committee elected by the Conference hold together for any length of time. Nevertheless, with the Russian example before his eyes, Lord Milner took alarm at these clarion calls. On 1st June he wrote to the Prime Minister in order to warn him about the Leeds meeting and to protest against Ramsay MacDonald's plan to attend the Petrograd Conference. In order to make his fears seem more valid, he included with his letter another report written by Victor Fisher. Milner explained to Lloyd George:[1]

My dear Prime Minister,   1.6.17
    . . . It is now too late to stop R.M. going to Russia, or the Leeds meeting. In any case I should not have stopped the latest. But I think there is still time to instruct the Press . . . not to "boom" the Leeds proceedings too much.
    And I fear the time is very near at hand, when we shall have to take some strong steps in this country, unless we wish to "follow Russia" into impotence and dissolution.
                                        Yours very sincerely,
                                                M.

Victor Fisher's report was concerned with MacDonald's plan to attend the Petrograd Conference in company with other "minority" Socialist leaders. Fisher's Memorandum, entitled "Mission of the Independent Labour Party and British Socialist Party Leaders to Russia", explained the significance of the Leeds Convention and the plans of the "minority" Socialists in dramatic terms:[2]

    . . . If I thought that the proposed Mission could affect the fighting value of the Russian Army in the interests of the Allies, I admit that I should be prepared to waive the strong objection which I am about

---

[1] Lloyd George Papers, Milner to Lloyd George, 1st June 1917. In the event, MacDonald did not go to Russia, though he tried to do so.
[2] Undated memorandum, enclosed with Milner's letter of the 31st May 1917, to Lloyd George.

to place before you. I am however profoundly convinced that this cannot be the case. That on the contrary the whole policy, opinions, and intentions of these people are in the directly opposite direction . . .

I now ask you to read the enclosed cutting from this week's "Labour Leader" in regard to the dangerous Convention that is being called at Leeds. . .

No language that I could use could comment too severely on the Government ignoring this Convention. . .

Speaking as a democrat and as one jealous for civil liberties I do not hestitate to express the opinion that . . . this Convention should never have been allowed. . .

. . . Mr MacDonald and his colleagues will now go to Russia not as the delegates of the small factions of the I.L.P. and B.S.P., but as the delegates of a frankly revolutionary gathering nominally representing many tens of thousands of British working men. They will in my judgment do unutterable mischief while they are in Russia. They will return from Russia with an immense prestige in the eyes of their followers here, they will feed the Syndicalist Press in England . . . with articles purporting to express at first hand the views of our Russian "brothers" and they will form the nucleus of a dangerous revolutionary movement in this country. . .

Governments most frequently do not realise that they are on the brink of a revolution until it is too late . . . yet I deliberately venture to assure your Lordship that we are heading straight towards a popular outburst in this country in favour of what I shall now call a Russian Peace, which is being brilliantly engineered by Mr MacDonald and his associates.

Lord Milner probably did not believe that Britain was "on the brink of a revolution". However, he had already lost faith in Russia's capacities as an Ally in war. In addition, Victor Fisher's warnings reinforced him in his opinion that Russia, by her example, menaced the internal security of this country and its unity in the struggle against Germany. These impressions served to convince him that Britain was no longer bound by any commitments to the Revolutionary regime in Russia.

Lord Milner now proceeded to act upon this assumption. In the late summer of 1917 he gave his "blessing" to a plan for the overthrow of the democratic Government in Russia, and the establishment of a military dictatorship there.

By the summer of 1917 Alexander Kerensky had taken the place of Prince Lvov, as head of the Provisional Government. His position was threatened by the Bolsheviks upon the one hand, and by conservative elements in the country upon the other. Early in September General Lavr Kornilov was plotting to overthrow Kerensky, as part of a counter revolutionary design. Many Russians supported Kornilov as a prospective dictator who could restore order and tranquillity. Lord Milner believed that a strong man in Russia might be able to re-impose discipline there, and thus revive Russia's military capacities. In order to further these objects, Milner "gave his blessing" to Kornilov's treasonable enterprise. Kerensky has written in this connection that:[1]

. . . At about this time, Aladin, a former labour member of the Duma, arrived from England, whither he had fled in 1906. . . This discredited man brought to General Korniloff a letter from Lord Milner, British War Minister, expressing his approval of a military dictatorship in Russia and giving his blessing to the enterprise. This letter naturally served to enourage the conspirators greatly.

Kornilov's coup ended in failure. However, in order to defeat him Kerensky was forced to appeal to the Bolsheviks for help. As a result, their prestige increased by leaps and bounds. Lenin saw that his opportunity was at hand. After Kornilov's attack upon the Government, the life of the democratic regime in Russia was practically over. And in the opinion of Alexander Kerensky, the Milner letter had played a part of some significance in the development of Kornilov's fateful plans.

[1] Alexander F. Kerensky, *The Catastrophe* (New York, 1925), p. 315. See also Ullman, *op. cit.*, p. 11, n. 30, who states: "Milner's papers . . . contain no trace of this letter". Anyone familiar with the Milner Papers knows that the collection is far from complete and that many of Milner's letters are no longer preserved in it. Aside from any other reasons, Lady Milner removed certain documents from the Milner Papers before they were sent to New College. This statement is based upon Private Information given to the present writer by a number of different persons who were in a position to know.

XI

By the late autumn of 1917 political circles in London were beginning to say that Lord Milner was the most ardent advocate, inside the War Cabinet, of a negotiated peace with Germany. In October Dr. Thomas Jones, one of Lloyd George's closest henchmen, and a diligent gossip in his own right, told Sidney and Beatrice Webb of the attitude of the Cabinet:[1]

Tom Jones lunched here. . . The War Cabinet is much perturbed at the rumours of revoluntionary feeling among the working class. . . Milner is said to be the most alarmed and to be hankering after peace by agreement lest worse befall the British and German Junker class alike.

We need not depend upon the remarks of Dr. Jones in order to understand Lord Milner's attitude at this time. On 3rd November Milner spoke to W. H. Buckler, a Counsellor at the American Embassy in London. According to Buckler's report, which was forwarded to President Wilson by Colonel House, Milner thought that as a result of the March Revolution in Russia the Allies "ought to listen to every peace whisper."[2]

A few days later, on the 7th–8th November, the Bolsheviks seized power in Petrograd. Instantly, they urged upon the belligerents the "immediate opening of negotiations for a just and democratic peace". Lord Milner's anticipations about the course of the Revolutionary "fever" in Russia were fulfilled by the end of November, for at that time the Bolsheviks proposed an armistice to the Central Powers. Everyone was at once aware of the tremendous military significance of these developments. At the same time, the disaster of Caporetto threatened the Allied military position in the West.

[1] B. Webb, *Diaries,* pp. 96–7.
[2] See Arno J. Mayer, *op. cit.,* p. 282 and n. 47 for Buckler's report, preserved in the Wilson Papers.

In these circumstances Lord Milner sought out Sidney Low once again, in order to explain his impressions of the new situation. Low's diary for the 12th November 1917 declares in terms that are significant for our story that:[1]

... Talk with Lord Milner. Said Italian situation even worse than commonly understood...

Milner takes gloomy view of general position. Believes we can do little more in *West* for many months, if at all...

Milner gave me impression that he sees little prospect of military success for us. At the same time he does not see chance to conclude tolerable peace. Germans will not give back occupied territory on terms we could accept. They would certainly demand free hand in Poland and Russia; and restoration of their African colonies...

Milner almost seems to think that we can neither make successful war nor successful peace.

It is thus clear that despite Lord Milner's gloom he was not prepared to accept any conditions of peace from the German enemy. His gloomy outlook was not the despair of one prepared to bow to superior force. His object was to conclude a "tolerable" peace. He measured, without cant or self-deception, the terrible condition of the Allies in the late autumn of 1917. If he was prepared to consider a bargain with the enemy, he was not ready to give way to him. His object was to secure a "successful" peace for the Empire, and for the Allies. In his opinion it was more than ever necessary for the British Government and the Empire to decide exactly the terms and conditions of their war-aims; the reasons why it was necessary for them to continue the war. Conversely, they were also required to cast upon one side all those objects and aims of unthinking enthusiasts which were invalid, so far as the Empire was concerned in its conduct of the war.

Although Milner was prepared to consider some kind of

[1] Chapman-Huston, *The Lost Historian*, pp. 278–9. In this connection we should point out that Sidney Low's niece Ivy was married to M. Litvinov, the Bolshevik emissary in London at this time. According to E. H. Carr's *The Bolshevik Revolution*, vol. III, p. 25, n. 6 "There is ... no evidence that information percolated to Petrograd through this channel".

arrangement with the Germans, the reader should remember that exactly at this time he was risking his political life in order to help Lloyd George to create an efficient Allied Supreme War Council at Versailles, in the face of the hostility of the Generals. He was in no way ready to accept defeat in this period of the war. On the other hand, he recognised the impossibility of the "Knock-Out Blow" against Germany. In his opinion it was necessary for Britain to fight on for a time in order to be in a position to arrange a valid bargain with the enemy. In particular, something had to be done about the situation in the East if the war were not to be lost in the immediate future. It was to this area of the struggle that he now turned his attention. Unlike Lord Lansdowne, Milner, however conciliatory he may have been, did not argue in November of 1917, that the prolongation of the war would spell "ruin for the civilised world".[1]

XII

A terrible problem that confronted the Allied leaders in November 1917 was how to close the yawning breach in the Front against Germany, caused by the Bolshevik intention to seek an armistice. The defection of Russia provided the Central Powers with wonderful military opportunities. They were now in a position to replenish their stocks of food and fuel from the Russian corn producing areas and oilfields; at the same time they could withdraw troops from the East to the French and Italian fronts. Lord

---

[1] The phrase is taken from Lansdowne's famous peace letter published in the *Daily Telegraph* for 29th November 1917. Too often, scholars dealing with the plans or suggestions for peace link the proposals of Lansdowne, Milner, the Union of Democratic Control, and the Independent Labour Party too closely together. These various advocates of peace were often suspicious of each other's objects. The matter is dealt with concisely by A. J. P. Taylor in *The Trouble Makers*, p. 150, where he points out that to Lansdowne's "bewilderment" his peace letter was taken up by the Radicals. Writers who simply link Milner and Lansdowne together as two right-wing or "traditionalist" advocates of peace do less than justice to their separate attitudes. Lord Milner was made of sterner stuff than Lansdowne.

Milner played a significant part in the earliest plans of the Allies to intervene in Russia in order to thwart these designs of the Germans and Austrians.

The matter was taken up by the British War Cabinet on the 29th November. "There could be no doubt", Lloyd George has written, "that Russia meant to desert her Allies. France, Britain and Italy had to face a new and exceedingly dangerous situation."[1]

As a result of more than one discussion, the Cabinet decided to send Milner and Lord Robert Cecil to Paris in order to discuss with the French the attitude to be adopted and the arrangements to be made by the Allies in the new condition of affairs in Russia. After full discussion in the Cabinet, Milner and Lord Robert prepared a Memorandum to be submitted to the French. Certain points in this document deserve our close attention. The Milner-Cecil Memorandum suggested that each country should appoint "unofficial agents" in order to establish relations with the Bolsheviks. The paper also advised that the Allies should explain to the Bolsheviks that they had no desire to interfere with internal politics in Russia, but that they felt it necessary to "keep in touch" with the Cossack lands, with the Ukraine, with Finland, and with Siberia. These semiautonomous areas represented a very large proportion of the strength of Russia, and were not yet under the control of the regime in Petrograd. The Memorandum went on to say:[2]

Most important of all, the Bolsheviks should prevent . . . the wheat districts of Russia . . . falling into the control of or being made available for the Central Powers. . .

In Southern Russia our principal object must be . . . to save Roumania. Next we must aim at preventing Russian supplies from reaching Germany. . .

If we could induce the Southern Russian armies to resume the fight,

---

[1] Lloyd George, *War Memoirs,* vol. II, p. 1543.
[2] The document is printed in Lloyd George, *War Memoirs,* vol. II, pp. 1550-1.

that would be very desirable. . . . To secure these objects the first thing is money to reorganise the Ukraine, to pay the Cossacks and Caucasian forces, and to subsidise the Persians. . . If the French could undertake the finance of the Ukraine, we might find the money for the others. . . Beside finance, it is important to have agents and officers to advise and support the provincial Governments and their armies. It is essential that this should be done as quietly as possible so as to avoid the imputation . . . . that we are preparing to make war on the Bolsheviks.

We would suggest that the Ukraine should be again, in this matter, dealt with by the French, while we would take the other south-eat provinces. A general officer from each country would be appointed to take charge of our respective activities. . .

When Milner and Cecil presented this Memorandum to the French in Paris on the 23rd December, it was accepted in full. In effect, this secret Anglo-French Convention divided Russia into spheres of influence. Britain was allotted the Cossack territories, the Caucasus, Armenia, Georgia, and Kurdistan; France was assigned the Ukraine, Crimea, and Bessarabia. This pattern was later followed exactly when the Allies intervened in Russia with military forces.

Lord Milner's object in these arrangements was clear enough. In his opinion if the Germans were allowed to exploit the riches of the East, the Allies might easily lose the war. It was therefore necessary to stop them from securing the oil and foodstuffs of Russia.

On the other hand, if Milner entertained the idea of a negotiated peace with Germany by giving her a "free hand" in the East his plan would only be valid, during the period of the war, if the Germans did not yet dominate and control the key areas of Russia. In order to make his proposed bargain a possibility of war-time diplomacy, Milner was required to do what he could to prevent the Germans from fastening upon the resources of Russia which seemed most attractive to them. There would be less chance to conclude a bargain if the Germans already possessed all that they desired in the Ukraine, in the Crimea, in Bessarabia, and in the Caucasus. From this time Lord Milner played an important part in the efforts of the Allies to restore some kind of Front in the East.[1]

Milner was prepared to tolerate any condition of affairs in Russia in order to prevent the Germans from gaining their objects there. On 23rd December he reported to the Prime Minister from Paris that:[2]

> There is just one point about the Russian question, to which Wilson attaches great importance... This is the effect of the terms of the armistice already concluded upon the supply to Germany of foodstuffs etc. from Russia. One of the clauses of *the armistice provides* for *free commercial intercourse on the Black Sea.* This is particularly dangerous because, while railway disorganisation, lack of coal, etc. may make it difficult to Germans for a long time to supply themselves overland, there is nothing to prevent grain being shipped in quantities from Odessa to the mouth of the Danube, once Odessa is under the control of the Bolsheviks. The same applies to oil from Batoum...
>
> It therefore becomes of particular importance to us, even if we cannot ultimately prevent, *to delay as long as possible* the establishment of an authority favourable to trade with the Central Powers in *parts of Southern Russia.* Civil War, or even the mere continuance of chaos and disorder, would be an advantage to us from this point of view.
>
> ... Anything we can do to prevent Germany and Austria getting relief from Russia—and it is only from Southern Russia, and chiefly by sea that they can get it—during this critical period is of the greatest value.

XIII

By the end of the year 1917 the Bolsheviks, from Petrograd and from Brest-Litovsk, were calling upon the Allied Governments to define their war-aims in clear and definite terms. The Central Powers had made statements of their own upon the subject. In Britain, Lord Lansdowne's counsel

[1] Milner played a leading part in February 1918 in the selection of R. H. Bruce Lockhart as one of the "unofficial agents" to be sent to the Bolsheviks, as suggested by the terms of the Milner-Cecil Memorandum reproduced above. See Ullman, *op. cit.*, p. 61. Later, in June 1918, Milner was influential in causing American troops to be sent to Russia. See Ullman, *op. cit.*, pp. 195 ff. Milner also concerned himself with the employment of Czech troops in Russia—Ullman, *op. cit.*, p. 155.

[2] Lloyd George Papers, Milner to Lloyd George, 23rd December 1917, marked "Personal".

of moderation had been welcomed by important sections of the Liberal Press, and also by certain leaders of the Labour movement. Lord Milner still desired peace upon those "moderate terms" he had explained to Sidney Low. During that winter the Prime Minister and the War Cabinet decided that a re-statement of war-aims was required of the British Government.

In particular, the peace discussions at Brest-Litovsk between the Russians and the Germans exerted a powerful influence upon Labour circles in Britain. Lloyd George has emphasised the unrest of working men in this country, caused by pacifist propaganda. "Amongst the workmen", he has written, "there was an unrest that was disturbing and might at any moment become dangerous".[1]

At this time the War Cabinet was planning a drastic "comb-out" of industry in order to gather in recruits for the 1918 campaign. This new recruiting scheme violated certain pledges already made to the Trade Unions. Would the Labour leaders accept these new proposals? Lloyd George was convinced that it was necessary for him to explain to British working men why renewed sacrifices were being asked of them. A clear pronouncement upon British war-aims was needed, for the sake of the more efficient prosecution of the war.

The matter was discussed in the War Cabinet; intensive talks were arranged with representatives of the Labour Party and the trade unions; Asquith and Grey, as the spokesmen of the Liberals, were applied to by the Prime Minister; discussions were held with the leaders of the Dominions. On the 5th January 1918, after these extensive preparations, Lloyd George took the extraordinary step of appearing before a Conference of the Trade Unions Congress, in order to define the objects of the British Government in its conduct of the war. *The Times* of 7th January 1918 called the Prime Minister's speech the "most important State document issued since the declaration of war".

[1] Lloyd George, *War Memoirs*, vol. II, p. 1491.

We need not concern ourselves with the details of the Prime Minister's discourse. For the purposes of our story it is only necessary to ask if Lloyd George gave any genuine indication in his address that the British Government proposed to abandon Russia to the Central Powers, as part of a scheme for a negotiated peace. We must also seek to discover Lord Milner's role in the matter. It should be stated at once, in this connection, that much must be left to conjecture, though not all.

In one of the talks preliminary to his great speech of the 5th January, Lloyd George saw C. P. Scott of the *Manchester Guardian* and Lord Buckmaster, representatives of the Liberals. On that occasion, the 28th December 1917, the Prime Minister said: ". . . I am in a very pacifist temper. . . There is a good deal of feeling in the War Cabinet towards peace—Balfour is not opposed—Milner is the most inclined to peace of anybody. Carson is nothing like so violent as he seems. . ." Some time later after another talk with the Prime Minister, Scott wrote in his diary: ". . . The rather startling fact became quite patent to me that . . . George . . . was now bent on giving effect to the policy . . . of paying the Germans in the East in order to square them in the West. . ."[1]

Certain passages in Lloyd George's speech of the 5th January have generally been looked upon as being "not inconsistent" with the policy of a negotiated peace with Germany at the expense of Russia. Lloyd George told the trade unions leaders that:

I will not attempt to deal with the question of the Russian territories now in German occupation . . . The present rulers of Russia are now engaged, without any reference to the countries whom Russia brought into the war, in separate negotiations with the common enemy. I am indulging in no reproaches. I am merely stating facts with a view to making it clear why Britain cannot be held accountable for decisions

[1] J. L. Hammond, *C. P. Scott*, pp. 223–232; Hammond has also written of this plan at p. 214 that "It was generally believed that Milner and his followers looked for some solution of this kind . . ."

taken in her absence and concerning which she has not been consulted
. . . We shall be proud to fight to the end side by side with the new
democracy of Russia . . . But if the present rulers of Russia take action
which is independent of their Allies we have no means of intervening
to avert a catastrophe which is assuredly befalling their country.
Russia can only be saved by her own people. . .

These careful references to the Russo-German peace
negotiations at Brest-Litovsk assumed great significance
with the passage of time, although Trotsky was instantly
convinced that they meant the sacrifice of Russia. On 6th
January the American Ambassador in Petrograd telegraphed to his Secretary of State that: "Trotsky gone to
Brest to meet German peace commission but told one man
at noon yesterday and another at 5 p.m. that Lloyd George
had expressed hope that Russia would be compelled to
make disgraceful peace and Trotsky said on both occasions
that policy of Allies was to have German demands satiated
in the East so her requirements be minimised in the West."[1]

At Brest-Litovsk in the period January–March 1918 the
opposition of the Russians was beaten aside. By the 3rd
March the Russians were compelled to sign the Germans'
treaty of peace. The Revolutionary "fever", to use Lord
Milner's phrase, had now run its full course. Russia was
out of the war. Those in the West who desired a negotiated
peace with Germany were now presented with a perfect
pretext for the sacrifice of Russia, in an Allied-German
bargain.

Exactly at this time Lloyd George sought out Sidney and
Beatrice Webb in order to discover if co-operation between
the Government and the Labour Party was possible, in
these circumstances. Beatrice Webb's diary furnishes us
with the most dramatic information about Milner's plan to
achieve peace at Russia's expense. On 1st March she
wrote:[2]

[1] The Ambassador's telegram is printed in *Papers Relating To The Foreign Relations
of The United States, 1918, Russia*, vol. I, (Washington, 1931), p. 425.
[2] For these extracts see B. Webb, *Diaries*, pp. 111–116.

We dined yesterday with Haldane to meet . . . the Prime Minister . . . His object in meeting us was . . . to find out whether any co-operation with the Labour Party was practicable . . . He made distinct advances—pressed us repeatedly to come and dine with him and meet Milner—apparently to discuss the terms of peace. . .

What was clear from our talk is that the P.M. and Milner are thinking of a peace at the expense of Russia. He repeated with more frankness and emphasis what he has said publicly, that the Russians must lie in the bed made by the Bolsheviks, that neither France nor England would fight on to restore Courland and Lithuania, leave alone to restore the lost Poland . . . I am not at all sure whether his desire to meet us and his desire that we should meet Milner is not connected with this possible sacrifice of Russia and her Revolution. He wants to know how the Labour Party would take such a peace—whether it would be considered a betrayal of . . . democracy. I gather that Haldane is also looking forward to a reconciliation between the Junkers of Germany and those of England over an agreed extension of both Empires. With Russia to cut up, the map of the world is capable of all sorts of rearrangements. . .

On 3rd March, after further discussions with Haldane, Beatrice Webb wrote in her diary:

The surmise that Haldane is at heart an aristocrat and an Imperialist and is working with Milner and Lloyd George was yesterday verified.

On the 7th March, Beatrice Webb summarised her impressions of the attitudes of Milner, Haldane, and the Prime Minister: Her comments reveal a profound insight, and deserve the reader's closest attention:[1]

On reflection, I think it is unfair to blame Milner and Haldane for wishing to make peace with the German Junkers. Haldane has always believed in the German governing class . . . Milner too, by birth, by training, and by temperament has an almost identical "make up" with that of the German imperialist—he admires and hates the same characteristics in men and states . . . But neither Haldane nor Milner

---

[1] *Ibid.*, pp. 115–116; for the opposition of Sir Henry Wilson to these plans, see Wilson, *Diaries*, vol. II, pp. 49–50. Wilson declared that he was made "uneasy" by the attitude of Milner and Lloyd George, though the reference in his Diary is made in January 1918. It seems clear that Clifford Sharp's letter to Steed, accusing Milner of seeking a negotiated peace at Russia's expense, was based in large part upon the Webb's report to him of the conversations reproduced above.

have the moral fastidiousness necessary to realise the sheer brutal devilry of the German world purpose. With the P.M. it is different . . . If he desires peace at the expense of democracy to the glorification of German autocratic efficiency and militarism throughout the world, it is mere cynical opportunism.

What will the professional pacifists say to a cynical peace? All the pacifists who are pacifists on account of the injury to property by war . . . the Lansdownes . . . will be made keener in their demand for peace by immediate negotiation with Germany—the consequent defeat of the Russian Revolution adding an agreeable zest to the endeavour to come to terms . . . But the men and women who are believers in democratic equality . . . will become more in favour of continuing the war. . .

It is, of course, conceivable that we may be forced to accept a German peace. But for the first time during the war I feel warlike.

XIV

It has generally been assumed that the plan for a nego-tiated peace at the expense of Russia remained alive as a possibility of diplomacy, during the period March–July 1918. At the same time, however, Lord Milner strained every nerve to improve the Allied military arrangements for the defiance of the Central Powers. Before and after the attack of the 21st of March he was diligent in urging greater vigour and efficiency upon the Prime Minister.

On the 20th March 1918, the very day before the Ger-man blow fell in the West, Milner advised the Prime Minister to establish an Eastern Committee; he believed that the problems caused by the "defection" of Russia were so serious and so varied, that one body should be created to deal with them. It is not without significance that he suggested Smuts, a Dominion representative who was less concerned with the fortunes of the people of Eastern Europe than some other British statesmen, as the "right man to co-ordinate on Eastern enterprises. . ." He wrote to Lloyd George:[1]

---

[1] Lloyd George Papers, Milner to Lloyd George, 20th March 1918, marked "Very Confidential"; see also Ullman, *op. cit.*, p. 307, and n. 16.

I am getting very anxious about the Eastern Front . . . We have a new campaign, which really extends from the Mediterranean shore of Palestine to the frontier of India . . . Whether or not Japan takes on Northern Asia—I doubt her doing it—we alone have got to keep Southern Asia. . .

. . . India has to be more used. The Ameer has to be thought of. The Persians and the Turks may perhaps yet be set by the ears. There may still be something to be done in the Caucasus . . . In any case the *essential inter-connection* of all these matters requires some one mind of grasp and imagination to be constantly directed upon them, as a whole.

. . . Who is going to be in charge of the business? I can only think of Smuts . . . Smuts is deeply interested, grasps the essentials . . . We thought of him before as the right man to co-ordinate on Eastern enterprises. . .

. . . The whole thing is widening our enormously. We can't afford to be slow in readjusting our efforts to the new conditions. . .

After Milner returned from the Doullens Conference, he wrote to the Prime Minister again, in order to urge upon him every kind of resistance, despite the apparent success of the Germans. We have already seen that he told Lloyd George, on the 27th March, that "If there is a great disaster, we are as a Govt. 'down and out' whatever we do, and we may as well fall gloriously over a big effort to retrieve the situation. . . We are in for a long and dragging fight. . . It is simply deluding ourselves to think that the Germans, after such success as they have had . . . *will not continue to press us for all they are worth*. . . Unless we can hold out another year . . . a bad peace is a certainty. I should prefer to let someone else make it. . ."[1]

In other words, there was for Lord Milner a vast difference between the moderate peace he desired as a practical statesman aware of realities, and the bad peace he refused to make.

According to the *History of The Times*, the authoritative work on "appeasement" in Britain, "secret appeasement plans"[2] were entertained in this country, especially after the

[1] See above, Chapter XIX, section VI. These extracts from Milner's letter are reproduced here, in this new context, for the convenience of the reader.
[2] This is the page title at p. 359 of vol. IV of *History of The Times*.

treaty of Brest-Litovsk was signed, and after the marvellous success of the German attacks of March and April 1918. One passage of that work, based so far as research may discover upon information adduced in this chapter, explains of the Chief Proprietor of *The Times* that:[1]

Northcliffe was probably unaware that . . . Lloyd George and Milner both entertained a view of the war and a definition of victory that was now at variance with that of *The Times* . . . Their new estimate of the possibility of the immediate future led Lloyd George and Milner to think of settling the war on what the latter had called 'moderate' terms in the spring of 1917 . . . Milner certainly, and Lloyd George probably, had been forced to the conviction that, with Russia not merely out of the war but in the hands of Germany, the Allies must abandon the hope of winning in the West. Germany, by possessing Russia, had, in a sense, already won the war . . . The three months from April to June were grim, equally for those who hoped to end the war by negotiation. . .

The disasters of the spring and the Russian defection had undoubtedly enlarged the number of those in Britain and France who were prepared to discuss the idea of ending the war by agreement . . . They were very discreet . . . The Editor and his chief colleagues were unaware in April that the Prime Minister, Ministers and ex-Ministers, including members of the War Cabinet and some members of the Labour Party, had privately discussed the possibility of ending the struggle in the West by giving the Germans a free hand in the East . . . How far, in fact, the peace plan had been carried during April and May is unknown.

This passage contains the strongest and most positive statements in the historical literature dealing with the matter of a negotiated peace at Russian expense, leaving aside the opinions of Lenin, Trotsky and other Communists who have argued *a priori* that it was the "natural" course for the capitalist powers to follow. In the light of present historical knowledge the statements in the *History of The Times* may be accepted as reasonably accurate; students of the period will not be in a position to say very much more upon the subject until that happy day when

[3] *History of The Times*, vol. IV, pp. 358–9.

the official archives are thrown open for *all* to see.[1]

The months from April to June 1918 were certainly grim for Lord Milner. He was, as we have seen, prepared to negotiate with the German enemy, but he would not give way to him. On 9th June 1918, at the very time that Clifford Sharp wrote in order to warn Steed and Northcliffe of Milner's plans for a negotiated peace, Milner urged the Prime Minister to consider nothing less than a new war against the Central Powers, in case France and Italy, in addition to Russia, fell out of the fight. His letter must be extensively reproduced:[2]

Very Confidential   9 . 6 . 18.
My dear Prime Minister,   17 Great College St., S.W.
... We must be prepared for France and Italy both being beaten to their knees. In that case the Germans-Austro-Turks-Bulgar bloc will be master of all Europe and Northern and Central Asia up to the point at which Japan steps in to bar the way, *if* she does step in. . .

In any case it is clear that, unless the remaining free peoples of the world, America, this country, and the Dominions, are knit together in the closest conceivable alliance and prepared for the maximum of sacrifice, the Central Bloc . . . will control not only Europe and most of Asia but the whole world.

To suppose that Germany, with such a prospect in view, will desist now, whatever her losses and hardships, seems quite out of the question.

If all these things happen, the whole aspect of the war changes. These islands become an *exposed outpost* of the Allied positions encircling the world—a very disadvantageous position for the brain centre of such a combination. That, however, can't be helped. What is quite evident, and most relevant to the immediate issue, is that the Dominions and India will have to play an even much bigger part. . .

... The fight will now be for Southern Asia and above all for Africa

---

[1] Contrast the positive account in the *History of The Times* with the more cautious statement in Arno J. Mayer, *op. cit.*, p. 325, n. 28, "Especially in Great Britain the project of settling the war at the expense of Russia . . . seemed to gain important adherents between the middle of March and the middle of July 1918". E. H. Carr, *The Bolshevik Revolution 1917–1923*, vol. III, pp. 23–25, and n. 6, explains that Trotsky and Lenin were "firmly convinced" that Germany was to have a free hand in the East, and that their conviction had strong empirical support.

[2] Lloyd George Papers, Milner to Lloyd George, 9th June 1918, marked very confidential.

. . . and success may depend on what supplies we can get from India and Australia. . .

All this is assuming the worst and looking far ahead. Perhaps I should not say "far". . .

Last year we discussed the terms of peace.[1] If this year *we were seriously to* consider the necessities of the New War, it would be more to the purpose.

One thing more—intimately connected with the above. Of course all this depends on what America may do. Is not the time approaching, when we should try to find out, what she *will* do in case of a collapse of the Continental campaign against Germany?

If so, there is only one way of doing it—by a . . . message from you . . . to Wilson. Unless he can be shaken out of his aloofness and drops "co-belligerancy" or whatever halfway house he loves to shelter himself in, for out and out alliance— . . . I don't see how the new combination can have sufficient cohesion and inner strength. Moreover, he will have to be made to see—*and so will the Dominions* who are just as stupid about this—that he must wholly alter his attitude to Japan, if that country is to be part of the New Alliance. . .

If the bonds with America and Japan are really tight, we could still win through, though our own position here will henceforth be one of constant and immediate peril, and the mastery of the sea more than ever absolutely vital.

Yours ever,

M

XV

Lord Northcliffe was incensed by the information Clifford Sharp sent to *The Times* concerning the plan to consider a negotiated peace at Russian expense. In his straightforward opinion Germany would be so strengthened by the resources of the East that she would be able, in her own time, to turn back to the West and accomplish the victory denied her so far. Northcliffe was shortly to emerge as the most implacable enemy of the idea. He at once caused Steed to write an article in the *Daily Mail* for 21st June 1918, warning Ministers and the public to "Watch Lansdowne And Others". He also suggested to Dawson that an article in *The Times* might make some reference to Lord

[1] The Imperial War Cabinet was meeting in London.

Milner's "German origins". This article appeared in due course. In Dawson's hands, however, it became a hymn of praise for Milner's father who was "still remembered as the head of a typically English household of the kind which existed . . . in Germany 50 years ago. . ." ("Lord Milner's 'German' Origins" in *The Times*, 26th July 1918).

By the end of July the march of military events in the West began to dominate the situation of all the belligerents. Foch was at last beginning to master the enemy in France. On the 20th July the Germans retired from the left bank of the Marne. Decisive success was won by Haig in August. In September a general Allied offensive was begun. Although the military experts were still cautious and even pessimistic, there could be no doubt that the flood tide of German military power was at last on the ebb. The German Army in the field had failed in its purpose. In September the Bulgarians asked for an armistice, and accepted an almost unconditional surrender; on the 4th October their King abdicated.

Serious developments now took place in Germany. There, Ludendorff's nerve had finally cracked. He believed that the war was lost, and he desired the representatives of the Reichstag to begin to govern Germany in this new and unhappy condition of affairs. A constitutional Government came into existence, upon the orders of the German High Command. The task of the new Chancellor, Prince Max of Baden, was to begin negotiations for peace.

Early in October Prince Max sent the first of several Notes upon this subject to President Wilson. The Germans were making desperate efforts to get peace. Their exchanges with Wilson were not at once referred to all the Allied Powers. Nevertheless, in the opinion of Lloyd George and the War Cabinet, the time had come for the British Government to make up its mind upon the terms and conditions of an armistice with the enemy.

In these circumstances, Lord Milner suddenly stepped forward in order to announce certain startling proposals of his own. Although they were not immediately accepted, these proposals and the ideas which lay behind them created a legacy that dominated the outlook of Milner's disciples in the 1930s, the age of "appeasement".

XVI

On 13th October, Lloyd George, Milner, Bonar Law, Churchill, Henry Wilson, Balfour, Hankey, Philip Kerr, Lord Reading, and Admiral Wemyss met at Danny, the country home of Lloyd George's friend, Lord Riddell. It was nothing less than a meeting of the British Supreme Comand. They met to discuss their reply to President Wilson's Peace Note.

Although there was some general discussion, Kerr, Hankey, Reading, Milner, and Balfour retired to separate rooms in order to prepare their own draft replies to President Wilson's letter.

It is important for us to notice that it was decided at the end of the meeting that Sir William Sutherland, the Prime Minister's Political Secretary, "should see the newspapers and explain the position".[1] Lord Riddell who often trafficked with the Press upon the Prime Minister's behalf, took care to tell Lord Milner that he had provided Sutherland with a list of the newspapers that were to be informed about the meeting.

We must take some notice of these details because it has been said that when Milner later spoke to a representative of the Press on the subject of an armistice with Germany, "he acted on instructions".[2]

There is, however, no definite evidence that Milner spoke

---

[1] See Riddell, *War Diary*, p. 372; and also Lord Riddell, *Intimate Diary of The Peace Conference and After* (London, 1933), pp. 33-4.

[2] *History of The Times*, vol. IV, p. 373. But this definite statement is qualified at two separate places in the text of that work. See p. 372, n. 1, where it is suggested that Lloyd George may have "disagreed" with Milner's views; and p. 383, "Possibly all that Lloyd George . . . meant . . . was that the War Minister should feel the public's pulse . . ."

as he did, upon the orders and instructions of the Prime Minister. Lord Riddell's accounts of the meeting at Danny make it clear that separate drafts were worked out upon that occasion, and that Sutherland was the man assigned to make the final decisions public property. We may conclude the Lord Milner's famous interview upon the subject was made in very large part upon his own initiative. The Prime Minister was certainly in a position to know that Milner proposed to speak out, but this does not mean that he required his colleague to speak.

When Milner left the assembly of Ministers on the evening of the 13th, he at once travelled up to London in order to see Geoffrey Dawson, but he was unable to find him. On the next day, however, there was a full and regular meeting of the Monday night cabal where Milner met F. S. Oliver, Carson, Dawson, and Waldorf Astor. There can be little doubt that the subject of peace terms and armistice negotiations was discussed upon this occasion. The views of the Monday night cabal upon the subject of a "moderate" peace, upon the significance of the Bolshevik Revolution in Russia, and upon the effect and influence of Russian ideas upon working men in this country were possible topics for discussion at this second assembly Lord Milner attended, before he made his opinions available to the public.

On the day following the meeting of the Monday night cabal, the 15th October, Arthur Mann of the *Evening Standard* was told by Sutherland that Lord Milner desired to see him. On the next day their interview took place, at Milner's home.

According to Arthur Mann's account of this conversation, Lord Milner began by pointing out that the Germans were not absolutely broken in the field. If they once began to fight behind prepared positions inside Germany itself, their resistance would almost certainly become much stronger. Milner believed that the Allies could win this new battle, but only at a very heavy cost in men. This was the first point he made in his conversation with Arthur Mann.[1]

The second main point in the talk was concerned with the danger of Bolshevism. We have already demonstrated in detail in this chapter that when Lord Milner considered the Russian Revolution in all its aspects, he was always concerned with the influence of that Revolution upon the labouring masses of industrial Britain. There is no need for anyone to doubt that this part of the problem was in his mind, however guarded were his phrases, in the conversation with Arthur Mann. Milner said in earnest and deliberate tones that : "Heavy fighting in Germany . . . would create in Central Europe a state of chaos, confusion and desperation congenial to the spread of Bolshevism. Would it not be better for an armistice to be concluded as soon as possible, so long as its conditions guaranteed the military supremacy of the Allies?" The point Milner seemed to be making was that a continuation of the war in Germany would lead to the "spread of Bolshevism". He assigned no limits to how far the Bolshevik movement might "spread" in such circumstances.

A third part of the talk was devoted to Milner's opinion of the German people. In his view they did not like the "Junker and the Jackboot". They merely tolerated these things. Milner argued that an armistice and Allied terms of peace would utterly discredit militarism in Germany. He held that a "complete transformation of the system of government in Germany was already in progress". He added that "we should not be in too great a hurry to denounce these changes as a sham".

When Milner's exposition was finished Mann asked if he had any objection to the publication of his views, a charming and very English touch, in the circumstances. The reply was that Lord Milner did not object, provided that he could

---

[1] Mann's account of the interview is printed in the *History of The Times*, vol. IV, part II, pp. 1091–2. Mann, in this account, describes Lord Milner as a Member of the War Cabinet, but this was not the case in October 1918.

"see the interview in proof before publication". Eventually, Lord Milner altered only two words in Arthur Mann's article, which was published on the front page of the *Evening Standard* for 17th October 1918.

XVII

In its published version, the interview in the *Evening Standard* sought to define what was meant by the term "Complete victory", and to suggest how it might be achieved in the shortest possible way. Milner's definition was quite clear. By complete victory he meant the *"destruction of Prussian militarism"*. In his opinion the complete victory could be gained in one of two ways—either by forcing the enemy to accept unconditional surrender, or by an armistice "under such conditions as to guarantee that the military supremacy of the Allies shall not be weakened . . . by the cessation of hostilities". Lord Milner favoured the second of these alternatives:

He is *inclined to think that if the Allies . . . attempt to dictate to Germany certain drastic changes in their own government both as regards constitution and personnel, the resistance of the German armies and people, already waning, may be stiffened.*

After all, Lord Milner points out, there must be a German Government to negotiate an armistice with . . . A complete transformation of the system . . . is already in progress.

The present holders of power are responsible to the Reichstag, and the Reichstag is the only popularly elected national assembly in Germany. It is in the interests of the Allies to see a stable Government of some sort maintained in Germany. As reparation has to be obtained, we do not wish to see Bolshevism and chaos rampant there.

The publication of this interview was responsible for a series of violent explosions, in the Press and in Parliament for weeks after the 17th October. The *Manchester Guardian* and the *Daily News* quickly took the field in Lord Milner's support, and reprinted the *Evening Standard* article in their own pages. The most hostile of Milner's critics was Lord

Northcliffe. Unlike the Secretary of State for War, he favoured a surrender without conditions. He was later charged by the Milnerites with seeking to exploit the incident in order to push himself forward. Lord Northcliffe was certainly a man with great ambitions at this time, but he had feared and suspected Germany for more than a decade before the outbreak of war, and he feared and suspected her still. On 22nd October he made a speech at an American officers' club in London (the Washington Inn) in which he warned his audience against Lord Milner's arguments. He pointed out that "We are in the presence of the great enemy peace offensive which we always knew would come when the enemy felt himself beaten. . ." He also warned that the way to create Bolshevism in England was to "let the Hun off". This was a theme he continued to stress during the controversy.

In Parliament, Bonar Law declared on the 23rd October that Milner's statements in the *Evening Standard* were made "on his own responsibility". There is no reason why we should doubt the veracity of Bonar Law's remark.

Ministers, however, were anxious to make this aspect of the situation as clear as crystal. On the 24th, David Davies, the Prime Minister's Parliamentary Secretary, raised the matter once again. The purpose of his intervention was to provide the Government with yet another opportunity to deny its responsibility for Milner's statements. Before any Ministerial answer could be given, John Dillon, the Irish leader, rose in order to criticise Milner in terms that were certain to prove popular among vast sections of the British community. Dillon said (*The Times*, 25th October 1918):

> Lord Milner has his views. . . He . . . was concerned that we should not disturb the *personnel* of the German Government . . . The Minister of War had no business to step into the place of the Foreign Minister or the Prime Minister to declare the policy of the country at a time of crisis . . . the American Press undoubtedly took it as a slap in the face to President Wilson, who throughout the whole of his historic utterances during this year laid special stress on the point that the main,

most fundamental, and important matter in this great controversy was that the German people should give an assurance of their good faith by changing their Government, and, if possible, the *personnel* of their Government. That was President Wilson's fundamental principle. But Lord Milner said it would be unwise for the government of this country to make any condition that Germany should change the *personnel* or form of her Government. What was the result? All the German Press immediately took notice of it . . . This was the response to President Wilson's great speech . . . To the solemn appeal which he then made, no response has been given, except the response of Lord Milner to save the Hohenzollerns and the autocratic power of Germany. . .

Dillon had struck hard upon a fundamental point. Since April 1917 President Wilson had urged a policy of inciting the peoples of the Central bloc against their constitutional rulers. He insisted that America would "not take the word of the present rulers of Germany". This course of policy was, at best, received with reluctance in London and in Paris. Statesmen there would not advocate a policy of "subversion". Although Lord Milner always strongly denied that his object was to "save the Hohenzollerns",[1] the matter is open to question. W. H. Buckler of the American Embassy in London, reported to Colonel House, as early as November 1917, that Milner was one of those who would have preferred that "the President had not insisted so strongly upon what amounted to a revolution in Germany, that is, upon an event almost impossible to bring about during war".[2]

Another line of attack upon Milner appeared in North-cliffe's *Evening News* of the 28th October which declared of Milner that "his German origin is not forgotten, and the man in the street declares that he is acting as a Prussian. Lord Milner should take care. If this impression were to spread the results might surprise him. . ."

Later, on the 4th November, the *Daily Mail* criticised

---

[1] In fairness to Milner his denial should be read at pp. 381–2 in the *History of The Times*, vol. IV.

[2] Arno, J. Mayer, *op. cit.*, p. 334, and n. 13.

another aspect of Milner's proposals, as explained in the *Evening Standard*. It was a matter that concerned Lord Northcliffe very deeply. An article from the Paris Correspondent of the *Daily Mail* declared ". . . The Germans rely on Allied disunion and Lord Milner's 'bogey' the spread of Bolshevism. Lord Milner's views cause disquiet here". The first leading article in the *Daily Mail* dealt with the matter at greater length:

> The news that Lord Milner is in Paris . . . has caused some uneasiness among those whose doubts were first aroused by the publication of the interview with him which appeared in the *Evening Standard* of October 17.
>
> . . . It was published immediately after President Wilson's downright declaration that we could have no faith in the present rulers of Germany. . .
>
> . . . If Lord Milner thought that he was serving the interests of any British institution his action was altogether uncalled for . . . If he was afraid of Bolshevism in Germany we need only say that we must leave such outbreaks . . . to be dealt with by those who have provoked them. If he fears "sympathetic" Bolshevism in Great Britain, then he does not, in our opinion, understand the people of this country.

The Milnerites were not prepared to tolerate such criticism. It was left to Sir Edward Carson to strike back at Northcliffe for his attacks upon Milner. Carson was well equipped for the purpose. On the 7th November he rose in the House in order to say in cutting tones that:[1]

> I am quite alive to the fact that it is almost high treason to say a word against Lord Northcliffe. I know his power . . .
>
> Within the last few days there has been an attack made by this Noble Lord's papers upon Lord Milner . . . Lord Milner seems to have given an interview to a rival paper. . .
>
> . . . I have a strong suspicion myself in this case that he is anxious to drive Lord Milner out of office, and, indeed, he does not cloak it because he heads his articles "Will he resign?" . . . day after day, come these attacks . . . upon Lord Milner to drive him out of his office. For what? In order the Lord Northcliffe may get it or may get into the War Cabinet . . . The whole thing is a disgrace to public life in England. . .

[1] Hansard, *Parliamentary Debates*, 7th November 1918, col. 2354. For the reaction of the other Milnerites, see the *History of The Times*, vol. IV, pp. 393 ff.

XVIII

Lord Northcliffe's battle with the Milnerites had more than a transitory significance. The basic elements of their quarrel involved matters of very high importance in the political life of the country.

Alfred Harmsworth, Lord Northcliffe, was a Titan among men, or at least among newspapermen. Of course, he was not without his faults, and these were often serious, but a chief source of the hostility that confronted him lay in the fact that he was so different from the other members of the ruling class of his time. They resented his power, his influence, his ability, and most of all, his refusal to conform to their standards. Like other Press Lords who came after him, the established classes were hostile to Northcliffe because he came from a different background, because he had clawed his way to the top, because he was required, as an outsider, to have recourse to different methods when he sought to clutch at authority and grasp for power. The ordinary rulers of Britain were ruthless enough but a man of Northcliffe's type had to be harder, tougher, more openly brutal, or else he would perish. He had no traditional base to stand upon. The essence of his success lay in the fact that he always avoided the ordinary course; he had beaten his way to a prominent position by novel means, and he was not prepared to abandon them in the hour of his ambition.

These factors played their part in his dispute with Milner and the Milnerites. In particular, Northcliffe always resented the influence of Milner, Oliver, and Waldorf Astor upon Geoffrey Dawson, the man he had chosen as editor of *The Times*. No one would suggest that as Chief Proprietor of the paper, Northcliffe had the right to dominate his editor's outlook, but he had valid cause for resentment. Milner often interfered with Dawson, after he became editor of *The Times*, and so did the other members of the Monday night cabal.

In 1914, for example, Milner hinted that he could help

Dawson to obtain a job in the City or else in the Civil Service, in case he found his relations with Northcliffe too unpleasant.[1] This was not merely the concern of a sympathetic friend. Milner had been anxious for Dawson to go to Printing House Square in the first place in order to "deal with Imperial matters"[2] in the way that he desired. Northcliffe certainly resented this tampering with the allegiance of his editor.

In Dawson's own account of his resignation from *The Times*, which occurred in February 1919, he points out that he began to keep notes upon the matter from the time of a "violent attack on Lord Milner in the *Daily Mail*."[3] According to the *History of The Times*, Dawson thought of resigning when Northcliffe attacked Milner for his plan for "Peace with the Hohenzollerns".[4]

When, after Northcliffe's death, Dawson was invited to return to *The Times* by R. H. Brand, he at once sought out Lord Milner to ask him for his advice. As a result, a Memorandum was drawn up, defining the status and condition of the editor of the paper. According to the *History of The Times*, "The Memorandum, it cannot be doubted, was a joint production of Milner and Dawson."[5] These "Milner-Dawson" conditions were eventually accepted by the new proprietors.

It seems clear enough, therefore, that when Dawson left *The Times* and when he returned to it, he was dominated by his relationship with Lord Milner. What, we may ask, was the effect of this legacy upon Dawson's mind?

Lord Northcliffe had desired a "hard" peace for Germany. Lord Milner had looked upon the matter in a completely different light. From an early period of the war he made it clear that he desired a "moderate" peace; that

---

[1] See Evelyn Wrench, *Geoffrey Dawson and Our Times* (London, 1955), p. 176, n. 1.
[2] *Ibid.*, p. 77.
[3] *Ibid.*, p. 176.
[4] *History of The Times*, vol. IV, p. 447.
[5] *Ibid.*, vol. IV, part II, p. 778.

Britain was not vitally concerned with the fate of the people of Eastern and Central Europe; that "We did not go to war for Czechoslovakia, Yugoslavia, Rumanians, or Poles. . ." Moreover, as a British Imperialist, Milner always explained that the hope of the Empire lay not in any entangling continental alliances, but in closer Imperial unity. Certainly, affairs in Europe could not be ignored by British statesmen. Were they to deal with Germany or with Russia, in the period after the war?

Once the "destruction of Prussian militarism" was accomplished, Milner clearly believed that Britain should deal with a "stable" government in Germany since "we do not wish to see Bolshevism and chaos rampant there. . ." When the Germans were beaten in the West and no longer threatened the Empire in an immediate sense, Milner had no objection to the conditions established at Brest-Litovsk, to the "free hand" in the East for Germany.[1]

Before the war the extreme conservatives in Britain, who placed their faith in Milner, feared and suspected the Germans. After the war, some of them—Dawson, Astor, and Lothian[2]—for example, were prepared to work with the Germans. This basic change of outlook occurred, in good part, as a result of Lord Milner's teaching. He not only emphasised the fact that it was in Britain's "interests" to deal with a stable German regime, he also stressed the dangers of the Revolution in Russia, and the influence of that Revolution in Britain. These were the factors and this the legacy that he left to his young men at a time when their influence and authority came to dominate the thinking of many people in this country. They form, in part at least, the background for any understanding of their motives and aspirations in the age of "appeasement".

[1] In this connection see the recent comment by A. J. P. Taylor in *The Origins of The Second World War* (London, 1961), pp. 69–70.

[2] Lothian was not a Liberal until after his association with Lloyd George in 1916. Before that time he considered standing for Parliament as a Conservative, or Unionist.

XXI. Colonial Secretary

Last months at the War Office – Milner asks for his dis-
charge – The coupon election – Appointed Colonial
Secretary – At the Paris Peace Conference – Work at the
Colonial Office – The situation in Egypt – Lord Milner's
Mission – Boycott – Milner's report to the Prime Minister –
Declaration of the 29th December – Milner's attitude to
Egypt – The Milner-Zaghlul "Agreement" – The waspish
attack of Dr. Jones – Milner plans to resign – Milner and
Empire organisation – End of the official career.

I

LORD Milner's last months as Secretary of State for
War were not happy. The vicious cynicism the Prime
Minister displayed to many of his colleagues now
that victory was in sight, the details of the work upon
which Milner was engaged, and his own physical exhaustion
combined to make office a burden for him. A wise and
sympathetic chief might have salved Milner's feelings; but
in the hour of his triumph Lloyd George saw no reason for
the exercise of sympathy, a sentiment he indulged in very
sparingly at the best of times.

On 6th September the Secretary of State gave expression
to his feelings in a pointed letter to the Prime Minister:[1]

Something must be done *at once* about the W.O. as we are all at
sixes and sevens. . .
Personally I feel I cannot attempt a complete reorganisation of the
W.O. The more I look at the problem . . . the more convinced I am
that to try a fresh reorganisation at this moment would be a fearful
blunder. I should shrink from it. . .
. . . The long and short of it is, as between you & me, a question

[1] Lloyd George Papers, Milner to Lloyd George, 6th September 1918.

of confidence... I keep your objects steadily in view, *but I don't bother you* with the hundred and one difficulties which have to be encountered in pursuing them. The *how* and the *when* must be left to my judgment and I must be judged by results...

This appeal for confidence met with no response from the Prime Minister. He made no reply. Milner was himself occupied by visits to various Headquarters in France and with other departmental tasks. He allowed the matter of War Office reform to mark time. Nevertheless, after the victory over Germany, the immediate problems of the War Office became very pressing.

A few days after the end of the war Milner wrote again to the Prime Minister about the War Office, almost in despairing tones: "I hope it may be possible to get the Cabinet, or yourself, to give one clear half-hour's attention, without delay, to the question of the future of the Army. Without some sort of line to go on, we shall be paralysed at the War Office..."[1]

This general situation led to an extraordinary scene in the following month. Lord Milner had been involved in a plan for the withdrawal of miners from the Army, as early as September 1918. Despite all his efforts he was unable to talk seriously to the Prime Minister about the matter until the 6th December. On that occasion Lloyd George suddenly attacked him for his "dilatoriness and neglect" of War Office affairs. The attack was made in the company of a crowd of railway and Board of Trade officials, who were present in Downing Street. It was outrageous for Lloyd George to berate a public servant of Milner's high standing in such terms, before such an audience. On the next day Milner wrote to the Prime Minister in order to ask for his "discharge". This letter explains in the clearest terms the nature and sources of Milner's loyalty to Lloyd George, and also his lack of enthusiasm for office at this time:[2]

[1] Lloyd George Papers, Milner to Lloyd George, 13th September 1918.
[2] Lloyd George Papers, Milner to Lloyd George, 7th December 1918, partly printed in Beaverbrook, *Men and Power*, p. 329–330, and in Wrench, *Milner*, p. 353.

Ever since it became evident that the war . . . was practically over, I have been anxious to ask you for my "discharge". During the two years that I have spent in your Ministry, I have till lately had the satisfaction of feeling, that I was of some real use to you and to the country, and I shall always be grateful to you for having given me the opportunity of doing such important work.

I am sure no one else in your position would have given me that chance, and I have sought to repay you by strenuous and loyal service.

But in itself official life has become very irksome to me in these days. I am extremely tired. . .

To be quite frank, and I know how you love frankness, my desire to withdraw from the arena has been quickened by the impatience, which you have of late frequently manifested of my conduct of affairs at the War Office. . .

What I am not willing to accept is a position, in which I am exposed to such vehement charges of dilatoriness and neglect as you made yesterday, in the presence of a large number of people, many of them not Ministers. . .

To submit to that sort of public rebuke without a protest, or to expose myself to a chance of its repetition is, I feel, not consistent with self-respect.

The last thing I wish to do is to add to your burdens . . . I am quite ready to carry on at the War Office until the election is over. . .

At the same time I should like you to feel that, if you found it convenient to make a change even before then, I am prepared at any moment to fall in with your wishes.

A few days later this incident was smoothed over, and Lord Milner consented to remain in office. Nevertheless, the tasks that still confronted him were not congenial. When the war ended there was a good deal of discontent in the Army. Some soldiers even rioted because they were disappointed at the slowness of their return to civilian life. These petty incidents occasionally threatened to become serious, but Milner's great talents were ill-used when they were bent to the soothing of an irate soldiery. Problems of this kind were not his *metier*. Lloyd George and other Ministers were dissatisfied with his conduct of the War Office, in its last phases.[1]

[1] See in this connection, Winston Churchill, *The Aftermath*, pp. 53–4.

II

Lord Milner played little part in the famous "coupon" election of December 1918. In Lloyd George's opinion Milner had no political "nostril"; furthermore, he was worn out by the cares of office; in particular, he longed to give up his place as Secretary of State for War.

In addition to these factors, we should notice another. At the time of the 1918 election Lloyd George relied very heavily upon Bonar Law in his calculations for the victory. When Lloyd George's first Administration was formed in 1916, he had been required, as we have seen, to mollify those Tory extremists who were uneasy under Bonar Law's leadership, but who respected Milner, Carson, and their friends. Now, the chief members of this extreme faction of the Tories had been swallowed up in the Government, or had been dispersed. The inefficiency of Asquith's wartime Administration no longer served as a target to bind them together. They were prepared, on the eve of an election, to follow the lead of Bonar Law. In 1916 Lloyd George had been required to balance between the Milner-Carson section of the Tories upon the one hand, and those who followed Bonar Law, upon the other. This was no longer the case. Lloyd George placed most of his confidence in Bonar Law when he planned the electoral victory of December 1918. There was no need for him to mollify Milner's friends.

Although Milner was displeased by the general tone of the election campaign, he did what he could to help the Prime Minister. As early as the beginning of September Lloyd George applied to him for advice about the technical question of Tariff Reform and Imperial Preference. Lloyd George was flirting with the idea as a part of his general policy. He realised that the Tories had lost several elections because of their Tariff programme, but he understood that Milner could make valuable suggestions in this general field. In September Milner prepared some notes for the

Prime Minister's guidance. On the 9th he wrote to Lloyd George to explain how the terrible stigma of the "Food Taxes" could be avoided, in case a scheme of preference were adopted:[1]

My dear P.M.   9 . 9 . 18
    Thinking over my notes about Preference, which were written in a hurry, I want to make one addition . . . It is with regard to Preference in Tariffs . . . I do not think a Tariff is essential to the practice of Preference . . . But I do think . . . that it is essential that on existing duties, and such as we may from time to time see fit to impose, there should be some reduction for goods of British origin. . .
    . . . as long as we maintain the principle . . . that we should be guided in the matter of tariff by our own interest , . . there is no reason why we should not give this advantage to the Dominions. . .
    . . . For obviously, the fact that we imposed on goods of British origin a lower rate than on similar imported goods, could not raise the price, or in any way increase the cost of living. If we are afraid of "taxing the food of the people" all we need do is not to impose any duty on imported articles of food. If, on the contrary, we do, as I hope, continue to tax *certain* imported articles of food, like sugar, tea, cocoa, then it is not an increase but if anything an alleviation of the burdens of the consumer, to admit these imports from our Dominions at a somewhat lower rate.
                                                      Yours very sincerely,
                                                                Milner.

Less valid than this advice was Milner's conduct of a scheme to provide newspapers for the troops in France, as a part of the election campaign. Early in December arrangements were made by the War Office to send out to the Army, in addition to the ballot papers, large numbers of newspapers. The object was to arouse interest in the election. The idea was to distribute these newspapers, of every political complexion, free of charge to the soldiers. As Milner explained to Lloyd George, "The stuff can be got out and distributed, if only it can be provided".[2]
    Unfortunately, the provision of the papers fell woefully

---

[1] Lloyd George Papers, Milner to Lloyd George, 9th September, 1918.
[2] Lloyd George Papers, Milner to Lloyd George, 4th December 1918.

short of the promises made by the publishers. The *Daily Chronicle* and the *Daily Mirror*, for example, furnished no newspapers at all, upon one occasion. Milner wrote to the Prime Minister that the scheme was a complete "wash-out" and Lord Beaverbrook has described it as a "fiasco".[1]

Despite this contretemps, the election resulted in a tremendous victory for the Lloyd George Coalition. Shortly after the results were announced Milner wrote to the Prime Minister in order to ask that he be allowed to give up the War Office. On this occasion he did not suggest his retirement from the Government but only that he should relinquish a post no longer congenial to him.[2] When the new Ministry was announced on the 10th January 1919, it was learned that Winston Churchill was the new War Minister, and that Lord Milner had been appointed Secretary of State for the colonies.

Thus ended Lord Milner's period of service at the War Office. Although the conditions of the time provided him with no opportunity to reform that Department, his tenure was notable. It witnessed the triumph of Britain over a formidable enemy, after a terrible and unprecedented war. His greatest War Office reform lay in the field of Army education, where he did a great deal to modernise that aspect of British military organisation. Although his last months as Secretary of State were tedious, Lord Milner could look back upon his work at the War Office with feelings of genuine pride and accomplishment.

III

As Secretary of State for the Colonies Lord Milner was at once beset by a host of detailed but important matters, both in the conduct of his Department and at the Peace Conference in Paris. After a brief holiday he took up his new burdens.

[1] Beaverbrook, *Men and Power*, p. 329.
[2] Lloyd George Papers, Milner to Lloyd George, 4th January 1919.

Many of his devoted admirers believed that his tenure of the Colonial Office would rival that of Joseph Chamberlain, but this did not turn out to be the case. Milner was often required to leave London in order to go to Paris, and later he travelled to Egypt as head of a special Mission to that country. Although he was Colonial Secretary for two years, many months of that period of service were spent away from Whitehall, in the discharge of tasks assigned him by the Cabinet. It was a gruelling succession of duties that fell to his lot; they would have taxed the energies of a much younger and more vigorous man.

One incident of January 1919 deserves our notice because it reveals the extent of Lord Milner's concern for and loyalty to subordinates. It had been arranged that Leo Amery should join him as Under-Secretary of State at the Colonial Office. At the last moment, however, Milner learned that Lloyd George and Bonar Law had dropped Amery in order to find a place for another of their friends. Milner refused to go until this decision was altered. He held out until Amery was invited, by the Prime Minister, to accept the position he had been promised. We can scarcely wonder at the devotion Milner inspired in his young men in the face of incidents of this kind. Few ordinary politicians would have acted as Milner did, in the circumstances.[1]

The British Empire Delegation at the Paris Peace Conference was entitled to five principal delegates, as its representatives. Lord Milner was not one of these five. He spoke and acted at Paris, for the most part, only as head of his Department, although he was sometimes assigned specific tasks by the Conference. The Milnerites were disappointed by the nature of his position; they have suggested that Lloyd George would have acted more wisely had he "put the peace-making in the hands of a man like Milner."[2] In practice; however, the negotiations were left almost exclusively to Lloyd George and Balfour.

[1] The story is told in Amery, *My Political Life*, vol. II, p. 176.
[2] Wrench, *Milner*, p. 360. See also Amery, *op. cit.*, p. 179.

As a result of the Prime Minister's decision with regard to the delegates, Milner was usually concerned with technical details at Paris, though his personal influence occasionally permitted him to play a large and general part in the proceedings.

Before and after the delegates of the Powers met at Paris Milner insisted that the Germans should be effectively disarmed, and that the burden of reparations placed upon them should not be made too heavy. His object in urging these policies was two-fold. He desired to destroy the menace of Germany for the British Empire; at the same time he wanted to be certain that the terms of the Peace Treaty were not so harsh that Germany would be driven to Bolshevism. In a discussion about reparations in the Imperial Cabinet he pointed out that "the most certain way of 'bolshevising' Germany would be to put an excessive burden on her".[1]

Lord Milner was placed in charge of some of the most important sections of the Peace Treaties. He presided over the Mandates Commission which defined the nature of the control over the former German colonies; he dealt with the Italian demands for territorial compensation outside Europe; he sought to help the Zionists to make their proposals about Palestine valid; he was, in Lloyd George's phrase, a fervent believer in and an advocate of the League of Nations. Milner was also required to deal with the situation in Syria, where the French and Arabs were involved in mortal disagreement. This phase of his work at Paris brought down upon him the wrath and anger of both Lloyd George and Clemenceau.

Lloyd George has complained that the delay in delimiting spheres of military occupation in Syria occurred because of Milner's lethargy. He had written of the Syrian situation that:[2]

... There was delay ... For this Clemenceau blamed Milner ... For this charge there was a certain amount of justification. Ever since the

[1] Lloyd George, *Truth About The Peace Treaties*, vol. I, p. 477; see also pp. 714–15.
[2] *Ibid.*, pp. 1075–6.

spring of 1918—since Lord Milner went to the War Office—his energy
seemed to have sagged . . . there was a nervous lassitude which
appeared to have descended upon him and affected his fine faculties
with the supineness of fatigue . . . It was of no avail to point out to
him that putting off decisions was exasperating the French and fostering
their suspicions. . .

On 14th May 1919 Lloyd George wrote to Milner in rude
and cavalier terms that:[1]

I earnestly hope that you will not find it necessary a second time to
leave Paris without achieving a decision on the important questions
entrusted to your charge. There are at least five matters essential to the
peace settlement which you alone can pilot to a conclusion. Togoland,
Kameroons, German East Africa, Nauru and Somaliland.

You can forgive me for saying emphatically that there can be no
colonial business which more urgently presses for treatment than these
affairs. . .

The business of his Department that sometimes required
Milner to absent himself from Paris was as varied as his
work at the Peace Conference. In general, the Secretary of
State sought to establish at the Colonial Office a rational
and logical system, designed to take the place of the haphazard and thoroughly English organisation of the past.
Milner always deplored the lack of method and order
which, in his opinion, was too often characteristic of the
great Departments of State in Whitehall.

He sought to create a Colonial Development Council
whose business was to survey the economic resources and
possibilities of every part of the Colonial Empire. The
experts of the Council were required to devise plans for the
efficient exploitation of these resources. Milner also helped
to work out schemes for emigration from Britain to various
parts of the Empire; he was always interested in placing
people of British stock in those distant possessions upon
which so much depended for the Imperial future. He
helped to work out schemes for native education in the

[1] Lloyd George Papers, Lloyd George to Milner, 14th May 1919; printed in
Beaverbrook, *Men and Power*, pp. 330–1.

Colonies, and plans for the creation of colleges of tropical agriculture. He raised funds for the London School of Tropical Diseases. One scheme especially dear to him was a plan to extend the construction of railways in every part of the Empire.

Although some of these proposals prospered under his hand, the situation in Egypt early in 1919 became so dangerous that Milner was required to leave London to visit that country as head of a special Mission. For a period of several months Amery took the place of his chief in Whitehall, in order to serve as an acting Secretary of State.

IV

By the end of the war the situation in Egypt was boiling up to one of those periodic crises which have regularly marred that country's relations with Great Britain. Certain statements of the Allies made during the war had aroused in Egyptian breasts ardent hopes; and now a movement began to turn these hopes into political reality.

At the end of 1914 a British Protectorate which abolished Turkish suzerainty was declared over Egypt. This change of status included the novel idea of incorporating Egypt in the British Empire. The plan was not merely to maintain British control over the country but also to develop self-governing institutions which, in the happy fulness of time, might lead to responsible government. By 1918, however, the Allies announced their intention of enfranchising the peoples oppressed by Turkish rule. The idea of self-determination was in the air. The Egyptians believed that their title to manage their own affairs was equal to that of the Arabs. A deputation led by Zaghlul Pasha, a Nationalist politician of long experience, presented itself before the High Commissioner, Sir R. Wingate, and asked for permission to proceed to London to submit the case for Egyptian independence to the British Government. Eventually, their proposal was reported to London, but it was rejected by the Secretary of State. Zaghlul and his extremist friends were not allowed to leave the country.

There now followed the first of a series of blunders that led to a worsening of the relations between Britain and Egypt. The suggestion was made that certain moderate leaders should be permitted to go to London, in Zaghlul's room. Had this request been accepted, the moderates would have captured the attention of the Egyptian public. When it was refused, Zaghlul's status was enhanced; his country-men came to look upon him as the only man who might achieve results. His followers proceeded to organise the national elements in the country, and an agitation was begun.

When the British Government refused to allow any Egyptians to proceed to London or Paris, they confined the trouble to Egypt itself, where Zaghlul was rapidly becoming master. In March 1919 he and certain of his col-leagues were arrested, placed upon a British destroyer, and removed to Malta. This arrest of the Pasha resulted in an explosion of violence. Riots, murder, acts of sabotage, and strikes culminated in a situation that has been accurately described as a rebellion. By early April the military had managed to restore a semblance of order but the condition of Egypt was still troubled and dangerous. It was clear that something had to be done if further chaos and bloodshed were to be avoided.

General Sir Edmund Allenby, the Commander-in-Chief in Egypt, was ordered to return to the country from a sojourn in Paris, to take up the post of special High Com-missioner. He proceeded to restore law and order; at the same time he invited responsible Egyptians to discuss matters with him. They pointed out that the situation could not be eased until the exiles on Malta were released. On the 7th April Allenby agreed to their demands. Zaghlul and his friends were set free, and left Malta for Paris. This decision has been severely criticised as a surrender to the forces of disorder. The Egyptians were taught that violence or the threat of it might succeed where constitutional and orderly methods were bound to fail. By Allenby's proclamation of the 7th April, the British in effect recognised Zaghlul and his agitators as the spokesmen of Egypt.

At the same time General Allenby began to press the Government at home to announce that a Royal Commission under Lord Milner would proceed to Egypt in order to review the entire situation. It seemed obvious that if further troubles were to be avoided, the Milner Mission should set out at once. However, the authorities in Cairo and in London hesitated to act. They were unable to decide upon the correct course. For a period of several months Lord Milner was unable to discover exactly when the Government desired him to leave for Egypt.

Finally, in November, the High Commissioner at last recommended to authority that the Mission should be sent. Early in December 1919 Lord Milner and his colleagues, J. A. Spender, Sir Rennell Rodd, General Maxwell, Sir Cecil Hurst, and Sir Owen Thomas arrived in Cairo. The terms of reference of their special Mission read as follows:

To enquire into the causes of the late disorders in Egypt and to report on the existing situation in the country and the form of the Constitution which, under the Protectorate, will be best calculated to promote its peace and prosperity, the progressive development of self-governing institutions, and the protection of foreign interests.

V

Unlike the British Government, the nationalists in Egypt had not wasted their time in the period between the release of Zaghlul and the arrival of Lord Milner and his party. They organised a boycott of the Mission which proved very effective. They made certain that few Egyptians of consequence trafficked with any members of the Mission. These nationalists argued that discussions with Lord Milner might prejudice Egyptian prospects in the Peace Conference at Paris.

The result was a deadlock. The British Government had made it clear that they proposed to maintain the Protectorate. Zaghlul and his friends refused to accept a Protectorate and demanded complete independence for their country. Milner and his colleagues sat impotent in the Semiramis Hotel in Cairo.

J. A. Spender has recalled that Milner, in particular, was determined to achieve something.[1] After three weeks in the country he planned a radical change of course for his Mission. At the same time he sent the Prime Minister a long report which surveyed the entire situation and may serve us as a background for the developments which followed. On the 28th December 1919 Milner wrote to Lloyd George:[2]

... Egypt is in a much worse state than I imagined ... Indeed I think we have been going bad ever since Cromer, though not so rapidly as in quite recent days.

The present position is this: Order has been ... almost completely restored ... The Fellaheen have had a lesson and are indisposed to give further trouble, especially with cotton 5 times its old price! ...

As against this, I am bound to admit that ... the whole of the middle and upper classes—the landowners, the "intelligenzia", the officials, the religious leaders—are all out to give us all the trouble they can. The agitation for "complete independence" has swept right over the country ... it is evident that, till there is some change in the temper of the people, Egypt will continue to be a thorn in our side and will exercise a disturbing influence in our position in the whole of the near East and to some extent also in India.

This is a serious danger, which by hook or by crook we must try to overcome. It will take time, but I don't mean to say that, if we can get our policy here on to better lines ... the problem is insoluble. Evidently the first thing to do is to try and create a better atmosphere ... we are trying hard to explain to all and sundry, that it is not Britain's wish or interest, to subjugate Egypt ... It is clear that, if the Moderates are successfully to resist the Extremists, we must have something to give to the Moderates; they must be able to hold out some attractive prospect of "self-government" to the people— beautiful phrase this, but the Orientals live on phrases and camouflage ... even more than we do.

[1] J. A. Spender, *Life, Journalism and Politics* (London, 1927), vol. II, p. 90.
[2] Lloyd George Papers, Milner to Lloyd George, 28th December 1919, marked "Confidential".

It is the appearance they care about more than the substance. The difficulty is to find a way of making Egypt's relation to Great Britain *appear* a more independent and dignified one than it ever really can be without our abandoning the degree of control which, in view of native incompetence and corruption we are constrained to keep.

This is the *crux*. I hope to get over it, but, in order to do so, we are bound to allow a very large amount of latitude to the native "spouters" ... As a mission of enquiry without executive functions *we* can afford to be much more indulgent ... than the High Commissioner ... our policy here must be directed in relation to what we are going to do in other parts of the Near East...

In order to escape the effect of the nationalist boycott; to create a "better atmosphere" in Egypt; to strengthen the "Moderates"; and to find some way of making Anglo-Egyptian relations appear more "dignified", the Milner Mission issued a far-reaching declaration on the 29th December. This declaration explained that: "The Mission has been sent out by the British Government, with the approval of Parliament, to reconcile the aspirations of the Egyptian people with the special interests which Great Britain has in Egypt and with a maintenance of the legitimate rights of all foreign residents in the country".[1]

It has been pointed out that this declaration was a complete misstatement of the facts. The original terms of reference of the Milner Mission had not been to reconcile the aspirations of the Egyptian people with the special interests of Great Britain in Egypt, but with the maintenance of the British Protectorate. By the terms of this declaration of the 29th December the maintenance of the Protectorate had been relinquished as an object of policy, by the Milner Mission at least.[2]

The immediate result of this declaration was only partially successful, from Lord Milner's point of view. The boycott of the Mission, despite the concessions of the declaration of the 29th December, was only partially broken. In order

[1] Spender, *op. cit.*, p. 90 says that the idea of issuing the proclamation was his.
[2] For the most serious criticism and the best account, see Lord Lloyd, *Egypt Since Cromer* (London, 1934), vol. II, pp. 15 ff., and *passim*.

to collect the information upon which to base its report, the Mission was forced to rely upon official and non-Egyptian sources of information. Early in March 1920 it returned to London.

We should notice that Milner and his colleagues differed from their critics in one important particular, in their analysis of the Egyptian situation. Milner, especially, believed that a settlement of some kind was necessary, for the sake of Britain's position in the Near East. Moreover, as an old Egyptian official he did not look upon Egypt as a part of the British Empire. Subject to certain safeguards, he believed that independence was the proper status for the country. According to Spender, Milner's view was that "if the Egyptians did not want us to govern them and could keep order and maintain solvency without us, we were under no obligation to undertake the ... task of governing them against their will. I may add ... that the Mission took very special pains to obtain a careful estimate of the steps which would have to be taken, if a settlement could not be obtained".[1]

VI

The Milner Mission arrived back in London in April 1920. Their labours were far from finished. In their opinion, one fact dominated the Egyptian situation. This was Zaghlul Pasha's position as the hero and "father" of his people. There could be no settlement of Egyptian affairs unless Zaghlul were involved in it. After negotiation, Zaghlul and certain of his colleagues arrived in London from their exile in Paris, for a series of conversations with the Mission. These deliberations, which were exhausting for Lord Milner, resulted in the so-called Milner-Zaghlul Agreement, a document which abandoned completely the idea of a British Protectorate over Egypt. Although Zaghlul's behaviour in the talks has been properly described

[1] Spender, *op. cit.*, p. 91. For the opposite view, see Lord Lloyd, *op. cit.*, pp. 15 ff.

as "monstrous", Lord Milner was convinced that the "Agreement" could serve as a basis for lasting peace and amity between the two countries.[1] It was concluded in August 1920, although Zaghlul, devious as always, refused to commit himself to it until the Egyptian people declared their approval of its terms.

In effect, the Mission now suggested a new method of dealing with Egypt, the method of a "free bilateral agreement". The Mission was prepared to acknowledge the independence of Egypt by means of a Treaty, subject only to the safeguarding of certain British and foreign interests in the country. These safeguards .under the proposed Treaty, included Britain's right to maintain military forces on Egyptian soil, her right to be consulted in the selection of the Egyptian Financial and Judicial Advisers, and her right to intervene to protect foreigners in Egypt.

This "Agreement" with Zaghlul has been subjected to severe but just criticism. It has been referred to as an example of "that failure of nerve, that weakening of the will to rule, which began to afflict the British ruling classes in the aftermath of the first World War, and which was to make the dissolution of the British Empire so ugly and ruinous, for subjects and rulers alike".[2]

We should notice, however, that the conclusions of the Milner Mission were not definite in themselves, but merely one stage in the developments which led to the abolition of the Protectorate over Egypt. On the 28th February 1922, when Milner had disappeared from the political scene, Lord Allenby made public a declaration which explained that the British Protectorate over Egypt was at an end, and that Egypt would thereafter be looked upon as an independent Sovereign State. Certain matters were reserved to the discretion of the British Government until they could be decided by "free discussion and friendly accommodation

---

[1] See the account in E. Kedourie, *"Sa'ad Zaghlul and the British"*, published in *St. Antony's Papers, No. 11, passim.*

[2] See Kedourie, *op. cit.*, and Lord Lloyd, *op. cit., passim.*

on both sides". These included the security of Empire communications in Egypt, the defence of the country, the question of the Sudan, and the protection of foreign minorities.

Lord Allenby's statement did not result from the "bilateral" Treaty or Agreement which had been suggested by the Milner Mission. It was a unilateral decision, based in part at least upon the opinion that such an expression of confidence could in itself lead to a lasting settlement.

It has been said that the inability of the Lloyd George Government to act promptly on the recommendations of the Milner Mission was the "tragedy of Egypt's later history".[1] In any case the Foreign Secretary, Lord Curzon, believed that "had the Milner memorandum been accepted by the British Government as the basis of a final treaty . . . the whole Egyptian question might have been solved in 1920".[2] Perhaps the best defence of Milner and his colleagues has been adduced by J. A. Spender, who later wrote that:[3]

> The publication of the Report was, of course, a decisive event which changed the direction of British policy, but most of these efforts seemed wasted in the confusion of the next two years. When the Report was finished, Milner seemed tired and exhausted, and after he had retired from the Government it was left without a champion . . . By ill luck the Egyptian question had collided with the Irish, and the Coalition Government was, I imagine, in no mind to couple its Irish settlement with what its Tory supporters would have called a surrender to Egyptian Nationalists . . . Allenby, backed by his officials in Egypt, put on pressure which resulted in the proclamation of March, 1922. Some decision had by this time become imperative . . . But the granting of Independence by Proclamation with the "reserved questions" unsettled was a far worse solution than the Treaty recommended by the Commission, which would have settled the "reserved questions" prior to or simultaneously with the grant of Independence. This we regarded as the essence of our plan. . .

---

[1] See the article on "Egypt" in the *Encyclopaedia Britannica*, p. 83.
[2] This is the argument in Harold Nicolson, *Curzon: The Last Phase* (London, 1934), p. 176.
[3] Spender, *op. cit.*, vol. II, pp. 99–100.

The harshest public criticism of Lord Milner's Egyptian endeavours has come from a curious source which merits our attention. Dr. Thomas Jones wrote a letter to a correspondent which purported to give Stanley Baldwin's opinion of Milner's handling of Egyptian affairs. According to Jones, Baldwin "recalled to me the disastrous effect of Milner's senility in the Egyptian negotiations as a warning of what happens when old and tired men carry on too long."[1]

How are we to explain this waspish attack upon Lord Milner's memory? We should notice that although the Milner Mission was the last of Lord Milner's major services to the State, his resignation which shortly followed was only accomplished over the objections of the Prime Minister, who desired him to continue as a member of the Administration. The decision to resign was Milner's, and it was opposed by his colleagues. Furthermore, although Milner was tired out by his duties in connection with Egypt, this condition of nervous exhaustion, as we have seen, was a handicap that had afflicted him from the days of his youth. Despite it, he was able to discharge duties of every kind, whatever the personal cost. Senility was certainly a singular word to employ, in such a connection.

We may explain Dr. Jones's letter by referring to his own condition at the time that he wrote it, in 1936. Then, he was acting as the guide and adviser of Waldorf Astor, the owner of *The Observer*. Like J. L. Garvin before him, Dr. Jones was sometimes jealous of the influence exerted upon Astor by the Milnerites. On occasion, he resented the power of men like Curtis, Lothian, and Dawson over his wealthy friend. It seems probable that in an effort to strike back at them he condemned their old chief in a phrase that has been applied to him by no other observer of recent political life in this country.[2]

---

[1] Thomas Jones, *A Diary With Letters* (London, 1954), p. 175.
[2] For an example of Dr. Jones's jealousy of the Milnerites, see Jones, *op. cit.*, p. 173.

VII

By the autumn of 1920 Lord Milner was determined to leave the Government. He was still dominated by feelings of loyalty to the Prime Minsiter, but his will to continue in office no longer existed. It was not merely that he was tired out: He felt that he had done enough; his private affairs now required his undivided attention; since he looked upon himself primarily as an "emergency man" to be called in by the State at a moment of dire crisis he did not believe, in the circumstances of 1920, that there was any valid reason for him to carry on.

His last months in the Government were devoted to the preparations for the holding of an Imperial Conference in 1921, a subject always dear to his heart. On the 8th October 1920 he wrote the Prime Minister his last letter dealing with Imperial matters. This paper reveals his attitude to the organisation of the Empire in the evening of his days as an Imperial leader:[1]

... we have been drifting rather, and we and the Dominions are all at sixes and sevens about "Imperial Cabinet", "Imperial Conference", etc. etc. etc. Everybody feels that something is wanted, yet nobody quite knows what...

Yet the matter is really simple...

We do not, in my humble opinion, want a "Constitutional" or other "Conference", viz. a big pow-wow to discuss the "constitutional relations" of the Mother Country and the Dominions.

That may have to come some day, but it is too soon; nobody has the leisure or disposition for it and in 1921 it would end in smoke.

What we do want is to keep in touch, so profitably established during the war between the Governments, not to evolve a new Imperial constitution but to *discuss and settle* on the basis of our existing institutions, the various *practical and urgent* problems, which affect the Dominions as well as the Mother Country, and to ensure harmony and co-operation between them. That is to say we want very soon to have a meeting of what we once called the Imperial War Cabinet", or of some body very like it. The only essential thing is to get the different Prime

[1] Lloyd George Papers, Milner to Lloyd George, 8th October 1920, marked "Very Confidential".

Ministers together under your Presidency. More business can be done like that in a week than in months and years of telegrams flying backwards and forwards.

In the following month Lord Milner warned the Prime Minister that he proposed to retire from office at the end of the year. He promised that he would always be at Lloyd George's service, even in his retirement; and he expressed his appreciation for the kindness and consideration he had received from Lloyd George and from their colleagues in the Administration.[1]

Despite this clear explanation of his purpose the Prime Minister, early in January 1921, proposed that Milner should organise a Committee to deal with the transfer of Palestine and Mesopotamia to the jurisdiction of the Colonial Office. On 3rd January 1921 Milner wrote to Lloyd George in order to decline this proposal, and to make his decision about resignation absolutely final. He explained that "I will not discuss the scheme, with which I do not agree. It is a Government decision and has to be carried out by members of the Government. But not by me, who am on the very eve of retirement, and only hanging on from day to day . . . I do beg that we may soon come to a final understanding as to the actual date when I may count upon being free from official duties".[2]

Lloyd George at last realised that Milner was fixed in his intention to withdraw. On the 24th March 1921, after more than one attempt, he sent a graceful letter acquiescing in Milner's decision and expressing his own regret and that of their colleagues:[3]

March 24th 1921   10 Downing Street
My dear Milner,

The Cabinet at a recent meeting asked me unanimously to explain to you their deep regret that you have felt it necessary to relinquish office, and their huge appreciation of the counsel and assistance you

---

[1] Lloyd George Papers, Milner to Lloyd George, 27th November 1920.
[2] Lloyd George Papers, Milner to Lloyd George, 3rd January 1921.
[3] Lloyd George Papers, Lloyd George to Milner, 24th March 1921.

have given them during the last four years. They earnestly hope that the services you have given so unstintingly and so selflessly will not be lost to the Empire and that after a rest you will be able to devote time and energy to public affairs for many years to come. . . .

May I also say personally how much I regret your resignation. I could not have had a more hard-working, a wiser or a stauncher colleague during the War Cabinet days . . . They were great days to have lived through and I shall never forget your loyal and most efficient co-operation which contributed enormously to the victory of the Allies. . .

Yours ever sincerely,
(signed) D. Lloyd George.

Rt. Hon. The Viscount Milner, G.C.B., G.C.M.G.

Thus there came to an end the long official career which had begun in the eighties of the previous century. It was a career of truly selfless service, however over-worked that phrase may be, and was recognised by authority with the high award of the Garter. Lord Milner, despite the bitter vagaries of his official life, could look back content upon this second period of his service to the State, the period which began during the crisis of the World War and ended only after the achievement of victory.

XXII.   The Religio Milneriana

Lord Milner's Marriage – Politics and Journalism – A
South African Visit – Sleepy Sickness – The Man of no
illusions – Not a Prussian autocrat – Some flaw in him –
Rejects the British system – The example of the Irish –
crisis – The example of the Dardanelles – Other factors –
Lord Milner's death – The *Religio Milneriana* revived – Fear
not to sow.

I

A few weeks after he retired from the Government
Lord Milner, for so long a confirmed bachelor,
married a devoted friend, Violet Maxse, the Lady
Edward Cecil. By this alliance he won to his side a staunch
and loyal wife, a wife who shared a genuine interest in all
his public work. Her vigorous devotion to Milner's status
as a politician and statesman while he lived, and to his memory after his death, did much to enhance a reputation that
was already being puffed up by the Milnerites in the Press,
in official circles, and in that narrow society frequented
by the English ruling class.

After a honeymoon in Europe Milner returned to
London, revived in spirit. Though he was delighted to be
relieved of office, he still retained a keen interest in public
affairs. There was much for him to do in his new role of
elder statesman. In particular, in the public sphere, he
determined to do what he could to further the cause of a
united Empire. The various *Round Table* clubs which were
set up in nearly all the British territories, and similar
organisations in London, could look to him for help,
counsel, and inspiration.

In the autumn of 1922 when Bonar Law formed his Government Lord Milner was asked to join, but the invitation was refused in very strong terms. Although he would not be involved in party politics as such, Lord Milner turned to journalism in order to make public some of his views and opinions upon the national requirements of the day. For the entire month of January 1923 Waldorf Astor's *Observer* was dominated by a series of brilliant articles written by Milner. Some of these papers, together with certain other essays, were published in book form in that year under the title *Questions of the Hour,* a volume that was reprinted two years later. One of Lord Milner's last excursions in active politics occurred in 1924. After the General Election of December 1923, which resulted in the first Labour Government in this country, Milner, Amery and Neville Chamberlain decided to form an organisation for the purpose of educating the country on the subjects of protection and Imperial Preference. Stanley Baldwin, the leader of the Conservatives, was also involved in the plan. At his request, Milner consented to preside over a tariff committee. This development might have had profound consequences in the politics of that time but the scheme was allowed to dwindle into insignificance. The plan for a great campaign for Tariff Reform and Imperial Preference, despite a certain initial promise, was largely stillborn.

In 1924 Lord and Lady Milner decided to visit South Africa to observe once again the scenes of earlier trials and triumphs. The visit was in large part successful. However, it was marred much later by Lady Milner's publication of the impressions of her visit. The tone and details of these published impressions caused offence. They revealed that lack of felicity of touch which sometimes characterised the actions of her husband in his dealings with those who were not especially close to him. J. C. Smuts, the son of the South African leader, later wrote in this connection that:[1]

[1] J. C. Smuts, *Jan Christian Smuts* (Cape Town, 1952), p. 285.

... the Earl of Athlone brought Lord and Lady Milner out to the farm for lunch. Lady Milner mentions this visit in a publication of her diaries ... She refers to my mother as a "plump Boer woman", though at the time my mother weighed only 107 pounds. She says we seemed awed by the presence of a great man (Milner). Doornkloof has seen many great men, and we are not easily awed. And the "scrub cattle" she saw were prize studbook Frieslands. However, my father was very pleased to see Milner and to show him hospitality ...

In 1925 the travellers returned to London. In March of that year Lord Milner's name was put forward to become Chancellor of Oxford University, in succession to Lord Curzon. He was not destined to receive this honour, however. On the 30th April tragedy struck when Milner's doctor discovered that he was suffering from a mortal disease, sleepy sickness, probably contracted on the South African tour. It was a terrible and completely capricious development.

II

Alfred Milner was sometimes described as the "man of no illusions".[1] We may wonder as he lay on his sick bed, as his vital forces ebbed away, if he ever thought of the phrase of another famous Imperialist, Benjamin Disraeli, the Earl of Beaconsfield, who often liked to murmur in the hour of crisis that "All is illusion". Most probably he did not.

Lord Milner was too intense, too involved, too desperately devoted to the cause of Britain to indulge in Disraeli's cynical levities. The Radical journalists who liked to attack Milner as an unfeeling Prussian autocrat were wrong in one sense; Milner felt intensely about all things concerned with the fate of his country, the fate of the "race" to which he belonged, and the future of the Empire, the tangible expression of that "race" in the world of nations.

He was not a Bismarck who could rise above feeling and sentiment. The key to much of his political life in the two decades after his return from South Africa lies in the completely different fact that he was passionately and personally

---

[1] This is the subtitle of Sir Evelyn Wrench's biography of Milner.

moved by developments other British political men could look upon as mere phases in the game waged between parties. It was anathema for him, an accursed thing, that the British future should be decided by the players of games— the Balfours, Churchills, Walter Longs—short-sighted, narrowly ambitious, crafty, momentary men, "Mandarins" without the training or ability or inclination to weigh in the statesman's balance the courses they proposed and pursued.

III

A second aspect of his career after his return from South Africa was more obvious. This was that essence of disappointment and failure that clung round him, despite marvellous accomplishments. In his opinion and in that of his disciples he was fitted for the first place in the State, but there was never even a remote chance for him to become Prime Minister, despite the highest capacity. Why was this so?

It has been said that there was some flaw in him, that things always went wrong for Milner at the point of triumphant success. It has been pointed out that when he manoeuvred Kruger into war the British Army was not ready; that when he worked the reconstruction of South Africa the election of 1906 ruined the purpose and force of his accomplishment; that within a month of the victory of 1918, for which he had done so much, he was publicly humiliated by Lloyd George; that when he was selected to become Chancellor of Oxford he died a fortnight before his tenure was to have begun. It has been suggested that the flaw in Lord Milner was that he despised everyone less able than himself.[1]

It is certain that Milner could not tolerate the actions of those with whom he did not agree, and that he lacked the guile or patience required to mask his attitude. There were

[1] See an article by A. J. P. Taylor in *The Observer*, 24th August, 1958.

other reasons also. As an Imperialist he desired to preserve the British system over vast areas of the world. But a basic thing about him was that he disliked the British system, and British politics, and British democracy. And the alternative he had to offer, rule by men like himself and his friends was unthinkable, however valid many of his plans were.

Winston Churchill has pointed out with pride that the British Constitution has "grown up as the most thorough and practical mechanism yet devised in the modern world for bringing the force of public opinion to bear upon the conduct of affairs".[1] For Lord Milner, such a development had no valid meaning.

Intellectually, he lacked respect for the British Constitution, for the British way of doing things in political life. As we have seen in an earlier chapter, he once described himself as a "wrecker". His description was dismissed by his friend, F. S. Oliver, as a paradox, but Oliver was an extremely clever man prone to see paradoxes where they did not exist. Lord Milner may well have been correct in his description of himself, so far as active politics were concerned.

For example, as we have seen, at the time of the Irish crisis in 1914 he advocated violent policies which could not be accepted even by men so extreme as Sir Edward Carson or Captain Craig, the forceful and thoroughly defiant leaders of the Ulstermen. They respected the practices and the customs and the meaning of the British Constitution in a way that Lord Milner did not. He could, for a purpose that seemed valid to him, contemplate the wreck and ruin of that system while Carson and Craig refused to do so.[2] And many of their colleagues were made uneasy by the vehemance of Milner's counsel.

In the same way, at the time of the Dardanelles crisis, Milner's violence aroused suspicion and uneasiness. At that time he was distressed by the dilatoriness of the Asquith

---

[1] Churchill, *The Aftermath*, p. 60.
[2] For their differences, see above Chapter IX, "Crime and Treason".

Government which could not make up its mind at a moment of desperate military danger. In the autumn of 1915 Ministers were required to decide upon the evacuation or the reinforcement of troops at the Dardanelles, but definite action was postponed for a period of several weeks. Lord Milner was outraged by the Prime Minister's procrastination. He decided to force him to act. In order to do so he spoke out in the House of Lords, in a manner that was without precedent.[1] His speeches furnished the enemy with information of a very secret nature, information they could not otherwise have obtained. It was the method of a man who is lacking in moderation and even in balance simply because he has no faith in the value of the system he is attacking. Years after the event, the official historian, Brigadier C. F. Aspinall-Oglander, condemned Milner's outbursts as those of a "wrecker", although he did not mention his name. In his official work, *Military Operations Gallipoli*, he wrote:[2]

> Secrecy was indeed the first essential if evacuation was to have the smallest chance of success . . . the matter had been openly discussed in London, and in the latest papers from London the officers charged with devising a plan for that . . . delicate operation had read with astonishment and dismay the report of a recent debate in the House of Lords. There, reckless of the additional dangers to which their words were subjecting the lives of the troops, two well-known peers had pressed the Government to announce whether or not they were contemplating the "withdrawal from an enterprise, the successful completion of which is now hopeless". Later, on the 18th November, at a still more critical juncture, one of these two noblemen again returned to the charge . . . In view of these unfortunate public utterances it may well be imagined that the officers responsible for arranging the evacuation were almost bereft of the hope of averting a massacre on the beaches. Only after the war was it learnt that the Germans and Turks alike, unable to take these questions at face value, had regarded them as propaganda to hide the preparations for a further British attack.

[1] See above Chapter XII, "A Tiger is Let Loose".
[2] C. F. Aspinall-Oglander, *Military Operations Gallipoli* (London, 1932), pp. 410–11.

In addition to these significant political imperfections there were other factors that we have already noticed, which help to explain Lord Milner's disappointment. His disciples early realised that he could not "put himself across" to a popular audience, while he himself understood that he was unfitted to become a popular leader. Even many of those extreme Tories who were eventually attracted by his uncompromising attitude did not look upon him as a potential Prime Minister, but as a champion of the second class, as a brilliant intellectual who could serve best in the Administration of some more cautious and practical leader. In other words, despite his capacity, Lord Milner did not really fit in to the British political system.

IV

After a fortnight of illness Milner died on the 13th May 1925. He was buried at Salehurst at a private ceremony, attended only by Lady Milner and a few very close friends. On the 16th the Archbishop of Canterbury, Dr. Davidson, conducted a service in Milner's memory at Canterbury Cathedral. Two days after, a memorial service was held in the chapel of New College, Oxford. On that day also, another service was celebrated in Westminster Abbey, attended by the Prime Minister and all the members of the Cabinet. Lord Milner's passing was widely mourned. In particular, his "young men" felt the death of their old chief as a terrible loss.

After Milner's death there occurred a singular and remarkable development. Most statesmen leave behind them a body of adherents and a corpus of accomplishment that, taken together, serve to preserve and enhance their memory. In Milner's case, however, something almost unique in recent British political history occurred.

We have seen that in the years 1905–6 Sir Henry Campbell Bannerman had succeeded in stamping out of the Liberal Party the *Religio Milneriana,* that blind belief and faith in

Milner and in all his works, that dominated the outlook of Asquith, Gray, and Haldane. However, after 1925 the *Religio Milneriana* was revived by the fervour of Lady Milner and the loyalty of a score of faithful disciples. In the 1920's and after, these disciples were no longer his young men only. In that period they were men who possessed power and authority in their own right, men who dominated the thought and outlook of their fellows. Geoffrey Dawson of *The Times,* Lord Astor of *The Observer*, R. H. Brand, Lord Lothian, L. S. Amery, Basil Williams, Lionel Curtis, Basil Worsfold, F. S. Oliver, and others of their company were men who did much to mould and fashion the opinion of a generation. In their rapture they were responsible for the creation and propagation of a number of myths about Milner, which we have already noticed in the course of this history. It became the fashion for them to praise every action of their old chief, and to denigrate the motives and courses of those who had disagreed with him. Their high and particular opinions of Lord Milner's life swayed the attitude of contemporaries to a remarkable degree. Dr. Thomas Jones, the grey eminence of their time, and a maker of reputations in his own right, noted in sour terms with Lord Milner's career in his mind, that "the Round Tablers are good at collecting any credit there is going, like the Scotch".[1]

It is no denigration of Lord Milner's fine services to remark upon the exaggerations of those who were too warmly devoted to his memory. However, the extent of their devotion, as we have seen, served merely to falsify and pollute the mainstream of recent British political history.

What further judgment, what final analysis remains? It may be said that unlike so many politicians, there was not a scrap of narrow personal ambition in Lord Milner's make-up. The master desire of his life, the reason he sought power, was to serve, to serve Britain and the Empire. His

[1] Jones, *op. cit.*, p. 173.

chief contribution to the political thought of his generation, without any doubt, was his emphasis upon the need for Imperial Unity. He desired not a Liberal or a Labour or a Conservative policy, but a British policy—rational, logical, thoroughly planned. Unfortunately, he lacked the varied qualities of a great political leader. His rigid sincerity, and his inability to appreciate an opponent's point of view, made it impossible for him to compromise, at any time. He believed too ardently that he perceived the truth and that others who could not agree with him did not. If his perspective was larger than that of his contemporaries this alone, especially in England, did not fit him for the role of successful politician. His objects he kept clearly in mind always, but he lacked the qualities that might have helped him to dominate and control the means required to accomplish these objects: "He was . . . always more aware of what the Empire needed than of what the British people could be brought to accept". Given this general outlook, it was only in the last years of his life, when it was too late, that he could genuinely appreciate the motto and maxim of Canon Barnett, his friend of Toynbee Hall days, which was— "Fear not to sow because of the birds".

Index

Asquith, Herbert Henry—*continued*
336–9, 341–4; appointed Kitchener as
War Secretary, 240, 241; indulgence to
Wilson, 244; waning of authority,
249, 250; relations with Generals, 251;
formed Coalition Government (1915)
255–73, 277, 297, 320; supported by
King, 281–3, 372; rejected plan of
Committee for increasing food production, 289; agreed to send troops
to Egypt, 303; and Carson's resignation, 304, 310, 311, 315; agreed
evacuation of Dardanelles, 312, 313,
603, 604; loyalty of Bonar Law to,
314, 329, 358, 360, 361; Milnerites'
determination to destroy, 321, 322,
324, 329–35, 345–8, 359; agreed to
enquiries into campaigns that failed,
349; tried to associate Milner with
Government, 353, 354; and Lloyd
George's ideas of War Council, 356,
357, 362; Cabinet crisis that led to
resignation of, 362–4; and relations
with Lloyd George, 384, 385, 406;
Lloyd George's method of Government foreshadowed by reforms of,
394; opposed Lloyd George's Government, 380, 458, 463, 474, 518;
Haig's comment on, 495; alleged
meeting of, with General Robertson,
518; supported entry to War, 540;
and war aims statement, 558; author
of *Memories and Reflections* (q.v.), 25 n,
etc.; mentioned, 3, 175, 227, 248, 280,
316, 319, 350, 389, 391, 399
Asquith, Margot, Countess of Oxford
and Asquith, 25, 65, 99 n
Asquith Papers, 316 n, 353 n
Astor, Nancy, Viscountess, 164, 327 n
Astor, Waldorf (2nd Viscount), member
of Round Table, 164, 167; payment of
funds by, to aid Ulster, 188, 200;
adulation of Milner, 251; member of
Monday Night Cabal, 324–8, 569; as
owner of *Observer*, 327, 595, 606;
suggested Milner as Premier, 345, 347;
post in Government suggested for,
376; in Lloyd George's secretariat,
378, 379; relations with Garvin, 329
and n; exposed Colonel Repington,
516, 517 and n; associated with F. V.
Fisher, 546; influence on Dawson,
575; prepared to work with Germans

after War, 577; published Milner's
articles, 600
Astor, William Waldorf (1st Viscount),
326, 327
Astors, The, 326 n
Athlone, Earl of, 601
Atlantic Monthly, 537
Australia, 566
Austria, 301, 306, 449, 526, 536, 557

Bailey, Sir Abe, 162, 164, 166
Balcarres, Lord, *see* Crawford, 27th Earl
of
Baldwin, Stanley, 595, 600
Balfour, Arthur James, 1st Earl of,
Prime Minister, 42–4, 70–2, 74, 98;
opinion of Churchill, 82; in debate on
Chinese labour in South Africa, 85,
89, 92, 93; and Tariff Reform, 86,
108, 109–116, 147, 148, 168; and
Imperialism, 122, 148; and 1909
Budget, 157, 159; resigned as Conservative leader, 169; enemy of Irish
nationalism, 208, 212, 214; pressure
on, for despatch of expeditionary
force, 239, 240; criticised by Milner,
280, 364, 602; at conference on conscription, 282; relationship with
Garvin, 325; considered for Premiership, 330, 331; member of Lloyd
George's Government, 376, 419, 559;
discussed Carson with Haig, 431;
prepared to resign from Government,
454, 455; views on Robertson as
C.I.G.S., 483–5; considered President
Wilson's Peace Note, 568; at Peace
Conference, 584; mentioned, 3, 32,
120, 326, 386, 407 n
Balfour of Burleigh, 6th Baron, 158, 187
Balfour Papers, 44 n, etc.
Balliol College, Oxford, 8, 10, 12, 19, 20,
39, 55
Bangor, 209
Bank of British West Africa, 53
Barnes, George, 407 n, 446, 483, 485
Barnett, Canon, 607
Batoum, 557
Beaconsfield, 1st Earl of, *see* Disraeli,
Benjamin
Beatrice Webb's Diaries 1912-24, 524 n,
525 n, 552 n
Beaverbrook, 1st Baron (formerly Sir
W. Max Aitken), discussed Irish crisis,